D1536778

JavaScript

DEVELOPER'S DICTIONARY

 201 West 103rd Street, Indianapolis, Indiana 46290

JavaScript Developer's Dictionary

Copyright © 2002 by Sams Publishing

International Standard Book Number: 0-672-32201-3

Library of Congress Catalog Card Number: 2001094226

Printed in the United States of America

First Printing: June 2002

04   03   02   6   5   4   3

Trademarks

Warning and Disclaimer

Acquisitions Editors
Patricia Barnes
Shelley Johnston

Development Editor
Jonathan Steever

Managing Editor
Charlotte Clapp

Project Editors
Sheila Schroeder
Tricia Liebig

Copy Editor
Kate Givens

Indexer
Becky Hornyak

Proofreader
Linda Seifert

Technical Editors
Martin Honnen
Jason Byars
Andrew Watt

Team Coordinator
Amy Patton

Interior Design
Gary Adair

Cover Design
Alan Clements

Production
Ayanna Lacey

R0177800707 MB

Contents at a Glance

Table of Contents

About the Author

Alexander James Vincent is a 24-year-old Web design expert based in Vallejo, CA. Born and raised in Seattle, WA, he served 23 months in the United States Navy as a Seaman Journalist. Following his tour of duty, he returned to the field of computers he grew up around and discovered JavaScript. Since then he has become a standards evangelist for Web design, and works to encourage best practices in coding for all Web languages, client- and server-side. He moderates the JavaScript Programming Help forum and writes tutorials for Website Abstraction at http://www.wsabstract.com. He also contributes Quality Assurance efforts to the Mozilla.org project. He is currently in the process of completing the design of his JavaScript Laboratory site at http://www.jslab.org, a project he set aside for the *JavaScript Developer's Dictionary*. He is a huge fan of the Seattle Mariners, and hopes to see them in a World Series one day soon.

Dedication

To the Nathan Hale High School faculty members; particularly, Principal Eric Benson, and Language Arts teacher Victoria Carver. Also, the Mathematics team at Nathan Hale—particularly Mr. Dong, Mr. Coon, and Mr. Wiegand.

Numerous other departments (and the lunchroom cooks) may never forgive me for leaving them out. But I will say what I told Mr. Benson a couple years after my graduation; Nathan Hale High School was an average school when I entered it as a freshman, in Mr. Benson's first year as a principal. By the time I had left four years later, it was a first-class high school.

Acknowledgments

There are a number of people I wish to say "Thank You" to. First on that list is God. It may sound trite, but it isn't. I would have died at sea were it not for Him, before this book even became an idea in my head.

Next would be Arun Ranganathan at Netscape, for pointing me to those IDL files at `lxr.mozilla.org`. Without his help in at least pointing me to them, this book would have died halfway through.

Then there are the numerous people on the Sams Publishing team: Shelley Johnston-Markanday, Jon Steever, Patricia Barnes, the Technical Editors for this book, Martin Honnen and Jason Byers, and several other behind-the-scenes people I haven't yet met or e-mailed.

John Krutsch, a longtime friend and fellow moderator at Website Abstraction, for his work on cookies.

Jason Karl Davis, Ryan Frishberg (a.k.a. "Arielladog"), and Andrew Shults (a.k.a. "thejavaman1"), for second opinions on my occasional guessing.

Several Mozilla.org engineers and QA people whose names I can't even begin to recall. What goes around comes around, ladies and gentlemen, and I'll be coming around quite a bit in the future.

George Chiang, owner and operator of Website Abstraction (`http://www.wsabstract.com`), the first place I found a home in Web site design.

The various journalism instructors at Defense Information School at Fort Meade, MD. Particularly then-Gunnery Sergeants Beyer and Roberts of the United States Marine Corps, in the radio and public affairs departments respectively, and Sergeant 1st Class Sizer who put up with my attitudes (barely) in print journalism class in the winter of 1996–1997. I don't think I could have written this book as well as I did without your teachings, and you've definitely impacted my writing style. The same applies to all the non-commissioned officers, petty officers, and chief petty officers at DINFOS during that time.

James LeBlance at Smart Scents, and Dimple Sayles at D & R Hauling, for doing everything they could to keep a roof over my head and food in my stomach.

Who could forget Mom and Dad, who will be celebrating 25 years of marriage in April 2002? I couldn't.

Tell Us What You Think!

As the reader of this book, *you* are our most important critic and commentator. We value your opinion and want to know what we're doing right, what we could do better, what areas you'd like to see us publish in, and any other words of wisdom you're willing to pass our way.

You can e-mail or write me directly to let me know what you did or didn't like about this book—as well as what we can do to make our books stronger.

Please note that I cannot help you with technical problems related to the topic of this book, and that due to the high volume of mail I receive, I might not be able to reply to every message.

When you write, please be sure to include this book's title and author as well as your name and phone or e-mail address. I will carefully review your comments and share them with the author and editors who worked on the book.

E-mail: webdev@samspublishing.com

Mail: Mark Taber
            Associate Publisher
            Sams Publishing
            201 West 103rd Street
            Indianapolis, IN 46290 USA

Introduction

JavaScript. The term itself implies a scripting language, a "patchwork" for whatever Web page you have in mind. But, like many scripting languages, it's not necessarily a simple one.

What Is JavaScript?

The word "JavaScript" is really a name for a language with several different flavors. Microsoft Internet Explorer (IE) implements JavaScript under the name "JScript," and with browser-specific code in certain areas. Netscape Navigator 4 (Nav4) interacts with Web documents quite differently than Netscape 6 (Nav6), its successor. There have been six revisions of JavaScript alone for Netscape, which invented the language. Within the next few years, JavaScript 2.0 will enter the World Wide Web.

With all these variants on the same theme, Netscape and Microsoft leave a lot of developers scrambling to write code that works in all the major browsers. Furthermore, documentation can be found from a variety of sources in various formats, some of which may be incomplete or outdated. The result is a lot of developers who cannot easily find the information for which they are looking.

A Brief History of Time (or This Project, Anyway)

This book, or at least the concept behind it, truly started in 1999, when I asked for documentation on the current Mozilla.org JavaScript Engine and Document Object Model. This was long before Netscape 6 began its beta releases and before 6.0 was released. At the time, Mr. Steve Rudman asked me if I was willing to work for him, for hire, to do the documentation on JavaScript 1.5. I refused, feeling I was not up to the task.

Eight months later, I remembered some of the words of inspiration of several professionals in life changes, notably Anthony Robbins. (Thanks, Tony, though we've never met and I've yet to attend one of your seminars. "Awaken the Giant Within" was very interesting.) Effectively, I realized I had thrown away an opportunity for which I was very competent. I replied to the newsgroup, offering my services, but it was too late.

Sams Publishing's Acquisitions department, however, watches the newsgroups as well. After numerous unspeakable delays, the result is the *JavaScript Developer's Dictionary*. (I've also discovered about 15 errata in the JavaScript 1.5 Core documentation I refused to do…)

In a sense, this book is for me as well as for you. You'd be surprised how much you learn about a language by writing and researching a book about it. One fact I can take pride in about this book is I could regularly turn back to earlier draft chapters in this book when I needed to build a code listing in later chapters—without going to the official references I used as starting points.

Nonetheless, in our modern age, even a book such as this is a work in progress. Therefore, before we get into the chapters themselves, I have already set up a directory on my Web site for errata, new discoveries, and so on that I, you, or other readers may discover as copies of this book get around. Visit `http://www.jslab.org/jsdd` for the latest details on this book and its contents.

XHTML as HTML: The Dictionary Standard

In the process of editing chapters, I made a decision to re-create each listing as XHTML 1.0 Transitional documents whenever possible. When you examine and reproduce these listings, please save them as `.htm` or `.html` files, *not* `.xml` files.

XHTML 1.0 is a "reformulation of HTML as XML," as the W3C puts it. This means that HTML follows a very rigid structure, from which you should not deviate. Keeping to this structure gives you a solid, reproducible, and uniform DOM for each document, and subsequently each listing in this book.

However, why Transitional, and why as `.htm` or `.html`? The answer lies in the current state of affairs. Even now, we are still very much in a transition from pre-standards browsers to post-standards browsing. Internet Explorer, upon receiving an XHTML document as XML, treats it as XML and ignores the HTML features entirely. (I reference a workaround for this in Chapter 33, "Styling for HTML Elements.") As HTML, Internet Explorer often expects closing tags when an empty element tag would be appropriate (`<title></title>` instead of `<title />`, for example).

Netscape 6 treats it as XML, running it through the XML parser, but also does not expose the full HTML DOM for the document. This is even true when you serve the document through the official XHTML mime-type, `application/xhtml+xml`.

For your own coding efforts, I strongly recommend you get into the habit of writing valid XHTML code as soon as possible, not only because it works in a wide variety of browsing platforms, but also because it makes your DOM much more stable and predictable. If you already know HTML (pretty much a prerequisite to this book), learning XHTML is not difficult at all. First, you learn how to write valid HTML 4.01 Transitional code (somewhat easy), and then you learn to write XHTML 1.0 Transitional code from HTML 4.01 Transitional (easy, once you get the hang of it). The HTML Validation Service at `http://validator.w3.org` is the only one you should trust.

What Does this Book Cover?

JavaScript Developer's Dictionary is a reference to complete and enhance the documentation for the JavaScript language. As the vast majority of Internet users use Nav4, IE4, and later generations of these two browsers, the *Dictionary* shall focus on JavaScript, starting primarily at this level: JavaScript 1.2 for Netscape browsers, and JScript version 3 for Internet Explorer browsers. I also cover the added and deprecated features of Internet Explorer 5.0, Internet Explorer 5.5, and Netscape 6, to JScript version 5.5 and JavaScript 1.5.

This book covers every object available to the developer in typical client-side use. It covers Core JavaScript object constructors, such as `Object()`, `RegExp()`, and `Function()`, in Part I.

In Part II, we enter an area of JavaScript for which there are no standards per se, but which the two browser companies mentionned previously have paralleled each other on quite closely: the `window` object, the `navigator` object, and the `screen` object.

Part III covers the Document Object Model for HTML documents—both within the standards defined by W3C and proprietary, non-standard definitions of each HTML element. It begins with core DOM definitions as provided by the W3C DOM for nodes, attributes, document fragments, and the like. Then the book dives into the specific properties and methods associated with each element of the HTML language. Finally, we explore events and event handlers, styling, cookies, and the DOM Level 2 Range specification.

I wrap it up in Part IV with styling several significant XML-based technologies to keep an eye on. (As you'll see, you can use JavaScript with XML documents as well.)

This book does not cover signed scripts, the security model of either browser, or server-side scripts in the JavaScript language. For the most part, these features are often far more trouble than they are worth. Signed scripts and the security model involve a fairly intimidating warning for Web site visitors, who often deny permission for what the scripts request. These areas are insignificant for most JavaScripters, and thus this book offers no emphasis on the limited features these subsets of JavaScript provide.

One feature of JavaScript I want to emphasize quite heavily at this point is the inheritance of properties and methods of some objects in other objects. For instance, every HTML element inherits the properties and methods of the `HTMLElement` interface, described in the `HTMLElement` chapter.

Likewise, the `HTMLElement` interface inherits properties and methods of the `Element` interface, which inherits properties and methods of the `Node` interface. I have organized the chapters of this book to present fundamental object chapters before objects inheriting their properties. For each element I note specifically what element it inherits properties and methods from. Finally, each chapter (except the `Object()` chapter) indicates from which object it descends.

In case you're wondering, there will be examples of each object in active use. Many times, these examples will cover innovative concepts I find extremely useful and under-used. More than that, the examples are not written for the novice JavaScripter.

This book assumes you have some familiarity with the JavaScript language, and is not intended to teach you JavaScript. The examples are just that: examples. Sometimes the examples demonstrate good coding practices, and sometimes they may be quite impractical. Nonetheless, if you are just beginning to learn JavaScript, I recommend you read *Sams Teach Yourself JavaScript in 24 Hours* from Sams Publishing before you read this book.

Formatting of Script Examples

Throughout the rest of this book, you will notice several conventions. Netscape Navigator 4 and Netscape 6 browsers are abbreviated Nav4 and Nav6, respectively. Internet Explorer browsers are abbreviated IE4, IE5, IE5.5, and IE6, depending on the version of browser. Other abbreviations you see frequently in this book include W3C for the World Wide Web Consortium, DOM for Document Object Model, and ECMA for ECMAScript.

In any event, you may notice indentation of code blocks:

```
function myFunc() {
   if (1 == 1) {
      alert("Hello World")
      } else {
      alert("Goodbye, cruel world")
      }
   return false
   }
```

The primary reason for this is visual formatting, to ensure you can follow the code examples within. The browser ignores such formatting, but it makes code far easier to read. I generally do not have anything that is not indented, except for function and object definitions belonging to the window object itself. (You'll see what I mean in Chapters 1 and 15, "Object( )" and "window".)

I introduce each feature of the language with a table indicating what browsers implement it, and in which standard, if any, a feature also belongs to: ECMAScript or the DOM. Features that are implemented in DOM Level 2 (DOM-2) but not in DOM Level 1 (DOM-1) are noted as such. Likewise, if a basic constructor or node has been deprecated, the table notes this. The primary focus of this book is on JavaScript 1.2 and JScript version 3.0 and later, but earlier versions of JavaScript receive mention as well.

All this being said, welcome to the *JavaScript Developer's Dictionary*. Prepare for a few surprises, and a lot of fun.

"The first step to confirming there is a bug in someone else's work is confirming there are no bugs in your own."

–Alexander J. Vincent

PART I

Core JavaScript

CHAPTER 1

Object()

Browser/JavaScript Version	Created By
Nav4/JavaScript 1.2	`x = new Object()`
	`x = {}`
IE4/JScript 3.0	`x = new Object()`
	`x = {}`
IE5/JScript 5.0	`x = new Object()`
	`x = {}`
IE5.5/JScript 5.5	`x = new Object()`
	`x = {}`
Nav6/JavaScript 1.5	`x = new Object()`
	`x = {}`
ECMAScript 1st edition	`x = new Object()`
ECMAScript 3rd edition	`x = new Object()`
	`x = {}`

> **Note**
> Implemented in Nav2+, IE4+

Description

The `Object()` object constructor is fundamental to the entire JavaScript language for two separate reasons: it defines properties and methods that all ECMAScript-based objects in JavaScript inherit, and it provides a context for creating user-defined ECMAScript objects. (DOM objects for Netscape support inheritance of these properties and methods as well; Internet Explorer excludes them. The creation of DOM objects I cover in Chapter 20, "Core DOM Objects.")

Creating a New Object

You can create an object using the following syntax:

```
[var] x = new Object()
```

The left side, *x*, defines the object name. The equal sign (=), covered in Chapter 12, "Operators," indicates an assignment. The right side includes the new operator, also covered in Chapter 12, and the object constructor function, `Object()`. The result is JavaScript creates a new object and assigns a reference to it to *x*. (There are other constructor functions as well, defined later in this chapter and in Chapter 2, "Function().")

Another way of defining an instance of `Object()` is the literal syntax:

```
x = {}
```

This is not as well known as other literals, but useful as a shorthand. Defining properties and methods in the literal syntax is simple:

```
x = {prop1:value1, prop2:value2}
```

where `prop1` and `prop2` are the property and method names, and `value1` and `value2` are the values you assign to them.

> **Note**
> The literal syntax for objects is not available to Netscape browsers prior to version 4, or Internet Explorer browsers prior to version 4.0.

Getters and Setters of Netscape 6

Netscape 6 supports the capability for you to use getter and setter functions to set and retrieve properties of objects at will. With these functions, you can modify any other properties of the object simultaneously, and still return the correct result.

Defining a getter is simple. You first define the function you want to act as a getter function to return the value you want the function to get, and then use the `__defineGetter__()` method of the object to activate it. The first argument of `__defineGetter__()` is the property name the object is getting, in quotes. The second is the function you want to assign as a getter, without parentheses or arguments. Listing 1.1 shows the `__defineGetter__()` function.

Alternatively, you could use the function operator, which I cover in Chapter 2, "Function()" and a little in Chapter 12. This operator would allow you to define the getter function directly as the second argument. (I prefer not to do this, but it can be smarter to code this way.)

Defining a setter is equally simple. You first define the function you want to act as a setter function by assigning values to other properties as appropriate, and then use the `__defineSetter__()` method of the object to activate it. The first argument of __defineSetter__() is the property name the object is setting, in quotes. The second is the function you want to assign as a setter, without parentheses or arguments.

In Listing 1.1 the setter function returns the value it sets to the given reference.

Listing 1.1   *Getters and Setters Demonstrated (Netscape 6 Only)*

```
<?xml version="1.0" ?>
<!DOCTYPE html PUBLIC "-//W3C//DTD XHTML 1.0 Transitional//EN" "
    DTD/xhtml1-transitional.dtd">
<html xmlns="http://www.w3.org/1999/xhtml" >
<head><title></title>
</head>
<body>
<script language="JavaScript1.5" type="text/javascript">
<!--
function book_getName() {
    return this._author
    }

function book_setName(x) {
    this._author = x
    return this._author
    }

var book = { _author: "Alex Vincent"};
book.__defineSetter__('author', book_setName);
book.__defineGetter__('author', book_getName);


document.write("<p>The author is "+ book.author + ".</p>")
book.author = "Alexander J. Vincent"

document.write("<p>The author is "+ book.author + ".</p>")

//-->
</script>
<!-- Results
The author is Alex Vincent.
The author is Alexander J. Vincent.
//-->
</body>
</html>
```

Adding Properties and Methods to an Object

Whenever you create an object using the `Object()` constructor function or any other JavaScript-defined constructor, you will find you can add and change properties and methods of the object at will. For instance, if you were to say:

```
myArray = new Array()
```

you could still add properties and methods to the array object at will:

```
myArray.color = "red"
```

The addition of methods, in particular, can be very useful when the methods use the `this` keyword, as I discuss in Chapter 12. However, for many literals (covered in Chapter 13, "JavaScript Syntax"), you cannot add properties and methods so easily. There are two ways to defeat this, which the `Object()` function provides. One is through the `Object.prototype` property, and the other is through the `Object.constructor()` method.

Objects Are Typically Unique

Note the following code:

```
var x = new Object()
var y = new Object()
alert(x == y) // returns false
```

The reason the preceding alert returns `false` is simple. Unless two variables are explicitly set to reference one another, or a common value, they are unequal. You could say `y = x`, and then the alert would return `true`.

This becomes useful in a few situations. For instance, any object I create using the `Object()` constructor I can use as a flag. The word "flag" is a term programmers and scripters use to indicate an object the programmer uses to indicate some status or special use, but which has no meaning outside its context. Like all other arguments and variables in a function, they indicate to the function what it should do; unlike other arguments and variables in a function, flags relevant to the function they are applied against are largely irrelevant to the script and other functions at large. (To put it in perspective, consider: In a `for` loop, the looping variable is easily a flag within the loop. Would that variable have any meaning outside the loop?)

Returning New Objects Outside of a Function

A constructor function is a function specifically designed to return an object to the outside world, where the object returned can then be assigned a name outside the function. (Technically, because all functions called with the new keyword return this unless a return statement is included, all functions are constructor functions. However, this book will refer to constructor functions as functions following the first definition.) JavaScript allows you to create constructor functions using the this keyword, covered in Chapter 12. Listing 1.2 builds instances of Fruit() with certain properties. (The exception is when Fruit() receives an invalid set of arguments; I have designed the constructor with a rudimentary validation of its arguments. An invalid set will return {} instead.)

Listing 1.2   *A Constructor Function for* Fruit() *Objects*

```
<?xml version="1.0" ?>
<!DOCTYPE html PUBLIC "-//W3C//DTD XHTML 1.0 Transitional//EN"
    "DTD/xhtml1-transitional.dtd">
<html xmlns="http://www.w3.org/1999/xhtml" >
<head><title></title>
</head>
<body>
<script language="JavaScript" type="text/javascript">
<!--
function Fruit(color) {
   var response = this
   this.constructor = Fruit
   if (arguments.length > 0) {
      response.color = arguments[0]
      } else {
      response = {}
      }
   return response
   }

Apple = new Fruit("red") // returns object with color property set to "red"
Grape = new Fruit("purple") // returns object with color property set to
"purple"
Kibitz = new Fruit() // returns Object() object
document.write("<p>The apple's color is "+Apple.color+".</p>")
//-->
</script>
<!-- Result:
The apple's color is red.
-->
</body>
</html>
```

Those familiar with the `this` keyword used as a constructor may wonder why I include the command `var response = this`. The reason is simple: if I want to return a different kind of object, I can simply set `response` to some other object.

The `return` statement within the function and `new` operator outside the function make all the difference. When you omit the `return` statement from a constructor, JavaScript automatically returns the `this` object to whatever called the function. When you give it a `return` statement with an object you name (in this case, `response`), it returns the named object instead of the `this` object. (The `return` statement I cover in Chapter 11, "The Global Object and Statements.") The `new` keyword ensures it is a new object, and I cover this operator in Chapter 12.

Preparing Your Objects for Others

Listing 1.2, while it works, does not prepare its fruits for general consumption. If another developer adds the line

```
document.write(I would like to eat a " + Apple + ".")
```

the result, in your document, is

```
I would like to eat a [object Object].
```

`[object Object]` doesn't sound too tasty. This illustrates a point about object creation: what you do with the object and what others do with them may be totally different, and you should be ready. Part of this includes private objects, which I will cover in the next chapter. Another part involves making sure your objects are always ready to respond to the outside world.

Later in this chapter, I explain the `toString()` and `toSource()` methods. (If you are not already familiar with them, you may want to glance at their definitions for a moment.) It is vitally important for you to define `for` instances of your constructor function's methods which return string and source-code representations. When you define them, attach them as properties of the constructor function's `prototype` property. (This property I define later in this chapter, though it applies best to functions.)

I'd like to be able to say the `Apple` object is an apple, and the `Grape` object is a grape. Unfortunately, object creation doesn't quite work that way. Unless I provide the actual variable name I intend to create as an argument, it's excessively difficult to get the name "Apple" back. (For instance, what if `Apple` was a property of a `FruitBasket` object, which was a property of a `GroceryStore` object? The `for...in` statement won't find it easily with so many other objects to look through.)

So I settle for the next best thing. I simply say, "Okay, an apple with a red color I can call a red fruit." By the definition of toString(), I have enough to create a toString() method specific to instances of Fruit().

The definition of toSource(), in this case, is also similar. It's simply a requirement to generate a source-code representation that, if I ever execute it, would create an exact clone of the original. Listing 1.3 shows how to create and attach specific toString() and toSource() methods to a constructor's prototype, and thus by implication, to all instances of the constructor.

Listing 1.3   Fruit.prototype, toString(), *and* toSource()

```
<?xml version="1.0" ?>
<!DOCTYPE html PUBLIC "-//W3C//DTD XHTML 1.0 Transitional//EN"
    "DTD/xhtml1-transitional.dtd">
<html xmlns="http://www.w3.org/1999/xhtml" >
<head><title></title>
</head>
<body>
<script language="JavaScript" type="text/javascript">
<!--
function Fruit() {
    var response = this
    this.constructor = Fruit
    if (arguments.length > 0) {
        response.color = arguments[0]
        } else {
        response = new Object()
        }
    return response
    }

function Fruit_toString() {
    return this.color + " fruit"
    }
Fruit.prototype.toString = Fruit_toString

function Fruit_toSource() {
    return 'new Fruit("' + this.color + '")'
    }
Fruit.prototype.toSource = Fruit_toSource
```

Listing 1.3 *(continued)*

```
Apple = new Fruit("red") // returns object with color property set to "red"
Grape = new Fruit("purple") // returns object with color property set to
"purple"
Kibitz = new Fruit() // returns Object() object
document.write("<p>The apple's color is " + Apple.color + ".</p>")
document.write("<p>I would like to eat a " + Apple + ".</p>")
document.write("<p>You can create a new Apple object with ")
document.write("<code>" + Apple.toSource() + "</code>.</p>")

//-->
</script>

<!-- returns
The apple's color is red.
I would like to eat a red fruit.
You can create a new Apple object with new Fruit("red").
-->

</body>
</html>
```

Most Objects You Create Have a Parent Object

When you create a global variable in JavaScript, and append properties to it, the properties have a parent object. For instance,

```
var k = {}
k.p = 4
```

The parent of k.p is k. But the parent object of k isn't as obvious. The parent of k is the window object you built k in. Or, more correctly, the variable k is a property of the window object, and the variable holds a pointer to the object we call k.

Any object you create is a property of another object through whatever variable name you assign to it. (If there is no variable name, which can happen in a few odd cases, there is no parent object.) Eventually, no matter how many objects you create, you can trace each custom object's parentage all the way back to the window object. Even the Object() function is a property of the window object, at least as far as the browser program is concerned. Too bad JavaScript doesn't provide a function for tracking such a hierarchy from one object all the way back to window. (I'm working on it...)

Properties

Object().__proto__

JavaScript 1.2+

Nav4+

Syntax

```
var x = objname.__proto__
```

The __proto__ property of Object() objects is a unique feature of Netscape browsers that Netscape documents in its Client Side JavaScript 1.5 Guide, but not its Reference. Essentially, when you create a new object, it includes a __proto__ property referring to the constructor function's prototype property. Listing 1.4 shows the connection between a constructor function's prototype property and the __proto__ property of objects the function constructs.

Listing 1.4   *A Demonstration of the* __proto__ *Property (Netscape Only)*

```
<?xml version="1.0" ?>
<!DOCTYPE html PUBLIC "-//W3C//DTD XHTML 1.0 Transitional//EN" "DTD/xhtml1-
transitional.dtd">
<html xmlns="http://www.w3.org/1999/xhtml" >
<head><title></title>
</head>
<body>
<p>
<script language="JavaScript" type="text/javascript">
<!--
function myFunc() {
    }

k = new myFunc()
document.write("k.__proto__ == myFunc.prototype:   ")
document.write(k.__proto__ == myFunc.prototype) // true
</script>
<!-- Result:
k.__proto__ == myFunc.prototype:   true
-->
</p>
</body>
</html>
```

Object().prototype

JavaScript1.1+, JScript3.0+

Nav3+, IE4+

Syntax

```
var x = objname.prototype
```

The `prototype` property of instances of `Object()` is primarily useful in setting basic properties and methods for a constructor function. Listing 1.5 takes a blank constructor function and "prototypes in" a property that all objects the constructor creates inherit.

Listing 1.5   *An Object Constructor Named* `myFunc`

```
<?xml version="1.0" ?>
<!DOCTYPE html PUBLIC "-//W3C//DTD XHTML 1.0 Transitional//EN"
    "DTD/xhtml1-transitional.dtd">
<html xmlns="http://www.w3.org/1999/xhtml" >
<head><title></title>
</head>
<body>
<p>
<script language="JavaScript" type="text/javascript">
<!--
function myFunc() {
    }
myFunc.prototype.author = "Alex Vincent"

var o1 = new myFunc()
var o2 = new myFunc()
document.write('o1.author: ' + o1.author + '<br />')
document.write('o2.author: ' + o2.author + '<br />')

myFunc.prototype.author = "Alexander J. Vincent"
document.write("After changing myFunc.prototype.author, o2.author is " +
o2.author)
//-->
</script>
<!-- Results:
o1.author:  Alex Vincent
o2.author:  Alex Vincent
```

Listing 1.5   *(continued)*

```
After changing myFunc.prototype.author, o2.author is Alexander J. Vincent
-->
</p>
</body>
</html>
```

In this design, all instances of `myFunc()` have access to a property named `author`, equal to my short name. In all cases, every instance of `myFunc()` descends from the `Object()` constructor function.

In addition, if two such constructors descend directly from `Object()`, you can have one constructor descend from the other, instead:

```
myFunc.prototype = new myObj()
```

This means all instances of `myFunc()` will inherit the properties and methods of an instance of `myObj()` as well, unless specifically overridden in the `myFunc.prototype` object's properties.

Further, if you want all objects descended from the `Object()` constructor to access a `language` property equal to `"JavaScript"`, you could say:

```
Object.prototype.language = "JavaScript"
```

Note this forces all objects, including instances of `Array()`, `Function()`, and so on, to have access to a common `language` property. This is because each of these objects descends from the `Object()` constructor, and possesses references to the properties of `Object.prototype` as well. If you want to add a `language` property to instances of `myFunc()` only, use the following instead:

```
myFunc.prototype.language = "JavaScript"
```

You can also ensure all objects except instances of `myFunc()` have access to a common `language` property of `"JavaScript"`, and `myFunc()` objects have access to a common `language` property of `"English"`:

```
Object.prototype.language="JavaScript"
myFunc.prototype.language="English"
```

The `myFunc` prototype takes priority over the more remote `Object` prototype, but for instances of `myFunc()` only.

The `prototype` property is also extremely useful for affecting native-type literals, ensuring they can access the property you prototyped to its counterpart constructor.

```
Number.prototype.add = add // a function I define elsewhere
x = 3
alert(x.add) // returns the add function
```

As a result of this code, all numbers and instances of `Number()` would now have access to the `add()` function as a method.

Methods

__defineGetter__()

JavaScript 1.5+

Nav6

Syntax

objname.__defineGetter__('*propname*',*getterFunc*)

The __defineGetter__() method of instances of `Object()` allows you to identify a function *getterFunc()* to return the value for *objname.propname* whenever the latter is referenced. Usually you accomplish this by retrieving other properties and performing some calculations on them. Listing 1.1 demonstrates the use of the __defineGetter__() function in some detail.

__defineSetter__()

JavaScript 1.5+

Nav6

Syntax

objname.__defineSetter__('*propname*',*getterFunc*)

The __defineSetter__() method of instances of `Object()` allows you to identify a function *setterFunc()* to intercept a value being assigned to *objname.propname*. With this method and __defineGetter__(), you can force the value which the object will return later to reflect any value you want, and also change other properties of *objname* at the same time.

I recommend you include a return value for your setter functions. Specifically, return the value you set if the operation of setting a value is successful. Listing 1.1 demonstrates the use of the __defineSetter__() function and the returned value in some detail.

constructor()

JavaScript 1.1+, JScript 3.0+

Nav3+, IE4+

Syntax

```
var x = objname.constructor
```

Both Netscape and Internet Explorer refer to the constructor() object belonging to all objects as a property. However, because the constructor() object is a function, you can consider it a method of each object, though one that does not affect its this object. In any case, it merely is a reference to the constructor function, which either generated the object or represents the type of literal it is. (Every literal can be constructed as an object type with the same value.)

```
var x = new Object()
alert(x.constructor) // returns Object constructor function
var y = new String("Hello World")
alert(y.constructor) // returns String constructor function
var z = 3.14159
alert(z.constructor)
// returns Number constructor function for the literal
```

The constructor() method is useful in two ways: identifying what function builds an object, and rebuilding the object to add properties. In the Fruit() example earlier, you may have noticed the constructor() method changed to the Fruit() function. This is because unless you use the this keyword, your constructor() method will not automatically reflect the function returning the object. (Even so, if you override the function's prototype property, you must set the constructor() method of the this object to the function.)

```
var k = new myObj()
alert(k.constructor) // returns myObj constructor function
```

Using constructor() in this fashion, you can distinguish all instances of myObj() from all other objects. Note this function is referred to without parentheses in finding the constructor() method. This creates a reference to the function, instead of whatever object the function may return if executed. Functions always execute when you attach parentheses to them. Without parentheses, they are `Function()` objects (see Chapter 2).

The other nice feature about constructors is they allow you to reconstruct a literal as an object so you can attach properties and methods to the object. Note the following code:

```
obj = "x"
obj.temp = new Object()
alert(obj.temp) // returns undefined
```

This is not good. However, `obj` does have a `constructor` method, the `String()` function object. If you add the following code,

```
if (!obj.temp) {
    obj = new obj.constructor(obj)
    obj.temp = new Object()
    }
alert(obj.temp) // returns [object Object]
```

the results are drastically different, and you can add any property you wish. (This is because the `obj` object is no longer a "string" type, but an "object" type, according to the `typeof` operator. If you change the value of `"x"`, perhaps saying `obj += "y"`, you lose the `temp` property again.)

Note you use the `obj` object three times in one line: first to assign a new value to the object, second to grab a reference to its `constructor()` method, and third to tell the constructor function what data source it should use (its argument). The result is to eliminate the need for a `prototype` property, which may affect more objects than you intend.

Use `prototype` to add references to properties and methods in all objects descending from a constructor function. Use `constructor()` to re-initialize specific objects for adding properties and methods, and only if it cannot accept properties and methods naturally.

eval()

JavaScript 1.1

Implemented in Nav3

Deprecated in Nav4

Removed in Nav6

See the `eval()` method in Chapter 11; it's identical. Do not use it as a method of any object. Internet Explorer has never supported it as a method of objects in general, but has supported it as a method of the `window` object.

hasOwnProperty()

JavaScript 1.5+, JScript 5.5+

Nav6, IE5.5

Syntax

```
var x = objname.hasOwnProperty(propname)
```

The `hasOwnProperty()` method of all objects checks for the existence of a property or method within the object. If you give the property or method name within quotes, like this:

```
alert(x.hasOwnProperty('propname')
```

it will return `true` if the property exists, or `false` if the property does not exist in the object.

isPrototypeOf()

JavaScript 1.5+, JScript 5.5+

Nav6, IE5.5

Syntax

```
var boolValue = objname.isPrototypeOf(constructor)
```

The `isPrototypeOf()` method of instances of `Object()` checks to see if another object is in the prototype chain of the first argument's object. The prototype chain refers to the `prototype` properties of each function object used to build an object.

This function will only return `true` for objects that are prototypes of other objects. Typically, you want to use this as a method of constructor functions' `prototype` properties:

```
alert(Object.isPrototypeOf(Object)) // returns false
alert(Object.prototype.isPrototypeOf(Object)) // returns true
```

The method returns true for any object earlier in the prototype chain, and regardless of any changes to earlier prototype objects. Note how the Object.prototype property appears in Listing 1.6.

Listing 1.6 *The Prototype Chain of an Object Discovered*

```
<?xml version="1.0" ?>
<!DOCTYPE html PUBLIC "-//W3C//DTD XHTML 1.0 Transitional//EN"
    "DTD/xhtml1-transitional.dtd">
<html xmlns="http://www.w3.org/1999/xhtml" >
<head><title></title>
</head>
<body>
<p>
<script language="JavaScript" type="text/javascript">
<!--
function myObj() {
    }

function myFunc() {
    }
myFunc.prototype = new myObj()
myFunc.prototype.language = "JavaScript"

k = new myFunc()
alert(myFunc.prototype.isPrototypeOf(k)) // returns true

myFunc.prototype.color = "red"

document.write("myObj.prototype.isPrototypeOf(k) = ")
document.write(myObj.prototype.isPrototypeOf(k)+ "<br />")
document.write("Object.prototype.isPrototypeOf(myObj) = ")
document.write(Object.prototype.isPrototypeOf(myObj) + "<br />")
document.write("Object.prototype.isPrototypeOf(k) = ") // returns true
document.write(Object.prototype.isPrototypeOf(k) + "<br />") // returns true
//-->
</script>
</p>
</body>
</html>
```

propertyIsEnumerable()

JavaScript 1.5+, JScript 5.5+

Nav6, IE5.5

Syntax

```
var boolValue = objname.propertyIsEnumerable(propertyName)
```

The propertyIsEnumerable() method of instances of Object() returns true if the object's property is meant to be detected by JavaScript via the for...in statement and is a property not inherited by prototype. It accesses the object behind the scenes to detect a hidden attribute (which JavaScript cannot change, apparently). Most objects would not possess this attribute. A few native objects, such as the window.open() method, do possess this attribute, and the function returns false.

Listing 1.7 shows the results of the propertyIsEnumerable() method in action.

Listing 1.7   *Custom Properties Are Enumerable on the Object to Which You Attach Them*

```
<?xml version="1.0" ?>
<!DOCTYPE html PUBLIC "-//W3C//DTD XHTML 1.0 Transitional//EN"
"DTD/xhtml1-transitional.dtd">
<html xmlns="http://www.w3.org/1999/xhtml" >
<head><title></title>
</head>
<body>
<p>
<script language="JavaScript" type="text/javascript">
<!--
Object.prototype.k = 3
var x = {}
for (property in x) {
    document.write("property: "+property+"<br />")
    }
var HTML = ""
HTML += ("x.propertyIsEnumerable('k') == ")
HTML += (x.propertyIsEnumerable('k') + "<br />")
HTML += ("Object.prototype.propertyIsEnumerable('k') == ")
HTML += (Object.prototype.propertyIsEnumerable('k') + "<br />")
HTML += ("x.propertyIsEnumerable('toString') == ")
HTML += (x.propertyIsEnumerable('toString') + "<br />")
```

Listing 1.7 *(continued)*

```
HTML += ("Object.prototype.propertyIsEnumerable('toString') == ")
HTML += (Object.prototype.propertyIsEnumerable('toString') + "<br />")
document.write(HTML)

//-->
</script>
<!-- Results:
property:  k
x.propertyIsEnumerable('k') == false
Object.prototype.propertyIsEnumerable('k') == true
x.propertyIsEnumerable('toString') == false
Object.prototype.propertyIsEnumerable('toString') == false
-->
</p>
</body>
</html>
```

This will return `true` if the hidden attribute, named `DontEnum`, does not apply to the property, and `false` if it does or if it is a property inherited from a prototype.

toLocaleString()

JavaScript 1.5+, JScript 5.5+

Nav6, IE5.5

Syntax

```
var x = objname.toLocaleString()
```

Aside from instances of `Date()`, this method of all objects simply returns the result of calling the `toString()` method. Neither Microsoft's nor Netscape's documentation lists the `toLocaleString()` method except for instances of `Date()`, but it is clearly supported. (`Date.prototype` has its own `toLocaleString()` method.)

toString()

JavaScript 1.1+, JScript 3.0+

Nav3+, IE4+

Syntax

```
var x = objname.toString()
```

The `toString()` method of all objects returns a string representation of the `this` object. Many of JavaScript's core object constructors override the `toString()` method of `Object.prototype` with their own. (The constructors that do are `Array()`, `Boolean()`, `Date()`, `String()`, `Number()`, and `Function()`. Internet Explorer's `Error()` object does as well. Netscape overrides the `toString()` method in its `RegExp()`, `JavaArray()` and `LiveConnect()` objects. See the appropriate chapters for details.)

If you do not replace the `toString()` method, and your object descends directly from a native object not listed above or from `Object()`, this method returns a string with the value "`[object objectType]`", where *objectType* is the name of the object type.

```
function myFunc() {
    }

x = new myFunc()
alert(x.toString()) // returns [object Object]
```

Listing 1.3 covers the importance of custom `toString()` method writing.

toSource()

JavaScript 1.3+

Nav4.06+

Syntax

```
var x = objName.toSource()
```

The `toSource()` method of all objects returns a string in most instances indicating how you can reconstruct the `this` object if you were to take the string as a piece of program code.

Listing 1.3 covers the importance of custom `toSource()` method writing.

valueOf()

JavaScript 1.1+, JScript 3.0+

Nav3+, IE4+

Syntax

```
var x = objname.valueOf()
```

The `valueOf()` method of all objects returns a literal form of the `this` object if possible, or the `this` object if not. Again, most core object constructors in JavaScript override this method. (`Array()`, `Boolean()`, `Date()`, `Function()`, `Number()`, and `String()`—again, see the appropriate chapters. Internet Explorer's `Error()` object does not have this method.)

For instances of `Object()`, and all other objects not overriding this method, the `valueOf()` method returns the object itself as a literal. Most of the time you won't notice a difference, but sometimes you will. Listing 4.2 in Chapter 4, "String()," gives an example.

unwatch()

JavaScript 1.2+

Nav4+

Syntax

`objname.unwatch("propname")`

This method of all objects clears a watchpoint set upon the this object. The single argument of this function is a property of the object for which a `watch()` function was called. Clearing the watch set for a property `obj.watch('propname',functionName)` is identical to the syntax listing for this method.

watch()

JavaScript 1.2+

Nav4+

Syntax

`objname.watch(propname, watchfunction)`

The `watch()` method for all objects sets a watchpoint on a particular property to intercept changes to the property. This highly valuable feature is available only for Netscape browsers. At this time, Internet Explorer features an `onpropertychange` event handler for DOM objects, but I have discovered no comparable feature for core objects.

The `watch()` method works quite simply. The first argument is a string containing the property name for the browser to observe. When a change happens to the property, the function listed as the second argument of watch() is called, with three arguments: the property name, the old value, and the new value.

In Listing 1.8, JavaScript assigns to the watched property in question the value the function returns.

Listing 1.8   *Forcing an Object to Remain Constant in Netscape Browsers*

```
<?xml version="1.0" ?>
<!DOCTYPE html PUBLIC "-//W3C//DTD XHTML 1.0 Transitional//EN"
    "DTD/xhtml1-transitional.dtd">
<html xmlns="http://www.w3.org/1999/xhtml" >
<head><title></title>
</head>
<body>
<p>
<script language="JavaScript" type="text/javascript">
<!--
myObj = new Object()
myObj.language="JavaScript"
myObj.color = "red"

function checker(propname, lastValue, currValue) {
    alert(this.language) // returns "JavaScript"
    return lastValue
    }

myObj.watch('color', checker)

myObj.color = "blue" // watch function "checker" called
document.write("myObj.color = " + myObj.color)
//-->
</script>
<!-- Results:
alerts "JavaScript"

writes:
myObj.color = "red"
-->

</p>
</body>
</html>
```

One thing Netscape doesn't mention in its documentation is you can treat a watching function as a method of the object it watches over; the `this` keyword in the function refers to the object calling it as a watch. In the preceding example, the `myObj` object has a `language` property, which `checker()` can refer to freely.

The power of the watch is evident: by returning the old value of the property, you can force an object to remain constant. Or, if you change one property or method of an object, you can update as many other properties or methods of the object as you need to. With arrays, a simple self-check becomes powerful, as Listing 1.9 demonstrates.

Listing 1.9   *Giving an Array's Element List Properties for Their Siblings*

```
<?xml version="1.0" ?>
<!DOCTYPE html PUBLIC "-//W3C//DTD XHTML 1.0 Transitional//EN"
    "DTD/xhtml1-transitional.dtd">
<html xmlns="http://www.w3.org/1999/xhtml" >
<head><title></title>
</head>
<body>
<p>
<script language="JavaScript" type="text/javascript">
<!--
function resetSiblings(propName, lastValue, currValue) {
    var flag = true
    for (var res = 0; (res < this.length)&&(flag); res++) {
        if (lastValue == this[res]) {
            var resLast = res - 1
            flag = false
            this.watch(res + 1, resetSiblings)
            }
        }
    this[resLast].next = currValue
    currValue.prev = this[resLast]
    return currValue
    }

myArray = new Array()
myArray[0] = new Number(0)
myArray.watch('1',resetSiblings)

myArray[1] = new Number(1)
document.write('[0].next is :' + myArray[0].next + "<br />")
document.write('[1].prev is :' + myArray[1].prev + "<br />")
```

Listing 1.9   *(continued)*

```
myArray[2] = new Number(2)
document.write("[1].next is :" + myArray[1].next)
//-->
</script>
<!-- Results:
[0].next is 1
[1].prev is 0
[1].next is 2
-->
</p>
</body>
</html>
```

The preceding code sets some rules in place. It defines a watch function named `resetSiblings()`. Two features about this function make it significant: it sets properties for `.next` and `.prev`, and it sets a new watch in place for each new element of its `this` object, the `myArray` object. Then, it adds a few elements to the array, and a few things happen behind the scenes.

Whenever you change the array's elements, it reflexively updates the `.next` and `.prev` properties of its elements. It's as if you defined `next()` and `prev()` functions to point to the respective elements, but without the parentheses. The "pseudo-functions" `next` and `prev` return the correct element of the array automatically.

Deleting a property directly affected by the `watch()` has no effect on the `watch()` attached. Resetting the property later will fire the `watch()`.

Example: Creating a Persistent Reference to `this`

Until recently, I believed the `prototype` property of objects meant a new copy of prototyped-in properties and methods would exist, instead of a reference to a common object. Though I was wrong, the reference allows me to finally solve a problem that has vexed me for more than two years.

In Chapter 15, "window," I cover the `setTimeout()` and `setInterval()` methods. Essentially, these allow you to create JavaScript commands the browser will execute later. The catch is you cannot use the keyword `this` in these string commands:

```
function one(arg) {
    if (arg) {
```

```
    setTimeout("alert(this.two(false))", 100) // throws exception
    }
  return 3
  }
y = {}
y.two = one
y.two(true)
```

The reference to this ends when the function ends. Likewise with the following code:

```
setTimeout("alert(" + this + ".toString())", 100) // throws exception
```

Now, you could easily have this end up saying "[object Object]".

After a fashion, it gets quite annoying.

So what I need is a common reference that you could find anywhere, but at the same time wouldn't create a conflict of object names. The prototype property allows you to create a reference in all objects to the common objects you designate, without generating new top-level object names.

Listing 1.10 demonstrates two functions to solve the problem, first by creating a reference, and then by attaching a method to always get the reference.

Listing 1.10 *Persistent References to "Instances"*

```
<?xml version="1.0" ?>
<!DOCTYPE html PUBLIC "-//W3C//DTD XHTML 1.0 Transitional//EN"
    "DTD/xhtml1-transitional.dtd">
<html xmlns="http://www.w3.org/1999/xhtml" >
<head><title></title>
</head>
<body>
<p>
<script language="JavaScript" type="text/javascript">
<!--
Object.prototype.instances = [""]

function addInstance() {
    if (!this.instanceIndex) {
        this.instanceIndex = this.instances.length
        this.instances[this.instanceIndex] = this
        }
    }
```

Listing 1.10   *(continued)*

```javascript
Object.prototype.addInstance = addInstance

function getInstanceName() {
   return "Object.instances["+this.instanceIndex+"]"
   }
Object.prototype.getInstanceName = getInstanceName

function testObj() {
   this.value = 0
   this.addInstance()
   }

function test(x) {
   if (x.value < 100) {
      x.value += 10
      HTML += x.value + "<br />"
      setTimeout("test(" + x.getInstanceName() + ")")
      } else {
      HTML += "Pass"
      document.write(HTML)
      }
   }

HTML = ""
k = new testObj()
test(k)

//-->
</script>

<!-- Results:
10
20
30
40
50
60
70
80
90
Pass
```

Example: Creating a Persistent Reference to `this`

Listing 1.10   *(continued)*

```
-->
</p>
</body>
</html>
```

First, you run the `addInstance()` method of any object to which you want a reference. If `this` doesn't have `instanceIndex` as a property, it creates the property as the `length` of the `instances` array.

In truth, `this` doesn't have an `instances` array. But each object can now reference the `instances` array, which I prototyped to `Object()`.

Armed with the `instances` array, `this` then attaches itself to the end of the array, so its `instanceIndex` property points directly to its own position in the `instances` array.

The `getInstanceName()` method is straightforward. It returns the `instances` array element corresponding to the `this` object's `instanceIndex` property—in other words, `this`. You can then safely use `getInstanceName()` in constructing the string:

```
setTimeout("alert(" + this.getInstanceName() + ".toString()", 100)
```

CHAPTER 2

Function()

Browser/JavaScript Version	Created By
Nav4/JavaScript 1.2	`function functionName(arguments) {source}` `functionName = new Function(arguments, source)`
IE4/JScript 3.0	`function functionName(arguments) {source}` `functionName = new Function(arguments, source)`

IE5/JScript 5.0	`function functionName(arguments) {source}`
	`functionName = new Function(arguments, source)`
	`functionName = function(arguments) {source}`

IE5.5/JScript 5.5	`function functionName(arguments) {source}`
	`functionName = new Function(arguments, source)`
	`functionName = function(arguments) {source}`

Nav6/JavaScript 1.5	`function functionName(arguments) {source}`
	`functionName = new Function(arguments, source)`
	`functionName = function(arguments) {source}`

ECMAScript 1st edition	`function functionName(arguments) {source}` `functionName = new Function(arguments, source)`

ECMAScript 3rd edition	`function functionName(arguments) {source}`
	`functionName = new Function(arguments, source)`
	`functionName = function(arguments) {source}`

> **Note**
> Implemented in Nav2+, IE3+
> Descends from `Object` object

Description

`Function` objects, or functions, are prepackaged sequences of code that must be called in order to execute. Applied as properties of an object, they become methods of the object. In the preceding chapter, you saw several examples of functions, including the `ineq` function.

Executing a Function

To execute a `Function()` object, you attach parentheses to the object, and any arguments you want passed to the function. To refer to the `Function()` object without executing the function, omit the parentheses and arguments. Listing 2.1 shows the difference between a function and its use as a constructor to create new objects.

Listing 2.1   *The Difference Between a Function and Its Executed Results*

```
<?xml version="1.0" ?>
<!DOCTYPE html PUBLIC "-//W3C//DTD XHTML 1.0 Transitional//EN"
➥"DTD/xhtml1-transitional.dtd">
<html xmlns="http://www.w3.org/1999/xhtml">
<head><title></title></head>
<body>
<script language="JavaScript" type="text/javascript">
<!--
function myFunc() {
    }
myObj = new myFunc()
alert(myObj.constructor) // returns myFunc function
myAlt = myFunc
alert(myAlt.constructor) // returns Function function
//-->
</script>
</body>
</html>
```

Declaring Objects Inside Functions

When declaring objects inside functions, the object can be local or global. If you omit var or const keywords before an object definition, you will find the object definition is global—that is, it can be found anywhere. Because many functions may use the same object names for different objects (I almost always use the name response for an object I want to return), you should prefix objects you want to remain only within the function with the var or const keywords. (See Chapter 11, "Global Object and Statements," for details.)

Browser Differences in Properties Returned

Listing 2.2 returns different results for Netscape 4 and 6, and Internet Explorer 5.

Listing 2.2   *The Object Model Rules for Inner Functions*

```
<?xml version="1.0" ?>
<!DOCTYPE html PUBLIC "-//W3C//DTD XHTML 1.0 Transitional//EN"
➥"DTD/xhtml1-transitional.dtd">
<html xmlns="http://www.w3.org/1999/xhtml">
<head><title></title></head>
<body>
<script language="JavaScript" type="text/javascript">
<!--
```

Listing 2.2   *(continued)*

```
function outer() {
   var response = this
   function inner() {
      return "inner"
      }
   response.inner = inner
   response.language = "JavaScript"
   return response
   }

for (property in outer) {alert(property)}
alert("Done")
alert(outer.inner)
alert(outer.response)
//-->
</script>
</body>
</html>
```

Netscape 4 returns `response` and `inner` as properties of the `outer` object. It returns the `inner` `Function()` object when asked for `outer.inner`, but returns `undefined` for `outer.response`.

Internet Explorer 5 returns no properties of the `outer` object. It also returns undefined for `outer.inner` and `outer.response`.

Netscape 6 returns "response" as the only property of the `outer` object. However, it returns undefined for `outer.response`. `outer.inner` is also undefined.

In light of this, it is far easier to use the `toString` method of `Function()` objects than `for...in` statements to determine what exactly is a property of a function.

Functions Defined Within Functions

Functions defined within functions are always local. Thus in Netscape 4 and 6, and Internet Explorer 5, `alert(inner)` throws an exception. `inner` exists as a function only within the `outer` function. The object that `outer` returns does have the `inner` method, but only because of the code `response.inner = inner`.

Functions Can Call Themselves: Recursion

One of the nice things about JavaScript is that when you call a function to execute, the code that executes is not the same as the `Function()` object. `Function()` objects are static sections of code. The function call is the function's code block being passed to the browser for execution.

This means the Function() object in question is actually independent of the code block it contains. It thus becomes fair game for a function's code block to call the function again. This is a concept called *recursion*.

One of the most common examples of recursion is the factorial () function. In mathematics, a factorial is n! = (n) * (n–1) * (n–2) * ... 2 * 1. To see this in JavaScript, refer to Listing 2.3.

Listing 2.3   *A Factorial Function by Recursion*

```
<?xml version="1.0" ?>
<!DOCTYPE html PUBLIC "-//W3C//DTD XHTML 1.0 Transitional//EN"
➥"DTD/xhtml1-transitional.dtd">
<html xmlns="http://www.w3.org/1999/xhtml">
<head><title></title></head>
<body>
<script language="JavaScript" type="text/javascript">
<!--
function factorial(n) {
   if (n > 1) {
      return n * factorial(n - 1)
      } else {
      return 1
      }
   }
//-->
</script>
</body>
</html>
```

If you call factorial(4), the code block calls factorial(3). This in turn calls factorial(2), which calls factorial(1). The factorial(1) function returns 1 to factorial(2). Then factorial(2) returns 2 * (1), or 2, to factorial(3). Now, factorial(3) returns 3 * (2), or 6, to factorial(4), and factorial(4) returns 4 * (6), or 24, to you.

Using recursion can backfire. If the function did not check for the value of n being greater than one, but simply returned n * factorial(n - 1), there is no point at which factorial(n - 1) will return an actual number before calling factorial (n - 2). The result is a series of factorial function calls, for which the browser will eventually throw an exception.

Programming for recursion is much like the idea of mathematical induction. Mathematical induction rests on the concept of finding a value when a condition n = 1, and then finding the value for any n = k + 1, given a value n = k. Thus, if you have the solution for n = 1, you can find the solution for n = 2. But then, you can also find the solution for n = 3. And then n = 4, and n = 5, and so on, and so forth. All you have to do is determine which value of n you want to look at.

Incidentally, the `factorial` function can be accomplished without recursion, by using a `for-` loop (see Listing 2.4).

Listing 2.4   A Factorial Function Without Recursion

```
<?xml version="1.0" ?>
<!DOCTYPE html PUBLIC "-//W3C//DTD XHTML 1.0 Transitional//EN"
➥"DTD/xhtml1-transitional.dtd">
<html xmlns="http://www.w3.org/1999/xhtml">
<head><title></title></head>
<body>
<script language="JavaScript" type="text/javascript">
<!--
function factorial(n) {
   var response = 1
   for (var k = 1; k <= n; k++) {
      response *= k
      }
   return response
   }
//-->
</script>
</body>
</html>
```

Most other functions that use recursion to find a value can also be rewritten to be as effective by using a loop instead of recursion. I personally suggest using an array, which gets more elements added to it as the search progresses, and a `for-` loop tied to the array's `length` property. Again, you have to determine where to break out of the loop (see Listing 2.5).

Listing 2.5   Another factorial() Function, Using Arrays in a Self-Expanding Loop

```
<?xml version="1.0" ?>
<!DOCTYPE html PUBLIC "-//W3C//DTD XHTML 1.0 Transitional//EN"
➥"DTD/xhtml1-transitional.dtd">
<html xmlns="http://www.w3.org/1999/xhtml">
```

Listing 2.5   *(continued)*

```
<head><title></title></head>
<body>
<script language="JavaScript" type="text/javascript">
<!--
function factorial(n) {
   var myArray = new Array()
   myArray[0] = 1
   for (k = 1; (k == myArray.length)&&(k <= n); k++) {
      myArray[k] = myArray[k - 1] * k
      }
   return myArray[n]
   }
//-->
</script>
</body>
</html>
```

Exiting from a Function Gracefully

The third edition of ECMAScript adds a `try...catch` statement for handling exceptions.
I will cover this statement in Chapter 12, "Evaluation and Comparison Operators," but
users of JavaScript prior to Netscape 6 and Internet Explorer 5 are not as fortunate.

One thing about functions is that once they start, they do not always stop halfway—
they may execute all the lines of code, as best they can. This means that if an error
happens in one line of code in a function, the next line typically will still execute. The
result is often an avalanche of errors, where one error causes the next. For users who
don't have `try...catch`, error handling is limited to the `onError` event handler,
described in Chapter 31 "Programmable Elements." This event handler is not
designed to repair damage or exit a function early.

However, emulating a `try...catch` for conditions that will cause errors (but aren't
errors themselves) is not terribly difficult. It merely involves a bit of logic. Note the
sample function in Listing 2.6.

Listing 2.6   *Emulating a* `try...catch` *Statement for Error-Causing Conditions*

```
<?xml version="1.0" ?>
<!DOCTYPE html PUBLIC "-//W3C//DTD XHTML 1.0 Transitional//EN"
➥"DTD/xhtml1-transitional.dtd">
<html xmlns="http://www.w3.org/1999/xhtml">
<head><title></title></head>
<body>
```

Listing 2.6   *(continued)*

```
<script language="JavaScript" type="text/javascript">
<!--
function myFunc() {
   varmyFunc_error = 0
   var response = this
   myFunc_label:
   if (1 == 1) {
/* main function body */
      }
   switch (myFunc_error) {
      case 0:
      break;
      default:
      alert("Function-specific error thrown, no error-handling defined")
      break;
      }
   return response
   }
//-->
</script>
</body>
</html>
```

Then, wherever you could experience a condition that would cause a function error in the following statements, you can include a check for that condition:

```
// code lines preceding
if (isNaN(x)) {
   myFunc_error = 1
   break myFunc_label
   }
alert(Math.sin(x))
// code lines following
```

The Math.sin method, as implemented naturally by JavaScript, can only accept numbers for arguments. By detecting first if x really isn't a number, I can set a custom error flag for the function, and break out of the if (1 == 1) {...} code block entirely. (That condition is there simply to force JavaScript to have a code block to break out of.)

The function then follows directly into the switch statement, and if the myFunc_error variable was changed, the relevant myFunc error code case (which you define) executes. From there, you can do anything you want. You could even insert a function call before or in place of `break myFunc_label` to execute special internal error handling (see Listing 2.7).

Listing 2.7   *Handling an Error-Causing Condition Within a Function*

```
<?xml version="1.0" ?>
<!DOCTYPE html PUBLIC "-//W3C//DTD XHTML 1.0 Transitional//EN"
➡"DTD/xhtml1-transitional.dtd">
<html xmlns="http://www.w3.org/1999/xhtml">
<head><title></title></head>
<body>
<script language="JavaScript" type="text/javascript">
<!--
function outer() {
   var response = this
   function inner() {
      response.value = 3
      }
   var outer_error = 0
   outer.inner = inner
   outer_label:
   if (1 == 1) {
      if (!response.value) {
         outer_error = 1
         outer.inner()
         break outer_label
         }
      outer.language = "JavaScript"
      }
/* appropriate switch and case statements */
   return response
   }
//-->
</script>
</body>
</html>
```

The `return` Statement Exits a Function

Whenever you use a `return` statement, it forces a function to end automatically; any following code does not execute. This can be useful if you've got your result already and want to avoid processing other code.

As well as simply using the `return` statement to exit a function it may also be used to return a value from the function.

Properties

Function().arity

JavaScript 1.2+

Nav4

Deprecated in Nav6

Syntax

```
functionname.arity
```

The `arity` property of the `Function()` object returns the number of parameters expected by the function and is essentially identical to the `Function().length` property. One wonders why Netscape included it at all, considering it was added after `Function().length`, and does the same thing. Netscape's removal of this extraneous function for Netscape 6 was a sensible action.

Function().arguments

JavaScript 1.1+, JScript 1.0+

Nav3+, IE4+

Syntax

arguments (within the function)

The `arguments` property of the `Function()` object is an array representing the arguments passed to the function, in order. (Note Netscape Navigator 4 gives the `arguments` property the properties and methods of `Array()` objects; Internet Explorer 5 and Netscape Navigator 6 do not.) I find this useful in naming certain default arguments of a function (see Listing 2.8).

Listing 2.8   *Determining the Length of the Arguments Property*

```
<?xml version="1.0" ?>
<!DOCTYPE html PUBLIC "-//W3C//DTD XHTML 1.0 Transitional//EN"
➥"DTD/xhtml1-transitional.dtd">
```

Listing 2.8   *(continued)*

```
<html xmlns="http://www.w3.org/1999/xhtml">
<head><title></title></head>
<body>
<script language="JavaScript" type="text/javascript">
<!--
function myFunc() {
    if (arguments.length > 0) {
        var language = arguments[0]
        } else {
        var language = "JavaScript"
        }
    // ...
    }
//-->
</script>
</body>
</html>
```

As you may have noticed, the arguments property exists as a local object, not needing a reference to its parent Function() object. The arguments property has a few properties of its own:

arguments.callee

JavaScript 1.2, JScript 5.5

Nav4, IE5.5

Syntax

```
arguments.callee
```

The arguments property of the Function() object is available only within the function, and refers to the function itself. It's a great way to get properties belonging to the Function() object.

arguments.caller

JavaScript 1.1

Nav3—4.05

Deprecated in Nav4.06+

Syntax

```
arguments.caller
```

The `caller` property of the `Function()` object refers to the `Function()` object which called the `Function()` object currently running. If the function was not called from another function, this returns `null` (and thus is not a method). Internet Explorer 5 and Netscape 4.06–4.75 support the same through the `Function()`.
`caller` property. Netscape 6 dZoes not support this property in any form.

> **Note**
> Netscape 6.01 recently reinstated the `Function().caller` syntax.

arguments.length

JavaScript 1.1+, JScript 2+

Implemented in Nav3+, IE4+

Syntax

```
arguments.length
```

The `length` property of the `Function()` object refers to the number of arguments actually passed to the function.

Function().caller

JavaScript 1.2, JScript 1.0+

Nav4.06—4.75, IE4+

Deprecated in Nav6

Syntax

```
functionname.caller
```

The `caller` property of the `Function()` object refers to the `Function()` object that called the `Function()` object currently running. If the function was not called from another function, this returns `null` (and thus is not a method). Netscape 3–4.05 support the same through the `arguments.caller` property.

> **Note**
> Netscape 6.01 recently reinstated the `Function().caller` syntax.

Function().length

JavaScript 1.1+, JScript 2.0+

Nav3+, IE4+

Syntax

```
functionname.length
```

The `length` property of the `Function()` object refers to the minimum number of arguments in a function definition. If you define `myFunc` to have two arguments:

```
myFunc = new Function(arg1, arg2, "")
alert(myFunc.length) // returns 2
```

Note carefully the difference between `arguments.length` and `Function().length` in this instance. The `length` property of the `Function()` object returns the number of arguments specified in the function definition. The `length` property of the `Function().arguments` object returns the actual number of arguments received. This difference is illustrated in Listing 2.9.

Listing 2.9   *The Difference Between* `Function().length` *and* `arguments.length`

```
<?xml version="1.0" ?>
<!DOCTYPE html PUBLIC "-//W3C//DTD XHTML 1.0 Transitional//EN"
➥"DTD/xhtml1-transitional.dtd">
<html xmlns="http://www.w3.org/1999/xhtml">
<head><title></title></head>
<body>
<script language="JavaScript" type="text/javascript">
<!--
function test() {
   alert(length) // returns 0
   alert(arguments.length) // returns 1 on the following function call
   }
test(3)
//-->
</script>
</body>
</html>
```

Methods

Function().apply

JavaScript 1.3+, JScript 5.5+

Nav4.06+, IE5.5

Syntax

```
functionname.apply(thisobj, argumentsArray)
```

The `apply()` method of the `Function()` object allows you to apply most functions as if they were methods of other objects. The first argument of this function is an object passed to the function as its `this` object. The second argument is an array passed to the function as its `arguments` property. You could easily say the following for a function that simply forwards the exact same conditions to `myFunc` as the calling function receives:

```
myFunc.apply(this, arguments)
```

Or you could define your own array, which you pass to the function as the `arguments` object.

Function().call

JavaScript 1.3+, JScript 5.5+

Nav4.06+, IE5.5

Syntax

```
functionname.call(thisobj, arg0, arg1, arg2...)
```

The `call()` method of the `Function()` object executes a method of one object in the context of the object that calls the method and is similar to the `Function().apply` method. The only difference between this method and `Function.apply()` is you pass the arguments of the function as individual arguments of this method, instead of condensed into an array:

```
myFunc.call(this, arguments[0], arguments[1], arguments[2]) // etc., etc.
```

You can pass whatever arguments you want using either method—it's mainly a difference in style.

Function().toString

JavaScript 1.2+, JScript 2.0+

Nav3+, IE4+

Overrides `Object().toString()`

Syntax

```
functionname.toString()
```

The `toString()` method of the `Function()` object returns a string representing the source code of the `Function()` object in question. If you use the `Function()` object constructor to construct a function, it will return the following:

```
function anonymous(argumentlist) {
// source code of the function
}
```

If you define the function using the `function` statement, it will return the following:

```
function functionname() {
// source code of the function
   }
```

If you define the function using the `function` operator (`myFunc = function() {}`), it will return the following:

```
function (argumentlist) {
// source code of the function
   }
```

Finally, if you call this for a function which JavaScript defines for you (such as `Object()` or `Function()`), you get the following:

```
function functionname() {
     [native code]
}
```

Sorry, you can't see the source code behind these functions. But you can most likely replace the function, as an example later in this chapter will demonstrate.

You may notice no indentation on the final bracket for the first form of the `toString()` method. This is because the browsers are building your function dynamically, from a string source code.

Note you cannot execute a `Function` (`myFunc.toString()`) command and expect to get the same `myFunc` object back. The reason for this is the first and last lines received back from the `toString()` method: the function statement with name, argument list, and opening bracket, and the function's closing bracket. If you were to execute the statement in the first line of this paragraph, you would get something like this:

```
function anonymous() {
function myFunc(argumentlist) {
// source code
    }
}
```

At the end of this chapter, I provide a quick little function to retrieve the source code for the function, let you call an additional function to edit that source, and re-initialize the function under its original name.

Function().toSource

JavaScript 1.3+

Nav4.06+

Overrides `Object.toSource()`

Syntax

```
functionname.toSource()
```

The `toSource()` method of the `Function()` object returns a string containing the source code of the `Function()` object. Equivalent to `Function.toString()`.

Function().valueOf

JavaScript 1.1+, JScript 2.0+

Nav3+, IE4+

Overrides `Object.valueOf()`

Syntax

```
functionname.valueOf()
```

The `valueOf()` method of the `Function()` object returns the `Function()` object itself. The difference between this method and the `toString()` method is that `toString()` always returns a `String` object.

Example: Using the Function() Objects' Source Codes

Most functions, including all user-defined functions, can be replaced with other Function() objects. This unique feature allows us to emulate two different procedures: editing the source code of a function, and also a concept known as *method overloading*.

The first listing can be used to prepare a Function() object to have its source code edited. The first argument of this function is the Function() object you want to edit. The second is a function you define to edit the source code (see Listing 2.10).

Listing 2.10   *The* SourceEdit() *Function and Sample Code*

```
<?xml version="1.0" ?>
<!DOCTYPE html PUBLIC "-//W3C//DTD XHTML 1.0 Transitional//EN"
➥"DTD/xhtml1-transitional.dtd">
<html xmlns="http://www.w3.org/1999/xhtml">
<head><title></title></head>
<body>
<script language="JavaScript" type="text/javascript">
<!--
function SourceEdit(source, editor) {
   var SEString = source.toString()
   var SEBrack = SEString.indexOf("{")
   var SECode = SEString.substring(SEBrack+1, SEString.length - 2)
   return new Function(editor(SECode))
   }

function test() {
   alert("yellow")
   }

function myEdit(mySource) {
   mySource+= "\n"
   mySource+= "alert('green')\n"
   return mySource
   }

test = SourceEdit(test, myEdit)
test() // returns two alerts:  yellow, green
//-->
</script>
</body>
</html>
```

The first statement in the `SourceEdit()` function converts the `Function()` object to a string. The second statement finds the first opening brace in the source code string—which is where the function will begin.

The third statement is the most important. It extracts a string slice, starting one character after the brace, and ending two characters before the original function's source code ends. You might wonder why `SourceEdit()` removes two characters instead of one. The reason is to ensure both Netscape and Internet Explorer get the full source code without the closing brace. (They return slightly different results for the `toString()` method—so slight it's barely worth mentioning.)

The fourth statement calls the `editor` argument function with the source code as its argument. You must define the editor function passed to the `SourceEdit()` function. Finally, `SourceEdit()` returns a new `Function()` object, initialized after your changes.

Outside the `SourceEdit()` function, the `test` object is redefined to equal the response of the `SourceEdit()` function. It still is a `Function()` object, but now it is a new one, reflecting the changes introduced by your editor function (in this case, `myEdit`).

This is somewhat useful if you run into a function someone else writes and you want to update it dynamically before it gets called. However, for some functions you can't do this—such as native code functions, like `Math.sin()`.

One of the scripts I've created is a script for creating what I believe are known as *arbitrary-precision numbers*. Basically, these are numbers that can have any number of digits you want—and perform the arithmetic correctly. The Java language from Sun Microsystems has an equivalent class called `java.math.BigDecimal`. Accordingly, I call my custom number objects `BigDecimal()` objects. (These objects are part of the eXtensible Number System, available via `http://mozcalc.mozdev.org`.)

Much as I like these new `BigDecimal()` objects, I can't pass them to `Math.sin()` or any other `Math` object method. This is because `Math.sin()` and other methods of the `Math` object will accept only `Number()` objects for their arguments. (You can find information on the `Number()` object constructor and the `Math` object in Chapters 7 and 8, respectively.) I also can't edit the source code for the `Math` object or its methods because these are native to JavaScript.

However, as I've noted before, I can replace most methods and functions with other functions. (Be very careful tampering with native code functions if you do decide to do this—you can cause some unintended effects if your code is awry. If you do decide to alter native code functions, have a very good reason for doing so, and leave a backup of the object behind, as I do.)

Example: Playing Around with Function() Objects' Source Codes

So let me define a new function which I want to call in place of `Math.sin()`, to intercept a function call. This is an equivalent of "method overloading" in some object-oriented languages (see Listing 2.11).

Listing 2.11   *A Function to Redirect to Other Functions, Based on Arguments*

```
<?xml version="1.0" ?>
<!DOCTYPE html PUBLIC "-//W3C//DTD XHTML 1.0 Transitional//EN"
➥"DTD/xhtml1-transitional.dtd">
<html xmlns="http://www.w3.org/1999/xhtml">
<head><title></title></head>
<body>
<script language="JavaScript" type="text/javascript">
<!--
function BigD_Math_sin_int(arg) {
    if ((arg.constructor == BigDecimal)) {
        return Math.BigD.sin(arg)
        } else {
        return Math.old.sin(arg)
        }
    }
Math.old = new Object()
Math.old.sin = Math.sin

Math.sin = BigD_Math_sin_int
//-->
</script>
</body>
</html>
```

Ignore for now the nonexistence of the `Math.BigD.sin` object. At first you might wonder how I can call on `Math.old.sin()` before `Math.old.sin()` is defined. However, I do not do this. I define a function which calls on `Math.old.sin()`, yes. But the function does not execute right away. The `Math.old` and `Math.old.sin` objects are defined before anyone has a chance to call on the `Math.sin()` function. Thus they are in place when the function does get called.

Finally, to make sure my function redirect executes every time, no matter who is using my script, I include a statement that replaces `Math.sin` with `BigD_Math_sin_int`, the redirect function.

> **Caution**
>
> Do not replace native code functions like this unless it is absolutely necessary—and then only to extend their power for specific cases. Always leave the default methods in place and accessible through any such redirecting function as if the redirection never took place. If you define a replacement for the `Math.sin` function and then call `Math.sin(Math.PI/2)`, it should still return 1. Failure to ensure your redirection function will respond correctly to the default functions guarantees other people using your scripts will run into errors and bugs they cannot trace to their own code—and much frustration for them as well.

CHAPTER 3

Array()

Browser/JavaScript Version	Created By

Nav4/JavaScript 1.2	`x = new Array(argument1, argument2...)`
	`x = new Array(length)`
	`x = new Array() // for zero-length arrays`
	`x = []`

IE4/JScript 3.0	`x = new Array(argument1, argument2...)`
	`x = new Array(length)`
	`x = new Array() // for zero-length arrays`

IE5/JScript 5.0	`x = new Array(argument1, argument2...)`
	`x = new Array(length)`
	`x = new Array() // for zero-length arrays`
	`x = []`

IE5.5 / JScript 5.5	`x = new Array(argument1, argument2...)`
	`x = new Array(length)`
	`x = new Array() // for zero-length arrays`
	`x = []`

Nav6/JavaScript 1.5	`x = new Array(argument1, argument2...)`
	`x = new Array(length)`
	`x = new Array() // for zero-length arrays`
	`x = []`

ECMAScript 1st edition	`x = new Array(argument1, argument2...)`
	`x = new Array(length)`
	`x = new Array() // for zero-length arrays`

ECMAScript 3rd edition	`x = new Array(argument1, argument2...)`
	`x = new Array(length)`
	`x = new Array() // for zero-length arrays`
	`x = []`

> **Note**
> Implemented in Nav3+, IE4+
> Descends from `Object()`

Description

Arrays, simply put, are objects that can have a series of properties ordered by an index number. Sometimes it matters to have a specific order to these properties, called elements of the array. Sometimes it does not, except to give you a grouping of common elements. (Do not confuse these elements with HTML elements, discussed in Part III, "Document Object Model for HTML Documents.")

Arrays are among the most useful features in JavaScript, simply for their flexibility. In the preceding two chapters, you saw a few examples of them. You will continue to see arrays throughout this book, in many of the examples. You will also see a few properties within this book that are special instances of Array(), as generated from strings and regular expressions.

Numbered and Unnumbered Properties of Arrays

Suppose you have an object myArray which is an array. Elements of the myArray object, the numbered properties, you can reach by referring to myArray[x], where x is the index number of the array indicating which element you want to reach.

(Only nonnegative integers less than 2^{32} - 1 qualify as index numbers for an array's elements.)

The first element of myArray is myArray[0]. The second is myArray[1]. The nth array element is myArray[n-1]. This is true for all arrays: they begin their element list at 0. The element list for myArray is the collection of all numbered elements, from myArray[0] to myArray[myArray.length-1]. The element list for any array object is defined similarly.

You can always add members to an array's element list. The most common way to do so is to refer to the length property of the array as an element list index number. (The length property, as I will note later in this chapter, is tied to the number of elements in the array; changes to one will reflect in the other.) For example:

```
myFunc = new Array()
// myFunc.length == 0
myFunc[myFunc.length] = new Object() // myFunc[0] is now an object
// myFunc.length == 1
myFunc[myFunc.length] = new Object() // myFunc[1] is now an object
// myFunc.length == 2
```

This assigns a value to myFunc[x] for a particular x (in the previous example, x = myFunc.length). At the same time, it extends the length of the array.

Although all elements of the array are properties of the array, not all properties of the array are elements of the array. You can add properties to an array that will not show up in the array's element list. For instance, you can add a method to any array much like you would add a method to other objects:

```
myArray.myMethod = myFunc
```

myArray will have the `myMethod` property, but it will not be between `myArray[0]` and `myArray[myArray.length-1]` unless you specifically add it as a member of the element list.

You cannot refer directly to an element's index number:

```
alert(myArray.0) // throws exception
```

This can get a bit confusing when you see an error message like this in IE: `myArray.0.constructor is not an object`. A numbered property like this is always an array's index number. Netscape's error message is clearer: `myArray[0] has no properties`.

An Array's Elements Can Be Any Object or Value

A new array begins only with the elements explicitly defined in the constructor or literal notation. You can assign to every element of the array whatever object or literal you wish. This includes objects, numbers, strings...whatever you want.

A common practice among JavaScripters is to create two-dimensional arrays by creating arrays as elements of a parent array:

```
myArray = new Array()
myArray[0] = new Array()
myArray[0][0] = new Object()
myArray[0][1] = new Object()
// ...
```

I have come up with a number of uses for arrays. One of them is the emulation of `java.math.BigDecimal()` objects, mentioned briefly in the preceding chapter. Each `BigDecimal()` object as I implement has an array of four-digit numbers, with an optional minus sign and a mandatory decimal point somewhere in the array's element list, which I designate as properties. By attaching various methods for comparison and arithmetic, I make it possible for JavaScript to handle numbers with any length of digits. (The script and its mathematics are beyond the scope of this book.)

Another use, featured as the example at the end of this chapter, is an extensible version of the `switch` statement, which is covered in Chapter 11, "The Global Object and Statements." By "extensible," I mean a developer can add cases to the switch at will. A similar concept allows developers to implement an emulation of method overloading, an advanced concept I covered in a limited fashion as the example in Chapter 2, "Function()." Still another use of arrays is my Basket of Windows script, which I feature as the example in Chapter 15, "window."

Populating an Array Automatically

You can define a few elements in the array (populate the array) as you define the array. The first way is to include the elements as arguments in the `Array()` constructor:

```
var myArray = new Array("red", "green", "blue")
```

This makes `myArray[0]` equal to `"red"`, `myArray[1]` equal to `"blue"`, and `myArray[2]` equal to `"green"`. Another way to populate an array is to use the array literal:

```
var myArray = ["red", "green", "blue"]
```

The exception to this rule of populating an array is when you use the `Array()` function and give it a nonnegative integer as its only argument:

```
var myArray = new Array(3)
```

This will instead create an array with a `length` property of 3. On the other hand,

```
var myArray = new Array("3")
```

will create an array with a `length` property of 1, and `myArray[0]` equal to `"3"`.

Properties

index

JavaScript 1.2+, JScript 5.5

Nav4+, IE4+

Syntax

```
var x = arrayObj.index
```

The `index` property of arrays reflects a number (which I will call n) such that (n–1) is the character where the first match starts. If `myArray` is the result of a `string`'s `match()` method call, `myArray.input.charAt(myArray.index)` is the first character of the first match.

The `index` property only applies to arrays generated by a `match()` method call of a string or an `exec()` method call of a regular expression. (See Chapters 4, "String()," and 9, "RegExp()," for more information.)

input

JavaScript 1.2+, JScript 5.5

Nav4+, IE4+

Syntax

```
var x = arrayObj.input
```

The `input` property of arrays reflects the `string` against which the `match()` method call executed. If `myArray` is the result of a `String().match()` method call, `myArray.input.charAt(myArray.index)` is the first character of the first match.

This property only applies to arrays generated by a `match()` method call of a string or an `exec()` method call of a regular expression. (See Chapters 4, "String()," and 9, "RegExp()," for more information.)

length

Nav3+, IE4+

Syntax

```
[var x =] arrayObj.length [= newLength]
```

The `length` property of arrays typically indicates the number of elements in the array's element list. This is a property JavaScript updates any time the `array` changes.

If you reduce the `length` value, JavaScript crops the array until the actual length matches the length you set. If you increase it, you add more `undefined` elements to the array. But you can do the same by simply assigning an object to the last element you want to define —everything between the last defined value and your new defined value exists as `undefined`.

```
myArray = ["red", "green","blue"]
myArray.length = 2
alert(myArray) // returns Array() object containing "red", "green"
```

However, the `length` property is more valuable when you retrieve its value than when you set it. The two most common uses are to go through each element in an array's element list, and to add new elements to the end of the element list.

The first uses a `for` statement loop:

```
for (var loop = 0; loop < myArray.length; loop++) { /* ... */ }
```

The second simply assigns a value to the element index just past the last element in the array:

```
myArray[myArray.length] = new Object()
```

Setting the `length` property to less than zero is forbidden; it actually caused a crash in Netscape 4 during one of my tests. Likewise, the `length` property must be an integer; decimal values are not allowed.

Methods

concat()

JavaScript 1.2+, JScript 3+

Nav4+, IE4+

Syntax

```
var x = arrayObj.concat(arrayObj2 [, arrayObj3...])
var x = arrayObj.concat(Obj0 [,Obj1...])
```

The `concat()` method of instances of `Array()` returns a new instance of `Array()` with the arguments in the `concat()` method attached to the end, after the `this` array's elements. If the argument is an `Array()` object, the `Array()` object's members will be appended, instead of the `Array()` object itself. This does not mean a two-dimensional array's second dimension will bubble up to directly append its elements:

```
myArray = new Array("3","4")
myAlt = ["5"]
alert(myArray.concat("2",myAlt, "6")) // returns ["3","4","2","5","6"]
alert(myArray.concat("2",myAlt, "6")[3].constructor)
// returns String() constructor function

myObj = new Array("x")
myObj[0] = new Array("x")

alert(myArray.concat("2", myObj )[3].constructor)
// returns Array() constructor function
```

This method does not change the array which it references.

join()

JavaScript 1.1, JScript 3+

Nav3+, IE4+

Syntax

```
var x = arrayObj.join(joinString)
```

The join() method of instances of Array() returns a string containing the elements of the array in the order they held within their element list, separated by the first argument of the method. For instance, if the argument was ",", all elements would have a comma separating them from other elements, and nothing else—no spaces, no line returns, and so on.

This method does not change the array which it references.

pop()

JavaScript 1.2+, JScript 5+

Nav4+, IE5.5

Syntax

```
var x = arrayObj.pop()
```

The pop() method of instances of Array() extracts the last element of the array and returns it to the user. The last element is removed from the array.

Developers targeting earlier browsers may emulate this using the script shown in Listing 3.1.

Listing 3.1   *Emulating* Array().pop

```
<?xml version="1.0" ?>
<!DOCTYPE html PUBLIC "-//W3C//DTD XHTML 1.0 Transitional//EN"
➥"DTD/xhtml1-transitional.dtd">
<html xmlns="http://www.w3.org/1999/xhtml" >
<head><title></title></head>
<body>
<script language="JavaScript" type="text/javascript">
<!--
```

Listing 3.1   *(continued)*

```
function Array_pop() {
   var response = this[this.length - 1]
   this.length--
   return response
   }

if (typeof(Array.prototype.pop) == "undefined") {
   Array.prototype.pop = Array_pop
   }
//-->
</script>
</body>
</html>
```

push()

JavaScript 1.2+, JScript 5.5+

Nav4+, IE5.5

Syntax

arrayObj.push(arg0[, arg1[, arg2...]])

The push() method of instances of Array() appends the arguments provided in the method to the end of the array. For Netscape 4.00–4.05, this method returns the last new element of the array. For Netscape 4.06+ and Internet Explorer 5.5, it returns the new length property of the array.

Developers targeting earlier browsers may emulate this using the script shown in Listing 3.2.

Listing 3.2   *Emulating* Array().push

```
<?xml version="1.0" ?>
<!DOCTYPE html PUBLIC "-//W3C//DTD XHTML 1.0 Transitional//EN"
➥"DTD/xhtml1-transitional.dtd">
<html xmlns="http://www.w3.org/1999/xhtml" >
<head><title></title></head>
<body>
<script language="JavaScript" type="text/javascript">
<!--
```

PART I   Core JavaScript

Listing 3.2   *(continued)*

```
function Array_push() {
   var A_p = 0
   for (A_p = 0; A_p < arguments.length; A_p++) {
      this[this.length] = arguments[A_p]
      }
   return this.length
   }

if (typeof Array.prototype.push == "undefined") {
   Array.prototype.push = Array_push
   }
//-->
</script>
</body>
</html>
```

reverse()

JavaScript 1.1+, JScript 3+

Nav3+, IE4+

Syntax

arrayObj.reverse()

The reverse() method of instances of Array() reverses the ordering of elements in the array's element list. For example, the first element becomes the last element, and vice versa.

shift()

JavaScript 1.2+, JScript 5.5+

Nav4+, IE5.5+

Syntax

var *x* = *arrayObj*.shift()

The shift() method of instances of Array() extracts the first element in the array object's element list and returns it. The element returned is removed from the array altogether.

Developers targeting earlier browsers may emulate this using the script shown in Listing 3.3.

Listing 3.3   *Emulating* `Array().shift`

```
<?xml version="1.0" ?>
<!DOCTYPE html PUBLIC "-//W3C//DTD XHTML 1.0 Transitional//EN" "DTD/xhtml1-
transitional.dtd">
<html xmlns="http://www.w3.org/1999/xhtml" >
<head><title></title></head>
<body>
<script language="JavaScript" type="text/javascript">
<!--
function Array_shift() {
   var A_s = 0
   var response = this[0]
   for (A_s = 0; A_s < this.length-1; A_s++) {
      this[A_s] = this[A_s + 1]
      }
   this.length--
   return response
   }

if (typeof Array.prototype.shift == "undefined") {
   Array_prototype.shift = Array_shift
   }
//-->
</script>
</body>
</html>
```

slice()

JavaScript 1.2+, JScript 3+

Nav4+, IE4+

Syntax

```
var x = arrayObj.slice(startPos, endPos)
```

The `slice()` method of instances of `Array()` returns the elements of the `this` array between and including those elements whose index numbers of the array match the two arguments for this function.

If the second argument is negative, the method stops copying the array's elements x units from the end of the array, where x is the absolute value of the second argument.

This method does not change the array it references.

sort()

JavaScript 1.1+, JScript 3+

Nav3+, IE4+

Syntax

arrayObj.sort([*funcname*])

The sort() method of instances of Array() sorts the this array's element list according to a function you provide as the method's only argument. Your function receives two arguments, which represent elements in the array. Create rules describing the relationships between these two objects. If you want the first element to precede the second after sorting, return +1 (or any positive number). If you want the first element to come after the second, return -1 (or any negative number). If the order does not matter, return 0.

If you do not provide such a function, JavaScript will sort your array by characters according to the language's ASCII codes. (This is a term indicating a listing of characters assigned special codes. ASCII codes are covered in more depth in Chapters 4, "String()" and 31, "Programable Elements.") Each element of the array this method treats as a string. This can result in 415 coming before 5. Write your sort functions carefully.

A typical sort function for numbers in an array is found in Listing 3.4, as the sortNumbers() function.

Listing 3.4   *Sorting an Array of Numbers*

```
<?xml version="1.0" ?>
<!DOCTYPE html PUBLIC "-//W3C//DTD XHTML 1.0 Transitional//EN"
➥"DTD/xhtml1-transitional.dtd">
<html xmlns="http://www.w3.org/1999/xhtml" >
<head><title></title></head>
<body>
<p>
<script language="JavaScript" type="text/javascript">
<!--
```

Listing 3.4   *(continued)*

```
function sortNumbers(first, second) {
   return first-second
   }

var x = [0, -4, 2, 6, 1]

document.write("[" + x + "] ")
x.sort(sortNumbers)
document.write("sorts as ["+ x +"].")
//-->
</script>

<!-- Result:
[0,-4,2,6,1] sorts as [-4,0,1,2,6].
-->
</p>
</body>
</html>
```

splice()

JavaScript 1.2+, JScript 5.5+

Nav4+, IE5.5+

Syntax

```
var x = arrayObj.splice(startIndex, cutTotal [, arg0 [, arg1...]])
```

The powerful splice() method of instances of Array() both removes and inserts elements based on the arguments you feed it. The first argument is an index number of the element list indicating where the method begins its work. The second argument tells the function how many elements of the array to remove starting at the indexed element. The remaining arguments are elements to add to the array after its indexed element.

If only one element of the array is to be returned, Netscape 4.00–4.05 browsers will return the element. Netscape 4.06+ and Internet Explorer 5.5 browsers will return an array containing the element as its only element. If two or more elements are to be returned, regardless of the circumstances, the method will return an array containing their values.

Developers targeting earlier browsers can emulate this using the script shown in Listing 3.5.

Listing 3.5   *Emulating* splice()

```
<?xml version="1.0" ?>
<!DOCTYPE html PUBLIC "-//W3C//DTD XHTML 1.0 Transitional//EN"
➥"DTD/xhtml1-transitional.dtd">
<html xmlns="http://www.w3.org/1999/xhtml" >
<head><title></title></head>
<body>
<script language="JavaScript" type="text/javascript">
<!--
function Array_splice(index, delTotal) {
   var temp = new Array()
   var response = new Array()
   var A_s = 0
   for (A_s = 0; A_s < index; A_s++) {
      temp[temp.length] = this[A_s]
      }
   for (A_s = 2; A_s < arguments.length; A_s++) {
      temp[temp.length] = arguments[A_s]
      }
   for (A_s = index + delTotal; A_s < this.length; A_s++) {
      temp[temp.length] = this[A_s]
      }
   for (A_s = 0; A_s < delTotal; A_s++) {
      response[A_s] = this[index + A_s]
      }
   this.length = 0
   for (A_s = 0; A_s < temp.length; A_s++) {
      this[this.length] = temp[A_s]
      }
   return response
   }

if (typeof Array.prototype.splice == "undefined") {
   Array.prototype.splice = Array_splice
   }
//-->
</script>
</body>
</html>
```

toString()

JavaScript 1.1+, JScript 3+

Nav3+, IE4+

Overrides `Object.prototype.toString()`

Syntax

```
var x = arrayObj.toString()
```

The `toString()` method of instances of `Array()` simply returns the same as `this.join(",")`. See the `join()` method description for details.

toSource()

JavaScript 1.3+

Nav4.05+

Overrides `Object.prototype.toSource()`

Syntax

```
var x = arrayObj.toSource()
```

The `toSource()` method of instances of `Array()` provides a source-code breakdown of the array in question. Primarily this is for debugging purposes only, though you can look at it to see just what's in your array. The function returns the array as an array literal: `["red","green","blue"]`

unshift()

JavaScript 1.2+, JScript 5.5+

Nav4+, IE5.5

Syntax

```
[var x =] arrayObj.unshift(arg0 [, arg1 [, arg2...]])
```

The `unshift()` method of instances of `Array()` inserts the arguments provided to the method at the beginning of the array, moving all other elements later in the chain. In Netscape 4+, it returns the new length of the `Array()` object.

Developers targeting earlier browsers may emulate this using the script shown in Listing 3.6.

Listing 3.6   *Emulating* unshift()

```
<?xml version="1.0" ?>
<!DOCTYPE html PUBLIC "-//W3C//DTD XHTML 1.0 Transitional//EN"
➥"DTD/xhtml1-transitional.dtd">
<html xmlns="http://www.w3.org/1999/xhtml" >
<head><title></title></head>
<body>
<script language="JavaScript" type="text/javascript">
<!--
function Array_unshift() {
    var A_u = 0
    for (A_u = this.length-1; A_u >= 0; A_u--) {
        this[A_u + arguments.length] = this[A_u]
        }
    for (A_u = 0; A_u < arguments.length; A_u++) {
        this[A_u] = arguments[A_u]
        }
    return this.length
    }

if (typeof Array.prototype.unshift == "undefined") {
    Array.prototype.unshift = Array_unshift
    }
//-->
</script>
</body>
</html>
```

valueOf()

JavaScript 1.1+, JScript 3.0+

Nav3+, IE4+

Overrides `Object.prototype.valueOf()`

Syntax

```
var x = arrayObj.valueOf()
```

The `valueOf()` method of instances of `Array()` returns the array itself as a literal object.

Example: An Extensible switch Function

One of the nice things about JavaScript is it is an object-oriented language. It's built around the concept of objects, which makes it very easy to extend the language and add capabilities, if you choose to do so. (I choose to do so.)

The switch statement of Chapter 11 is one of the statements I like. It allows me to compare an unknown value against a set of known values, and at the first match, execute a code block. This makes it a very powerful feature of the language. The only thing I don't like about it is the inability to add new known values to the set of known values it checks against. I would have to replace the function containing the switch statement with another function or edit the function's source code (see Chapter 2's example for details on this). Either way is a bit long for simply adding one more known value.

Enter arrays. As you know, arrays can handle any kind of object or literal value you throw at them in an element list. So suppose I have a list of known values in an array to check an unknown value against, and a code block to execute for each match. Then it's merely a matter of checking each element in the array until I have a match, and if there is no match, executing the default code.

The xswitch() script, which I provide here as Listing 3.7, does precisely this. The xSwitchObj() function creates the array and attaches a few methods for accessing the array. The xswitch() function returns a code block, which you can use an eval() method call to execute. Basically, the results have the same scope as a switch statement would have, but also thanks to the object-oriented design they support the capability to add new cases as the user sees fit.

Listing 3.7   *The* xswitch() *Script with a Sample Use*

```
<?xml version="1.0" ?>
<!DOCTYPE html PUBLIC "-//W3C//DTD XHTML 1.0 Transitional//EN"
➥"DTD/xhtml1-transitional.dtd">
<html xmlns="http://www.w3.org/1999/xhtml" >
<head><title></title></head>
<body>
<script language="JavaScript" type="text/javascript">
<!--
function xswitch(xswitch_1, switchObj) {
    var cases = switchObj.cases
    var xswitch_k = 0;
    var xswitch_flag = true
    var response = ""
```

Listing 3.7   *(continued)*

```
    for (xswitch_k = 0; (xswitch_k < cases.length)&&(xswitch_flag);
➥xswitch_k++) {
        if (xswitch_1 == cases[xswitch_k].xswitch_2) {
            response = cases[xswitch_k].code
            xswitch_flag = false
            }
        }
    if (xswitch_flag) {
        response = switchObj.def
        }
    return response
    }


function xswitchObj() {
    function xaddCase(xswitch_2, code) {
        this.cases[this.cases.length] = new Object()
        this.cases[this.cases.length-1].xswitch_2 = xswitch_2
        this.cases[this.cases.length-1].code = code
        }
    function xdefCase(code) {
        this.def = code
        }
    this.cases = []
    this.addCase = xaddCase
    this.defCase = xdefCase
    }

myCases = new xswitchObj()
myCases.defCase("alert('default case')")
myCases.addCase(1, "alert('one')")
myCases.addCase(2, "alert('two')")
eval(xswitch(3, myCases))
// executes an alert for the phrase "default case"

myCases.addCase(3, "alert('three')")
eval(xswitch(3, myCases))
// executes an alert for the word "three"
//-->
</script>
</body>
</html>
```

Example: An Extensible switch Function

Using the xswitch function is actually fairly easy. You start by defining a basic xswitchObj() object.

```
myCases = new xswitchObj()
```

This is not much—but I can define a default case for the new xswitchObj() object easily:

```
myCases.defCase("alert('default case')")
```

Adding individual cases to read before the default is equally easy:

```
myCases.addCase(1, "alert('one')")
myCases.addCase(2, "alert('two')")
```

Then, to actually execute the xswitch() as intended, I simply call an eval() of the xswitch() function, with the first argument being the unknown value mentioned previously, and the second being the xSwitchObj() object it is being compared against:

```
eval(xswitch(3, myCases))
// executes "alert('default case')" and pops up an alert
```

The xswitch() function searches the element list of the xswitchObj() array passed to it for the matching value in one of its properties. At the first match, it returns the code and breaks out of the loop. The default case reflects here because no case has been defined for the number 3. This, however, is easily solved:

```
myCases.addCase(3, "alert('three')")
```

This time, when you call

```
eval(xswitch(3, myCases))
```

the eval() method receives "alert('three')", which it then executes.

CHAPTER 4

String()

Browser/JavaScript Version	Created By
Nav4/JavaScript 1.2	`x = new String(stringValue)` `x = "stringValue"`
IE4/JScript 3.0	`x = new String(stringValue)` `x = "stringValue"`
IE5/JScript 5.0	`x = new String(stringValue)` `x = "stringValue"`
IE5.5/JScript 5.5	`x = new String(stringValue)` `x = "stringValue"`
IE6	`x = new String(stringValue)` `x = "stringValue"`
Nav6/JavaScript 1.5	`x = new String(stringValue)` `x = "stringValue"`
ECMAScript 1st edition	`x = new String(stringValue)` `x = "stringValue"`
ECMAScript 3rd edition	`x = new String(stringValue)` `x = "stringValue"`

> **Note**
> Implemented in Nav2+, IE3+
> Descends from `Object()`

Description

Strings are, simply put, everywhere, and not just in JavaScript. A string, in its simplest definition, is an object that can hold one piece of information—and that information can be anything whatsoever.

Interestingly, both Netscape and Internet Explorer take strings and add a lot of nonstandardized methods to them. Most of these methods are identically named and perform the same actions, relating to the HTML implementation of strings. The method's section is thus organized to present standardized ECMAScript methods first, with nonstandardized but agreed-upon methods later.

HTML and Strings: The Connection

JavaScript began as a language to augment the power Web browsers could offer in terms of functionality without relying on the server. One of the biggest features of JavaScript was the capability to retrieve many form input values (by this, I refer to more than just the `<input/>` tag) as strings. For example, the contents of an HTML text area element could be retrieved as a string:

```
var TextAreaValue = document.forms.formname.textareaname.value
```

In the preceding string, *formname* refers to the `name` attribute of the text area's parent form, and *textareaname* refers to the `name` attribute of the text area.

The designers of JavaScript also foresaw the desire for JavaScripters to write their own HTML code directly. (Very wise of them—it remains one of the most powerful features of JavaScript.) To accommodate this, both browsers added a large number of methods which JavaScripters could use to construct HTML source code, with all the advantages hypertext had to offer, namely basic styling of the text. (This includes boldface, font size, and color changes, italics, and the now-infamous blink effect.) It also included a method of the `document` object, covered in Chapter 23, "HTMLDocument/document," known as the `write()` method, for directly serving that string as HTML code for the browser to render.

JavaScript and Strings: The Other Connection

HTML wasn't the only thing about strings in JavaScript that made them special. A little background here: before I began working with JavaScript, I tinkered around quite a bit with the BASIC family of languages, particularly QBASIC from MS-DOS 5.0. One of the things I really did not like about QBASIC was the inability for me to construct a command string and execute it as a statement within the program. JavaScript solved this problem two ways. The first is a method of the global pseudo-object (covered in Chapter 11, "The Global Object and Statements") known as `eval()`. The second is the capability to use braces to construct property names, as I discuss in Chapter 13, "JavaScript Syntax." Listing 4.1 uses this latter format.

If you've got a series of HTML input elements named similarly, like `myInput0` to `myInput99`, you can use a `for-` statement loop to access them all, and only them (see Listing 4.1).

Listing 4.1   *Using Strings to Access Properties*

```
<?xml version="1.0" ?>
<!DOCTYPE html PUBLIC "-//W3C//DTD XHTML 1.0 Transitional//EN"
➥"DTD/xhtml1-transitional.dtd">
```

Listing 4.1   *(continued)*

```html
<html xmlns="http://www.w3.org/1999/xhtml" >
<head><title></title></head>
<body>
<form name="myForm">
<input type="input" name="myInput0" />
<input type="input" name="myInput1" />
<input type="input" name="myInput2" />
<input type="input" name="myInput3" />
<input type="input" name="myInput4" />
<input type="input" name="myInput5" />
<input type="input" name="myInput6" />
<input type="input" name="myInput7" />
<input type="input" name="myInput8" />
<input type="input" name="myInput9" />
</form>
<script language="JavaScript" type="text/javascript">
<!--
for (var myLoop = 0; myLoop <= 9; myLoop++) {
    document.forms.myForm["myInput" + myLoop].value = "JavaScript"
    }
//-->
</script>
</body>
</html>
```

This loop basically initializes every element between `myInput0` and `myInput9` as having a `value` attribute of `"JavaScript"`.

String HTML-Related Methods Are Not XHTML-Compliant

Sadly, the two browser companies have not yet updated their HTML-related methods of strings to comply with the XHTML 1.0 Recommendation from the W3C. Netscape 6 and Internet Explorer 5 still return uppercase tags for these methods. As far as compliance with XHTML 1.0 goes, it's mainly a simple matter of forcing the opening and closing tags to be lowercase instead of uppercase. If you intend to use these methods for writing code, I recommend replacing them to return lowercase tags instead of uppercase. (The procedure for replacing a function I cover as the main example of Chapter 2, "Function()".)

> **Note**
> By the time you read this, Netscape 6.1 will be XHTML-compliant; it will return lowercase tags for HTML methods.

Errata in JScript Documentation Regarding Strings

Microsoft reports in its JScript documentation that if you attempt to add a property to a string value ("This means a string defined by being in quotes."), the property you add applies then to all string values. This is simply not true, at least in Internet Explorer 5+. The following code proves, instead, that the property does not apply to either the new string value or the one you originally applied it to. See Listing 4.2.

Listing 4.2   *The Inability to Add Properties to a String Value*

```
<?xml version="1.0" ?>
<!DOCTYPE html PUBLIC "-//W3C//DTD XHTML 1.0 Transitional//EN"
➥"DTD/xhtml1-transitional.dtd">
<html xmlns="http://www.w3.org/1999/xhtml" >
<head><title></title></head>
<body>
<p>
<script language="JavaScript" type="text/javascript">
<!--
var test1 = "Hello, World"
var test2 = "Goodbye, cruel world"
test1.language = "JavaScript"
document.write("test2.language = " + test2.language + "<br />")
document.write("test1.language = " + test1.language)
//-->
</script>
</p>
<!-- Results:
test2.language = undefined
test1.language = undefined
-->
</body>
</html>
```

You can actually add properties and methods to a value by converting the value to an object using the value's `constructor` method, as I describe in Chapter 1, "Object()."

Properties

length

JavaScript 1.0+, JScript 1.0+

Nav2+, IE3+

Syntax

```
var x = stringObj.length
```

The `length` property of strings, simply put, is the number of characters in the string.

```
x = "1+2"
alert(x.length) // returns 3
```

Special characters, covered in Chapter 13, can be made of more than one character when you express them. However, as far as the string itself is concerned, they are one character each.

```
x = "1\n2"
alert(x.length) // returns 3
```

You cannot change the `length` property of a `String()` object. Replacing one `String()` object with another is the only way to change the `length`.

Methods

anchor

JavaScript 1.0+, JScript 1.0+

Nav2+, IE3+

Syntax

```
var x = stringObj.anchor(anchor)
```

The `anchor()` method of strings returns a copy of `this` as a string value, with a prefix and a suffix. The prefix is `"<A NAME='"`, plus the argument of the `anchor()` function, plus `"'>"`. The suffix is simply `"</A>"`.

> **Note**
> By the time you read this, Netscape 6.1 will be XHTML-compliant; it will return lowercase tags for the `anchor()` method.

big()

JavaScript 1.0+, JScript 1.0+

Nav2+, IE3+

Syntax

```
var x = stringObj.big()
```

The `big()` method of strings returns a copy of `this` as a string value, with a prefix and a suffix. The prefix is `"<BIG>"`, and the suffix is `"</BIG>"`.

> **Note**
> By the time you read this, Netscape 6.1 will be XHTML-compliant; it will return lowercase tags for the `big()` method.

blink()

JavaScript 1.0+, JScript 1.0+

Nav2+, IE3+

Syntax

```
var x = stringObj.blink()
```

The `blink()` method of strings returns a copy of `this` as a string value, with a prefix and a suffix. The prefix is `"<BLINK>"`, and the suffix is `"</BLINK>"`.

What is most amusing about this particular method is that while Internet Explorer 5 supports this method, it does not support the `<blink>` tag at all. In effect, this method is quite useless in Internet Explorer 5+ browsers.

Furthermore, the W3C has never included the `<blink>` tag in its HTML or XHTML Recommendations. It is therefore a proprietary Netscape tag. That, and the overall annoyance of the blinking effect (one of the main reasons W3C did not endorse it—another is accessibility issues), makes this one special effect which you may want to avoid.

> **Note**
> By the time you read this, Netscape 6.1 will return lowercase tags for the `blink()` method. (The `<blink>...</blink>` tags are not valid XHTML; Netscape has included them, disabled, in its implementation.)

bold()

JavaScript 1.0+, JScript 1.0+

Nav2+, IE3+

Syntax

```
var x = stringObj.bold()
```

The `bold()` method of strings returns a copy of this as a string value, with a prefix and a suffix. The prefix is `"<B>"`, and the suffix is `"</B>"`.

> **Note**
> By the time you read this, Netscape 6.1 will be XHTML-compliant; it will return lowercase tags for the `bold()` method.

charAt()

JavaScript 1.0+, JScript 1.0+

Nav2+, IE3+

Syntax

```
var x = stringObj.charAt(index)
```

The `charAt()` method of strings normally returns a one-character string. It's much like splitting this into an array of one-character strings, and returning the element of the array corresponding to the argument of the method. The first character of `myString` is `myString.charAt(0)`. The last character of `myString` is `myString.charAt(myString.length - 1)`.

If you give the `charAt()` method an invalid argument, it returns an empty string (`""`).

It's worth noting Netscape allows you to use brackets in place of the `charAt()` method:

```
var x = "Hello"
document.write("x.charAt(0) = " + x.charAt(0))
// Netscape, Internet Explorer:  x.charAt(0) = H
document.write("x[0] = " + x[0])
// Netscape:  x[0] = H
// Internet Explorer:  x[0] = undefined
```

charCodeAt()

JavaScript 1.2+, JScript 3.0+

Nav4+, IE4+

Syntax

```
var x = stringObj.charCodeAt(index)
```

The `charCodeAt()` method of strings returns a Unicode character code number for the character at this method's first argument. For most cases, this will be a nonnegative integer less than 256; in all cases, it is a nonnegative integer less than 65,536.

Character code numbers less than 256 correspond to the ASCII set of keys, where 32 is a space, 65 is the capital letter A, and 13 is the Enter key. Formally, the ASCII key set is a 128-key subset of ISO-Latin-1, a 256-key subset of Unicode.

concat()

JavaScript 1.1+, JScript 3.0+

Nav3+, IE4+

Syntax

```
var x = stringObj0.concat(stringObj1)
```

The `concat()` method of strings returns a string starting with `this` and appending each argument string to the end of the returned string, in order of appearance.

```
var x = "a"
alert(x.concat("b","c")) // returns "abc"
```

String().fixed

JavaScript 1.0+, JScript 1.0+

Nav2+, IE3+

Syntax

```
var x = stringObj.fixed()
```

The `fixed()` method of strings returns a copy of `this` as a string value with a prefix and a suffix. The prefix is `"<TT>"`, and the suffix is `"</TT>"`.

> **Note**
> By the time you read this, Netscape 6.1 will be XHTML-compliant; it will return lowercase tags for the `fixed()` method.

String().fontcolor

JavaScript 1.0+, JScript 1.0+

Nav2+, IE3+

Syntax

```
var x = stringObj.fontcolor(color)
```

The `fontcolor()` method of strings returns a copy of `this` as a string value, with a prefix and a suffix. The prefix is `"<FONT COLOR='"`, plus the first argument you supply this function, plus `"'>"`. The suffix is `"</FONT>"`.

> **Note**
> By the time you read this, Netscape 6.1 will be XHTML-compliant; it will return lowercase tags for the `fontcolor()` method.

String().fontsize

JavaScript 1.0+, JScript 1.0+

Nav2+, IE3+

Syntax

```
var x = stringObj.fontsize(sizechange)
```

The `fontsize()` method of strings returns a copy of `this` as a string value with a prefix and a suffix. The prefix is `"<FONT SIZE='"`, plus the first argument you supply this function, plus `"'>"`. The suffix is `"</FONT>"`.

> **Note**
> By the time you read this, Netscape 6.1 will be XHTML-compliant; it will return lowercase
> tags for the `fontsize()` method.

String.fromCharCode()

JavaScript 1.2+, JScript 3.0+

Nav4+, IE4+

Syntax

```
var x = String.fromCharCode(code0 [, code1 [, ... ]])
```

The `fromCharCode()` method is specific to the `String()` function object, not strings in
general. It allows you to construct a string from Unicode character code numbers
exclusively.

```
alert(String.fromCharCode(72, 69, 76, 76, 79, 32, 87, 79,
    82, 76, 68, 33)) // returns "HELLO WORLD!"
```

Netscape 4.00–4.05 users are restricted to the ISO-Latin-1 code set (ASCII) and 256
characters. Unicode appears in more detail in Chapter 13.

indexOf()

JavaScript 1.0+, JScript 1.0+

Nav2+, IE3+

Syntax

```
var x = stringObj.indexOf(stringObj1 [, startIndex])
```

The `indexOf()` method of strings allows you to find the first occurrence of a string
within the `this` string starting from a particular point in the string. The first argument
is the string you are searching for. The second, optional, argument is a starting point
you may wish to give. If you omit the second argument, the starting point becomes the
first character.

The method returns the index number of the first character to match after and
including the starting point (see Listing 4.3).

Listing 4.3   *A Demonstration of the* indexOf() *Method*

```
<?xml version="1.0" ?>
<!DOCTYPE html PUBLIC "-//W3C//DTD XHTML 1.0 Transitional//EN"
➥"DTD/xhtml1-transitional.dtd">
<html xmlns="http://www.w3.org/1999/xhtml" >
<head><title></title></head>
<body>
<p>Positions of o:<br />
<script language="JavaScript" type="text/javascript">
<!--
var myString = "The quick fox jumped over the lazy brown dogs."
document.write(myString.indexOf("o") + "<br />") // returns 11
document.write(myString.indexOf("o", 5) + "<br />") // returns 11
document.write("ov:  " + myString.indexOf("ov", 5) + "<br />") // returns 21
document.write(myString.indexOf("o", 11) + "<br />") // returns 11
document.write(myString.indexOf("o", 12) + "<br />") // returns 21
document.write(myString.indexOf("o", 43)) // returns -1
//-->
</script>
</p>
<!-- Returns:
Positions of o:
11
11
ov:   21
11
21
-1
-->
</body>
</html>
```

The value of -1 on the last document.write() is because after character 43, there are no more matches for the string "o". If the indexOf method does not find a match, it returns -1.

italics()

JavaScript 1.0+, JScript 1.0+

Nav2+, IE3+

Syntax

```
var x = stringObj.italics()
```

The italics() method of strings returns a copy of this as a string value with a prefix and a suffix. The prefix is "<I>", and the suffix is "</I>".

> **Note**
> By the time you read this, Netscape 6.1 will be XHTML-compliant; it will return lowercase tags for the italics() method.

lastIndexOf()

JavaScript 1.0+, JScript 1.0+

Nav2+, IE3+

Syntax

```
var x = stringObj.lastIndexOf(stringObj1[, endIndex])
```

The lastIndexOf() method of strings is the reverse of the indexOf() method. It searches from the end of the string to the beginning, and returns the index number of the first character to match in this, starting from the endpoint marked in the second argument. Lacking a second argument, the method simply starts at the end of this (see Listing 4.4).

Listing 4.4   *A Demonstration of the* lastIndexOf() *Method*

```
<?xml version="1.0" ?>
<!DOCTYPE html PUBLIC "-//W3C//DTD XHTML 1.0 Transitional//EN"
➥"DTD/xhtml1-transitional.dtd">
<html xmlns="http://www.w3.org/1999/xhtml" >
<head><title></title></head>
<body>
<p>Positions of o:<br/>
<script language="JavaScript" type="text/javascript">
<!--
var myString = "The quick fox jumped over the lazy brown dogs."
document.write(myString.lastIndexOf("o") + "<br />")
document.write(myString.lastIndexOf("o", 44) + "<br />")
document.write("ov:  " + myString.lastIndexOf("ov", 44) + "<br />")
```

Listing 4.4   *(continued)*

```
document.write(myString.lastIndexOf("o", 21) + "<br />")
document.write(myString.lastIndexOf("o", 11) + "<br />")
document.write(myString.lastIndexOf("o", 10))
//-->
</script>
</p>
<!-- Returns:
Positions of o:
42
42
ov:  21
21
11
-1
-->
</body>
</html>
```

Again, lacking a match, the method will return -1.

link()

JavaScript 1.0+, JScript 1.0+

Nav2+, IE3+

Syntax

```
var x = stringObj.link(URI)
```

The link() method of strings returns a copy of this as a string value, with a prefix and a suffix. The prefix is "<A HREF='", plus the first argument you supply this function, plus "'>". The suffix is "</A>".

> **Note**
> By the time you read this, Netscape 6.1 will be XHTML-compliant; it will return lowercase tags for the link() method.

match()

JavaScript 1.2+, JScript 1.2+

Nav4+, IE4+

Syntax

```
var x = stringObj.match(regexpObj)
```

The match() method of strings returns an array of matches generated by comparing this to the match's first argument, a RegExp() object. This method is similar to the RegExp().exec method, except the String() object and the RegExp() object are switched. Chapter 9, "RegExp()," covers regular expressions in JavaScript.

Listing 4.5 shows the use of the match() method to retrieve particular results:

Listing 4.5   *The* match() *of a String and Regular Expression*

```
<?xml version="1.0" ?>
<!DOCTYPE html PUBLIC "-//W3C//DTD XHTML 1.0 Transitional//EN"
➥"DTD/xhtml1-transitional.dtd">
<html xmlns="http://www.w3.org/1999/xhtml" >
<head><title></title></head>
<body>
<p>
<script language="JavaScript" type="text/javascript">
<!--
var myString = "The quick fox jumped over the lazy brown dogs."
var check = /\s../gi // space followed by any two characters
document.write(myString.match(check))
//-->
</script>
</p>
<!-- Returns (spaces significant):
 qu, fo, ju, ov, th, la, br, do
-->
</body>
</html>
```

replace()

JavaScript 1.2+, JScript 3.0+

Nav4+, IE4+

Syntax

stringObj.replace(*regexpObj*, *newString*)

The replace() method of strings performs a search through the this object based on the RegExp() object in the first argument. The matches the RegExp() object generates by this method are then replaced with the string returned in the second argument (either a string or a function designed to return a string.) Chapter 9, offers the use of the replace() method of strings as its example.

search()

JavaScript 1.2+, JScript 3.0+

Nav4+, IE4+

Syntax

stringObj.search(*regexpObj*)

The search() method of strings performs a search through the this object based on the RegExp() object in the first argument. It returns the index number of the first character in this matching the RegExp() object. If there is no match, it returns –1. This method is similar to the test() method of regular expressions, except the string and the regular expression are switched, and test() returns a Boolean true or false value. Listing 4.6 shows the first index of the word "white" in a string.

Listing 4.6   *The First Occurrence Index of a Regular-Expression Match*

```
<?xml version="1.0" ?>
<!DOCTYPE html PUBLIC "-//W3C//DTD XHTML 1.0 Transitional//EN"
➥"DTD/xhtml1-transitional.dtd">
<html xmlns="http://www.w3.org/1999/xhtml" >
<head><title></title></head>
<body>
<p>The first index of white occurs at character
<script language="JavaScript" type="text/javascript">
<!--
var myString = "I love white wine and white sunsets."
var check = /white/gi // space followed by any two characters
document.write(myString.search(check))
//-->
</script>
</p>
```

Listing 4.6 *(continued)*

```
<!-- Returns:
The first index of white occurs at character 7
-->
</body>
</html>
```

slice()

JavaScript 1.0+, JScript 3.0+

Nav2+, IE4+

Syntax

```
var x = stringObj.slice(startIndex [, endIndex])
```

The slice() method of strings returns a partial copy of this, starting at the index number provided in the first argument. If there is a second argument, it is considered the index number of the first character after the starting index not for copying.

If the second argument is less than the first but at least 0, the slice() method returns "". If the second argument is less than 0, the slice() method returns to the end of the string, but then chops off the end by the number of characters indicated in the second argument. For example, -1 indicates chopping one character. -2 indicates chopping two characters (see Listing 4.7).

Listing 4.7   *Dice and* slice *Strings*

```
<?xml version="1.0" ?>
<!DOCTYPE html PUBLIC "-//W3C//DTD XHTML 1.0 Transitional//EN"
➡"DTD/xhtml1-transitional.dtd">
<html xmlns="http://www.w3.org/1999/xhtml" >
<head><title></title></head>
<body>
<p>
<script language="JavaScript" type="text/javascript">
<!--
var language="JavaScript"
document.write(language.slice(0,4) + "<br />") // returns "Java"
document.write(language.slice(4,9) + "<br />") // returns "Scrip"
document.write(language.slice(4,-1) + "<br />") // returns "Scrip"
document.write(language.slice(4,3) + "<br />") // returns ""
```

Listing 4.7   *(continued)*

```
//-->
</script>
</p>
<!-- Results:
Java
Scrip
Scrip

-->
</body>
</html>
```

small()

JavaScript 1.0+, JScript 1.0+

Nav2+, IE3+

Syntax

```
var x = stringObj.small()
```

The small() method of strings returns a copy of this with a prefix and a suffix. The prefix is "<SMALL>", and the suffix is "</SMALL>".

> **Note**
> By the time you read this, Netscape 6.1 will be XHTML-compliant; it will return lowercase tags for the small() method.

split()

JavaScript 1.0+, JScript 3.0+

Nav3+, IE4+

Syntax

```
var x = stringObj.split(splitStr)
```

The split() method of strings returns an array containing sections of the string, as split by the string contained as its argument. (Netscape 4+, and Internet Explorer 4+

also support splitting this by a RegExp() object.) It is essentially the inverse of the join() method of arrays described in Chapter 3, "Array()."

I like to use this to break up a URL's search-query section into name-value pairs. One of my "dirty little tricks" is to send a window commands via the location.search property (see Listing 4.8).

Listing 4.8 *Executing Statements Contained in the* location.search *Property*

```
<?xml version="1.0" ?>
<!DOCTYPE html PUBLIC "-//W3C//DTD XHTML 1.0 Transitional//EN"
➥"DTD/xhtml1-transitional.dtd">
<html xmlns="http://www.w3.org/1999/xhtml" >
<head><title></title></head>
<body>
<p>
<script language="JavaScript" type="text/javascript">
<!--
// assuming 04list08.htm?document.write(34)
var x = 0
mySearch = location.search.substr(1).split("&")
for (x = 0; x <= mySearch.length; x++) {
   eval(mySearch[x])
   }
//-->
</script>
</p>
<!-- Results, assuming 04list08.htm?document.write(34):
34
-->
</body>
</html>
```

With this function, I could easily have a URL like this: http://www.mysite.com/mypage.htm?SelfWin=1&ParentWin=0. By executing the function, SelfWin=1 and ParentWin=0. The standardized format for separating URL form query elements from each other is the ampersand (&) character. So by splitting the string based on this character, and running each element of the resulting array through an eval() statement, the script can receive a few short commands from an outside source. (There are better ways, which I discuss in other chapters, but few of which will work receiving commands from pages outside your domain name.)

strike()

JavaScript 1.0+, JScript 1.0+

Nav2+, IE3+

Syntax

```
var x = stringObj.strike()
```

The `strike()` method of strings returns a copy of `this` as a string value with a prefix and a suffix. The prefix is `"<STRIKE>"`, and the suffix is `"</STRIKE>"`.

> **Note**
> By the time you read this, Netscape 6.1 will be XHTML-compliant; it will return lowercase tags for the `strike()` method.

sub()

JavaScript 1.0+, JScript 1.0+

Nav2+, IE3+

Syntax

```
var x = stringObj.sub()
```

The `sub()` method of strings returns a copy of `this` as a string value with a prefix and a suffix. The prefix is `"<SUB>"`, and the suffix is `"</SUB>"`.

> **Note**
> By the time you read this, Netscape 6.1 will be XHTML-compliant; it will return lowercase tags for the `sub()` method.

substr()

JavaScript 1.0+, JScript 3.0+

Nav2+, IE4+

Syntax

```
var x = stringObj.substr(startIndex [, length])
```

The `substr()` method of strings returns a partial copy of `this` as a string value, starting at the first index number given as its first argument. If there is a second argument, it becomes the `length` of the returned string, designating how many characters the `substr()` method copies from `this`. If there is no second argument, the `substr()` method copies to the end of the `this` object.

```
var x = "World Wide Web"
alert(x.substr(6, 4)) // returns "Wide"
```

substring()

JavaScript 1.0+, JScript 1.0+

Nav2+, IE3+

Syntax

```
var x = stringObj.substring(startIndex [, endIndex])
```

The `substring()` method of strings accepts for its arguments two index numbers of `this`, and returns a partial copy of `this`. The first number indicates the index number of the starting character. The last number indicates an index number one greater than the ending character's index number. (In other words, the character at the last index number is not included.)

```
var x = "World Wide Web"
alert(x.substring(6, 12)) // returns "Wide W"
```

sup()

JavaScript 1.0+, JScript 1.0+

Nav2+, IE3+

Syntax

```
var x = stringObj.sup()
```

The `sup()` method of strings returns a copy of `this` as a string value with a prefix and a suffix. The prefix is `"<sup>"`, and the suffix is `"</sup>"`.

> **Note**
> By the time you read this, Netscape 6.1 will be XHTML-compliant; it will return lowercase tags for the `sup()` method.

toLowerCase()

JavaScript 1.0+, JScript 1.0+

Nav2+, IE3+

Syntax

```
var x = stringObj.toLowerCase()
```

The `toLowerCase()` method of strings returns a new string matching this exactly, except that every character returned is a lowercase character (no capital letters).

```
var myString = "HELLO WORLD"
alert(myString.toLowerCase()) // returns "hello world"
```

toSource()

JavaScript 1.3+

Nav4.06+

Overrides `toSource()` method of `Object.prototype`

Syntax

```
var x = stringObj.toSource()
```

The `toSource()` method of strings returns a string value of the string you can use to reconstruct the string as an instance of `String()`.

```
var x = "Alex Vincent"
var y = x.toSource()
alert(y) // returns '(new String("Alex Vincent"))'
```

toString()

JavaScript 1.1+, JScript 3.0+

Nav3+, IE4+

Overrides `toString()` method of `Object.prototype`

Syntax

```
var x = stringObj.toString()
```

The `toString()` method of strings returns a string value of the string.

toUpperCase()

JavaScript 1.0+, JScript 1.0+

Nav2+, IE3+

Syntax

```
var x = stringObj.toUpperCase()
```

The `toUpperCase()` method of strings returns a new string matching `this` exactly, except that every character returned is an uppercase character (all capital letters).

```
var myString = "hello world"
alert(myString.toUpperCase()) // returns "HELLO WORLD"
```

valueOf()

JavaScript 1.1+, JScript 3.0+

Nav3+, IE4+

Overrides `valueOf()` method of `Object.prototype`

Syntax

```
var x = stringObj.valueOf()
```

The `valueOf()` method of strings returns a string value of the string.

Example: Strings in HTML

Earlier in this chapter, I demonstrated how the `location.search` object is a string by first taking a `substr()` of the object, and then applying `split()` to the results. However, many HTML elements, especially form elements, support `value` attributes. These attributes expose themselves to JavaScript in the form of strings.

With that in mind, it becomes very easy to construct a simple testbed for any JavaScript or HTML code you want to debug. All you really need is a few basic form elements and some JavaScript.

This listing is a simplified version of my own JavaScript Laboratory (JSLab) project's main editing page. I have deliberately removed all the bells and whistles for this example. Nonetheless, it is a handy tool for editing source code on-the-fly (see Listing 4.9).

Listing 4.9   *The JSLab Short Text Area View Page (Condensed)*

```
<?xml version="1.0" ?>
<!DOCTYPE html PUBLIC "-//W3C//DTD XHTML 1.0 Transitional//EN"
➥"DTD/xhtml1-transitional.dtd">
<html xmlns="http://www.w3.org/1999/xhtml" >
<head>
<title>JavaScript Laboratory Short TextArea Editing view</title>
<meta name="Author" content="Alexander J. Vincent">
<!-- TA-Short currently optimized for 640x480 resolution. -->

<script language="JavaScript" type="text/javascript">
<!--
function oneLiner() {
// executes the one-line JavaScript command
    eval(document.forms.JS.oneLine.value)
    }

function runCombo() {
    JSL = document.forms.JS
    eval(JSL.choice[JSL.choice.selectedIndex].value)
    }

function lab() {
    var testHTM = JSL.testScript.value

// check to see if popup is an open window; if not, open it
    if ((!window.popup)||(popup.closed)) {
        popup = window.open()
        }

    popup.document.write(testHTM)
    popup.document.close()
    popup.focus()
    }

//-->
</script>
</head>

<body>
<form name="JS">
<input type="text" size="30" name="oneLine" />
```

Listing 4.9   *(continued)*

```
<input type="button" onclick="runCombo()" value="Go!" size="5" />
<select name="choice">
    <option selected value="oneLiner()">Execute Command Line</option>
    <option value="location.href='javascript:'"
➥>JavaScript console (javascript:)</option>
    </select>
<input type="button" onclick="lab()" value="Execute!" />
<br />
<textarea rows="14" cols="60" name="testScript"></textarea>
</body>
</html>
```

What this does is first build a page with a text input area, a select box, two buttons, and an empty text area. Figure 4.1 shows what the page looks like.

Figure 4.1
Short text area editing page of JSLab.

When you set the combo box to Execute Command Line and click the Go! button, it executes the runCombo() function, which executes the selected option's value (namely, oneLiner()). The oneLiner() function executes, which basically runs one line of code:

```
eval(document.forms.JS.oneLine.value)
```

The string contained in the `oneLine` `<input />` element now becomes a statement for JavaScript to execute immediately. This comes in very handy for testing brief statements quickly.

If you don't like that and you're using Netscape 4+, you can change the combo box to JavaScript Console and click the Go! button again. This pops up Netscape's JavaScript Console, used for spelling out JavaScript errors and giving you another one-line input box.

The `lab()` function, activated `onClick` of the "Execute!" button, is a bit more complex. First, it checks to see if a particular pop-up window is open. If not, the function opens the pop-up window. Then it takes the text area's value attribute (again, a string) and uses a `popup.document.write()` method to transfer the value attribute's contents to the pop-up window. Close the data stream using `popup.document.close()` and transfer view to the pop-up using `popup.focus()`, and you can see the HTML source code you spent a few minutes making small changes to update instantly!

This minimal design is easily extensible. By using a check box, a user can indicate whether the text area contains HTML markup or a JavaScript, and the developer can permit this by adding HTML prefixes and suffixes to wrap the JavaScript in HTML code. You can activate Event handlers such as `window.onFocus`, `window.onBlur`, and `window.onLoad` as well. With a server-side database, you could even build an entire code-editing platform.

Note

In case you're wondering, JSLab is an implementation of a code-editing platform using this basic text area editing concept. One of its features is the capability to permit editing and revision of its own code.

Plus, in a pinch, if you're looking to debug something really quick, it comes in handy in avoiding multiple file saves.

CHAPTER 5

Boolean()

Browser/JavaScript Version	Created By
Nav4/JavaScript 1.2	`x = new Boolean()` `x = (comparison)`
IE4/JScript 3.0	`x = new Boolean()` `x = (comparison)`
IE5/JScript 5.0	`x = new Boolean()` `x = (comparison)`
IE5.5/JScript 5.5	`x = new Boolean()` `x = (comparison)`
Nav6/JavaScript 1.5	`x = new Boolean()` `x = (comparison)`
ECMAScript 1st edition	`x = new Boolean()` `x = (comparison)`
ECMAScript 3rd edition	`x = new Boolean()` `x = (comparison)`

> **Note**
> Implemented in NN3+, IE4+
>
> Descends from `Object()`

Description

There are really only two native instances of `Boolean()` from a JavaScript point of view: the `true` value and the `false` value. JavaScript provides the `Boolean()` constructor function for three reasons. The first is to give a simple conversion function into a true/false setting. The second is to associate certain properties and methods via prototyping with the `true` and `false` values, in order to make them true objects in the language. The third is to provide for the construction of instances of `Boolean()` that can accept new properties.

Defining Boolean() Objects by Comparison

Whenever you ask JavaScript to compare two items in an `if...else` statement, you create a `boolean` value that determines which branch of the `if...else` statement executes.

Description

```
if (y == 3) { alert("true") } else { alert("false") }
```

In this code, y == 3 becomes a boolean value. It's either true or false. If it is true, the branch following the if statement executes. If it is false, the branch following the optional else statement executes.

The code y == 3 is a comparison. Using a comparison operator like this (or others I describe in Chapter 12, "Operators"), you create a new boolean value you can assign to an object name. Listing 5.1 clarifies this.

Listing 5.1   *Assigning a Variable a Boolean Value by Comparison*

```
<?xml version="1.0" ?>
<!DOCTYPE html PUBLIC "-//W3C//DTD XHTML 1.0 Transitional//EN"
➥"DTD/xhtml1-transitional.dtd">
<html xmlns="http://www.w3.org/1999/xhtml" >
<head><title></title></head>
<body>
<script language="JavaScript" type="text/javascript">
<!--
y = 4
x = (y == 3) // false in this case
alert(x.constructor) // returns Boolean() constructor function
//-->
</script>
</body>
</html>
```

Technically, you do not need the parentheses around a definition. In Listing 5.1, you would be fine with:

```
x = y == 3
```

I personally recommend you use the parentheses anyway. It helps others to see what's a comparison and what's an assignment. (For instance, the beginner to JavaScript might think x and y were receiving the value 3.)

Defining Boolean() Object Values by the Boolean() Function

If you want to see what your objects look like to if...else statements without a comparison, the Boolean() function is tailored for you. Most values (including all objects), when applied as the first argument of the Boolean() function, return true. A few notable exceptions can be seen in Listing 5.2.

Listing 5.2   *A* `Boolean()` *Function Call Returning* `false`, *Based on Arguments*

```
<?xml version="1.0" ?>
<!DOCTYPE html PUBLIC "-//W3C//DTD XHTML 1.0 Transitional//EN"
➥"DTD/xhtml1-transitional.dtd">
<html xmlns="http://www.w3.org/1999/xhtml" >
<head><title></title></head>
<body>
<script language="JavaScript" type="text/javascript">
<!--
var a = Boolean(false)
var b = Boolean(0)
var c = Boolean(null)
var d = Boolean(Number.NaN)
var e = Boolean("")
var f = Boolean()

alert(a + "\n" + b + "\n" + c + "\n" + d + "\n" + e + "\n" + f)
// returns false six times
//-->
</script>
</body>
</html>
```

All other objects passed to the `Boolean()` function return `true`, including:

```
var g = Boolean("false")
```

The reason this returns `true` is that you aren't passing `false` to the `Boolean()` function; you are passing a string. The string is not empty, and by the ECMAScript standards, the function must return `true`.

Properties

Instances of `Boolean()` inherit the properties of the `Object.prototype` object, and do not override any of them.

Methods

toSource()

JavaScript 1.3+

Nav4.06+

Overrides `Object.prototype.toSource()`

Syntax

```
var x = BoolObj.toSource()
```

The `toSource()` function of `boolean` values returns a source-code representation of a new `Boolean()` object as a string, for later construction. If the `boolean` value is `true`, this function returns the string `"(new Boolean(true))"`. If the `Boolean()` object is `false`, this function returns the string `"(new Boolean(false))"`.

toString()

JavaScript 1.1+, JScript 3.0+

Nav3+, IE4+

Overrides `Object.prototype.toString()`

Syntax

```
var x = BoolObj.toString()
```

The `toString()` method of `boolean` values returns a string representation of the actual value. If the `boolean` value is `true`, this method returns the string `"true"`. If the `boolean` value is `false`, this method returns the string `"false"`.

valueOf()

JavaScript 1.1+, JScript 3.0+

Nav3+, IE4+

Overrides `Object.prototype.valueOf()`

Syntax

```
var x = BoolObj.valueOf()
```

The valueOf() method of boolean values returns the explicit value of the this object, either true or false, depending on the value the Boolean() object assumed upon creation.

Example: Shorthand for an if Statement

Sometimes code expressions get very long. To me, this can be a bit irritating, especially when I'm trying to debug something that just stretches out. More than that, when attempting to evaluate a compounded true or false statement, keeping track of the parentheses becomes a bit of a hassle.

However, because you can assign true or false values to objects before an if statement, and use the if statement based on their values, you can save some horizontal space by adding a few lines of code just before an if statement (see Listing 5.3).

Listing 5.3   *An if Statement Based on Pre-existing Conditions*

```
<?xml version="1.0" ?>
<!DOCTYPE html PUBLIC "-//W3C//DTD XHTML 1.0 Transitional//EN"
➥"DTD/xhtml1-transitional.dtd">
<html xmlns="http://www.w3.org/1999/xhtml" >
<head><title></title></head>
<body>
<script language="JavaScript" type="text/javascript">
<!--
var a = 3
var b = 4
var c = 3

var p = (a == b) // false
var q = (a == c) // true

if (p && q) {
   alert("p and q")
   } else {
   alert("not p or not q")
   } // returns "not p or not q"

if (p || q) {
   alert("p or q")
```

Example: Shorthand for an `if` Statement

Listing 5.3   *(continued)*

```
   } else {
   alert("not p and not q")
   } // returns "p or q"
//-->
</script>
</body>
</html>
```

What happens here is simple. First, you establish values for p and q, namely, `false` and `true` respectively. Then, your `if` statement takes the values from these values and compares their values, first in a "this and that" situation (the && operator) and then in a "this or that" situation (the || operator)—covered in Chapter 12, "Operators").

If you do not keep up with changes in your underlying conditions, the situation found in Listing 5.4 may occur.

Listing 5.4   *A Flawed `if` Statement Caused by Pre-existing Conditions*

```
<?xml version="1.0" ?>
<!DOCTYPE html PUBLIC "-//W3C//DTD XHTML 1.0 Transitional//EN"
➥"DTD/xhtml1-transitional.dtd">
<html xmlns="http://www.w3.org/1999/xhtml" >
<head><title></title></head>
<body>
<script language="JavaScript" type="text/javascript">
<!--
var a = 3
var b = 4
var c = 3

var p = (a == b)
var q = (a == c)

if (p && q) {
   alert("p and q")
   } else {
   alert("not p or not q")
   } // returns "not p or not q"

b = 3

if (p && q) {
```

Listing 5.4 *(continued)*

```
    alert("p and q")
    } else {
    alert("not p or not q")
    } // returns "not p or not q"
//-->
</script>
</body>
</html>
```

In this case, one of the prerequisites changes, but the condition evaluated does not. You must re-evaluate any such conditions immediately before the if statement to which they apply.

CHAPTER 6

Date()

Browser/JavaScript Version	Created By
Nav4/JavaScript 1.2	x = new Date()
IE4/JScript 3.0	x = new Date()
IE5/JScript 5.0	x = new Date()
IE5.5/JScript 5.5	x = new Date()
Nav6/JavaScript 1.5	x = new Date()
ECMAScript 1st edition	x = new Date()
ECMAScript 3rd edition	x = new Date()

> **Note**
> Implemented in Nav2+, IE3+

Description

When JavaScripters talk about getting a date, often we aren't referring to the kind involving a gourmet restaurant. Instead, we may be talking about getting a date from the browser, via the `Date()` object. JavaScript provides this kind of object specifically for us to have a reference to moments of time as objects in the browser.

A Special Number Line for Time

The nice thing about JavaScript is the designers knew Web page developers would want some way to reference dates and times in JavaScript. Therefore, the designers of the language created a special application of the number line for handling time. 0 in the context of this number line referred to precisely January 1st, 1970, at midnight: the start of that particular year. They also declared increments of 1 along this number line to be increases of one millisecond. (A millisecond is 1/1000th of a second.) Thus, 1,000 would indicate 12:00:01 a.m. on January 1st, 1970 in GMT (Greenwich Mean Time) time, precisely.

At this rate, midnight on January 2nd, 1970, GMT would be equal to 86,400,000 on this timeline. In case you wonder how JavaScript can evaluate time on the scale of decades, bear in mind JavaScript supports number values greater than 9 quadrillion (9 with 15 zeroes after it). This translates to over 250,000 years on either side of 1970 A.D. At the time I write this, the current number on the current instance of `Date()`'s number line has just passed 983,946,267,970 (early March, 2001).

JavaScript's Interpretation of This Timeline

JavaScript provides an almost complete interface for reading, setting, and adjusting instances of Date(). (Note this does not mean adjusting actual time on the computer). The time the instance of Date() receives is based on the computer's clock, and JavaScript cannot change the computer's clock under any circumstances. For the most part, you can get or set any information about a particular instance of Date() (not what happened then) you want: UTC (Universal Coordinated Time), local time, day of the month or week, month, year, hour, minute, second, millisecond, time zone.

About the only information about a particular instance of Date() you can't get directly is whether Daylight Savings Time is in effect on the client computer. (But you can get this information indirectly—see the example at the end of this chapter.)

Determining a Specific Date

If you use the Date() constructor function with no arguments, the browser returns the current date and time in the returned instance of Date(). JavaScript assumes (correctly) that you as the developer cannot possibly know when one of your scripts executes. So in the instance where you provide no arguments, it just defaults to "now."

On the other hand, you can provide certain arguments to construct a particular instance of Date() (millisecond in time). If you give a single numeric argument, that indicates the number index on the special time number line mentioned earlier; the number of milliseconds elapsed since January 1st, 1970, at midnight.

```
var y = new Date(1000) // returns January 1st, 1970 at 12:00:01 a.m.
```

You can also specify a date by giving numeric arguments for year, month, and day in that order. Additional arguments can be hour, minute, second, and millisecond, respectively, but these are not required.

```
var z = new Date(2001, 2, 8, 21, 0, 1) // 2001, March, 8, at 22:00:01
```

Notice the month says 2. This is because the month starts from a zero-based index: January is the "0th" month. If you omit any optional arguments for a time of day, the arguments missing are assumed to equal 0.

The month value should be between 0 and 11. The day value must be between 1 and 31. The hour value must be between 0 and 23. The minute and second values must be between 0 and 59. The millisecond value must be between 0 and 999. (All the preceding ranges include the ends of the range: a month value of 11 or 0 is acceptable, for instance.)

Part I Core JavaScript

Caution

If you exceed the common calendar definitions for a piece of the instance of `Date()`, it does not throw any exceptions. It simply rolls over:

```
var w = new Date(2000, 12, 1, 0, 0, 0) // January 1, 2001 at midnight
```

Finally, you can pass a string containing a correctly formatted UTC date string to the `Date()` function to create its corresponding `Date()` object.

```
var x = new Date("Thu Mar 8 21:00:01 PST 2001"))
```

Instances of Date() Obey the Rules of Number Arithmetic

The comparison and arithmetic operators apply to instances of `Date()` as of JavaScript1.1. This proves quite useful when you want to evaluate how long a particular piece of code takes to run, using the `Date()` function to build a stopwatch function.

Note that for most JavaScript scenarios, this is not terribly useful: most JavaScript functions execute in less than one millisecond. Thus, they cannot be measured accurately for execution time. However, it is useful if you wish to find out how long a Web page takes to load (see Listing 6.1).

Listing 6.1 *Calculating Load Time for a Web Page*

```
<?xml version="1.0" ?>
<!DOCTYPE html PUBLIC "-//W3C//DTD XHTML 1.0 Transitional//EN"
➥"DTD/xhtml1-transitional.dtd">
<html xmlns="http://www.w3.org/1999/xhtml" >
<head><title></title></head>
<body onLoad='stopClock();loaded = true'>
<script language='JavaScript' type='text/javascript'>
<!--
startDate = new Date()

function stopClock() {
   var stopDate = new Date()
   msElapsed = stopDate-startDate
   document.getElementById("Timer").write(msElapsed)
   }
//-->
</script>
<!-- Results are a positive integer of elapsed milliseconds -->
```

Listing 6.1 *(continued)*

```
<div id="Timer"></div>
</body>
</html>
```

This source code begins by defining the stopClock() function and startDate as an instance of Date(). Then, onload, the stopClock() function executes, building the stopDate object. Finally, the script treats the two instances of Date() as numbers, and the earlier (lesser) one is subtracted from the later (larger) one. Because both are measured in milliseconds, the result is an expression of how many milliseconds elapsed between the startClock() function call and the onLoad event firing.

In this script, you may notice the defer="defer" attribute has been omitted; this is deliberate, to ensure the startDate object is created as soon as possible. Also, if you do use a script like this, place the script as early in the document as you can, again to get the most accurate count on the loading time. Despite all this, it will probably be a few milliseconds short of the actual load time: after all, loading the script into the browser is not a zero-time operation. The script gives the best possible estimate under the circumstances.

Properties

All instances of Date() inherit the properties of the Object.prototype object through the Date.prototype object, and do not override any of them.

Methods

getDate()

JavaScript 1.0+, JScript 3.0+

Nav2+, IE4+

Syntax

```
var x = dateObj.getDate()
```

The getDate() method of instances of Date() returns the this object's day of the month value. For the date of March 8, 2001, at 10:51:00 p.m., this returns 8.

getDay()

JavaScript 1.0+, JScript 3.0+

Nav2+, IE4+

Syntax

```
var x = dateObj.getDay()
```

The getDay() method of instances of Date() returns the this object's day of the week as a number value, with 0 as Sunday through 6 as Saturday. For the date of March 8, 2001, at 10:51:00 p.m., this returns 4, for Thursday.

getFullYear()

JavaScript 1.3+, JScript 3.0+

Nav4.06+, IE4+

Syntax

```
var x = dateObj.getFullYear()
```

The getFullYear() method of instances of Date() returns the this object's year value. For the date on March 8, 2001, at 10:51:00 p.m., this returns 2001.

Because of the infamous Y2K bug, this method supersedes the getYear() method call of instances of Date(), which you must use in Netscape Navigator 2–4.05 and Internet Explorer 3. (See the getYear() method later in this chapter for details.)

getHours()

JavaScript 1.0+, JScript 3.0+

Nav2+, IE4+

Syntax

```
var x = dateObj.getHours()
```

The getHours() method of instances of Date() returns the this object's hour value. For the date of March 8, 2001, at 10:51:00 p.m., this returns 22 (10 p.m. == 10 + 12).

getMilliseconds()

JavaScript 1.3+, JScript 3.0+

Nav4.06+, IE4+

Syntax

```
var x = dateObj.getMilliseconds()
```

The getMilliseconds() method of instances of Date() returns the this object's milliseconds value. For the date of March 8, 2001, at 10:51:00 p.m., this returns 0.

getMinutes()

JavaScript 1.0+, JScript 3.0+

Nav2+, IE4+

Syntax

```
var x = dateObj.getMinutes()
```

The getMinutes() method of instances of Date() returns the this object's minutes value. For the date of March 8, 2001, at 10:51:00 p.m., this returns 51.

getMonth()

JavaScript 1.0+, JScript 3.0+

Nav2+, IE4+

Syntax

```
var x = dateObj.getMonth()
```

The getMonth() method of instances of Date() returns the this object's month as a number value, with 0 as January, through 11 as December. For the Date() object on March 8, 2001, at 10:51:00 p.m., this returns 2, for March.

getSeconds()

JavaScript 1.0+, JScript 3.0+

Nav2+, IE4+

Syntax

```
var x = dateObj.getSeconds()
```

The method of instances of Date() returns the this object's seconds value. For the date of March 8, 2001, at 10:51:00 p.m., this returns 0.

getTime()
JavaScript 1.0+, JScript 3.0+

Nav2+, IE4+

Syntax

```
var x = dateObj.getTime()
```

The getTime() method of instances of Date() returns the this object's total number of milliseconds since January 1st, 1970 at midnight, UTC (Universal Coordinated Time). This is equivalent to returning the position of the date on the special time number line.

getTimezoneOffset()
JavaScript 1.0+, JScript 3.0+

Nav2+, IE4+

Syntax

```
var x = dateObj.getTimezoneOffset()
```

The getTimezoneOffset() method of instances of Date() returns the this object's offset from UTC (Universal Coordinated Time) to local time in minutes. For instance, Pacific Standard Time (eight time zones to the west) will return 480, 8 hours * 60 minutes/hour behind UTC time. East of UTC's time zone, the number is negative, until the International Date Line.

As UTC itself is not adjusted for Daylight Savings Time, this will increase by 60 minutes for countries where and when Daylight Savings Time is in effect. Not every country in the world uses Daylight Savings Time, so watch out for this.

getUTCDate()

JavaScript 1.3+, JScript 3.0+

Nav4.06+, IE4+

Syntax

```
var x = dateObj.getUTCDate()
```

The getUTCDate() method of instances of Date() returns the this object's day of the month value according to UTC (Universal Coordinated Time). Similar to the getDate() method.

Listing 6.2, later in this chapter, covers the difference between UTC time and local time (from where I'm writing this, Pacific time zone).

getUTCDay()

JavaScript 1.3+, JScript 3.0+

Nav4.06+, IE4+

Syntax

```
var x = dateObj.getUTCDay()
```

The getUTCDay() method of instances of Date() returns the this object's day of the week value according to UTC (Universal Coordinated Time). Similar to the getDay() method.

Listing 6.2, later in this chapter, covers the difference between UTC time and local time (from where I'm writing this, Pacific time zone).

getUTCFullYear()

JavaScript 1.3+, JScript 3.0+

Nav4.06+, IE4+

Syntax

```
var x = dateObj.getUTCFullYear()
```

The getUTCFullYear() method of instances of Date() returns the this object's year value according to UTC (Universal Coordinated Time). Similar to the getFullYear() method.

Listing 6.2, later in this chapter, covers the difference between UTC time and local time (from where I'm writing this, Pacific time zone).

getUTCHours()

JavaScript 1.3+, JScript 3.0+

Nav4.06+, IE4+

Syntax

```
var x = dateObj.getUTCHours()
```

The `getUTCHours()` method of instances of `Date()` returns the `this` object's hour value according to UTC (Universal Coordinated Time). This method is similar to the `getHours()` method.

Listing 6.2, later in this chapter, covers the difference between UTC time and local time (from where I'm writing this, Pacific time zone).

getUTCMilliseconds()

JavaScript 1.3+, JScript 3.0+

Nav4.06+, IE4+

Syntax

```
var x = dateObj.getUTCMilliseconds()
```

The `getUTCMilliseconds()` method of instances of `Date()` returns the `this` object's milliseconds value, according to UTC (Universal Coordinated Time). This method is similar to the `getMilliseconds()` method.

Listing 6.2, later in this chapter, covers the difference between UTC time and local time (from where I'm writing this, Pacific time zone).

getUTCMinutes()

JavaScript 1.3+, JScript 3.0+

Nav4.06+, IE4+

Syntax

```
var x = dateObj.getUTCMinutes()
```

The getUTCMinutes() method of instances of Date() returns the this object's minutes value according to UTC (Universal Coordinated Time). This method is similar to the getMinutes() method.

Listing 6.2, later in this chapter, covers the difference between UTC time and local time (from where I'm writing this, Pacific time zone).

getUTCMonth()

JavaScript 1.3+, JScript 3.0+

Nav4.06+, IE4+

Syntax

```
var x = dateObj.getUTCMonth()
```

The getUTCMonth() method of instances of Date() returns the this object's day of the month index value according to UTC (Universal Coordinated Time). This method is similar to the getMonth() method.

Listing 6.2, later in this chapter, covers the difference between UTC time and local time (from where I'm writing this, Pacific time zone).

getUTCSeconds()

JavaScript 1.3+, JScript 3.0+

Nav4.06+, IE4+

Syntax

```
var x = dateObj.getUTCSeconds()
```

The getUTCSeconds() method of instances of Date() returns the this object's seconds value, according to UTC (Universal Coordinated Time). This method is similar to the getSeconds() method.

Listing 6.2, later in this chapter, covers the difference between UTC time and local time (from where I'm writing this, Pacific time zone).

getYear()

JavaScript 1.0-1.2, JScript 1.0

Nav2-Nav4.05, IE3

Deprecated in Nav4.06, IE4

Syntax

```
var x = dateObj.getYear()
```

The `getYear()` method of instances of `Date()` returns the `this` object's year as a number value. For years in the twentieth century (1900–1999), it returns a two-digit number, for the last two digits in the year number. For all others, it returns varying results.

For Internet Explorer 3 and Netscape Navigator 2–4, this method returns a number equal to the actual year number minus 1900. For Internet Explorer 4+, it returns the four-digit year number, as if a `this.getFullYear()` method call executed.

This method has been deprecated, due to the infamous Y2K bug. Use `getFullYear()` instead.

Date.parse()

JavaScript 1.0+, JScript 1.0+

Nav2+, IE3+

Syntax

```
var x = Date.parse(dateString)
```

This method acts directly on the `Date()` constructor function. It accepts a string representation of a date and returns the number of milliseconds elapsed from January 1st, 1970 at midnight to that date. The returned value is a number, not a date.

setDate()

JavaScript 1.0+, JScript 3.0+

Nav2+, IE4+

Syntax

```
dateObj.setDate(dayValue)
```

The setDate() method of instances of Date() sets the this object's day of the month value to match the first argument of this function. This is set according to the client computer's time. This is the inverse of the getDate() method.

This method returns the new value of the this object in milliseconds since January 1st, 1970, UTC time.

setFullYear()

JavaScript 1.3+, JScript 3.0+

Nav4.06+, IE4+

Syntax

```
dateObj.setFullYear(yearValue[, monthValue[, dayValue]])
```

The setFullYear() method of instances of Date() sets the this object's year value to match the first argument of this function. This is set according to the client computer's time. This is the inverse of the getFullYear() method.

If you provide two or three arguments, the second argument is set as the month of the year for the this object. The third argument is likewise set as the day of the month. These two arguments are optional.

This method returns the new value of the this object in milliseconds since January 1st, 1970, UTC time. This method supersedes the setYear() method call, which you must use in Netscape 2–4.05 and Internet Explorer 3.

setHours()

JavaScript 1.0+, JScript 3.0+

Nav2+, IE4+

Syntax

```
dateObj.setHours(hoursValue[, minutesValue[, secondsValue[, msValue]]])
```

The setHours() method of instances of Date() sets the this object's hour value to match the first argument of this function. This is set according to the client computer's time. This is the inverse of the getHours() method.

If you provide two, three, or four arguments, the second, third, and fourth arguments, respectively, set the minutes, seconds, and milliseconds of the this object. This is in effect for Netscape 4.06+ and Internet Explorer 5+.

This method returns the new value of the this object in milliseconds since January 1st, 1970, UTC time.

setMilliseconds()

JavaScript 1.3+, JScript 3.0+

Nav4.06+, IE4+

Syntax

`dateObj.setMilliseconds(msValue)`

The `setMilliseconds()` method of instances of `Date()` sets the `this` object's milliseconds value to match the first argument of this function. This is set according to the client computer's time. This is the inverse of the `getMilliseconds()` method.

This method returns the new value of the `this` object in milliseconds since January 1st, 1970, UTC time.

setMinutes()

JavaScript 1.0+, JScript 3.0+

Nav2+, IE4+

Syntax

`dateObj.setMinutes(minutesValue[, secondsValue[, msValue]])`

The `setMinutes()` method of instances of `Date()` sets the `this` object's minutes value to match the first argument of this function. This is set according to the client computer's time. This is the inverse of the `getMinutes()` method.

If you provide two or three arguments, the second and third arguments, respectively, set the seconds and milliseconds of the `this` object. This is effective in Netscape 4.06+ and Internet Explorer 5+.

This method returns the new value of the `this` object in milliseconds since January 1st, 1970, UTC time.

setMonth()

JavaScript 1.0+, JScript 3.0+

Nav2+, IE4+

Syntax

dateObj.setMonth(*monthValue*[, *dayValue*])

The setMonth() method of instances of Date() sets the this object's month value to match the first argument of this function. This is set according to the client computer's time. This is the inverse of the getMonth() method.

If you provide a second argument, the second argument is set as the day of the month.

This method returns the new value of the this object in milliseconds since January 1st, 1970, UTC time.

setSeconds()

JavaScript 1.0+, JScript 3.0+

Nav2+, IE4+

Syntax

dateObj.setSeconds(*secondsValue*[, *msValue*])

The setSeconds() method of instances of Date() sets the this object's day of the month value to match the first argument of this function. This is set according to the client computer's time. This is the inverse of the getDate() method.

If a second argument is provided, it is set as the milliseconds value of the this object. This is effective in Netscape 4.06+ and Internet Explorer 5+.

This method returns the new value of the this object in milliseconds since January 1st, 1970, UTC time.

setTime()

JavaScript 1.0+, JScript 3.0+

Nav2+, IE4+

Syntax

dateObj.setTime(*timeValue*)

The setTime() method of instances of Date() sets the this object's milliseconds since January 1st, 1970 at midnight, UTC (Universal Coordinated Time), to match the first argument of this function. This is the inverse of the getTime() method. It is also equivalent to creating a new instance of `Date()` using the first argument of the method as the only argument of the `Date()` constructor function.

This method returns the new value of the `this` object in milliseconds since January 1st, 1970, UTC time.

setUTCDate()

JavaScript 1.3+, JScript 3.0+

Nav4.06+, IE4+

Syntax

`dateObj.setUTCDate(dayValue)`

The `setUTCDate()` method of instances of `Date()` sets the `this` object's day of the month value to match the first argument of this function. This is set according to UTC (Universal Coordinated Time). This is the inverse of the `getUTCDate()` method, and is similar to the `setDate()` method.

This method returns the new value of the `this` object in milliseconds since January 1st, 1970, UTC time.

Listing 6.2, later in this chapter, covers the difference between UTC time and local time (from where I'm writing this, Pacific time zone).

setUTCFullYear()

JavaScript 1.3+, JScript 3.0+

Nav4.06+, IE4+

Syntax

`dateObj.setUTCFullYear(yearValue[, monthValue[, dayValue]])`

The `setUTCFullYear()` method of instances of `Date()` sets the `this` object's day of the month value to match the first argument of this function. This is set according to UTC (Universal Coordinated Time). This is the inverse of the `getUTCFullYear()` method, and is similar to the `setFullYear()` method.

This method returns the new value of the `this` object in milliseconds since January 1st, 1970, UTC time.

Listing 6.2, later in this chapter, covers the difference between UTC time and local time (from where I'm writing this, Pacific time zone).

setUTCHours()

JavaScript 1.3+, JScript 3.0+

Nav4.06+, IE4+

Syntax

dateObj.setUTCHours(*hoursValue*[, *minutesValue*[, *secondsValue*[, *msValue*]]])

The setUTCHours() method of instances of Date() sets the this object's hour value to match the first argument of this function. This is set according to UTC (Universal Coordinated Time). This is the inverse of the getUTCHours() method, and is similar to the setHours() method.

This method returns the new value of the this object in milliseconds since January 1st, 1970, UTC time.

Listing 6.2, later in this chapter, covers the difference between UTC time and local time (from where I'm writing this, Pacific time zone).

setUTCMilliseconds()

JavaScript 1.3+, JScript 3.0+

Nav4.06+, IE4+

Syntax

dateObj.setUTCMilliseconds(*msValue*])

The setUTCMilliseconds() method of instances of Date() sets the this object's milliseconds value to match the first argument of this function. This is set according to UTC (Universal Coordinated Time). This is the inverse of the getMilliseconds() method, and is similar to the setMilliseconds() method.

This method returns the new value of the this object in milliseconds since January 1st, 1970, UTC time.

Listing 6.2, later in this chapter, covers the difference between UTC time and local time (from where I'm writing this, Pacific time zone).

setUTCMinutes()

JavaScript 1.3+, JScript 3.0+

Nav4.06+, IE4+

Syntax

`dateObj.setUTCMinutes(minutesValue[, secondsValue[, msValue]])`

The `setUTCMinutes()` method of instances of `Date()` sets the `this` object's minutes value to match the first argument of this function. This is set according to UTC (Universal Coordinated Time). This is the inverse of the `getUTCMinutes()` method, and is similar to the `setMinutes()` method.

This method returns the new value of the `this` object in milliseconds since January 1st, 1970, UTC time.

Listing 6.2, later in this chapter, covers the difference between UTC time and local time (from where I'm writing this, Pacific time zone).

setUTCMonth()

JavaScript 1.3+, JScript 3.0+

Nav4.06+, IE4

Syntax

`dateObj.setUTCMonth(monthValue[, dayValue])`

The `setUTCMonth()` method of instances of `Date()` sets the `this` object's day of the month value to match the first argument of this function. This is set according to UTC (Universal Coordinated Time). This is the inverse of the `getUTCMonth()` method, and is similar to the `setMonth()` method.

This method returns the new value of the `this` object in milliseconds since January 1st, 1970, UTC time.

Listing 6.2, later in this chapter, covers the difference between UTC time and local time (from where I'm writing this, Pacific time zone).

setUTCSeconds()

JavaScript 1.3+, JScript 3.0+

Nav4.06+, IE4+

Syntax

dateObj.setUTCSeconds(*secondsValue*[, *msValue*])

The setUTCSeconds() method of instances of Date() sets the this object's day of the month value to match the first argument of this function. This is set according to UTC (Universal Coordinated Time). This is the inverse of the getUTCSeconds() method, and is similar to the setSeconds() method.

This method returns the new value of the this object in milliseconds since January 1st, 1970, UTC time.

Listing 6.2, later in this chapter, covers the difference between UTC time and local time (from where I'm writing this, Pacific time zone).

setYear()

JavaScript 1.0-1.2, JScript 1.0

Nav2+, IE3

Deprecated in Nav4.06, IE4

Syntax

dateObj.setYear(*yearValue*[, *monthValue* [, *dayValue*]])

The setYear() method sets the this object's year as a number value from the method's first argument. For one- or two-digit numbers, it sets a year in the twentieth century (1900–1999) by adding 1900 to the argument. For all others, it returns varying results.

Given a four-digit argument, for Internet Explorer 3 and Netscape 2–3, it sets a year equal to the first argument value plus 1900. For Internet Explorer 4+ and for Netscape Navigator 4.0x, it sets the four-digit year number from the first argument, as if a setFullYear() method call executed.

This method returns the new value of the this object in milliseconds since January 1st, 1970, UTC time. This method has been deprecated, due to the infamous Y2K bug. Use setFullYear() instead.

toDateString()

JavaScript 1.5, JScript 5.5+

Nav6.01, IE5.5

Syntax

```
dateObj.toDateString()
```

The `toDateString()` method of instances of `Date()` returns a string representation of the `this` object in a human readable form, containing the month, day of month, and year in local time.

toGMTString()/toUTCString()

JavaScript 1.0-1.2, JScript 1.0

Nav2–4.05, IE3 as `toGMTString()`

JavaScript 1.3+, JScript 3.0+

Nav4.06+, IE4+ as `toUTCString()`

Syntax

```
dateObj.toUTCString()
```

The `toUTCString()` and `toGMTString()` methods, which are identical but have different names, return a string representation of the `this` object in a human-readable form, containing the month, day of month, year, hour, minute, and second in GMT (Greenwich Mean Time), or UTC (Universal Coordinated Time). (These two are the same thing, with different names.)

Listing 6.2 covers the difference between UTC time and local time (from where I'm writing this, Pacific time zone).

Listing 6.2   *UTC Time and Local Time*

```
<?xml version="1.0" ?>
<!DOCTYPE html PUBLIC "-//W3C//DTD XHTML 1.0 Transitional//EN"
➥"DTD/xhtml1-transitional.dtd">
<html xmlns="http://www.w3.org/1999/xhtml" >
<head><title></title></head>
<body>
<p>
<script language="JavaScript" type="text/javascript">
<!--
var x = new Date("Thu Mar 8 21:00:01 PST 2001")
document.write(x.toString() + "<br />")
document.write(x.toUTCString())
//-->
```

```
</script>
</p>
<!-- Results
Thu Mar 8 21:00:01 PST 2001
Fri, 9 Mar 2001 05:00:01 UTC
-->
</body>
</html>
```

toLocaleDateString()

JavaScript 1.5, JScript 5.5+

Nav6+, IE5.5+

Syntax

```
dateObj.toLocaleDateString()
```

The `toLocaleDateString()` method returns a string representation of the `this` object in a human readable form, containing the month, day of month, and year in local time.

toLocaleString()

JavaScript 1.0+, JScript 3.0+

Nav2+, IE3+

Overrides `Object.prototype.toLocaleString()`

Syntax

```
dateObj.toLocaleString()
```

The `toLocaleString()` method of instances of `Date()` returns a string containing the breakdown of the `this` object in a shorthand human readable form, containing the month, day of month, year, hour, minute, and second in local time.

```
var x = new Date()
alert(x.toLocaleString())
// returns "Friday, March 09, 2001 10:39:09" in Nav
// returns "03/09/2001 10:42:45" in IE
```

Your `toLocaleDateString()` results may differ, based on which country and time zone you are in.

toLocaleTimeString()

JavaScript 1.5, JScript 5.5+

Nav6+, IE5.5+

Syntax

dateObj`.toLocaleTimeString()`

The `toLocaleTimeString()` method of instances of `Date()` returns a string representation of the `this` object in a human readable form, containing the hour, minutes, and seconds in local time, on a 24-hour clock.

toSource()

JavaScript 1.3+

Nav4.06+

Overrides `Object.prototype.toSource()`

Syntax

dateObj`.toSource()`

The `toSource()` method of instances of `Date()` returns a source-code representation of the `this` object: the `Date()` constructor function with a given number of milliseconds elapsed since January 1st, 1970 at midnight, local time.

```
var x = new Date()
alert(x.toSource()) // returns approximately "(new Date(984163879810))"
// argument of the Date() function may differ.
```

toString()

JavaScript 1.1+, JScript 3.0+

Nav3+, IE4+

Overrides `Object.prototype.toString()`

Syntax

dateObj`.toString()`

The `toString()` method of instances of `Date()` returns a string containing the breakdown of the `Date()` object in a human-readable form, breaking it down by weekday, month, day of month, hour, minute, second, time zone offset from UTC (Universal Coordinated Time), time zone, and year, in that order.

```
var x = new Date()
alert(x.toString())
// returns "Fri Mar 09 10:36:54 GMT-0800 (Pacific Standard Time) 2001" in Nav
// returns "Friday, March 09, 2001 10:39:09" in IE
// string results may differ by date.
```

toTimeString()

JavaScript 1.5, JScript 5.5+

Nav6.01+, IE5.5+

Syntax

```
dateObj.toTimeString()
```

This method returns a string representation of the `this` object in a human readable form, containing the hour, minutes, and seconds in local time, on a 24-hour clock.

toUTCString()

See `toGMTString()` earlier in this chapter.

Date.UTC()

JavaScript 1.0+, JScript 3.0+

Nav2+, IE3+

Syntax

```
Date.UTC(year, month, day[, hrs[, min[, sec[, ms]]]])
```

This method returns a number of milliseconds elapsed in a date string representation since January 1st, 1970 at midnight, UTC (Universal Coordinated Time). You can use this to accept a series of arguments indicating year, month, day of month, hour, minute, second, and millisecond (optional after day of month). Then, by feeding it to the `Date()` constructor function, you can get a `Date()` object centered on UTC time.

```
var x = new Date(Date.UTC(2001, 02, 08, 12))
// returns UTC-based date of March 8, 2001, noon
```

Listing 6.2, earlier in this chapter, covers the difference between UTC time and local time (from where I'm writing this, Pacific time zone).

valueOf()

JavaScript 1.1+, JScript 3.0+

Nav3+, IE4+

Overrides `Object.prototype.valueOf()`

Syntax

dateObj`.valueOf()`

The `valueOf()` method of instances of `Date()` returns a number containing the number of milliseconds elapsed since January 1st, 1970 at midnight, UTC (Universal Coordinated Time).

Example: Detecting Daylight Savings Time

ECMAScript does not by definition include a method of instances of `Date()` for exposing to developers whether the client is on Daylight Savings Time (DST). The language itself calculates if DST is in effect, but it doesn't tell us directly. I personally think this is an oversight, but a minor one, and easily corrected.

This function uses the `Date()` constructor function twice: once in January, when DST is never in effect, and once in July, when DST is in effect in every area that supports it. The time zone offsets from UTC (Universal Coordinated Time) for these two instances of `Date()` can give us a hint as to whether DST is in effect for part of the year. The time zone offset of "now" as compared to the January and July dates can tell us whether DST is in effect "now" if DST is also in effect in one month and not another (see Listing 6.3).

Listing 6.3   *Finding* `isDaylightSavings` *or Not*

```
<?xml version="1.0" ?>
<!DOCTYPE html PUBLIC "-//W3C//DTD XHTML 1.0 Transitional//EN"
➥"DTD/xhtml1-transitional.dtd">
<html xmlns="http://www.w3.org/1999/xhtml" >
<head><title></title></head>
<body>
```

Example: Detecting Daylight Savings Time

Listing 6.3   *(continued)*

```
<script type="text/javascript">
<!--
function Date_isDaylightSavings() {
   var StTime = new Date("January 1, 2001")
   var DLTime = new Date("July 1, 2001")
   var DLOffset = StTime.getTimezoneOffset() -
➥ DLTime.getTimezoneOffset()
   var ThisOff = this.getTimezoneOffset() -
➥ StTime.getTimezoneOffset()
   return Boolean(DLOffset * ThisOff)
   }

Date.prototype.isDaylightSavings = Date_isDaylightSavings

var x = new Date("March 1, 2001")
alert(x.isDaylightSavings()) // returns false

var y = new Date("June 30, 2001")
alert(y.isDaylightSavings()) // returns true
//-->
</script>
</body>
</html>
```

The first part of this function establishes times when DST would definitely be off and on, respectively. Each has an offset from UTC time, which DST never affects. If the two offsets are equal, `DLOffset` is set to `0`. If the two are unequal, DST is in effect at one of these times.

The next part compares the offsets of standard time to the offset of the `this` object's time. If the two offsets are unequal, something is shifting an extra offset into place. The only such extra offset that can exist is Daylight Savings Time.

The `return` statement gets a `Boolean` value by multiplying together the two offset differences. In effect, if either of the two is zero, the function will return `false`. But if both of them are non-zero, the result is non-zero, and the `Boolean()` function must return `true`. This result then returns out of the function. Finally, the script adds the `isDaylightSavings` method to `Date.prototype` and executes a couple of quick tests to demonstrate.

CHAPTER 7

Number()

Browser/JavaScript Version	Created By
Nav4/JavaScript 1.2	`x = new Number()` `x = number`
IE4/JScript 3.0	`x = new Number()` `x = number`
IE5/JScript 5.0	`x = new Number()` `x = number`
IE5.5/JScript 5.5	`x = new Number()` `x = number`
Nav6/JavaScript 1.5	`x = new Number()` `x = number`
IE6	`x = new Number()` `x = number`
ECMAScript 1st edition	`x = new Number()` `x = number`
ECMAScript 3rd edition	`x = new Number()` `x = number`

> **Note**
> Nav2 (number values), Nav3+ (number objects), IE4+
>
> Descends from `Object()`

Description

JavaScript includes a special function for giving all numbers in the language access to properties and methods. It also allows us to create a few numbers not contained in the decimal number system JavaScript supports, such as `+Infinity` and `-Infinity`.

Numbers Are Everywhere in JavaScript

Already you've seen several examples of numbers being used in this book: the `factorial` functions, the `length` property of strings, functions, and arrays, in `for` statement loops, as arguments fed to `Boolean()` constructor functions, and so on. The list goes on and on.

Numbers can be compared to one another or manipulated using many of the operators discussed in Chapter 12, "Operators." But there are also a few things you can do using the properties and methods of the `Number()` constructor function.

JavaScript, however, doesn't cover all numbers. This is because JavaScript restricts itself to terminating decimal numbers. For instance, JavaScript cannot exactly cover 1/3. If you feed JavaScript 1/3, it returns 0.3333333333333333. This is an approximation of 1/3. The actual value for 1/3 continues on in an endless stream of threes. In mathematics, this is called a nonterminating decimal. JavaScript simply cuts the fraction's evaluation off at 16 digits. (More precisely, the IEEE 754 standard for binary floating point arithmetic is the model ECMAScript and JavaScript use. This standard defines a number system using 64 bits, or 8 bytes.)

For the same reasons, JavaScript does not support irrational numbers ($\sqrt{2}$) exactly or complex numbers ($a + b\sqrt{-1}$) at all. Its number system is limited strictly to decimals. The example at the end of this chapter defines a complex number constructor function Complex(), and rules for handling numbers and corresponding Complex() objects.

JavaScript's mathematics aren't always perfect, either (see Listing 7.1).

Listing 7.1 *Inaccuracies in JavaScript Number Handling*

```
<?xml version="1.0" ?>
<!DOCTYPE html PUBLIC "-//W3C//DTD XHTML 1.0 Transitional//EN"
➡ "DTD/xhtml1-transitional.dtd">
<html xmlns="http://www.w3.org/1999/xhtml" >
<head><title></title></head>
<body>
<p>
<script language="JavaScript" type="text/javascript">
<!--
for (x = 0; x < 1; x += .1) {
   document.write(x + "<br />")
   }

/* This returns the following:
0
0.1
0.2
0.30000000000000004
0.4
0.5
0.6
0.7
0.7999999999999999
0.8999999999999999
0.9999999999999999
```

Listing 7.1   *(continued)*

```
*/
//-->
</script>
</p>
</body>
</html>
```

What happened? Each time through the loop, x should have added 0.1 to its value. Apparently, it didn't add exactly 0.1. (The inherent design of the IEEE 754 standard causes this; it is not a design flaw in JavaScript. Technically, it's not considered a design flaw in IEEE 754 either. It's more of an inconvenience than anything else.)

You can fix this using the `Math.round()` method, described in Chapter 8, "Math." Simply use it to adjust *x* as needed (see Listing 7.2).

Listing 7.2   *Rounding* x *to the Correct Value*

```
<?xml version="1.0" ?>
<!DOCTYPE html PUBLIC "-//W3C//DTD XHTML 1.0 Transitional//EN"
➥ "DTD/xhtml1-transitional.dtd">
<html xmlns="http://www.w3.org/1999/xhtml" >
<head><title></title></head>
<body>
<p>
<script language="JavaScript" type="text/javascript">
<!--
for (x = 0; x < 1; x += .1) {
   x = Math.round(x * 10) / 10
   document.write(x + "<br />")
   }

/* This returns the following:
0
0.1
0.2
0.3
0.4
0.5
0.6
0.7
0.8
```

Listing 7.2 *(continued)*

```
0.9
*/
//-->
</script>
</p>
</body>
</html>
```

Note also one round gets chopped off the execution. (The .999999 value doesn't appear, which is correct: 10 numbers are returned instead of 11.) So in some small effects, rounding can actually help your scripts a little in larger functions.

> **Note**
> A lot of people get mad at Microsoft and Netscape for these rounding errors. Their anger is misplaced; Netscape and Microsoft are simply following the ECMAScript standard, which specifies numbers should be handled using the IEEE 754 standard. This is a binary (base-2) digit representation of numbers, which cannot exactly handle decimal numbers (base-10, or 2 * 5). The binary representation is optimized for the computer, not for the human.

JavaScript Supports Scientific Notation

A number literal for most people is simply the digits of the number. For example, 5 is a number literal. However, JavaScript also allows you to define a number literal in scientific notation.

Scientific notation is simple: it is a decimal number between 1 and 10, including possibly 1, multiplied by a power of 10. $2.7 * 10^1$ is 27 in scientific notation. $1 * 10^3$ is 1,000 in scientific notation. The idea is any decimal number can be represented in scientific notation by factoring out a power of 10.

You can define a number literal in scientific notation by giving the coefficient (the decimal part), followed by an e, followed by the exponent of the power of 10. No spaces are allowed. For example, 5e+03 is 5,000. 1e-01 is 0.1. It is preferable to include a plus sign (+) after the e if the exponent is positive or zero, but not absolutely required.

Accessing Properties and Methods of Number Literals

JavaScript presents a peculiar problem for object-oriented numbers. A period (.) is used commonly in English-speaking countries and English-based languages (such as JavaScript) to indicate the separation of whole numbers and portions of a number.

However, in JavaScript, the period also indicates a break between a parent object and its child objects. The problem arises when you try to reference a method or property of instances of `Number()` to a number literal which is an integer:

```
var x = 5.toString() // throws exception
```

JavaScript expects a numeric digit (0–9) immediately following the period. Instead, it gets a letter (t).

You can fix this by inserting a space before the period. This tells JavaScript the number literal is done, and the space allows you in this instance to access the method of the number literal.

```
var x = 5 .toString() // returns "5"
```

Another way is to enclose the number literal in parentheses. This transforms it to a number value before executing the method call:

```
var x = (5).toString() // returns "5"
```

Technically, if there is already a decimal point in the number literal, the space is not required. However, it is a good practice to include it anyway.

Another thing to note is when you call a method of a number value that isn't an object, JavaScript automatically (and temporarily) converts the value to an object long enough to execute the method call. After the method call, it reverts to its native number type. For instance, x = 2; y = x.toString(16) temporarily converts x into an instance of `Number()`, applies the `toString()` method, and then reverts x's type to `"number"`.

The Number() Function Performs a Type Change

If you call the `Number()` function without the `new` keyword, the value it returns is a number equal in value to its first argument.

```
var x = Number("5")
alert(x) // returns 5
alert(typeof x) // returns "number"
```

If the first argument is not a number, this function call will return `Number.NaN`:

```
var x = Number("x")
alert(x) // returns Number.NaN
alert(typeof x) // returns "number"
```

Properties

Number.MAX_VALUE

JavaScript 1.1+, JScript 3.0+

Nav3+, IE4+

Syntax

```
var x = Number.MAX_VALUE
```

The `MAX_VALUE` property of `Number()` is a number indicating the largest positive value JavaScript will accept below `+Infinity`. Any number larger than this number JavaScript automatically translates to `+Infinity`.

As of ECMAScript 3rd edition, `Number.MAX_VALUE` is set approximately to `1.7976931348623157e+308`. (Number enthusiasts take note: this is bigger than one googol cubed!) You do not call `Number.MAX_VALUE` as a property of any number you create, but as a property of the `Number()` constructor function.

Number.MIN_VALUE

JavaScript 1.1+, JScript 3.0+

Nav3+, IE4+

Syntax

```
var x = Number.MIN_VALUE
```

The `MIN_VALUE` property of `Number()` is a number indicating the smallest positive value JavaScript will accept above `0`. Any positive number smaller than this number JavaScript automatically translates to `0`.

As of ECMAScript 3rd edition, `Number.MIN_VALUE` is set approximately to `5e-324`. Note this number does not indicate the smallest number JavaScript will accept without returning `-Infinity`. You do not call `Number.MIN_VALUE` as a property of any number you create, but as a property of the `Number()` constructor function.

Number.NaN

JavaScript 1.1+, JScript 3.0+

Nav3+, IE4+

Syntax

```
var x = Number.NaN
```

The value `Number.NaN` is a special constant to indicate a value which is not a number.

This may sound like a contradiction in the definition of JavaScript numbers, but there is a place for it. For instance, if you try to execute `Math.sin(new Object())`, what is it supposed to return? There is no decimal value for an instance of `Object()`, so `Math.sin` would normally throw an error. Instead, `Math.sin` returns `Number.NaN` because it cannot return a number.

Likewise, if you wish to return an invalid number value from your functions, you can return `Number.NaN`.

`Number.NaN` cannot be compared against any other object, including itself. It is not equal to every other number, and likewise is not greater than or less than any other number. To give you an example, `Math.sqrt(-1)` returns `Number.NaN`. This imaginary number, commonly known as *i* or *j*, is not greater than or less than any other number. The only difference between this example and JavaScript's `Number.NaN` is *i* == *i*. `Number.NaN` != `Number.NaN`.

To find out if a value is a valid JavaScript number, use the `isNaN()` function, described in Chapter 11, "The Global Object and Statements."

Likewise, you cannot use arithmetic operations on `Number.NaN` (see Listing 7.3).

Listing 7.3   *Adding to* `Number.NaN` *Results in* `Number.NaN`

```
<?xml version="1.0" ?>
<!DOCTYPE html PUBLIC "-//W3C//DTD XHTML 1.0 Transitional//EN"
➥ "DTD/xhtml1-transitional.dtd">
<html xmlns="http://www.w3.org/1999/xhtml" >
<head><title></title></head>
<body>
<p>
<script language="JavaScript" type="text/javascript">
<!--
var x = Number.NaN
x++
document.write(x)
//-->
</script>
```

Listing 7.3 *(continued)*

```
</p>
<!-- Results:
NaN
-->
</body>
</html>
```

`Number.NaN.toString()`returns `"NaN"`. `Number.NaN.toSource()` returns `"(new Number(NaN))"` for Netscape browsers. You do not call `Number.NaN` as a property of any number you create, but as a property of the `Number()` constructor function.

Number.NEGATIVE_INFINITY

JavaScript 1.1, JScript 3.0+

Nav3+, IE4+

Syntax

```
var x = Number.NEGATIVE_INFINITY
```

The `NEGATIVE_INFINITY` property of `Number()` is a number representing `-Infinity` to JavaScript. (I discuss `Infinity` in Chapter 11, "The Global Object and Statements.")

Number.POSITIVE_INFINITY

JavaScript 1.1+, JScript 3.0+

Nav3+, IE4+

Syntax

```
var x = Number.POSITIVE_INFINITY
```

The `POSITIVE_INFINITY` property of `Number()` is a number representing `+Infinity` to JavaScript. (I discuss `Infinity` in Chapter 11, "The Global Object and Statements.")

`+Infinity` and `-Infinity` react almost identically to mathematical infinity (positive and negative). Specifically, Tables 7.1 and 7.2 show what happens when you multiply and divide, respectively, one JavaScript number by another. (I use shorthand in this table. When a column says $x > 0$, for example, that means the value x is a finite positive number.)

Table 7.1　*Multiplication Involving Real Numbers and Infinity*

x * y = z	x = 0	x > 0	x < 0	x = +Infinity	x = -Infinity
y = 0	z = 0	z = 0	z = 0	z = 0	z = 0
y > 0	z = 0	z > 0	z < 0	z = +Infinity	z = -Infinity
y < 0	z = 0	z < 0	z > 0	z = -Infinity	z = +Infinity
y = +Infinity	z = Number.NaN	z = +Infinity	z = -Infinity	z = +Infinity	z = -Infinity
y = -Infinity	z = Number.NaN	z = -Infinity	z = +Infinity	z = -Infinity	z = +Infinity

Table 7.2　*Division Involving Real Numbers and Infinity*

x / y = z	x = 0	x > 0	x < 0	x = +Infinity	x = Infinity
y = 0	z = Number.NaN	z = +Infinity	z = -Infinity	z = +Infinity	z = -Infinity
y > 0	z = 0	z > 0	z < 0	z = +Infinity	z = -Infinity
y < 0	z = 0	z < 0	z > 0	z = -Infinity	z = +Infinity
y = +Infinity	z = 0	z = 0	z = 0	z = Number.NaN	z = Number.NaN
y = -Infinity	z = 0	z = 0	z = 0	z = Number.NaN	z = Number.NaN

Attempting to add +Infinity to -Infinity results in Number.NaN, as does subtracting +Infinity from itself or subtracting -Infinity from itself. Adding or subtracting any other number from +Infinity or -Infinity returns +Infinity and -Infinity, respectively.

Methods

toExponential()

JavaScript 1.5+, JScript 5.5+

Nav6, IE5.5+

Syntax

```
var x = num.toExponential(digits)
```

The `toExponential()` method of numbers returns a string representation of a number in scientific notation.

```
alert(5180 .toExponential()) // returns "5.18e+3"
```

If you set the first argument as a number between 0 and 20 for the `toExponential()` method, it returns a number of digits after the decimal point of the scientific notation in the number equal to the first argument.

```
alert(5180 .toExponential(1)) // returns "5.2e+3"
```

toFixed()

JavaScript 1.5+, JScript 5.5+

Nav6, IE5.5+

Syntax

```
var x = num.toFixed(digits)
```

The `toFixed()` method of numbers returns a string representation of the number. The representation is cut off after the number of digits past the decimal point given as the first argument of the method call. With no argument given, it cuts off all digits after the decimal point. There may be some rounding, based on the first digit removed, and the translation by JavaScript from its internal binary number system to our decimal system.

```
alert(51.815 .toFixed()) // returns "52"
alert(51.815 .toFixed(1)) // returns "51.8"
alert(51.815 .toFixed(2)) // returns "51.82"
```

toPrecision()

JavaScript 1.5+, JScript 5.5+

Nav6, IE5.5+

Syntax

```
var x = num.toPrecision(digits)
```

The `toPrecision()` method of numbers returns a string representation of the number, but only with a certain number of significant digits, followed by zeroes.

Significant digits are digits at the start of a number, except for initial zeroes. 592 has three significant digits. 0.00592 also has three significant digits. 5092 has four significant digits. 5920 also has four significant digits.

If you omit the argument of the `toPrecision()` method, it returns the same as `toString()` would for that number. If the argument of `toPrecision()` is greater than the number of significant digits, the method appends zeroes (and a decimal point, if necessary) to ensure the number it returns is equal to the `this` object and with the correct number of significant digits. Typically, the method will return a number in standard notation when this happens.

If the argument of `toPrecision()` is less than the number of significant digits, only the number of significant digits specified as the argument will pass into the string returned. Typically, the method will return a number in scientific notation when this happens.

The argument must be an integer greater than 0 and less than 22.

```
alert(59201 .toPrecision(6)) // returns "59201.0"
alert(59201 .toPrecision(5)) // returns "59201"
alert(59201 .toPrecision(4)) // returns "5.920e+4"
alert(59201 .toPrecision(3)) // returns "5.92e+4"
alert(59201 .toPrecision(2)) // returns "5.9e+4"
alert(59201 .toPrecision(1)) // returns "6e+4"
alert(59201 .toPrecision()) // returns "59201"
```

toSource()

JavaScript 1.3+

Nav4.06+

Overrides `Object.prototype.toSource()`

Syntax

```
var x = num.toSource()
```

The `toSource()` method of instances of `Number()` returns the `this` object in a source-code breakdown.

```
alert(5 .toSource()) // returns "(new Number(5))"
```

toString()

JavaScript 1.1+, JScript 3.0+

Nav3+, IE4+

Overrides `Object.prototype.toString()`

Syntax

`var x = num.toString([base])`

The `toString()` method of instances of `Number()` returns a string containing the `this` object. If you provide an integer between 2 and 36 (including these values) as the first argument, it converts the number to a number with a base equal to the argument. For example, if you call `toString(2)` on a number, it returns the `this` object to base 2, which means the binary representation of the number. If you call `toString(16)` on a number, it returns the hexadecimal representation of the number.

```
alert(255 .toString()) // returns "255"
alert(255 .toString(2)) // returns "11111111"
alert(255 .toString(16)) // returns "ff"
alert(255 .toString(10)) // returns "255"
```

valueOf()

JavaScript 1.1+, JScript 3.0+

Nav3+, IE4+

Overrides `Object.prototype.valueOf()`

Syntax

`var x = num.valueOf()`

The `valueOf()` method of `Number()` returns `this` as a number value (as opposed to a number object).

Example: Implementing Complex Numbers in JavaScript

I noted earlier in this chapter JavaScript's inability to directly handle numbers outside the decimal number system. This is one aspect about JavaScript I actually dislike. I have experimented quite a bit with creating new extensions to JavaScript's decimal number system, and recently I have begun formalizing these extensions under the MozCalc project at `http://mozcalc.mozdev.org`. Those of you who are curious may look it up under the eXtensible Number System, or XNS.

Although the scope of my work is far beyond the simple example here, I can give demonstrations of how to implement complex numbers in JavaScript without too much technical wizardry. A complex number, in the simplest terms, is a number of the form $(a + b * i)$, where i = `Math.sqrt(-1)`.

We already know we cannot actually evaluate a value for i, but if we can create arithmetic and comparison operations for objects in this form which match the rules of handling complex numbers, we have emulated the complex number in JavaScript, and that's all we need to define i.

The first step is to create a generic `Complex()` constructor function as shown in Listing 7.4.

Listing 7.4   *The* `Complex()` *Constructor Function*

```
<?xml version="1.0" ?>
<!DOCTYPE html PUBLIC "-//W3C//DTD XHTML 1.0 Transitional//EN"
➥"DTD/xhtml1-transitional.dtd">
<html xmlns="http://www.w3.org/1999/xhtml" >
<head><title></title></head>
<body>
<p>
<script language="JavaScript" type="text/javascript">
<!--
function Complex() {
   if (arguments.length > 0) {
      this.real = arguments[0]
      } else {
      this.real = 0
      }
   if (arguments.length > 1) {
      this.imag = arguments[1]
      } else {
      this.imag = 0
      }
   }

Complex.prototype.toString = function() {
   return this.real + " + " + this.imag + "i"
   }
```

Example: Implementing Complex Numbers in JavaScript

Listing 7.4   *(continued)*

```
Complex.prototype.toSource = function() {
    return "(new Complex(" + this.real + ", " + this.imag + "))"
    }

var i = new Complex(0, 1)
document.write("<em>i</em> = " + i)
//-->
</script>
</p>
<!-- Results:
i = 0 + 1i
-->
</body>
</html>
```

This is simple enough. Calling `Complex()` with one argument returns a number with a `real` property set to the argument, and an `imag` property set to `0`. Likewise, calling `Complex()` with no arguments returns `real` and `imag` properties equal to `0`. Given two arguments, `Complex()` returns an object with `real` and `imag` properties equal to the first and second arguments, respectively.

However, we cannot just add a JavaScript number to a `Complex()` object, using the plus sign (+). JavaScript does not support an operation needed to achieve this, called *operator overloading*. Fortunately, we can define methods of numbers to do this for us (see Listing 7.5).

Listing 7.5   *Addition Defined as a Method of Numbers*

```
<?xml version="1.0" ?>
<!DOCTYPE html PUBLIC "-//W3C//DTD XHTML 1.0 Transitional//EN"
➥"DTD/xhtml1-transitional.dtd">
<html xmlns="http://www.w3.org/1999/xhtml" >
<head><title></title></head>
<body>
<script language="JavaScript" type="text/javascript">
<!--
function Number_add(that) {
    if (that.constructor == Number) {
        var response = this + that
        }
```

Listing 7.5   *(continued)*

```
    if (that.constructor == Complex) {
        var response = new Complex(this)
        response = response.add(that)
        }
    return response
    }
Number.prototype.add = Number_add
//-->
</script>
</body>
</html>
```

This creates a new method of all numbers titled add(). If the first argument is a number, it returns this + that. But if the first argument is a Complex() object, it creates a response beginning with the Complex() form of this. Then it calls the response's add() method to add the first argument.

There's only one catch: we haven't defined the response's add() method, or any add() method for Complex() objects. Listing 7.6 shows the appropriate code:

Listing 7.6   *Addition Defined as a Method of* Complex() *Objects*

```
<?xml version="1.0" ?>
<!DOCTYPE html PUBLIC "-//W3C//DTD XHTML 1.0 Transitional//EN"
➥"DTD/xhtml1-transitional.dtd">
<html xmlns="http://www.w3.org/1999/xhtml" >
<head><title></title></head>
<body>
<script language="JavaScript" type="text/javascript">
<!--
function Complex() {
    if (arguments.length > 0) {
        this.real = arguments[0]
        } else {
        this.real = 0
        }
    if (arguments.length > 1) {
        this.imag = arguments[1]
        } else {
        this.imag = 0
        }
    }
```

Example: Implementing Complex Numbers in JavaScript

Listing 7.6   *(continued)*

```
function Complex_add(that) {
   var response = new Complex(this.real, this.imag)
   if (that.constructor == Number) {
      response.real += that
      }
   if (that.constructor == Complex) {
      response.real += that.real
      response.imag += that.imag
      }
   return response
   }
Complex.prototype.add = Complex_add
//-->
</script>
</body>
</html>
```

This method checks to see if the first argument received is a JavaScript number or a
`Complex()` object. (First, it initializes `response` as a new `Complex()` object.) If it is
a JavaScript number, it adds the first argument directly to `response.real`. If it is
a `Complex()` object, it adds together the `real` properties, and the `imag` properties. Then
it returns `response` to the outer world. Finally, the `add` method is added to all
`Complex()` objects.

You can define similar methods for JavaScript numbers, following the rules for
numbers. (The idea is to create a system of methods common to both JavaScript
numbers and custom complex numbers.) The `Complex()` object can have
corresponding methods. Note in particular the `Complex().multiply` method shown in
Listing 7.7.

Listing 7.7   *Multiplication Defined as a Method of* `Complex()` *Objects*

```
<?xml version="1.0" ?>
<!DOCTYPE html PUBLIC "-//W3C//DTD XHTML 1.0 Transitional//EN"
➥"DTD/xhtml1-transitional.dtd">
<html xmlns="http://www.w3.org/1999/xhtml" >
<head><title></title></head>
<body>
<p>
<script language="JavaScript" type="text/javascript">
```

Listing 7.7 *(continued)*

```
<!--
function Complex() {
   if (arguments.length > 0) {
      this.real = arguments[0]
      } else {
      this.real = 0
      }
   if (arguments.length > 1) {
      this.imag = arguments[1]
      } else {
      this.imag = 0
      }
   }

function Complex_multiply(that) {
   var response = new Complex()
   if (that.constructor == Number) {
      response.real = this.real * that
      response.imag = this.imag * that
      }
   if (that.constructor == Complex) {
      response.real = this.real * that.real
      response.real+= -(this.imag * that.imag)
      response.imag = this.real * that.imag
      response.imag+= this.imag * that.real
      }
   return response
   }
Complex.prototype.multiply = Complex_multiply

Complex.prototype.toString = function() {
   return this.real + " + " + this.imag + "i"
   }

Complex.prototype.toSource = function() {
   return "(new Complex(" + this.real + ", " + this.imag + "))"
   }

var i = new Complex(0, 1)
document.write("<em>i</em> * <em>i</em> = " + i.multiply(i))
//-->
```

Example: Implementing Complex Numbers in JavaScript

Listing 7.7 *(continued)*

```
</script>
</p>
</body>
</html>
```

This obeys the rules $(a + bi)*(c) = (a*c + b*ci)$ and $(a + bi)*(c + di) = (a*c - b*d) + (a*d + b*c)i$, as defined for complex numbers.

CHAPTER 8

Math

Description

The Math object, unlike other objects ECMAScript defines, is not an object you can create. Instead, it is a container object for basic mathematics functions common to most programming and scripting languages.

Accordingly, the methods and properties of the Math object have been almost unchanged since JavaScript was born, certainly before ECMAScript 1st Edition. The only difference between the Math object as it is today and the Math object in JavaScript 1.0 is the implementation of Math.random on all platforms for Netscape browsers in Netscape 3+ (JavaScript 1.1+).

This chapter will briefly touch on the mathematics behind the properties and methods the Math object exposes. For instance, many of the functions JavaScript provides deal with trigonometry. Figure 8.1 shows a triangle you can use as a reference throughout the chapter for the trigonometric functions.

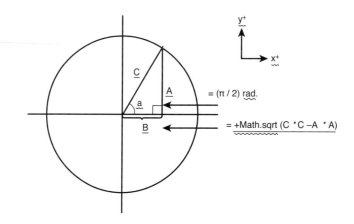

Figure 8.1
A sample triangle for trigonometric functions.

Properties

E

JavaScript 1.0+, JScript 1.0+

Nav2+, IE3+

Syntax

```
var e = Math.E
```

The E property of the Math object is a representation of Euler's number, the natural logarithm base (e). It is approximately equal to 2.718281828459045. The natural logarithm base is exactly equal to the limit of $(1 + h)^{1/h}$ as h approaches 0 from above. (For those of you who are unfamiliar with calculus, $(1 + 10^{-6})^{1,000,000}$ = 2.718280469096; $(1 + 10^{-9})^{1,000,000,000}$ = 2.718282052012. As h gets closer to zero, the number approaches the value for e.) Math.E ties in with logarithmic and exponential functions.

LN2

JavaScript 1.0+, JScript 1.0+

Nav2+, IE3+

Properties

Syntax

```
var x = Math.LN2
```

The `LN2` property of the `Math` object is a representation of the natural logarithm of 2. This number is approximately 0.6931471805599453. Equivalent to `Math.log(2)`.

LN10

JavaScript 1.0+, JScript 1.0+

Nav2+, IE3+

Syntax

```
var x = Math.LN10
```

The `LN10` property of the `Math` object is a representation of the natural logarithm of 10. This number is approximately 2.302585092994046. Equivalent to `Math.log(10)`.

LOG2E

JavaScript 1.0+, JScript 1.0+

Nav2+, IE3+

Syntax

```
var x = Math.LOG2E
```

The `LOG2E` property of the `Math` object is a representation of the logarithm of e to the base 2. This number is approximately 1.4426950408889633. Equivalent to `1 / Math.log(2)`.

LOG10E

JavaScript 1.0+, JScript 1.0+

Nav2+, IE3+

Syntax

```
var x = Math.LOG10E
```

The `LOG10E` property of the `Math` object is a representation of the logarithm of e to the base 10. This number is approximately 0.4342944819032518. Equivalent to `1 / Math.log(10)`.

PI

JavaScript 1.0+, JScript 1.0+

Nav2+, IE3+

Syntax

```
var pi = Math.PI
```

The `PI` property of the `Math` object is a representation of π, the ratio of a circle's circumference to its diameter. π is approximately 3.141592653589793. `Math.PI` ties in with trigonometric functions.

SQRT1_2

JavaScript 1.0+, JScript 1.0+

Nav2+, IE3+

Syntax

```
var x = Math.SQRT1_2
```

The `SQRT1_2` property of the `Math` object is a representation of the positive square root of 0.5, equal to `Math.SQRT2 / 2`. This number is approximately 0.7071067811865476. Equivalent to `Math.sqrt(0.5)`.

SQRT2

JavaScript 1.0+, JScript 1.0+

Nav2+, IE3+

Syntax

```
var x = Math.SQRT2
```

The `SQRT2` property of the `Math` object is a representation of the positive square root of 2. This number is approximately 1.4142135623730951. Equivalent to `Math.sqrt(2)`.

Methods

abs()

JavaScript 1.0+, JScript 1.0+

Nav2+, IE3+

Syntax

```
var y = Math.abs(x)
```

The abs() method of the Math object takes the first argument given and returns a number. If the argument is x, and $x \geq 0$, the method returns x. If $x < 0$, the method returns $-x$. If x is not a number, this method returns Number.NaN.

acos()

JavaScript 1.0+, JScript 3.0+

Nav2+, IE3+

Syntax

```
var x = Math.acos(y)
```

The acos() method of the Math object returns the inverse cosine of a real number. In Figure 8.1 Math.acos(B / C) is equal to a. The value acos() returns is an angle expressed in radians.

asin()

JavaScript 1.0+, JScript 1.0+

Nav2+, IE3+

Syntax

```
var x = Math.asin(y)
```

The asin() method of the Math object returns the inverse sine of a real number. In Figure 8.1 Math.asin(A / C) is equal to a. The value asin() returns is an angle expressed in radians.

atan()

JavaScript 1.0+, JScript 1.0+

Nav2+, IE3+

Syntax

```
var x = Math.atan(y)
```

The atan() method of the Math object returns the inverse tangent of a real number (used as a ratio of two sides). In Figure 8.1 Math.atan(A / B) is equal to a. The value atan() returns is an angle expressed in radians.

atan2()

JavaScript 1.0+, JScript 1.0+

Nav2+, IE3+

Syntax

```
var z = Math.atan2(x, y)
```

The atan2() method of the Math object returns the inverse tangent of a number you do not specify directly. The first argument is divided by the second argument, and the result is used to get the inverse tangent. In Figure 8.1 Math.atan2(A, B) is equal to a. The value atan2() returns is an angle expressed in radians.

ceil()

JavaScript 1.0+, JScript 1.0+

Nav2+, IE3+

Syntax

```
var y = Math.ceil(x)
```

The ceil() method of the Math object takes the first argument and returns the next higher integer. Basically, given a number $x = k + c$ such that k is an integer and $0 < c \le 1$, the method returns $k + 1$. If the method's first argument is not a number, this method returns Number.NaN.

For example, Math.ceil(3.49) returns 4. Math.ceil(4) returns 4. Math.ceil(-3.5) returns –3. Math.ceil(-3) returns –3. Math.ceil(-4) returns –4.

cos()

JavaScript 1.0+, JScript 1.0+

Nav2+, IE3+

Syntax

```
var y = Math.cos(x)
```

The `cos()` method of the `Math` object returns the cosine of a real number expressed in radians. In Figure 8.1 `Math.cos(a)` is equal to `B / C`.

exp()

JavaScript 1.0+, JScript 1.0+

Nav2+, IE3+

Syntax

```
var y = Math.exp(x)
```

The `exp()` method of the `Math` object takes the first argument x and returns the value of Euler's number to the power of x. Basically, for every real number x, there is a value y such that $e^x = y$. The method returns y.

If $x == 0$, the method returns 1. If $x == 1$, the method returns `Math.E`.

floor()

JavaScript 1.0+, JScript 1.0+

Nav2+, IE3+

Syntax

```
var y = Math.floor(x)
```

The `floor()` method of the `Math` object takes the first argument and returns the next lower integer. Basically, given a number $x = k + c$ such that k is an integer and $0 < c <= 1$, the method returns k. If the method's first argument is not a number, this method returns `Number.NaN`.

For example, `Math.floor(3.49)` returns 3. `Math.floor(4)` returns 4. `Math.floor(-3.5)` returns –4. `Math.floor(-3)` returns –3. `Math.floor(-4)` returns –4.

log()

JavaScript 1.0+, JScript 1.0+

Nav2+, IE3+

Syntax

```
var y = Math.log(x)
```

The `log()` method of the `Math` object takes the first argument x and returns the natural logarithm of x. Basically, for every positive real number x, there is a value y such that $e^y = x$. The method returns y.

If $x == 0$, this method returns `-Infinity`. If $x < 0$ or not a number, the method returns `Number.NaN`. If $x == 1$, the method returns `0`. If $x ==$ `Math.E`, the method returns `1`.

max()

JavaScript 1.0+, JScript 1.0+

Nav2+, IE3+

Syntax

```
var z = Math.max(x, y)
```

The `max()` method of the `Math` object returns the largest argument given to it. If no arguments are given, it returns `-Infinity`. If any argument is not a number, it returns `Number.NaN`. Netscape 2.x through 4.x only consider the first two arguments, however, so watch out for this.

For example, `Math.max(3, 4)` returns 4. `Math.max(-3, -4)` returns –3. `Math.max(0, 3, 4)` returns 4, except for Netscape 2 through Netscape 4 (these return 3). `Math.max(0, -3, -4)` returns 0.

min()

JavaScript 1.0+, JScript 1.0+

Nav2+, IE3+

Syntax

```
var z = Math.min(x, y)
```

The `min()` method of the `Math` object returns the smallest argument given to it. If no arguments are given, it returns `+Infinity`. If any argument is not a number, it returns `Number.NaN`. Netscape 2.x through Netscape 4.x only consider the first two arguments, however, so watch out for this.

For example, `Math.min(3, 4)` returns 3. `Math.min(-3, -4)` returns –4. `Math.min(0, 3, 4)` returns `0`. `Math.min(0 , -3, -4)` returns –4, except for Netscape 2 through Netscape 4 (these return –3).

pow()

JavaScript 1.0+, JScript 1.0+

Nav2+, IE3+

Syntax

```
var z = Math.pow(x, y)
```

The `pow()` method of the `Math` object takes the first argument x, the second argument y, and returns x^y. If y is equal to 2, this equals $x * x$. If y is equal to 3, this equals $x * x * x$. If y is equal to –1, this equals $1 / x$. Integer values for y return powers of x.

If y is not a whole number, this is equal to `Math.exp(Math.log(x) * y)`. (It is anyway, but finding the power with an integer exponent is easier using multiplication.)

random()

JavaScript 1.0 (Unix), JavaScript 1.1+, JScript 3.0+

Nav2 (Unix version), Nav3+ (all versions), IE3+

Syntax

```
var x = Math.random()
```

The `random()` method of the `Math` object returns a "pseudo-random" number x such that $0 \leq x < 1$. The "pseudo" indicates a number that appears random, but really isn't. JavaScript attempts to deliver a number that appears random, based on an algorithm each browser provides. However, because it is based on an algorithm, it really isn't a random number.

This is useful in creating objects that appear just as random, such as dice or a card deck. One of the simpler examples of a die roll is shown in Listing 8.1.

Listing 8.1   *A Single Die Roll in JavaScript* (`dieroll()` *function*)

```
<?xml version="1.0" ?>
<!DOCTYPE html PUBLIC "-//W3C//DTD XHTML 1.0 Transitional//EN"
➡"DTD/xhtml1-transitional.dtd">
<html xmlns="http://www.w3.org/1999/xhtml" >
<head><title></title></head>
<body>
<p>
<script language="JavaScript" type="text/javascript">
<!--
function dieroll() {
   var response = Math.random()
// 0 <= response < 1
   return Math.floor(response * 6) + 1
// 0 <= response * 6
// 0 <= Math.floor(response * 6) <= 5
// 1 <= Math.floor(response * 6) + 1 <= 6
   }
document.write("This time you received a die roll of " + dieroll() + ".")
//-->
</script>
</p>
<!-- Results are one of the following lines.
This time you received a die roll of 1.
This time you received a die roll of 2.
This time you received a die roll of 3.
This time you received a die roll of 4.
This time you received a die roll of 5.
This time you received a die roll of 6.
-->
</body>
</html>
```

By multiplying by 6, you assure a pseudo-random number between zero and five (because $x < 1$, $6 * x < 6$). By taking the `Math.floor` of this number, you get a much more random number, which is 0, 1, 2, 3, 4, or 5. Then, you add one and return the result, which is 1, 2, 3, 4, 5, or 6. This number is not purely random, either, but it's closer, and close enough for us.

I could not have used the following code instead:

```
return Math.ceil(response * 6)
```

The reason is response could still be 0, and `Math.ceil(0 * 6)` is still 0.

round()

JavaScript 1.0+, JScript 1.0+

Nav2+, IE3+

Syntax

```
var y = Math.round(x)
```

The `round()` method of the `Math` object takes the first argument and returns the nearest integer. Basically, given a number $x = k + c$ such that k is an integer and $-0.5 \leq c < 0.5$, the method returns k. If the method's first argument is not a number, this method returns `Number.NaN`.

For example, `Math.round(3.49)` returns 3. `Math.round(3.5)` returns 4. `Math.round(-3.49)` returns –3. `Math.round(-3.5)` returns –3. `Math.round(-3.51)` returns –4.

sin()

JavaScript 1.0+, JScript 1.0+

Nav2+, IE3+

Syntax

```
var y = Math.sin(x)
```

The `sin()` method of the `Math` object returns the sine of a real number, expressed in radians. In Figure 8.1 `Math.sin(a)` is equal to `A / C`.

sqrt()

JavaScript 1.0+, JScript 1.0+

Nav2+, IE3+

Syntax

```
var y = Math.sqrt(x)
```

The `sqrt()` method of the `Math` object takes the first argument and returns the positive square root of that argument. For example, if the argument is x, it returns `Math.pow(x, 0.5)`.

If the first argument is a negative number or not a number, this method returns `Number.NaN`. (For an example of square roots of negative numbers, see Chapter 7, "Number().")

tan()

JavaScript 1.0+, JScript 1.0+

Nav2+, IE3+

Syntax

```
var y = Math.tan(x)
```

The `tan()` method of the `Math` object returns the tangent of a real number (used as an angle), expressed in radians. In Figure 8.1 `Math.tan(a)` is equal to `A / B`.

Example: A Logarithm Function for Multiple Bases

In Chapter 2, "`Function()`," I replaced one of the `Math` object's methods with an alternative as the example. However, the `Math` object itself can contain any additional properties and methods you care to create directly.

One of my favorites is a logarithm function that responds with a different base than Euler's number, e. For instance, $\log_{10} 1,000 = 3$ because $10^3 = 1,000$. JavaScript does not provide this functionality natively (see Listing 8.2).

Listing 8.2   *Logarithms of a Number to a Base*

```
<?xml version="1.0" ?>
<!DOCTYPE html PUBLIC "-//W3C//DTD XHTML 1.0 Transitional//EN"
➥"DTD/xhtml1-transitional.dtd">
<html xmlns="http://www.w3.org/1999/xhtml" >
<head><title></title></head>
<body>
<p>
<script language="JavaScript" type="text/javascript">
<!--
function Math_logbase(num, base) {
    return Math.round(Math.log(num) / Math.log(base) * 1000000) / 1000000
/* Rounding to the nearest millionth
This is done because of JavaScript's handling of decimal numbers.
```

Listing 8.2   *(continued)*

```
See Chapter 7, "Number()," for details.
*/
    }
Math.logbase = Math_logbase
document.write("The base 10 log of 1000 is " + Math.logbase(1000, 10)
➥]+ ".<br />")
document.write("The base 2 log of 64 is " + Math.logbase(64, 2) + ".<br />")
document.write("The base 3 log of 3 is " + Math.logbase(3, 3) + ".<br />")
document.write("The base 10 log of 1 is " + Math.logbase(1, 10) + ".")
//-->
</script>
</p>
<!-- Results:
The base 10 log of 1000 is 3.
The base 2 log of 64 is 6.
The base 3 log of 3 is 1.
The base 10 log of 1 is 0.
-->
</body>
</html>
```

With logarithms, a common rule applies: $\log_b(n) = \log(n) / \log(b)$. It's therefore quite simple to apply. (You could even replace the main logarithm function directly if you desire, making the second argument optional.)

Similarly, you can define secant, cosecant, and cotangent functions (reciprocals of the cosine, sine, and tangent functions, respectively) and apply them to the Math object.

CHAPTER 9

RegExp()

Browser/JavaScript Version	Created By
Nav4/JavaScript 1.2	`x = new RegExp("`*`regular-expression`*`", "`*`flags`*`")`
	`x = /`*`regular-expression`*`/`*`flags`*
IE4/JScript 3.0	`x = new RegExp("`*`regular-expression`*`", "`*`flags`*`")`
	`x = /`*`regular-expression`*`/`*`flags`*
IE5/JScript 5.0	`x = new RegExp("`*`regular-expression`*`", "`*`flags`*`")`
	`x = /`*`regular-expression`*`/`*`flags`*
IE5.5/JScript 5.5	`x = new RegExp("`*`regular-expression`*`", "`*`flags`*`")`
	`x = /`*`regular-expression`*`/`*`flag`*
Nav6/JavaScript 1.5	`x = new RegExp("`*`regular-expression`*`", "`*`flags`*`")`
	`x = /`*`regular-expression`*`/`*`flags`*
ECMAScript 1st edition	(not implemented)
ECMAScript 3rd edition	`x = new RegExp("`*`regular-expression`*`", "`*`flags`*`")`
	`x = /`*`regular-expression`*`/`*`flags`*

> **Note**
> Implemented in Nav4+, IE4+
> Descends from `Object()` object

Regular expressions, or `RegExp()` objects, easily qualify as among the most intimidating expressions for new JavaScripters to master. They intimidate new JavaScripters for the same reason computers intimidate new owners: they are so complex and powerful that we don't know what to do with them.

It doesn't help much to understand JavaScript inherited regular expressions from the Perl language. It does help to understand you use regular expressions to search through `String()` objects.

In mathematics, we have an algebra of variables and numbers. Regular expressions describe an algebra of text: a way of establishing rules for searching through a text, and rearranging the text as necessary. This chapter includes lots of simple code for you to see what happens.

Description

In the simplest form, a regular expression is nothing more than a specific string of text you expect to search for. Without any modifier codes, you could write a regular expression /Hello/ and it would be useful in searching a string for the specific phrase "Hello" (see Listing 9.1).

Listing 9.1 *A Sample of Searching Through a String Using Regular Expressions*

```
<?xml version="1.0" ?>
<!DOCTYPE html PUBLIC "-//W3C//DTD XHTML 1.0 Transitional//EN"
➥"DTD/xhtml1-transitional.dtd">
<html xmlns="http://www.w3.org/1999/xhtml">
<head><title></title></head>
<body>
<script language="JavaScript" type="text/javascript">
<!--
var x = "The user has typed 'Hello World' into his computer."
var y = /Hello/

document.write(x.match(y) + "<br>") // displays the string "Hello"
document.write(y.exec(x)) // displays the string "Hello"
//-->
</script>
</body>
</html>
```

When match() or exec() are called in this example, they return the matched expression as an array of strings. In each case there is only one match, hence when you run the example, you will see "Hello" twice in the window. The fun (and fear) begins when you try to add more power to a regular expression.

The Special Characters of Regular Expressions

Those of you familiar with type definitions for XML documents will recognize the *, +, and ? special characters. These specify "zero or more matches," "one or more matches," and "less than two matches," respectively. Likewise, the | character lets the regular expression match either the preceding or following strings (see Listing 9.2).

Listing 9.2 *And/Or Operators in Regular Expressions*

```
<?xml version="1.0" ?>
<!DOCTYPE html PUBLIC "-//W3C//DTD XHTML 1.0 Transitional//EN"
➥"DTD/xhtml1-transitional.dtd">
<html xmlns="http://www.w3.org/1999/xhtml">
<head><title></title></head>
```

Listing 9.2   *(continued)*

```
<body>
<script language="JavaScript" type="text/javascript">
<!--
var w = "The user has typed 'Hello World Hee hee' into his computer."
var x = /el?/gi
var y = /or*/gi
var z = /he+/gi
var p = /el?|or*/gi

document.write(w.match(x) + "<br>") // returns
["e","e","e","el","e","e","e","e","e"]
document.write(w.match(y) + "<br>") // returns ["o","or","o","o"]
document.write(w.match(z) + "<br>") // returns ["he","He","Hee","hee"]
document.write(w.match(p))
// returns ["e","e","e","el","o","or","e","e","e","e","o","o","e"]
//-->
</script>
</body>
</html>
```

In this example, the calls to the `match()` method return an array of strings for all the matches. When arrays with multiple elements are printed, they are separated by commas by default. From the output, it is fairly obvious what the individual expressions are searching for, but what might not be obvious is what the `g` and `i` flags are for. `g` is the global flag and tells the search to find all matches in the string. `i` is the ignore case flag. When `true`, the search does not match by case.

The caret (^) character—not in brackets—tells a regular expression to match the next character with the first character of a line in the string to check. The dollar sign `$` character used in a regular expression (not as a property) tells a regular expression to match the next character with the last character of a line in the string to check. The `\w` you see in both expressions tells a regular expression to match one letter, numeral, or underscore (see Listing 9.3).

Listing 9.3   *Matching Beginning and Ending Characters*

```
<?xml version="1.0" ?>
<!DOCTYPE html PUBLIC "-//W3C//DTD XHTML 1.0 Transitional//EN"
➥"DTD/xhtml1-transitional.dtd">
<html xmlns="http://www.w3.org/1999/xhtml">
<head><title></title></head>

<body>
<script language="JavaScript" type="text/javascript">
```

Listing 9.3   *(continued)*

```
<!--
var x = "abac"
var y = /^a\w/gi
var z = /\wc$/gi

document.write(x.match(y) + "<br>") // returns ab
docment.write(x.match(z)) // returns ac
//-->
</script>
</body>
</html>
```

The period . character tells a regular expression to match any character that isn't a new line (\n) character (see Listing 9.4). Thus the a\nc portion of the string does not match. However, abc, a c, and a1c" do match the search a.c.

Listing 9.4   *Matching Characters Which Aren't New Line Characters*

```
<?xml version="1.0" ?>
<!DOCTYPE html PUBLIC "-//W3C//DTD XHTML 1.0 Transitional//EN"
➥"DTD/xhtml1-transitional.dtd">
<html xmlns="http://www.w3.org/1999/xhtml">
<head><title></title></head>

<body>
<script language="JavaScript" type="text/javascript">
<!--
var x = "abc\na\nc\na c\na1c"
var y = /a.c/gi

document.write(x.match(y)) // returns the array [abc, a c, a1c]
//-->
</script>
</body>
</html>
```

Braces {} indicate when there are a minimum and optional maximum number of characters to match. If the first number is followed by a comma, it indicates a minimum number of digits to match. One argument and no comma means an exact number of characters to match. Two arguments separated by a comma indicates a minimum and maximum number of characters to match (see Listing 9.5).

Listing 9.5   *Matching Characters Following a Starting Character*

```
<?xml version="1.0" ?>
<!DOCTYPE html PUBLIC "-//W3C//DTD XHTML 1.0 Transitional//EN"
➡"DTD/xhtml1-transitional.dtd">
<html xmlns="http://www.w3.org/1999/xhtml">
<head><title></title></head>
<body>
<script language="JavaScript" type="text/javascript">
<!--
var w = "ab123bc\nb"
var x = /b.{1}/g   // match b and exactly one additional character
var y = /b.{1,}/g  // match b and at least one additional character
var z = /b.{1,2}/g // match b and one or two additional characters

document.write(w.match(x) + "<br>") // returns ["b1","bc"]
document.write(w.match(y) + "<br>") // returns ["b123bc"]
document.write(w.match(z)) // returns ["b12", "bc"]
//-->
</script>
</body>
</html>
```

Effective in Netscape 6 and Internet Explorer 5.5, a question mark following a *, +, ?, or braces {} causes the pattern to search in what is known as a non-greedy manner. This means it returns matches of the smallest length possible. The greedy manner returns matches of the largest length possible (see Listing 9.6).

Listing 9.6   *Greedy Versus Non-Greedy Pattern Matching*

```
<?xml version="1.0" ?>
<!DOCTYPE html PUBLIC "-//W3C//DTD XHTML 1.0 Transitional//EN"
➡"DTD/xhtml1-transitional.dtd">
<html xmlns="http://www.w3.org/1999/xhtml">
<head><title></title></head>
<body>
<script language="JavaScript" type="text/javascript">
<!--
var x = "mm"
var y = /m+?/g // non-greedy
var z = /m+/g  // greedy

document.write(x.match(y) + "<br>") // returns ["m", "m"]
document.write(x.match(z)) // returns ["mm"]
//-->
</script>
</body>
</html>
```

Brackets [] indicate a range of characters to match against the character specified. If you include a dash, the character before the dash and the character after the dash define the endpoints in part of the range: [a-d] is the same as [abcd] (see Listing 9.7).

Listing 9.7   *Matching Characters in a Range*

```
<?xml version="1.0" ?>
<!DOCTYPE html PUBLIC "-//W3C//DTD XHTML 1.0 Transitional//EN"
➥"DTD/xhtml1-transitional.dtd">
<html xmlns="http://www.w3.org/1999/xhtml">
<head><title></title></head>
<body>
<script language="JavaScript" type="text/javascript">
<!--
var w = "Holy zamboni machines, Batman!!  "
w+= "That man was as quaint as pink lightning!"
var x = /[qz]../g   // match q or z and 2 additional characters
var y = /[m-qz]../g // match m through q or z and 2 additional characters

document.write(w.match(x) + "<br>") // returns ["zam", "qua"]
document.write(w.match(y))
// returns ["oly", "zam", "oni", "mac", "nes", "man", "man",
➥ "qua", "nt ", "pin", "nin"]
//-->
</script>
</body>
</html>
```

A caret included at the start of the brackets [^...] indicates the inverse: match any character that isn't in the range (see Listing 9.8).

Listing 9.8   *Matching Characters Not in a Range*

```
<?xml version="1.0" ?>
<!DOCTYPE html PUBLIC "-//W3C//DTD XHTML 1.0 Transitional//EN"
➥"DTD/xhtml1-transitional.dtd">
<html xmlns="http://www.w3.org/1999/xhtml">
<head><title></title></head>
<body>
<script language="JavaScript" type="text/javascript">
<!--
var w = "Holy zamboni machines, Batman!!  "
w+= "That man was as quaint as pink lightning!"
```

Listing 9.8   *(continued)*

```
var x = /[^a-z]..../g       // match anything not lower case and 4 more
characters
document.write(w.match(x)) // returns the following array of matching strings:
// ["Holy "," mach",", Bat","!!  T"," man "," as q"," as p"," ligh"]
//-->
</script>
</body>
</html>
```

A pair of parentheses (...) containing a piece of a regular expression indicates matches for the RegExp() object to remember as a property of the regular expression. The first match is the $1 property and also the $+ property. These and other possibilities are covered in more detail in the properties section.

Effective in Netscape 6 and Internet Explorer 5.5, the following additional features have been added: A pair of parentheses beginning with a question mark and a colon (?:...) does not remember a match. A pair of parentheses beginning with a question mark and an equal sign (?=...) matches only if the expression following the equal sign follows the expression preceding the parentheses. In these cases, whatever the parentheses contain is not included in the match. Likewise, a pair of parentheses beginning with a question mark and an exclamation point (?!...) matches only if the string does not follow whatever precedes the parentheses with the expression that follows the exclamation point.

The Literal Notation of RegExp() Objects

Finally, any of the preceding characters you can actually search for by adding a backslash (\) before them. Searching for a backslash involves writing two backslashes: (\\). (Note you must also include a second backslash to get one backslash in a string. This is covered in Chapter 13, "JavaScript Syntax.") See Listing 9.9.

Listing 9.9   *Matching Characters Which Have Meaning in* RegExp() *Objects*

```
<?xml version="1.0" ?>
<!DOCTYPE html PUBLIC "-//W3C//DTD XHTML 1.0 Transitional//EN"
➥"DTD/xhtml1-transitional.dtd">
<html xmlns="http://www.w3.org/1999/xhtml">
<head><title></title></head>
<body>
<script language="JavaScript" type="text/javascript">
<!--
var w = "Kenneth Blanchard wrote a book entitled 'Who Moved My Cheese?'"
```

Listing 9.9   *(continued)*

```
var x = "filename:  c:\\myfile.txt"

var y = /......\?/g   // match 6 characters and a question mark
document.write(w.match(y) + "<br>") // returns ["Cheese?"]

var z = /\\....../g   // match a \ followed by 6 characters
document.write(x.match(z)) // returns ["\myfile"]
//-->
</script>
</body>
</html>
```

Regular expressions get a bit more confusing because some characters when prefixed by a backslash take on a totally different meaning. One of the better-known combinations, the \n combination, means a check for new lines in the string. RegExp() objects obtain several other such combinations from their matching literals, covered in Chapter 13 (specifically, \f, \t, \b, \r, \\, \", and \'). Others are more obscure…

In these characters, a capitalized letter preceded by a backslash usually indicates to match the inverse. For instance, \s matches a single whitespace, while \S matches a single nonwhitespace.

The \d character matches any digit, like [0-9]. The \D character matches any character which is *not* a digit, like [^0-9]. See Listing 9.19.

Listing 9.10   *Checking for Digits in a String*

```
<?xml version="1.0" ?>
<!DOCTYPE html PUBLIC "-//W3C//DTD XHTML 1.0 Transitional//EN"
➥"DTD/xhtml1-transitional.dtd">
<html xmlns="http://www.w3.org/1999/xhtml">
<head><title></title></head>
<body>
<script language="JavaScript" type="text/javascript">
<!--
var w = "3.14159"
var x = /\d/g  // match a numeral
var y = /\D/g  // match anything but a numeral

document.write(w.match(x) + "<br>") // returns ["3","1","4","1","5","9"]
document.write(w.match(y)) // returns ["."]
//-->
```

Listing 9.10   *(continued)*

```
</script>
</body>
</html>
```

The \v character defines a vertical tab. Neither Netscape 4 nor Internet Explorer 5 renders this character in any way that indicates a whitespace. Nonetheless, it is a character you can search for.

The \w character tells the RegExp() object to look at word characters. This means it returns any single letter, uppercase, lowercase, an underscore, or any digit. In regular expression syntax, this means [A-Za-z0-9_]. The inverse returns matches that are not letters, digits, or underscores: \W is equivalent to [^A-Za-z0-9_]. See Listing 9.11.

Listing 9.11   *Checking for Normal Word Characters*

```
<?xml version="1.0" ?>
<!DOCTYPE html PUBLIC "-//W3C//DTD XHTML 1.0 Transitional//EN"
➥"DTD/xhtml1-transitional.dtd">
<html xmlns="http://www.w3.org/1999/xhtml">
<head><title></title></head>
<body>
<script language="JavaScript" type="text/javascript">
<!--
var x = "Hey!"
var y = /\w/g  // match a letter, number, or underscore
var z = /\W/g  // match anything but a letter, number, or underscore

document.write(x.match(y) + "<br>") // returns ["H", "e", "y"]
document.write(x.match(z)) // returns ["!"]
//-->
</script>
</body>
</html>
```

The \s character matches any *whitespace* characters: characters that take up space on the screen but don't have anything to show, such as spaces, tabs, carriage returns, and so on. This is equivalent to [\n\t\r\f\v].

The \b character matches any *word boundary*. This means a location in the string that either is preceded by a space and a \w ("b") or followed by a space and preceded by a \w ("b "). The only exception is if the string is one word, in which case it will also match. Note this isn't an actual character of the string; it lies between characters, and restricts the search terms of the `RegExp()` object. (Also note `[\b]` means a backspace character.)

Likewise, the `\B` character matches any non-word boundary. This means a location in the string surrounded on both sides by characters that are not spaces (see Listing 9.12).

Listing 9.12   *Word Boundaries in* `RegExp()` *Objects*

```
<?xml version="1.0" ?>
<!DOCTYPE html PUBLIC "-//W3C//DTD XHTML 1.0 Transitional//EN"
➥"DTD/xhtml1-transitional.dtd">
<html xmlns="http://www.w3.org/1999/xhtml">
<head><title></title></head>
<body>
<script language="JavaScript" type="text/javascript">
<!--
var x = "Hey, batter!"
var y = /\b./g  // match a word boundary followed by one character
var z = /\B./g  // match a non-word boundary followed by one character

var p = /.\b/g  // match a character followed by a word boundary
var q = /.\B/g  // match a character followed by a non-word boundary

document.write("original string: " + x + "<br>")
document.write("matching: " + y + "<br>")
document.write(x.match(y) + "<br>") // ["H", ",", "b", "!"]
document.write("matching: " + p + "<br>")
document.write(x.match(p) + "<br>") // ["y", " ", "r"]

document.write("matching: " + z + "<br>")
document.write(x.match(z) + "<br>") // ["e", "y", " ", "a", "t", "t", "e", "r"]
document.write("matching: " + q + "<br>")
document.write(x.match(q)) // ["H", "e", ",", "b", "a", "t", "t", "e", "!"]
//-->
</script>
</body>
</html>
```

The `\c` character allows a `RegExp()` object to search for control characters—Ctrl+I, for instance, would be caught by `\cI`.

The `\x` character allows a `RegExp()` object to search for ASCII code characters in hexadecimal format of two digits. For instance `\x41` represents the letter "A."

Similarly, the \u character allows a RegExp() object to search for Unicode characters, in hexadecimal format of four digits (see Listing 9.13).

Listing 9.13   *Matching a Character by Hexadecimal Code*

```
<?xml version="1.0" ?>
<!DOCTYPE html PUBLIC "-//W3C//DTD XHTML 1.0 Transitional//EN"
➥"DTD/xhtml1-transitional.dtd">
<html xmlns="http://www.w3.org/1999/xhtml">
<head><title></title></head>
<body>
<script language="JavaScript" type="text/javascript">
<!--
var x = "abc"
var y = /\x61b/g // match ab

document.write(x.match(y)) // returns ["ab"]
//-->
</script>
</body>
</html>
```

Internet Explorer introduces a somewhat confusing notation for octal numbers as well (base-8 numbers; decimal is base-10, hexadecimal base-16). If there are no preceding parentheses submatches ($*n* properties), *kkk* matches an ASCII code character, where *kkk* is an octal number of up to three digits less than 400 (256 in decimal). It is supported in Internet Explorer 5.0+. Netscape 4 uses the octal format \0*kkk*. At the time of this writing neither format appears to work in Netscape 6. (see Listing 9.14).

Listing 9.14   *Matching a Character by Octal ASCII Code (Internet Explorer Only)*

```
<?xml version="1.0" ?>
<!DOCTYPE html PUBLIC "-//W3C//DTD XHTML 1.0 Transitional//EN"
➥"DTD/xhtml1-transitional.dtd">
<html xmlns="http://www.w3.org/1999/xhtml">
<head><title></title></head>
<body>
<script language="JavaScript" type="text/javascript">
<!--
var x = "ABC"
var y = /\101B/g // 101 in octal stands for "A"

document.write(x.match(y)) // returns ["AB"]
//-->
</script>
```

Listing 9.14   *(continued)*

```
</body>
</html>
```

Because this can be confused with the $n properties of Internet Explorer's RegExp object, I do not recommend you use this notation.

The Flags of Regular Expressions

In Chapter 1, "Object()," I mentioned a concept of flags. I did not invent this concept; it has been around for a long time. RegExp() objects also have flags, some of which you've seen in the previous code examples. Specifically, there are three flags: the global flag g, the ignore-case flag i, and the multiline flag m.

> **Note**
> These are not predefined objects, nor are they objects you cannot use. They are in place for compliance with the ECMAScript specifications, and do not affect the operation of JavaScript in any other way.

These flags always come after the RegExp() object's main body. In the literal notation, they come after the second forward slash. In the RegExp() constructor function, they come in as a string in the second argument.

The g flag specifies a global search. Without this flag, JavaScript returns only the first successful match of a string against the regular expression. With this flag, JavaScript returns all successful matches of a string and the regular expression (see Listing 9.15).

Listing 9.15   *Global Searches Turned On and Off*

```
<?xml version="1.0" ?>
<!DOCTYPE html PUBLIC "-//W3C//DTD XHTML 1.0 Transitional//EN"
➥"DTD/xhtml1-transitional.dtd">
<html xmlns="http://www.w3.org/1999/xhtml">
<head><title></title></head>

<body>
<script language="JavaScript" type="text/javascript">
<!--
var x = 'Hey, batta batta batta swing batta'
var y = /batta/    // match the first instance of "batta"
var z = /batta/g  // match all instances of "batta"

document.write(x.match(y) + "<br>") // returns ["batta"]
document.write(x.match(z)) // returns ["batta", "batta", "batta", "batta"]
```

Listing 9.15   *(continued)*

```
//-->
</script>
</body>
</html>
```

The i flag specifies a search that doesn't care if letters are uppercase or lowercase. Without this flag, JavaScript will only return matches which share match the case of the regular expression. With this flag, JavaScript returns all matches that have the same spelling as the regular expression implies (see Listing 9.16).

Listing 9.16   *Ignore-Case Searches Turned On and Off*

```
<?xml version="1.0" ?>
<!DOCTYPE html PUBLIC "-//W3C//DTD XHTML 1.0 Transitional//EN"
➥"DTD/xhtml1-transitional.dtd">
<html xmlns="http://www.w3.org/1999/xhtml">
<head><title></title></head>
<body>
<script language="JavaScript" type="text/javascript">
<!--
var x = "DAY-O day-o... daylight come and we want to go home..."
var y = /day\-o/g  // match exactly "day-o"
var z = /day\-o/gi // match "day-o" ignoring case

document.write(x.match(y) + "<br>") // returns ["day-o"]
document.write(x.match(z)) // returns ["DAY-O", "day-o"]
//-->
</script>
</body>
</html>
```

The m flag is new to Netscape 6 and Internet Explorer 5.5. It causes each new line to be treated as a separate string in the regular expression match (see Listing 9.17).

Listing 9.17   *Multiline Searches Turned On and Off*

```
<?xml version="1.0" ?>
<!DOCTYPE html PUBLIC "-//W3C//DTD XHTML 1.0 Transitional//EN"
➥"DTD/xhtml1-transitional.dtd">
<html xmlns="http://www.w3.org/1999/xhtml">
<head><title></title></head>
```

Listing 9.17 *(continued)*

```
<body>
<script language="JavaScript" type="text/javascript">
<!--
var x = "I'm gonna send thee 1 by 1:\n"
x+= "1 for the itty-bitty baby"

var y = /^\d/  // match a numeral
var z = /^\d/m // match a numeral on any line

document.write(x.match(y) + "<br>") // returns []
document.write(x.match(z)) // returns ["1"]
//-->
</script>
</body>
</html>
```

Properties

> **Note**
> Internet Explorer adds a lot of properties to the RegExp object itself, based on the most
> recent RegExp() object's searches as a group. Netscape 4 browsers did implement many of
> these features, but Netscape 6 has generally deprecated most of them, retaining a few as
> properties of RegExp() objects. The reason for such confusion is because RegExp() objects
> were not formally defined as part of the ECMAScript standard until the third edition.

RegExp().global

JavaScript 1.2+, JScript 3+

Nav4+, IE4+

Syntax

regexpObj.global

The global property of the regular expression object indicates whether the g flag of
the this object is in effect (see Listing 9.18). If it is, all matches for the expression will
be returned.

Listing 9.18   *The* global *Property of* RegExp() *Objects*

```
<?xml version="1.0" ?>
<!DOCTYPE html PUBLIC "-//W3C//DTD XHTML 1.0 Transitional//EN"
➥"DTD/xhtml1-transitional.dtd">
<html xmlns="http://www.w3.org/1999/xhtml">
<head><title></title></head>
<body>
<script language="JavaScript" type="text/javascript">
<!--
var x = /Hello/
var y = /Hello/g
alert(x.global) // returns false
alert(y.global) // returns true
//-->
</script>
</body>
</html>
```

RegExp().ignoreCase

JavaScript 1.2+, JScript 3+

Nav4+, IE4+

Syntax

regexpObj.ignoreCase

The ignoreCase property of the regular expression object indicates whether the i flag of the this object is in effect. Similar in design to RegExp().global.

RegExp.index

JScript 3+

IE4+

Syntax

RegExp.index

The index property of a regular expression object returns the character index of the last executed match's first matched character in its string. In Internet Explorer 5.5, this changed to reflect cumulative matching as seen in Listing 9.19.

Listing 9.19   *The* index *and* lastIndex *Properties of* RegExp

```
<?xml version="1.0" ?>
<!DOCTYPE html PUBLIC "-//W3C//DTD XHTML 1.0 Transitional//EN"
➥"DTD/xhtml1-transitional.dtd">
<html xmlns="http://www.w3.org/1999/xhtml">
<head><title></title></head>
<body>
<script language="JavaScript" type="text/javascript">
<!--
var x = "Hey, batta batta batta swing batta"
var y = /batt/
y.exec(x)
document.write("original string: " + x + "<br>")
document.write("RegExp.index: " + RegExp.index + "<br>") // returns 5
document.write("RegExp.lastIndex: " + RegExp.lastIndex + "<br>") // returns 9
document.write("RegExp.charAt: " + x.charAt(RegExp.index) + "<br>") // returns
"b"
document.write("x.charAt: " + x.charAt(RegExp.lastIndex) + "<br>") // returns
"a"
y.exec(x)
document.write("y.exec(x) <br>")
document.write("RegExp.index: " + RegExp.index + "<br>") // returns 5
document.write("RegExp.lastIndex: " + RegExp.lastIndex + "<br>") // returns 9
y = /batt/g
y.exec(x)
document.write("y.exec(x) <br>")
document.write("RegExp.index: " + RegExp.index + "<br>") // returns 5
document.write("RegExp.lastIndex: " + RegExp.lastIndex + "<br>") // returns 9
y.exec(x)
document.write("y.exec(x) <br>")
document.write("RegExp.index: " + RegExp.index + "<br>") // returns 11 in IE5.5,
5 in IE4-5
document.write("RegExp.lastIndex: " + RegExp.lastIndex)
// returns 15 in IE5.5, 9 in IE4-5
//-->
</script>
</body>
</html>
```

Note

The differences in the output of Listing 9.19 above comes from what some consider a bug in Internet Explorer 4/5 that causes the g flag to be ignored with repeated exec calls. It is definitely something to remember to avoid an unpleasant afternoon of debugging.

RegExp.input / RegExp.$_

JScript 3+

IE4+ (`RegExp.input`)

JScript 5.5+

IE5.5 (`RegExp.$_`)

Syntax

```
RegExp.input
```

The `input` property of a regular expression object returns the string used in the last regular expression match.

RegExp.lastIndex

JScript 3+

IE4+

Syntax

```
RegExp.lastIndex
```

The `lastIndex` property of a regular expression object returns the character index of the last executed match's first character after the matched character set in its string. In Internet Explorer 5.5, this changed to reflect cumulative matching (see Listing 9.19).

RegExp().lastIndex

JavaScript 1.2+, JScript 5.5

Nav4+, IE5.5

Syntax

```
regexpObj.lastIndex
```

The `lastIndex` property of the regular expression object returns the index of the first character after the last match of the `this` object in the string last matched.

RegExp.$*n* (1 <= n <= 9)

JavaScript 1.2+, JScript 3+

Nav4+, IE4+

Syntax

```
RegExp.$n
```

The `$n` property of a regular expression returns the last remembered matches (those in parentheses) of the last `RegExp()` object search. These properties do not apply as properties of `RegExp()` objects, but as properties of the `RegExp` constructor function. As you can see in Listing 9.20 there are other matches, but only the ones in parentheses are remembered.

Listing 9.20   *The* `$n` *Properties of* `RegExp`

```
<?xml version="1.0" ?>
<!DOCTYPE html PUBLIC "-//W3C//DTD XHTML 1.0 Transitional//EN"
➥"DTD/xhtml1-transitional.dtd">
<html xmlns="http://www.w3.org/1999/xhtml">
<head><title></title></head>
<body>
<script language="JavaScript" type="text/javascript">
<!--
var w = "Testing, testing, one, two, three"
var x = "When I say jump, you jump!!"
var y = /(test)(ing)/gi   // remember matching "test" and "ing"
var z = /(j)(u)m(p)/gi  // remember matching j, u, m, or p
alert(y.exec(w))   // returns ["Testing", "test", "ing"]
alert(RegExp.$1+"\n"+RegExp.$2+"\n"+RegExp.$3+"\n"+RegExp.$4+"\n"+RegExp.$5)
/* returns
Test
ing
*/
alert(z.exec(x)) // returns ["jump","j","u","p"]
alert(RegExp.$1+"\n"+RegExp.$2+"\n"+RegExp.$3+"\n"+RegExp.$4+"\n"+RegExp.$5)
/* returns
j
u
```

Listing 9.20 *(continued)*

```
p
*/
//-->
</script>
</body>
</html>
```

RegExp.lastMatch

JavaScript 1.2+, JScript 5.5+

Nav4+, IE5.5

Syntax

```
RegExp.lastMatch
```

The `lastMatch` property of a regular expression object returns the last match of the regular expression.

RegExp.lastParen

JavaScript 1.2+, JScript 5.5+

Nav4+, IE5.5

Syntax

```
RegExp.lastParen
```

The `lastParen` property of a regular expression object returns the last parenthesized match of the regular expression (see Listing 9.21).

Listing 9.21 *The* `input`, `lastMatch`, *and* `lastParen` *Properties of* `RegExp`

```
<?xml version="1.0" ?>
<!DOCTYPE html PUBLIC "-//W3C//DTD XHTML 1.0 Transitional//EN"
➥"DTD/xhtml1-transitional.dtd">
<html xmlns="http://www.w3.org/1999/xhtml">
<head><title></title></head>
<body>
<script language="JavaScript" type="text/javascript">
<!--
```

Listing 9.21   *(continued)*

```
x = "The ox met the ax, and was vexed."
y = /(.)x/g  //remember any character followed by an x
x.match(y)
document.write(RegExp.input + "<br>")
// returns x, not supported under Netscape
document.write(RegExp.$_ + "<br>") // returns x, not supported under Netscape
document.write (RegExp.lastMatch + "<br>") // returns "ex"
//alert(RegExp.$&) // breaks script
document.write (RegExp.lastParen + "<br>") // returns "e"
x.match(y)
document.write (RegExp.lastMatch + "<br>") // returns "ex"
document.write (RegExp.lastParen + "<br>") // returns "e"
//-->
</script>
</body>
</html>
```

RegExp.leftContext

JavaScript 1.2+, JScript 5.5

Nav4+, IE5.5

Syntax

```
RegExp.leftContext
```

The leftContext property of a regular expression object returns all characters preceding the final match returned from the last string that it was matched against. See Listing 9.22 for a test case.

RegExp.rightContext

JavaScript 1.2+, JScript 5.5

Nav4+, IE5.5

Syntax

```
RegExp.rightContext
```

The rightContext property of a regular expression object returns all characters following the final match returned from the last string that was matched against (see Listing 9.22).

Listing 9.22   *The* `leftContext` *and* `rightContext` *Properties of* `RegExp`

```
<?xml version="1.0" ?>
<!DOCTYPE html PUBLIC "-//W3C//DTD XHTML 1.0 Transitional//EN"
➥"DTD/xhtml1-transitional.dtd">
<html xmlns="http://www.w3.org/1999/xhtml">
<head><title></title></head>
<body>
<script language="JavaScript" type="text/javascript">
<!--
x = "The ox met the ax, and was vexed."
y = /(.)x/g  // remember any character followed by an x
x.match(y)
document.write(RegExp.leftContext + "<br>") // returns "The ox met the ax, and
was v"
document.write(RegExp.rightContext + "<br>") // returns "ed."
//alert(RegExp.$`) // breaks script
//alert(RegExp.$') // breaks script
//-->
</script>
</body>
</html>
```

RegExp().source

JavaScript 1.2+, JScript 3+

Nav4+, IE4+

Syntax

```
regexpObj.source
```

The source property of the regular expression object returns the source of the `this` object in text form. This property is read-only (see Listing 9.23).

Listing 9.23   *The* `lastIndex` *Property of* `RegExp()` *Objects*

```
<?xml version="1.0" ?>
<!DOCTYPE html PUBLIC "-//W3C//DTD XHTML 1.0 Transitional//EN"
➥"DTD/xhtml1-transitional.dtd">
<html xmlns="http://www.w3.org/1999/xhtml">
<head><title></title></head>
<body>
<script language="JavaScript" type="text/javascript">
```

Listing 9.23 *(continued)*

```
<!--
var x = "Show me the money!!"
var y = /mo/g
z = y.exec(x)
alert(y.lastIndex + "\n" + x.charAt(y.lastIndex)) // IE5.5:  returns 14, "n"
alert(y.source) // returns "mo"
//-->
</script>
</body>
</html>
```

RegExp.multiline

JavaScript 1.2

Nav4.00—4.75

Deprecated in Nav6

Syntax

```
RegExp.multiline
```

The multiline property of a regular expression object indicates whether the last search executed over several lines within a string.

RegExp().multiline

JavaScript 1.5, JScript 5.5

Nav6, IE5.5

Syntax

```
regexpObj.multiline
```

The multiline property of the regular expression object indicates whether the m flag of the this object is in effect. Similar in design to RegExp().global.

Methods

RegExp().compile()

JavaScript 1.2+, JScript 3+

Nav4+, IE4+

Syntax

regexpObj.compile(pattern [, flags])

The compile() method of the regular expression object method allows you to take one RegExp() object and redefine it as a new one in compiled form. The first argument is the regular expression pattern you want this to become; the second optional argument specifies flags (see Listing 9.24).

Listing 9.24   *The Compile Method of* RegExp() *Objects*

```
<?xml version="1.0" ?>
<!DOCTYPE html PUBLIC "-//W3C//DTD XHTML 1.0 Transitional//EN"
➥"DTD/xhtml1-transitional.dtd">
<html xmlns="http://www.w3.org/1999/xhtml">
<head><title></title></head>
<body>
<script language="JavaScript" type="text/javascript">
<!--
var x = new RegExp("Hello","g")
alert(x) // returns /Hello/g
x.compile("Goodbye")
alert(x) // returns /Goodbye/
x.compile("Ciao", "gi")
alert(x) // returns /Ciao/ig
//-->
</script>
</body>
</html>
```

RegExp().exec()

JavaScript 1.2+, JScript 3+

Nav4+, IE4+

Syntax

```
regexpObj.exec(strObj)
```

The exec() method of the regular expression object returns the results of matching the this object against the first argument, a String() object. Similar to the String().match() method call. exec() returns an array of strings that match the expression, or null if there are no matches. If the g flag is set, repeated calls to exec() will step through the string and return each individual match.

RegExp().test()

JavaScript 1.2+, JScript 3+

Nav4+, IE4+

Syntax

```
regexpObj.test(strObj)
```

The test() method of the regular expression object returns a Boolean() value telling if there is at least one match between the this object and the first argument, a String() object. Similar to the String().search() method call.

Listing 9.25 *The* test *and* exec *Methods in a Demonstration*

```
<?xml version="1.0" ?>
<!DOCTYPE html PUBLIC "-//W3C//DTD XHTML 1.0 Transitional//EN"
➥"DTD/xhtml1-transitional.dtd">
<html xmlns="http://www.w3.org/1999/xhtml">
<head><title></title></head>
<body>
<script language="JavaScript" type="text/javascript">
<!--
var x = "Hello World"
var y = "Goodbye, cruel world"
var z = new RegExp("Hello","g")
alert(z.test(x)) // returns true
alert(z.test(y)) // returns false
alert(z.exec(x)) // returns "Hello"
alert(z.exec(y)) // returns null
//-->
</script>
</body>
</html>
```

RegExp().toSource()

JavaScript 1.2+

Nav4+

Overrides `Object().toSource()`

Syntax

`regexpObj.toSource()`

The `toSource()` method of the regular expression object returns a source-code representation of the `this` object.

RegExp().toString()

JavaScript 1.2+, JScript 3+

Nav4+, IE4+

Overrides `Object().toString()`

Syntax

`regexpObj.toString()`

The `toString()` method of the regular expression object returns the `this` object in literal notation as a string.

```
var x = new RegExp("Hello", "g")
alert(x.toString()) // returns "/Hello/g"
```

RegExp().valueOf()

JavaScript 1.2+, JScript 3+

Nav4+, IE4+

Overrides `Object().valueOf()`

Syntax

`regexpObj.valueOf()`

The `valueOf()` method of the regular expression object returns the unchanged literal notation of the `this` object.

```
var x = new RegExp("Hello", "g")
alert(x.valueOf()) // returns /Hello/g
```

Example: Regular Expressions and Text Exercises

With a little practice using the regular expressions tools explained earlier in the chapter, you can achieve rather impressive results. The remaining examples demonstrate some rather complex string manipulation. Shakespeare, anyone?

Listing 9.26   *Hamlet, JavaScript Style*

```
<?xml version="1.0" ?>
<!DOCTYPE html PUBLIC "-//W3C//DTD XHTML 1.0 Transitional//EN"
➥"DTD/xhtml1-transitional.dtd">
<html xmlns="http://www.w3.org/1999/xhtml">
<head><title></title></head>
<body>
<script language="JavaScript" type="text/javascript">
<!--
var a = "((BB)||!(BB))==?"
var b = /\(B{2}\)/g
var c = /\|{2}/
var d = /!/
var e = /\(/
var f = /\)==\?/

alert(a) // returns "((BB)||!(BB))==?"
var m = a.replace(b, "to be")
var n = m.replace(c, " or ")
var o = n.replace(d, "not ")
var p = o.replace(e, "")
var q = p.replace(f, "\n that is the question")
alert(q)
// returns "to be or not to be\n that is the question"
//-->
</script>
</body>
</html>
```

Of course, regular expressions are useful in more ways than prose. You can use them to scramble text (including source code, if you so desired) so that the browser can read the source code, but the user would have a tougher time.

Unicode is an extended character set of some 65,536 characters, but JavaScript source code is restricted to the first 256 characters thereof. So you could render a source code somewhat harder to read by shifting all the characters in its source up the Unicode scale by more than 256, but all the same distance. (A similar procedure was one of the first codes ever used in history.) See Listing 9.27.

Listing 9.27   *Encoding in Its Simplest Form*

```
<?xml version="1.0" ?>
<!DOCTYPE html PUBLIC "-//W3C//DTD XHTML 1.0 Transitional//EN"
➥"DTD/xhtml1-transitional.dtd">
<html xmlns="http://www.w3.org/1999/xhtml">
<head><title></title></head>
<body>
<script language="JavaScript" type="text/javascript">
<!--
var shift = Math.ceil(Math.random() * 256)
var str = "The quick red fox jumped over the lazy brown dog."
for (loop = "z".charCodeAt(0); loop >= "a".charCodeAt(0); loop--) {
   var check = new RegExp(String.fromCharCode(loop),"g")
   str = str.replace(check, String.fromCharCode(loop+shift))
   }

for (loop = "Z".charCodeAt(0); loop >= "A".charCodeAt(0); loop--) {
   var check = new RegExp(String.fromCharCode(loop),"g")
   str = str.replace(check, String.fromCharCode(loop+shift))
   }

for (loop = "9".charCodeAt(0); loop >= "0".charCodeAt(0); loop--) {
   var check = new RegExp(String.fromCharCode(loop),"g")
   str = str.replace(check, String.fromCharCode(loop+shift))
   }

alert(str) // returns human-illegible string (we hope)
//-->
</script>
</body>
</html>
```

Example: Regular Expressions and Text Exercises

This code is easily crackable by any advanced JavaScripter; do not use this in your own projects. It is merely another demonstration of the power of regular expressions.

One final bit of information that might be of interest is Netscape allows regular expressions to be used directly as function calls. For example,

```
/foo/("A string with foo")
```

is perfectly acceptable and will match "foo". However, this does not work under Internet Explorer and as such, should be avoided for cross-browser compatibility.

CHAPTER 10

Error()

Browser/JavaScript Version	Created By
Nav4/JavaScript 1.2	(Not implemented)
IE4/JScript 3.0	(Not implemented)
IE5/JScript 5.0	x = new Error(*message*)
IE5.5/JScript 5.5	x = new Error(*message*)
Nav6/JavaScript 1.5	x = new Error(*message*)
IE6	x = new Error(*message*)
ECMAScript 1st edition	(Not implemented)
ECMAScript 3rd edition	x = new Error(*message*)

> **Note**
> Implemented in Nav6, IE5+
> Descends from `Object()`

Description

Errors, or exceptions, exist in every programming language—not errors of the language, but features of the language to handle errors in various programs and scripts. JavaScript has its own version of errors as well. However, the latest push toward JavaScript standardization means that even errors are considered objects.

Error-handling has been part of JavaScript since Netscape 4 and Internet Explorer 4. The third edition of ECMAScript defines special statements for handling errors (`try...catch...finally` and `throw`, which I cover in Chapter 11, "The Global Object and Statements"), and prior to that, we have the `window.onerror` event handler for at least documenting errors.

You can create custom errors any time you want, but before you do that, you should understand how the various browsers implement their instances of `Error()`. The example will thus describe custom errors you can create for these browsers. See Listing 10.1.

> **Note**
> Instances of `Error()` are not the same as the `event` objects passed via the `window.onerror` event handler.

Listing 10.1   *Forcing an Error to Find Out How It Works (Internet Explorer 5+, Netscape 6)*

```
<?xml version="1.0" ?>
<!DOCTYPE html PUBLIC "-//W3C//DTD XHTML 1.0 Transitional//EN"
➥"DTD/xhtml1-transitional.dtd">
<html xmlns="http://www.w3.org/1999/xhtml" >
<head><title></title></head>
<body>
<p>
<script language="JavaScript" type="text/javascript">
<!--
try {
   var x = "A".toNumber()
   }
catch (exception) {
   document.write(exception + "<br />")
   for (property in exception) {
      document.write(property + " = " + exception[property] + "<br />")
      }
   }
//-->
</script>
</p>
<!-- Results in Netscape 6.00
TypeError: "A".toNumber is not a function
message = "A".toNumber is not a function
fileName = file:///C:/WIN95/DESKTOP/Book/2013/Lab.htm
lineNumber = 7
name = TypeError
-->
</body>
</html>
```

Properties

description

JScript 5.0+

IE5.0+

Syntax

```
var x = errObj.description
```

The `description` property of instances of `Error()` represents the error message behind the `this` object. Note ECMAScript third edition replaces this property with the `message` property of instances of `Error()` in Internet Explorer 5.5, but it remains for backward-compatibility.

fileName

JavaScript 1.5

Nav6

Syntax

```
var x = errObj.fileName
```

The `fileName` property of instances of `Error()` is one of the nice things about Netscape's implementation of JavaScript: they always tell you what filename caused an error. This becomes highly useful in a frameset, when the frames may have different filenames than the main frameset. The `fileName` gives a URI direct to the name of the file that causes the exception.

(Internet Explorer also has this information, but does not incorporate it into its `Error()` objects.)

lineNumber

JavaScript 1.5

Nav6

Syntax

```
var x = errObj.lineNumber
```

The `lineNumber` property of instances of `Error()` returns the line number where the error originated at. Although neither Netscape nor Internet Explorer provides any way of seeing what line number is what without counting, this can help you narrow it down a bit. (Internet Explorer also has the line number information, but does not incorporate it into its `Error()` objects.)

What I like to do to help narrow down an error is add in a diagnostic alert box and move it around. If the error line number shifts down, I know the alert box happens before the error. If the error line number is unaffected, I know the alert box happens after the error. Refer to Listings 10.2 and 10.3 to help you see the concept.

Listing 10.2   Alert Box Before the Error

```
<?xml version="1.0" ?>
<!DOCTYPE html PUBLIC "-//W3C//DTD XHTML 1.0 Transitional//EN"
➥"DTD/xhtml1-transitional.dtd">
<html xmlns="http://www.w3.org/1999/xhtml" >
<head><title></title></head>
<body>
<p>
<script language="JavaScript" type="text/javascript">
<!—
try {
    alert("Hello")
    var x = "A".toNumber() // lineNumber == 7
    }
catch (exception) {
    document.write(exception+"<br />")
    for (property in exception) {
       document.write(property+"    " + exception[property] + "<br />")
       }
    throw exception
    }
//—>
</script>
</p>
</body>
</html>
```

Listing 10.3   Alert Box After the Error

```
<?xml version="1.0" ?>
<!DOCTYPE html PUBLIC "-//W3C//DTD XHTML 1.0 Transitional//EN"
➥"DTD/xhtml1-transitional.dtd">
<html xmlns="http://www.w3.org/1999/xhtml" >
<head><title></title></head>
<body>
<p>
```

Listing 10.3   *(continued)*

```
<script language="JavaScript" type="text/javascript">
<!--
try {
   var x = "A".toNumber() // lineNumber == 6
   alert("Hello")
   }
catch (exception) {
   document.write(exception+"<br />")
   for (property in exception) {
      document.write(property+"    " + exception[property] + "<br />")
      }
   throw exception
   }
//-->
</script>
</p>
</body>
</html>
```

By moving the alert box up and down in the file, I can actually narrow down where the error is, until there's only one line on which it can be. However, you can usually find the results much quicker by using an editor with line number support. I almost never do, so I developed this technique for times when I don't actually have line numbering. (If you don't like the numerous alerts, you could always use void(null) instead.)

(Incidentally, the error numbers in Listings 10.2 and 10.3 may not reflect the exact line numbers of the error that you may get if you run the these scripts; they are used as a demonstration.)

message

JavaScript 1.5, JScript 5.5+

Nav6, IE5.5

Syntax

```
var x = errObj.message
```

The message property of instances of Error() represents the error message behind the this object, describing exactly what happened to throw the error.

name

JavaScript 1.5, JScript 5.5+

Nav6, IE5.5

Syntax

```
var x = errObj.name
```

The `name` property of instances of `Error()` represents the type of error thrown, similar to the `constructor` method detailed in Chapter 1, "`Object()`." However, this is not a function; it just gives the type of error as a string.

One feature ECMAScript third edition defines is various types of errors. One is the `EvalError`, used when you feed an `eval()` method an inappropriate string command. Another is the `TypeError`, which happens when a function expects one type for `this` or an argument and gets another. The `RangeError` describes when a number is not in the acceptable range. The `SyntaxError` is a syntax error (likely a missing quote or closing parenthesis or closing bracket). The `URIError` describes a URI-handling function used improperly. The `ReferenceError` describes an improper reference.

If instead you get `"Error"` as the `name` property, you probably have a custom-defined error.

number

JScript 5.0+

IE5.0+

Syntax

```
var x = errObj.number
```

The `number` property of instances of `Error()` represents a custom error number you assign to the `this` object. You might expect Internet Explorer to assign error numbers to its native errors, but as of versions 5.0 and 5.5, it does not. (According to Microsoft's JScript documentation, each native run-time error has an error number in the 5,000 range.)

Incidentally, the error number is a 32-bit number, which can be somewhat confusing to decipher. Microsoft's JScript documentation was kind enough to provide this formula for retrieving the number code:

```
var errNum = (errObj.number & 0xFFFF)
```

Microsoft's documentation provides some of the error codes; for instance, its own documentation lists error code 5009 for an undefined variable. However, for the `"A".toNumber()` scenario throughout this chapter, Microsoft Internet Explorer's error code is 438. The JScript documentation lists no such error code.

Methods

toString()

JavaScript 1.5, JScript 5.0+

Nav6, IE5.0+

Overrides `Object.prototype.toString()`

Syntax

```
var x = errObj.toString()
```

In Netscape 6, the `toString()` method of instances of `Error()` returns a string representation of the exception's message, prefixed by the type of error it was. Changing the `message` and `name` properties does not affect the method's returned string. In the error I use in Listings 10.1–10.3, Netscape 6 returns `'TypeError: "A".toNumber is not a function'`.

Internet Explorer 5.0+ has this method as well, but it returns `"[object Error]"`.

toSource()

JavaScript 1.5

Nav6

Overrides `Object.prototype.toSource()`

Syntax

```
var x = errObj.toSource()
```

The `toSource()` method of instances of `Error()` returns a source code representation of the `this` object—the exact function used to create an error. Because there is more than one type of error (see "`name`" earlier in this chapter), it names the function used to create an error. In the error I use in Listings 10.1–10.3, Netscape 6 returns:

```
(new TypeError(""A".toNumber is not a function",
➥"file:///C:/WIN95/DESKTOP/Book/2013/Lab.htm", 7))
```

> **Note**
> This code, which Netscape 6 returns, has a known bug—the adjacent double quotes. Recent Mozilla builds may fix the bug. See `http://bugzilla.mozilla.org/show_bug.cgi?id=96284` for details.

Example: Creating and Using Errors

Internet Explorer 5.0 supports only the `Error()` constructor function; Internet Explorer 5.5 and Netscape 6 support all the constructor functions named in the `name` property definition. For backward-compatibility and simplicity, however, let's stick with `Error()`.

> **Note**
> Internet Explorer 4 and Netscape 4 do not support `Error()` as defined by ECMAScript third edition. However, you can create an `Error()` constructor as I demonstrate in Chapter 1, "`Object()`." If you choose to do so, please do so in compliance with ECMAScript third edition. You will not be able to create the `try...catch` and `throw` statements, however.

The `Error()` constructor function, as defined by ECMAScript third edition, accepts one argument for properties. The first argument, if given, becomes the `message` property of the instance of `Error()`. (In Internet Explorer 5.0, it becomes the `description` property.)

With instances of `Error()`, you can set any properties or methods you want after the fact:

```
var y = new Error()
y.message = "I'm having a bad hair day"
```

As I've noted in Chapter 2, "`Function()`," you can often avoid the need for errors to be thrown and caught explicitly by using `break` statements and labels. However, they won't help much in catching errors in syntax. Netscape, as of JavaScript 1.3+, will not pop up an error box right away. Instead, without a `window.onerror`, your script will simply stop working and you won't see anything outside the JavaScript console.

Therefore, when debugging in Internet Explorer 5.5 and Netscape 6, you can use the code in Listing 10.4.

Listing 10.4   *Complete Error-Handling in Internet Explorer 5.0+, Netscape 6*

```
<?xml version="1.0" ?>
<!DOCTYPE html PUBLIC "-//W3C//DTD XHTML 1.0 Transitional//EN"
➡"DTD/xhtml1-transitional.dtd">
<html xmlns="http://www.w3.org/1999/xhtml" >
<head><title></title></head>
<body>
<script language="JavaScript" type="text/javascript">
<!--
function myFunc() {
   try {
      myFunc_label:
      if (true) {
         // error-handling and normal operation as per Chapter 2
         }
      switch (interror) {
         // error-handling and normal operation as per Chapter 2
         }
      }
   catch (exception) {
      var errormsg = exception.toString()
      for (property in errormsg) {
         errormsg += "\n" + property + ":   " + eval("errormsg."+property)
         }
      alert(errormsg)
      }
   return response // if necessary
   }
//-->
</script>
</body>
</html>
```

The main body of the function takes place in the if (true) section. You handle custom errors not thrown using the throw statement as I describe in Chapter 2. Errors you throw using the throw statement, and those which the browser throws for your typos, get caught after the fact in the catch statement, which immediately breaks down the error and gives you an alert in a formatted manner. Finally, if you desire to return a response, you do so after all error-handling has finished.

One thing I mentioned in Chapter 2 should be re-emphasized here. It is preferable for you to handle error-causing conditions before a browser acts on them, creating an error. Once an error gets thrown using the `throw` statement, there is no way to go back to the line of code that threw the exception, and thus no way to continue execution of the function normally. This is the reason for the error "pre-interception" routine in Chapter 2.

CHAPTER 11

The Global Object and Statements

The Global object is an object which ECMAScript defines, but which you cannot access directly. It is a wrapper for functions and objects available throughout the JavaScript language.

Netscape refers to these functions and objects as *top-level*. In a way, this is appropriate—you don't access them as properties of any given object. The window object is the Global object as far as client side JavaScript is concerned, so it has all objects and functions this chapter covers as properties and methods, respectively.

There are also several statements in the JavaScript language that have the same scope as these top-level objects, but are not objects themselves. These statements, such as if...else and var define the structure of the language.

Top-Level Objects

Infinity

JavaScript 1.2+, JScript 3+

Nav4.06+, IE4+

Syntax

```
Infinity
```

The `Infinity` property of the `Global` object is equal to the `Number.POSITIVE_INFINITY` value. See Chapter 7, "Number()," for the `Number.POSITIVE_INFINITY` value.

NaN

JavaScript 1.2+, JScript 3+

Nav4.06+, IE4+

Syntax

```
NaN
```

The `NaN` property of the `Global` object is equivalent (but not equal to) the `Number.NaN` value. See Chapter 7 for the `Number.NaN` object.

undefined

JavaScript 1.2+, JScript 5.5+

Nav4.06+, IE5.5+

Syntax

```
undefined
```

The `undefined` property of the `Global` object is a value provided to define the "undefined" type. Any variable that has not been assigned a value is undefined. Keep in mind the undefined value has been around for a long time in JavaScript. This is just a convenient way to access it.

Interestingly, Internet Explorer 5.0 provides this as an empty property. In Internet Explorer 5.0, the following throws an exception, but not on `undefined`, as you might expect:

```
alert(undefined == x) // exception:  'x' is undefined
```

Under conditions like this, it's usually better to use the `typeof` operator described in Chapter 12, "Operators."

Top-Level Functions

decodeURI( )

JavaScript 1.5, JScript 5.5

Nav6, IE5.5

Syntax

```
decodeURI(URIString)
```

The `decodeURI()` method of the `Global` object takes a URI string and decodes it as a regular string. Effectively, it is an inverse to the `encodeURI` function.

```
alert(decodeURI(encodeURI(x)) == x) // returns true
```

decodeURIComponent( )

JavaScript 1.5, JScript 5.5

Nav6, IE5.5

Syntax

```
decodeURIComponent(URIComponentString)
```

The `decodeURIComponent()` method of the `Global` object takes a URI component string and decodes it as a regular string. Effectively, it is an inverse to the `encodeURIComponent` function.

encodeURI( )

JavaScript 1.5, JScript 5.5

Nav6, IE5.5

Syntax

```
encodeURI(NormalString)
```

The encodeURI() method of the Global object accepts a string for its first argument and returns the string reformatted according to the W3C's URI definition. It assumes you are passing it a complete URI. Thus, it does not encode colons, slashes, question marks, hash marks, and so on. An example of this method can be seen in Listing 11.1.

encodeURIComponent( )

JavaScript 1.5, JScript 5.5

Nav6, IE5.5

Syntax

```
encodeURIComponent(NormalString)
```

The encodeURIComponent() method of the Global object accepts a string for its first argument and returns the string reformatted according to the W3C's URI definition. It assumes you are passing it a portion of a complete URI, which does not contain more than one component of a URI (query string, target, directory, domain name, and so on). An example of this method can also be seen in Listing 11.1.

escape( )

JavaScript 1.0+, JScript 1+

Nav2+, IE3+

Syntax

```
escape(NormalString)
```

The escape() method of the Global object was provided to permit users a way to encode strings for use in URLs. For instance, a URL cannot have spaces or quotes in it natively: http://yoursite.com/yourpage.htm?info="Bad URL". Instead, the developer must say http://yoursite.com/yourpage.htm?info=%22Good%20URL%22.

The first argument, a string, is transformed such that every character that cannot be safely passed in a URL is encoded using an escape code (the % sign, followed by a hexadecimal number of the ASCII equivalent for each character). This includes colons, question marks, hash marks, and so on (",","?:). For this reason, only pass the part you want encoded to the string, or else you may get this, an invalid URL:

```
http%3A//yoursite.com/yourpage.htm%3Finfo%3D%22Bad%20URL%22
```

This function exists in the ECMAScript 1st edition specifications, but has been removed from the ECMAScript 3rd edition specifications. Netscape 6 and Internet Explorer 5.5 still support it, but it may have been deprecated in these versions. (Microsoft's documentation implies this, and Netscape's is silent on the matter.)

To demonstrate the differences between these three methods, observe Listing 11.1.

Listing 11.1   *The Three URI Encoding Functions Compared*

```
<?xml version="1.0" ?>
<!DOCTYPE html PUBLIC "-//W3C//DTD XHTML 1.0 Transitional//EN"
➡"DTD/xhtml1-transitional.dtd">
<html xmlns="http://www.w3.org/1999/xhtml">
<head><title></title></head>
<body>
<script language="JavaScript" type="text/javascript">
<!--
var x = "http://Hello.htm?info=Hello: World"
document.write(escape(x)+"<br />")
// returns "http%3A//Hello.htm%3Finfo%3DHello%3A%20World"
document.write(encodeURI(x)+"<br />")
// returns "http://Hello.htm?info=Hello:%20World"
document.write(encodeURIComponent(x)+"<br />")
// returns "http%3A%2F%2FHello.htm%3Finfo%3DHello%3A%20World"

var y = "Hello: World"
var z = "http://Hello.htm?info="
z = encodeURI(z)
z += encodeURIComponent(y)
document.write(z)
// returns "http://Hello.htm?info=Hello%3A%20World"
//-->
</script>
</body>
</html>
```

Note the last returned string is a correctly formatted URI. Encode the main parts of the URI first with the `encodeURI()` function, and then append the components encoded using the `encodeURIComponent()` function. Be careful not to encode parts which must not be encoded (such as "?info=").

eval( )

JavaScript 1.0+, JScript 1+

Nav2+, IE3+

Syntax

```
eval(CodeBlock)
```

The `eval()` method of the `Global` object was briefly covered in Chapter 4, "String()." Basically, you can take any string you feed to the `eval()` function as its first argument, and it will execute the string as if it were a code block actually belonging to the script.

A simple example is creating references to existing objects:

```
y = 4
var x = eval("myObj" + y) // x = myObj4
```

The other use is in telling JavaScript what to do:

```
x = "alert('Hello World')"
eval(x) // alerts "Hello World"
```

The only caveat about the `eval()` function is when you use it on an object, which is not a literal. The fix is to refer to the object via its `valueOf` method. (Refer to Listing 4.2 for a demonstration.)

isFinite( )

JavaScript 1.2+, JScript 3+

Nav4.06+, IE4+

Syntax

```
isFinite(object)
```

The `eval()` method of the `Global` object returns `true` if the first argument given will convert to a number and is not equal to `Number.POSITIVE_INFINITY` or `Number.NEGATIVE_INFINITY`. Otherwise, this function returns `false`.

isNaN( )

JavaScript 1.0

Nav2 (Unix)

JavaScript 1.1+, JScript 1+

Nav3+, IE3+ (all platforms)

Syntax

```
isNaN(object)
```

The `isNaN()` method of the `Global` object tries to convert the first argument to a number. If the value returned is `NaN`, the `isNaN()` returns `true`. If the argument can be evaluated as a number, this returns `false`. (If the string is `"3"` this function will return as `false`.)

parseFloat( )

JavaScript 1.0+, JScript 1+

Nav2+, IE3+

Syntax

```
parseFloat(object)
```

The `parseFloat()` method of the `Global` object takes the first argument and returns a floating-point number representation of the argument. If the argument is not a number, it returns `Number.NaN`. This function is similar to `Number(arguments[0])`, however it will ignore trailing characters and return a number. `Number(arguments[0])` would return `NaN`. (Note: Netscape 2 for platforms besides Solaris and Unix will return `0`, if the argument is not a number.)

parseInt( )

JavaScript 1.0+, JScript 1+

Nav2+, IE3+

Syntax

```
parseInt(object [, base])
```

The `parseInt()` method of the `Global` object takes the first argument, usually a string, and parses it for an integer value. Leading whitespace and any trailing non-numerical characters are ignored. However, the argument may not be a base-10 number (a decimal). Therefore, if you provide a second argument indicating the base of the number, it converts the first number from that base to base-10 and returns the value as an integer. Else it assumes the number is base-10.

This function is thus an inverse to the `Number().toString` method, covered in Chapter 7.

```
alert(parseInt("FF",16)) // returns 255
```

If the argument cannot be parsed for an integer, it returns `Number.NaN`. (Note: Netscape 2 for platforms besides Solaris and Unix will return `0`, if the argument is not a number.)

taint( ), untaint( )

JavaScript 1.1

Nav3

Deprecated and removed in Nav4

Do not use!

The `taint()` and `untaint()` method of the `Global` object were briefly a part of the JavaScript language as the early implementation of security in JavaScript. The signed script model of Netscape 4 replaced these functions. Do not use them.

unescape( )

JavaScript 1.0+, JScript 1+

Nav2+, IE3+

Syntax

```
unescape(URIString)
```

The `unescape()` method of the `Global` object takes a URI string and decodes it as a regular string. Effectively, it is an inverse to the `escape` function.

```
alert(unescape(escape(x)) == x) // returns true
```

This function exists in the ECMAScript 1st edition specifications, but has been removed from the ECMAScript 3rd edition specifications. Netscape 6 and Internet Explorer 5.5 still support it, but it may have been deprecated in these versions. (Microsoft's documentation implies this, and Netscape's is silent on the matter.)

Interestingly, `decodeURIComponent` and `unescape` return correct inverses of Listing 11.1, while `decodeURI` is slightly off. See Listing 11.2.

Listing 11.2   *The Three URI Decoding Functions Compared*

```
<?xml version="1.0" ?>
<!DOCTYPE html PUBLIC "-//W3C//DTD XHTML 1.0 Transitional//EN"
➥"DTD/xhtml1-transitional.dtd">
<html xmlns="http://www.w3.org/1999/xhtml">
<head><title></title></head>
<body>
<script language="JavaScript" type="text/javascript">
<!--
var x = "http://Hello.htm?info=Hello%3A%20World"
document.write(unescape(x) + "<br />")
// returns "http://Hello.htm?info=Hello: World"
document.write (decodeURI(x) + "<br />")
// returns "http://Hello.htm?info=Hello%3A World"
document.write (decodeURIComponent(x) + "<br />")
// returns "http://Hello.htm?info=Hello: World"
//-->
</script>
</body>
</html>
```

Statements

break

JavaScript 1.0+, JScript 1+

Nav2+, IE3+

Syntax

`break [label]`

Simply put, break tells JavaScript to exit a loop or conditional statement immediately. If *label* is given, it exits out of the loop or conditional statement immediately following the *label* statement. (Labeled statements are covered in Chapter 12.) The break statement will exit from switch, for, for...in, do...while, and while statements.

const

JavaScript 1.5

Nav6

Reserved word in JavaScript

Syntax

```
const constantName [ = value]
```

const allows you to force a value to be a constant in JavaScript. If used within a function, the value is local to the function. If used outside all functions, it is a global value (see Listing 11.3).

Listing 11.3   *The const Statement in Netscape 6*

```
<?xml version="1.0" ?>
<!DOCTYPE html PUBLIC "-//W3C//DTD XHTML 1.0 Transitional//EN"
➥"DTD/xhtml1-transitional.dtd">
<html xmlns="http://www.w3.org/1999/xhtml">
<head><title></title></head>
<body>
<script language="JavaScript" type="text/javascript">
<!--
const x = 3
function myFunc() {
  x++ // does absolutely nothing
  const y = 4
  alert(x) // returns 3
  }
myFunc()
alert(window.y) // returns undefined because y is out of scope
//-->
</script>
</body>
</html>
```

This throws exceptions in Internet Explorer because const is a word reserved for future use within the language as far as Internet Explorer is concerned. For the same reason, Netscape 4 or earlier will throw exceptions.

In Netscape 4 or earlier, you can implement the same effect via the Object().watch method, by having it return the original value every time. The only disadvantage is the watch can be cleared by an Object().unwatch method call.

continue

JavaScript 1.0+, JScript 1+

Nav2+, IE3+

Syntax

```
continue [label]
```

Simply put, continue tells JavaScript to restart a loop that it is in immediately, without executing the remaining statements in a loop. If *label* is given, it restarts the loop immediately following the *label* statement. The continue statement will restart the for, for...in, do...while, and while statement loops.

Listing 11.4 demonstrates break and continue.

Listing 11.4   *To* break *and* continue *Loops*

```
<?xml version="1.0" ?>
<!DOCTYPE html PUBLIC "-//W3C//DTD XHTML 1.0 Transitional//EN"
➡"DTD/xhtml1-transitional.dtd">
<html xmlns="http://www.w3.org/1999/xhtml">
<head><title></title></head>
<body>
<script language="JavaScript" type="text/javascript">
<!--
for (x = 1; x <= 5; x++) {
  if (x == 2) {
    continue
    }
  if (x == 4) {
    break
    }
  alert(x) // returns 1, 3
  }
alert(x) // returns 4
```

Listing 11.4   *(continued)*

```
//-->
</script>
</body>
</html>
```

do...while

JavaScript 1.2+, JScript 3+

Nav4+, IE4+

Syntax

```
do {codeBlock} while (condition)
```

The do...while statement starts a loop executing first the code block within the brackets. Then it tests `condition`. If `condition` evaluates to `true`, it restarts the code block again, to test `condition` again upon completion. Until `condition` evaluates to `false` or a `break` or `continue` statement takes the executing code out of the loop, the code block will continue to execute over and over again.

The code block will execute at least once, even if `condition` evaluates to `false` after the code block executes.

By executing the code block, hopefully the conditions that `condition` checks for will change. The idea is eventually the code block will force `condition` to evaluate as `false`, but not necessarily right away.

for

JavaScript 1.0+, JScript 1+

Nav2+, IE3+

Syntax

```
for (startcond; testcond; loopcode) {codeBlock}
```

The `for` loop starts a loop by executing the statements in `startcond`, then as long as `testcond` evaluates to `true`, it executes the code block within the brackets. Then it executes `loopcode` and checks `testcond` again, to see if it should repeat the code block. Until the `testcond` evaluates to `false` or a `break` or `continue` statement takes the executing code out of the loop, the code block will continue to execute over and over again.

If *testcond* initially evaluates to `false`, the code block does not execute.

By executing *loopcode* or the code block, the conditions with which *startcond* began the `for` statement hopefully change. The idea is eventually the *loopcode* will force *testcond* to evaluate as `false`, but not necessarily right away.

for...in...

JavaScript 1.0+, JScript 5+

Nav2+, IE5.0+

Syntax

```
for (property in object) {codeBlock}
```

The `for...in` statement iterates through all properties and in an object which you define, and all properties which the browser intends to let you see. Most properties will show up, but a few may not (such as `join` in `Array()` objects). This is primarily dependent on the ECMAScript specifications and browser implementation of proprietary features.

```
x = {owner:"me"}
for (property in x) {
  alert(property)
  // returns "owner", but not anything else
  }
```

All properties and methods of *object* that a JavaScript developer defines will appear as one of the *property* selections.

function

JavaScript 1.0+, JScript 1+

Nav2+, IE3+

Syntax

```
function [functionname] (arguments) {codeBlock}
```

The `function` statement defines a `Function` object and creates a property of the `Global` object to which the `Function` object is assigned. See Chapter 2, "Function()," for details.

if...[else {...}]

JavaScript 1.0+, JScript 1+

Nav2+, IE3+

Syntax

```
if (condition) {codeBlock} [else {codeBlock2} ]
```

The `if...else` statement evaluates the condition given. If the condition evaluates to `true`, it executes the first statement block immediately following the condition (the first set of brackets). If the condition evaluates to `false` and the `else` keyword is included, it executes the first statement block immediately following the `else` keyword (the second set of brackets).

The brackets are necessary only if you have two or more lines of code to execute for an `if...else` statement. The following is valid:

```
if (1 == 2) alert("Contradiction"); else alert("false");
```

However, I prefer to code using the brackets, with each line of code isolated from the `if...else` statement keywords and condition. One never knows when one has to add more lines of code.

```
if (1 == 2) {
  alert("Contradiction")
  } else {
  alert("false")
  }
```

Also see Chapter 12 for a shorthand version of the `if...else` statement, using question marks and colons.

return

JavaScript 1.0+, JScript 1+

Nav2+, IE3+

Syntax

```
return expression
```

The `return` statement causes a `Function` object to return *object* to any object calling the function, and then exit the function. Without this statement, the `Function` object

will automatically return `undefined` upon execution. See Chapter 2 for more on the
`return` statement.

switch...case...default

JavaScript 1.2+, JScript 3+

Nav4+, IE4+

Syntax

```
switch(expression) {case (compare): codeBlock;
    [case (compare): codeBlock; ]
    [case (compare): codeBlock; ]

    [... ]

    [default:...]}
```

The `switch` statement defines a statement block where various `case` objects are
compared against the `switch` expression value. Users familiar with the BASIC family
of languages can compare this statement to the "select case" statement.

Essentially, for each `case` sub-statement, it performs an `if (expression == compare)`
match. If the two objects match, it executes the code block beginning immediately
after the `case` sub-statement.

If no match exists for the `switch` statement's expression before a `default` code section
is given, JavaScript executes the code block beginning immediately after the `default`
substatement.

A `break` statement terminates execution of the `switch` statement's code block. This
becomes important to prevent a function from overlapping (see Listing 11.5).
Forgetting a `break` statement is a common source of irritating errors, so don't forget
to include it.

Listing 11.5   *A* `switch` *Statement without an Effective* `break` *Statement*

```
<?xml version="1.0" ?>
<!DOCTYPE html PUBLIC "-//W3C//DTD XHTML 1.0 Transitional//EN"
➥"DTD/xhtml1-transitional.dtd">
<html xmlns="http://www.w3.org/1999/xhtml">
<head><title></title></head>
<body>
<script language="JavaScript" type="text/javascript">
```

Listing 11.5   *(continued)*

```
<!--
x = 2
switch (x) {
  case 2:
  x++
  //break
  //the preceding line commented out means continue on
  case 5:
  x++
  }
alert(x)
// we may want x == 3, but x == 4 because the break statement is missing
//-->
</script>
</body>
</html>
```

throw

JavaScript 1.5, JScript 5+

Nav6, IE5.0+

Syntax

```
throw exception
```

The throw statement lets you throw exceptions to be caught by a catch statement later in the code. Note you can actually throw any kind of data you wish, including custom-built objects. However, I recommend you throw custom Error() objects since this is what throw is designed for—for dumping errors quickly, complete with error messages and other information (see Listing 11.6).

Listing 11.6   *Throwing an Exception Manually*

```
<?xml version="1.0" ?>
<!DOCTYPE html PUBLIC "-//W3C//DTD XHTML 1.0 Transitional//EN
➥"DTD/xhtml1-transitional.dtd">
<html xmlns="http://www.w3.org/1999/xhtml">
<head><title></title></head>
<body>
<script language="JavaScript" type="text/javascript">
```

Listing 11.6   *(continued)*

```
<!--
try {
  var x = new Error()
  x.message = "Bad Hair Day!!"
  throw x
  }
catch (e) {
  alert(x.message) // returns "Bad Hair Day!!"
  }
//-->
</script>
</body>
</html>
```

try...catch...finally

JavaScript 1.5, JScript 5+

Nav6, IE5.0+

Syntax

```
try {codeBlock} catch (exception [if (condition)] )
    {codeBlock2} [catch... ] [finally {codeBlock3}]
```

The try statement lets you test a section of code for exceptions within the language. If an exception occurs, it immediately jumps out of the try statement's code block directly to the first catch statement that matches an *exception* value. (Netscape 6 permits conditional catch statements using the if statement following the *exception* variable. Internet Explorer does not.) After any catch statement that matches the exception execute, if a finally statement is given, the code in that block will execute.

Chapter 10, "Error()," uses the try...catch statement fairly extensively; however, this example may clarify the impact of the finally statement:

```
try {
  x = 1
  }
catch (e) {
  alert("Hello") // does not execute
  }
finally {
  alert("Goodbye") // returns "Goodbye"
  }
```

var

JavaScript 1.0+, JScript 1+

Nav2+, IE3+

Syntax

```
var varName [ = value] [, object [ = value] [, ...] ]
```

The var statement defines a variable that can be local to a function or global to a script. Within a function, the variable defined exists; outside the function, it does not (see Listing 11.7).

Listing 11.7   *The* var *Statement and Its Effect on a Variable*

```
<?xml version="1.0" ?>
<!DOCTYPE html PUBLIC "-//W3C//DTD XHTML 1.0 Transitional//EN"
➥"DTD/xhtml1-transitional.dtd">
<html xmlns="http://www.w3.org/1999/xhtml">
<head><title></title></head>
<body>
<script language="JavaScript" type="text/javascript">
<!--
var k;
function myFunc() {
  var response = new Object()
  k = new Object()
  alert(response) // returns "[object Object]"
  alert(k) // returns "[object Object]"
  }
myFunc()
alert(k) // returns "[object Object]"
alert(response) // throws exception:  "response is undefined"
//-->
</script>
</body>
</html>
```

Note with the var statement, you are not required to define an initial value for an object. The following is perfectly legitimate:

```
var response;
```

---

while

JavaScript 1.0+, JScript 1+

Nav2+, IE3+

Syntax

```
while (condition) {...}
```

The while statement starts by evaluating *condition*. If *condition* evaluates to true, it executes the code block, to test *condition* again upon completion. Until *condition* evaluates to false or a break or continue statement takes the executing code out of the loop, the code block will continue to execute over and over again.

If *condition* initially evaluates to false, the code block does not execute.

By executing the code block, hopefully the conditions that *condition* checks for will change. The idea is eventually the code block will force *condition* to evaluate as false, but not necessarily right away.

Listing 11.8 demonstrates uses of the for, do...while, and while statements.

Listing 11.8   *The Looping Statements Examined*

```
<?xml version="1.0" ?>
<!DOCTYPE html PUBLIC "-//W3C//DTD XHTML 1.0 Transitional//EN"
➥"DTD/xhtml1-transitional.dtd">
<html xmlns="http://www.w3.org/1999/xhtml">
<head><title>
<script language="JavaScript" type="text/javascript">
<!--
document.write("for (x = 1; x <= 3; x++) <br />")
for (x = 1; x <= 3; x++) {
  document.write(x + "<br />") // returns 1, 2, 3
  }
// x == 4
document.write("do <br />")
do {
  document.write(x + "<br />") // returns 4, 3, 2
  x--
  } while (x > 1)
document.write("while (x > 1) <br />")
while (x > 1) {
// x == 1
```

Listing 11.8   *(continued)*

```
  document.write("Hello <br />") // does not execute
  }
document.write("while (x < 3) <br />")
while (x < 3) {
  document.write(x + "<br />") // returns 1, 2
  x++
  }
//-->
</script>
</title></head>
<body>
</body>
</html>
```

with

JavaScript 1.0+, JScript 1+

Nav2+, IE3+

Syntax

```
with (object) {codeBlock}
```

The with statement establishes a default object within the code block. This allows you to access properties and methods of the object without having to repeat the object name again and again (see Listing 11.9).

Listing 11.9   *Using the* with *Statement*

```
<?xml version="1.0" ?>
<!DOCTYPE html PUBLIC "-//W3C//DTD XHTML 1.0 Transitional//EN"
➥"DTD/xhtml1-transitional.dtd">
<html xmlns="http://www.w3.org/1999/xhtml">
<head><title></title></head>
<body>
<script langauge="JavaScript" type="text/javascript">
<!--
x = [3, 4]
  alert(x.join("*")) // normal call to join returns "3*4"
with (x) {
  alert(join("*")) // equivalent to x.join("*")
```

Listing 11.9 *(continued)*

```
  // which returns "3*4"
  }
//-->
</script>
</body>
</html>
```

Controlling How a Script Runs

In various parts of this book, ranging from `document.write` to event and error handling, I discuss various options for guiding your script to do what you want it to do. However, there are a few techniques you can use for driving your scripts in the right direction. I collect a couple of them here, though in reading other parts of this book, you will certainly pick up a few more.

As far as the statements covered in this chapter exclusively, many of them relate to one another. You can use `break` and `continue` to exit loops. You can use `throw` to exit quickly out of a `try` code block directly to the `catch` or `finally` code blocks. You can nest loops and conditional statements, one within another, as necessary. You can use flags to communicate between one loop and another, as the `ineq` function example does in Chapter 1, "Object()." The `var` statement, although optional in many cases, is recommended to declare all variables as a matter of good programming practice. The `const` keyword is a powerful tool, but should be understood before using. Otherwise, you may find you have created a constant in a way that was not intended.

The best way to really learn how to use your scripts and how to control them is to analyze the flow of statements from top to bottom.

A script starts out by executing every command you give it outside a function. If it runs into a function call, it "splices in" the commands in the function, adjusted for the arguments given to the function. The statements given in this chapter often just test a condition and tell the browser which code block to execute next (see Listing 11.10).

Listing 11.10 *Reading the Flow of a Script*

```
<?xml version="1.0" ?>
<!DOCTYPE html PUBLIC "-//W3C//DTD XHTML 1.0 Transitional//EN"
➡"DTD/xhtml1-transitional.dtd">
<html xmlns="http://www.w3.org/1999/xhtml">
```

Listing 11.10   *(continued)*

```
<head><title></title></head>
<body>
<script langauge="JavaScript" type="text/javascript">
<!--
var a = 1 // Thirdcommand executed
function y() { // define function first action taken
  var m;
  for (m = 0; m < 2; m++) {
    alert(5) // Eighth, tenth commands executed
    } // m++ ninth, eleventh commands executed
  }
function x() { // define function second action taken
  if (1 == 1) {
    alert(4) // Sixth command executed
    y() // Seventh command executed
    } else {
    z() // not executed
    }
  alert(0) // Twelfth command executed
  }
var b = 2 // Fourth command executed
x() // Fifth command executed
var c = 3 // Thirteenth command executed
//-->
</script>
</body>
</html>
```

Looking at this example you may notice that all function declarations are processed first. That's why you can call a function before declaring it in many cases, though it is ill-advised to do so. After all functions are defined, the normal commands of the script proceed to execute in order, including the function calls.

The only way I can really teach you how to control your scripts better than this is for you to observe the various code examples throughout this book. If you care to look at this issue specifically, I encourage you to browse through the book, analyzing the flow from top to bottom, jumping in and out of functions as the scripts progress. If nothing else, Listing 11.10 can give you advice on charting the progress of your scripts, until you begin reading them without needing to chart.

It's not hard to break beyond this low-level version of a flowchart, but sometimes detailed analysis such as this can reveal where a script begins to fail and produces the avalanche of errors I mentioned in Chapter 2. You'll be able to follow, line by line, what changes happen to your objects (and which ones are in place). It also helps to think in this way occasionally when your script's bugs erupt only from certain events in a certain order. Reproducing a bug in an exact and documented pattern of actions is an essential feature to debugging any script.

CHAPTER 12

Operators

Operators in JavaScript define rules by which objects and primitive values change. Some of them perform basic mathematic or logical calculations; others involve affecting objects directly. It is no lie to say objects could not exist without operators.

Unless otherwise noted, all operators are in effect for Netscape 2+ and Internet Explorer 3+.

The Primary Assignment Operator

The assignment operator takes the form a = b, where a would be the left side, and b the right side.

=

JavaScript 1.0+, JScript 1+

Nav2+, IE3+

The assignment expression is made up of a left side expression, the = operator, and a right side expression. First the left expression is evaluated, usually determining the storage location of the results of the operator. Typically, this is a variable name or object property. Then the right side expression is evaluated to determine its value. Finally the value from the right side is assigned to the property on the left side. If you think about it, the value is always assigned to a property, given that all variables are really properties of the window/global object.

This operator you can use successively several times in defining multiple properties identically.

```
var a = b = c = d = Math.PI
```

This evaluates as

```
var a = (b = (c = (d = Math.PI)));
```

In the preceding, b, c, and d have global scope (beyond their own function), while a is local to its function. Unfortunately, you cannot use it later on:

```
var a = var b = 3 // throws exception
```

Use commas instead, covered later in this chapter.

Arithmetic Operators

+

JavaScript 1.0+, JScript 1+

Nav2+, IE3+

The + operator adds the values on the left and right sides of the operator in the format x + y and returns the result. It is important to realize the + operator exists as both a unary and binary operator and is overloaded. Unary form would be +y where it tries to covert the right operand to a number. This is important because if y is a string you will find it happily coverts to `Number.NaN` without throwing any errors. As a binary operator, in addition to adding numbers, operator + can add booleans and concatenate strings. Keep in mind though the + operator will try to convert many operands into numbers in certain situations like `true + true = 2`!

+=

Javascript1.0+, JScript 1+

Nav 2+, IE3+

The += operator adds the value on the right side of the operator to the object on the left side of the operator, and assigns the result to the left side. If either is a string, the object or primitive on the left side becomes a string value of the left side concatenated with a string value of the right side. `x += y` is the same as `x = x + y`.

-

JavaScript 1.0+, JScript 1+

Nav2+, IE3+

The - operator subtracts the value on the right side from the value on the left side of the operator in the format `x - y`. In addition to this binary format, the - operator is available in a unary form like `-y`. This is equivalent to `0 - y` and effectively negates y.

-=

JavaScript 1.0+, JScript 1+

Nav2+, IE3+

The -= operator subtracts the value on the right side of the operator from the object or primitive on the left side of the operator, and assigns the result to the left side. Simply put `x -= y` is the same as `x = x - y`.

*

JavaScript 1.0+, JScript 1+

Nav2+, IE3+

The * operator converts the values on the left and right sides of the operator into numbers and then multiplies them. The format for the * operator is x * y.

*=

JavaScript 1.0+, JScript 1+

Nav2+, IE3+

The = operator multiplies the value on the right side of the operator by the property on the left side of the operator, and assigns the result to the left side. Simply put x *= y is the same as x = x * y.

/

JavaScript 1.0+, JScript 1+

Nav2+, IE3+

The / operator converts its operands to numbers and then divides the value on the left side of the operator by the value on the right side. The format of the / operator is x / y.

/=

JavaScript 1.0+, JScript 1+

Nav2+, IE3+

The /= operator converts its operands to numbers and then divides the value on the left side of the operator by the value on the right side of the operator, and assigns the result to the left side. Simply put x /= y is the same as x = x / y.

%

JavaScript 1.0+, JScript 1+

Nav2+, IE3+

The % operator converts its operands to numbers and returns the modulus of the left side of the operator by the right side of the operator. The format of the modulus operator is x % y. The modulus operator gives you the remainder of x divided by y.

%=

JavaScript 1.0+, JScript 1+

Nav2+, IE3+

The %= operator converts all its operands to numbers and divides the value on the left side of the operator by the value on the right side of the operator, and assigns the whole number remainder to the left side. x %= y is the same as x = x % y.

++

JavaScript 1.0+, JScript 1+

Nav2+, IE3+

The ++ operator increments the property being affected by one. If this is immediately following the object, the object's current value is returned before the increment. If this is immediately preceding the object, the object's current value is incremented before it is returned. If the argument to ++ is not a number, it will try to convert it to a number and then increment it. (See Listing 12.1.)

Listing 12.1 *A Demonstration of the ++ Operator*

```
<?xml version="1.0" ?>
<!DOCTYPE html PUBLIC "-//W3C//DTD XHTML 1.0 Transitional//EN
➥"DTD/xhtml1-transitional.dtd">
<html xmlns="http://www.w3.org/1999/xhtml">
<head><title></title></head>
<body>
<script language="JavaScript" type="text/javascript">
<!--
var x = 3
alert(x) // returns 3
alert(x++) // returns 3
alert(x) // returns 4

var y = 3
alert(y) // returns 3
alert(++y) // returns 4
alert(y) // returns 4
//-->
</script>
</body>
</html>
```

--

JavaScript 1.0+, JScript 1+

Nav2+, IE3+

The decrement operator decrements the property being affected by one. If this is immediately following the object, the object's current value is returned before the decrement. If this is immediately preceding the object, the object's current value is decremented before it is returned. If the argument to -- is not a number it will try to convert it to a number before performing the operation. See Listing 12.1 for a similar implementation using the ++ operator.

Comparison Operators

==

JavaScript 1.0+, JScript 1+

Nav2+, IE3+

The equality operator returns `true` if the object or primitive on the left side of the operator is equal to the object or primitive on the right side of the operator. Otherwise, it returns `false`.

The implementation of this operator is somewhat confusing. For Netscape 2, 3, and 4.06+, if the two values are of different types it converts them to the same type before performing the comparison. (`-5 == '-5'`, for example.) For Netscape 4.00–4.05, it does not attempt to convert types; the preceding code would return `false`. This behavior may also occur in Netscape 4.06+ and Netscape 6+ if the script language specified is "Javascript1.2". Internet Explorer attempts to convert types for this operator.

In Chapter 1, "Object()" I stated objects are typically unique. This applies to all objects. Hence, comparing two objects whose properties are equal should return `false`.

```
var x = new String("s")  // object
var y = new String("s")
alert(x == y) // returns false

x = "s"  // primitive value
y = "s"
alert(x == y) // returns true
```

!=

JavaScript 1.0+, JScript 1+

Nav2+, IE3+

The inequality operator returns `false` if the object or primitive on the left side of the operator is equal to the object or primitive on the right side of the operator. Otherwise, it returns `true`.

The implementation of this operator is somewhat confusing. For Netscape 2, 3, and 4.06+, if the two values are of different types it converts them to the same type before performing the comparison. (`-5 != '-5'`, for example.) For Netscape 4.00–4.05, it does not attempt to convert types; the preceding code would return `true`. This behavior may also occur in Netscape 4.06+ and Netscape 6+ if the script language specified is "Javascript1.2". Internet Explorer attempts to convert types for this operator.

In Chapter 1, I stated objects are typically unique. This applies especially to all objects. In the first case in the following example you are comparing to see if the two object references are the same object. Of course they are not, so it returns `true`. The second example compares two primitive values that are the same. Because they are equal, `false` is returned.

```
var x = new String("s")  // object
var y = new String("s")
alert(x != y) // returns true

x = "s"
y = "s"
alert(x == y) // returns false
```

===

JavaScript 1.2+, JScript 5+

Nav4.06+, IE5+

The `===` operator returns `true` only if the left and right sides have matching types and values. (`-5 === '-5'`) returns `false`.

!==

JavaScript 1.2+, JScript 5+

Nav4.06+, IE5+

The !== operator returns true only if the left and right sides do not have matching types and values. (-5 !== '-5') returns true.

<

JavaScript 1.0+, JScript 1+

Nav2+, IE3+

The less than operator returns true if the left side has a lower value than the right side. Otherwise, this returns false. For numbers this is obvious. However, strings can also be compared by the Unicode alphabet for alphabetical order. ("A" < "a") returns true.

> **Note**
> String comparison only occurs if both arguments are strings.

>

JavaScript 1.0+, JScript 1+

Nav2+, IE3+

The greater than operator returns true if the left side has a greater value than the right side. Otherwise, this returns false. For numbers this is obvious. However, strings can also be compared by the Unicode alphabet for alphabetical order. ("a" > "A") returns true.

> **Note**
> String comparison only occurs if both arguments are strings.

<=

JavaScript 1.0+, JScript 1+

Nav2+, IE3+

The less than equal to operator returns true if the left side has a lower or equal value than the right side. Otherwise, this returns false. For numbers this is obvious. However, strings can also be compared by the Unicode alphabet for alphabetical order. ("A" <= "a") returns true.

> **Note**
> String comparison only occurs if both arguments are strings.

>=

JavaScript 1.0+, JScript 1+

Nav2+, IE3+

The greater than equal to operator returns `true` if the left side has a greater or equal value than the right side. Otherwise, this returns `false`. For numbers this is obvious. However, strings can also be compared by the ASCII alphabet for alphabetical order. (`"a" >= "A"`) returns `true`.

> **Note**
> String comparison only occurs if both arguments are strings.

Boolean Operators

!

JavaScript 1.0+, JScript 1+

Nav2+, IE3+

The negation operator returns the Boolean inverse of the expression it is attached to—if the Boolean expression returns `true`, this forces it to return `false`.

&&

JavaScript 1.0+, JScript 1+

Nav2+, IE3+

The Boolean and operator is normally thought to return a Boolean result. However, in JavaScript it returns one of the operands. It converts the first operand to a Boolean. If that Boolean is true it returns the second operand. If it was `false`, it returns the first operand. Although this may seem weird at first from a Boolean standpoint it is very efficient and logical. All the traditional Boolean behavior works and because it returns the operands instead of just `true` or `false`, you have the capability to be far more creative.

If the first operand evaluates as `false`, the second operand is not evaluated. This allows for certain expressions that would otherwise be dangerous.

```
if ((window.x)&&(!x.closed)) alert("x is an open window")
```

If `window.x` returns `false`, there is no need to check for `!x.closed`. This saves us from encountering an exception for the nonexistence of x and thus of properties of x.

||

JavaScript 1.0+, JScript 1+

Nav2+, IE3+

The Boolean or operator in JavaScript, like the Boolean and operator, returns one of its arguments as a result. Basically it evaluates the first operand expression and converts it to a Boolean. If the resulting Boolean evaluates to `true`, the first operand is returned. If it evaluates to `false` the second argument is returned. This works fine for Boolean logic and again, allows the programmer more options with the results.

A handy thing to remember too is if the first operand evaluates to `true`, the second operand is not evaluated.

One other use of this operator is in defining objects initially:

```
var x = arguments[0] || "JavaScript"
```

If `arguments[0]` returns `false` (as it would if it were `undefined`), then `"JavaScript"` gets assigned to x.

?:

JavaScript 1.0+, JScript 1+

Nav2+, IE3+

The conditional operator is very similar to the `if...else` statement of JavaScript. An expression precedes the `?`, followed by a code block to execute if the expression evaluates to `true`. This is then followed by a colon, and a code block to execute if the condition evaluates to `false`. Ultimately, the result of the code block that is evaluated is returned.

Often this provides a shorthand for defining a quick function for returning an object based on the condition. In the following code, based on the value of x, the string y gets either `"script"` or `"program"` returned to it. (The expression gets placed within parentheses to isolate it. It is not a `Function()` object.)

```
y = "This is a " + ((x == "Java") ? "script" : "program")
```

JavaScript 1.0+, JScript 1+

Nav2+, IE3+

The comma operator allows you to use multiple expressions within a single expression definition. Although this is commonly used to list similar repetitive expressions, it is important to remember it does return the value of the last operand in the list. One common use is in `for` loops:

```
for (x = 0, y = 0; x < 5; x++, y++) {
   alert(x * y) // returns 0, 1, 4, 9, 16
   }
```

Bitwise Operators

These require a bit of explanation. You can feed any number in base-10 and perform operations using bitwise operators. What happens is the number is converted to a base-2 number as a string, and then logical operators apply to each character in the string. If two operators are involved, the corresponding characters are evaluated according to the operator. The result is then translated back to a base-10 number, according to ECMAScript's numbering system.

In base-2, 7 becomes "111." 16 becomes "10000." 5 becomes "101." The right edges of the numbers line up for any operations, and empty slots are filled with zeroes, up to 32 digits total for all operands.

JavaScript 1.0+, JScript 1+

Nav2+, IE3+

The bitwise negation operator inverts each character within a bitwise comparison: ones become zeroes, and vice versa.

```
"0000 0000 0000 0000 0000 0000 0001 0000" // 16

~    "1111 1111 1111 1111 1111 1111 1110 1111" // -17
```

&

JavaScript 1.0+, JScript 1+

Nav2+, IE3+

The bitwise and operator returns bits equal to 1 where both corresponding bits of the two operands also equal 1; otherwise, it returns 0.

```
    "0000 0000 0000 0000 0000 0000 0000 0000 0101" // 5
&   "0000 0000 0000 0000 0000 0000 0000 0000 1100" // 12

=   "0000 0000 0000 0000 0000 0000 0000 0000 0100" // 4
```

|

JavaScript 1.0+, JScript 1+

Nav2+, IE3+

The bitwise or operator returns bits equal to 1 where either of the corresponding bits of the two operands equals 1; otherwise, it returns 0.

```
    "0000 0000 0000 0000 0000 0000 0000 0000 0101" // 5
|   "0000 0000 0000 0000 0000 0000 0000 0000 1100" // 12

=   "0000 0000 0000 0000 0000 0000 0000 0000 1101" // 13
```

^

JavaScript 1.0+, JScript 1+

Nav2+, IE3+

The bitwise xor operator returns bits equal to 1 where exactly one corresponding bit of the two operands equals 1; otherwise, it returns 0.

```
    "0000 0000 0000 0000 0000 0000 0000 0000 0101" // 5
&   "0000 0000 0000 0000 0000 0000 0000 0000 1100" // 12

=   "0000 0000 0000 0000 0000 0000 0000 0000 1001" // 9
```

&=

JavaScript 1.0+, JScript 1+

Nav2+, IE3+

The &= operator returns bits equal to 1 where both corresponding bits of the two operands also equal 1; otherwise, it returns 0. The finished bitwise number is then assigned to the left side object. Simply put, x &= y is the same as x = x &= y.

|=

JavaScript 1.0+, JScript 1+

Nav2+, IE3+

The |= operator returns bits equal to 1 where either of the corresponding bits of the two operands equals 1; otherwise, it returns 0. The finished bitwise number is then assigned to the left side object. Simply put, x |= y is the equivalent of x = x | y.

=

JavaScript 1.0+, JScript 1+

Nav2+, IE3+

The ^= operator returns bits equal to 1 where exactly one corresponding bit of the two operands equals 1; otherwise, it returns 0. The finished bitwise number is then assigned to the left side object. Simply put, x ^= y is the same as x = x ^ y.

<<

JavaScript 1.0+, JScript 1+

Nav2+, IE3+

The bitwise left shift operator shifts each bit in the left side bitwise number x bits to the left, dropping the x leftmost bits and inserting x zeroes at the rightmost bit. x in this case equals the right side operand.

```
"0000 0000 0000 0000 0000 0000 0001 0000"  // 16

<< 2    "0000 0000 0000 0000 0000 0000 0100 0000"  // 64
```

>>

JavaScript 1.0+, JScript 1+

Nav2+, IE3+

The bitwise right shift operator shifts each character in the left side bitwise number x bits to the right, dropping the x rightmost bits and inserting x copies of the leftmost bit to the far left. x in this case equals the right side operand.

```
"0000 0000 0000 0000 0000 0000 0001 0000" // 16

>> 2    "0000 0000 0000 0000 0000 0000 0000 0100" // 4
```

>>> returns the same, except instead of inserting x copies of the leftmost bit, it inserts x zeroes unconditionally.

<<=

JavaScript 1.0+, JScript 1+

Nav2+, IE3+

The <<= operator shifts each character in the left side bitwise number x bits to the left, dropping the x leftmost bits and inserting x zeroes at the rightmost bit. x in this case equals the right side operand, and the returned bitwise number is assigned to the left side bitwise operand. Equivalent to `left = left << shift`.

>>=

JavaScript 1.0+, JScript 1+

Nav2+, IE3+

The >>= operator shifts each character in the left side bitwise number x bits to the right, dropping the x rightmost bits and inserting x copies of the leftmost bit to the far left. x in this case equals the right side operand, and the returned bitwise number is assigned to the left side bitwise operand. Equivalent to `right = right>> shift`.

>>>= returns the same, except instead of inserting x copies of the leftmost bit, it inserts x zeroes unconditionally.

Word Operators

delete

JavaScript 1.2+, JScript 3+

Nav4+, IE4+

The `delete` operator deletes the following object property if it is possible. If the operation is successful, it returns `true`; otherwise it returns `false`.

function

JavaScript 1.5, JScript 3+

Nav6+, IE4+

The `function` operator allows you to define an unnamed function in a localized setting. See Chapter 2, "Function( )," for more details.

in

JavaScript 1.5+, JScript 1+

Nav6+, IE3+

The `in` operator allows you to determine if the property or method named on the left side of the operator exists in the object named on the right side. It's similar to `for...in`, except it doesn't iterate through, it just tests for the existence of the object.

Developers for Netscape 4.x and earlier must use `typeof(`*`object.propertyname`*`)` != `"undefined"` to prove if an object exists.

instanceof

JavaScript 1.5+, JScript 5+

Nav6+, IE5.0+

The `instanceof` operator determines whether an object or primitive descends from a constructor function. Primitive values automatically return `false` under this operator, except if being checked as an instance of `Object`. Because they are primitives the only possible result is `false`. Every object in JavaScript that is user-defined or defined in ECMAScript is an instance of `Object`. By this operator, you can officially determine every constructor involved in an object's construction. Once you've determined this, a simple search of various `prototype` properties can determine the order of inheritance if it ever becomes necessary. See Listing 12.2. An important thing to note is `instanceof` expects a function for the right operand. If it is not given one, it will throw an error in Internet Explorer 5+.

Listing 12.2   *The* `instanceof` *Operator Explored*

```
<?xml version="1.0" ?>
<!DOCTYPE html PUBLIC "-//W3C//DTD XHTML 1.0 Transitional//EN"
➥"DTD/xhtml1-transitional.dtd">
<html xmlns="http://www.w3.org/1999/xhtml">
<head><title></title></head>
<body>
```

Listing 12.2   *(continued)*

```
<script language="JavaScript" type="text/javascript">
<!--
function High() {
    }

function Low() {
    }
Low.prototype = new High()

x = new High()
y = new Low()
z = new Object()
w = ""

//alert(y instanceof x) // returns false (will cause an error in IE5+)
alert(y instanceof Low) // returns true
alert(y instanceof High) // returns true
alert(y instanceof Object) // returns true

alert(x instanceof Low) // returns false
alert(x instanceof High) // returns true
alert(x instanceof Object) // returns true

alert(z instanceof High) // returns false
alert(z instanceof Object) // returns true

alert(w instanceof String) // returns false
alert(w instanceof Object) // returns true
//-->
</script>
</body>
</html>
```

new

JavaScript 1.0+, JScript 1+

Nav2+, IE3+

The new operator returns a new instance of an object, as opposed to simply copying whatever it returns. You can see examples of this operator used at the beginning of Chapters 1–10. Its usage follows.

```
x = new ConstructorFunction()
```

this

JavaScript 1.0+, JScript 1+

Nav2+, IE3+

The this operator returns the object that has the current function as a method.

The this operator has a few different contexts. As a method of an object already defined, you can call other methods and properties of the object:

```
function AObject() {
   this.language = 'foo'
   alert(this.language)
   }
```

If you haven't specified a prototype for the function being called, then the function is a method of the Global object. In client side JavaScript, this refers to the window object (see Listing 12.3).

Listing 12.3   *The* this *Object as the* window *Object*

```
<?xml version="1.0" ?>
<!DOCTYPE html PUBLIC "-//W3C//DTD XHTML 1.0 Transitional//EN"
➥"DTD/xhtml1-transitional.dtd">
<html xmlns="http://www.w3.org/1999/xhtml">
<head><title></title></head>
<body>
<script language="JavaScript" type="text/javascript">
<!--
function go() {
   this.setTimeout("alert('Hello')",100)
   }
go() // sets alert to fire in 100 milliseconds
//-->
</script>
</body>
</html>
```

If you are using the this keyword to represent an object which the function is constructing, you can define properties for this within the function. Constructor functions are covered in more detail in Chapters 1 and 2.

Finally, you cannot replace the object which this represents directly within a function.

```
var this = 3 // throws exception
```

typeof

JavaScript 1.1+, JScript 1+

Nav3+, IE3+

The `typeof` operator returns the data type of a primitive, based on what type of data it is. It's a more primitive way to identify data, as data types are not a strongly enforced concept in JavaScript. ECMAScript 3rd edition defines six data types: `object`, `string`, `number`, `boolean`, `undefined`, and `function`. I prefer the `constructor` method and the `instanceof` operator to determine more specifically what an object is, but this could easily be a matter of taste.

void

JavaScript 1.0+, JScript 1+

Nav2+, IE3+

The `void` operator is simply one which makes the result of any expression undefined, replacing what is actually returned with `undefined`, while not affecting anything returned. The `void` operator can actually be used as a function (`void(null)` is the best-known usage), but the parentheses are optional (see Listing 12.4).

Listing 12.4 *The* void *Operator Examined*

```
<?xml version="1.0" ?>
<!DOCTYPE html PUBLIC "-//W3C//DTD XHTML 1.0 Transitional//EN"
➡"DTD/xhtml1-transitional.dtd">
<html xmlns="http://www.w3.org/1999/xhtml">
<head><title></title></head>
<body>
<script language="JavaScript" type="text/javascript">
<!--
function x() {
    return 3
    }
alert(x())// returns 3
alert(void(x()))
// returns undefined even though x() returns 3
//-->
</script>
</body>
</html>
```

CHAPTER 13

JavaScript Syntax

In elementary school, they teach you about punctuation: how to use periods, commas, question marks, quote marks, and so on correctly. In JavaScript, you also have to learn about punctuation, but in a different style. Punctuation in JavaScript is less forgiving, however. A typographical error in JavaScript means an exception, often of the kind which occurs before any code executes. It's therefore important to use punctuation correctly in JavaScript.

In this chapter, I'm going to cover several elements of the syntax behind JavaScript. A few of these you will have seen in earlier chapters. Sometimes, I'll be able to offer advice on ensuring correct counts of these characters.

Parentheses, Square Brackets, and Curly Braces

Prominent among the aspects of JavaScript syntax where it is easy to introduce inadvertent errors are parentheses, square brackets, and curly braces.

Parentheses ( )

You normally see parentheses in two contexts: in enclosing the arguments of a statement or function, and in pre-evaluating one expression as part of another. For example:

```
var x = 3 + 4 * 5 // x = 23
```

Without parentheses, the multiplication operator acts first. Thus we add 3 to the result of 4 times 5 (20). The sum of 3 plus 20 is 23. But by using parentheses, you have the option to change the order of operations:

```
var x = (3 + 4) * 5 // x = 35
```

The parentheses cause 3 to be added to 4 producing a result of 7. Then 7 is multiplied by 5 giving a final result of 35, which is assigned to the variable x.

Every opening parenthesis (must have a matching closing parenthesis), and vice versa. (() and ()) are illegitimate uses of parentheses. Sometimes you can have so many parentheses in a statement (especially in diagnostic `alert()` method calls and `if` statements) that you lose one. What I do in cases like these when I'm unsure of the parentheses in a single statement is count a virtual sum: every opening parenthesis adds one and every closing parenthesis subtracts one (see Listing 13.1).

Listing 13.1   *Counting Parentheses*

```
<?xml version="1.0" ?>
<!DOCTYPE html PUBLIC "-//W3C//DTD XHTML 1.0 Transitional//EN"
➥"DTD/xhtml1-transitional.dtd">
<html xmlns="http://www.w3.org/1999/xhtml">
<head><title>
<script language="javascript" type="text/javascript">
alert((3/2)+(5/2);
/* Note that there is one more opening than closing parentheses.
     12    1 2   1 */

</script>
</title></head>
```

Listing 13.1   *(continued)*

```
<body>
</body>
</html>
```

If you examine the `alert()` statement in Listing 13.1 you will see that there is one more opening parenthesis than closing parenthesis. Within the comment I show the count of the parentheses. At the end of a statement the count should be zero. If it is not you need to examine the statement to determine whether a parenthesis has been omitted or an extra one inserted inadvertently.

If you run the code in Listing 13.1 you may receive no error message—the alert box is simply not displayed. If you add a single closing parenthesis immediately before the semicolon at the end of the alert statement the alert box will be displayed.

Any time the count drops below zero, you've got an automatic exception for too many closing parentheses marks. If the count is not equal to zero at the end of the line, you've got an automatic exception for missing some closing parentheses marks.

An additional context where matching parentheses is important is in defining regular expressions. See Chapter 9, "RegExp()," for details.

Square Brackets []

A common use of braces (sometimes referred to as "square brackets") is with `Array()` objects—either in accessing the elements of an `Array()` object or defining one. See Chapter 3, "Array()," for details. I use a similar counting method to the one in Listing 13.1 to confirm that opening and closing square brackets are correctly balanced.

A further use of square brackets is to reference properties of an object with a syntax such as

```
objectName['propertyName']
```

This syntax is an alternative to the form with which you are possibly more familiar,

```
objectName.propertyName
```

Curly Braces {}

These you can find in two different contexts. The first is in defining an `Object()` object literal. See Chapter 1, "Object()," for details.

The second is in defining a code block for execution. To JavaScript, anything within a code block is one line outside the code block. You've seen code blocks in `Function()` objects, and in the looping and condition statements of Chapter 12, "Operators."

In the Introduction, I mentioned my peculiar indenting style. Other JavaScripters may shake their heads in dismay, but I do have a reason for this. Each code block I indent by a certain number of spaces, typically a tab. This includes the closing bracket of any code block. It helps me in two ways. The first is to isolate that code block from every other statement in the script.

```
if (1 == 1) {
        // indented code belonging only to the if statement
        } // indented to indicate close to if statement code block
    void(null) // indented to the same level as the if statement
// this is to show it belongs to the same code block as the if statement
```

The second is to help me track down a missing closing bracket fairly quickly.

```
function myFunc() {
    try {
        if (1 == 1) {
            alert("Hello World")
            }
    catch (e) {
        alert(e)
        }
    }
}
```

Without the tabbing, I would not be able to see the missing closing bracket that JavaScript requires to close the `try` statement's code block.

Quote Marks

Quote marks come in two different sets, the single quote ', and the double quote ". Typically, they come in pairs: a pair of double quotes or a pair of single quotes. You can safely nest one single quote within two double quotes, or vice versa:

```
var x = "'" // valid single quote mark as a string
```

Quotes define `string` literals. Every opening single quote must be balanced by a closing single quote, unless escaped (see the section "Literals," later in this chapter), or enclosed between double quotes. Likewise, every opening double quote must be answered by a closing double quote, unless escaped or enclosed between single quotes.

Usually, to ensure I have the right arrangement of quotes in a line, I start with a logical number of 0. A single quote mark changes 0 to 1, or 1 to 0. A double quote mark changes 0 to 2, or 2 to 0. There are no changes directly between 1 and 2. If at the end of the line my logical number is not 0, I've got an extra quote or I'm missing one.

```
var x = " ' " + ' " ' + " ' " + ' ' + " '
/* the above code returns the following quote count:
        2   0   1   0   2   0   1 0   2
missing quote character:   "
*/
```

The only time when this method is not perfect is when the string constructed will be used in an `eval()` method call. In cases like that, I simply `alert()` the string that `eval()` normally executes and recheck the executable string for typos before `eval()` executes it.

Semicolons, Colons, Commas, and Periods

Let's move on to look at basic punctuation marks—semicolons, colons, commas and periods.

Semicolons ;

Semicolons have two uses. The first is an optional one, in separating commands within a code block from each other. (It is a requirement if two or more commands are on the same line.)

```
var x = 3; var y = 4
```

The preceding line is equivalent to

```
var x = 3
var y = 4
```

and:

```
var x = 3;
var y = 4;
```

The other use for semicolons is separating statements in a `for` loop:

```
for (x = 0; x < 2; x++) { ... }
```

Commas ,

Commas have a number of uses in JavaScript. One is to separate arguments in a function definition:

```
myFunction(firstArgument, secondArgument)
```

and, similarly, in a function call:

```
myFunc(3, 4)
```

Additionally, the comma can be used as a separator when a list of variables is being declared:

```
var a, b, c;
```

A further use of the comma is as an operator, as described in Chapter 12.

Colons :

Colons have three uses in JavaScript. The first is to create a labeled statement. The labeled statement immediately precedes a statement whose code block you may want to break out of later, by referring to the labeled statement.

```
function myFunc() {
   y = 0
   myFunc_label: // labeled statement
   for (x = 0; x < 2; x++) {
      y++
      break myFunc_label
      }
// resumes here
   alert(y) // returns 1
   }
```

The second use of colons is as part of the conditional operator as described in Chapter 12. The third use of colons is in defining properties of `Object()` object literals as described in Chapter 1.

Periods .

Periods have two uses in JavaScript. The first is to separate an object from its properties and methods (sometimes called a *member expression*). For example, `Math.sin` is the sine function because the sin method is a method of the `Math` object.

The second use is as a decimal point, to separate a Number() object's integer portion from its decimal portion. In 3.14, "3" is the integer portion and "14" is the decimal portion. When attempting to apply a property or method of a Number() object literal, a period immediately following the whole number portion with no space in-between is interpreted as the decimal point. See the next section, "Literals," and also Chapter 7, "Number ()," for more details.

Literals

JavaScript supplies a number of literals for use within the language, known as special characters. JavaScript also supplies syntax for defining literals of various object types. The literals, and what they translate into, are shown in Table 13.1.

Table 13.1   *Literals in JavaScript*

Literal Notation	Result
\'	'
\"	"
\\	\
\n	New line character
\t	Tab character
\r	Carriage return (Enter key)
\v	Vertical tab
\b	Backspace
\f	Form feed
\x##	ASCII hexadecimal code of character
\u####	Unicode hexadecimal code of character
\###	ASCII octal code of character
{propname:propval}	New Object() (literal, see Chapter 1)
["element0", "element1"]	New Array() (literal, see Chapter 3)
[-]####[.]####[e[-]##]	New Number() (literal, see Chapter 7)
0###	Octal number (literal, see Chapter 7)
0x###	Hexadecimal number (literal, see Chapter 7)
/expression/flags (literal, see Chapter 9)	New RegExp("expression", "flags")
"string" 'string'	New String(string) (literal, see Chapter 4)

ASCII and Unicode

Several years ago, the ASCII standard defined 128 basic character codes for standardized use on any computer platform. This included the character code 65 for the letter "A", the code 32 for a space, the code 13 for a carriage return, and so on. The ASCII code has been a mainstay of computer coding for years, and in JavaScript appears in escaped characters and character codes extracted from strings or keyboard events.

However, in recent years, the ASCII format has proved insufficient to express common characters in languages other than English. For instance, there is zero support in ASCII for Japanese characters, or mathematical symbols. A partial solution, specialized fonts, arose to alleviate the problem. (The Symbol and Wingdings fonts have been the best-known such fonts.)

Specialized fonts were not a complete solution, and so the Unicode Consortium has created a new character set with 65,536 characters instead of ASCII's 128. This character set is commonly known as Unicode, and only in the more recent versions of Netscape and Internet Explorer have Unicode characters begun to appear. (Many character sets within this range remain undefined, reserved for future definitions.)

Unicode's first 256 characters, ranging from 0 to 255, match the ISO-Latin-1 font, which is arranged according to the old ASCII format. Thus, there are no characters in ASCII that Unicode does not cover.

You can explicitly create ASCII and Unicode characters by using one of two notations. The first is to use the `String.fromCharCode` method, described in Chapter 4, "String ()." The second is to use a hexadecimal number format with a prefix. If the prefix is `\x`, you can use two hexadecimal digits to return an ASCII character. If the prefix is `\u`, you can use up to four hexadecimal digits to return a Unicode character. You can get Unicode character charts from the Unicode Consortium's Web site at `http://www.unicode.org`.

Comment Lines //, /* ... */

There are two kinds of comment markers in JavaScript. One is the single line comment `//`, which you see numerous times throughout this book. Whenever you encounter this character pair active in JavaScript, any characters following on that line (including semicolons and other comment markers) are considered characters that the JavaScript engine must ignore.

The other kind of comment markers, /* and */, define regions of text that the
JavaScript engine must ignore. Anything between these two markers the engine
ignores.

```
x = 3; /* x++; // */ alert(x) // returns 3
```

These two markers do not have to be on the same line. However, each active /*
marker (meaning not commented out) must be answered by a closing */ marker. The
first */ marker following a /* marker ends the comment section. A */ marker may not
be found alone, nor may an opening /* marker. A couple of examples of /* ... */
commenting can be found earlier in this chapter.

CHAPTER 14

Conditional Compilation
in Internet Explorer

Browser/JavaScript Version	Opened By
Nav4/JavaScript 1.2	(Not implemented)
IE4/JScript 3.0	/*@cc_on*/
IE5/JScript 5.0	/*@cc_on*/
IE5.5/JScript 5.5	/*@cc_on*/
Nav6/JavaScript 1.5	(Not implemented)
ECMAScript 1st edition	(Not implemented)
ECMAScript 3rd edition	(Not implemented)

> **Note**
> Implemented in IE4+

Description

Conditional compilation is a feature that Internet Explorer makes available for its browsers. For JavaScripters, it provides the capability to define custom code blocks that run only within the Internet Explorer browser. You can also use it to write code that will not run in Internet Explorer 4+, but will run otherwise.

Conditional compilation supports a few variables that are not otherwise available to the user. Some of these are about the version of JScript in place; others are about the kind of central processing unit (CPU) the client computer has. A couple identify the operating system as 16-bit or 32-bit. (The information in predefined conditional compilation objects can be deduced from the navigator object in Chapter 18, "navigator," in every case.)

The syntax of conditional compilation is slightly different. Conditional compilation statements and variables begin with @. When you comment them out, as I describe later in this chapter, you have to end them with the @ sign.

Conditional compilation appears to ignore event handlers entirely, as seen in Listing 14.1.

Listing 14.1   *Conditional Compilation Executes Immediately, Regardless of Where It Is in a Script*

```
<?xml version="1.0" ?>
<!DOCTYPE html PUBLIC "-//W3C//DTD XHTML 1.0 Transitional//EN"
➥"DTD/xhtml1-transitional.dtd">
<html xmlns="http://www.w3.org/1999/xhtml">
```

Listing 14.1 *(Continued)*

```
<head><title>
<script language="JavaScript" type="text/javascript">
<!--
/*@cc_on
@set @x = 3
@*/
//-->
</script>
</title></head>
<body onLoad="alert(eval(document.forms.myForm.test.value));
@set @x = 4@*/;
alert(eval(document.forms.myForm.test.value))">
<!-- alerts 4 onLoad twice -->
<form name="myForm">
<input type="hidden" value="@x" value="2" name="test" />
</form>
</body>
</html>
```

Statements

@cc_on

Syntax

```
/*@cc_on@*/
```

This statement is useful only if you use conditional compilation without creating any new objects (see @set) or testing objects (see @if).

```
@cc_on
alert(@_jscript_version)
```

Without the @cc_on statement, this code would throw an exception. Instead, it tells the browser, "Hey, wake up. I need some conditional compilation objects right now." The browser complies.

@if and @set activate conditional compilation at the first instance of their use automatically.

@if...[@elif... [@elif...]] [@else...] @end

Syntax

```
@if (cond1) codeBlock...[ @elif (cond2) codeBlock2... ]
➥[@else codeBlock3...] @end
```

The `@if` syntax is somewhat different from conventional JavaScript `if` statement syntax. The equivalent JavaScript syntax is

```
if (cond1) {
   codeBlock
   } else if (cond2) {
   codeBlock2
   } else {
   codeBlock3
   }
```

In one way, it emulates the ?: syntax of Chapter 13, "JavaScript Syntax."

```
alert(@if (@_jscript) "Conditional Compilation On!" @else "This will not run"
@end )
```

You can have as many `@elif` clauses as you want in one of these statements:

```
@if (!@_x86) alert("Do you have any Grey Poupon?")
@elif (@_win16) alert("Short filenames")
@elif (@_win32) alert("Good call!")
@else alert("Umm...")
@end
```

Note there are no brackets {} in the preceding code. For some reason, conditional compilation does not like them. In the syntactic structure of this statement, they are not necessary anyway.

If a variable doesn't exist, its value is `Number.NaN`. Because `Number.NaN != Number.NaN`, you can check for its existence like this:

```
@if (@x == @x) alert("Hi") @else alert("Bye") @end // alerts "Bye"
```

@set

Syntax

```
@set @objname = value
```

This allows you to create variables that are either `Number()` or `Boolean()` literals only. You can use an expression for the right side *value* to arrive at an appropriate literal.

```
@set @x = ((3 * 3) + (4 * 4))
alert(@if (@x) @x @else !@_jscript @end ) // returns 25
```

Objects

@_alpha

This is a `Boolean()` object indicating whether the client is running a DEC Alpha CPU.

@_jscript

This is a `Boolean()` object indicating whether the client is running the JScript engine at the time. (Obviously, because the language is JavaScript/JScript, the value is `true`.)

@_jscript_build

This is a `Number()` object indicating the build number of the JScript engine.

@_jscript_version

This is a `Number()` object indicating the version number of the JScript engine. (For Internet Explorer 5.01, it reports 5.1, which is not a valid JScript version number. JScript went directly from 5.0 to 5.5.)

@_mac

This is a `Boolean()` object indicating whether the client is running on a Macintosh platform.

@_mc680x0

This is a `Boolean()` object indicating whether the client is running on a Motorola 680x0 platform.

@_PowerPC

This is a `Boolean()` object indicating whether the client is running on a PowerPC platform.

@_win16

This is a `Boolean()` object indicating whether the client is running on a 16-bit version of Windows.

@_win32

This is a `Boolean()` object indicating whether the client is running on a 32-bit version of Windows.

@_x86

This is a `Boolean()` object indicating whether the client is running on an Intel 80x86 processor or an Intel Pentium processor (which followed in the 80x86 series of processors; the first Pentium CPU was frequently called the 80586).

Compatibility with Netscape Browsers

Netscape under no circumstances allows an object to start with the @ symbol. Microsoft recognized this, and allows us to write conditional compilation statements enclosed in JavaScript comments, as seen in Listing 14.2.

Listing 14.2   *Commenting Out Conditional Compilation*

```
<?xml version="1.0" ?>
<!DOCTYPE html PUBLIC "-//W3C//DTD XHTML 1.0 Transitional//EN"
➥"DTD/xhtml1-transitional.dtd">
<html xmlns="http://www.w3.org/1999/xhtml">
<head><title></title></head>
<body>
<script language="JavaScript" type="text/javascript">
<!--
/*@cc_on@*/
/*@if (@_win32) alert("Politically Correct");
 @else@*/alert("Return of the Mac");
/*@end@*/
//-->
</script>
</body>
</html>
```

When commenting out conditional compilation code, all such comments must begin with `/*@` and end with `@*/`. Also, watch for spacing; an ill-placed space can wreck your code, unlike in other areas of JavaScript.

Personally, I avoid conditional compilation. Microsoft provides similar information through its `navigator` object (which I detail in Chapter 18). There does not seem to be any particular need for conditional compilation that other well-established and better-known procedures do not also have. I expect Microsoft will retain it for backward-compatibility, but conditional compilation does not appear to be a necessary part of the JavaScript language to know.

PART II

Window and Client Objects

CHAPTER

CHAPTER 15

window

Browser/JavaScript Version	Created By
Nav4/JavaScript 1.2	`// Browser starting new window` `window.open()`
IE4/JScript 3.0	`// Browser starting new window` `window.open()`
IE5/JScript 5.0	`// Browser starting new window` `window.open()`
IE5.5/JScript 5.5	`// Browser starting new window` `window.open()`
IE6	`// Browser starting new window` `window.open()`
Nav6/JavaScript 1.5	`// Browser starting new window` `window.open()`

> **Note**
> Implemented in Nav2+, IE3+
> Equivalent to Global object (Chapter 11, "Global Objects and Statements")

Description

The `window` object is as fundamental to client-side JavaScript as any of the core objects of JavaScript. It is a container for all objects you create, both directly via JavaScript and indirectly through the DOM. However, it is also the first object where standards developed by the W3C and the ECMA do not truly apply. Thus, while the `window` object has many objects common to both Netscape and Internet Explorer browsers, each browser adds its own proprietary properties and methods as well.

Common `window` **Object Names**

You can have several `window` objects simultaneously in a master window: the topmost window, framesets, framed windows, pop-up windows, and inline frames are all considered `window` objects. In addition, there is a legitimate concern for calling `Layer()` objects (discussed in Chapter 28, "Text Elements") `window` objects, though these are considered properties of the `document.layers` object.

Description

A window object can refer to itself typically through its window and self properties. If a window object is in a frameset, parent refers to the frameset window object; else parent also refers to window. If a window object is the topmost window in a frameset chain (that is, it is not framed in any way), top refers to window; else, it refers to the highest frameset in a window structure. See Listing 15.1.

Listing 15.1   *The* top, parent, window, *and* self *Objects*

```
<?xml version="1.0" ?>
<!-- 15lst01a.htm -->
<!DOCTYPE html PUBLIC "-//W3C//DTD XHTML 1.0 Frameset//EN"
➥"DTD/xhtml1-frameset.dtd">
<html xmlns="http://www.w3.org/1999/xhtml" >
<head><title></title>
<script language="JavaScript" type="text/javascript">
<!--
obj = "Hello"
//-->
</script>
</head>
<frameset rows="*,0" onload="frames[0].frames[0].frames[0].test()">
    <frame src="15lst01b.htm" />
    <frame />
    </frameset>
</html>


<?xml version="1.0" ?>
<!-- 15lst01b.htm -->
<!DOCTYPE html PUBLIC "-//W3C//DTD XHTML 1.0 Frameset//EN"
➥"DTD/xhtml1-frameset.dtd">
<html xmlns="http://www.w3.org/1999/xhtml" ><head><title></title>
<script language="JavaScript" type="text/javascript">
<!--
obj = "Greetings"
//-->
</script>
</head>
<frameset rows="*,0">
    <frame src="15lst01c.htm" />
    <frame />
    </frameset>
</html>
```

Listing 15.1   *(continued)*

```
<?xml version="1.0" ?>
<!-- 15lst01c.htm -->
<!DOCTYPE html PUBLIC "-//W3C//DTD XHTML 1.0 Frameset//EN"
➥"DTD/xhtml1-frameset.dtd">
<html xmlns="http://www.w3.org/1999/xhtml" >
<head><title></title>
<script language="JavaScript" type="text/javascript">
<!--
obj = "Bonjour"
//-->
</script>
</head>
<frameset rows="*,0">
   <frame src="15lst01d.htm" />
   <frame />
   </frameset>
</html>


<?xml version="1.0" ?>
<!-- 15lst01d.htm -->
<!DOCTYPE html PUBLIC "-//W3C//DTD XHTML 1.0 Transitional//EN"
➥"DTD/xhtml1-transitional.dtd">
<html xmlns="http://www.w3.org/1999/xhtml" >
<head><title></title></head>
<body>
<script language="JavaScript" type="text/javascript">
<!--
obj = "Howdy"
function test() {
   var ta = document.forms.myForm.ta
   ta.value += "top.obj == " + top.obj + "\n"
   ta.value += "parent.obj == " + parent.obj + "\n"
   ta.value += "parent.parent.obj == " + parent.parent.obj + "\n"
   ta.value += "parent.parent.parent.obj == " + parent.parent.parent.obj + "\n"
   ta.value += "window.obj == " + window.obj + "\n"
   ta.value += "self.obj == " + self.obj + "\n"
   ta.value += "obj == " + obj
   }
//-->
</script>
<form name="myForm" action="javascript:void(null)">
```

Description

Listing 15.1 *(continued)*

```
<textarea rows="7" cols="60" name="ta"></textarea>
</form>
<!-- Results:
top.obj == Hello
parent.obj == Bonjour
parent.parent.obj == Greetings
parent.parent.parent.obj == Hello
window.obj == Howdy
self.obj == Howdy
obj == Howdy
-->
</body>
</html>
```

Also, if you run 15lst01d.htm as a standalone file and call on test(), you get seven lines of text, each ending in "Howdy".

Pop-up windows can refer to the window objects that create them by the opener property, discussed later in this chapter.

Order of Operations in Loading Scripts

Any time you have window objects that must share information, you invite trouble. For instance, frames can safely refer to each other as parent.*otherFrameName* or parent.frames.*otherFrameName*, if the other frame has finished loading. Imagine the scenario shown in Listing 15.2.

Listing 15.2 *A Basic Frameset, Flawed*

```
<?xml version="1.0" ?>
<!-- 15lst02a.htm -->
<!DOCTYPE html PUBLIC "-//W3C//DTD XHTML 1.0 Frameset//EN"
➥"DTD/xhtml1-frameset.dtd">
<html xmlns="http://www.w3.org/1999/xhtml" >
<head><title></title></head><frameset rows="50%,*">
   <frame name="page1" src="15lst02b.htm" />
   <frame name="page2" src="15lst02c.htm" />
   </frameset>
</html>

<?xml version="1.0" ?>
```

Listing 15.2   *(continued)*

```
<!-- 15lst02b.htm -->
<!DOCTYPE html PUBLIC "-//W3C//DTD XHTML 1.0 Transitional//EN"
➥"DTD/xhtml1-transitional.dtd">
<html xmlns="http://www.w3.org/1999/xhtml" >
<head><title></title></head>
<body>
<script language="JavaScript" type="text/javascript">
<!--
a = 3
alert(parent.page2.b)
//-->
</script>
</body>
</html>


<?xml version="1.0" ?>
<!-- 15lst02c.htm -->
<!DOCTYPE html PUBLIC "-//W3C//DTD XHTML 1.0 Transitional//EN"
➥"DTD/xhtml1-transitional.dtd">
<html xmlns="http://www.w3.org/1999/xhtml" >
<head><title></title></head>
<body>
<script language="JavaScript" type="text/javascript">
<!--
b = 3
alert(parent.page1.a)
//-->
</script>
</body>
</html>
```

Although `15lst02b.htm` and `15lst02c.htm` both define objects on which the other calls, they aren't both in place before the respective `alert()` method calls fire. Neither are their global values, which JavaScript would make available as properties of their respective `window` objects. Suppose `15lst02a.htm` loads first. Here's the order of operations, then:

1. `15lst02a.htm` loads

2. `a = 3`

3. `alert(parent.page2.b) // returns undefined`

4. 15lst02b.htm loads

5. b = 3

6. alert(parent.page1.a) // returns 3

It doesn't matter if you fire the variable definitions and alerts onload. One page will probably load and execute before the other can get its object in place. In this case, you have two options: rely on the frameset's onload event handler, or force each page's script to wait until the other script has finished loading.

Because window objects can change documents, I prefer the second solution. I recommend you begin using <body onload="loaded = true">. You can use the setTimeout() method of window objects to check for the value of the loaded object in any other window object you can reference from your own domain name.

> **Caution**
> JavaScript specifically denies access to the objects and values of any window object not from your domain without the user's permission.

In Chapter 5, "Boolean()," I mentioned the undefined value always evaluates to false in a conditional test. Thus, if I check for the value of window.loaded in an if...else statement, I get false if it is undefined. On the other hand, I can set loaded, and thus window.loaded for that particular window, to be true. See Listing 15.3.

Listing 15.3   *A Basic Frameset, with Checking for* onload *Event Firing*

```
<?xml version="1.0" ?>
<!-- 15lst03a.htm -->
<!DOCTYPE html PUBLIC "-//W3C//DTD XHTML 1.0 Frameset//EN"
➥"DTD/xhtml1-frameset.dtd">
<html xmlns="http://www.w3.org/1999/xhtml" >
<head><title></title></head>
<frameset rows="50%,*">
   <frame name="page1" src="15lst03b.htm" />
   <frame name="page2" src="15lst03c.htm" />
   </frameset>
</html>


<?xml version="1.0" ?>
```

Listing 15.3 *(continued)*

```html
<!-- 15lst03b.htm -->
<!DOCTYPE html PUBLIC "-//W3C//DTD XHTML 1.0 Transitional//EN"
➥"DTD/xhtml1-transitional.dtd">
<html xmlns="http://www.w3.org/1999/xhtml" >
<head><title></title></head>
<body onload="loaded=true">
<script language="JavaScript" type="text/javascript">
<!--
a = 3
function page1_init() {
   if (parent.page2.loaded) {
      alert(parent.page2.b)
      } else {
      setTimeout("page1_init()",100)
      }
   }
page1_init()
//-->
</script>
</body>
</html>


<?xml version="1.0" ?>
<!-- 15lst03c.htm -->
<!DOCTYPE html PUBLIC "-//W3C//DTD XHTML 1.0 Transitional//EN"
➥"DTD/xhtml1-transitional.dtd">
<html xmlns="http://www.w3.org/1999/xhtml" >
<head><title></title></head>
<body onload="loaded=true">
<script language="JavaScript" type="text/javascript">
<!--
b = 3
function page2_init() {
   if (parent.page1.loaded) {
      alert(parent.page1.a)
      } else {
      setTimeout("page2_init()",100)
      }
   }
page2_init()
```

Description

Listing 15.3   *(continued)*

```
//-->
</script>
</body>
</html>
```

What happens here is significantly different: each page creates its `window.loaded` value `onload`, and then a function checks for the value of the `window.loaded` value in the other window. Initially, we expect the value to be `undefined` and read `false` to the `if...else` statement. Whenever that happens, a `setTimeout()` method call schedules the function to execute again in 100 milliseconds.

When the other frame finally loads and sets `loaded = true`, the function in the first frame detects that, and fires the `alert()` method call as we originally intended. This time, we guarantee both frames have created their objects (a, b) before either frame references them.

Sending Objects and Values Between Windows

In Listing 15.2, we have three `window` objects. The `onload` event handlers for `page1.htm` and `page2.htm` will fire before the `onload` event handler for `Frameset.htm`. The same applies to child layers and inline frame elements (but not necessarily pop-up windows). Listing 15.2 involves `window` objects getting values from one another, but you can also set objects in other `window` objects from your native `window` object.

```
parent.book.author = "Alex Vincent"
```

Thus, if you have a frame named `book`, it will then have a property named `author` with my name in it. To the `book` frame, `author` is a top-level property of the window because `window.x == x` for all `window` objects.

This comes in very handy when you have objects with lots of specific properties and methods to pass along. However, what makes this interesting is `window` objects can receive properties from other `window` objects that survive their originating windows. See Listing 15.4.

Listing 15.4   *An Object Surviving the* window *Object That Created It*

```
<?xml version="1.0" ?>
<!-- 15lst04a.htm -->
<!DOCTYPE html PUBLIC "-//W3C//DTD XHTML 1.0 Frameset//EN"
➥"DTD/xhtml1-frameset.dtd">
<html xmlns="http://www.w3.org/1999/xhtml" >
```

Listing 15.4   *(continued)*

```
<head><title></title></head>
<frameset rows="50%,*">
    <frame name="page1" src="15lst04b.htm" />
    <frame name="page2" src="15lst04c.htm" />
    </frameset>
</html>

<?xml version="1.0" ?>
<!-- 15lst04b.htm -->
<!DOCTYPE html PUBLIC "-//W3C//DTD XHTML 1.0 Transitional//EN"
➥"DTD/xhtml1-transitional.dtd">
<html xmlns="http://www.w3.org/1999/xhtml" >
<head><title></title></head>
<body>
<script language="JavaScript" type="text/javascript">
<!--
book = new Object()
book.author = "Alex Vincent"
parent.frames.page2.book = book
location.href = "15lst04d.htm"
//-->
</script>
</body>
</html>

<?xml version="1.0" ?>
<!-- 15lst04c.htm -->
<!DOCTYPE html PUBLIC "-//W3C//DTD XHTML 1.0 Transitional//EN"
➥"DTD/xhtml1-transitional.dtd">
<html xmlns="http://www.w3.org/1999/xhtml" >
<head><title></title></head>
<body></body>
</html>

<?xml version="1.0" ?>
<!-- 15lst04d.htm -->
<!DOCTYPE html PUBLIC "-//W3C//DTD XHTML 1.0 Transitional//EN"
➥"DTD/xhtml1-transitional.dtd">
<html xmlns="http://www.w3.org/1999/xhtml" >
<head><title></title></head>
<body>
```

Description

Listing 15.4   *(continued)*

```
<script language="JavaScript" type="text/javascript">
<!--
book = parent.frames.page2.book
alert(book.author) // returns "Alex Vincent"
//-->
</script>
</body>
</html>
```

Had the `book` object reacted as JavaScript typically does, calling the `book.author` property would have thrown an exception. Instead, we retrieve the property correctly and without error. This rather interesting factoid about JavaScript is put to good use in the example at the end of this chapter.

The `window` Object, Event Handlers, and the W3C DOM

The W3C defines quite a few event handlers in its DOM-2 Events Recommendation. However, some of these event handlers do not apply directly to the `HTMLDocument` interface they use, but to the `window` object, which the DOM does not attempt to define. These event handlers I list at the end of the Methods section. The actual event handler definitions come in Chapter 32, "DOM-2 Events and Event Handlers."

Windows Have Two Names

One confusing fact to a lot of developers is that `window` objects can have an HTML name and a JavaScript name. By HTML name I refer to the `target` attribute of a link or form. By JavaScript name I refer to the object handle given a window by either the user or by the browser's DOM implementation.

```
JSWindowName = window.open("about:blank","HTMLWindowName")
```

The name `JSWindowName` is a JavaScript object container for the new window. `HTMLWindowName` refers to the window's `name` HTML attribute. See Listing 15.5.

Listing 15.5   *HTML and JavaScript Window Names Demonstrated*

```
<?xml version="1.0" ?>
<!DOCTYPE html PUBLIC "-//W3C//DTD XHTML 1.0 Transitional//EN"
➥"DTD/xhtml1-transitional.dtd">
<html xmlns="http://www.w3.org/1999/xhtml" >
<head><title></title></head>
<body onload="self.focus()">
```

Listing 15.5   *(continued)*

```
<script language="JavaScript" type="text/javascript">
<!--
crosshairs = window.open("about:blank","bullseye")
//-->
</script>
<form target="bullseye" action="http://www.jslab.org/jsdd" method="get" >
<input type="text" name="myName" value="great"  />
<input type="submit" onclick="crosshairs.focus();return true" />
<!--
```

The `onClick` event handler of the submit button brings the pop-up window to focus.

The second argument of the `window.open()` method call matches the target attribute of the form, and specifies the pop-up window to change URI to the action attribute given, with `"?myName=great"` attached.

```
-->
</form>
</body>
</html>
```

Personally, I recommend using the exact same values for the HTML window name and the JavaScript window name. This makes it easier for you as a developer to refer to the same object by the same name in both HTML and JavaScript.

Properties

_content

JavaScript 1.5

Nav6

Syntax

```
window._content
```

The `_content` property of `window` objects refers to the main content section of the browser window. This is primarily used in Netscape's proprietary "XML-Based User Interface Language", and is beyond the scope of this book.

Properties

clientInformation

JScript 3.0+

IE4+

Syntax

```
var x = clientInformation
```

The `clientInformation` property of `window` objects is a synonym for the `navigator` object. See Chapter 18, "navigator," for more details.

clipboardData

JScript 5.0+

IE5+

Syntax

```
var x = clipboardData
```

The `clipboardData` property of `window` objects is an object that groups a few methods together to interact with the operating system's Clipboard.

clearData( )

JScript 5.0+

IE5+

Syntax

```
clipboardData.clearData(dataType)
```

The `clearData()` method of `clipboardData` objects clears the data in the Clipboard according to the first argument, a string. If the argument is "Text," it clears the text formatting of the Clipboard. Similarly, it will clear HTML, images, files, and URLs stored in the given arguments of "HTML", "Image", "File", and "URL", respectively.

getData( )

JScript 5.0+

IE5+

Syntax

```
var x = clipboardData.getData(outputType)
```

The getData() method of clipboardData objects returns the contents of the Clipboard. If you feed the method "Text" as an argument, it returns the value unconditionally. If you feed the method "URL" as an argument, it will return the Clipboard value if and only if the Clipboard contains an URL. Otherwise, it will return null.

setData( )

JScript 5.0+

IE5+

Syntax

```
[var x =] clipboardData.setData(dataType, data)
```

The setData() method of clipboardData objects sets the second argument, a string, as the data the Clipboard contains. The first argument is either "Text" or "URL," indicating what kind of data the Clipboard stores: plain text or a link, respectively.

closed

JavaScript 1.0+, JScript 3.0+

Nav2+, IE4+

Syntax

```
var x = windowObj.closed
```

The closed property of window objects is a true or false value indicating whether the this object has been closed. I use it all the time in determining if I need to create a new pop-up window, or if I can just continue normally:

```
if ((typeof(windowobj) != "undefined")&&(!windowobj.closed)) {
```

However, it doesn't work perfectly. Internet Explorer has a known bug when you try to reference the `window.closed` property. You can find the bug at `http://support.microsoft.com/support/kb/articles/Q241/1/09.ASP`.

Components

JavaScript 1.5

Nav6

Syntax

```
window.Components
```

The `Components` property of `window` objects is another object that belongs to XPCOM and XPConnect. It is a wrapper for all XPCOM objects, written in both native (C++) and JavaScript code. It has several properties that are beyond the scope of this book. More information may be found at this URI: `http://www.mozilla.org/scriptable/components_object.html`.

controllers

JavaScript 1.5

Nav6

Syntax

```
window.controllers
```

The `controllers` property of `window` objects works with XUL controllers. Controllers determine the actions to be taken within an XUL document; which ones are enabled, which ones are disabled, and so on.

Once again, XUL is beyond the scope of this book.

crypto

JavaScript 1.2+

Nav4+

Syntax

```
window.crypto
```

The `crypto` property of `window` objects holds one property and a few methods for use when encrypting information for transmission to a server. Netscape 6 does not support any of these standalones without throwing an exception. Typically, a JavaScript developer never needs to call these functions.

Although signed scripts are beyond the scope of this book, there is one method of the `crypto` object worth explaining in detail. (The others are `crypto.signText()`, in Netscape 4+, and in Netscape 6, `crypto.version`, `crypto.generateCRMFRequest()`, `crypto.importUserCertificates()`, `crypto.popChallengeResponse()`, `crypto.alert()`, `crypto.logout()`, and `crypto.disableRightClick()`.)

crypto.random( )

Nav4+

JavaScript 1.2+

Syntax

```
var x = crypto.random(totChars)
```

The `random()` method of `window.crypto` returns a string of n characters, where n is a number and the first argument. The characters in the string are randomly chosen from the first 256 characters of the Unicode set. If you can translate from the "base-256" number to standard base-10 (decimal) numbers, you can then get random numbers with as many digits as you want.

defaultStatus

JavaScript 1.0+, JScript 1.0+

Nav2+, IE3+

Syntax

```
[var x = ] defaultStatus [= msgString]
```

The `defaultStatus` property of `window` objects allows you to retrieve or set a default status bar message in the browser window. (Typically, the status bar is at the bottom of a window.) Unless you override it, the `defaultStatus` value typically is "Document: Done" in Netscape, and an empty string in Internet Explorer. See the `status` property later in this chapter for details.

directories

JavaScript 1.5

Nav6

Syntax

```
window.directories
```

See `window.personalbar.`

document

JavaScript 1.0+, JScript 1.0+

Nav2+, IE3+

Syntax

```
document
```

The `document` property of `window` objects is a reference to the current `document` object of a page. See Chapter 23, "HTMLDocument/document," and the `Document` section of Chapter 20, "Core DOM Objects," for details.

external

JScript 3.0+

IE4+

Syntax

```
external
```

The `external` property of `window` objects wraps access to objects available to the browser and Web page that are not standard Web page components. It also allows modification of the Web browser through its methods.

Because of its connections to the Component Object Model, this book will not explain more than the immediately relevant methods.

AutoScan( )

JScript 5.0+

IE5+

Syntax

```
external.AutoScan(siteName0, altURL, [targetWin])
```

The `AutoScan()` method of `window.external` attempts to find a Web site matching a particular group of names. If you give it "microsoft" for the first argument, it will try www.microsoft.com, www.microsoft.net, www.microsoft.org, and so on until it finds a match. If it does not find a match, it jumps to the URL found in the second argument. The optional third argument specifies a window by HTML name where the page should load (without it, the page loads in the current window).

addFavorite( )

JScript 3.0+

IE4+

Syntax

```
external.addFavorite(URIString, title)
```

The `addFavorite()` method of the `window.external` object pops up the Add Favorites dialog box, offering the user a chance to add the first argument (URL) to his or her Favorites list. The second argument becomes the default title of the bookmark.

frameElement

JScript 5.5+

IE5.5

Syntax

```
var x = window.frameElement
```

The `frameElement` property of framed `window` objects allows the frame to access the `<frame />` or `<iframe />` element in the parent window directly. Thus, any properties of the `HTMLFrameElement` or `HTMLIFrameElement` (both described later in this chapter) you can access or change. Listing 15.6 shows the relationship between an `HTMLFrameElement` and its corresponding `window` object.

Listing 15.6   *The* frameElement *and* contentWindow *Objects*

```
<?xml version="1.0" ?>
<!-- 15lst06a.htm -->
<!-- IE 5.5+ only.  -->
<!DOCTYPE html PUBLIC "-//W3C//DTD XHTML 1.0 Frameset//EN"
➥"DTD/xhtml1-frameset.dtd">
<html xmlns="http://www.w3.org/1999/xhtml" >
<head><title></title></head>
<frameset rows="50%,*">
    <frame src="15lst06b.htm" />
    <frame src="about:blank" />
    </frameset>
</html>


<?xml version="1.0" ?>
<!-- 15lst06b.htm -->
<!DOCTYPE html PUBLIC "-//W3C//DTD XHTML 1.0 Transitional//EN"
➥"DTD/xhtml1-transitional.dtd">
<html xmlns="http://www.w3.org/1999/xhtml" >
<head><title></title></head>
<body>
<script language="JavaScript" type="text/javascript">
<!--
alert(window.frameElement.contentWindow == self)
// returns true
//-->
</script>
</body>
</html>
```

frames

JavaScript 1.0+, JScript 1.0+

Nav2+, IE3+

Syntax

```
frames
```

This returns a special array whose elements are child frames within the current document.

In Netscape 4, the `length` property reflects the number of frames within one document for which the `src` attribute has been defined. Internet Explorer returns the total number of frames within the document. (Note this does not include framesets and frames defined within the various frame documents. If a frame loads a frameset HTML page, that is not part of the total `frames.length` count of the topmost frameset, as I describe in Listing 15.1.)

In Netscape 6 and Internet Explorer 4.0+, if the document is not a frameset document, the `<iframe />` elements in the document populate this array.

If a frame has a `name` property, you can refer to the frame as having that `name` property's value. Also, the members of this array are arranged based on their ordering in the document. You can refer to the frame as a member of the `frames` array as I describe in Chapter 3, "Array( )," in the section "Numbered and Unnumbered Properties of Arrays."

```
alert(window.frames["framename"] == window.frames.framename) // returns true
```

See `HTMLFramesetElement`, `HTMLFrameElement`, and `HTMLIFrameElement` later in this chapter for more information.

history

JavaScript 1.1+, JScript 1.0+

Nav3+, IE3+

Syntax

```
history
```

The `history` property of `window` objects is a reference to the current `history` object of a window. See Chapter 17, "history," for details.

innerHeight

JavaScript 1.2+

Nav4+

Syntax

```
[var y =] innerHeight [= pixelHeight]
```

The innerHeight property of window objects retrieves from the client how many pixels, vertically, the browser can render without scrolling. This is the height of the content window. When used to set a value, it resizes the window to force the new innerHeight value.

The equivalent property in Internet Explorer 4 is document.body.clientHeight.

innerWidth

JavaScript 1.2+

Nav4+

Syntax

```
[var x =] innerWidth [= pixelWidth]
```

The innerWidth property of window objects retrieves from the client how many pixels, horizontally, the browser can render without scrolling. This is the width of the content window. When used to set a value, it resizes the window to force the new innerWidth value.

The equivalent property in Internet Explorer 4 is document.body.clientWidth.

length

JavaScript 1.0+, JScript 3.0+

Nav2+, IE4+

Syntax

```
var x = length
```

The length property of window objects is identical to window.frames.length. See window.frames for more detail.

location

JavaScript 1.1+, JScript 1.0+

Nav3+, IE3+

Syntax

```
location
```

The `location` property of `window` objects is a reference to the current `location` object of a window. See Chapter 16, "location," for details.

locationbar

JavaScript 1.2+

Nav4+

Syntax

```
var x = locationbar
```

The `locationbar` property of `window` objects represents the physical presence of the location bar within the window. The location bar is the section where the URI of a page displays. It has one property, `visible`, indicating whether the location bar is visible within the window. The script may change the visibility of this object only when it successfully requests the `UniversalBrowserWrite` privilege. For Web pages, this is generally only possible when the script is signed or the page is served via the `https://` protocol. The `UniversalBrowserWrite` privilege is beyond the scope of this book, however.

You can choose whether it is visible in a pop-up window, using the `window.open()` method, discussed later in this chapter.

menubar

Nav4+

Syntax

```
var x = menubar
```

The `menubar` property of `window` objects represents the physical presence of the menu bar within the window. The menu bar is the section where the drop-down command menus (such as File and Help) reside. It has one property, `visible`, indicating whether the menu bar is visible within the window. The script may change the visibility of this object only when it successfully requests the `UniversalBrowserWrite` privilege. For Web pages, this is generally only possible when the script is signed or the page is served via the `https://` protocol. The `UniversalBrowserWrite` privilege is beyond the scope of this book, however.

(You can choose whether it is visible in a pop-up window, using the `window.open()` method, discussed later in this chapter.)

name

JavaScript 1.0+, JScript 1.0+

Nav2+, IE3+

Read-only in Nav2, replaceable in Nav3+

Syntax

```
[var x = ] name [= HTMLWindowName]
```

The `name` property of `window` objects represents the HTML name of the `this` object. Because each `window` object has two possible names, an HTML name and a JavaScript name, this becomes significant to the browser for form processing and other actions a markup language calls upon. Listing 15.5 and the immediately preceding paragraphs go over this in some detail.

navigator

JavaScript 1.0+, JScript 1.0+

Nav2+, IE3+

Syntax

```
navigator
```

The `navigator` property of `window` objects is a synonym for the `navigator` object. See Chapter 18, "navigator," for more details.

offscreenBuffering

JavaScript 1.2-JavaScript 1.3, JScript 3.0+

Nav4, IE4+

Removed in Nav6

Syntax

```
[var x = ] offscreenBuffering [= "booleanVal"]
```

The `offscreenBuffering` property of `window` objects is one you can use to force the browser to either store page elements outside the viewable screen in a buffer, or to automatically render them. If you decide to set this to `false`, you may see smoother page loads that take up more memory. If you decide to set this to true, you may see pages that take up less memory but load a bit more unsteadily. It's usually best to leave this property alone and let the browser decide whether to buffer, although you may want to tinker with this in your Web pages to see what really loads best and renders smoothest.

opener

JavaScript 1.0+, JScript 3.0+

Nav3+, IE4+

Syntax

```
opener
```

The opener property of window objects refers to the window object that created this. In Internet Explorer and Netscape 4, it reflects the opening window only if you use window.open(). Netscape 6 reflects the opener property regardless of how you open this, whether by window.open() or by an HTML action, such as a click on a link.

If there is no direct opener window, the property returns null in Netscape, and undefined in Internet Explorer. Listing 15.7 demonstrates this.

Listing 15.7   *Framed Pages Do Not Respect window.opener*

```
<?xml version="1.0" ?>
<!-- 15lst07a.htm:  Opener window -->
<!DOCTYPE html PUBLIC "-//W3C//DTD XHTML 1.0 Transitional//EN"
➥"DTD/xhtml1-transitional.dtd">
<html xmlns="http://www.w3.org/1999/xhtml" >
<head><title></title></head>
<body onload="go()">
<script language="JavaScript" type="text/javascript">
<!--
function go() {
   window.open("15lst07b.htm")
   return false
   }
//-->
</script>
</body>
</html>
```

Listing 15.7   *(continued)*

```
<?xml version="1.0" ?>
<!-- 15lst07b.htm:  Frameset window -->
<!DOCTYPE html PUBLIC "-//W3C//DTD XHTML 1.0 Frameset//EN"
➥"DTD/xhtml1-frameset.dtd">
<html xmlns="http://www.w3.org/1999/xhtml" >
<head><title></title></head>

<frameset rows="*,0" >
   <frame src="15lst07c.htm" />
   <frame src="about:blank" />
   </frameset>
</html>


<?xml version="1.0" ?>
<!-- 15lst07c.htm:  Framed window -->
<!DOCTYPE html PUBLIC "-//W3C//DTD XHTML 1.0 Transitional//EN"
➥"DTD/xhtml1-transitional.dtd">
<html xmlns="http://www.w3.org/1999/xhtml" >
<head><title></title></head>
<body onload="go()">
<script language="JavaScript" type="text/javascript">
<!--
function go() {
   document.write("<p>opener = " + opener + "</p>")
   document.write("<p>opener = " + parent.opener + "</p>")
   }
//-->
</script>
</body>
</html>
```

outerHeight

JavaScript 1.2+

Nav4+

Syntax

```
[var y =] outerHeight [= pixelHeight]
```

The `outerHeight` property of `window` objects retrieves from the client how many pixels, vertically, the browser occupies of the viewable screen. When used to set a value, it resizes the window to force the new `outerHeight` value.

outerWidth

JavaScript 1.2+

Nav4+

Syntax

```
[var x =] outerWidth [= pixelWidth]
```

The `outerWidth` property of `window` objects retrieves from the client how many pixels, horizontally, the browser occupies of the viewable screen. When used to set a value, it resizes the window to force the new `outerWidth` value.

pageXOffset

JavaScript 1.2+

Nav4+

Syntax

```
var x = pageXOffset
```

The `pageXOffset` property of `window` objects retrieves how far from the left edge of the document the currently visible portion of the document is. For instance, if you've scrolled 100 pixels to the right within the document from the left edge, `pageXOffset` is equal to 100.

The equivalent property in Internet Explorer 4 is document.body.scrollLeft.

pageYOffset

JavaScript 1.2+

Nav4+

Syntax

```
var y = pageYOffset
```

The pageYOffset property of window objects retrieves how far from the top edge of the document the currently visible portion of the document is. For instance, if you've scrolled 100 pixels down within the document from the top edge, pageYOffset is equal to 100.

The equivalent property in Internet Explorer 4 is document.body.scrollTop.

parent

JavaScript 1.0+, JScript 1.0+

Nav2+, IE3+

Syntax

```
parent
```

The parent property of window objects refers to the window object containing this as a framed window. If there is no direct parent window, the property returns the same as this. Listing 15.1 demonstrates the use of the parent object.

personalbar

JavaScript 1.2+

Nav4+

Nav6: Also known as window.directories

Syntax

```
window.personalbar
```

The personalbar property of window objects represents the physical presence of the directories bar within the window. The directories bar is the section where items such as "What's New" and "What's Cool" appear. It has one property, visible, indicating whether the location bar is visible within the window. The script may change the visibility of this object only when it successfully requests the UniversalBrowserWrite privilege. For Web pages, this is generally only possible when the script is signed or the page is served via the https:// protocol. The UniversalBrowserWrite privilege is beyond the scope of this book, however.

You can choose whether it is visible in a pop-up window, using the `window.open()` method, discussed later in this chapter.

prompter

JavaScript 1.5

Nav6

Syntax

```
window.prompter
```

The `prompter` property of `window` objects is an XPConnect prompt control feature for XPCOM objects. In short, it allows a particular engine that imports Gecko (the browser engine behind Netscape 6) to define its own dialog boxes.

window.screen

JavaScript 1.2+, JScript 3.0+

Nav4+, IE4+

Syntax

```
screen
```

The `screen` property of `window` objects is a synonym for the `screen` object. See Chapter 19, "screen" for more details.

screenX (Nav), screenLeft (IE)

JavaScript 1.2+, JScript 5.0+

Nav4+, IE5+

Read-only as `screenLeft`

Syntax

```
[var x =] (window.screenX || window.screenLeft) [= screenXPixels]
```

This property in both of its names tells the distance from the left edge of the viewable screen to the left edge of the browser window in pixels. For instance, if the browser window's upper-left corner is at (200, 300), this returns 200.

screenY (Nav), screenTop (IE)

JavaScript 1.2+, JScript 5.0+

Nav4+, IE5+

Read-only as `screenTop`

Syntax

```
[var y =] (window.screenY || window.screenTop) [= screenYPixels]
```

This property tells the distance from the top edge of the viewable screen to the top edge of the browser window in pixels. For instance, if the browser window's upper-left corner is at (200, 300), this returns 300.

scrollbar

JavaScript 1.2+

Nav4+

Syntax

```
window.scrollbar
```

The `scrollbar` property of `window` objects represents the physical presence of the scrollbars within the window. It has one property, `visible`, indicating whether the scrollbars are visible within the window. The script may change the visibility of this object only when it successfully requests the `UniversalBrowserWrite` privilege. For Web pages, this is generally only possible when the script is signed or the page is served via the `https://` protocol. The `UniversalBrowserWrite` privilege is beyond the scope of this book, however.

You can choose whether it is visible or not in a pop-up window, using the `window.open()` method, discussed later in this chapter.

self

JavaScript 1.0+, JScript 3.0+

Nav2+, IE3+

Syntax

```
var winObj = self
```

The `self` property of `window` objects refers literally to itself. Listing 15.1 demonstrates the use of the `self` object.

status

JavaScript 1.0+, JScript 1.0+

Nav2+, IE3+

Syntax

```
[var x =] window.status [= msgString]
```

The `status` property of `window` objects sets the status bar's current value. It immediately overrides the `defaultStatus` value and replaces any current status bar value. This is useful in links `onmouseover` (you must `return true` in these for it to work), to override the standard `href://www.yoursite.com/yourdir/yourpage.htm?yourquery=`data URI string. When your `onmouseout` event fires, the status bar reverts to the `defaultStatus` message. See Listing 15.8.

Listing 15.8   *The* `status` *and* `defaultStatus` *Properties*

```
<?xml version="1.0" ?>
<!DOCTYPE html PUBLIC "-//W3C//DTD XHTML 1.0 Transitional//EN"
➥"DTD/xhtml1-transitional.dtd">
<html xmlns="http://www.w3.org/1999/xhtml" >
<head><title></title></head>
<body onload="defaultStatus='Hello World'">
<p>
<a href="#" onmouseover="status='I said HELLO WORLD!!';
return true">Test</a>
</p>
</body>
</html>
```

statusbar

JavaScript 1.2+

Nav4+

Syntax

```
window.statusbar
```

The `statusbar` property of `window` objects represents the physical presence of the status bar within the window. The status bar is the section where the browser tells you primarily what your document's status is, or where short messages from the user or identifying links may appear. (See `window.status` and `window.defaultStatus`.) It has one property, `visible`, indicating whether the location bar is visible within the window. The script may change the visibility of this object only when it successfully requests the `UniversalBrowserWrite` privilege. For Web pages, this is generally only possible when the script is signed or the page is served via the `https://` protocol. The `UniversalBrowserWrite` privilege is beyond the scope of this book, however.

You can choose whether it is visible in a pop-up window, using the `window.open()` method, discussed later in this chapter.

toolbar

JavaScript 1.2+

Nav4+

Syntax

```
window.toolbar
```

The `toolbar` property of `window` objects represents the physical presence of the main toolbar within the window. The main toolbar is the section where items such as Back and Stop appear. It has one property, `visible`, indicating whether the location bar is visible within the window. The script may change the visibility of this object only when it successfully requests the `UniversalBrowserWrite` privilege. For Web pages, this is generally only possible when the script is signed or the page is served via the `https://` protocol. The `UniversalBrowserWrite` privilege is beyond the scope of this book, however.

You can choose whether it is visible in a pop-up window, using the `window.open()` method, discussed later in this chapter.

top

JavaScript 1.2+, JScript 1.0+

Nav2+, IE3+

Syntax

```
top
```

The `top` property of `window` objects refers to the topmost frameset that contains `this` object. It is where the chain of `parent.parent.parent.parent...` ends. Listing 15.1 demonstrates the use of the `top` and `parent` objects.

window

JavaScript 1.0+, JScript 1.0+

Nav2+, IE3+

Syntax

```
window
```

The `window` property of `window` objects refers literally to itself. It is much like the `valueOf()` method return of Core JavaScript objects. Listing 15.1 demonstrates the use of the `window` object.

Methods

alert( )

JavaScript 1.0+, JScript 1.0+

Nav2+, IE3+

Syntax

```
alert(alertMsg)
```

The `alert()` method of `window` objects generates a miniature pop-up window containing only two items. The first is the value of the first argument, rendered directly into the window. The second is an OK button to close the alert pop-up window.

The pop-up window renders the message based on JavaScript syntax, not HTML syntax. For instance, `alert("a\nb")` will render the letter `"b"` on the second line, instead of `alert("a<br />b")`. Alert windows are modal dialog boxes, something I explain a little later in this chapter; basically, they stop execution of the script.

I like to use alerts quite a bit for diagnostic purposes, to tell me what a script is doing. However, you should probably avoid alerts in the final version of a page you present to users. They can be annoying, especially if they are simply sending a message.

A lot of people like to use alerts to intercept and cancel right-clicks of the mouse. However desirable it may be to you to protect your content, a determined person will already have a copy of it in their cache before they can right-click. You can look at `http://continue.to/hope` for more details on this issue.

atob( )

JavaScript 1.2-1.3

Nav4

Deprecated in Nav6

Syntax

```
var x = atob(ASCIIStr)
```

The `atob()` method of `window` objects provides for translation from a base-64 encoding to standard text. The encoding is based of RFC 2045, section 6.8 from `www.ietf.org`, but has been removed from Netscape 6. Netscape's documentation says it is particularly useful for translating control characters, and any ASCII character less than 32.

attachEvent( )

JScript 5.0+

IE5+

Syntax

```
attachEvent(eventName, handler)
```

The `attachEvent()` method of `window` objects causes the event handler given as the first argument to pass any events fired on it to the second argument, a function. The function is called after the event handler fires. See Chapter 32, "DOM-2 Events and Event Handlers," for details.

back( )

JavaScript 1.2+

Nav4+

Syntax

```
back()
```

The `back()` method of `window` objects is the same as clicking the Back button on a browser. It's usually better to use the `history.back()` method described in Chapter 17, "history," as you can target that for specific `window` objects' history values.

For example, if you take two frames in a frameset, advance the first frame to a new document, and then the second frame to a new document, to set the first frame back without changing the second frame, you'd say `frames[0].history.back()`. To just take a step back, no matter how the browser's current window reached its current status, use `window.back()`.

> **Note**
> The behavior for `history` changed in Netscape 6; it is now associated with the `top` object.

blur( )

JavaScript 1.0+, JScript 3.0+

Nav2+, IE4+

Syntax

```
self.blur()
```

The `blur()` method of `window` objects forces the browser window to lose focus. What this means is it tells the operating system "I'm not important; let some other window take center stage." The operating system reacts by either moving another window to the forefront of the viewing screen and making it active, or if there are no other windows, just letting the window run in the background.

btoa( )

JavaScript 1.2-1.3

Nav4

Deprecated in Nav6

Syntax

```
var x = btoa(base64String)
```

The btoa() method of window objects provides for translation to a base-64 encoding from standard text. The encoding is based on RFC 2045, section 6.8 from www.ietf.org, but has been removed from Netscape 6. Netscape's documentation says it is particularly useful for translating control characters, and any ASCII character less than 32.

captureEvents( )

JavaScript 1.2+

Nav4+

Syntax

```
captureEvents(eventName0 [| eventName1 ...])
```

The captureEvents() method of window objects in Netscape intercepts all events of the types specified in the first argument, which you separate by | marks; multiple events combine to form a logical OR statement: (Event.CLICK | Event.FOCUS). (Typically, these events are referred to as Event.EVENTNAME, where the event name is capitalized.) Using this method, you catch the events thrown or fired before the object they apply to catches them. See Chapter 32, "DOM-2 Events and Event Handlers" for details.

clearInterval( )

JavaScript 1.2+, JScript 3.0+

Nav4+, IE4+

Syntax

```
clearInterval(repeater)
```

The `clearInterval()` method of `window` objects cancels a repeating function call set by the `window.setInterval()` method call. The repeating function call you identify as the first argument.

As an example, note the code in Listing 15.9.

Listing 15.9   `setInterval` *and* `clearInterval` *Demonstrated*

```
<?xml version="1.0" ?>
<!DOCTYPE html PUBLIC "-//W3C//DTD XHTML 1.0 Transitional//EN"
➥"DTD/xhtml1-transitional.dtd">
<html xmlns="http://www.w3.org/1999/xhtml" >
<head><title></title></head>
<body>
<script language="JavaScript" type="text/javascript">
<!--
function begin() {
    y++
    html += y + "<br />"
    }

function end() {
    clearInterval(x)
    document.write(html)
    document.close()
    }

html = ""
y = 0
x = setInterval("begin()",10)
setTimeout("end()",1000)

//-->
</script>
</body>
</html>
```

Here, the *x* variable is set as a handler for executing the `begin()` function every 10 milliseconds. Then, 1000 milliseconds later (one second later), the `end()` function executes. The first command in the `end()` function is `clearInterval(x)`. In other words, cancel the repeating function call named x.

clearTimeout( )

JavaScript 1.0+, JScript 1.0+

Nav2+, IE3+

Syntax

```
clearTimeout(timeout)
```

The `clearTimeout()` method of `window` objects cancels a scheduled function call set by the `window.setInterval()` method call. The scheduled function call you identify as the first argument.

This is similar to the `window.clearInterval()` method, the only difference being this works on values set by the `window.setTimeout()` method, whereas `window.clearInterval()` works on values set by the `window.setInterval()` method.

close( )

JavaScript 1.0+, JScript 1.0+

Nav2+, IE3+

Syntax

```
self.close()
```

The `close()` method of `window` objects attempts to close the `window` object entirely, removing it from existence.

Generally, without the `window` object prefix, the script calls the `document.close()` method instead. The most notable exception is when an event-handling function calls on `close()`. In either case, it's definitely safer to specify from which object you are calling the `close()` method.

Depending on the context, it may close automatically, or it may call a pop-up dialog box to get the user's permission:

- If the window opens via a `window.open()` method call, it automatically closes. If it opened some other way, it requests confirmation from the user.

- If an event handler calls a function containing the `close()` method for the window, the window attempts to close.

- If an event handler itself calls `close()`, to close the window the `window` or `self` prefix must be given (`window.close()` instead of `close()`). Omitting the prefix results in the browser interpreting it as `document.close()`.

- Applying `close()` to a `window` object that is not a top-level `window` (for instance, the window object is a frame) has zero effect. For frames, use `top.close()`. Listing 15.10 demonstrates this.

Listing 15.10   *The* `window.close()` *Method in Frames Does Not Work*

```
<?xml version="1.0" ?>
<!-- 15lst10a.htm:  Frameset page -->
<!DOCTYPE html PUBLIC "-//W3C//DTD XHTML 1.0 Frameset//EN"
➥"DTD/xhtml1-frameset.dtd">
<html xmlns="http://www.w3.org/1999/xhtml" >
<head><title></title></head>
<frameset rows="*,0">
   <frame src="15lst10b.htm" />
   <frame src="about:blank" />
   </frameset>
</html>

<?xml version="1.0" ?>
<!-- 15lst10b.htm:  Framed page -->
<!DOCTYPE html PUBLIC "-//W3C//DTD XHTML 1.0 Transitional//EN"
➥"DTD/xhtml1-transitional.dtd">
<html xmlns="http://www.w3.org/1999/xhtml" >
<head><title></title></head>
<body onload="window.close()">
<a href="javascript:top.close()">Close the window!</a>
</body>
</html>
```

confirm( )

JavaScript 1.0+, JScript 1.0+

Nav2+, IE3+

Syntax

```
var boolValue = confirm(msg)
```

The confirm() method of window objects opens a miniature pop-up window with three parts. The first is the value of the first argument, written out as a JavaScript string. The second is an OK button, and the third is a Cancel button. If the user clicks OK, the method returns true. If the user clicks Cancel, the method returns false.

Confirm windows are modal dialog boxes, something I explain a little later in this chapter; basically, they stop execution of the script.

Either way, when the user clicks a button, the pop-up window closes and script execution resumes.

The pop-up window renders the message based on JavaScript syntax, not HTML syntax. For instance, confirm("a\nb") will render the letter "b" on the second line, instead of confirm("a
b").

I like to use confirm pop-ups for diagnostic purposes, to give me an option to exit a function or loop early in case I run into something I don't anticipate. You may remember the error-interception routines of Chapters 2, "Function()," and 10, "Error()." In Listing 15.11, something will cause a glitch if I don't stop it.

Listing 15.11   *Using* confirm() *to Verify Proceeding*

```
<?xml version="1.0" ?>
<!DOCTYPE html PUBLIC "-//W3C//DTD XHTML 1.0 Transitional//EN"
➥"DTD/xhtml1-transitional.dtd">
<html xmlns="http://www.w3.org/1999/xhtml" >
<head><title></title></head>
<body>
<script language="JavaScript" type="text/javascript">
<!--
var x = [3, 4, 5]
var z = 0
looplabel:
    for (y = 2; y > -2; y-=1) {
        if (confirm("x[" + y + "]")) {
            z += x[y]
            } else {
            break looplabel
            }
        }
alert(z)
//-->
```

Listing 15.11   *(continued)*

```
</script>
</body>
</html>
```

The `confirm()` alerts the user to `x[2]`, `x[1]` and `x[0]`, which I expect. But then it alerts me to `x[-1]`, which I know is an invalid array element. If I click the Cancel button, I can avoid trying to add `x[-1]`, which would normally result in `Number.NaN`. Instead, I get 12 for the value of `z`. This comes in very handy in situations where, for instance, `z` must be a number to prevent an avalanche of errors.

createPopup()

JScript 5.5+

IE5.5+

Syntax

```
var x = createPopup()
```

The `createPopup()` method of `window` objects creates a special kind of dialog pop-up window used for dialog boxes (alerts, confirms, and so on). You can access certain properties of the pop-up window that have been created specifically for the dialog pop-up.

One interesting thing about these dialog pop-up windows is when focused, they do not cause their opener windows to lose focus. Another is that they directly float over frame borders. This is in direct conflict with standard window operations, but fits the effects of alert boxes in Internet Explorer.

document

JScript 5.5+

IE5.5+

Syntax

```
popupWin.document
```

The `document` property of dialog boxes reflects the `document` object of the newly created dialog pop-up. See Chapters 20, "Core DOM Objects," and 23, "HTMLDocument/document," for more information.

isOpen

JScript 5.5+

IE5.5+

Syntax

popupWin.isOpen

The isOpen property of dialog boxes is an inverse of the standard window.closed property, and is specific to dialog pop-up windows. If the value reads true, the pop-up is still open. If the value reads false, the pop-up has been closed.

hide( )

JScript 5.5+

IE5.5+

Syntax

popupWin.hide()

The hide() method of dialog pop-up windows hides the dialog pop-up window.

show( )

JScript 5.5+

IE5.5+

Syntax

popupWin.show()

The show() method of dialog boxes renders the dialog pop-up window visible.

detachEvent( )

JScript 5.0+

IE5+

Syntax

detachEvent(*eventName*, *handler*)

The `detachEvent()` method of `window` objects causes the event handler given as the first argument to stop passing any events fired on it to the second argument, a function. This method works only if the `window.attachEvent()` method was called with the exact same arguments. See Chapter 32, "DOM-2 Events and Event Handlers" for details.

execScript( )

IE4+

Syntax

```
execScript(source, language)
```

The `execScript()` method of `window` objects accepts two arguments. The first is a source code string to execute in a particular scripting language. The second is a string identifying what language the source code is to execute in.

```
execScript("MsgBox('Hello World.')", "VBScript")
```

This script pops up a message box in VBScript that says "`Hello World.`"

find( )

JavaScript 1.2+

Nav4

Deprecated in Nav6

Syntax

```
find(string [, caseSens, fromEnd])
```

The `find()` method of `window` objects searches through the text of the window's document, much like regular expressions search through strings. The first argument is a string you are asking the browser to find among the rendered text of the window. If the text is found, the method returns `true` and selects the matched text; else, the method returns `false`.

The second and third arguments are either included together or omitted together. The second argument is a `true` or `false` value indicating whether to perform a case-sensitive search; it is equivalent to omitting the `i` flag of regular expressions. The third argument, if `true`, specifies the search must go from the current selected text or the end of the document, whichever is earlier, backward. If `false`, it proceeds forward from the beginning of the document or the selected text, whichever is later.

One of the worst-kept secrets about browsers is the `about:mozilla` URI. Microsoft, no friend of Netscape and its mozilla.org project, gives a rendition of the "blue screen of death" when you type `about:mozilla` into Internet Explorer's location bar. Netscape gives a couple mock-biblical passages prophesying about the downfall of nonstandard code: one in Netscape 6, and another in Netscape 4. It's actually quite hilarious, but we can also use it to demonstrate `window.find()` in Netscape 4.

In Netscape 4, type `about:mozilla` into the location bar. Then, type the following into the location bar:

```
javascript:void(window.find("the"))
```

Each time you press the Enter key to execute the URI again, you find it advancing through the text of the page, moving to the next "the" or "The" in the page. On the last "The," it stalls.

You can try a couple variations, such as:

```
javascript:void(window.find("the", true, true))
```

In this variation, it will look backward and skip every instance of "The." If you do a search for "body," however, which exists in the HTML tag but not in the document, the method returns `false`.

focus( )

JavaScript 1.0+, JScript 3.0+

Nav2+, IE4+

Syntax

```
self.focus()
```

The `focus()` method of `window` objects forces the browser window to gain focus. What this means is it tells the operating system "Hey! I'm taking over this computer." (Not literally. The user retains control.) The operating system reacts by moving this window to the forefront and making it the active window, the one directly responding to user actions such as typing or clicking the mouse.

You most often see this one in pop-up advertising banners. Using it unconditionally can cause problems. For instance, if you say `<body onblur="self.focus()">`,your pop-up will indeed remain the active window, but it also means the user cannot use another browser window until the pop-up closes. This is very annoying, and most advertising banner companies don't even do this. It effectively interferes with the user's control of his own computer.

On the other hand, too many times I find myself clicking on a link in one frame to see another frame change. I then expect I can just scroll down the second frame using my Page Down key. Instead, it scrolls down the first frame. Here is a clearly beneficial use of the `window.focus()` method call that many Web page developers overlook entirely: use the `focus()` method aimed at your second frame for any link that changes it.

forward( )

JavaScript 1.2+

Nav4+

Syntax

```
forward()
```

The `forward()` method of `window` objects is the same as clicking the Forward button on a browser. It's usually better to use the `history.forward()` method described in Chapter 17, "history," as you can target that for specific `window` objects' history values.

For example, if you take two frames in a frameset, advance the first frame to a new document, and then the second frame to a new document, and click your Back button twice, to advance the second frame again without changing the first frame, you'd say `frames[1].history.forward()`. To just take a step forward, no matter how the browser's current window reached its current status, use `window.forward()`.

> **Note**
> The behavior for `history` changed in Netscape 6; it is now associated with the `top` object.

handleEvent( )

JavaScript 1.2+

Nav4+

Syntax

`handleEvent(`*`eventObj`*`)`

The `handleEvent()` method of `window` objects in Netscape assigns all events of the type given as the first argument to the `this` object. (Typically, these events are referred to as `Event.`*`EVENTNAME`*, where the event name is capitalized.) Using this method, you force the events thrown or fired to report to a particular object's event handler. See Chapter 32, "DOM-2 Events and Event Handlers," for details.

home( )

JavaScript 1.2+

Nav4+

Syntax

`home()`

The `home()` method of `window` objects forces the browser window to go immediately to the page marked in its preferences as its home page. It is equivalent to clicking the Home button on the browser.

moveBy( )

JavaScript 1.2+, JScript 3.0+

Nav4+, IE4+

Syntax

`self.moveBy(`*`rightPixels, downPixels`*`)`

The `moveBy()` method of `window` objects accepts two arguments. The first tells how many pixels `this` is to move to the right. The second tells how many pixels `this` is to move down. (Negative values are acceptable, telling how far to move to the left and up, respectively.)

In Netscape, the script may change the visibility of this object only when it successfully requests the `UniversalBrowserWrite` privilege. For Web pages, this is generally only possible when the script is signed or the page is served via the `https://` protocol. The `UniversalBrowserWrite` privilege is beyond the scope of this book, however. Internet Explorer does not require any such special treatment.

moveTo( )

JavaScript 1.2+, JScript 3.0+

Nav4+, IE4+

Syntax

```
self.moveTo(horizPixels, vertPixels)
```

The moveTo() method of window objects accepts two arguments. The first tells how far from the left edge of the screen the window must be. The second tells how far from the top edge of the screen the window must be.

The script may change the visibility of this object only when it successfully requests the UniversalBrowserWrite privilege. For Web pages, this is generally only possible when the script is signed or the page is served via the https:// protocol. The UniversalBrowserWrite privilege is beyond the scope of this book, however.

Internet Explorer does not require any such special treatment.

navigate( )

JScript 1.0+

IE3+

Syntax

```
self.navigate(URIString)
```

The navigate() method of window objects takes the first argument (a URL) and tells the browser to load that URL into this.

Because this is functionally similar to setting location.href directly, and both Netscape and Internet Explorer support the location.href property, I recommend you do not use this method in preference over location.href.

open( )

JavaScript 1.0+, JScript 1.0+

Nav2+, IE3+

Syntax

```
window.open(URLString, HTMLWindowName, featureString [, historyOn])
```

The open() method of window objects is, quite arguably, the most important method in all of JavaScript. Because it sets the initial rules of a new window object, many of which cannot be changed by JavaScript later without a signed script, a full understanding of this method is critical.

The first argument given to this method is the URI you want the window to load. If you don't have one, you can enter an empty string, and about:blank will load.

The second argument given to this method is the HTML name for the browser window. Listing 15.5 demonstrates this at some length. The JavaScript name for the browser window is what you assign the returned object of window.open() to.

The third argument given to this method is a string containing many optional features you can turn on and off. The features you specify you separate with commas, and in *name* = *value* format. I list them as follows. (For yes, you can always substitute 1, and for no, you can substitute 0.)

> **Note**
> There is also an option for simply using *name* instead of *name* = *value* as your format in certain yes/no options. However, this is not a generally advisable approach.

> **Caution**
> Microsoft's own documentation is not clear as to when these features take effect. I have been able to test them in Internet Explorer 5.0 and higher. Please check my Dictionary Web site at http://www.jslab.org/jsdd for any additional details on earlier versions of Internet Explorer.

alwaysLowered

Nav4+, signed scripts only

Yes: Window always floats below other windows.

No: No significant change.

alwaysRaised

Nav4+, signed scripts only

Yes: Window always floats above other windows.

No: No significant change.

> **Note**
> Internet Explorer 5.0+ provides the `showModelessDialog()` method, which I describe later in this chapter, as an equivalent.

channelMode

IE5.0+

Yes: Sets a special "theater mode." Equivalent to full-screen mode in the browser.

No: No significant change.

dependent

Nav4+

Yes: When `opener` closes, window closes.

No: Window may be operated independently of opener's closed status.

directories

Nav4+, IE5.0+

Yes: Includes standard browser feature buttons like "What's New," "What's Cool," and so on.

No: Window omits feature buttons.

fullscreen

IE5.0+

Yes: Window opens with no toolbars or buttons at all. (This includes no Close button and no taskbar, so include instructions to your users on how to close the window.)

No: Window opens standard size.

height

Nav2 to Nav3, IE5.0+

Deprecated but retained in Nav4+

Number given indicates height of window in pixels. Must be no less than 100 without a signed script.

hotKeys

Nav4+

Yes: No significant change.

No: If `menubar = no`, disables all hot keys (keyboard commands to the browser) except security and quit keys. (The quit key on a Windows platform, for example, is Alt+F4.)

innerHeight

Nav4+

Number given indicates height of content area of window. Must be no less than 100 without a signed script.

innerWidth

Nav4+

Number given indicates width of content area of window. Must be no less than 100 without a signed script.

left

Nav4+, IE5.0+

Number given indicates distance from left edge of screen to left edge of window.

location

Nav4+, IE5.0+

Yes: Includes location bar in window.

No: Does not include location bar in window.

menubar

Nav4+, IE5.0+

Yes: Includes main menu bar (File, Edit, Help, and so on).

No: Does not include main menu bar.

outerHeight

Nav4+

Number given indicates height of window, including all components. Must not be less than 100 without a signed script.

outerWidth

Nav4+

Number given indicates width of window, including all components. Must not be less than 100 without a signed script.

personalbar

Nav4+

Same as directories.

resizable

Nav4+, IE6

Yes: User may resize window.

No: Window size remains constant.

screenX

Nav4+

Number given indicates distance between left edge of window and left edge of screen. Moving a window offscreen requires a signed script.

screenY

Nav4+

Number given indicates distance between top edge of window and top edge of screen. Moving a window offscreen requires a signed script.

scrollbars

Nav4+, IE5.0+

Yes: Window includes horizontal and vertical scrollbars.

No: No scrollbars included in new window.

status

Nav4+, IE5.0+

Yes: Window includes status bar.

No: Window omits status bar.

titlebar

Nav4+

Yes: Window includes title bar.

No: Window omits title bar. Requires a signed script to set as no.

toolbar

Nav4+, IE5.0+

Yes: Window includes standard toolbar, with back, forward, print, home, stop, and other buttons.

No: Window omits standard toolbar.

top

Nav4+, IE5.0+

Number given indicates distance from top edge of screen to top edge of window.

width

Implemented in Nav2-3, IE5.0+

Deprecated but retained in Nav4+

Number given indicates width of window in pixels. Must be no less than 100 without a signed script.

z-lock

Nav4+, signed scripts only

Yes: Window cannot rise above other windows when it receives focus.

No: No significant change.

By default, if you set any of the yes/no values for window features, all other yes/no values you do not explicitly set have a value of no. (Netscape makes an exception for title bar and hotkeys, setting these to yes by default when you specify any window features.) Otherwise, all yes/no features retain a yes value, except those that require signed scripts.

Internet Explorer supports an optional fourth argument in the `window.open()` method call. If you set the fourth argument to `true`, it replaces the current URL with the new one in the history. If you set the fourth argument to `false`, it appends the current URL to the end of the history.

print( )

JavaScript 1.2+, JScript 5.0+

Nav4+, IE5+

Syntax

```
print
```

The `print()` method of `window` objects calls on the browser to print the current window's contents to the printer. The standard print page dialog will appear, giving the user options to control how the window's contents will appear on the printout. (Note this method call does not stop execution of the page's scripts in any fashion.)

To print a frame, place focus on the frame and use the `print()` method of the frame. Internet Explorer requires this.

prompt( )

Nav2+, IE3+

Syntax

```
var x = prompt(question [, default])
```

The `prompt()` method of `window` objects generates a miniature pop-up window that contains only two items. The first is the value of the first argument, rendered directly into the window. The second is a text input element that the method call returns to JavaScript—for example, `myValue = window.prompt("What is your name?")`.

If you provide a second argument, it becomes a default value for the input to return. The user may override the default value with a custom value, or select the `"Cancel"` button for the prompt to return `null`.

> **Note**
> True to form, if you omit the second argument, JavaScript treats it as `undefined`. The prompt would then use the string value of `undefined`, which is `"undefined"`.
>
> Thus, it's generally a good idea to provide a second argument, even an empty string, instead of seeing `"undefined"` in the prompt input field...

The pop-up window renders the message based on JavaScript syntax, not HTML syntax. For instance, `prompt("a\nb")` will render the letter "b" on the second line, instead of `prompt("a<br />b")`.

Prompts like this can be useful as the simplest kind of form available, but usually it's best to use a full-fledged form instead. Prompt values cannot be directly submitted back to a server, unless transferred to a form first. They are good for one-time inputs.

releaseEvents( )

JavaScript 1.2+

Nav4+

Syntax

```
releaseEvents(eventName0 [| eventName1...])
```

The `releaseEvents()` method of `window` objects in Netscape effectively cancels the `window.captureEvents()` method call for all events specified in the first argument (which you separate by | marks; multiple events combine to form a logical OR statement: (`Event.CLICK | Event.FOCUS`). (Typically, these events are referred to as `Event.EVENTNAME`, where the event name is capitalized.) Using this method, you cause the events thrown or fired to bubble up through the event handler chain normally in Netscape 6. See Chapter 32, "DOM-2 Events and Event Handlers," for details.

resizeBy( )

JavaScript 1.2+, JScript 3.0+

Nav4+, IE4+

Syntax

```
resizeBy(rightPixels, downPixels)
```

The `resizeBy()` method of `window` objects resizes the window by moving the bottom-right corner of the window. The corner moves to the right by the number of pixels in the first argument. It moves down by the number of pixels in the second argument.

Netscape and Internet Explorer prohibit using this method to force the window's edges to be less than 100 pixels in length.

window.resizeTo( )

JavaScript 1.2+, JScript 3.0+

Nav4+, IE4+

Syntax

```
resizeTo(horizPixels, vertPixels)
```

The `resizeTo()` method of `window` objects resizes the window by moving the bottom-right corner of the window. The corner adjusts the outer width to match the number of pixels in the first argument. It adjusts the outer height to match the number of pixels in the second argument.

Netscape and Internet Explorer prohibit using this method to force the window's edges to be less than 100 pixels in length.

routeEvent( )

JavaScript 1.2+

Nav4+

Syntax

```
routeEvent(eventObj)
```

The `routeEvent()` method of `window` objects in Netscape sends the event object specified in the first argument to the next event handler in its chain. Using this method, you cause the events thrown or fired to proceed to the next scheduled event handler for that event. See Chapter 32, "DOM-2 Events and Event Handlers," for details.

scroll( )

JavaScript 1.0-JavaScript 1.1, JScript 3.0

Nav2-Nav3, IE4

Deprecated in Nav4+, IE5+

Syntax

```
scroll(horizPixels, vertPixels)
```

The `scroll()` method of `window` objects scrolls the window's document such that the left edge of the visible document portion is to the right of the document's left edge by x pixels. x is the first argument, a number, of this function. The document is also scrolled such that the top edge of the visible document portion is below the document's top edge by y pixels. y is the second argument, a number, of this function.

The `window.scrollTo()` method supersedes this method call.

scrollBy( )

JavaScript 1.2+, JScript 3.0+

Nav4+, IE4+

Syntax

```
scrollBy(rightPixels, downPixels)
```

The `scrollBy()` method of `window` objects scrolls the window's document. It scrolls the document to the right by the number of pixels specified in the first argument. It scrolls the document down by the number of pixels specified in the second argument.

Negative arguments cause scrolling in the opposite directions, as a negative value to the right is a positive value to the left. Likewise, a negative value downward is a positive value upward. You cannot force scrolling off the page, however.

scrollByLines( )

JavaScript 1.5

Nav6

Syntax

```
scrollByLines(numLines)
```

The `scrollByLines()` method of `window` objects in Netscape 6 allows you to scroll down a page a given number of lines, the number being the first argument. It's essentially the same as pressing the down arrow on a Web page a number of times equal to the argument.

Negative arguments cause scrolling in the opposite direction, as a negative value downward is a positive value upward. You cannot force scrolling off the page, however.

scrollByPages( )

JavaScript 1.5

Nav6

Syntax

```
scrollByPages(pageDowns)
```

The `scrollByPages()` method of `window` objects in Netscape 6 allows you to scroll down a page a given number of viewable pages, the number being the first argument. It's essentially the same as pressing the page-down button on a Web page a number of times equal to the argument.

Negative arguments cause scrolling in the opposite direction, as a negative value downward is a positive value upward. You cannot force scrolling off the page, however.

scrollTo( )

JavaScript 1.2+, JScript 3.0+

Nav4+, IE4+

Syntax

```
scrollTo(horizPixels, vertPixels)
```

The scrollTo() method of window objects scrolls the window's document such that the left edge of the visible document portion is to the right of the document's left edge by *x* pixels. *x* is the first argument, a number, of this function. The document is also scrolled such that the top edge of the visible document portion is below the document's top edge by *y* pixels. *y* is the second argument, a number, of this function.

setInterval( )

JavaScript 1.2+, JScript 3.0+

Nav4+, IE4+

Syntax

```
[var repeater =] setInterval(evalStr, msec)


[var repeater =] setInterval(funcObj, msec)
```

The setInterval() method of window objects sets a repeating function call. There are two syntaxes for this method in Netscape; because Internet Explorer supports only one of these, I will recommend only one.

The first argument to this method call is a string containing the code block you want to execute on a repeating basis. The second argument is the number of milliseconds you want to elapse between each execution of the first argument.

Often the first argument is merely a function call with arguments preset. However, there is a faulty design you can run into. Listing 15.12 details the problem.

Listing 15.12   setInterval *in a Function: Bad Design*

```
<?xml version="1.0" ?>
<!DOCTYPE html PUBLIC "-//W3C//DTD XHTML 1.0 Transitional//EN"
➥"DTD/xhtml1-transitional.dtd">
<html xmlns="http://www.w3.org/1999/xhtml" >
<head><title></title></head><body>
<script language="JavaScript" type="text/javascript">
<!--
function begin(x) {
    var m = setInterval("x++",10)
    }

var k = 0
begin(k)
```

Listing 15.12   *(continued)*

```
// throws exception 10 milliseconds later.

//-->
</script>
</body>
</html>
```

The problem is the value for *x* disappears after the function `begin()` stops executing. But the `setInterval` continues to call for *x*. A similar oversight can occur for the `setTimeout` method, referring to an object whose name is local to a function.

An ideal solution to this would be to give each object a way to find its full object name (example: `this == window.objName.propName`).

An interim, less object-oriented way is to create an object with a global name reflecting the argument by reference. If the argument or local variable is named x, this means:

```
globalObject = x
```

Note the absence of a `var` keyword. I dislike this procedure because if you call the function more than once, you automatically destroy the reference to the first x argument, and you may have multiple `setInterval` or `setTimeout` method calls operating on the same object. (Plus, it throws a JavaScript strict warning, a subject I discovered far too late to include in this book. You can find a link to my article on it at `http://www.jslab.org/jsdd`.)

setResizable( )

JavaScript 1.2+

Nav4, Nav6.1+

Syntax

```
setResizable(boolValue)
```

The `setResizable()` method of `window` objects overrides the current setting for a window's `resizeable` attribute. If the first argument is `true`, the window may be resized. If the first argument is `false`, the window's size remains fixed.

setTimeout( )

JavaScript 1.0+, JScript 3.0+

Nav2+, IE4+

Syntax

```
[var timeout =] setTimeout(evalStr, msec)
```

```
[var timeout =] setTimeout(funcObj, msec [, arg0, arg1...])
```

The setTimeout() method of window objects sets a delayed function call. There are two syntaxes for this method; because Internet Explorer supports only one of these, I will recommend only one.

The first argument to this method call is a string containing the code block you wish to execute on a repeating basis. The second argument is the number of milliseconds you want to elapse before the execution of the first argument.

Often the first argument is merely a function call with arguments preset. However, there is a faulty design you can run into. Listing 15.12 details the problem.

The second syntax, which I personally recommend against, is using a function as the first argument instead of a string. In Netscape 4+, you can append arguments for the function as additional arguments for the setTimeout() method call. Internet Explorer 5.0+ supports this syntax as well, but does not pass on additional arguments to functions.

showHelp( )

JScript 3.0+

IE4+

Syntax

```
showHelp(CHMString)
```

The showHelp() method of window objects calls on an HTML file or a ".chm" file specified in the first argument and loads it into a help window. Microsoft recommends you use this on HTML Help files.

You can provide a second, optional argument as a string identifying the context in the help file, in order to open the right page of the help file.

window.showModalDialog( ) or window.showModelessDialog( )

JScript 3.0+

IE4+

Syntax

```
[var x =] showModalDialog(URLString, [arguments,] [featString])

[var x =] showModelessDialog(URLString, [arguments,] [featString])
```

Internet Explorer provides two methods for creating miniature help boxes that float above their respective windows and are intimately tied to them. The only real difference is a "modeless" dialog box can lose focus to the main window, while still remaining above the window. The "modal" dialog box retains focus over the main window, so whenever you try to focus on the main window, it instead goes to the modal window. When you close the master window, typically the new dialog window closes as well.

The first argument gives a URL of the page to load into the dialog box. You can then include arguments (objects) you want passed to the dialog box. Finally, like the `window.open()` method, you can include a list of features which you can specify in a string with semicolons (;) separating each feature. (Number values must have explicit units associated with them.)

center

Yes: Centers the dialog box on the screen.

No: Does not affect the positioning of the dialog box.

dialogHeight

This number specifies the height of the dialog box.

dialogLeft

This number specifies the distance from the left edge of the screen to the left edge of the dialog box.

dialogTop

This number specifies the distance from the top edge of the screen to the top edge of the dialog box.

dialogWidth

This number specifies the width of the dialog box.

edge

"sunken" or "raised," indicating how the border of the box appears. Defaults to "raised."

help

Yes: Displays the Help icon for the dialog box. Default.

No: Omits the Help icon for the dialog box.

resizable

Yes: The dialog box can be resized.

No: The dialog box cannot be resized. Default.

scroll

Yes: Shows scroll bars in the dialog box. Default.

No: Hides scroll bars in the dialog box.

status

Yes: Shows status bar in the dialog box. Default.

No: Hides status bar in the dialog box.

These dialog box objects also have specific properties that you can use.

popup.dialogArguments

Returns all arguments passed to the dialog box. Read-only.

popup.dialogHeight

This returns or allows you to set the height of a dialog pop-up.

popup.dialogLeft

This returns or allows you to set the distance between the left edge of the screen and the left edge of a dialog pop-up.

popup.dialogTop

This returns or allows you to set the distance between the top edge of the screen and the top edge of a dialog pop-up.

popup.dialogWidth

This returns or allows you to set the width of a dialog pop-up.

popup.returnValue

This returns or allows you to set the value the dialog pop-up is to return to the main window.

For more information on dialog pop-ups, see Microsoft's documentation at `http://msdn.microsoft.com/workshop/author/dhtml/reference/methods/showModalD ialog.asp`.

stop( )
Nav2+, (IE3+)

Syntax

```
stop()
```

The `stop()` method of `window` objects, in Netscape 2+, forces the browser to stop all activity, as if you clicked on the Stop button on the main toolbar.

I find a delicious irony in Internet Explorer's explicit lack of support for this method. Unless you define a `stop()` function (not advisable, thanks to its usage in Netscape browsers), calling `stop()` throws an exception. Without error handling, this pops up a small dialog box explaining the error…and stops the script from running. So in a way, you get the same effect in Internet Explorer as you do in Netscape. It's just less transparent to the user, giving them an error that is a side effect. (This is why Internet Explorer 3+ support for this is in parentheses above.)

> **Note**
>
> In IE5+ you can achieve the same effect without an exception using the
> `document.execCommand('Stop')` statement.

Some have claimed the `document.close()` method can substitute for `window.stop()` in Internet Explorer. Listing 15.13 debunks this theory completely.

Listing 15.13   *The* `document.close()` *Method Does Not Stop a Script*

```
<?xml version="1.0" ?>
<!DOCTYPE html PUBLIC "-//W3C//DTD XHTML 1.0 Transitional//EN"
➥"DTD/xhtml1-transitional.dtd">
<html xmlns="http://www.w3.org/1999/xhtml" >
<head><title></title></head><body>
<script language="JavaScript" type="text/javascript">
<!--
function go() {
    x = 0
    for (y = 0; y <= 50000; y++) {
        x += y
        if (y == 3) {
            document.close()
            }
        }
    }
go()
//-->
</script>
<a href="javascript:alert(x)">alert(x)</a>
</body>
</html>
```

If the `document.close()` method had been successful in stopping the script, the link would return a fairly small number—maybe not 6 as you might expect, but a number likely no higher than 1,000,000. Instead, the script continues to execute and *x* reaches its full value of 1,250,025,000. (Replacing `document.close()` with `window.stop()` in Netscape yields a script which stops before reaching this height.)

Event Handlers

Netscape supports the following event handlers for the `window` object:

```
onblur

onchange

onclose

ondragdrop

onerror

onfocus

onload

onmove

onpaint

onresize

onscroll

onunload
```

Internet Explorer supports the following event handlers for the `window` object:

```
onactivate

onafterprint

onbeforedeactivate

onbeforeprint

onbeforeunload

onblur

oncontrolselect

ondeactivate

onerror

onfocus

onhelp
```

onload

onmove

onmoveend

onmovestart

onresize

onresizeend

onresizestart

onscroll

onunload

HTMLFrameSetElement /<frameset>...</frameset>

Browser/JavaScript Version	Created By
Nav4/JavaScript 1.2	`<frameset>...</frameset>`
IE4/JScript 3.0	`<frameset>...</frameset>`
IE5/JScript 5.0	`<frameset>...</frameset>`
	`document.createElement("frameset")`
IE5.5/JScript 5.5	`<frameset>...</frameset>`
	`document.createElement("frameset")`
IE6	`<frameset>...</frameset>`
	`document.createElement("frameset")`
Nav6/JavaScript 1.5	`<frameset>...</frameset>`
	`document.createElement("frameset")`

Note
Implemented in Nav2+, IE3+

Child of `HTMLHtmlElement`, `HTMLFramesetElement`.

Descends from `HTMLElement`, `window` objects

Description

> **Note**
> This element inherits a lot of properties from `HTMLElement`, which I cover in a later chapter. However, because framesets and frames are also closely related to windows, I have decided to keep this element near the `window` element. See Chapter 20, "Core DOM Objects," and Chapter 21, "HTMLElement," for other properties and methods this element possesses, and for a description of the Document Object Model.
>
> Also, adding this element to a document by script currently has no effect.

Framesets simply describe collections of `window` objects that are unique and distinct from one another. But they also are `window` objects themselves.

We've already discussed frames and framesets to some length in this chapter, but I want to emphasize one other lesson. JavaScripters as a whole tend to pass objects directly between frames in a frameset, and usually overlook the frameset as a window object.

I, on the other hand, love to assign new properties to the `parent` or `top` objects of a frame, namely, their framesets. There's nothing that says I can't, and as long as the document doesn't change, I'm all right. (Many developers use frames of zero pixels in height, but I don't see a need to when I can just use the frameset.)

My JavaScript Laboratory project (`http://www.jslab.org`) uses this extensively. The `top` object is a one-frame frameset, which I use to store common objects. The frame of that frameset is another frameset document, which I can change to suit the needs I have for framed pages.

According to the W3C HTML 4.0 Recommendation, `HTMLFramesetElement` objects can only be children of `HTMLHtmlElement` objects, and can only have `HTMLFrameElement`, `HTMLFramesetElement`, and `HTMLNoFramesElement` objects as their children.

For accessing attributes of a particular frameset tag, I recommend you look up the `document` object of Chapters 20, "Core DOM Objects," and 23, "HTMLDocument/document." Listing 15.14 gives an example of one way to do this, through the `document.getElementById` method.

Properties

border

JScript 3.0+

IE4+

Syntax

HTMLFramesetElement.border [= *pixels*]

The border property of frameset objects refers to the border attribute of framesets. The outermost frameset this is set on determines the border width between all frames.

borderColor

JScript 3.0+

IE4+

Syntax

HTMLFramesetElement.borderColor [= "*color*"]

The borderColor property of frameset objects refers to the Internet Explorer-proprietary borderColor attribute of framesets. An inner frameset may override the borderColor attribute of an outer frameset for its own borders using its own. See Listing 15.14.

Listing 15.14   *Framesets with Varying* borderColor *Attributes*

```
<!-- IE5.0+ only. Not XHTML 1.0.   -->
<html>
<head><title></title></head>
<frameset id="myFrameset" rows="*,*" borderColor="red"
onload="document.getElementById('myFrameset').borderColor = 'blue'">
   <frame src="about:blank" />
   <frameset cols="*,*" borderColor="green" >
      <frame src="about:blank" />
      <frame src="about:blank" />
      </frameset>
   </frameset>
</html>
```

In Listing 15.14, the horizontal border color appears blue `onload`, while the vertical border color is green.

cols

JavaScript 1.5, JScript 3.0+

Nav6, IE4+

Exactly one `cols` or `rows` attribute must exist for this element.

Syntax

HTMLFramesetElement.cols [= *colsString*]

The `cols` property of frameset objects reflects on the `<frameset>` tag's `cols` attribute. By definition, it defines the width of frames arranged from left to right.

You can set *colsString* to be a series of values separated by commas. The values must be either percentages (of the viewable screen), pixel widths, or an asterisk (which means remaining screen space). The following is perfectly valid: `"50%, 120, *"`. (Netscape 6 does not currently resize the frameset's contents when you set the `cols` property.) You can also specify the "remaining screen space" divides into equal parts, and each frame has a certain number of them: `<frameset cols="*, 2*">...</frameset>` means the second frame occupies two-thirds of the available horizontal space.

frameBorder

JScript 3.0+

IE4+

Syntax

HTMLFramesetElement.frameBorder [= *booleanVal*]

The `frameBorder` property of frameset objects, which can be either "yes", "no", "1" or "0", indicates to the browser whether it should render a border between frames. (A "0" or "no" value indicates it should not; otherwise, it does.)

Interestingly, the `frameBorder` attribute of a `<frameset>` tag does not affect its child `<frame />` tags when you explicitly set them, and vice versa. This can lead to some rather interesting effects in Internet Explorer, such as the hollow border between the frames, shown in Listing 15.15.

Listing 15.15   *Explicit Defining of Frame Border Attributes*

```
<!-- IE4.0+ only. Not XHTML 1.0.  -->
<html>
<head><title></title></head><frameset rows="*,*" frameborder="0">
    <frame src="about:blank" frameborder="1" />
    <frame src="about:blank" frameborder="1" />
    </frameset>
</html>
```

frameSpacing

IE4+

Syntax

HTMLFramesetElement.frameSpacing [= *number*]

The frameSpacing property of frameset elements sets a default number of pixels to add to a `<frame />` tag's rendered borders. (Adjusting this value does not adjust the `<frame />` tag's border attribute.)

Internet Explorer's default spacing is two pixels.

rows

JavaScript 1.5, JScript 3.0+

Nav6, IE4+

Exactly one cols or rows attribute must exist for this element.

Syntax

HTMLFramesetElement.rows [= *rowsString*]

The rows property of frameset objects reflects on the `<frameset>` tag's rows attribute. By definition, it defines the height of frames arranged from top to bottom.

You can set *rowsString* to be a series of values separated by commas. The values must be either percentages (of the viewable screen), pixel widths, or an asterisk (which means remaining screen space). The following is perfectly valid: "50%, 120, *". (Netscape 6 does not currently resize the frameset's contents when you set the rows property.) You can also specify the "remaining screen space" divides into equal parts, and each frame has a certain number of them: `<frameset rows="*,` `2*">...</frameset>` means the second frame occupies two-thirds of the available horizontal space.

---

width

JScript 3.0+

IE4+

Syntax

```
HTMLFramesetElement.width [= widthValue]
```

The `width` property of frameset objects, for Internet Explorer, should set a width of the object. I was unable to generate a working example of this:

```
<?xml version="1.0" ?>
<!-- altered from 15lst10b.htm:  Framed page -->
<!DOCTYPE html PUBLIC "-//W3C//DTD XHTML 1.0 Transitional//EN"
➡"DTD/xhtml1-transitional.dtd">
<html xmlns="http://www.w3.org/1999/xhtml" >
<head><title></title></head>
<frameset rows="*,*" width="50" >
    <frame src="about:blank"  />
    <frame src="about:blank"  />
    </frameset>
</html>
```

It's better to use `cols` instead.

Methods

HTMLFrameSetElement objects do not possess any methods beyond those inherited from the HTMLElement object.

Event Handlers

Internet Explorer supports the following event handlers for the HTMLFrameSetElement object:

    onactivate

    onafterprint

onbeforedeactivate

onbeforeprint

onbeforeunload

onblur

oncontrolselect

ondeactivate

onfocus

onload

onmove

onmoveend

onmovestart

onresizeend

onresizestart

onunload

HTMLFrameElement/<frame />

Browser/JavaScript version	Created By
Nav4/JavaScript 1.2	<frame />
IE4/Jscript 3.0	<frame />
IE5/JScript 5.0	<frame />
	document.createElement("frame")
IE5.5/JScript 5.5	<frame />
	document.createElement("frame")
IE6	<frame />
	document.createElement ("frame")
Nav6 / JavaScript 1.5	<frame />
	document.createElement("frame")

> **Note**
>
> Implemented in Nav2+ (HTML), Nav6 (JS), IE3+ (HTML), IE4+ (DOM)
>
> Child of `HTMLFrameSetElement`
>
> Descends from `HTMLElement`, `window` objects

Description

A frame is a `window` object designated to hold one page in a contained space within another viewable page. You can set them to hold whatever you wish: images, XML documents, HTML documents, and so on.

A `<frame />` element, on the other hand, is how the parent document refers to the frame, and builds it for the page. Through this, both a frame and an element corresponding to that frame in the parent document exist.

According to the W3C HTML 4.0 Recommendation, `HTMLFrameElement` objects are only allowed as children of `HTMLFrameSetElement` objects.

allowTransparency

JScript 5.5+

IE5.5+

Syntax

HTMLFrameElement.allowTransparency [= *booleanVal*]

The `allowTransparency` property of `<frame />` elements, when set to `true`, implies to the browser that if the framed page is itself transparent, to render the frame as having the same background as the parent window. Microsoft's documentation says this attribute must be set to `true` in order to force transparency; Listing 15.16 disagrees.

Listing 15.16   *The `allowTransparency` Attribute Demonstrated*

```
<!-- 15lst16a.htm
Not XHTML 1.0. -->
<html>
<head><title></title></head>
<frameset rows="*,*,*,*,*,*,*,*,*" width="50" STYLE="background-color: red" >
    <frame allowtransparency="false" style="background-color: blue"
src="15lst16b.htm" />
```

Listing 15.16   *(continued)*

```
    <frame allowtransparency="true" style="background-color: blue"
src="15lst16b.htm" />
    <frame style="background-color: blue" src="15lst16b.htm" />
    <frame allowtransparency="false" src="15lst16b.htm" />
    <frame allowtransparency="true" src="15lst16b.htm" />
    <frame allowtransparency="false" style="background-color: blue"
src="15lst16c.htm" />
    <frame allowtransparency="true" style="background-color: blue"
src="15lst16c.htm" />
    <frame allowtransparency="false" src="15lst16c.htm" />
    <frame allowtransparency="true" src="15lst16c.htm" />
    <frame src="15lst16c.htm" />
     </frameset>
</html>


<?xml version="1.0" ?>
<!-- 15lst16b.htm -->
<!DOCTYPE html PUBLIC "-//W3C//DTD XHTML 1.0 Transitional//EN"
➥"DTD/xhtml1-transitional.dtd">
<html xmlns="http://www.w3.org/1999/xhtml" >
<head><title></title></head>
<body style="background-color: transparent">
<p>Hello World</p>
</body>
</html>


<?xml version="1.0" ?>
<!-- 15lst16c.htm -->
<!DOCTYPE html PUBLIC "-//W3C//DTD XHTML 1.0 Transitional//EN"
➥"DTD/xhtml1-transitional.dtd">
<html xmlns="http://www.w3.org/1999/xhtml" >
<head><title></title></head>
<body style="background-color: orange">
<p>Hello World</p>
</body>
</html>
```

When you render the frameset in Listing 15.16, the first two frames are blue. In other words, you can set the value to `false` and Internet Explorer 5.5 will act as if it is `true`.

Microsoft's documentation contradicts this. The third is white, indicating setting transparency in the framed page will lead to a white background when you attempt to set a background color. The fourth and fifth are gray, indicating an absent background color style in the frameset forces the transparent frame to render gray.

Frames 6–10 are all orange; the local framed page's background color overrides all frameset page settings.

contentDocument

JavaScript 1.5+

Nav6

Syntax

HTMLFrameElement.contentDocument

The contentDocument property of <frame /> elements reflects the document object of the <frame /> tag. In Internet Explorer 5.5, you can achieve the same by saying *HTMLFrameElement*.contentWindow.document. See Listing 15.17.

Listing 15.17   *The* contentDocument *Property in Context*

```
<?xml version="1.0" ?>
<!DOCTYPE html PUBLIC "-//W3C//DTD XHTML 1.0 Frameset//EN"
➥"DTD/xhtml1-frameset.dtd">
<html xmlns="http://www.w3.org/1999/xhtml" >
<head>
<script language="JavaScript" type="text/javascript">
<!--
function go() {
   alert(document.getElementById('myFrame').contentDocument.URL)
// returns the URL for 15lst16c.htm
   }
//-->
</script>
<title></title></head>
<frameset rows="*,*" onload="go()">
   <frame src="15lst16c.htm" id="myFrame" />
   <frame src="15lst16c.htm" />
   </frameset>
</html>
```

Description

contentWindow

JScript5.5+

IE5.5+

Syntax

HTMLFrameElement.contentWindow

The contentWindow property of <frame /> elements is a reference from the <frame /> element to the window object it contains. See Listing 15.18.

Listing 15.18   *The* contentWindow *Property in Context*

```
<?xml version="1.0" ?>
<!DOCTYPE html PUBLIC "-//W3C//DTD XHTML 1.0 Frameset//EN"
➥"DTD/xhtml1-frameset.dtd">
<html xmlns="http://www.w3.org/1999/xhtml" >
<head>

<script language="JavaScript" type="text/javascript">
<!--
function go() {
   alert(document.getElementById('myFrame').contentWindow.location)
   // returns the URL for 15lst16c.htm
   }
//-->
</script>
<title></title></head>
<frameset rows="*,*" onload="go()">
   <frame src="15lst16c.htm" id="myFrame" />
   <frame src="15lst16c.htm" />
   </frameset>
</html>
```

dataFld

JScript 3.0+

IE4+

Syntax

HTMLFrameElement.dataFld [= *fieldName*]

The `dataFld` property of `<frame />` elements, in data binding, sets the field to which the frame is bound. There must be a `datasrc` attribute included as well in this element if you include `datafld`. Data binding is beyond the scope of this book; you can find more information on it at

`http://msdn.microsoft.com/workshop/author/databind/data_binding.asp`.

dataSrc

JScript 3.0+

IE4+

Syntax

`HTMLFrameElement.dataSrc [= srcURL]`

The `dataSrc` property of `<frame />` elements, in data binding, sets the field to which the frame is bound. Data binding is beyond the scope of this book; you can find more information on it at

`http://msdn.microsoft.com/workshop/author/databind/data_binding.asp`.

frameBorder

JScript 3.0+

IE3+ (HTML), IE4+ (JS)

Syntax

`HTMLFrameElement.frameBorder = flagValue`

The `frameBorder` property of `<frame />` objects is a value which can be either "yes", "no", "1", or "0", indicates to the browser whether it should render a border for the frame. (A "0" or "no" value indicates it should not render a border; otherwise, it does.)

longDesc

Nav6, IE5.5

Syntax

`HTMLFrameElement.longDesc [= descURI]`

The longDesc property of <frame /> elements should be used to give a link to a URI describing what the frame is for. It is similar to the alt attribute for images, but allows for much longer details than the alt attribute can contain.

marginHeight
Nav3+ (HTML), Nav6 (JS), IE3+ (HTML), IE4+ (JS)

Syntax

```
HTMLFrameElement.marginHeight [= margValue]
```

The marginHeight property of <frame /> elements sets a margin of white space above and below the contents of a frame. It takes away from the viewable space of the frame; it doesn't push the frame outward, but pushes the content inward.

marginWidth
Nav3+ (HTML), Nav6 (JS), IE3+ (HTML), IE4+ (JS)

Syntax

```
HTMLFrameElement.marginWidth [= margValue]
```

The marginWidth property of <frame /> elements sets a margin of white space to the left and right of the contents of a frame. It takes away from the viewable space of the frame; it doesn't push the frame outward, but pushes the content inward.

noResize
JavaScript 1.5, JScript 3.0+

Nav3+ (HTML), Nav6 (JS), IE3+ (HTML), IE4+ (JS)

Syntax

```
[var x =] HTMLFrameElement.noResize [= booleanVal]
```

The noResize property of <frame /> elements, when you set it to true, forces the frame to remain the same size. The client cannot resize the frame by dragging it or through any other means. (They could do so by disabling this attribute via JavaScript in Internet Explorer 5 and Netscape 6.)

For XHTML compliance, you set this to noresize="noresize". But for HTML compliance prior to XHTML, simply use the word noresize.

recordNumber

JScript 3.0+

IE4+

Syntax

```
var x = HTMLFrameElement.recordNumber
```

The recordNumber property of <frame /> elements gets the record number of the frame. This only exists if the frame is a data-bound object. Data binding is beyond the scope of this book; you can find more information on it at http://msdn.microsoft.com/workshop/author/databind/data_binding.asp.

readyState

JScript 5.5+

IE5.5+

Syntax

```
var x = HTMLFrameElement.readyState
```

The readyState property of <frame /> elements indicates to the client how far along the frame is in being loaded and ready to accept commands. There are five states, strings, which this may equal. The "uninitialized" state indicates it's just getting started. The "loading" state indicates it is loading its page. The "loaded" state indicates a fully loaded page, which is going through final checks. The "interactive" state means the user can play around with it, while it finishes loading. The "complete" state means a fully activated frame.

scrolling

JavaScript 1.5, JScript 3.0+

Nav3+ (HTML), Nav6 (JS), IE3+ (HTML), IE4+ (JS)

Syntax

```
HTMLFrameElement.scrolling [= "scrollValue"]

<frame scrolling="scrollValue" />
```

The scrolling property of <frame /> elements can have a value that is one of three choices: "yes" for telling the browser to provide scrollbars, "no" for telling the browser not to provide scrollbars, or "auto" to let the browser use its best judgement. Typically, if "auto" is set, the browser will provide scrollbars when the content area exceeds the viewable area of the frame. The "auto" setting is the default, provided when you leave it out.

src

JavaScript 1.1 (window.frames), JavaScript 1.5 (DOM), JScript 3.0+

Nav2+ (HTML), Nav3+ (JS by window.frames), Nav6 (JS by DOM), IE3+ (HTML), IE4+ (JS)

Syntax

HTMLFrameElement.src = *"URIString"*

The src property of <frame /> elements and frame objects sets or retrieves the URL of the document or image the frame contains. A simple example is shown in Listing 15.19.

Listing 15.19   *Two Ways to Set a Frame's* src *Attribute*

```
<?xml version="1.0" ?>
<!-- Nav6, IE5+ only -->
<!DOCTYPE html PUBLIC "-//W3C//DTD XHTML 1.0 Frameset//EN"
➡"DTD/xhtml1-frameset.dtd">
<html xmlns="http://www.w3.org/1999/xhtml" >
<head><title></title></head>
<frameset cols="*,*"
onload="document.getElementById('myFrame').src='about:blank';
alert('Hello')">
    <frame src="about:blank" />
    <frame src="about:mozilla" id="myFrame" />
    </frameset>
</html>
```

Methods

HTMLFrameElement objects do not possess any methods beyond those inherited from the HTMLElement object, which I discuss in Chapter 21, "HTMLElement."

Event Handlers

Internet Explorer supports the following event handlers for the `HTMLFrameElement` object:

`onactivate`

`onafterupdate`

`onbeforedeactivate`

`onbeforeupdate`

`onblur`

`oncontrolselect`

`ondeactivate`

`onerrorupdate`

`onfocus`

`onload`

`onmove`

`onmoveend`

`onmovestart`

`onresize`

`onresizeend`

`onresizestart`

HTMLIFrameElement/<iframe />

Browser/JavaScript Version	Created By
Nav4/JavaScript 1.2	Not implemented
IE4/Jscript 3.0	`<iframe />`
IE5/JScript 5.0	`<iframe />`
IE5.5/JScript 5.5	`<iframe />`
	`document.createElement("iframe")`

IE6   `<iframe />`

                                 `document.createElement("iframe")`

Nav6/JavaScript 1.5   `<iframe />`

                                 `document.createElement("iframe")`

Note
Implemented in Nav6, IE4+

Child of `HTMLBodyElement`

Descends from `HTMLFrameElement` object

Description

Inline frames, or iframes (no relation to iMac computers) are frames which, instead of belonging to a frameset, lie directly embedded in a Web page. In many ways they are exactly like layers for Netscape 4. The major difference is the `iframe` is a W3C standard supporting all the major attributes these two browsers require for effective use, including the valuable `src` attribute.

For compatibility with Netscape, I recommend you enclose `<ilayer>`...`</ilayer>` (inline layer) tags inside `<iframe>`...`</iframe>` tags, with both having the same `src` attribute. Netscape 4 will ignore the `iframe` tags, and Internet Explorer 4+/Netscape 6 will ignore the `ilayer` tags. This will cost you HTML 4.01 compliance, however.

```
<iframe src="myPage.htm">
<ilayer src="myPage.htm">
</ilayer></iframe>
```

Properties

align
Nav6 (deprecated), IE4

Deprecated in Nav6, IE5

Syntax

HTMLIFrameElement.align = "*alignString*"

The align property of inline frame elements determines the alignment of the iframe relative to surrounding text. This attribute, though supported by the DOM, has been deprecated from the HTML 4.0 and XHTML 1.0 Recommendations. Avoid use of this attribute; use CSS styling as I describe in Chapter 33, "Styling for HTML Elements."

height

JScript 3.0+

IE4+

Syntax

```
HTMLFrameElement.height = pixelValue
```

The height property of inline frame elements specifies the height of the frame element, the physical distance in pixels from top to bottom.

Microsoft does not document this for iframe elements, but it's there. (I mention it here because <iframe /> elements inherit from <frame /> elements.) See Listing 15.20.

Listing 15.20   *Height of an* iframe

```
<?xml version="1.0" ?>
<!DOCTYPE html PUBLIC "-//W3C//DTD XHTML 1.0 Transitional//EN"
➡"DTD/xhtml1-transitional.dtd">
<html xmlns="http://www.w3.org/1999/xhtml" >
<head><title></title></head><body>
<p>Hello, World</p>
<iframe height="400" src="about:mozilla" />
<p>Goodbye</p>
</body>
</html>
```

hspace, vspace

JScript 3.0+

IE4+

Syntax

```
HTMLIFrameElement.hspace = spacePixels
```

The hspace and vspace properties of inline frames set margins horizontally and vertically, respectively, from the edges of the frame to the content they contain. However, these attributes have officially been deprecated. Use CSS styling as I describe in Chapter 33, "Styling for HTML Elements", instead.

Methods

HTMLIFrameElement objects do not possess any methods beyond those inherited from the HTMLFrameElement object.

Event Handlers

Internet Explorer supports the following event handlers for the HTMLIFrameElement object:

```
onactivate

onafterupdate

onbeforedeactivate

onbeforeupdate

onblur

oncontrolselect

ondeactivate

onerrorupdate

onfocus

onload

onmove

onmoveend

onmovestart

onreadystatechange

onresizeend

onresizestart

ontimeerror
```

Example: A Basket of Windows

Earlier in the chapter I mentioned sending values between `window` objects. In that instance, I showed a procedure using framesets and frames. But what about sending values between top-level windows?

One way to send information between top-level windows is through the `location` object, covered in Chapter 16, "location." This script uses that to establish itself, but it also plugs a hole in communicating between windows.

Suppose you have Window0 as your master window. Window0 opens Window1 and Window2. So far, so good. Window1 opens Window3. No problem. Each window can talk to other windows through openers and JavaScript window containers. (See the section titled "Windows Have Two Names" near the beginning of this chapter for details.)

But it gets thorny when Window1 closes. Window3 is totally cut off from Window0 and Window2, and vice versa.

The obvious solution is to assign Window3 as a property of the other windows before Window1 closes:

```
Window1.Window3 = window.open('win3.html', 'Window3')
Window0.Window3 = Window1.Window3
Window2.Window3 = Window1.Window3
```

Although this works, it's not very elegant. I find it better to have a common object that can hold this information together. I call it the `Basket` object.

In case you're wondering, the `Basket` object isn't just for holding windows. So I create a `Windows` array property of the `Basket` object specifically for that purpose. I also assign the first element of the `Windows` array as the container window.

```
Basket = new Object()
Basket.Windows = new Array()
Basket.Windows[0] = self
```

Although this may seem a bit weird, this is totally valid. It's worth noting `Basket.Windows[0].Basket == Basket`. However, note what happens when I want to open a new window, a clone of the current window:

```
Basket.Windows[Basket.Windows.length] = window.open(location.href)
```

Example: A Basket of Windows

Automatically, I've added a new window to the `Basket`. The new window, however, only has a direct reference to its `opener` window, not to any other window I open in this manner. So, from the newest window, I arrange the following:

```
Basket = opener.Basket
```

This means the new window has a complete reference to the opener window's `Basket` object. What makes this so remarkable is any properties I add to one copy of the `Basket` will show up in all other copies of the `Basket`. Which means that if `Basket.Windows[0]` opens up `Basket.Windows[2]`, the one in between, `Basket.Windows[1]`, already knows about Window2. And better than that, Window2 knows about Window1.

That's the gist of it. I did have to hard-code a few special features into the Basket of Windows script. For instance, the known bug in the `window.closed` property I built a workaround for. I had to test for pages reloading (firing the `onunload` event handler while still existing) as opposed to closing (firing the `onunload` handler and disappearing).

I used the `location.search` property to indicate to a window which window it was in the `Basket` object. In retrospect, I could have avoided this with a bit of logic. Plus, there is a known bug I could not fix, one belonging to Internet Explorer 5.0 and earlier versions. If a person right-clicks on the taskbar as if to close the program, the script throws a series of exceptions that brings the `Basket` object's synchronization to a halt.

In any case, here is the entire Basket of Windows script. Don't worry if you don't understand it, I explain it in Listing 15.21.

Listing 15.21   *The Basket of Windows Script*

```
<?xml version="1.0" ?>
<!DOCTYPE html PUBLIC "-//W3C//DTD XHTML 1.0 Transitional//EN"
➥"DTD/xhtml1-transitional.dtd">
<html xmlns="http://www.w3.org/1999/xhtml" >
<head><title></title></head>
<body>
<script language="JavaScript" type="text/javascript">
<!--
/* Basket of Windows script
Copyright 1999 by Alexander J. Vincent
Permission to reuse and distribute freely at your discretion.
Please contact me at jscript@pacbell.net before making changes.
```

Listing 15.21   *(continued)*

```
*/
loaded = false

function cloneMe() {
   var newWin = location.protocol+"\/\/"+location.host+location.pathname
   newWin += "?SelfWin="+Basket.Windows.length
   Basket.Windows[Basket.Windows.length] = window.open(newWin)
   Basket.WinClosed[Basket.WinClosed.length] = false
   r = checkLoaded(Basket.Windows.length-1)
   }

function BasketStart() {
   loaded = true

   if ((window.opener)&&(!window.opener.closed)&&(window.opener.Basket)) {
      Basket = window.opener.Basket
      findSelfWin()
      Basket.WinClosed[SelfWin] = false // useful for reloaded windows
      } else {
      setTimeout("createBasket()",1000)
      }
   }

function createBasket() {
   if (!window.Basket) {
      Basket = new Object()
      Basket.Windows = new Array()
      Basket.Windows[0] = self
      Basket.WinClosed = new Array()
      Basket.WinClosed[0] = false
      SelfWin = 0
      }
   }

function checkLoaded(checkWin) {
   if (!window.Basket.WinClosed[checkWin]) {
      r = setTimeout("checkLoaded("+checkWin+")",300)
      } else {
      r = null
      Basket.Windows[checkWin].Basket = Basket
      findSelfWin()
```

Example: A Basket of Windows

Listing 15.21   *(continued)*

```
      }
   }

function getFromSearch() {
   var x = 0
   mySearch = location.search.substr(1).split("&")
   for (x=0;x<=mySearch.length;x++)  {
      eval(mySearch[x])
      }
   }

function findSelfWin() {
   SelfWin = 0
   if (location.search!=null) {
      getFromSearch()
      }
   if ((window.opener)&&(!window.opener.closed)) {
// attempting to define an OpenerWin variable
      for (temp=0;temp<SelfWin;temp++) {
         if (Basket.WinClosed[temp]==false) {
// preventing closed windows errors
            if (Basket.Windows[temp]==window.opener) {
               OpenerWin = temp
               checkOpener = setInterval("isReloadOpener("+OpenerWin+")",100)
               }
            }
         }
      }
   }

isReloadFlag = false
function isReloadOpener(thisWin) {
   if ((isReloadFlag==true)&&(window.opener.closed==false)) {
      isReloadFlag = false
      Basket.Windows[thisWin].Basket = Basket
      Basket.WinClosed[thisWin] = false
      Basket.Windows[thisWin].findSelfWin()
      findSelfWin()
      }
   if ((isReloadFlag==true)&&(window.opener.closed==true)) {
      clearTimeout(checkOpener)
```

Listing 15.21 *(continued)*

```
        }
    if ((isReloadFlag==false)&&(Basket.WinClosed[thisWin]==true)) {
        isReloadFlag = true
        }
    }

// This covers the creation of windows.
//-->
</script>

<script language="JavaScript" type="text/javascript">
<!--
window.onload = function() {
    document.forms.tester.SelfWin.value = SelfWin
    document.forms.tester.OpenerWin.value = OpenerWin
    }
//-->
</script>
<form name="tester" action="javascript:void()">
<input type="button" onclick="cloneMe()" value="cloneMe()" />
<input type="button" onclick="self.close()" value="closeMe()" />
This Window Number:<input type="text" size="3" name="SelfWin" />
This Window's Opener Number:<input type="text" size="3" name="OpenerWin" />
</form>

</body>
</html>
```

Listing 15.21 includes a simple form with four fields. Two of them load with appropriate opener and self window numbers.

One nice thing about this script is the Basket object. Basically, it doesn't have to hold just Windows and WinClosed arrays. Any property you add to or change in one copy of Basket will reflect in all the copies instantly. Even when you close all but one window holding that Basket, the Basket will retain all properties and methods you attach to it.

Its ability to survive and maintain consistency across several window objects makes the Basket object what I call a "universal" object—an object with a larger scope (lifespan) than a global object, which you define outside a function as a property of one particular window. It also has a larger scope than a local object you define within a function using the var statement.

CHAPTER 16

location

Browser/JavaScript Version	Created By
Nav4/JavaScript 1.2	window object
IE4/JScript 3.0	window object
IE5/JScript 5.0	window object
IE5.5/JScript 5.5	window object
Nav6/JavaScript 1.5	window object

> **Note**
> Implemented in Nav2+, IE3+
>
> Property of window object (Nav2+, IE3+), document object (IE3+)

Description

The location object describes, quite simply, the current document's location on the World Wide Web or the client computer. It includes methods for reloading or replacing a page, and properties for the protocol, server, directories, filename, page target, and query-string.

Internet Explorer and Netscape support it as a property of the document object. While this seems a more logical place for it, Netscape and Internet Explorer support the same object (not a copy of it; the same one) as a property of the window object. I recommend you refer to it as window.location, or just location. Using window.location may solve some problems for setting the location of frames currently displaying a page from another host.

When you use the location object itself in a string context, such as alert(location), the value of location.href is used. Another important thing to be aware of is assignment to the location is possible, such as location = 'some.html', but the value will be assigned to location.href, not the location property itself.

Properties

hash

JavaScript 1.0+, Jscript 1.0+

Nav2+, IE3+

Syntax

```
[var x =] location.hash [= "targetName"]
```

The hash property of the location object identifies the target or anchor of the URL loaded in the document. The browser uses targets to load a page and scroll it to a particular place in the document automatically. Targets you define with HTMLAnchorElement or by simply assigning an element an ID, as in the following:

```
<a name="myTarget"></a>
or
<p id="myTarget">…<p>
```

Then you can just to the preceding location with

```
location.hash = "myTarget"
```

Typically, the anchor in this sense does not have an href property. The hash refers to the part of the URI following (and including) the pound sign (#) but preceding (and not including) the question mark (?). If the URI

```
http://jslab.isamillionaire.com/mydir/mypage.htm#mySpot?owner="AlexVincent"
```

existed, the location.hash property is equal to "#mySpot".

You can set the location.hash property explicitly to force the browser to scroll automatically to the given target; however,using the scroll methods of the window object of Chapter 15, "window" is generally safer.

Setting this property is the only way you can affect the location property of the window without forcing the browser to call the page from the server again.

host

JavaScript 1.0+, Jscript 1.0+

Nav2+, IE3+

Syntax

```
[var x =] location.host [= "domainNameStr"]
```

The host property of the location object joins the location.hostname and location.port properties in one string. You can explicitly set both properties at the same time by setting the host property directly.

Given a URI `http://jslab.isamillionaire.com:80/mypage.htm`, `location.host` is usually `"jslab.isamillionaire.com:80"`. However, in most cases the `location.port` property is an empty string. Most of the time, the URI may return `"jslab.isamillionaire.com"`. Thus, `location.host` is often a synonym for `location.hostname`. However, `location.host` can also be set to an IP address just as easily as a hostname.

For files local to the client machine, this is an empty string.

hostname

JavaScript 1.0+, Jscript 1.0+

Nav2+, IE3+

Syntax

```
[var x =] location.hostname [= "domainNameStr"]
```

The `hostname` property of the `location` object represents the server domain name from which the user called the current document. This includes any subdomains attached to the domain name. Given a URI `http://jslab.isamillionaire.com/mypage.htm`, `location.hostname` equals `"jslab.isamillionaire.com"`.

For files local to the client machine, this is an empty string.

href

JavaScript 1.0+, Jscript 1.0+

Nav2+, IE3+

Syntax

```
[var x =] location.href [= "URIString"]
```

The `href` property of the `location` object reflects the entire URI of a page, including protocol, server, directories, filename, target, and query-string.

This is the preferred object for directly changing the URI of a page without using a method of the location object. Fortunately, you can specify relative URIs as well. `"/mydir/mypage.htm"` is a perfectly valid setting for a relative URI. The JavaScript engine will redirect the browser to the page you requested and return the absolute URI of the new page to `location.href`.

pathname

JavaScript 1.0+, Jscript 1.0+

Nav2+, IE3+

Syntax

```
[var x =] location.pathname [= "dirString"]
```

The pathname property of the location object retrieves the filename path from the server to the filename and extension. It excludes any targets and query strings, and does not include a server name.

I like to use this property sometimes to get the actual filename itself. See Listing 16.1.

Listing 16.1   *Getting a Filename from the Pathname*

```
<html>
<body>
<script language="JavaScript" type="text/javascript">
<!--
function location_getFilename() {
   with (location.pathname) {
      // local files use \ and remote files use / so we have to test
      if (lastIndexOf("/") == 0) {
        return substr(lastIndexOf("\\")+1)
      } else {
        return substr(lastIndexOf("/")+1)
      }
    }
}
location.getFilename = location_getFilename
alert(location.getFilename())
//-->
</script>
</body>
</html>
```

port

JavaScript 1.0+, Jscript 1.0+

Nav2+, IE3+

Syntax

```
[var x =] location.port [= portNum]
```

The `port` property of the `location` object returns the port number of the server the page came through, if the server provided it. Usually, servers offer pages through specific ports: HTTP-served pages normally go through port 80, and FTP-served pages go through port 21.

However, rarely do you see the port number specified in URIs anymore. So in all likelihood, this particular property will be an empty string.

Setting the port number can cause unusual effects if you do not set it to a port number from which pages are served. Most of the time, if you do not set it to the default port number, you will get some form of a "browser can't connect" error.

protocol

JavaScript 1.0+, Jscript 1.0+

Nav2+ (read/write), IE3+ (read-only)

Syntax

```
[var x =] location.protocol [= "protString"]
```

The `protocol` property of the `location` object refers to what `protocol` the client called the page. Usually it's `"http:"` for the HyperText Transfer Protocol. Others you may see frequently are `"ftp:"` for File Transfer Protocol or `"news:"` for newsgroup readings.

What a few of you will also see, which technically aren't protocols, are `"javascript:"`, for sending JavaScript commands to the browser, `"mailto:"` for e-mails, and `"about:"`, which provides information about the browser. One I particularly like is `"view-source:"`, which tells the browser to display the source code to a file.

Netscape makes this property a read/write property; Microsoft holds it as read-only. However, there is rarely any reason to tinker with this particular property. The various protocols for Internet access are not interchangeable.

search

JavaScript 1.0+, Jscript 1.0+

Nav2+, IE3+

Syntax

```
var x =] location.search [= "queryString"]
```

The `search` property of the `location` object describes the query-string of the page's URI. This includes the question mark of a URI and everything following.

When setting this property, be aware of correct URI syntax. For this, I strongly recommend you use the `encodeURI()` top-level function of Netscape 6 and Internet Explorer 5.5. For browsers prior to Netscape 6 and Internet Explorer 5.5, avoid placing spaces, question marks, colons, # characters, @ characters, & characters, and percentage marks in the query-string without very good reason. If you have queries that require the & character or any of the other above characters, it is advisable to use `encodeURIComponent` or the escape function on the string to avoid problems.

I personally like using this property to send information from one page to another which follows it. The example at the end of this chapter will demonstrate this technique.

Methods

assign

JavaScript 1.0+, Jscript 3.0+

Nav2+, IE3+

Syntax

```
location.assign(URIString)
```

The `assign` method of the `location` object acts as if you set the `location.href` property to the value of the first argument; it calls the new page and adds an entry to the `history` array. Because it is relatively new, I recommend you use the `location.href` property directly instead.

reload

JavaScript 1.1+, Jscript 3.0+

Nav3+, IE4+

Syntax

```
location.reload([boolValue])
```

The `reload` method of the `location` object tells the browser to reload the current page. Without an argument or with a `false` value, it simply reloads from the cache. (The user's preferences may force the browser to call the page again from the server.) However, if you supply the first argument as `true`, it automatically tells the browser to call the page again, fresh from the server.

replace

JavaScript 1.1+, Jscript 3.0+

Nav3+, IE4+

Syntax

```
location.replace(URIString)
```

The `replace` method of the `location` object tells the browser to call the page at the first argument into the current window. However, unlike other methods of calling pages, this one overwrites the current page's entry in the window's `history` array. (You'll learn about `history` in Chapter 17, "history.") This means the current page effectively disappears from the browser's history of pages.

Example: Sending Information from One Page to Another

At Website Abstraction (`http://www.wsabstract.com`), one of the sites I contribute to, I've written a tutorial called "Sending objects from one page to another." It continues to be one of the questions we get very frequently, so the lesson bears repeating. In Chapter 15, I discussed sending objects by framesets and by pop-up windows. In this chapter, I discuss using the `location.search` property.

Let's say you have a form that decides what data to send on. (Using a link is only slightly different.) In this example we just send the contents of an input box, but the principle is the same for other data. See Listing 16.2.

Example: Sending Information from One Page to Another

Listing 16.2   *The Sending Page Source Code*

```
<html>
<body>
<script language="JavaScript" type="text/javascript">
<!--
function valSubmit() {
    if (document.forms.myForm.myData.value.length > 0) {
        var URI = "16list03.htm?";
        for (var val=0; val<document.forms.myForm.length; val++) {
            var elName = document.forms.myForm[val].name
            var elValue = document.forms.myForm[val].value
            if (elName != "") {
                URI += escape(elName) + ".value='" + escape(elValue) + "'&"
                }
            }
        URI = URI.substr(0,URI.length - 1)
        location.href = URI
        }
    }
//-->
</script>
<form name="myForm" method="get">
<input type="text" name="myData" value="Hello" />
<input type="button" onclick="valSubmit()" value="Submit!" />
</form>
</body>
</html>
```

Listing 16.2 starts by creating a URI string I called, appropriately enough, URI. The URI string references the page I intend to load. Then, for each element of the form, it attempts to find a name and value property. Keep in mind the value property does not work for all elements in Netscape 4 so there are compatibility issues to consider using this example.

If the name property (matching the name attribute of the same element) is not an empty string, it attaches the name property, plus ".value" to URI. Then it attaches "='" and the value property, followed by "'&". The single quotes are to ensure the receiving page receives a syntactically correct string that is easier to parse. The .value part ensures it is getting passed to a form value on the following page. The & character prepares the URI variable to receive another form value.

When we're done going through all the form properties, we need merely to chop off the last & character (which is not necessary or desirable) and pass URI to `location.href`. This tells the browser to call on the next file, with the appropriate query string attached, as shown in Listing 16.3.

Listing 16.3   *The Receiving Page Source Code*

```
<html>
<body onload="setData()">
<script language="JavaScript" type="text/javascript">
<!--
function setData() {
   var query = location.search.substr(1).split("&")
   for (var setD = 0; setD < query.length; setD++) {
      eval("document.forms.myForm."+unescape(query[setD]))
      }
   }
//-->
</script>
<form name="myForm">
<input type="text" name="myData" value="Test" />
<input type="text" name="normal" value="World" />
<input type="button" value="Continue!" />
</form>
</body>
</html>
```

The receiving page is pretty simple. After the page loads, it gets the `location.search` property and chops off the first character (the question mark). Then it splits the resulting string by the & characters, leaving an array of `"objName.value='objValue'"` strings behind for the query object to pick up.

The next step is to take each of these strings and prefix them with `"document.forms.myForm."`. Thus each string becomes `"document.forms.myForm.objName.value='objValue'"`. This is a valid JavaScript command, which I pass to the global `eval` function as its first argument. Thus, the statement executes. The `objName` field's value is set to `objValue`. Keep in mind this example only makes sense for passing text values for input elements like `text`, `password`, and `textarea`. Passing values for check boxes and other elements would require additional processing code for meaningful results.

Example: Sending Information from One Page to Another

At the time I write this, I ask myself if this is an entirely safe procedure. HTTP GET methods use the location.search property as well, but on the server. It may be wise to check for the existence of the client-side form element on the receiving page before attempting to assign a value to it, assuming the existence of certain form fields you do not wish to pass on.

CHAPTER 17

history

Browser/JavaScript Version	Created By
Nav4/JavaScript 1.2	window object
IE4/JScript 3.0	window object
IE5/JScript 5.0	window object
IE5.5/JScript 5.5	window object
Nav6/JavaScript 1.5	window object

> **Note**
> Implemented in Nav2+, IE3+
> Property of window object

Description

The history object describes, to a limited extent, the history of pages visited by the current browser window. I say limited because each document, without having a signed script with permission, may not be able to read any of the entries in the history array. This depends on how the page was loaded and often on an individual's browser preferences. If the page loads from file: or https: it should be able to request the necessary privileges, while an http request usually requires a signed script. In these days of Web virus paranoia, make sure you have a signature to sign the scripts with that requires special privileges, or do not expect Web users to run your script.

This book does not cover properties that require signed scripts, and so you will not see them here. In case you are wondering, you will see full descriptions of these properties at http://devedge.netscape.com/docs/manuals/js/client/jsref/history.htm.

Properties

length

JavaScript 1.0+, JScript 3.0+

Nav2+, IE3+

Syntax

```
[var x =] history.length
```

The length property of the history object tells the total number of pages in the history array. For details on the length property, see Chapter 3, "Array()." However, you should know that this property, unlike the Array() object's length properties, is read-only.

Methods

back()
JavaScript 1.0+, JScript 1.0+

Nav2+, IE3+

Syntax

```
history.back([pageNumber])
```

This method forces the current window to go back one page in the last frame changed, as if the user clicked the browser's Back button.

In Internet Explorer, if you provide an argument, it goes back by the number of pages specified in the argument. Otherwise for Internet Explorer (and regardless of arguments in Netscape), it goes back exactly one page.

forward()
JavaScript 1.0+, JScript 1.0+

Nav2+, IE3+

Syntax

```
history.forward()
```

This method forces the current window to go forward one page in the last frame changed, as if the user clicked the browser's Forward button.

go()
JavaScript 1.0+, JScript 1.0+

Nav2+, IE3+

Syntax

```
history.go(pageString)
```

This method forces the current window to go forward or back by the number of pages indicated in the first argument. The window goes forward if the first argument is a positive number; back if the first argument is a negative number. The number of pages moved is equal to the absolute value (see `Math.abs` in Chapter 8, "Math") of the first argument.

Using `history.go(0)` is the same as saying `location.reload()`. The first argument may also be a URL string. Internet Explorer requires a complete URL from the history, while Netscape will try to match a substring.

Example: Moving a Separate Frame Back

One of the things which I find most annoying about many framed Web sites is the need to click the Back button over and over again, backing up one frame when I want to back up the other. There's a rather easy workaround, though. Note Listing 17.1, which has five separate HTML files.

Listing 17.1   *Moving Through Frames*

```html
<!-- 17lst01a.htm -->
<html>
<frameset cols="25%,*">
    <frame name="framea" src="17lst01b.htm" />
    <frame name="frameb" src="17lst01c.htm" />
    </frameset>
</html>


<!-- 17lst01b.htm -->
<html>
<body>
Start page.
</body>
</html>


<!-- 17lst01c.htm -->
<html>
<body>
```

Example: Moving a Separate Frame Back

Listing 17.1   *(continued)*

```
<a href="17lst01d.htm" target="framea">Move frame A forward</a>
</body>
</html>


<!-- 17lst01d.htm -->
<html>
<body>
<p>Forward in Frame A.  <a href="17lst01e.htm"
target="frameb">Move frame B forward</a></p>
</body>
</html>


<!-- 17lst01e.htm -->
<html>
<body>
<a href="javascript:history.go(-2);">
Let's move the other frame back.</a>
</body>
</html>
```

Load the first file (17lst01a.htm) into a browser. Keep in mind the frame on the left is framea and the frame on the right is frameb. The second and third files are displayed in the frames, with the frame on the right offering to change the frame on the left. Clicking the link on the right causes the fourth file to load in framea on the left. Its link loads the fifth file into frameb on the right. Finally, the new link in frameb loads the first file back in framea. If you try this in Netscape 4 you will find the last link doesn't work. That is because the history object in Netscape 3 and 4 is frame-related, not frameset-related. For that matter there are subtle differences in the history object's behavior between versions of Netscape. The window.back method acts more like Internet Explorer and may be an alternative.

CHAPTER 18

navigator

Browser/JavaScript Version	Created By
Nav4/JavaScript 1.2	Browser
IE4/Jscript 3.0	Browser
IE5/Jscript 5.0	Browser
IE5.5/JScript 5.5	Browser
Nav6/JavaScript 1.5	Browser

> **Note**
> Implemented in Nav2+, IE3+
>
> Property of `window` object
>
> This object and all predefined properties/methods are read-only

Description

The `navigator` object describes to JavaScript the client browser's details. This includes such things as the operating system, the computer it runs on, plug-ins the browser has available, and what kind of documents the browser can accept. However, the specifics of the navigator object can vary significantly between browsers. It is important to note that in Netscape 4 and probably previous versions the `navigator` object was a global object with one instance for all browsers. In Internet Explorer 4+ and Netscape 6 each window has its own `navigator` object.

In Microsoft Internet Explorer, as of version 4, the `window.clientInformation` property refers to the same object as the `navigator` property.

Browser Sniffing, the Incorrect Way

A common practice by many Web designers is to detect a browser by the objects it supports. For instance, if you are running Netscape 4, it has the `document.layers` object. If you are running Internet Explorer 4+, it has the `document.all` object.

Many people have assumed this means a browser having the `document.layers` object is a Netscape browser. Likewise, they have assumed a browser having the `document.all` object is a Microsoft Internet Explorer browser (see Listing 18.1).

Browser Sniffing, the Incorrect Way

Listing 18.1   *How Most JavaScripters (Incorrectly) Identify a Browser*

```
<html>
<body>
<script language="JavaScript" type="text/javascript">
<!--
if (document.layers) {
   // Netscape-specific code
   alert("Netscape browser")
   }
if (document.all) {
   // Internet Explorer-specific code
   alert("Internet Explorer browser")
   }
//-->
</script>
</body>
</html>
```

However, this is a fallacy. If all cars are vehicles, are all vehicles cars? Yes, 99.9 percent of browsers currently are Netscape or Microsoft browsers. But there's still that 1/10 of a percent, which may support *one or the other* of these object *names* in their version of JavaScript, *but not the same object sets as the major browsers*. How many people are using the Internet? Multiply that by 0.001 and you still get a sizable number of people for whom your page is broken. Why have a Web site up at all? Or is that 0.1 percent so insignificant to you? That 0.1 percent could easily have among it a multimillionaire who could save or seriously grow your business.

Not only that, but experience by thousands of Web developers has shown the code in Listing 18.1 is not reliable. Netscape 6 *did not support either proprietary object*. So when Netscape rolled out its latest version of the popular browser, people en masse blamed Netscape for lazy and incorrect coding logic.

Naturally, within a few weeks, someone found an object combination that distinctly "identified" Netscape 6. The latest code includes checking for `document.getElementById` existing and `document.all` *not* existing. It's a lazy and incorrect way to code. What's going to happen when Internet Explorer 6 hits the streets (currently in preview release at the time of this writing)? All those short object-detection scripts are going to break again. Who knows what future browsers will support and won't support?

So getting your code right is, in my humble opinion, fairly important. Even my colleagues at Website Abstraction disagree about this. Netscape, however, recommends using a browser detection script sniffing the `navigator` object, which is an unofficial standard across JavaScript-enabled browsers such as Opera. I vote with Netscape on this one: the `navigator` object has all the information you need to conclusively identify the browser and platform on which your JavaScripts run. Remember that some rather sneaky things were done to the `navigator` object during the browser wars, so still check your browser detection code when a new browser version comes out, or you may be in for a nasty surprise.

Netscape, through `mozilla.org`, provides a free script for explicitly detecting on which browser your scripts run. I have obtained permission from Netscape to reprint that script in this book, and I will do so as the example for this chapter.

Properties

appCodeName
JavaScript 1.0+, JScript 1.0+

Nav2+, IE3+

Syntax

```
[var x =] navigator.appCodeName
```

The `appCodeName` property of the `navigator` object, in theory, represents a unique code name for a browser within the browser's company. Netscape named its code "Mozilla" as of version 2.0. Microsoft, for reasons of its own, also called its code name "Mozilla," apparently implying compatibility with pages written for Netscape browsers. (Incidentally, this was before the 4.x browser war and the fourth-generation browser issues of styling.)

appMinorVersion
JScript 3.0+

IE4+

Syntax

```
[var x =] navigator.apppMinorVersion
```

The `appMinorVersion` property of the `navigator` object retrieves a small amount of information about the browser—what service pack it is, and some relatively meaningless text.

appName

JavaScript 1.0+, JScript 1.0+

Nav2+, IE3+

Syntax

```
[var x =] navigator.appName
```

The `appName` property of the `navigator` object, simply put, is the official name of the browser. Microsoft Internet Explorer returns `"Microsoft Internet Explorer"`, and Netscape returns `"Netscape"`. Opera, depending on its settings, may return either value. So there is still no conclusive property to test with.

appVersion

JavaScript 1.0+, JScript 1.0+

Nav2+, IE3+

Syntax

```
[var x] = navigator.appVersion
```

The `appVersion` property of the `navigator` object returns the browser version and a couple other details. Microsoft and Netscape differ slightly on the syntax for this property.

Netscape returns the version number of the software, followed by the language code in brackets, followed by the platform abbreviation and a one-letter code in parentheses. For instance, Netscape 4.72 returns `"4.7 [en] (Win95; U)"` on a Windows 95 computer set to the English language. However, Netscape 6 returns `"5.0 (Windows; en-US)"`, so this is not a miracle cure either.

Internet Explorer returns the stored version number of the software, followed by the word `"compatible"`, followed by the actual browser abbreviation (MSIE) and exact version number, followed by the platform name. Internet Explorer 5.5 on a Windows 98 system returns `"4.0 (compatible; MSIE 5.5; Windows 98)"`.

You may notice Internet Explorer 5.5 returned 4.0 at first. This is a known "feature" in Internet Explorer for which the script at the end of this chapter accounts. Although I'm sure it was meant to specify backward compatibility, it creates another issue to deal with.

browserLanguage/language

JavaScript 1.2+, JScript 3.0+

Nav4+ (language), IE4+ (browserLanguage)

Syntax

```
[var x =] navigator.browserLanguage
```

The browserLanguage property of the navigator object returns the appropriate language to use. In Internet Explorer 4 and Netscape 4+, this returns a language code for the instance of the browser in use. In Internet Explorer 5+, this returns the language code for the operating system.

Language codes are abbreviations of a language's name, typically in that language. English is en. German is de. Japanese is ja. You can learn more about language codes at http://msdn.microsoft.com/workshop/author/dhtml/reference/language_codes.asp.

cookieEnabled

JavaScript 1.5+, JScript 3.0+

Nav6, IE4+

Syntax

```
[var x =] navigator.cookieEnabled
```

The cookieEnabled property of the navigator object will tell you if you can store cookies on the client. When this property is true, the browser confirms for you the ability for it to accept and store cookies on the client machine. (Cookies I cover in Chapter 23, "HTMLDocument/document.")

> **Note**
> Versions prior to Netscape 4 did not implement this feature, although versions through
> Netscape 4 by default enabled cookies.
>
> ```
> if (!navigator.cookieEnabled) {
> ```
>
> This line is inconclusive for Netscape 4 browsers. The only way to know if cookies are
> enabled for Netscape 4 is to set a cookie and see if you can retrieve it.

cpuClass

JScript 3.0+

IE4+

Syntax

```
[var x =] navigator.cpuClass
```

This simply tells what kind of CPU chip the system is running on—"x86" for Intel-compatible chips, "Alpha" for Digital chips, "68K" and "PPC" for Motorola chips (two separate brands). If the chip is not one of these chips, the property is equal to "Other".

mimeTypes

JavaScript 1.1+

Nav3+

Syntax

```
navigator.mimeTypes[index]
```

The mimeTypes property of the navigator object is a special array Netscape makes available for identifying what mime-types the browser knows how to handle. Technically Internet Explorer provides mimeTypes, but it is just an empty array. Also, be aware that Netscape 6 lists the mime-types it supports, while Netscape 3 and 4 list all supported mime-types. This may seem like a hassle just to find out if Flash or some other feature is supported, but remember you can index by name. So to check for flash all you would have to do is

```
Navigator.mimeTypes['application/x-shockwave-flash']
```

Each element of the array is a MimeType object, and possesses the following properties:

description

JavaScript 1.1+

Nav3+

Syntax

mimeType.description

The description property of the mimeType object provides a description for you and I of what the mime-type is about. It's a version meant for us to read.

enabledPlugin

JavaScript 1.1+

Nav3+

Syntax

mimeType.enabledPlugin

The enabledPlugin property of the mimeType object describes the plugin object for the mime-type object. If there is no plugin for a given mime-type, this property is null. Plugin objects are covered in detail in Chapter 31, "Programmable Elements."

suffixes

JavaScript 1.1+

Nav3+

Syntax

mimeType.suffixes

The suffixes property of the mimeType object is a comma-delineated string containing valid filename suffixes for the given mime-type. For example, "svg,svgz" would be a valid entry in the suffixes property for the Adobe SVG Viewer plug-in for Netscape 4.

type

JavaScript 1.1+

Nav3+

Syntax

mimeType.type

The type property of the mimeType object is what mime-types are all about. Briefly, this is a two-part string. The first part describes what class of file it fits into: text, application, image, and so on. The second part describes the exact file type. "image/svg-xml" is the official mime-type for SVG.

onLine

JScript 3+

IE4+

Syntax

[var *boolValue* =] navigator.onLine

The onLine property of the navigator object returns true if the user is not in offline browsing mode (meaning he or she can look at pages on the World Wide Web). Otherwise, this property returns false.

platform

JavaScript 1.2+, JScript 3.0+

Nav4+, IE4+

Syntax

[var *x* =] navigator.platform

The platform property of the navigator object gives some basic information about the type of operating system on the computer. (It does not name the operating system.) A 32-bit version of Windows (Win9x, WinNT, Win2k, WinME, WinXP) will return "Win32". Likewise, a 16-bit version of Windows (Windows 3.1, for example) will return "Win16". Others include "Mac68k" for Macintosh, "SunOS" for Solaris, "MacPPC" for PowerPC, and "HP-UX" for Hewlett-Packard Unix.

plugins

JavaScript 1.1+, Jscript 3.0+

Nav3+, IE4+

Syntax

```
[var x =] navigator.plugins[index]
```

The `plugins` property of the `navigator` object is a special array containing the `Plugin` objects attached to the client's browser. Technically this property is supported by Internet Explorer 4+, but it is only an empty array that will not tell you much. You can use this array to search for a particular plug-in, and if it is not installed, warn the user ahead of time to go get the plug-in. (This is actually a very common task for JavaScript.)

plugins.length

JavaScript 1.1+, JScript 3.0+

Nav3+, IE4+

Syntax

```
[var x =] navigator.plugins.length
```

The `length` property of the `plugins` array reflects the number of plug-ins attached to the browser. Remember, because this is an empty array in Internet Explorer, expect length to be 0.

plugins.refresh()

JavaScript 1.1+

Nav3+

Syntax

```
navigator.plugins.refresh(boolean)
```

The `refresh` method of the `plugins` array is a less well-known method. So many times early in my browsing the World Wide Web, I would install a plug-in and the program would ask me to restart my browser. You don't have to with this method.

Anytime you install a plug-in, calling this method refreshes the entire plug-in system—so your newly installed plug-in lands and you can go to work with it right away. If you call `refresh` with a value of `true`, it refreshes the array and any documents with an `EMBED` tag. If called with a value of `false`, it will only refresh the `plugins` array.

systemLanguage

JScript 3.0+

IE4+

Syntax

```
[var x =] navigator.systemLanguage
```

The systemLanguage property of the navigator object reflects the language code
(described earlier in this chapter) for the operating system.

userAgent

JavaScript 1.0+, JScript 1.0+

Nav2+, IE3+

Syntax

```
[var x =] navigator.userAgent
```

The userAgent property of the navigator object combines the appCodeName property
of the browser with the appVersion property to return a string (theoretically) unique
to a particular version (and for Netscape/Mozilla, build date) of a browser. For
example, the userAgent property of Netscape 6 is "Mozilla/5.0 (Windows; U; Win95;
en-US; m18) Gecko/20001108 Netscape6/6.0". Later versions of Netscape 6 have
different userAgent properties. However, because this is used as part of the http
request header, most of this information is spoofed along the Mozilla/x.y format to
ensure sites will not exclude their users.

userLanguage

JScript 3.0+

IE4+

Syntax

```
[var x =] navigator.userLanguage
```

The userLanguage property of the navigator object retrieves the user's local language
setting from his Internet Options control panel, Regional Options section.

userProfile

JScript 3.0+

IE4+

Syntax

```
[var x =] navigator.userProfile
```

The userProfile property of the navigator object is a container for gathering information from the client machine's user preferences in Internet Explorer and passing it to the server, with permission. Basically, it requests the user to authorize the release of certain (generally nonsensitive) information. If the user authorizes such a release, the browser releases only the requested information.

Generally, you fill up a queue of requests, call for all the information at once with the doReadRequest() method, and get the information the user provides, assigning various pieces to object names. Microsoft calls this the AutoComplete feature, which is fairly closely related to the vCard standard. (Outlook Express 5 supports vCard, and Internet Explorer 5 is very closely related to Outlook Express 5. In my research, I found multiple clues that hinted at Internet Explorer 5 conforming to vCard, but no definitive statements.) Interestingly, uppercase versus lowercase does not matter in naming vCard attributes. Listing 18.2 shows a usage of the userProfile object, while Figure 18.1 shows the results of that usage.

Listing 18.2   *The* navigator.userProfile *Object in Context*

```
<html>
<body onLoad="go()">
<script language="JavaScript" type="text/javascript">
<!--
function go() {
   navigator.userProfile.clearRequest()
   navigator.userProfile.addReadRequest("Vcard.displayname")
   navigator.userProfile.doReadRequest(1, "JavaScript Laboratory")
   document.forms.myForm.myName.value =
      navigator.userProfile.getAttribute("Vcard.displayname")
navigator.userProfile.clearRequest()
   }
//-->
</script>
<form name="myForm">
```

Listing 18.2   *(continued)*

```
<input type="text" name="myName" />
</form>
</body>
</html>
```

Figure 18.1
Listing 18.2 after the `doReadRequest()` *call.*

addReadRequest()

JScript 3.0+

IE4+

Syntax

```
navigator.userProfile.addReadRequest(attName)
```

This allows you to add a request for vCard information to the queue of requests. Microsoft documentation (in the `getAttribute` property of the `userProfile` object) states you may request any of the following in your scripts:

vCard.Business.City	vCard.Business.Country	vCard.Business.Fax
vCard.Business.Phone	vCard.Business.State	vCard.Business.StreetAddress
vCard.Business.URL	vCard.Business.Zipcode	vCard.Cellular
vCard.Company	vCard.Department	vCard.DisplayName
vCard.Email	vCard.FirstName	vCard.Gender

vCard.Home.City	vCard.Home.Country	vCard.Home.Fax
vCard.Home.Phone	vCard.Home.State	vCard.Home.StreetAddress
vCard.Home.Zipcode	vCard.Homepage	vCard.JobTitle
vCard.LastName	vCard.MiddleName	vCard.Notes
vCard.Office	vCard.Pager	

Listing 18.2 adds the vCard.DisplayName to the queue of requests.

ClearRequests()

JScript 3.0+

IE4+

Syntax

```
navigator.userProfile.clearRequests()
```

This method empties the current list of queued requests. It is generally a good idea to call this method twice: once to empty the queue before your script gets it, and once after.

doReadRequest()

JScript 3.0+

IE4+

Syntax

```
navigator.userProfile.doReadRequest(code [, siteName [, domain [, path] ] ] )
```

This method executes a request for all information the queue of requests wants. (See addReadRequest, earlier in this chapter, for more information.) The result is a pop-up window like the one in Figure 18.1. It lists each item the queue wants to get, and if the user answers Yes, the browser may gather that information. (If the user answers No, the browser returns an empty string for any attempt to get information from the queue.)

The first argument is a code you must use to indicate how you will use the information (see Table 18.1). (These messages are at the bottom of the pop-up request window.

Table 18.1 `doReadRequest()` *Usage Codes*

Code	Message
0	Used for system administration.
1	Used for research and product development.
2	Used for completion and support of the current transaction.
3	Used to customize the content and design of a site.
4	Used to improve the content of a site that includes advertisements.
5	Used for notifying visitors about updates to the site.
6	Used for contacting visitors for marketing of services or products.
7	Used for linking other collected information.
8	Used by a site for other purposes.
9	Disclosed to others for customization or improvement of the content and design of the site.
10	Disclosed to others, who may contact the user, for marketing of services or products.
11	Disclosed to others, who may contact the user, for marketing of services or products. The user can ask a site not to do this.
12	Disclosed to others for any other purpose.

The second, third, and fourth arguments are all optional. The second argument gives a company or individual name for the site that requests the information. The third argument gives domain names this request applies for (like cookies, described in Chapter 23). The fourth argument gives a path from the domain to the filename requesting the information.

getAttribute

JScript 3.0+

IE4+

Syntax

`[var x =] navigator.userProfile.getAttribute(attString)`

Similar to the `getAttribute` method of the `Document` interface in Chapter 20, "Core DOM Objects," this value accepts a vCard object name as its first argument, a `String()` value. See `addReadRequest`, slightly earlier in this chapter, for details on valid vCard names.

If the first argument is not a valid vCard name, or the user denied permission to the latest approved request, or the userProfile queue has been cleared, this method returns an empty string.

Listing 18.2 demonstrates, briefly, the use of this method.

setAttribute

JScript 3.0+

IE4+

Syntax

```
navigator.userProfile.setAttribute(attString, valueString [, flags])
```

See the setAttribute method of the Node interface in Chapter 20. This method is identical. In this case it maybe useful for setting temporary attributes in the userProfile object, but it should not be able to permanently change anything.

Methods

javaEnabled()

JavaScript 1.1+, JScript 3.0+

Nav3+, IE4+

Syntax

```
[var boolValue =] navigator.javaEnabled()
```

The javaEnabled() method of the navigator object returns true if the browser's Java Virtual Machine is available. Otherwise it returns false.

taintEnabled()

JavaScript 1.1, JScript 3.0+

Implemented in Nav3, IE4+

Removed in Nav4+

Syntax

```
navigator.taintEnabled(boolean)
```

The `taintEnabled` method of the navigator object reflects a short-lived security model named data tainting. Microsoft has never supported it except possibly in Internet Explorer 5.5, and Netscape experimented with it in Netscape 3. In Netscape 4, the revised security model, involving signed scripts, rendered this method obsolete. It is advisable to avoid using the `taintEnabled()` method.

Example: Browser Sniffing, the Correct Way

Earlier in this chapter, I ranted quite a bit about using object detection to identify a browser. The `navigator` object provides 95 percent of what a JavaScript needs to identify a browser accurately. Here I include a script to identify the browser fairly accurately. Keep in mind this only works on current browsers, as newer versions keep coming out I'm sure this script will have to be adapted to handle the spoofing. Also even in the extensive script later in this chapter a lot of assumptions were made. For instance, Internet Explorer 5.5 is associated with JavaScript 1.3, when JavaScript 1.5 might be more appropriate.

Although this chapter probably sounds like it discourages use of object detection, that is not the intent. Object detection has its uses, but detecting a single object when you need to identify a specific browser is a really bad idea. However, in many cases you really don't care about the "exact" browser the user is using. You only need to know if a certain method or property is supported so that your script will work. In those cases object detection makes a lot more sense than using the massive script that follows.

Incidentally, I did not write this script. The original source is `http://www.mozilla.org/docs/web-developer/sniffer/browser_type_oo.html`, and it is copyright 2001, Netscape Communications Corporation. (I've added the requisite <HTML> and <BODY> tags to ensure this can work in your browser natively.) If you are thinking about using this script it would be a good idea to check for an updated version. See Listing 18.3.

Listing 18.3   *The Netscape Ultimate Client Sniffer Script, Version 3.02*

```
<html>
<body>
<script language="JavaScript" type="text/javascript">
<!-- hide JavaScript from non-JavaScript browsers
```

Listing 18.3 *(continued)*

```
// Ultimate client-side JavaScript client sniff. Version 3.02
// (C) Netscape Communications 1999-2001.
// Permission granted to reuse and distribute.
// Revised 17 May 99 to add is.nav5up and is.ie5up (see below).
// Revised 21 Nov 00 to add is.gecko and is.ie5_5 Also Changed is.nav5
// and is.nav5up to is.nav6 and is.nav6up
// Revised 22 Feb 01 to correct Javascript Detection for IE 5.x, Opera 4,
//                   correct Opera 5 detection
//                   add support for winME and win2k
//                   synch with browser-type-oo.js
//                   add is.aol5, is.aol6
// Revised 26 Mar 01 to correct Opera detection


// Everything you always wanted to know about your JavaScript client
// but were afraid to ask ... "Is" is the constructor function for "is" object,
// which has properties indicating:
// (1) browser vendor:
//     is.nav, is.ie, is.opera, is.hotjava, is.webtv, is.TVNavigator, is.AOLTV
// (2) browser version number:
//     is.major (integer indicating major version number: 2, 3, 4 ...)
//     is.minor (float   indicating full  version number: 2.02, 3.01, 4.04 ...)
// (3) browser vendor AND major version number
//     is.nav2, is.nav3, is.nav4, is.nav4up, is.nav6, is.nav6up, is.gecko,
is.ie3,
//     is.ie4, is.ie4up, is.ie5, is.ie5up, is.ie5_5, is.ie5_5up,
//     is.hotjava3, is.hotjava3up,
//     is.opera2, is.opera3, is.opera4, is.opera5, is.opera5up, is.aol3,
//     is.aol4, is.aol5, is.aol6
// (4) JavaScript version number:
//     is.js (float indicating full JavaScript version number: 1, 1.1, 1.2 ...)
// (5) OS platform and version:
//     is.win, is.win16, is.win32, is.win31, is.win95, is.winnt,
//     is.win98, is.winme, is.win2k
//     is.os2
//     is.mac, is.mac68k, is.macppc
//     is.unix
//     is.sun, is.sun4, is.sun5, is.suni86
//     is.irix, is.irix5, is.irix6
//     is.hpux, is.hpux9, is.hpux10
//     is.aix, is.aix1, is.aix2, is.aix3, is.aix4
//     is.linux, is.sco, is.unixware, is.mpras, is.reliant
```

Example: Browser Sniffing, the Correct Way

Listing 18.3   *(continued)*

```
//      is.dec, is.sinix, is.freebsd, is.bsd
//      is.vms
//
// See http://www.it97.de/JavaScript/JS_tutorial/bstat/navobj.html and
// http://www.it97.de/JavaScript/JS_tutorial/bstat/Browseraol.html
// for detailed lists of userAgent strings.
//
// Note: you don't want your Nav4 or IE4 code to "turn off" or
// stop working when Nav5 and IE5 (or later) are released, so
// in conditional code forks, use is.nav4up ("Nav4 or greater")
// and is.ie4up ("IE4 or greater") instead of is.nav4 or is.ie4
// to check version in code which you want to work on future
// versions.


function Is ()
{   // convert all characters to lowercase to simplify testing
    var agt=navigator.userAgent.toLowerCase();

    // *** BROWSER VERSION ***
    // Note: On IE5, these return 4, so use is.ie5up to detect IE5.

    this.major = parseInt(navigator.appVersion);
    this.minor = parseFloat(navigator.appVersion);

    // Note: Opera and WebTV spoof Navigator.  We do strict client detection.
    // If you want to allow spoofing, take out the tests for opera and webtv.
    this.nav  = ((agt.indexOf('mozilla')!=-1) && (agt.indexOf('spoofer')==-1)
                && (agt.indexOf('compatible') == -1) && (agt.indexOf('opera')==-
1)
                && (agt.indexOf('webtv')==-1) && (agt.indexOf('hotjava')==-1));
    this.nav2 = (this.nav && (this.major == 2));
    this.nav3 = (this.nav && (this.major == 3));
    this.nav4 = (this.nav && (this.major == 4));
    this.nav4up = (this.nav && (this.major >= 4));
    this.navonly     = (this.nav && ((agt.indexOf(";nav") != -1) ||
                            (agt.indexOf("; nav") != -1)) );
    this.nav6 = (this.nav && (this.major == 5));
    this.nav6up = (this.nav && (this.major >= 5));
    this.gecko = (agt.indexOf('gecko') != -1);
```

Listing 18.3   *(continued)*

```javascript
this.ie      = ((agt.indexOf("msie") != -1) && (agt.indexOf("opera") == -1));
this.ie3     = (this.ie && (this.major < 4));
this.ie4     = (this.ie && (this.major == 4) && (agt.indexOf("msie 5")==-1) );
this.ie4up   = (this.ie  && (this.major >= 4));
this.ie5     = (this.ie && (this.major == 4) && (agt.indexOf("msie 5.0")!=-1) );
this.ie5_5   = (this.ie && (this.major == 4) && (agt.indexOf("msie 5.5") !=-1));
this.ie5up   = (this.ie  && !this.ie3 && !this.ie4);
this.ie5_5up =(this.ie && !this.ie3 && !this.ie4 && !this.ie5);

// KNOWN BUG: On AOL4, returns false if IE3 is embedded browser
// or if this is the first browser window opened.  Thus the
// variables is.aol, is.aol3, and is.aol4 aren't 100% reliable.
this.aol     = (agt.indexOf("aol") != -1);
this.aol3    = (this.aol && this.ie3);
this.aol4    = (this.aol && this.ie4);
this.aol5    = (agt.indexOf("aol 5") != -1);
this.aol6    = (agt.indexOf("aol 6") != -1);

this.opera = (agt.indexOf("opera") != -1);
this.opera2 = (agt.indexOf("opera 2") != -1 || agt.indexOf("opera/2") != -1);
this.opera3 = (agt.indexOf("opera 3") != -1 || agt.indexOf("opera/3") != -1);
this.opera4 = (agt.indexOf("opera 4") != -1 || agt.indexOf("opera/4") != -1);
this.opera5 = (agt.indexOf("opera 5") != -1 || agt.indexOf("opera/5") != -1);
    this.opera5up = (this.opera && !this.opera2 && !this.opera3 &&
!this.opera4);

this.webtv = (agt.indexOf("webtv") != -1);

this.TVNavigator =
      ((agt.indexOf("navio") != -1) || (agt.indexOf("navio_aoltv") != -1));
this.AOLTV = this.TVNavigator;

this.hotjava = (agt.indexOf("hotjava") != -1);
this.hotjava3 = (this.hotjava && (this.major == 3));
this.hotjava3up = (this.hotjava && (this.major >= 3));
```

Example: Browser Sniffing, the Correct Way

Listing 18.3   *(continued)*

```
// *** JAVASCRIPT VERSION CHECK ***
if (this.nav2 || this.ie3) this.js = 1.0;
else if (this.nav3) this.js = 1.1;
else if (this.opera5up) this.js = 1.3;
else if (this.opera) this.js = 1.1;
else if ((this.nav4 && (this.minor <= 4.05)) || this.ie4) this.js = 1.2;
else if ((this.nav4 && (this.minor > 4.05)) || this.ie5) this.js = 1.3;
else if (this.hotjava3up) this.js = 1.4;
else if (this.nav6 || this.gecko) this.js = 1.5;
// NOTE: In the future, update this code when newer versions of JS
// are released. For now, we try to provide some upward compatibility
// so that future versions of Nav and IE will show they are at
// *least* JS 1.x capable. Always check for JS version compatibility
// with > or >=.
else if (this.nav6up) this.js = 1.5;
// note ie5up on mac is 1.4
else if (this.ie5up) this.js = 1.3

// HACK: no idea for other browsers; always check for JS version with > or
>=
else this.js = 0.0;

// *** PLATFORM ***
this.win    = ( (agt.indexOf("win")!=-1) || (agt.indexOf("16bit")!=-1) );
// NOTE: On Opera 3.0, the userAgent string includes "Windows 95/NT4" on all
//       Win32, so you can't distinguish between Win95 and WinNT.
this.win95 = ((agt.indexOf("win95")!=-1) || (agt.indexOf("windows 95")!=-
1));

// is this a 16 bit compiled version?
this.win16 = ((agt.indexOf("win16")!=-1) ||
              (agt.indexOf("16bit")!=-1) || (agt.indexOf("windows 3.1")!=-1) ||
              (agt.indexOf("windows 16-bit")!=-1) );

this.win31 = ((agt.indexOf("windows 3.1")!=-1) || (agt.indexOf("win16")!=-1)
||
              (agt.indexOf("windows 16-bit")!=-1));

// NOTE: Reliable detection of Win98 may not be possible. It appears that:
//       - On Nav 4.x and before you'll get plain "Windows" in userAgent.
//       - On Mercury client, the 32-bit version will return "Win98", but
```

Listing 18.3   (continued)

```
//          the 16-bit version running on Win98 will still return "Win95".
this.win98 = ((agt.indexOf("win98")!=-1) || (agt.indexOf("windows 98")!=-
1));
this.winnt = ((agt.indexOf("winnt")!=-1) || (agt.indexOf("windows nt")!=-
1));
this.win32 = (this.win95 || this.winnt || this.win98 ||
            ((this.major >= 4) && (navigator.platform == "Win32")) ||
            (agt.indexOf("win32")!=-1) || (agt.indexOf("32bit")!=-1));

this.winme = ((agt.indexOf("win 9x 4.90")!=-1));
this.win2k = ((agt.indexOf("windows nt 5.0")!=-1));

this.os2   = ((agt.indexOf("os/2")!=-1) ||
            (navigator.appVersion.indexOf("OS/2")!=-1) ||
            (agt.indexOf("ibm-webexplorer")!=-1));

this.mac   = (agt.indexOf("mac")!=-1);
// hack ie5 js version for mac
if (this.mac && this.ie5up) this.js = 1.4;
this.mac68k = (this.mac && ((agt.indexOf("68k")!=-1) ||
                        (agt.indexOf("68000")!=-1)));
this.macppc = (this.mac && ((agt.indexOf("ppc")!=-1) ||
                        (agt.indexOf("powerpc")!=-1)));

this.sun   = (agt.indexOf("sunos")!=-1);
this.sun4  = (agt.indexOf("sunos 4")!=-1);
this.sun5  = (agt.indexOf("sunos 5")!=-1);
this.suni86= (this.sun && (agt.indexOf("i86")!=-1));
this.irix  = (agt.indexOf("irix") !=-1);      // SGI
this.irix5 = (agt.indexOf("irix 5") !=-1);
this.irix6 = ((agt.indexOf("irix 6") !=-1) || (agt.indexOf("irix6") !=-1));
this.hpux  = (agt.indexOf("hp-ux")!=-1);
this.hpux9 = (this.hpux && (agt.indexOf("09.")!=-1));
this.hpux10= (this.hpux && (agt.indexOf("10.")!=-1));
this.aix   = (agt.indexOf("aix") !=-1);        // IBM
this.aix1  = (agt.indexOf("aix 1") !=-1);
this.aix2  = (agt.indexOf("aix 2") !=-1);
this.aix3  = (agt.indexOf("aix 3") !=-1);
this.aix4  = (agt.indexOf("aix 4") !=-1);
this.linux = (agt.indexOf("inux")!=-1);
this.sco   = (agt.indexOf("sco")!=-1) || (agt.indexOf("unix_sv")!=-1);
```

Example: Browser Sniffing, the Correct Way

Listing 18.3   *(continued)*

```
    this.unixware = (agt.indexOf("unix_system_v")!=-1);
    this.mpras    = (agt.indexOf("ncr")!=-1);
    this.reliant  = (agt.indexOf("reliantunix")!=-1);
    this.dec    = ((agt.indexOf("dec")!=-1) || (agt.indexOf("osf1")!=-1) ||
                  (agt.indexOf("dec_alpha")!=-1) ||
(agt.indexOf("alphaserver")!=-1) ||
                  (agt.indexOf("ultrix")!=-1) || (agt.indexOf("alphastation")!=-
1));
    this.sinix = (agt.indexOf("sinix")!=-1);
    this.freebsd = (agt.indexOf("freebsd")!=-1);
    this.bsd = (agt.indexOf("bsd")!=-1);
    this.unix  = ((agt.indexOf("x11")!=-1) || this.sun || this.irix || this.hpux
||
                  this.sco ||this.unixware || this.mpras || this.reliant ||
                  this.dec || this.sinix || this.aix ||
                  this.linux || this.bsd || this.freebsd);

    this.vms   = ((agt.indexOf("vax")!=-1) || (agt.indexOf("openvms")!=-1));
}

var is;
var isIE3Mac = false;
// this section is designed specifically for IE3 for the Mac

if ((navigator.appVersion.indexOf("Mac")!=-1) &&
    (navigator.userAgent.indexOf("MSIE")!=-1) &&
(parseInt(navigator.appVersion)==3))
        isIE3Mac = true;
else   is = new Is();

//--> end hide JavaScript
</script>

<script language="JavaScript" type="text/javascript">
<!--
if (isIE3Mac) {
    document.write("You are operating Internet Explorer 3 on a Macintosh.")
    } else {
    for (property in is) {
       document.write("is."+property+":  "+eval("is."+property)+"<br />")
       }
```

Listing 18.3   *(continued)*

```
    }
//-->
</script>
</body>
</html>
```

To use the sniffer script unaltered simply do two things:

- Test the `isIE3Mac` object. If it is `true`, you're done.

- If it is `false`, use the appropriately named properties of the `is` object as `Boolean()` values to determine your browser forks. Thus, instead of `document.layers`, use `is.nav4`. For Netscape 6, use `is.nav6`.

This is demonstrated in Listing 18.4. For a script that uses a lot of browser-specific features, the advantages of using the script in Listing 18.3 quickly become obvious.

Listing 18.4   *An Example Using the Sniffer Script*

```
<html>
<body>
<script language="JavaScript" type="text/javascript" src="sniffer.js"></script>
<!-- Ultimate client-side JavaScript client sniff. Version 3.02
(C) Netscape Communications 1999-2001.  Permission granted to reuse and
distribute.
Original URI:  http://www.mozilla.org/docs/web-
developer/sniffer/browser_type_oo.html
-->
<script language="JavaScript" type="text/javascript">
<!--
if (is.nav4) {
    // Netscape-specific code
    alert("Netscape Communica\tor 4.x")
    }
if (is.ie4up) {
    // Internet Explorer-specific code
    alert("Microsoft Internet Explorer 4.x+")
    }
if (is.nav6) {
    // Netscape 6-specific code
    alert("Netscape 6")
    }
```

Example: Browser Sniffing, the Correct Way

Listing 18.4   *(continued)*

```
// -->
</script>
</body>
</html>
```

CHAPTER 19

screen

Browser/JavaScript Version	Created By
Nav4/JavaScript 1.2	Browser
IE4/Jscript 3.0	Browser
IE5/Jscript 5.0	Browser
IE5.5/JScript 5.5	Browser
Nav6/JavaScript 1.5	Browser

Note

Implemented in Nav4+, IE4+

Property of `window` object

This object and all properties (except for `bufferDepth` and `updateInterval`) are read-only.

Description

The `screen` object describes the client computer's screen settings in detail. Although this object doesn't have much information in it, like the `navigator` object, what it does provide you can use to determine which page a client browser should go to, or which code to execute. It is important to realize that all windows objects have a screen property, but the screen object is unique for every `window` object. Also, although you typically can add properties to an object, adding properties to the `screen` object in Internet Explorer 5.5 will cause an error to be thrown.

Properties

availHeight

JavaScript 1.2+, JScript 3.0+

Nav4+, IE4+

Syntax

```
[var x =] screen.availHeight
```

The `availHeight` property of the `screen` object describes the number of pixels available from top to bottom that the browser may occupy on the visible screen. This includes the areas of the screen occupied by features such as the browser's title bar, navigation buttons, and the content window. It does not include areas of the screen the operating system reserves for itself on the screen (example: the Windows 95 taskbar, where the Start button resides). You can use `screen.height` to determine the size of a browser, but this will result in some content being obstructed and annoy users.

availLeft

JavaScript 1.2+

Nav4+

Syntax

```
[var x =] screen.availLeft
```

The `availLeft` property of the `screen` object describes the leftmost pixel on the viewable screen available for the browser to use. (Moving a browser left of this point can cause problems.) If a feature such as the Microsoft Office Shortcut Bar resides on the left side, this will increase `screen.availLeft` and decrease `screen.availWidth`, even when you use the Auto-Hide feature. This is because the Shortcut Bar does not allow a program to overlap its leftmost edge.

availTop

JavaScript 1.2+

Nav4+

Syntax

```
[var x =] screen.availTop
```

The `availTop` property of the `screen` object describes the topmost pixel on the viewable screen available for the browser to use. (Moving a browser above this point can cause problems.) If a feature such as the Microsoft Office Shortcut Bar resides at the top of the screen, this will increase `screen.availTop` and decrease `screen.availHeight`, even when you use the Auto-Hide feature. This is because the Shortcut Bar does not allow a program to overlap its topmost edge.

availWidth

JavaScript 1.2+, JScript 3.0+

Nav4+, IE4+

Syntax

```
[var x =] screen.availWidth
```

The availWidth property of the screen object describes the number of pixels available from left to right that the browser may occupy on the visible screen. This includes features such as the browser's sidebars and the content window. It does not include areas of the screen the operating system reserves for itself on the screen (example: the Windows 95 taskbar, where the Start button resides). Again you can use the screen.width property to size a window, but this can cause some content to be obstructed and annoy users.

bufferDepth

JScript 3.0+

IE4+

Syntax

```
[var x =] screen.bufferDepth [= depthNum]
```

The bufferDepth property of the screen object allows you to explicitly set the color depth of items stored in the browser window but not on the visible screen (think scrolling to understand this). The idea is you can set the buffer to one value, and when it appears on the visible screen, the browser can restore the intended color-depth. This can save time in graphics-intensive pages in rendering.

If you set this property to a value other than 0, 1, 4, 8, 16, or 32, the browser will reset it to –1 and execute default buffering at the normal color-depth. The default value is 0 and causes no buffering.

colorDepth

JavaScript 1.2+, JScript 3.0+

Nav4+, IE4+

Syntax

```
[var x =] screen.colorDepth
```

The colorDepth property of the screen object returns the number of bits the Web page currently has enabled in the browser. An 8-bit graphics card supports 256 colors.

16-bit graphics cards support 65,536 colors, the "high-color" setting on Win9x systems. 24-bit graphics cards support 16,777,216 colors: the "true-color" setting on Win9x systems. Some systems support 32-bit color depths: 4,294,976,296 colors.

For Netscape browsers, the use of a color palette overrides this setting. For Internet Explorer browsers, a setting to `bufferDepth` other than 0 or –1 matches `colorDepth` to the set `bufferDepth` value.

fontSmoothingEnabled

JScript 3.0+

IE4+

Syntax

```
[var boolValue =] screen.fontSmoothingEnabled
```

The `fontSmoothingEnabled` property of the `screen` object is primarily available for information purposes. For Win98 and later systems (and also Win95 Plus!), there is a setting in the Control Panel: Display for F/S (font smoothing). When the client has checked this option true, the property returns `true`. Otherwise, it returns `false`, including on computers that do not support this feature. (For instance, my Win95 system will return `undefined`, which in a conditional statement will evaluate to `false` anyway.)

height

JavaScript 1.2+, JScript 3.0+

Nav4+, IE4+

Syntax

```
[var y =] screen.height
```

The `height` property of the `screen` object describes the total height, in pixels, the operating system uses for the client machine's display. This includes the taskbar in Windows-based systems.

pixelDepth

JavaScript 1.2+

Nav4+

Syntax

```
[var x =] screen.pixelDepth
```

The `pixelDepth` property of the `screen` object tells the color-depth number of bits the operating system natively has enabled. See `colorDepth` earlier in this chapter for a more complete description.

Because Internet Explorer supports the `colorDepth` property and not the `pixelDepth` property, I recommend you use the `colorDepth` property.

updateInterval

JScript 3.0+

IE4+

Syntax

```
[var x =] screen.updateInterval [= mSec]
```

The `updateInterval` property of the `screen` object tells the browser to refresh the screen rendering of its Web page every certain number of milliseconds. You can explicitly set this value if you wish, but doing so may cause the page's quality of rendering to falter. Setting this value to 0, the default, lets Internet Explorer determine how often to "repaint" the Web page on the screen.

width

JavaScript 1.2+, JScript 3.0+

Nav4+, IE4+

Syntax

```
[var x =] screen.width
```

The `width` property of the `screen` object describes the total width, in pixels, the operating system uses for the client machine's display. This includes the taskbar in Windows-based systems.

Example: Redirecting Based on Screen Resolution

One of the scenarios I face in my JavaScript Laboratory is the layout of a page. For instance, I want my pages visible to the client computer without horizontal scrolling. However, I designed my system on an 800×600 screen resolution. Today, this is the standard, but many people still operate on a 640×480 resolution. (You may recall my rant in the previous chapter about supporting everybody; it applies to screen dimensions as well.)

So I need a special section for people who support a smaller resolution. Building a directory for it on my server is not hard. In my frameset directory, I can include a script so the URIs point to the directory appropriate for a user's resolution as seen in Listing 19.1.

Listing 19.1   *Detecting Screen Resolution and Redirecting Appropriately*

```
<html>
<script language="JavaScript" type="text/javascript">
<!--
if (screen.width < 800) {
    var baseDir = "http://jslab.isamillionaire.com/latest/x640/"
    } else {
    var baseDir = "http://jslab.isamillionaire.com/latest/x800/"
    }
//-->
// Note:
// This file just shows the script.
// Listing 19.3 is the one that works.
</script>
<frameset cols="25%,*">
    <frame name="tree" src="about:blank" >
    <frame name="main" src="about:blank" >
    </frameset>
</html>
```

With this script, I can use `javascript:` baseDir + URIs to change frame `location.href` properties appropriately as shown in Listing 19.2.

Listing 19.2   *Using the Screen Information to Link to the Appropriate Directory*

```
<html>
<body>
<p>
<a href="javascript:void 0" onclick="this.href=top.baseDir+'19list02.htm'"
 target="main">Click Here</a>
</p>
</body>
</html>
```

It doesn't get much simpler than this to ensure correct redirection. The first file determines which set of frames is appropriate and sets a variable for the appropriate path. All subsequent frame links can be automatically adjusted by using that variable. The second listing demonstrates this. Then just setting aside a special directory for the lesser resolution pages and redesigning their interfaces appropriately gets the job done.

If you want to test how this works on a local machine, try Listing 19.3 in place of Listing 19.1 and substitute the appropriate separation character for your machine. If you try this example on Netscape 4 you'll notice another browser opens instead of the file being loaded into the frame on the right as in Netscape 6 and Internet Explorer 5.5. So you still have to deal with the different ways the browsers handle frames.

Listing 19.3   *Local Machine Emulation of Directory Selection*

```
<html>
<script language="JavaScript" type="text/javascript">
<!--
baseDir = location.pathname.substr(0,location.pathname.lastIndexOf('\\')+1)
// Note: This is for IE, for Netscape or Linux use lastIndexOf("/")
// Likewise for Macs substitute the appropriate separation character
// for your browser
//-->
</script>
<frameset cols="25%,*">
   <frame name="tree" src="19list02.htm" />
   <frame name="main" src="about:blank" />
   </frameset>
</html>
```

PART III

Document Object Model for HTML Documents

CHAPTER

CHAPTER 20

Core DOM Objects

The Document Object Model (DOM) is a representation of each document as a hierarchy of objects. This includes the document itself as an object. This chapter explains the core features of the Document Object Model, implemented in Internet Explorer 5 and Netscape 6.

The DOM, in short, provides a standardized way for languages such as JavaScript to access and manipulate documents in general. This includes editing form fields (a feature available since the earliest days of JavaScript) and tables (a feature available only with the DOM). The DOM applies primarily to XML and HTML documents, with some XML languages (such as SVG and MathML) having their own object models which extend the Core DOM. (The Core DOM applies to all XML and HTML documents; the HTML DOM, covered in most later chapters, applies only to HTML documents.)

> **Note**
>
> The W3C created the standardized Document Object Model as a response to differences between Netscape and Internet Explorer in their own DOMs. Since then, both browser companies have attempted to comply with the W3C DOM. Netscape 6's DOM compliance is the strongest of the browsers, with Netscape 4 and Internet Explorer 5 as the weakest.
>
> In a couple of places, I discuss features not in the current browser DOMs. Future editions of Netscape or Internet Explorer may have them.

Unlike ECMAScript objects, you cannot construct these objects using the `var x = new Object()` syntax; that is, the `new` and constructor function arrangement does not work. Likewise, there are no literal representations of these objects. Instead, these objects exist as part of the document from which they derive, or you create them from the `document` object with specific methods for that purpose, such as `document.createElement()`.

Beginning with DOM Level 2, namespace support exists in the DOM. Namespaces are a way of embedding XML documents written in one XML language in XML documents written in another. I cover namespaces in far more detail in Chapter 36, "XML-Related Technologies and Their DOMs."

The W3C recommends against mixing namespace-designated properties and methods with DOM Level 1 properties and methods. Use either namespace-enabled methods or namespace-disabled methods within a document; do not use both in the same document.

> **Note**
>
> Internet Explorer 5.0 does not support namespace-enabled methods.

In this chapter, you will see a few XML documents. For these, having both Netscape 6 and Internet Explorer 5+ becomes very valuable. Without CSS or XSLT, Internet Explorer 5+ applies an internal default stylesheet to show you the structure of the XML document, color-coded for tags. The black sections represent what a browser would normally render as plain text. Netscape 6 literally renders the page according to the XML specification, showing nothing a CSS or XSLT stylesheet does not require. (The exception comes from using HTML-namespaced elements. See Chapter 36 for an introduction to this concept.)

Before I enter into descriptions of the various interfaces, I should note the most important ones are `Node` and `Document`. The `Document` interface is the skeleton of the DOM, and `Node` objects are the various bones and joints in that skeleton. Often interfaces in this chapter will refer to these two interfaces, and so I recommend you review them in particular.

Attr

JavaScript 1.5, JScript 5.0+

Nav6, IE5+

Descends from `Node` interface

`nodeName`: Attribute name

`nodeType`: 2

`nodeValue`: Attribute value

Description

The `Attr` interface represents attributes of elements. Each `Attr` node is an attribute of a particular element. You can use the various methods of the `Element` interface to reach an attribute's node (if the method has the word "Node" in its name), and from there correctly reach any entities or other properties of the attribute you so desire.

Some of the properties for `Attr` nodes are automatically `null`. For instance, `parentNode`, `nextSibling`, and `previousSibling` are all `null`. The reason for this is attributes technically do not fit in the tree of nodes for a document. (Elements isolate attributes in a separate `NamedNodeMap` object—the former's `attributes` property. See the `Node` interface later in this chapter for details.)

Properties

name

JavaScript 1.5

Nav6

Syntax

`var x = AttrNode.name`

The name property of Attr nodes refers to the name of the attribute. Attributes in XML and HTML take the form *name="value"*. The read-only name property is also a synonym for the Node interface's nodeName property as it applies to attributes. See nodeName under Node.

ownerElement

JavaScript 1.5

Nav6

Syntax

```
var x = AttrNode.ownerElement
```

The ownerElement property of Attr nodes is a read-only reference to the Element object which holds the this object as an attribute.

specified

JavaScript 1.5

Nav6

Syntax

```
var boolValue = AttrNode.specified
```

The specified property of Attr nodes is a read-only true or false value indicating whether the document or the client explicitly set the value of the this object to a specific value. If the client removes the attribute, this attribute is set to false. An attribute you create has this property set to true.

value

JavaScript 1.5

Nav6, IE6

Syntax

```
[var x =] AttrNode.value [= valueString]
```

The value property of Attr nodes returns a string value containing the value of the attribute. Optionally, you can set it by giving a string; this sets the this object's childNodes property (see the Node interface in this chapter) to a NodeList containing one node. The node is a Text node containing the string you fed to the property.

Methods

The Attr node provides no methods beyond those given in the Node interface.

CDATASection

JavaScript 1.5, JScript 5.0+

Nav6, IE5+

Descends from Text interface

nodeName: "#cdata-section"

nodeType: 4

nodeValue: All characters contained within the CDATA section

Description

CDATA sections describe areas where source code appears instead of what it symbolizes. This is much like the deprecated <xmp>...</xmp> tag of HTML. Literally nothing in these sections may be treated as markup; it is all plaintext to an XML parser.

A CDATA section has a prefix of <![CDATA[and a suffix of]]>, indicating where the CDATA section begins and ends, respectively.

Depending on the context, a CDATA section may render or it may not. Independent of any other markup, it will render.

CDATA sections do not exist in HTML 4.0, but they do exist in XHTML 1.0. Therefore, you must take care to note the document's mime-type (or for local files, the extension) when writing your source code.

Finally, although CDATA sections inherit from the Text interface, the Text interface inherits from the CharacterData interface. So I recommend you read the CharacterData interface (immediately after this one) before jumping halfway through the chapter.

Properties

The CDATASection interface provides no properties beyond those the Text interface defines.

Methods

The CDATASection interface provides no methods beyond those the Text interface defines.

CharacterData

JavaScript 1.5, JScript 3.0+

Nav6, IE5+

Descends from Node interface

Description

The CharacterData interface represents character data (such as scripts or text). As there is no createNode() method for creating a Node object, there is no createCharacterDataNode() method for creating a CharacterData object. This interface, like Node, defines a common group of characteristics for several objects.

Character data is simply anything that is not markup data. This includes <![CDATA[...]]>, known as CDATA sections (for character data sections) and Text nodes. Like the now-deprecated <xmp>...</xmp> tags, anything in these sections the browser must treat as plain text.

Properties

data

JavaScript 1.5, JScript 5.0+

Nav6, IE5+

Syntax

```
[var x =] cData.data [= dataString]
```

The data property of CharacterData nodes returns the contents of the node as a string value. If you so desire, you may change the contents of the node by setting this property to another string.

length

JavaScript 1.5, JScript 5.0+

Nav6, IE5+

Syntax

```
var x = cData.length
```

The `length` property of `CharacterData` nodes returns the number of characters in the character data section.

Methods

appendData()

JavaScript 1.5

Nav6

Syntax

```
cData.appendData(dataString)
```

The `appendData()` method of `CharacterData` nodes adds the first argument, a string value, to the end of the `this` object's contents. Similar to saying `this.data +=` `dataString`, where `dataString` is the first argument.

deleteData()

JavaScript 1.5

Nav6

Syntax

```
cData.deleteData(startIndex, length)
```

The `deleteData()` method of `CharacterData` nodes removes characters from the `this` object starting from a zero-based index equal to the first argument, a number. (By zero-based index, I mean the first character the engine refers to as 0.) You risk an exception if the first argument is not a valid index number for the `this` argument (for instance, if it is negative or at least the length.) The method removes a number of characters equal to the second argument.

insertData()

JavaScript 1.5

Nav6

Syntax

`cData.insertData(startIndex, newString)`

The `insertData()` method of `CharacterData` nodes splices in characters to the `this` object starting from a zero-based index equal to the first argument, a number. (By zero-based index, I mean the first character the engine refers to as 0.) The method adds in the contents of the second argument, a string value.

replaceData()

JavaScript 1.5

Nav6

Syntax

`cData.replaceData(startIndex, cutLength, newString)`

The `replaceData()` method of `CharacterData` nodes acts as a combination of the `deleteData()` and `insertData()` methods. First, it removes the characters from the `this` object starting from a zero-based index equal to the first argument, a number. (By zero-based index, I mean the first character the engine refers to as 0.) The method removes a number of characters equal to the second argument. Then it adds in, at the same index number, the contents of the third argument, a string value.

substringData

JavaScript 1.5

Nav6

Syntax

`cData.substringData(startIndex, length)`

The `substringData()` method of `CharacterData` nodes returns a portion of the `this` object's data, starting at the first zero-based index number given as its first argument. The second argument becomes the `length` of the returned string, designating how many characters the substringData() method copies from this. This method is similar to the substr() method of strings. (See Chapter 4, "String()," for details.)

Example: Manipulating Character Data

Listing 20.1 takes a simple character data string (in this case, a Text node), and edits it piece by piece, using each of the methods listed previously. Though I don't use them explicitly, the properties and methods of strings are available for use on the data property.

Listing 20.1   *A Few Uses of Character Data Nodes (Nav6)*

```
<?xml version="1.0" ?>
<!DOCTYPE html PUBLIC "-//W3C//DTD XHTML 1.0 Transitional//EN"
➥ "DTD/xhtml1-transitional.dtd">
<html xmlns="http://www.w3.org/1999/xhtml" >
<head><title></title></head>
<body>
<p id="me">red, green, blue</p>
<script language="JavaScript" type="text/javascript">
<!--
function go() {
   var cData = document.getElementById("me").childNodes[0]
   var pre = document.createElement("pre")
   var pre_text = "cData.data = " + cData.data + "\n"
   pre_text += "cData.data.length = " + cData.data.length + "\n"
   pre_text += "cData.length = " + cData.length + "\n"
   cData.appendData(", yellow")
   // "red, green, blue, yellow"
   cData.deleteData(5, 7) // removes "green, "
   cData.insertData(5, "purple, ")
   // "red, purple, blue, yellow"
   cData.replaceData(0, 4, "white,")
   // "white, purple, blue, yellow"
   pre_text += "After mutations, cData.substringData(15, 4) = "
   pre_text += cData.substringData(15, 4)
   pre.appendChild(document.createTextNode(pre_text))
   document.body.appendChild(pre)
   }
//-->
</script>
<a href="javascript:go()">Change colors</a>
<!-- Results:
```

Listing 20.1   *(continued)*

```
cData.data = red, green, blue
cData.data.length = 16
cData.length = 16
After mutations, cData.substringData(15, 4) = blue
-->
</body>
</html>
```

Comment

JavaScript 1.5, JScript 5.0+

Nav6, IE5+

Descends from `CharacterData` interface

nodeName: "#comment" ("!" in IE5, IE5.5)

nodeType: 8 (1 in IE5, IE5.5)

nodeValue: The text between the opening and closing comments (null in IE5)

Description

By now, you have seen comment tags everywhere throughout this book and in JavaScript development. (In case you haven't, it's <!--.....-->.)

Comments serve little other purpose than internal documentation in a Web page. In Chapter 13, "JavaScript Syntax," I covered the syntax for JavaScript comments; here I cover HTML and XML comments.

Nothing you put in a comment tag will render on the screen. HTML rendering ignores any such lines entirely. The DOM parser of the browser may decide to remove such comment lines. (Netscape 6 does, for XML documents. This book uses them in listings because the intent is for you to save the listings as HTML documents, even though technically they are HTML documents and XML documents simultaneously.) As a result, in certain cases, you may not even see comment nodes in a document's object tree.

Properties

The `Comment` interface provides no properties beyond those the `CharacterData` interface defines.

Methods

The Comment interface provides no methods beyond those the CharacterData interface defines.

Document

JavaScript 1.5, JScript 5.0+

Nav6, IE5+

Descends from Node interface

nodeName: "#document" (undefined in IE5)

nodeType: 9 (undefined in IE5)

nodeValue: null

Description

This object represents the HTML or XML document as a whole. This is the starting point for all access to a document from a JavaScript.

Chapter 23, "HTMLDocument/document," describes the document object, which is an extension of this object, in some detail. You cannot access the Document object as the W3C defines it, but you can access the document object of a window object, which is effectively the same thing.

This interface and the DOMImplementation interface are the only interfaces the DOM allows to create other nodes of any object type. (It does not allow the creation of a generic Node object; you must create specific types of nodes.)

Properties

doctype

JavaScript 1.5

Nav6.1+, IE6

Syntax

```
alert(document.doctype)
```

The doctype property of Document nodes reflects the DocumentType node of this document, which I describe later in this chapter. If the document has no DocumentType node or is served as text/html, this property returns null.

documentElement

JavaScript 1.5, JScript 5.0+

Nav6, IE5+

Syntax

```
var rootElement = document.documentElement
```

The `documentElement` property of `Document` nodes returns the root element of the document. In HTML documents, this is the `HTMLHtmlElement`, denoted by `<html>...</html>`. Likewise, SVG documents have a root element denoted by `<svg>...</svg>`. (However, it is not the language name but the `<!DOCTYPE ...>` tag that determines the root element.)

All XML and HTML documents must have exactly one top-level element; the following is not well-formed HTML:

```
<html>
<body>
<p>Hello World</p>
</body>
</html>
<script language="JavaScript" type="text/javascript">
<!--
window.open("adbanner.html")
//-->
</script>
```

The `<script />` element, according to HTML 4, must be contained within the `<head>...</head>` element (which is missing, another requirement of HTML 4), or the `<body>...</body>` element. There are other HTML requirements this document violates, but these are the most significant. (The W3C HTML Validator at `http://validator.w3.org` is the best source for validating HTML documents.)

implementation

JavaScript 1.5

Nav6, IE6

Syntax

```
var docDOMImplem = document.implementation
```

The `implementation` property of `Document` nodes returns the `DOMImplementation` object for the document. The `DOMImplementation` object I discuss later in this chapter.

Methods

createAttribute()

JavaScript 1.5

Nav6, IE6

Syntax

```
var AttrNode = document.createAttribute(attrName)
```

The `createAttribute()` method of `Document` nodes creates an `Attr` node for the document, with a `name` property equal to the first argument. See the `Attr` and `Element` objects for more details.

createAttributeNS()

JavaScript 1.5

Nav6

Syntax

```
var AttrNode = document.createAttributeNS(nsURI, attrName)
```

The `createAttributeNS()` method of `Document` nodes creates an `Attr` node for the document, with a `name` property equal to the second argument and a `namespaceURI` property equal to the first argument. See the `Attr` and `Element` objects for more details.

createCDATASection()

JavaScript 1.5

Nav6

Syntax

```
var xmp = document.createCDATASection(cdataString)
```

The createCDATASection() method of Document nodes creates a CDATA section (<![CDATA[...]]>) for the document, its contents being equal to the first argument. CDATA sections are like the now-deprecated <xmp>...</xmp> tags of HTML: everything, including markup, inside them renders as plain text. See the CDATASection object for more details.

> **Note**
> HTML documents do not support this feature. XML documents do. This is one case where the mime type of the document matters.

createComment()

JavaScript 1.5

Nav6, IE6

Syntax

```
var commentNode = document.createComment(contents)
```

The createComment() method of Document nodes creates a comment section (<!--...-->) whose contents are equal to the first argument of the method call. See the Comment object for more details.

createDocumentFragment()

JavaScript 1.5

Nav6, IE6

Syntax

```
var docFrag = document.createDocumentFragment()
```

The createDocumentFragment() method of Document nodes creates a blank DocumentFragment object. See the DocumentFragment object for more details.

createElement()

JavaScript 1.5, JScript 5.0+

Nav6, IE5+

Syntax

```
var newElement = document.createElement(tagName)
```

The `createElement()` method of `Document` nodes creates a new `Element` node, essentially a markup tag, with a tag name equal to the first argument. For example, `document.createElement('p')` creates `<p></p>` as an `Element` node and returns it to the script.

If the method's argument is a valid HTML element name and the document is an HTML document, the `Element` object this method creates inherits the properties and methods of its corresponding HTML DOM implementation. This applies in a more generic sense: if the document is a particular type of XML document and the first argument fits a valid element name in the document, the element this method creates inherits the properties and methods appropriate for the element name in the document's DOM.

createElementNS()

JavaScript 1.5

Nav6

Syntax

```
var newElement = document.createElementNS(nsURI, tagName)
```

The `createElementNS()` method of `Document` nodes creates a new `Element` node, essentially a markup tag, with a qualified name equal to the second argument, and a `namespaceURI` property equal to the first argument. For example, `document.createElementNS('http://www.w3.org/1999/xhtml','p')` creates a `<p></p>` element in the XHTML namespace and returns it to the script. (I explain namespaces in more detail in Chapter 36, "XML-Related Technologies and Their DOMs".)

If the method's second argument is a valid HTML element name and the first argument is an HTML namespace, the `Element` node this method creates inherits the properties and methods of its corresponding HTML DOM implementation. This applies in a more generic sense: if the first argument fits a namespace of the XML document and the second argument fits a valid element name in the namespace, the element this method creates inherits the properties and methods appropriate for the element name in the namespace's DOM.

See the `Element` node for more details.

createEntityReference()

JavaScript 1.5

Nav6

Syntax

```
var entityRef = document.createEntityReference(entityName)
```

The `createEntityReference()` method of `Document` nodes creates an `EntityReference` object, which refers to the entity the first argument names in the document. See the `Entity` and `EntityReference` objects for more details.

createProcessingInstruction()

JavaScript 1.5

Nav6

Syntax

```
var procIns = document.createProcessingInstruction(target, info)
```

The `createProcessingInstruction()` method of `Document` nodes creates a `ProcessingInstruction` node, with the first argument identifying the application for which the object is meant, and the second argument identifying what information to pass to the application. See the `ProcessingInstruction` object for more details.

> **Note**
> HTML documents do not support this feature. XML documents do. This is one case where the mime type of the document matters.

createTextNode()

JavScript1.5, JScript 5.0+

Nav6, IE5+

Syntax

```
var myText = document.createTextNode(text)
```

The createTextNode() method of Document nodes creates a Text node containing the value of the first argument. See the Text interface for more details.

getElementById()

JavaScript 1.5, JScript 5.0+

Nav6, IE5+

Syntax

```
var myElement = document.getElementById(idStr)
```

The getElementById() method of Document nodes returns the element within the document having the matching identification attribute value. (An identification attribute is an attribute the DTD or XML Schema names as such with the ID declaration. It is not necessarily the ID attribute.) Because identification attribute values are unique within a document, this method will return null or exactly one element from the document.

getElementsByTagName()

JavaScript 1.5, JScript 5.0+

Nav6, IE5+

Syntax

```
var elemList = document.getElementsByTagName(tagName)
```

The getElementsByTagName() method of Document nodes returns a NodeList object containing all elements within the document with a tagName property matching the first argument. If you use "*" as the argument for this method, it returns all elements in the document.

getElementsByTagNameNS()

JavaScript 1.5

Nav6

Syntax

```
var elemList = document.getElementsByTagNameNS(nameSpace, localTagName)
```

The `getElementsByTagNameNS()` method of `Document` nodes returns a `NodeList` object containing all elements within the document matching the namespace URI given in the first argument and the `localName` property given in the second argument. If you use `"*"` as the first argument for this method, it returns all elements within the document matching the second argument. If you use `"*"` as the second argument for this method, it returns all elements in the document for the chosen namespace.

importNode()

JavaScript 1.5

Nav6

Syntax

```
document.importNode(nodeObj, boolValue)
```

The `importNode()` method of `Document` nodes returns a clone of the first argument, which must be a `Node` object. The first argument belongs to a separate document. The second object, when set to `true`, tells the method to retrieve all child nodes as well—the entire tree, instead of just the one node. `Document` and `DocumentType` nodes may not be imported.

Example: Indenting All Paragraphs, the Hard Way

With Cascading Style Sheets, you can force any kind of styling changes you want. Though it's less efficient, you can also force styling changes through the Core DOM.

Listing 20.2 shows just such a procedure, by indenting each paragraph element of an HTML document. I use two features, the `getElementsByTagName` method of `Document` and the `setAttribute` and `getAttribute` methods of `Element`.

Listing 20.2   *Changing Element Properties, One by One (Netscape 6 Only)*

```
<?xml version="1.0" encoding="iso-8859-1"?>
<!DOCTYPE html PUBLIC "-//W3C//DTD XHTML 1.0 Transitional//EN"
    "http://www.w3.org/TR/xhtml1/DTD/xhtml1-transitional.dtd">
<html xmlns="http://www.w3.org/1999/xhtml">
<head>
<script language="JavaScript" type="text/javascript">
<!--
function go() {
    var paragraphs = document.getElementsByTagName("p")
    for (var y = 0; y < paragraphs.length; y++) {
```

Listing 20.2 *(continued)*

```
    paragraphs[y].setAttribute("style",paragraphs[y].getAttribute("style")+";
➡ text-indent: 30pt")
    alert(paragraphs[y].getAttribute("style")+"\n"+y)
    }
  }
//-->
</script>
</head>

<body>
<p>This is a test.</p>

<p style="text-indent: 15pt">This is an automatically indented paragraph.</p>

<pre>This is a false paragraph.</pre>

<p style="background-color:yellow">This is the last paragraph.</p>
<form>
<input type="button" onclick="go()" value="Indent paragraphs!" />
</form>
</body>
</html>
```

You may notice I set the style attribute of each p element by first getting the style attribute currently in place. This is to ensure I don't overwrite other styling attributes (such as the background color of the last paragraph).

In Chapters 24 and 33 ("Head Elements" and "Styling for HTML Elements," respectively), I will discuss other, better ways to implement styling changes.

DocumentFragment

JavaScript 1.5

Nav6

Descends from Node interface

nodeName: "#document-fragment"

nodeType: 11

nodeValue: null

Description

The DocumentFragment interface is almost identical to the Node interface, in that there are no additional methods or properties specific to DocumentFragment objects. The primary difference lies in how they attach nodes to a document's structure.

Any child nodes you append to a DocumentFragment node are, for all intents and purposes, held there. When you use a method to attach the DocumentFragment node to a master node in the document, the browser instead attaches the child nodes of the DocumentFragment node to the master node directly. The DocumentFragment node itself becomes irrelevant, and will not itself be attached. So what, you may ask. What good is the DocumentFragment interface then, anyway?

If you have a large group of nodes you want to attach to a single parent node, but you want to construct the group beforehand, use the DocumentFragment interface. Attach child nodes to the new object you create using the createDocumentFragment method of the Document interface, and then attach the new DocumentFragment object to your parent node. Instead of the DocumentFragment object being between the parent node and the object's child nodes, the object's child nodes then become child nodes of the parent node.

Properties

The DocumentFragment interface provides no properties beyond those the Node interface defines.

Methods

The DocumentFragment interface provides no methods beyond those the Node interface defines.

Example: Pasting a Series of Nodes Repeatedly

At this time, the following example does not work in Internet Explorer or Netscape 6, due to bugs in their software. I have verified this code is correct. (In the case of Internet Explorer, it simply hasn't been implemented yet.)

Listing 20.3 collects several nodes under one DocumentFragment object, and then posts two copies of the object as child nodes of two corresponding <p>...</p> elements. The idea is to keep code fragments reusable.

Listing 20.3   `DocumentFragment` *as a Container*

```
<?xml version="1.0" ?>
<!DOCTYPE html PUBLIC "-//W3C//DTD XHTML 1.0 Transitional//EN"
➥ "DTD/xhtml1-transitional.dtd">
<html xmlns="http://www.w3.org/1999/xhtml" >
<head><title></title></head>
<body>
<p id="one">One</p>
<p id="two">Two</p>
<script language="JavaScript" type="text/javascript">
<!--
var docFrag = document.createDocumentFragment()
var text1 = document.createTextNode("This is a text of the ")
var code2 = document.createElement("code")
var text2 = document.createTextNode("DocumentFragment ")
code2.appendChild(text2)
var text3 = document.createTextNode("interface.")

docFrag.appendChild(text1)
docFrag.appendChild(code2)
docFrag.appendChild(text3)

document.getElementById("one").appendChild(docFrag.cloneNode(true))
document.getElementById("two").appendChild(docFrag.cloneNode(true))
//-->
</script>
</body>
</html>
```

Note the use of the `cloneNode()` method from the `Node` interface, with a `true` argument. This ensures each paragraph element gets a fresh and complete copy of all nodes within the `DocumentFragment` object, without contaminating the `DocumentFragment` with information such as a `parentNode` property. You could do this a thousand times, and the original `DocumentFragment` object would not change.

DocumentType

JavaScript 1.5

Nav6

Descends from `Node` interface

nodeName: Document type name (`"html"`, `"svg"`, etc.) or `null`

nodeType: 10

nodeValue: `null`

Description

The `DocumentType` interface describes for us what kind of a document the local document is: an HTML document, an SVG document, another kind of XML document, and so on. It also provides a container for a read-only list of entities (see `Entity` and `EntityReference` for details) in the document.

The `DocumentType` object in each `Document` object is read-only; you may not change it. You can only set the document type of a document upon creation of the document. (See the `DOMImplementation` interface for details on creating `Document` and `DocumentType` objects.)

Properties

entities

JavaScript 1.5

Nav6

Syntax

```
var x = docType.entities
```

The `entities` property of `DocumentType` nodes is a `NamedNodeMap` object containing all first instances of entities the `DocumentType` defines. This object explicitly excludes parameter entities. (For more information, see `Entity` in this chapter.)

internalSubset

JavaScript 1.5

Nav6

Syntax

```
var x = docType.internalSubset
```

The `internalSubset` property of `DocumentType` nodes is a browser-dependent string describing the internal subset of the `this` object. (Note this is a new feature, and not very clearly defined. Mozilla 0.9, for instance, returns a blank string.)

name

JavaScript 1.5, JScript 5.0+

Nav6

Syntax

```
var x = docType.name
```

The `name` property of `DocumentType` nodes is a synonym for the `nodeName` of the `this` object. In the line

```
<!DOCTYPE html PUBLIC "-//W3C//DTD XHTML 1.0 Transitional//EN"
➥ "DTD/xhtml1-transitional.dtd">
```

the `name` property is `"html"`. See `nodeName` under the `Node` interface for details.

notations

JavaScript 1.5

Nav6

Syntax

```
var x = DocType.notations
```

The `notations` property of `DocumentType` nodes is a `NamedNodeMap` object containing all `Notation` nodes the document type definition provides. (See `Notation` for details.) In HTML this is `null`.

publicId

JavaScript 1.5

Nav6

Syntax

```
var x = DocType.publicId
```

The `publicId` property of `DocumentType` nodes refers to the public identification string, if one exists in the document type declaration, of the document. For the line

```
<!DOCTYPE html PUBLIC "-//W3C//DTD XHTML 1.0 Transitional//EN"
➥ "DTD/xhtml1-transitional.dtd">
```

the `publicId` property refers to `"-//W3C//DTD XHTML 1.0 Transitional//EN"`. This string basically summarizes what the DTD file of the system identifier defines.

systemId

JavaScript 1.5

Nav6

Syntax

```
var x = docType.systemId
```

The `systemId` property of `DocumentType` nodes refers to the system identification string of the document type declaration. For the line

```
<!DOCTYPE html PUBLIC "-//W3C//DTD XHTML 1.0 Transitional//EN"
➥ "DTD/xhtml1-transitional.dtd">
```

the system identifier is `"DTD/xhtml1-transitional.dtd"`. It basically points to the file containing the actual language definitions.

Methods

The `DocumentType` interface provides no methods beyond those the `Node` interface defines.

DOMImplementation

JavaScript 1.5

Nav6

Description

The `DOMImplementation` object provides an interface for determining what a browser supports of the DOM, and also allows for the creation of entirely new documents via the DOM. It is not a node in any way, but it is the `implementation` property of the `Document` object.

Properties

The DOMImplementation interface provides no properties.

Methods

createDocument()

JavaScript 1.5

Nav6

Syntax

```
var x = document.implementation.createDocument(namespaceURI, localName, docType)
```

The createDocument() method of DOMImplementation objects returns a new Document node. The first argument specifies the namespace the Document occupies. The second argument represents a local name for the root element of the Document node. The third argument is a DocumentType node you create using the createDocumentType() method I describe next.

createDocumentType()

JavaScript 1.5

Nav6

Syntax

```
var y = document.implementation.createDocumentType(localName, publicId,
➡ systemId)
```

The createDocumentType() method of DOMImplementation objects returns a new DocumentType node. The first argument specifies the root element the DocumentType node requires (the name property). The second and third arguments, respectively, are the public and system IDs of the returned DocumentType node.

hasFeature()

JavaScript 1.5

Nav6, IE5+

Syntax

```
var boolValue = document.implementation.hasFeature(featName, version)
```

The `hasFeature()` method of `DOMImplementation` objects returns `true` if the browser supports the feature named in the first argument, or `false` if it does not. The second argument allows for determining which levels of the DOM support the feature.

For example, the line

```
alert(document.implementation.hasFeature("HTML","1.0"))
```

returns `true` in Netscape 6. It's not quite a perfect barometer, however: Netscape returns `false` for the arguments `"Core"` and `"1.0"`.

Element

JavaScript 1.5, JScript 5.0+

Nav6, IE5+

Descends from `Node` interface

`nodeName`: Element tag name

`nodeType`: 1

`nodeValue`: null

Description

An element, in the simplest terms, is an opening markup tag and all attributes, and the closing markup tag matching the opening markup tag if there is one. For instance, `<html>...</html>` is an element, which in the HTML DOM is `HTMLHtmlElement`. If nodes define the basic building blocks, elements define the skeleton of a document.

Most elements, as you most certainly know, can (and often must) have child elements; `HTMLHtmlElement` requires `<head>...</head>` and `<body>...</body>`, or `<head>...</head>` and `<frameset>...</frameset>` for child elements. Such child elements are nodes in the parent element's `childNodes` property (described in the `Node` interface section).

HTML elements have special properties and methods beyond those described in this chapter; they all inherit properties and methods from the `HTMLElement` interface, described in Chapter 21, "HTMLElement." (`HTMLElement`, in turn, inherits from `Element`, so this section still applies.) Similarly, many XML languages such as MathML, SVG, and XSLT have their own extensions to `Element` for their specific elements.

The DOM specifications for XML documents recommend you access attributes as `Attr` nodes using the `getAttributeNode()`, `getAttributeNodeNS()`, `removeAttributeNode()`, `setAttributeNode()`, and `setAttributeNodeNS()` methods. For HTML and XHTML documents, it is perfectly safe to use `getAttribute()`, `getAttributeNS()`, `removeAttribute()`, `removeAttributeNS()`, `setAttribute()`, and `setAttributeNS()`—if the browser supports them.

Properties

tagName

JavaScript 1.5, JScript 3.0+

Nav6, IE4+

Syntax

```
var x = ElemNode.tagName
```

The `tagName` property of `Element` nodes is a synonym for the `Node` interface's `nodeName` property as it applies to elements. It's basically the name of the element. (In HTML, the `tagName` property is always uppercase; in XML, it matches the case of the element.) See `nodeName` under `Node`.

Methods

getAttribute()

JavaScript 1.5, JScript 3.0+

Nav6, IE5+

Syntax

```
var x = ElemNode.getAttribute(attName)
```

The `getAttribute()` method of `Element` nodes retrieves the attribute value of the attribute whose name matches the first argument, a string, and is also an attribute of the `this` object. The value this method returns is also a string, unless

- The attribute has no default value and was not explicitly set.
- The attribute has not been defined for the `this` object.

In either case, the method returns `""`, an empty string.

getAttributeNS()

JavaScript 1.5

Nav6

Syntax

```
var x = ElemNode.getAttributeNS(namespaceURI, attName)
```

The `getAttributeNS()` method of `Element` nodes retrieves the attribute value of the attribute whose namespace URI matches the first argument, a string, whose local name matches the second argument, a string, and is also an attribute of the `this` object. The value this method returns is also a string, unless

- The attribute has no default value and was not explicitly set.
- The attribute has not been defined for the `this` object.

In either case, the method returns `""`, an empty string.

getAttributeNode()

JavaScript 1.5

Nav6

Syntax

```
var x = ElemNode.getAttributeNode(attName)
```

The `getAttributeNode()` method of `Element` nodes retrieves the `Attr` node of the attribute whose name matches the first argument, a string, and is also an attribute of the `this` object. This method returns the `Attr` node object, unless the attribute has no default value and was not explicitly set. In this case, the method returns `null`.

getAttributeNodeNS()

JavaScript 1.5

Nav6

Syntax

```
var x = ElemNode.getAttributeNodeNS(namespaceURI, attName)
```

The getAttributeNodeNS() method of Element nodes retrieves the Attr node of the attribute whose namespace URI matches the first argument, a string, whose local name matches the second argument, a string, and is also an attribute of the this object. This method returns the Attr node object, unless the attribute has no default value and was not explicitly set. In this case, the method returns null.

getElementsByTagName()

JavaScript 1.5, JScript 5.0+

Nav6, IE5+

Syntax

```
var x = ElemNode.getElementsByTagName(tagName)
```

The getElementsByTagName() method of Element nodes retrieves all descendant elements of the this object that possess a tagName property equal to the first argument, a string. By descendant, I mean child elements, grandchild elements, great-grandchild elements, and so on. The retrieved collection of nodes it returns as a NodeList. If you use "*" as the argument for this method, it returns all elements in the document in Netscape 6.

Listing 20.5 shows the global reach of such a method.

getElementsByTagNameNS()

JavaScript 1.5

Nav6

Syntax

```
var x = ElemNode.getElementsByTagNameNS(namespaceURI, localName)
```

The getElementsByTagNameNS() method of Element nodes retrieves all descendant elements of the this object whose namespace URI matches the first argument, a string, and whose local name matches the second argument, a string. By descendant, I mean child elements, grandchild elements, great-grandchild elements, and so on. The retrieved collection of nodes it returns as a NodeList. If you use "*" as the argument for this method, it returns all elements in the document in Netscape 6.

hasAttribute()

JavaScript 1.5

Nav6

Syntax

```
var x = ElemNode.hasAttribute(attName)
```

The `hasAttribute()` method of `Element` nodes returns `true` if two conditions are met. The first is the `this` object must have an attribute whose name matches the first argument, a string. The second is that said attribute has been defined or has a default value. Otherwise, this method returns `false`.

hasAttributeNS()

JavaScript 1.5

Nav6

Syntax

```
var x = ElemNode.hasAttributeNS(namespaceURI, localName)
```

The `hasAttributeNS()` method of `Element` nodes returns `true` if the `this` object has a defined or default attribute whose namespace URI matches the first argument, a string, and whose local name matches the second argument, a string. Otherwise, this method returns `false`.

removeAttribute()

JavaScript 1.5, JScript 5.0+

Nav6, IE5+

Syntax

```
ElemNode.removeAttribute(attName)
```

The `removeAttribute()` method of `Element` nodes removes the attribute named in the first argument, a string. Afterward, if the attribute has a default value, the attribute's default value is set.

removeAttributeNS()

JavaScript 1.5

Nav6

Syntax

ElemNode.removeAttributeNS(*namespaceURI*, *localName*)

The removeAttributeNS() method of Element nodes removes the attribute with the namespace URI named in the first argument, a string, and the localname named in its second argument, also a string. Afterward, if the attribute has a default value, the attribute's default value is set.

setAttribute()

JavaScript 1.5, JScript 5.0+

Nav6, IE5+

Syntax

ElemNode.setAttribute(*attName*, *attValue*)

The setAttribute() method of Element nodes sets the attribute value of the attribute whose name matches the first argument, a string, and is also an attribute of the this object. The value this method sets is equal to the second argument, also a string. If this method replaces a current value, the method returns the old value of the attribute. Listing 20.1, earlier in this chapter, demonstrates this method.

setAttributeNS()

JavaScript 1.5

Nav6

Syntax

[var *x* =] *ElemNode*.setAttributeNS(*namespaceURI*, *qualifiedName*, *attValue*)

The setAttributeNS() method of Element nodes sets the attribute value of the attribute whose namespace URI matches the first argument, a string, whose local name matches the second argument, a string, and is also an attribute of the this object. The value this method sets is equal to the third argument, also a string.

setAttributeNode()

JavaScript 1.5

Nav6

Syntax

```
[var x =] ElemNode.setAttributeNode(AttrNode)
```

The setAttributeNode() method of Element nodes sets an Attr node, the first argument, under the this object's attributes according to the nodeName property. If this method replaces a current Attr node possessing the same nodeName property, the method returns the old Attr node.

> **Note**
> You must ensure the Attr node you attach does not already belong to another node; the cloneNode() method can help prevent this condition. (See cloneNode() under Node, earlier in this chapter.)

setAttributeNodeNS()

JavaScript 1.5

Nav6

Syntax

```
[var x =] ElemNode.setAttributeNodeNS(AttrNode)
```

The setAttributeNodeNS() method of Element nodes sets an Attr node, the first argument, under the this object's attributes according to the namespaceURI and localname properties. If this method replaces a current Attr node possessing the same namespaceURI and localname properties, the method returns the old Attr node.

Note you must ensure the Attr node you attach does not already belong to another node; the cloneNode method can help prevent this condition. (See cloneNode under Node, earlier in this chapter.)

Example: Descendant Nodes (Not Just Child Nodes)

Listing 20.4 takes advantage of the getElementsByTagName() method of Element objects to gather a listing of all <br /> elements under the <body>...</body> element.

The purpose here is not so much to do anything with them (
 elements are simply line breaks), but to count them. It is worth noting the getElementsByTagName() method does not stop at immediate child nodes, but goes to child nodes of the child nodes (grandchildren), and great-grandchildren, and so on.

Listing 20.4   *Descendant Nodes of an* Element *Node*

```
<?xml version="1.0" ?>
<!DOCTYPE html PUBLIC "-//W3C//DTD XHTML 1.0 Strict//EN"
➥   "DTD/xhtml1-strict.dtd">
<html xmlns="http://www.w3.org/1999/xhtml" >
<body id="one" onload="go()" >
<p id="two">This is a test<br />
 of how many
<code> break tags<br /> show up as </code>
 descendants of a <br />
 &lt;body> node.</p>
<script language="JavaScript" type="text/javascript">
<!--
function go() {
   var one = document.getElementById('one')
   alert(one.getElementsByTagName('br').length) // returns 3
   }
//-->
</script>
</body>
</html>
```

The <body>...</body> element has no <br /> child nodes, but through the <p>...</p> and <code>...</code> elements, it has three descendant <br /> nodes.

Entity

Not implemented in HTML (DOM 1)

Descends from Node interface

nodeName: Entity name

nodeType: 6

nodeValue: null

Description

Entities in XML and HTML are essentially shorthand abbreviations you can define in an XML language's DTD file for use elsewhere within either the DTD or a document written in that XML language. HTML 4.0 and XHTML 1.0 include a large number of entities in their DTD files.

Interestingly, an `Entity` node is not the same as its corresponding entity definition in the DTD. (Much like a `Function()` object is not the same as the function executing.) As far as the DOM concerns itself at this stage, entities fall into place in the document and DTD before the DOM parser gets to them.

Thus, all we have on `Entity` nodes is their identification strings and a reference to any given notation for the entity. Often, we cannot even find an `Entity` node in a document, where there may be thousands. This is because `Entity` nodes are outside the normal DOM tree, and have no parent nodes. (The idea is an entity should be transparent to a document's end-user.) The child nodes of an `Entity` node correspond to the entity's assigned value string.

So what kinds of entities are there, anyway? For a better definition, I suggest you read a book on XML. However, most Web developers are familiar with the `&lt;` entity, which in HTML produces a < character. This is known as a *general entity*. A *character entity* is the familiar Unicode designation of a character, such as `&#x41;` (which equals the letter A).

Parameter entities, used within a DTD for the DTD, are like strings in JavaScript: they hold a certain value for repeated use. The difference is parameter entities are read-only. One such parameter entity from XHTML 1.0 Transitional DTD is `<!ENTITY % heading "h1|h2|h3|h4|h5|h6">`. This defines for the DTD a common string named `%heading;` which contains `"h1|h2|h3|h4|h5|h6"`. Such entities can appear elsewhere in a DTD easily, even in other DTD entity definitions. For instance, another parameter entity from XHTML 1.0 Transitional DTD is

```
<!ENTITY % block
    "p | %heading; | div | %lists; | %blocktext; | isindex |fieldset | table">
```

Properties

notationName

Not implemented in HTML (DOM 1)

Syntax

```
var x = EntityNode.notationName
```

The notationName property of Entity nodes provides the name of the Notation node for this node's corresponding entity, if it has one. Otherwise, this property is equal to null.

publicId

Not implemented in HTML (DOM 1)

Syntax

```
var x = EntityNode.publicId
```

The publicId property of Entity nodes refers to the public identification string, if one exists in the document type declaration, of the corresponding entity. Otherwise, this property is equal to null.

The public identification string is a human-readable string summarizing what the entity describes.

systemId

Syntax

```
var x = EntityNode.systemId
```

The systemId property of Entity nodes refers to the system identification string, if one exists in the document type declaration, of the corresponding entity. Otherwise, this property is equal to null.

The system identification string is a URI reference to the document that the entity references.

Methods

The Entity interface provides no methods beyond those the Node interface defines.

EntityReference

Not implemented in HTML (DOM 1)

Descends from Node interface

nodeName: Entity name

nodeType: 5

nodeValue: null

Description

`EntityReference` objects define references to entities in a document. For instance, if you see `&lt;script&gt;` in an HTML document, you expect it to render the line "<script>" in the page, but not as an actual <script> tag.

You may not necessarily find any `EntityReference` objects in a document; DOM-compliant browsers may replace any such references with the value of the entity it references. This is just as well, for there are no properties or methods this object has that `Node` objects in general do not have.

If the browser does not replace `EntityReference` objects, their `childNodes` property matches that of the entity they reference.

Properties

The `EntityReference` interface provides no properties beyond those the `Node` interface defines.

Methods

The `EntityReference` interface provides no methods beyond those the `Node` interface defines.

Node

The `Node` interface is to the DOM what the `Object()` constructor function is to ECMAScript: it defines basic properties and methods all nodes in a document inherit.

You cannot create any object that is purely a `Node` object; each object in the DOM has its own features and definitions. There are element nodes (called `Element` objects), attribute nodes (called `Attr` objects), CDATA sections and comments (called `CDATASection` and `Comment` objects, respectively), `Document` nodes (for whole documents), and so on.

Nonetheless, the features the `Node` interface makes available ensure the DOM truly is object-oriented. It enables navigation throughout the document from any node to any other node, allows changes to child nodes of the node, and allows placement and removal of child nodes at will. A concrete understanding of this interface is a must for understanding the DOM.

> **Note**
> You cannot add an ancestor node of any node as a child node. For instance, you cannot add the root `<html>` element as a child of its child `<body>` element. This is unlike ECMAScript, where you can say `x.y.x = x`.

Properties

attributes

JavaScript 1.5, JScript 5.0+

Nav6, IE5+

Syntax

```
var x = NodeObj.attributes
```

The `attributes` property, for `Element` nodes, is a `NamedNodeMap` containing all attributes for the given element. Basically, it is an unordered collection of the attributes for the element. (See `NamedNodeMap` for more details.) For all other nodes, this property returns `null`.

childNodes

JavaScript 1.5, JScript 5.0+

Nav6, IE5+

Syntax

```
var x = NodeObj.childNodes
```

The `childNodes` property of `Node` objects is a `NodeList` containing all child nodes of the given node (the `this` object, in JavaScript terms). This includes text, comments, elements, CDATA sections, and so on. Listing 20.5 shows a sample of this.

Listing 20.5   *Seven Children in a Family of Nodes*

```
<html>
<body onload="go()">
<p id="test">This is a <br /> test of
<b>node length</b> in a sentence<!-- and should return 7-->.</p>
<script language="JavaScript" type="text/javascript">
```

Listing 20.5   *(continued)*

```
<!--
function go() {
    alert(document.getElementById("test").childNodes.length)
    }
//-->
</script>
</body>
</html>
```

How do you get seven child nodes out of one? Simple—you just have to break it down:

```
<p id="test">
This is a
<br />
 test of
<b>node length</b>
 in a sentence
<!-- and should return 7-->
 .
</p>
```

You don't count the opening and closing `<p>...</p>` tags, but each distinct type of content is a node. The first, third, fifth, and seventh nodes in this case are `Text` nodes. The second and fourth are `Element` nodes, and the sixth is a `Comment` node.

Caution

It's not quite as simple as that. Netscape and Mozilla have a very bad habit of inserting `Text` nodes between element tags on different lines. Internet Explorer does not do this.

To check it, simply ask each browser for `document.documentElement.childNodes.length` in a minimal XHTML document. Internet Explorer returns two: the `<head>...</head>` element and the `<body>...</body>` element. Netscape 6 returns three.

---

firstChild

JavaScript 1.5, JScript 5.0+

Nav6, IE5+

Syntax

```
var x = NodeObj.firstChild
```

The firstChild property of Node objects returns the first child node of the this object. This is equivalent to calling the childNodes[0] property of the this object.

If there are no child nodes to this node (for example, the node is an empty Element or a Text node), this returns null.

lastChild

JavaScript 1.5, JScript 5.0+

Nav6, IE5+

Syntax

```
var x = NodeObj.lastChild
```

The lastChild property of Node objects returns the last child node of the this object. This is equivalent to calling the childNodes[childNodes.length - 1] property of the this object.

If there are no child nodes to this node (for example, the node is an empty Element or a Text node), this returns null.

localName

JavaScript 1.5

Nav6

Syntax

```
var x = NodeObj.localName
```

The localName property of Node objects returns the local name of the element or attribute the this object represents. It works only with Element and Attr nodes, and then only those which existed previously in the document or which the client machine creates using DOM Level 2 methods. For Element nodes, these return the local tag name. In both of the following cases, the localName is "p" for XML documents, or "P" for HTML documents:

```
<p id="test">Hello</p>
<html:p id="test2">World</html:p>
```

(This is because HTML 4 is entirely uppercase; XHTML as XML is case sensitive.)

The rules apply identically to attribute nodes. If a client creates a node using DOM Level 1 methods, or the node is not an `Element` or `Attr` node, this property returns `null`.

namespaceURI

JavaScript 1.5

Nav6

Syntax

```
var x = NodeObj.namespaceURI
```

The `namespaceURI` property of `Node` objects works only with `Element` and `Attr` nodes, and then only those which existed previously in the document or which the client machine creates using DOM Level 2 methods. For `Element` and `Attr` nodes, these return the namespace URI, if you provide one. (For example, the namespace URI for XHTML 1.0 is `http://www.w3.org/1999/xhtml`.) If a client creates a node using DOM Level 1 methods, or the node is not an `Element` or `Attr` node, this property returns `null`.

nextSibling

JavaScript 1.5, JScript 5.0+

Nav6, IE5+

Syntax

```
var x = NodeObj.nextSibling
```

The `nextSibling` property of `Node` objects returns the node that is one node later than the current node in the parent node's `childNodes` array. If the current node is the last node in the parent's `childNodes`, this property is equal to `null`.

nodeName

JavaScript 1.5, JScript 5.0+

Nav6, IE5+

Syntax

```
var x = NodeObj.nodeName
```

The `nodeName` property of `Node` objects reflects a string specific to each node giving a name for the node. If an object supports `nodeName`, you will find its listing at the beginning of the object's section of this chapter.

For HTML documents, the `nodeName` of an `Element` node will be written in uppercase (for example, "HTML"). For XML documents, the `nodeName` of an `Element` node will be written in the case the document provided. For XHTML documents (HTML written as XML), it depends on whether you serve the document as an XML document or an HTML document (client-side, if the extension is `.html`/`.htm` or `.xml`, respectively; server-side, if the mime-type is `text/html` or `text/xml` or `application/xml`, respectively).

nodeType

JavaScript 1.5, JScript 5.0+

Nav6, IE5+

Syntax

```
var x = NodeObj.nodeType
```

The `nodeType` property of `Node` objects reflects a number specific to each node giving a type code for the node type. If an interface supports `nodeType`, you will find its listing at the beginning of the object's interface of this chapter.

Table 20.1 demonstrates the constant properties of `Node` objects to compare them against.

Table 20.1   Node *Interface Constants*

Property Name	Property Value	Property Name	Property Value
ELEMENT_ NODE	1	PROCESSING_ INSTRUCTION_ NODE	7
ATTRIBUTE_NODE	2	COMMENT_ NODE	8
TEXT_NODE	3	DOCUMENT_ NODE	9
CDATA_SECTION_ NODE	4	DOCUMENT_ TYPE_NODE	10
ENTITY_ REFERENCE_ NODE	5	DOCUMENT_ FRAGMENT_ NODE	11
ENTITY_NODE	6	NOTATION_ NODE	12

nodeValue

JavaScript 1.5, JScript 5.0+

Nav6, IE5+

Syntax

```
var x = NodeObj.nodeValue
```

The nodeValue property of Node objects reflects a string specific to each node giving the value for the node. Note some nodes do not have a value per se; these nodes will return null. If an interface supports nodeValue, you will find its listing at the beginning of the object's section of this chapter.

ownerDocument

JavaScript 1.5

Nav6

Syntax

```
var x = NodeObj.ownerDocument
```

The `ownerDocument` property of `Node` objects refers to the `Document` that contains this node. `Document` and `DocumentType` nodes not belonging to any particular document return `null`.

parentNode

JavaScript 1.5, JScript 5.0+

Nav6, IE5+

Syntax

```
var x = NodeObj.parentNode
```

The `parentNode` property of `Node` objects refers to the immediate ancestor of the current node in the document's node tree. Somewhere, `this ==` `this.parentNode.childNodes(x)`, where $0 < x < $ `this.parentNode.childNodes.length`.

Certain nodes, when you call this property, return `null`: `Attr`, `Document`, `DocumentFragment`, `Entity`, and `Notation`.

prefix

JavaScript 1.5

Nav6

Syntax

```
var x = NodeObj.prefix
```

The `prefix` property of `Node` objects works only with `Element` and `Attr` nodes, and then only those which existed previously in the document or which the client machine creates using DOM Level 2 methods. For `Element` and `Attr` nodes, these return the prefix of the node name, if you provide one. In a tag name like `<svg:circle />`, the prefix is `"svg"`. If a client creates a node using DOM Level 1 methods, or the node is not an `Element` or `Attr` node, this property returns `null`.

previousSibling

JavaScript 1.5, JScript 5.0+

Nav6, IE5+

Syntax

```
var x = NodeObj.previousSibling
```

The previousSibling property of Node objects returns the node that is one node earlier than the current node in the parent node's childNodes array. If the current node is the first node in the parent's childNodes, this property is equal to null.

Methods

appendChild()

JavaScript 1.5, JScript 5.0+

Nav6, IE5+

Syntax

```
NodeObj.appendChild(newChildNode)
```

The appendChild() method of Node objects adds the first argument, a node, to the end of the childNodes array. If the parent and child nodes are both renderable under the current styling rules, the newly appended node is rendered. If the given argument is already a child of the this object, the method moves it to the end of the child nodes.

DocumentFragment nodes, when you attach them, behave significantly differently; see the DocumentFragment interface section for details.

cloneNode()

JavaScript 1.5, JScript 5.0+

Nav6, IE5+

Syntax

```
var x = NodeObj.cloneNode([true])
```

The cloneNode() method of Node objects returns a clone of the this node. When you set the first argument to true, it copies all child nodes (and their child nodes, and the child nodes of those child nodes, and so on) as well. Without that argument, it copies only the node itself. Element nodes get copies of their attributes as well. The clone is not necessarily read-only, except in the case of cloning an EntityReference node.

hasAttributes()

JavaScript 1.5, JScript 5.0+

Nav6, IE5+

Syntax

```
var boolValue = NodeObj.hasAttributes()
```

The `hasAttributes()` method of `Node` objects returns `true` if the node has any attributes; else it returns `false`. (Note only `Element` nodes can have attributes, and not every element will have them.)

hasChildNodes()

JavaScript 1.5, JScript 5.0+

Nav6, IE5+

Syntax

```
var boolValue = NodeObj.hasChildNodes()
```

The `hasChildNodes()` method of `Node` objects returns `true` if the node has any child nodes; else it returns `false`. This is equivalent to returning `Boolean(NodeObj.childNodes.length)`, where `NodeObj` is the node object you are testing.

insertBefore()

JavaScript 1.5, JScript 5.0+

Nav6, IE5+

Syntax

```
NodeObj.insertBefore(newChildNode, currentChild)
```

The `insertBefore()` method of `Node` objects places the first argument before the second argument in the `childNodes` array, forcing the first argument to render before the second on the page. If the second argument is `null`, this method reacts like `appendChild`. When the first argument is a `DocumentFragment`, this method inserts its child nodes in order, instead.

isSupported()

JavaScript 1.5

Nav6

Syntax

NodeObj.isSupported(*featName* , *version*)

The isSupported() method of Node objects returns a true or false value dependent on whether the this object supports a feature the first argument names. The second argument asks the method to narrow it down to a particular version, when you supply the argument. For instance, supplying "2.0" as the argument tells the method to look only at properties and methods implemented in DOM Levels 1 and 2. Omitting the second argument, in Internet Explorer, asks the method to determine if the feature has ever been supported (via the current browser).

This method returns true if the feature is supported in the given version; false otherwise.

normalize()

JavaScript 1.5

Nav6, IE6

Syntax

NodeObj.normalize()

The normalize() method of Node objects reorganizes all descendants of its this object into the most DOM-compacted form.

Sometimes in the process of editing a document by the DOM, a document may not be as neatly organized as it was before. For example, if you remove the ... element in the following code, you get two adjacent Text nodes.

```
<p>This is a test.
<strong>This is a string with strong emphasis.</strong>
This is the end of the test.</p>
```

Text nodes, for neatness, generally should not be adjacent to each other; it is usually best to join them together. The `normalize()` method is just such a "clean-up" method.

I personally recommend running this method from the Document or HTMLHtmlElement nodes if you make serious changes to the document and your interactions with the DOM start becoming messy.

removeChild()

JavaScript 1.5, JScript 5.0+

Nav6, IE5+

Syntax

```
[var x =] NodeObj.removeChild(childNode)
```

The `removeChild()` method of Node objects drops the argument, one of the `this` object's child nodes, from the document and returns the dropped node to the script. The result is said node will no longer render on the page.

replaceChild()

JavaScript 1.5, JScript 5.0+

Nav6, IE5+

Syntax

```
[var x =] NodeObj.replaceChild(newChild, childNode)
```

The `replaceChild()` method of Node objects drops the second argument, one of the `this` object's child nodes, from the document and returns the dropped node to the script. The method also places the first argument, a Node object, where the second argument resided in the `childNodes` array. The result is the second argument node will no longer render on the page, but the first argument node will render in its place.

Example: Navigating a Tree of Nodes

The methods for manipulating a tree of nodes, or for that matter, visiting them, may not be entirely clear without a sample document to explore them. Therefore, I present to you in Listing 20.6 a sample XHTML document which, through scripting and the DOM, will look totally different when we're finished.

Listing 20.6   *XHTML Before the Document Changes*

```
<?xml version="1.0" ?>
<!DOCTYPE html PUBLIC "-//W3C//DTD XHTML 1.0 Strict//EN"
➥ "DTD/xhtml1-strict.dtd">
<html xmlns="http://www.w3.org/1999/xhtml" >
<body>
<p>One</p>
<p id="two">Two

<strong id="four">Four</strong>
<em>Five</em>
Six</p>
<script language="JavaScript" type="text/javascript" >
<!--
function go() {
   var two = document.getElementById('two')
   var seven = document.createElement('p')
   seven.setAttribute('id', 'seven')
   var seventext = document.createTextNode('Seven Of Nine')
   seven.appendChild(seventext)
   two.parentNode.appendChild(seven)

   var three = document.createElement('code')
   three.setAttribute('id', 'three')
   var threetext = document.createTextNode('Three ')
   three.appendChild(threetext)
   var four = document.getElementById('four')
   two.insertBefore(three, four)

   var link = document.getElementById('changeLink')
   link.parentNode.removeChild(link)


   }
//-->
</script>
<p><a href="javascript:void(null)" onclick="go()" id="changeLink" >Change
➥ Document</a></p>
</body>
</html>
```

When you click on the link, several things happen. First, you get a reference to the
<p>...</p> element labeled "two", and call it a JavaScript object named two. You
create a new <p>...</p> element (more correctly called HTMLParagraphElement) and
name it seven. A Text node comes next, containing "Seven Of Nine," and this node
the script appends to the new seven node as a child. Then, the parent node of two gets
seven attached to it at the end (it's the last of two's siblings).

Next, another node, three, comes into existence as an HTMLElement (<code>...</code>
in this specific instance). The document creates a Text node containing "Three " and
makes it a child of three. Then, using a reference to the node containing "four", it
inserts the three node prior to that node.

Finally, to lessen the chance of an accidental repeat, the script references and removes
the link node.

The resulting XHTML document, though unchanged in the source, renders exactly
like Listing 20.7 would.

Listing 20.7   XHTML Document Post-Transformation

```
<?xml version="1.0" ?>
<!DOCTYPE html PUBLIC "-//W3C//DTD XHTML 1.0 Strict//EN"
➥ "DTD/xhtml1-strict.dtd">
<html xmlns="http://www.w3.org/1999/xhtml" >
<body>
<p>One</p>
<p id="two">Two
<code>Three </code><strong id="four">Four</strong>
<em>Five</em>
Six</p>
<script language="JavaScript" type="text/javascript" >
<!--
function go() {
   var two = document.getElementById('two')
   var seven = document.createElement('p')
   seven.setAttribute('id', 'seven')
   var seventext = document.createTextNode('Seven Of Nine')
   seven.appendChild(seventext)
   two.parentNode.appendChild(seven)

   var three = document.createElement('code')
   three.setAttribute('id', 'three')
   var threetext = document.createTextNode('Three ')
```

Listing 20.7   *(continued)*

```
    three.appendChild(threetext)
    var four = document.getElementById('four')
    two.insertBefore(three, four)

    var link = document.getElementById('changeLink')
    link.parentNode.removeChild(link)


    }
//-->
</script>
<p></p>
<p>Seven Of Nine</p>
</body>
</html>
```

NamedNodeMap

JavaScript 1.5, JScript 5.0+

Nav6, IE5+

The NamedNodeMap interface describes an unordered collection of nodes. Normally these are useful within the DOM for collections not requiring a specific order (for instance, attributes of an element). Each node in a NamedNodeMap has the nodeName value (defined under the Node interface), which you can use to reference it.

You should be aware the NamedNodeMap does not hold the Node objects themselves, but references to them. Thus, when you change a Node, the changes reflect in the NamedNodeMap's property for that node.

Properties

length

JavaScript 1.5, JScript 5.0+

Nav6, IE5+

Syntax

```
var x = NodeMap.length
```

The `length` property of NamedNodeMap objects reflects the number of nodes contained in `this`.

Methods

getNamedItem()
JavaScript 1.5, JScript 5.0+

Nav6, IE6

Syntax

```
var x = NodeMap.getNamedItem(name)
```

The `getNamedItem()` method of NamedNodeMap objects returns a Node whose nodeName property matches the first argument, a string. The Node is a member of the NamedNodeMap. If no such node is found, this method returns `null`.

getNamedItemNS()
JavaScript 1.5

Nav6

Syntax

```
var x = NodeMap.getNamedItemNS(namespaceURI, localname)
```

The `getNamedItemNS()` method of NamedNodeMap objects returns a Node whose namespaceURI property matches the first argument, and whose localname property matches the second argument. Both arguments are strings. The Node is a member of the NamedNodeMap. If no such node is found, this method returns `null`.

item()
JavaScript 1.5, JScript 5.0+

Nav6, IE5+

Syntax

```
var x = NodeMap.item(y)
```

The `item()` method of NamedNodeMap objects returns a Node object which the `this` object references. Although NamedNodeMap objects do not have a predefined order for them, upon creation they index their `Node` objects in an implementation-dependent order. By supplying a number (specifically, a non-negative integer less than `this.length`) as the first argument, you can get a `Node` object from the `this` object representing that `Node`'s placement in the `NamedNodeMap` index. Any other argument you submit to this method results in the method returning `null`.

removeNamedItem()

JavaScript 1.5, JScript 5.0+

Nav6, IE6

Syntax

```
[var x =] NodeMap.removeNamedItem(name)
```

The `removeNamedItem()` method of `NamedNodeMap` objects removes a `Node` from the `this` object whose `nodeName` property matches the first argument, a string. If the `Node` object is an attribute and has a default value, the default value is set in its place. This method then returns the removed `Node` object to the user.

removeNamedItemNS

JavaScript 1.5

Nav6

Syntax

```
[var x =] NodeMap.removeNamedItemNS(namespaceURI, localname)
```

The `removedNamedItemNS()` method of `NamedNodeMap` objects removes a `Node` from the `this` object whose `namespaceURI` property matches the first argument, and whose `localname` property matches the second argument. Both arguments are strings. If the `Node` object is an attribute and has a default value, the default value is set in its place. This method then returns the removed `Node` object to the user.

setNamedItem

JavaScript 1.5

Nav6, IE6

Syntax

```
[var x =] NodeMap.setNamedItem(NodeObj)
```

The setNamedItem() method of NamedNodeMap objects adds or replaces a Node in the this object whose nodeName property matches the nodeName property of the first argument, a Node. The node added to the this object is the first argument. If the node replaces another Node, the method returns the one it replaces to the user; otherwise, it returns null.

setNamedItemNS

JavaScript 1.5

Nav6

Syntax

```
[var x =] NodeMap.setNamedItemNS(NodeObj)
```

The setNamedItemNS() method of NamedNodeMap objects adds or replaces a Node in the this object whose namespaceURI property matches the namespaceURI property of the first argument, a Node object, and whose localname property matches the localname property of the first argument. The node added to the this object is the first argument. If the node replaces another Node, the method returns the one it replaces to the user; otherwise, it returns null.

NodeList

In contrast to the NamedNodeMap interface, which provides for holding Node objects in an unordered collection, the NodeList interface provides for an ordered collection of Node objects. The comparison is similar to the one between generic objects and arrays; objects are, among other things, basic containers (like NamedNodeMap objects). Arrays hold values with numbered indexes (like NodeList objects).

The similarity ends there, however. Neither NodeList nor NamedNodeMap must comply with the ECMAScript specifications for their counterparts, and neither Netscape nor Microsoft has written their browser to do so.

However, there is one feature of arrays NodeList does implement: the access of numbered properties via brackets. (The W3C DOM does not cover calling numbered properties this way, but the shorthand is very convenient.)

Properties

length

JavaScript 1.5, JScript 5.0+

Nav6, IE5+

Syntax

```
var x = NodeList.length
```

The length property of NodeList objects reflects the number of nodes contained in this.

Methods

item

JavaScript 1.5, JScript 5.0+

Nav6, IE5+

Syntax

```
var x = NodeMap.item(y)
var x = NodeMap[y]
```

By supplying a number (specifically, a non-negative integer less than this.length) as the first argument, you can get a Node object from the this object representing that Node's placement in the this object's index. Any other argument you submit to this method results in the method returning null.

Notation

Not implemented in HTML (DOM 1)

Descends from Node interface

nodeName: File extension for notation

nodeType: 12

nodeValue: null

Description

For HTML documents, often you run into a mime-type the browser does not natively support. (A classic example is Adobe Acrobat PDF files.) HTML solved this problem with plug-ins; XML solves it with `Notation` nodes.

Notations, in short, describe a file type and the program the XML file recommends for the processor to use on that file type. `Notation` nodes are read-only.

Properties

publicId

Not implemented in HTML (DOM 1)

Syntax

```
var x = notation.publicId
```

The `publicId` property of `Notation` nodes refers to the public identification string, if one exists, in the notation. For the line,

```
<!NOTATION SVG "-//Adobe SVG Viewer 2.0//EN" "/adobe/svgview.exe ">
```

the `publicId` property refers to `"-//Adobe SVG Viewer 2.0//EN"`. This string basically summarizes what the DTD file of the system identifier defines.

systemId

Not implemented in HTML (DOM 1)

Syntax

```
var x = notation.systemId
```

The `systemId` property of `Notation` nodes refers to the system identification string of the document type declaration. For the line,

```
<!NOTATION SVG "-//Adobe SVG Viewer 2.0//EN" "/adobe/svgview.exe ">
```

the system identifier is `"/adobe/svgview.exe "`. It basically points to the program that interprets the file type (denoted by `"SVG"`).

Methods

The `Notation` interface provides no methods beyond those the `Node` interface defines.

ProcessingInstruction

JavaScript 1.5

Nav6 (XML only)

Descends from Node interface

`nodeName`: target of instruction

`nodeType`: 7

`nodeValue`: data of instruction

Description

Processing instructions, or PI's, are a special kind of XML tag that contains directions a particular application may accept. For instance, `<?php ?>` is a common (and best practice) way to insert PHP code in an HTML document. Processing instructions may not begin with the letters `x`, `m`, and `l` in that sequence, in any variation of uppercase and lowercase. The W3C has reserved that for its own definitions. (However, Netscape treats the optional `<?xml version="1.0" ?>` as a processing instruction.)

The W3C recommends using an `<?xml-stylesheet ?>` PI for XML documents to reference a stylesheet for the document. (You can read the W3C Recommendation for this at `http://www.w3.org/1999/06/REC-xml-stylesheet-19990629/`.) I also cover this in more detail in Chapter 33, "Styling for HTML Elements."

PIs come in two main parts: the *target* and the *data*. The target refers to all characters after the first question mark and before the first space. The data refers to everything following the first space until the `?>` characters.

Properties

target

JavaScript 1.5

Nav6 (XML only)

Syntax

```
var x = PI.target
```

The `target` property of `ProcessingInstruction` nodes reflects the target of the PI the `this` object corresponds to. In the PI `<?php echo("Hello World"); ?>`, the target is php.

---

data

JavaScript 1.5

Nav6 (XML only)

Syntax

```
var x = PI.data
```

The `data` property of `ProcessingInstruction` nodes reflects the data section of the PI the `this` object corresponds to. In the PI `<?php echo("Hello World"); ?>`, the data is `'echo("Hello World"); '`. (Note the last space is in the data section.)

Methods

The `ProcessingInstruction` interface provides no methods beyond those the `Node` interface defines.

Text

JavaScript 1.5, JScript 5.0+

Nav6, IE5+

Descends from `CharacterData` object

`nodeName`: `"#text"`

`nodeType`: 3

`nodeValue`: The contents of the text node

Description

`Text` nodes are the simplest nodes of all in that they describe "plaintext," text that is not markup of any sort. Because of this, they also have no child nodes of any sort;

where the document is the root of the tree, often `Text` nodes represent the outermost branches. (A few exceptions exist, namely CDATA sections and comments, but these are insignificant in most cases.)

As a matter of fact, this particular object has only one method to extend the `CharacterData` interface.

Properties

The `Text` interface provides no properties beyond those the `CharacterData` interface defines.

Methods

splitText()

JavaScript 1.5, JScript 5.0+

Nav6, IE5+

Syntax

```
var x = textNode.splitText(index)
```

The `splitText()` method of `Text` nodes chops `this` in two at the zero-based index number equaling the first argument. The method returns a new sibling `Text` node that will hold the text to the right of (and including the character at) this index. The text to the left of the index remains as the value for `this`.

Listing 20.8 gives a good example of this method.

Example: Inserting Hypertext Inside Plaintext

In the `CharacterData` interface section, I established character data does not hold markup as such. This means if you were to insert markup directly into a `Text` node's value, it would render as plaintext; the markup tags would show up and any contents of them would still be plain text.

The only way to force markup to render as markup in the middle of a `Text` node is to break up the node into two pieces and slide the markup node in between. See Listing 20.8 for how this works.

Listing 20.8   *Splitting a* Text *Node for Inserting Hypertext*

```
<?xml version="1.0" ?>
<!DOCTYPE html PUBLIC "-//W3C//DTD XHTML 1.0 Transitional//EN"
➥ "DTD/xhtml1-transitional.dtd">
<html xmlns="http://www.w3.org/1999/xhtml" >
<head><title></title></head>
<body>
<p id="no">I object to this arrangement.</p>
<script language="JavaScript" type="text/javascript">
<!--
    var text = document.getElementById('no')
    var newTextNode = text.childNodes[0].splitText(9)
    var bold = document.createElement('strong')
    var boldtext = document.createTextNode('very strongly ')
    bold.appendChild(boldtext)
    text.insertBefore(bold, newTextNode)
//-->
</script>
<!-- Result:
I object <strong>very strongly </strong>to this arrangement.
-->
</body>
</html>
```

CHAPTER 21

HTMLElement

> DOM1+
>
> Descends from `Element` interface (see Chapter 20, "Core DOM Objects")
>
> Applies to HTML documents only

Description

The `HTMLElement` object defines a basic set of properties for all HTML elements—from the <a> tag to the <var> tag. In fact, for many HTML elements, "the buck stops here"—the `HTMLElement` object defines the last properties of these elements.

One item you should realize about all HTML elements is their attributes are made accessible as object properties through the HTML module of the DOM spec. As you will see with the HTML elements discussed later, this is quite convenient.

Also, the Microsoft implementation of `HTMLElement` isn't totally clear. For instance, they don't have an `HTMLElement` listing in their DHTML Reference. I credit Jason K. Davis, a fellow moderator at Website Abstraction, with creating a script to find a list of properties and methods common to all Internet Explorer HTML elements. Even then, his script generates a long list of "false positives," properties and methods that apply without use to all elements. This chapter is thus the result of painstaking examination of the Microsoft documentation in particular, and may contain some slight inaccuracies even after editing.

Elements That Are HTMLElement Objects

The following elements supported by the listed browsers have no definitions in the HTML DOM beyond `HTMLElement`:

<abbr>...</abbr>
Nav6

This element contains an abbreviation such as "WWW" for the World Wide Web, or "JSLab" for JavaScript Laboratory. The W3C recommends you use the `title` attribute (described later in this chapter) for the full name of the object:

```
<abbr title="JavaScript Developer's Dictionary">JSDD</abbr>
```

<acronym>...</acronym>

Nav6, IE4+

This element is similar to the <abbr>...</abbr> element, except this one contains acronyms. See the <abbr>...</abbr> element for details.

<address>...</address>

Nav1+, IE3+

This element the W3C designates for holding general contact information. The W3C recommends you use these at the beginning or end of the <body>...</body> section of a document.

...

Nav1+, IE1+

This element designates a section of markup to render as boldface.

<bdo>...</bdo>

Nav6+, IE5+

This element identifies a section the browser should render in either normal or reversed order (like this or siht ekil). By setting the dir attribute to "rtl", you force the characters within this element to be written right-to-left, in reverse.

<big>...</big>

Nav2+, IE3+

This element designates a section of markup to render in a slightly larger font than the section containing the <big>...</big> element.

<center>...</center>

Nav1.1+, IE3+

Deprecated in HTML 4

This element designates a section of HTML markup to render centered horizontally on the page. Because of the align attribute of text elements such as <p>...</p> and <pre>...</pre>, the W3C has deprecated this element.

`<cite>...</cite>`

Nav1.1+, IE3+

This element designates a section of markup for references (for instance, acknowledging that a particular piece of information came from a particular source). Browsers typically render this as italicized.

`<code>...</code>`

Nav1+, IE3+

This element designates a section of markup containing a programming or scripting code fragment. Browsers typically render this in a monospace font (like the code listings throughout this book).

`<dd>...</dd>`

Nav1+, IE3+

This element contains a description of a definition's listing (which the `<dl>...</dl>` tags define) corresponding to a defined term (which the `<dt>...</dt>` tags define).

`<dfn>...</dfn>`

Nav6, IE3+

This element names its contents as a definition of a term to the reader.

`<dt>...</dt>`

Nav1+, IE3+

This element contains a phrase to define in a definition listing (which the `<dl>...</dl>` tags define) corresponding to a definition (which the `<dd>...</dd>` tags define).

`<em>...</em>`

Nav1+, IE3+

This element designates a section of markup containing hypertext that requires emphasis. Browsers typically render this in italic.

`<i>...</i>`

Nav1+, IE3+ (HTML), IE4+ (JS)

This element designates a section of markup to render as italic.

Elements That Are HTMLElement Objects

\<kbd\>...\</kbd\>

<kbd>...</kbd>

Nav1+, IE3+

This indicates to the reader text the reader should enter. This often corresponds to HTMLInputElement objects and form objects in general, which I will cover in Chapters 25, "Form Elements," and 26, "Form Input Elements: HTMLInputElement."

<noframes>...</noframes>

Nav1+, IE3+

This is markup the browser must render in place of any frameset or <iframe /> tags if framesets have been disabled.

<noscript>...</noscript>

Nav3+, IE4+

This is markup the browser must render in place of any scripts if scripts have been disabled.

<s>...</s> / <strike>...</strike>

Nav1+, IE3+

Deprecated in HTML 4

This element designates a section of markup to render with a single line striking it out. Because of Cascading Style Sheets, the W3C has deprecated this element.

<samp>...</samp>

Nav1+, IE3+

This indicates to the reader a sample piece of output text.

<small>...</small>

Nav2+, IE3+

This element designates a section of markup to render in a slightly smaller font than the section containing the <small>...</small> element.

<span>...</span>

Nav4+, IE3+

This element designates an inline block of text that as a group may have special styling properties. (The class and style attributes of this element become very important for this element.)

<strong>...</strong>

Nav1+, IE3+

This element designates a section of markup containing hypertext that requires strong emphasis. Browsers typically render this in boldface.

<sub>...</sub>

Nav2+, IE3+

This element designates a section of markup containing hypertext the browser should render at half the standard height and below the middle of the standard height. This is commonly known as a "subscript," hence the name of this element.

<sup>...</sup>

Nav2+, IE3+

This element designates a section of markup containing hypertext the browser should render at half the standard height and above the middle of the standard height. This is commonly known as a "superscript," hence the name of this element.

<tt>...</tt>

Nav1+, IE3+

This element designates a section of markup containing hypertext the browser should render as if it came from a typewriter or teletype. Effectively, this means a fixed-width font for the contents of this element.

<u>...</u>

Nav3+, IE1+

Deprecated in HTML 4

This element designates a section of markup with an underline. Because of Cascading Style Sheets, the W3C has deprecated this element.

<var>...</var>

Nav4+, IE3+

This element designates a section of markup to represent a variable to the reader. Typically, the browser will render this in italic.

Properties

accessKey

IE5+

Syntax

```
[var x = ] HTMLElement.accessKey [ = "c"]
```

The accessKey property of the HTMLElement designates a shortcut key to focus. When the user presses the designated key and the Alt key (on Windows) while the window for the this object has focus, the element gains focus. The nodeValue for this attribute must be one character in length. This may be a common property for all elements, but it does not make sense for some HTML elements to gain focus and consequently you may find the accessKey property does nothing for some elements.

all

IE4+

Syntax

```
[var x =] HTMLElement.all
```

The all collection of the HTMLElement object is a collection of all child and descendant elements of the this object. Although the all collection is not available under Netscape, you can retrieve the equivalent collection with the following call.

```
var all = HTMLElement.getElementsByTagName('*')
```

You can access these elements in a number of ways, as Listing 21.1 demonstrates.

Listing 21.1   *Four Ways to Access Elements in the* all *Property*

```
<?xml version="1.0" ?>
<!DOCTYPE html PUBLIC "-//W3C//DTD XHTML 1.0 Transitional//EN"
➥"DTD/xhtml1-transitional.dtd">
<html xmlns="http://www.w3.org/1999/xhtml" >
<head><title></title></head>
<body onload="go()">
<p id="one">Hello, World</p>
<h1>
<script language="JavaScript" type="text/javascript">
<!--
function go() {
    var HTML = ""
    HTML += "1)" + document.body.all.one.tagName + "<br />"
    HTML += "2)" + document.body.all["one"].tagName + "<br />"
    HTML += "3)" + document.body.all(1).tagName + "<br />"
    HTML += "4)" + document.body.all("one",0).tagName
    document.body.all.info.innerHTML = HTML
    document.close()
    }
//-->
</script>
</h1>
<div id="info"> </div>
<!-- Result:
Hello, World
1)P
2)P
3)H1
4)P
-->
</body>
</html>
```

In Listing 21.1 you may be wonder why I chose to set the innerHTML of a <div> tag instead of just using document.write(). Using document.write() would overwrite the content we are accessing. This way we can view both. Also, you may be wondering why number three returns H1. Remember, collections are zero based, so the <P> tag would be zero. Another interesting point is the fourth syntax for when you have multiple elements in the collection sharing the same ID or name attribute values. (XHTML documents do not have to worry about this.) In these cases, the second argument reflects which element in the zero-based index of matches it is.

Methods

item

IE4+

Syntax

```
var x = HTMLElement.all.item(index)
```

The item method of the all collection takes a number (specifically, a non-negative integer less than this.length) as the first argument. You can get a Node object from the this object representing that Node's placement in the this object's index. Any other argument you submit to this method results in the method returning null.

length

IE4+

Syntax

```
var x = HTMLElement.all.length
```

The length property of the all collection tells how many objects are in the collection.

tags

IE4+

Syntax

```
var x = HTMLElement.all.tags(tagName)
```

The tags method of the HTMLElement returns a collection of the this element comprising all elements whose tagName property matches the first argument. To get the same collection with Netscape you can use the following call:

```
var tags = HTMLElement.getElementsByTagName('tagName')
```

urns

IE5+

Syntax

```
var x = HTMLElement.all.urns(behaviorName)
```

The urns method of the HTMLElement returns a collection of the this element comprising all elements possessing a DHTML behavior whose name matches the first argument.

DHTML behaviors, an Internet Explorer proprietary extension to HTML, go far beyond the scope of this book. You can find information on them via Microsoft's Web site at http://msdn.microsoft.com/workshop/author/behaviors/overview.asp.

behaviorUrns

IE5+

Syntax

```
var x = HTMLElement.behaviorUrns
```

The behaviorUrns method of the HTMLElement returns an array of all behaviors of the this object.

DHTML behaviors, an Internet Explorer proprietary extension to HTML, go far beyond the scope of this book. You can find information on them via Microsoft's Web site at http://msdn.microsoft.com/workshop/author/behaviors/overview.asp.

item

IE5+

Syntax

```
var x = HTMLElement.behaviorUrns.item(index)
```

The item method of the behaviorUrns collection, takes a number (specifically, a non-negative integer less than this.length) as the first argument, you can get a behavior from the this object representing that behavior's placement in the this object's index. Any other argument you submit to this method results in the method returning null.

length

IE5+

Syntax

```
var x = HTMLElement.behaviorUrns.length
```

The `length` property of the `behaviorUrns` collection tells how many objects are in the collection.

canHaveChildren

IE5+

Syntax

```
var boolValue = HTMLElement.canHaveChildren
```

The `canHaveChildren` property of the `HTMLElement`, a boolean value, tells whether the `this` element can accept child nodes. If `true`, the element can have child nodes.

canHaveHTML

IE5.5+

Read-only

Syntax

```
var boolValue = HTMLElement.canHaveHTML
```

The `canHaveHTML` property of the `HTMLElement`, a boolean value, tells whether the `this` element can contain rich HTML markup. If `true`, the element can contain HTML markup.

Microsoft's documentation on this subject is somewhat amusing; it says the property is changeable except for a certain group of elements. I checked the list and it's the same list of elements that make up Internet Explorer's implementation of HTML.

children

IE4+

Syntax

```
var x = HTMLElement.children
```

The `children` collection of the `HTMLElement` returns a collection of child elements to the `this` element.

Though Microsoft's documentation lists this property only for some of its HTML elements, all elements have this property. However, certain elements (such as the `<input />` element) cannot have children. Hence, the `length` of these elements is always zero.

item

IE4+

Syntax

```
var x = HTMLElement.children.item(index)
```

The `item` method of the `children` collection takes a number (specifically, a non-negative integer less than `this.length`) as the first argument. You can get a element object from the `this` element representing that element's placement in the `this` element's index. Any other argument you submit to this method results in the method returning `null`.

length

IE4+

Syntax

```
var x = HTMLElement.children.length
```

The `length` property of the `children` collection tells how many objects are in the collection.

tags

IE4+

Syntax

```
var x = HTMLElement.children.tags(tagName)
```

The `tags` method of the `children` collection returns a collection of the `this` elements comprising all elements whose `tagName` property matches the first argument.

urns

IE5+

Syntax

```
var x = HTMLElement.children.urns(behaviorName)
```

The `urns` method of the `children` collection returns a collection of the `this` element comprising all elements possessing a DHTML behavior whose name matches the first argument, a string.

DHTML behaviors, an Internet Explorer proprietary extension to HTML, go far beyond the scope of this book. You can find information on them via Microsoft's Web site at `http://msdn.microsoft.com/workshop/author/behaviors/overview.asp`.

className

IE4+, Nav6

Syntax

```
var x = HTMLElement.className
```

The `className` property of the `HTMLElement` refers to the `class` attribute of the element, which identifies the particular styling associated with this element. See `HTMLStyleElement` under Chapter 24, "Head Elements," for more details. An important point to remember is under Internet Explorer 4, you are only allowed to specify a single class name, whereas Internet Explorer 5+ and Netscape 6 allow you to specify a comma separated listed of classes.

contentEditable

IE5.5

Syntax

```
var x = HTMLElement.contentEditable
```

The `contentEditable` property of the `HTMLElement` tells whether the information the `this` element contains is available for modification by the user. A setting of `false` indicates the contents are read-only. A setting of `true` indicates the user may write to it freely. Often, the setting is `"inherit"`, meaning the property inherits whatever setting its parent node has for `contentEditable`.

dir

Nav6, IE5+

Syntax

```
HTMLElement.dir="direction"
```

The property of the `HTML` Element reflects the `dir` attribute, which indicates to the browser whether text must read forward or backward as compared to the source code. See the `<bdo>...</bdo>` element earlier in this chapter for details.

disabled

IE5.5

Syntax

```
var boolValue = HTMLElement.disabled
```

The `disabled` property of the `HTMLElement` in Internet Explorer 5.5, allows you to disable every element via JavaScript. (For many elements, it is as early as Internet Explorer 4.) By setting this value to `true`, you ensure no one can tamper with your element without resetting the `disabled` property to `false` by script.

hideFocus

IE5.5

Syntax

```
var boolValue = HTMLElement.hideFocus
```

The hideFocus property of the HTMLElement determines whether a given object that has focus should be shown. Standard browser procedure is for an element to indicate—either by an outline around it or some other equally obvious way—whether it has the document focus. By setting this value to true, you prevent focus on the particular element from being visible.

Use at your own discretion. Although it can look good, if there isn't an obvious sign, your visitors can easily lose their place.

id

Nav6, IE4+

Syntax

```
var id = HTMLElement.id
```

The id property of the HTMLElement reflects the id attribute of the HTML element.

isContentEditable

IE5.5

Syntax

```
var x = HTMLElement.isContentEditable
```

The isContentEditable property of the HTMLElement is a read-only version of the contentEditable property, covered earlier in this chapter.

isDisabled

IE5.5

Syntax

```
var boolValue = HTMLElement.isDisabled
```

The isDisabled property of the HTMLElement is a read-only version of the disabled property, covered earlier in this chapter.

isTextEdit

IE4+

Syntax

```
var boolValue = HTMLElement.isTextEdit
```

The isTextEdit property of the HTMLElement is a read-only property that specifies whether the user can create a text range with the this element. I cover ranges in Chapter 34, "DOM-2 Range."

lang

Nav6, IE4+

Syntax

```
Var language = HTMLElement.lang
```

The lang property of the HTMLElement represents the abbreviated language code, such as "en-us" for English in the United States of America dialect. This object retrieves the code from the lang attribute.

parentElement

IE4+

Syntax

```
var x = HTMLElement.parentElement
```

The parentElement property of the HTMLElement returns the HTMLElement that matches the parentNode property, if there is one; otherwise, it returns null.

parentTextEdit

IE4+ (for most elements)

Syntax

```
var x = HTMLElement.parentTextEdit
```

The `parentTextEdit` property of the `HTMLElement` retrieves an elements ancestor, which is helpful in creating a text range. I cover ranges in Chapter 34, "DOM-2 Range."

readyState

IE5+

Syntax

`var x = HTMLElement.readyState`

The `readyState` property of the `HTMLElement` reflects five different values: uninitialized, loading, loaded, interactive, and complete. The first, uninitialized, means the HTTP call has gone out to retrieve the element's data source but the response has not begun yet. The loading value means the program has begun to download the information the element references (for example, a JavaScript in a library file using the `src` attribute). The loaded value means the browser has downloaded the requested information, but it hasn't finished processing it. The interactive setting means the user can interact with it, even as it's still downloading. Finally, the complete state indicates all is well.

The `<object>...</object>` element uses numeric values instead of string values: `0` for uninitialized, `1` for loading, `2` for loaded, `3` for interactive, and `4` for complete.

scopeName

IE5+

Syntax

`var x = HTMLElement.scopeName`

The `scopeName` property of the `HTMLElement` works only with elements that existed previously in the document or which the client machine creates using DOM Level 2 methods. This returns the prefix of the node name, if you provide one. In a tag name like `<svg:circle />`, the prefix is `"svg"`. If a client creates a node using DOM Level 1 methods, this property returns `null`. (This is identical to `prefix` under `Element` in Chapter 20, "Core DOM Objects.")

sourceIndex

IE4+

Syntax

```
var x = HTMLElement.sourceIndex
```

The sourceIndex property of the HTMLElement gives the index number for where in the document.all collection the this element resides. In short, the following is true:

```
this == document.all[this.sourceIndex]
```

tagURN

IE5+

Syntax

```
var x = HTMLElement.tagURN
```

The tagURN property of the HTMLElement works only with elements that existed previously in the document or which the client machine creates using DOM Level 2 methods. This returns the namespace URI of the node name, if you provide one. If a client creates a node using DOM Level 1 methods, this property returns null. (This is identical to namespaceURI under Element in Chapter 20, "Core DOM Objects.")

title

Nav6, IE4+

Syntax

```
[var x =] HTMLElement.title = titleString
```

The title property of the HTMLElement reflects the title attribute of the HTML element. This property is most commonly used to create tooltips, plaintext that becomes visible to users when their mouse moves over the this element's corresponding space in the document.

Methods

addBehavior( )

IE5+

Syntax

`[var x =] HTMLElement.addBehavior(behaviorURN)`

The `addBehavior()` method of the `HTMLElement` adds the behavior that the first argument references by URL to the `this` element. The optional assignment to a variable allows for later removal of the behavior, much like assigning a variable to a `setTimeout` allows for clearing the timeout by `clearTimeout`. The specific method to remove a behavior is `removeBehavior()`, which I mention later in this chapter.

DHTML behaviors, an Internet Explorer proprietary extension to HTML, go far beyond the scope of this book. You can find information on them via Microsoft's Web site at `http://msdn.microsoft.com/workshop/author/behaviors/overview.asp`.

applyElement( )

IE5+

Syntax

`HTMLElement.applyElement(element[, innerFlag])`

The `applyElement()` method of the `HTMLElement` inserts the first argument, an `Element` node, as a parent element of the `this` object, making the current parent element the "grandparent" element of `this`.

If you specify the second argument as `"inside"`, this method inserts the first argument as the child element of the `this` element, making all current child elements become children of the inserted element instead.

Either way, it usually renders identically. But the differences in the object model are easily discernible, as Listing 21.2 shows.

Listing 21.2 *The* `applyElement()` *Method and the Object Model*

```
<?xml version="1.0" ?>
<!DOCTYPE html PUBLIC "-//W3C//DTD XHTML 1.0 Transitional//EN"
➥"DTD/xhtml1-transitional.dtd">
<html xmlns="http://www.w3.org/1999/xhtml" >
<head><title></title>
<!-- for IE5+ only -->
<script language="JavaScript" type="text/javascript">
<!--
function makeBig() {
   var one = document.getElementById("one")
   var two = document.createElement("big")
   one.applyElement(two)
   var three = document.createElement("p")
   var threetext = "one.parentNode.tagName = " + one.parentNode.tagName
   var threetext = document.createTextNode(threetext)
   three.appendChild(threetext)
   one.parentNode.appendChild(three)

   var four = document.createElement("em")
   one.applyElement(four, "inside")
   var five = document.createElement("p")
   var fivetext = "one.childNodes[0].tagName = " + one.childNodes[0].tagName
   fivetext = document.createTextNode(fivetext)
   five.appendChild(fivetext)
   one.parentNode.appendChild(five)
   alert(document.body.innerHTML)
   }
//-->
</script>
</head>
<body onload="makeBig()">


<p id="one">The <strong>bold</strong> text is <strong>bigger</strong>.</p>

<!-- Results:
The bold text is bigger.
one.parentNode.tagName = big
one.childNodes[0].tagName = em
-->
</body>
</html>
```

attachEvent( )

IE5+

Syntax

HTMLElement.attachEvent(*eventName, handler*)

The attachEvent() method of all HTMLElement instances attaches an event handler for the event the first argument names to the this object. Should the event actually happen upon the given element (or it bubbles up from a child event), the function specified as the second argument will execute.

I cover events and event handlers in more detail in Chapter 32, "DOM-2 Events and Event Handlers."

blur( )

IE5+

Syntax

HTMLElement.blur()

The blur() method of all HTMLElement instances removes focus from the given element without reassigning focus elsewhere. In the process it also fires the onBlur event handler.

This method has been supported for form elements in particular for as long as JavaScript and forms have worked together. However, with the new DOM, it becomes much more ubiquitous.

clearAttributes( )

IE5+

Syntax

HTMLElement.clearAttributes()

The clearAttributes() method of HTML elements sets most attribute's values to an empty string from the this object. It will not remove an id attribute, nor event handlers or styling attributes.

Listing 21.3 shows the effects of clearing all nonessential attributes.

Listing 21.3   *Clearing Attributes of an* HTMLScriptElement

```
<?xml version="1.0" ?>
<!DOCTYPE html PUBLIC "-//W3C//DTD XHTML 1.0 Transitional//EN"
➥"DTD/xhtml1-transitional.dtd">
<html xmlns="http://www.w3.org/1999/xhtml" >
<head><title></title></head>
<body>
<p>
<script language="JavaScript" type="text/javascript">
<!--
document.write("The language is " + document.scripts[0].language + "<br />")
document.scripts[0].clearAttributes()
document.write("The language is " + document.scripts[0].language + "<br />")
//-->
</script>
</p>
<!-- Result:
The language is JavaScript
The language is
-->
</body>
</html>
```

click( )

IE4+

Syntax

HTMLElement.click()

The click() method of HTML elements tells the browser to simulate a mouse-click on the this element. However, the this element does not gain focus when you use click().

componentFromPoint( )

IE4+

Syntax

HTMLElement.componentFromPoint(*xcoord, ycoord*)

The `componentFromPoint()` method of HTML elements returns a string describing how a current point relates to the `this` element. The two arguments are the x- and y-coordinates of the point. There are several different responses this method may return, based on the coordinates given. Figure 21.1 shows all of them except one.

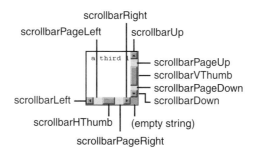

Figure 21.1

Features of a scrollable element.

The only one not shown is the setting for "outside." As you may guess, the method returns "outside" for any coordinate point outside the rendering of the `this` element.

contains( )

IE4+

Syntax

```
var boolValue = HTMLElement.contains(altHTMLElement)
```

The `contains()` method of the `HTMLElement` returns `true` if the first argument, an element in the document, is a descendant element of the `this` element. Otherwise, this method returns `false`. A common use for the `contains()` method is to determine whether an `onmouseover`/`onmouseout` event occurred because the mouse went in or out of the object, or in or out of a child object.

detachEvent( )

IE5+

Syntax

```
HTMLElement.detachEvent(eventName, handler)
```

The detachEvent() method of the HTMLElement causes the event handler given as the first argument to stop passing any events of the type named in the first argument and fired on the this element to the second argument, a function. This method works only if the attachEvent() method was called with the exact same arguments on the this element as well. See Chapter 32, "DOM-2 Events and Event Handlers," for details.

fireEvent( )

IE5.5+

Syntax

```
[var boolValue =] HTMLElement.fireEvent(eventName [, eventObj])
```

The fireEvent() method of the HTMLElement fires the event named as a string in the first argument upon the this element. The event object it actually passes to the event handler will begin as the second argument, if provided, or as a blank event object.

However, four properties of the event object this method passes are preset before the method delivers the event object to the event handler. The cancelBubble property becomes false, the returnValue property this method sets to true, the srcElement becomes this, and the type is the first argument of this method.

See Chapter 32, "DOM-2 Events and Event Handlers," for details on events.

focus( )

IE5+

Syntax

```
HTMLElement.focus()
```

The focus() method of all HTMLElement instances gives focus to the given element. In the process it also fires the onFocus event handler.

This method has been supported for form elements in particular for as long as JavaScript and forms have worked together. However, with the new DOM, it becomes much more ubiquitous.

getAdjacentText( )

IE5.0+

Syntax

```
var x = HTMLElement.getAdjancentText(strValue)
```

The `getAdjacentText()` method of all `HTMLElement` instances returns a string value of the closest `Text` node to a particular piece of the `this` element, based on the first argument, a string. If the argument is `"beforeBegin"`, it returns the contents of the closest `Text` node before the beginning tag of the element. If the argument is `"afterBegin"`, it returns the contents of the closest `Text` node after the beginning tag of the element. If the argument is `"beforeEnd"`, it returns the contents of the closest `Text` node before the ending tag of the element. If the argument is `"afterEnd"`, it returns the contents of the closest `Text` node after the ending tag of the element.

insertAdjacentElement( )

IE5.0+

Syntax

```
HTMLElement.insertAdjacentElement(strLocation, altHTMLElement)
```

The `insertAdjacentElement()` method of all `HTMLElement` instances inserts the second argument, an `HTMLElement` instance, in the document in a position relative to the `this` element. The first argument determines the position of the newly inserted element.

In a sense, this method is like many current Core DOM methods. If the first argument is `"beforeBegin"`, this acts the same as `this.parentNode.insertBefore` (`altHTMLElement, this`); just before the beginning of `this`. If the first argument is `"afterBegin"`, this acts the same as `this.insertBefore(altHTMLElement, this.childNodes[0]);` just at the beginning of `this`. If the first argument is `"beforeEnd"`, this acts the same as `this.appendChild(altHTMLElement);` just at the end of `this`. If the first argument is `"afterEnd"`, this acts the same as `this.parentNode.insertBefore(altHTMLElement, this.nextSibling);` just after the end of `this`. However, the DOM methods allow any arbitrary node to be inserted, while `insertAdjacentElement()` will throw an error if you pass it anything other than an `HTMLElement`. (See Chapter 20, "Core DOM Objects," for a description of all these properties and methods under the `Node` interface.)

insertAdjacentHTML( )

IE5.0+

Syntax

HTMLElement.insertAdjacentElement(*strLocation*, *altHTMLElement*)

The insertAdjacentHTML() method of all HTMLElement instances inserts the second argument, a string containing HTML code, in the document in a position relative to the this element. The first argument determines the position of the newly inserted element.

If the first argument is "beforeBegin", this inserts the HTML just before the beginning of this. If the first argument is "afterBegin", this inserts the HTML just at the beginning of this. If the first argument is "beforeEnd", this inserts the HTML just at the end of this. If the first argument is "afterEnd", this inserts the HTML just after the end of this.

The results of the insertion force the browser to re-render the this element.

mergeAttributes( )

IE5.0+

Syntax

HTMLElement.mergeAttributes(*altHTMLElement*, [*allFlag*])

The mergeAttributes() method of all HTMLElement interfaces imports the changeable attributes of the first argument, another HTMLElement instance, and applies them to the this element. This includes styling and event handlers. The imported attributes overwrite any corresponding attributes in this.

For Internet Explorer 5.5+, if the second argument is included and is false, all attributes, including the id attribute, will be imported into the this element.

removeBehavior( )

IE5+

Syntax

[var *x* =] *HTMLElement*.removeBehavior(*varName*)

The `removeBehavior()` method of the `HTMLElement` removes the behavior that the first argument references by variable name from the `this` object. (Typically, the behavior has been attached using the `addBehavior()` method, which I describe earlier in this chapter.)

DHTML behaviors, an Internet Explorer proprietary extension to HTML, go far beyond the scope of this book. You can find information on them via Microsoft's Web site at `http://msdn.microsoft.com/workshop/author/behaviors/overview.asp`.

removeNode( )

IE5.0+

Syntax

`HTMLElement.removeNode([childFlag])`

The `removeNode()` method of all `HTMLElement` instances is like a self-destruct system; by calling this method, the `this` element disappears from the document entirely. If you provide the first argument as `true`, this method removes all child nodes of the `this` element as well.

This method returns a reference to `this`.

replaceAdjacentText( )

IE5.0+

Syntax

`[var x =] HTMLElement.replaceAdjacentText(strLocation, altText)`

The `replaceAdjacentText()` method of all `HTMLElement` instances inserts the second argument, a string containing replacement text, in the document in a position relative to the `this` element. The first argument determines the position of the newly inserted element.

If the first argument is `"beforeBegin"`, this inserts the HTML just before the beginning of `this`. If the first argument is `"afterBegin"`, this replaces the text just at the beginning of `this`. If the first argument is `"beforeEnd"`, this replaces the HTML just at the end of `this`. If the first argument is `"afterEnd"`, this replaces the HTML just after the end of `this`.

This method returns the text the method replaces.

Listing 21.4 provides an example of the `replaceAdjacentText()` method at work; as you can see, the `"beforeBegin"` button performs an insertion instead of a replacement as Microsoft's documentation would have you believe. It is important to be aware of this unusual behavior or you could be in for some rather unpleasant debugging time.

Listing 21.4   *Replacing Adjacent Text*

```
<?xml version="1.0" ?>
<!DOCTYPE html PUBLIC "-//W3C//DTD XHTML 1.0 Transitional//EN"
➥"DTD/xhtml1-transitional.dtd">
<html xmlns="http://www.w3.org/1999/xhtml" >
<head><title></title></head>
<body>
<p>One</p>
<p>Two<b>Three</b>Four</p>
<p id="test">Five<b>Six</b>Seven</p>
<p>Eight<b>Nine</b>Ten</p>
<script language="JavaScript" type="text/javascript">
<!--
function go(arg0) {
    test.replaceAdjacentText(arg0,arg0)
    }
//-->
</script>
<form action="javascript:void(null)" method="post">
<input type="button" value="beforeBegin" onclick="go('beforeBegin')" />
<input type="button" value="afterBegin" onclick="go('afterBegin')" />
<input type="button" value="beforeEnd" onclick="go('beforeEnd')" />
<input type="button" value="afterEnd" onclick="go('afterEnd')" />
</form>
<!-- No specific results available; the test is flexible. -->
</body>
</html>
```

replaceNode( )

IE5.0+

Syntax

```
[var x =] HTMLElement.replaceNode(newNode)
```

The `replaceNode()` method of all `HTMLElement` instances replaces the `this` element in the document with the first argument, another `HTMLElement` interface. This method returns a reference to the `this` element.

scrollIntoView( )

IE5.0+

Syntax

HTMLElement`.scrollIntoView(`*boolValue*`)`

The `scrollIntoView()` method of all `HTMLElement` instances automatically scrolls the window so the desired element will appear as close to the left as possible and within view. If the first argument is omitted or set to `true`, the element appears as close to at the top of the visible portion of the window as possible. If the first argument is `false`, the element appears as close to the bottom of the visible portion of the window as possible.

Listing 21.5 demonstrates the use of the `scrollIntoView()` method, with an absurdly large document space.

Listing 21.5   *Using* `scrollIntoView()` *to Scroll a Window*

```
<?xml version="1.0" ?>
<!DOCTYPE html PUBLIC "-//W3C//DTD XHTML 1.0 Transitional//EN"
➥"DTD/xhtml1-transitional.dtd">
<html xmlns="http://www.w3.org/1999/xhtml" >
<head><title></title></head>
<body>
<div id="div0" style="color:red;position:absolute;top:800px;left:1500px;">
<p>Hello World</p>
</div>
<div id="div1" style="position:absolute;top:1600px;left:3000px">.</div>
<form action="javascript:void(null)" method="post">
<input type="button" value="toTop" onclick="moveDiv(true)" />
<!-- Click the onTop button; "Hello World" moves to the upper-left corner. -->

<input type="button" value="toBottom" onclick="moveDiv(false)" />
<!-- Click the onBottom button; "Hello World" moves to the lower-left corner. --
>

</form>
```

Listing 21.5   *(continued)*

```
<script language="JavaScript" type="text/javascript">
<!--
function moveDiv(arg) {
   document.all.div0.scrollIntoView(arg)
   }
//-->
</script>
<!-- No printed results.  The window scrolls upon a button click. -->
</body>
</html>
```

swapNode()

IE5.0+

Syntax

HTMLElement.swapNode(*altHTMLElement*)

The swapNode() method of all HTMLElement instances merely swaps one element, given as the first argument, in the document with the this element, switching their positions entirely.

Event Handlers

Internet Explorer supports the following event handlers for HTML elements:

onactivate	oncellchange	ondrag
onafterupdate	oncontextmenu	ondragend
onbeforecopy	oncontrolselect	ondragenter
onbeforecut	oncopy	ondragleave
onbeforedeactivate	oncut	ondragover
onbeforeeditfocus	ondataavailable	ondragstart
onbeforepaste	ondatasetchanged	ondrop
onbeforeupdate	ondatasetcomplete	onerrorupdate
onblur	ondblclick	onfilterchange
onclick	ondeactivate	onfocus

onhelp

onkeydown

onkeypress

onkeyup

onlayoutcomplete

onlosecapture

onmousedown

onmouseenter

onmouseleave

onmousemove

onmouseover

onmouseout

onmouseup

onmove

onmoveend

onmovestart

onpage

onpaste

onpropertychange

onreadystatechange

onresizestart

onrowenter

onrowexit

onrowsinserted

onresize

onresizeend

onrowsdelete

onselectstart

onscroll

CHAPTER 22

HTMLHtmlElement

Part III   Documents Object Model for HTML Documents

Browser/JavaScript Version	Created By
Nav4/JavaScript 1.2	`<html>...</html>`
IE4/JScript 3.0	`<html>...</html>`
IE5/JScript 5.0	`<html>...</html>`
IE5.5/JScript 5.5	`<html>...</html>`
Nav6/JavaScript 1.5	`<html>...</html>`
IE6	`<html>...</html>`

> **Note**
>
> Implemented in Nav1+ (HTML), IE1+ (HTML), Nav6 (DOM), IE4+ (DOM)
>
> Descends from `HTMLElement` interface (see Chapter 21, "HTMLElement")
>
> Parent elements: None

Description

The `HTMLHtmlElement` is the root element of any HTML or XHTML document. This element has no parent element (its parent node is the `HTMLDocument`). The only siblings this element may have are processing instructions, document type declarations, and comments. A convenient way to access the root element with the DOM is `document.documentElement`.

The DOM Level 1 defines one property of the `HTMLHtmlElement` that does not exist in the `HTMLElement` interface. This property, the `version` property, has been deprecated in favor of version information that the document type declaration stores (see Chapter 20 for the `DocumentType` interface).

Properties

clientHeight
Read-only IE5+

Syntax

```
[var x =] document.documentElement.clientHeight
```

The `clientHeight` property of the `HTMLHtmlElement` retrieves the height of the object, including padding. This property does not have a default value and is read-only.

clientWidth

Read-only IE5+

Syntax

```
[var x =] document.documentElement.clientWidth
```

The `clientWidth` property of the `HTMLHtmlElement` retrieves the width of the object, including padding. This property does not have a default value and is read-only.

innerHTML

Nav6, IE5+

Read-only in IE5+

Syntax

```
[var x =] document.documentElement.innerHTML [= HTMLString]
```

The `innerHTML` property of `HTMLHtmlElement` interfaces retrieves or sets the HTML source code contained between, but not including, the starting and ending tags.

I personally recommend against using `innerHTML` to set the HTML inside a tag. This forces the browser to re-render some or all the contents of the page. New browsers may be more efficient with this tag, but this will still most likely result in unnecessary work for the browser.

I strongly recommend against using `innerHTML` to append to the contents of an HTML tag:

```
elem.innerHTML += "<div><p>Hello World</p></div>" // DO NOT DO THIS
```

This forces the browser to retrieve the current `innerHTML` value, add new markup to it, and re-render the entire page. There are ways to have `innerHTML` re-render less, but it will still most likely re-render more than you want it to.

I do like the handiness of the `innerHTML` property for retrieving HTML source code at a glance, as a companion method to the W3C Document Object Model. (The DOM provides an object structure for the source code; `innerHTML` provides the corresponding source code.)

innerText

IE5+

Syntax

```
var x = document.documentElement.innerText
```

The `innerText` property of `HTMLHtmlElement` interfaces retrieves or sets the text contained between, but not including, the starting and ending tags.

For other elements this property is read/write; for `HTMLHtmlElement` it is read-only.

The `innerText` property can be useful, but the DOM Level 2 `Range` interface provides far more flexibility. See Chapter 34, "DOM-2 Range," for details on text ranges.

outerHTML

IE5+

Syntax

```
var x = document.documentElement.outerHTML
```

The `outerHTML` property of `HTMLHtmlElement` interfaces retrieves or sets the HTML source code contained between, and including, the starting and ending tags.

For other elements this property is read/write; for `HTMLHtmlElement` it is read-only.

I do like the handiness of the `outerHTML` property for retrieving HTML source code at a glance, as a companion method to the W3C Document Object Model. (The DOM provides an object structure for the source code; `outerHTML` provides the corresponding source code.)

outerText

IE5+

Syntax

```
var x = document.documentElement.outerText
```

The `outerText` property of `HTMLHtmlElement` interfaces retrieves or sets the text contained between, but not including, the starting and ending tags.

For other elements this property is read/write; for `HTMLHtmlElement` it is read-only.

The outerText property can be useful, but the DOM Level 2 Range interface provides far more flexibility. See Chapter 34, "DOM-2 Range," for details on text ranges.

scrollHeight

Read-only IE5+

Syntax

```
[var x =] document.documentElement.scrollHeight
```

The scrollHeight property of the HTMLHtmlElement retrieves the height of the object's content without padding. This property does not have a default value and is read-only.

scrollWidth

Read-only IE5+

Syntax

```
[var x =] document.documentElement.scrollWidth
```

The scrollWidth property of the HTMLHtmlElement retrieves the width of the object's content without padding. This property does not have a default value and is read-only.

uniqueID

IE5.0+

Syntax

```
var x = document.documentElement.uniqueID
```

The uniqueID property of the HTMLHtmlElement returns a string unique to the given document. Reloading the document changes this property. Note it does not exist within the this element until you actually call it.

version

Nav6, IE6

Syntax

```
var x = document.documentElement.version
```

This property reflects the `version` attribute of HTML, which corresponds to the version of the HTML document. Document type declarations have superseded the need for the `version` attribute, so you may not expect to see this property in widespread use.

Methods

The `HTMLHtmlElement` interface provides no methods beyond those the `HTMLElement` interface defines.

CHAPTER 23

HTMLDocument/ document

Browser/JavaScript Version	Created By
Nav4/JavaScript 1.2	HTML document
IE4/JScript 3.0	HTML document
IE5/JScript 5.0	HTML document
IE5.5/JScript 5.5	HTML document
Nav6/JavaScript 1.5	HTML document
IE6	HTML document
DOM 1 HTML	HTML document

> **Note**
>
> Implemented in Nav2+ (`document`), IE3+ (`document`), Nav6+ (`HTMLDocument`), IE5+ (`HTMLDocument`)
>
> Descends from `Document` interface in Chapter 20, "Core DOM Objects" (`HTMLDocument` only)
>
> Property of `window` object (`window.document`)

Description

The `HTMLDocument` object represents the current document loaded into the window. In earlier browsers, the `<body>...</body>` element defines the document whereas the `<html>...</html>` element defines the root of the document. Thanks to the Document Object Model, the `HTMLDocument` is an independent and superior (in the hierarchy) object to any other object in the tree of nodes.

One Method, Two Properties, and Compatibility with Three Browsers

In Chapter 20, "Core DOM Objects," I discussed the `document.getElementById()` method. In this chapter I explain the `document.layers` and `document.all` properties. Two of these are very similar, and the third works the same as the other two in regards to positioned content (for instance, a `<div>...</div>` element with style attributes designating where on the document it goes). This similarity of objects doing the same thing (almost) and having different names reminds us of the headaches we all have in writing for 4.x browsers. For those of you fortunate enough to write for Internet Explorer 5+ and Netscape 6 exclusively, a little background is necessary.

One of the biggest considerations the W3C DOM working group (WG) had in creating the DOM was ensuring compatibility with the "DOM Level 0"—meaning common features in Netscape Navigator 3.0 and Internet Explorer 3.0. Although the fourth-generation browsers were significantly different, most of the JavaScript-related changes dealt with positioning and styling issues. These issues fell outside the purview of the DOM working group for the immediate time, and so for all intents and purposes the DOM WG ignored 4.x browsers. The confusion all developers saw in coding for these 4.x browsers vindicated their decision—and the styling issues of JavaScript I will cover in Chapters 24, "Head Elements," (under `HTMLStyleElement`) and 33, "Styling for HTML Elements," (the entire chapter).

Meanwhile, the two major browser companies waged an advertising battle for WWW browser share. At first, the two browsers looked somewhat equal. Microsoft held a few advantages over Netscape, and Netscape held a few advantages over Microsoft. Neither browser held any real dominance over the other, and JavaScripters accepted a need for writing JavaScript code for both browsers.

It would have been far less difficult if the two browsers supported the same procedures for position and styled content. They did not, and the result was a massive series of discrepancies in browsers. Netscape, for example, went with the `<layer>...</layer>` tag; Internet Explorer used the `<div>...</div>` tag . Lots of JavaScript developers faced frustration (or at least rising paychecks) as they struggled to write code that would work in both browsers equally well. Dynamic HTML, and the First Browser War, were born for not entirely unrelated reasons.

The Impact of the Standards

Microsoft won a major fight in the first browser war by declaring its 5.x generation of browser was standards-compliant. (Netscape was still well over a year away from making a similar claim.) However, most advanced JavaScripters know better. Netscape 6, released at the end of 2000, was far more standards-compliant, in respect to W3C and ECMA standards, but still falls short in certain areas. Perhaps no browser will ever be fully standards-compliant.

I have noticed an interesting trend in the Website Abstraction Help Forum. Developers new to JavaScript strongly prefer Microsoft Internet Explorer, by far the most popular browser on the Internet. However, the more advanced developers favor Netscape 6 and especially its uncle, Mozilla. The reason is simple: most new people start out in Internet Explorer, but advanced developers like standards, and Mozilla is an open-source project that promotes standards heavily.

The irony in all this is far more people use Netscape Navigator 4.x than use Mozilla and Netscape 6 combined. So now instead of coding for two browsers, we typically code for three, aware that one of them has been deprecated….

The standards reshaped the entire approach of browsers to HTML (and now XML) documents, especially in terms of JavaScript. With an official roadmap, the focus for browser debugging became not "what they support that we don't", but "what we don't do correctly." The W3C promotes their standards so Web pages will (theoretically) render identically in any browser. The browser companies are responsible for correct rendering according to the standards.

The Second Browser War: 6.x

Yes, I do believe we will see a second round of browser wars. The standards, aside from XML-based ones, only define minimums. Each browser is free to implement features above and beyond the minimums—and both Netscape and Microsoft do that. Microsoft has long supported VML, literally "Vector Markup Language," which the SVG standard (a W3C recommendation) will eventually supersede. The `<marquee>...</marquee>` tag is an Internet Explorer-proprietary element, which XHTML does not permit. Netscape, of course, returns the favor with XBL and XUL, neither of which do I pretend to understand. (XHTML currently does not support multiple namespaces in a document officially as "strictly conforming.")

Collections: A Holdover from 3.x Browsers

The `document.layers` and `document.all` objects are arrays that are sometimes called collections. Essentially, a collection is an array of elements all of a certain type within the current document and will typically have methods to access elements in the collection such as `item` or `namedItem`. For instance, `document.images` is a collection of all `HTMLImageElement` objects within the document. (See Chapter 30, "Image Elements," for an explanation of the `HTMLImageElement`.)

You can access a particular element of a collection by name (`document.images.`*`imageName`* or `document.images["`*`imageName`*`"]`) or by its appearance in the document (`document.images[`*`x`*`]`, where x is a nonnegative integer).

Technically, with the `document.getElementsByTagName()` method, you really don't need these collections—the method retrieves collections of a particular element type automatically.

The Body and Document Are Now Separate

Part of the new Document Object Model splits pieces of the old document object into the new document object and the HTMLBodyElement element. The Document Object Model also defines several features that traditionally belong to the window object. The W3C acknowledges this, and such features have already been covered in Chapter 15, "window."

This book separates the HTMLBodyElement objects from the revised document object, but wherever a property existed earlier in the document object I will note so.

Properties

activeElement

JScript 3.0+

IE4+

Read-only

Syntax

```
var x = document.activeElement
```

The activeElement property of document returns the element that possesses focus relative to the window and document. Only one window may have focus at any given time. Within each window, only one element may have focus at any given time. You can have an activeElement from a window that does not currently have focus; in cases like this, typically the activeElement is the last element to have focus when the window also had focus.

alinkColor

JavaScript 1.0+, JScript 1.0+

Nav2+, IE3+

Read-only in Nav2-Nav4, IE3

Transferred to HTMLBodyElement in Nav6

Syntax

```
[var x =] document.alinkColor [= "colString"]
```

The `alinkColor` property of `document` reflects the active-link color setting of the document. An active link is a link on which the user is clicking (the link is only active during the click, not after).

all

JScript 3.0+

IE4+

Syntax

```
[var x =] document.all
```

The `all` property of `document` is a collection of all descendant elements of the `this` object. You can access these elements in a number of ways, as Listing 21.1 demonstrates.

item

JScript 3.0+

IE4+

Syntax

```
var x = document.all.item(index[, iSubindex])
```

The `item()` method of the `document.all` object takes a nonnegative integer less than `this.length` as the first argument. You can get a `Node` object from the `this` object representing that `Node`'s placement in the `this` object's index.

length

JScript 3.0+

IE4+

Syntax

```
var x = document.all.length
```

The `length` property of `document.all` tells how many objects are in the collection.

tags

JScript 3.0+

IE4+

Syntax

```
var x = document.all.tags(tagName)
```

The `tags()` method of `document.all` returns a collection of those elements in the `document.all` collection whose `tagName` property matches the first argument of the method.

urns

JScript 5.0+

IE5+

Syntax

```
var x = document.all.urns(behaviorName)
```

The `urns` method of `document.all` returns a subset of the `this` element comprising all elements possessing a DHTML behavior whose name matches the first argument.

DHTML behaviors, an Internet Explorer proprietary extension to HTML, go far beyond the scope of this book. You can find information on them via Microsoft's Web site at `http://msdn.microsoft.com/workshop/author/behaviors/overview.asp`.

anchors

JavaScript 1.0+, JScript 1.0+

Nav2+, IE3+

Syntax

```
[var x =] document.anchors
```

The `anchors` property of `document` is a collection of `HTMLAnchorElement` objects, or anchors, in the document. An anchor is an `<a>...</a>` element with a "name" attribute. See Chapter 28, "Text Elements," for more details.

applets

JavaScript 1.1+, JScript 3.0+

Nav3+, IE4+

Syntax

```
[var x =] document.applets
```

The `applets` property of `document` is a collection of all `HTMLObjectElement` and `HTMLAppletElement` objects in the document. Object elements and applets I discuss in greater detail in Chapter 31, "Programmable Elements."

bgColor

Nav2+, IE3+

Transferred to `HTMLBodyElement` in Nav6

Deprecated in IE5.5

Syntax

```
[var x =] document.bgColor [= "colString"]
```

The `bgColor` property of `document` reflects the background color setting of the document.

body

JavaScript 1.5, JScript 3.0+

Nav6, IE4+

Syntax

```
var x = document.body
```

The `body` property of `document` refers to the body section of the document, contained in `<body>...</body>` tags. See "`HTMLBodyElement`" later in this chapter.

characterSet/charset

JavaScript 1.5, JScript 3.0+

Nav6 (`characterSet`), IE4+ (`charset`)

Syntax

```
var x = document.charset
var x = document.characterSet
```

This property reflects the character set encoding (basically, a designation of the document's alphabet and what characters are in said alphabet) of the document. You define the character set via an `HTMLMetaElement`.

children

JScript 3.0+

IE4+

Syntax

```
var x = document.children
```

The `children` property contains the child elements of the document object. Note the difference from `childNodes` in the DOM where text, comment, and other nodes are also included. See `childNodes` under the DOM `Document` object in Chapter 20, "Core DOM Objects."

classes

JavaScript 1.2

Nav4

Removed in Nav6

Syntax

```
[var x =] document.classes
```

The `classes` property of `document` is a property that collects all classes in the document into an array. You can alter a class, and thus the styling of any element having that class name as an attribute, by altering the property of the `document.classes` object matching that class name. Because it is now abandoned I suggest you avoid its use.

cookie

JavaScript 1.0+, JScript 1.0+

Nav2+, IE3+

Syntax

```
[var x =] document.cookie [= cookieString]
```

The `cookie` property of `document` sets the current cookie value for the current document. If you read `document.cookie` you get all cookies for the document.

Cookies are a special feature of browsers and are specific to one domain and a path within it. Thus, if the cookie was on `www.example.com` with a path of `/` other servers should have no access to that cookie. They allow a document to store up to 4KB of information based on the URL of the document. Thus, a different document at the same URL (usually an update to the original document) can access the stored information.

In terms of data storage, cookies occupy a middle ground many find uncomfortable or undesirable. They do persist after the document has unloaded, for a certain length of time. However, because certain companies have used cookies in the past to collect information they wouldn't otherwise have, privacy advocates have for the most part condemned cookies. Likewise, many people disable cookies in their browsers.

There is a special kind of cookie called a "session variable" that servers can use to store information during one browser session.

defaultCharset

JScript 3.0+

IE4+

Syntax

```
var x = document.defaultCharset
```

The `defaultCharset` property of `document` reflects the default character set encoding (basically, a designation of the document's alphabet and what characters are in said alphabet) for the browser. This character set comes from the operating system controls.

designMode

JScript 5.0+

IE5+

Syntax

```
[var x =] document.designMode [ = desString]
```

The `designMode` property of `document` allows you to determine (or set) whether Internet Explorer is in a special design mode. The property may take the values of `"on"`, `"off"`, or `"inherit"`.

dir

JScript 5.0+

IE5+

Syntax

```
[var x =] document.dir
```

The `dir` property of `document` controls the direction of text, either from left to right (forwards), or right to left (backward—siht ekil). See the `BDO` tag definition in Chapter 21, "HTMLElement," for more details.

domain

JavaScript 1.1+, JScript 3.0+

Nav3+, IE4+

Syntax

```
[var x =] document.domain [= "domainString"]
```

The `domain` property of `document` reflects the domain name of the server that sent this document to the browser. This is similar to the `location.hostName` property.

You can set this property without ill effects, but there are restrictions on what you can set this to. Specifically, you can only set it to a less complex domain name, and to one of which the current domain name is a subdomain. For instance, any document at `jslab.isamillionaire.com` could set `document.domain` to `isamillionaire.com`, but not in reverse or to `yahoo.com`.

Setting this property helps your scripts gain access to information from each other, even if they are technically on different servers.

embeds

JavaScript 1.1+, JScript 3.0+

Nav3-Nav4.75, IE4+

Syntax

```
[var x =] document.embeds
```

The embeds property of document is a collection of all `<embed>...</embed>` elements in a page. Such elements have actually been removed from HTML 4, in favor of the HTMLObjectElement instead. See Chapter 31, "Programmable Elements," for details.

expando

JScript 3.0+

IE4+

Syntax

```
[var x =] document.expando [= boolValue]
```

When this property is true (the default), the document can accept user-defined properties. When this property is false, the document cannot accept new properties.

fgColor

JavaScript 1.0+, JScript 1.0+

Nav2+, IE3+

Read-only Nav2-4, IE3

Transferred to HTMLBodyElement in Nav6

Syntax

```
[var x =] document.fgColor [= colString]
```

The `document.fgColor` property of `document` reflects the foreground, or default text, color of the document.

fileCreatedDate

JScript 3.0+

IE4+

Syntax

```
var x = document.fileCreatedDate
```

The `fileCreatedDate` property contains the date a file was created if the server is kind enough to provide the date the file was created. Otherwise, the property usually reflects today's date.

fileModifiedDate

JScript 3.0+

IE4+

Syntax

```
var x = document.fileModifiedDate
```

The `fileModifiedDate` property contains the date a file was last modified if the server is kind enough to provide the date the file was last modified. Otherwise, the property usually reflects today's date.

fileSize

JScript 3.0+

IE4+

Syntax

```
var x = document.fileSize
```

The `fileSize` property of `document` reflects the length of the file in bytes.

forms

JavaScript 1.1+, JScript 1.0+

Nav3+, IE3+

Syntax

```
[var x =] document.forms
```

The `forms` property of `document` is a collection of all `HTMLFormElement` elements in the document, identified by name (`document.forms.myForm`) or by their order of appearance in the document structure (`document.forms[0]`). Although Netscape and Internet Explorer allow you to refer to a form by name directly as a property of `document`, I find it slightly better to refer to it as a property of `document.forms`. (This is more of a preference issue than a serious one. Most JavaScripters at Website Abstraction omit the `forms` property and deal directly with forms by name. I almost never do.)

frames

JScript 3.0+

IE4+

Syntax

```
var x = document.frames
```

The `frames` property of `document` is the same as the `window.frames` object in Chapter 15, "window."

height

JScript 3.0+

Nav4+

Syntax

```
[var x =] document.height
```

The `height` property of the `document` object tells you how many pixels within a window the document occupies vertically.

ids

JavaScript 1.2-1.3

Nav4-4.5Removed in Nav6

Syntax

```
[var x =] document.ids
```

The `ids` property of `document` is an array that contains the ID values of Netscape style sheets. For DOM-1 compliant browsers, use the `document.getElementById` method instead (covered in Chapter 20, "Core DOM Objects," under `Document`).

images

JavaScript 1.1+, JScript 3.0+

Nav3+, IE4+

Syntax

```
[var x =] document.images
```

The `images` property of `document` is a collection of all `HTMLImageElement` objects in a document. `HTMLImageElement` objects I discuss in more detail in Chapter 30, "Image Elements."

lastModified

JavaScript 1.0+, JScript 1.0+

Nav2+, IE3+

Syntax

```
var x = document.lastModified
```

The `lastModified` property of the `document` object contains the date on which a file was last modified, if the server provides the last-modified date of the file, this property reflects it. Otherwise, this property reflects `new Date(0)`.

layers

JavaScript 1.2-1.4

Nav4-4.7

Removed in Nav6

Syntax

```
[var x =] document.layers
```

The `layers` property of `document` is a collection of all `<layer>...</layer>` elements and `<ilayer>` elements within a page that are not themselves contained within another positioned element. See Chapter 28, "Text Elements," under `Layer` for specific features of these elements.

linkColor

JavaScript 1.0+, JScript 1.0+

Nav2+, IE3+

Read-only Nav2-4, IE3

Transferred to `HTMLBodyElement` in Netscape 6

Syntax

```
[var x =] document.linkColor [= colString]
```

The `linkColor` property of `document` reflects the unvisited link color setting of the document.

links

JavaScript 1.0+, JScript 1.0+

Nav2+, IE3+

Syntax

```
var x = document.links
```

The `links` property of `document` is a collection of `HTMLAnchorElement` objects, specifically links, in the document. A link is an `<a>...</a>` element with an `href` attribute. See Chapter 28, "Text Elements," for more details.

location

JavaScript 1.0+, JScript 1.0+

Nav2+, IE3+

Syntax

```
[var x =] document.location
```

See Chapter 16, "location."

namespaces

JScript 5.5+

IE5.5+

Syntax

```
var x = document.namespaces
```

The `namespaces` property of `document` returns a collection of namespaces belonging to the document.

parentWindow

JScript 3.0+

IE4+

Syntax

```
var x = document.parentWindow
```

The `parentWindow` property of `document` returns the `window` object containing the document. There appears to be no need for this object, as we can reference the `window` object the document resides in with the `self` object.

plugins

JavaScript 1.1-1.4

Nav3-Nav4.7x

Removed in Nav6

Syntax

```
[var x =] document.plugins
```

The `plugins` property of `document` is a collection of plug-ins the document references.

protocol

JScript 1.0+

IE3+

Syntax

```
var x = document.protocol
```

The `protocol` property of `document` is similar to the `location.protocol` property I covered in Chapter 17, "location," except instead this explains the acronym's value. FTP returns "File Transfer Protocol," for instance.

readyState

JScript 3.0+

IE4+

Syntax

```
var x = document.readyState
```

The `readyState` property of `document` reflects five different values: "uninitialized", "loading", "loaded", "interactive", and "complete". The first, "uninitialized", means the HTTP call has gone out to retrieve the document's data source but the response has not begun yet. The "loading" value means the program has begun to download the information the document references. The "loaded" value means the browser has downloaded the requested information, but it hasn't finished processing it. The "interactive" setting means the user can interact with it, even as it's still downloading…. Finally, the "complete" state indicates all is well.

referrer

JavaScript 1.0+, JScript 1.0+

Nav2+, IE3+

Syntax

```
[var x =] document.referrer
```

The `referrer` property of the `document` object contains the URL of the page you visited before the current one, if the server is kind enough to provide to the browser the URL of the last page the browser visited. Otherwise, this is an empty string.

scripts

JScript 3.0+

IE4+

Syntax

```
var x = document.scripts
```

The `scripts` property of `document` is a collection of `HTMLScriptElement` objects, specifically JavaScripts, VBScripts, and so on, in the document.

selection

JScript 3.0+

IE4+

Syntax

```
var x = document.selection
```

The `selection` property of `document` reflects the currently selected text of the document. Similar to, but more powerful than, Netscape's `document.getSelection()` method.

styleSheets

JavaScript 1.5, JScript 3.0+

Nav6, IE4+

Syntax

```
[var x =] document.styleSheets
```

The `styleSheets` property of `document` is a collection of `HTMLStyleElement` and `HTMLLinkElement` objects, specifically stylesheets, in the document. See Chapter 33, "Styling for HTML Elements," for more details.

tags

JavaScript 1.2

Nav4

Removed in Nav6

Syntax

```
[var x =] document.tags
```

The `tags` property of `document` collects all element names in the document into an array after the document has been rendered.

title

JavaScript 1.0+, JScript 3.0+

Nav2+, IE4+

Read-only Nav2-4

Syntax

```
var x = document.title
```

The `title` property of `document` retrieves the title of the document, which HTML defines as the contents of the `HTMLTitleElement`. I cover `HTMLTitleElement` in Chapter 24, "Head Elements."

uniqueID

JScript 5.0+

IE5.0+

Syntax

```
var x = document.uniqueID
```

The `uniqueID` property of `document` returns a string unique to the given document. Reloading the document changes this property. Note it does not exist within the `this` element until you actually call it.

URL

JavaScript 1.0+, JScript 3.0+

Nav2+, IE4+

Syntax

```
[var x =] document.URL
```

The `URL` property of `document` reflects the current Web location (URL) of the document. This property is very similar to `location.href`.

URLUnencoded

JScript 5.5+

IE5.5+

Syntax

```
var x = document.URLUnencoded
```

The `URLUnencoded` property of `document` is equivalent to `decodeURI(document.URL)`. See `decodeURI()` in Chapter 11, "The Global Objects and Statements."

vlinkColor

JavaScript 1.0+, JScript 1.0+

Nav2+, IE3+

Read-only Nav2-4, IE3

Transferred to `HTMLBodyElement` in Netscape 6

Syntax

```
[var x =] document.vlinkColor [= "colString"]
```

The `vlinkColor` property of `document` reflects the visited-link color setting of the document.

width

JavaScript 1.2+

Nav4+

Syntax

```
[var x =] document.width
```

The `width` property of `document` tells you how many pixels within a window the document occupies horizontally. The Internet Explorer equivalent is `document.body.scrollWidth`.

Methods

attachEvent()

JScript 5.0+

IE5.0+

Syntax

```
document.attachEvent(eventName, handler)
```

The `attachEvent()` method of `document` attaches an event handler for the event the first argument names to the document. Should the event actually happen upon the document (or it bubbles up from a child event), the function the second argument names without parentheses will execute.

I cover events and event handlers in more detail in Chapter 32, "DOM-2 Events and Event Handlers."

captureEvents()

JavaScript 1.2+

Nav4+

Syntax

```
document.captureEvents(eventType)
```

```
captureEvents(eventName0 [, eventName1 ...])
```

The captureEvents()is a method of Netscape that intercepts all events of the types given as arguments. (Typically, these events are referred to as Event.*EVENTNAME*, where the event name is capitalized.) Using this method, you catch the events thrown or fired before the object they apply to catches them. See Chapter 32, "DOM-2 Events and Event Handlers," for details.

close()

JavaScript 1.0+, JScript 3.0+

Nav2+, IE4+

Syntax

```
document.close()
```

The close() method of document closes a stream of HTML that JavaScript generates for the browser. You use this method only after use of the document.write() method, to force the browser to render whatever the write() method feeds to the browser. See the write() method and Listing 23.2, later in this chapter, for details.

contextual()

JavaScript 1.2+

Nav4+

Syntax

```
var x = document.contextual([[...,] GrandParentStyle,] ParentStyle, style)
```

The contextual() method of document takes an array of HTML elements in the last argument and filters it according to which HTML elements in the last argument are descendant elements of the preceding argument. It then proceeds to filter it further, removing elements that are not descendant elements of the preceding argument. It repeats this process for each argument it receives. It returns the results to the client. In the process, none of the original arguments change.

createEventObject()

JScript 5.5+

IE5.5+

Syntax

```
var x = document.createEventObject([eventObj])
```

The `createEventObject()` method of `document` creates and returns a new event object for use by the `fireEvent()` method of elements. If you provide an event object as the first argument, it bases the event object it creates on that argument. (The idea is to be able to create your own instances of an event, to contain specific information about the source of your event. You do this by attaching properties and methods to the object in question.)

See Chapter 32, "Events and Event Handlers," for details on events.

createStyleSheet()

JScript 3.0+

IE4+

Syntax

```
var x = document.createStyleSheet([optArg0, [optArg1]])
```

The `createStyleSheet()` method of `document` creates and returns a new `styleSheet` object (either an `HTMLStyleElement` or an `HTMLLinkElement`, based on the arguments).

You may provide up to two arguments for this method. If you provide the first argument as a string containing a URL, the new style sheet is an `HTMLLinkElement` element. If you provide the first argument as a string containing styling information, it will be appended to one of the document's current `HTMLStyleElements`.

After the optional string argument, you can include an integer telling where in the `document.styleSheets` collection to insert the returned style sheet. (You can omit the string argument and still include the integer argument as the first argument.) See Chapter 33, "Styling for HTML Elements."

detachEvent()

JScript 5.0+

IE5+

Syntax

```
document.detachEvent(oneventName, handler)
```

The detachEvent() method of document causes the event handler given as the first argument to stop passing any events of the type named in the first argument and fired on the document to the second argument, a function. This method works only if the attachEvent() method was called with the exact same arguments on the document as well. See Chapter 32, "Events and Event Handlers," for details.

elementFromPoint()

JScript 3.0+

IE4+

Syntax

```
var x = document.elementFromPoint(xcoord, ycoord)
```

The elementFromPoint() method of document returns the element which, on the client computer, exists at the coordinate set given as the arguments. The first argument is the distance from the left edge of the document. The second argument is the distance from the top edge of the document.

My experiments show this method may be somewhat sporadic. When I called this method in an onload event handler, it would throw an exception. When I called it as a command line in my textarea-based editing script (the example in Chapter 4, "String()"), it worked perfectly.

execCommand()

JScript 3.0+

IE4+

Syntax

```
[var x =] document.execCommand(commandName [, userGUI] [, assignValue])
```

The execCommand() method of document executes a special command, named in the first argument. If the command works correctly, the method returns true; else, it returns false.

You may have up to three arguments in this function. The second argument, if it is a Boolean value (true or false), indicates whether the user interface for the command, if there is one, should be available to the user. The other argument is a value you are assigning by the command.

There are a number of command names available to the document object. Table 23.1 shows the various commands for document, and acceptable values for the arguments.

Table 23.1   *Valid Argument Sets for* execCommand()

commandName	userGUI version	assignValue	action
2D-Position	false IE5.5+	true for dragging, false for stationary	Allows user to move a positioned div.
BackColor	false IE4+	Color name or hexadecimal representation	Sets background color of selection to assignValue.
Bold	IE4+		If selection is boldfaced, turn off boldface; else, turn it on.
Copy	IE4+		Copies the selection into the operating system Clipboard.
CreateBookmark	IE4+		Creates a bookmark anchor or retrieves a bookmark anchor for the current insertion point.
CreateLink	true or false IE4+	URL for link to create (optional)	If userGUI is false, or link given, sets link automatically; otherwise, prompts user for URL.
Cut	IE4+		Cuts the current selection from the document and moves it to the Clipboard.
Delete	IE4+		Removes the current selection from the document.
FontName	false IE4+	List of font names, in order of preference	Sets the font name of the selection to match the first font in the assignValue value, which the client supports.
FontSize	false IE4+	Integer between 1 and 7, including 1 or 7.	Sets a font-size attribute for the text.
ForeColor	false IE4+	Color name or hexadecimal representation	Sets text/foreground color of selection to assignValue.

Table 23.1   *(continued)*

commandName	userGUI version	assignValue	action
FormatBlock	false IE4+	Opening HTML block text tag (no closing tag)	Changes the text of the selection to render in the assignValue element type.
Indent	false IE4+		Indents the text inward by about one tab space.
InsertButton	false IE4+	Optional id attribute for the button	Replaces the selection with a <button></button> tag pair; no text on the button.
InsertFieldset	false IE4+	Optional id attribute for the box	Replaces the selection with a fieldset box.
InsertHorizontalRule	false IE4+	Optional id attribute for the horizontal rule	Replaces the selection with a <hr/> tag.
InsertIFrame	false IE4+	Optional id attribute for the iframe	Replaces the selection with a <iframe/> tag.
InsertImage	true or false IE5.0+	URL for image to download (optional)	Replaces the selection with an <image/> tag.
			If userGUI is false, or link given, sets image URL automatically; otherwise, prompts user for URL.
InsertInputButton	false IE4+	Optional id attribute for the button	Replaces the selection with an <input type="button" /> tag; no text on the button.
InsertInputCheckBox	false IE4+	Optional id attribute for the box	Replaces the selection with an <input type="checkbox" /> tag.
InsertInputFileUpload	false IE4+	Optional id attribute for the box	Replaces the selection with an <input type="file" /> tag.
InsertInputHidden	false IE4+	Optional id attribute for the tag	Replaces the selection with an <input type="hidden" /> tag.
InsertInputImage	false IE4+	Optional id attribute for the box	Replaces the selection with an <input type="image" /> tag.
InsertInputPassword	false IE4+	Optional id attribute for the box	Replaces the selection with an <input type="password" /> tag.

Table 23.1   *(continued)*

commandName	userGUI version	assignValue	action
InsertInputRadio	false IE4+	Optional `id` attribute for the box	Replaces the selection with an `<input type="radio" />` tag.
InsertInputReset	false IE4+	Optional `id` attribute for the box	Replaces the selection with an `<input type="reset" />` tag.
InsertInputSubmit	false IE4+	Optional `id` attribute for the box	Replaces the selection with an `<input type="submit" />` tag.
InsertInputText	false IE4+	Optional `id` attribute for the box	Replaces the selection with an `<input type="text" />` tag.
InsertInputMarquee	false IE4+	Optional `id` attribute for the marquee	Replaces the selection with a `<marquee></marquee>` tag pair.
InsertOrderedList	false IE4+	Optional `id` attribute for the ordered list	If the selection is in an ordered-list format (`<ol><li>...</li></ol>`), it removes the ordered-list format from the selection. Otherwise, it adds ordered-list format.
InsertParagraph	false IE4+	Optional `id` attribute for the paragraph	Replaces the selection with a `<p></p>` tag pair.
InsertSelectDropDown	false IE4+	Optional `id` attribute for the select box	Replaces the selection with a `<select>...</select>` tag pair.
InsertSelectListBox	false IE4+	Optional `id` attribute for the select box	Replaces the selection with a `<select multiple="multiple">...</select>` tag pair.
InsertTextArea	false IE4+	Optional `id` attribute for the textarea	Replaces the selection with a `<textarea>...</textarea>` tag pair.

Table 23.1 *(continued)*

commandName	userGUI version	assignValue	action
InsertUnorderedList	false IE4+	Optional `id` attribute for the ordered list	If the selection is in an unordered-list format (`<ul><li>...</li></ul>`), it removes the unordered-list format from the selection. Otherwise, it adds unordered-list format.
Italic	false IE4+		If selection is italicized, turns off italic; else, turns it on.
JustifyCenter	false IE4+		Centers the text block containing the selection horizontally.
JustifyLeft	false IE4+		Aligns the text block containing the selection on the left edge of the block's rendering area.
JustifyRight	false IE4+		Aligns the text block containing the selection on the right edge of the block's rendering area.
LiveResize	false IE5.5+		Resizes a `div` as user drags mouse.
MultipleSelection	false	`true` or `false`	When `assignValue` set to `true`, allows multiple elements to be selected simultaneously.
Outdent	false IE4+		Removes indentation of the text by about one tab space.
Overwrite	false IE4+	`true` or `false`	When `assignValue` is `true`, Overstrike mode is on (typing replaces characters). When `false`, Insert mode is on (typing inserts characters).
Paste	false IE4+		Overwrites the selection with the contents of the operating system Clipboard.

Table 23.1   *(continued)*

commandName	userGUI version	assignValue	action
Print	true IE5.5+		Opens the print dialog box, but for the selection.
Refresh	false IE4.0+		Same as `location.reload()`.
RemoveFormat	false IE4.0+		Removes any HTML formatting tags (`<b>`, `<i>`, and so on) from the selection.
SaveAs	true or false IE4+	String containing file path and name or null	If userGUI is false and assignValue is null, saves with no parameters. Otherwise, pops up a confirmation box for the user to confirm.
SelectAll	false IE4+		Selects everything in the document at once.
UnBookMark	false IE4+		Removes any bookmark from the current selection.
Underline	false IE4+		If selection is underlined, turns off underline; else, turns it on.
Unlink	false IE4+		Removes any link you've placed on the selection.
Unselect	false IE4+		This sets the selection as unselected; by this, nothing in the document will be selected.

Microsoft warns against using this method before the `onload` event handler fires.

Most of these commands you can execute using DOM-compliant methods already. The exceptions include most notably the `SaveAs` command. Listing 23.1 shows how you can use this method to ask the user to save the page.

Listing 23.1   *Saving a Page via JavaScript*

```
<?xml version="1.0" ?>
<!DOCTYPE html PUBLIC "-//W3C//DTD XHTML 1.0 Transitional//EN"
➥ "DTD/xhtml1-transitional.dtd">
<html xmlns="http://www.w3.org/1999/xhtml" >
<head><title></title></head>
<body>
<p>Saving the page...</p>
<script language="JavaScript" type="text/javascript">
<!--
// IE 4.0+ only
if (confirm("Do you want to save this page?")) {
   document.execCommand("SaveAs", true, "test.xhtml")
   }
//-->
</script>
<!-- Results:
After a confirm window gets approval, Internet Explorer pops up a
"Save Page As" dialog box.
It's then up to the user to approve it.
(The confirm window is mainly to let the user know ahead of time
what to expect.)
-->
</body>
</html>
```

focus()

JScript 3.0+

IE4+

Syntax

```
document.focus()
```

The focus() method of document is identical to window.focus() (see Chapter 15, "window").

getSelection()

JavaScript 1.2+

Nav4+

Syntax

```
var x = document.getSelection()
```

The `getSelection()` method of `document` returns a string containing the currently selected text of the document. This method is similar to Internet Explorer's `document.selection.createRange().text` property.

mergeAttributes()

JScript 5.0+

IE5.0+

Syntax

```
document.mergeAttributes(altHTMLElement, [allFlag])
```

The `mergeAttributes()` method of `document` imports the changeable properties corresponding to the attributes of the first argument, an `HTMLElement` instance, and applies them to the `this` element. This includes styling and event handlers. The imported attributes overwrite any corresponding attributes in `this`.

For Internet Explorer 5.5+, if the second argument is included and is `false`, all attributes, including the `id` attribute, will be imported into the `this` element.

open()

JavaScript 1.0+, JScript 3.0+

Nav2+, IE4+

Syntax

```
document.open()
```

The `open()` method of `document` opens a stream of HTML that JavaScript generates for the browser. Technically, this method is unnecessary, as the `document.write()` method will open a data stream automatically. See the `write()` method, later in this chapter, and Listing 23.2 for details on writing pages.

queryCommandEnabled()

JScript 3.0+

IE4+

Syntax

```
var x = document.queryCommandEnabled(commandName)
```

The queryCommandEnabled() method of document allows the developer to check if a particular command the execCommand() method executes has been enabled. See execCommand() earlier in this chapter for details on the commands document supports.

Microsoft notes document.queryCommandEnabled("delete") will return false, although the delete command does work.

queryCommandIndeterm()

JScript 3.0+

IE4+

Syntax

```
var x = document.queryCommandIndeterm(commandName)
```

The queryCommandIndeterm() method of document allows the user to check whether a particular command is indeterminate. Every command I have included in the document listing works, so you can expect these methods to return false.

queryCommandState()

JScript 3.0+

IE4+

Syntax

```
var x = document.queryCommandState(commandName)
```

The queryCommandState() method of document allows the user to check whether a particular command has been executed on the selection. If the command, given as a string in the first argument, has executed, the method returns true; otherwise, it returns false. See execCommand() earlier in this chapter for details on the commands document supports.

queryCommandSupported()

JScript 3.0+

IE4+

Syntax

```
var x = document.queryCommandSupported(commandName)
```

The `queryCommandSupported()` method of `document` returns `true` if the `document` object will support the first argument, a command to execute with the `execCommand()` method. Otherwise, the method returns `false`. See `execCommand()` earlier in this chapter for details on the commands `document` supports.

queryCommandValue()

JScript 3.0+

IE4+

Syntax

```
var x = document.queryCommandValue(commandName)
```

The `queryCommandValue()` method of `document` will return the current value for the command named in the first argument, a string.

Some commands, which cannot accept values, will throw an exception for this method. Those for which you can set a value will return a value. `FontSize` is one such command.

See `execCommand()` earlier in this chapter for details on the commands `document` supports.

recalc()

JScript 3.0+

IE4+

Syntax

```
document.recalc()
```

The recalc() method of document is somewhat like refreshing the screen without reloading the document; it forces the browser to recalculate dynamic HTML content (such as animations or special effects, including JavaScript-driven changes to a document).

When the first argument to this function is true, all elements of the document are recalculated. When the first argument is false, only the elements that have changed are recalculated.

releaseCapture()

JScript 5.0+

IE5+

Syntax

```
var x = document.releaseCapture()
```

The releaseCapture() method of document releases all mouse capturing events from the document which the document has set using the setCapture() method on any element that supports this method.

releaseEvents()

JavaScript 1.2+

Nav4+

Syntax

```
document.releaseEvents(eventName0)
```

The releaseEvents() method of document effectively cancels the document.captureEvents() method call for all events named as arguments. (Typically, these events are referred to as Event.EVENTNAME, where the event name is capitalized.) Using this method, you cause the events thrown or fired to bubble up through the event handler chain normally. See Chapter 32, "DOM-2 Events and Event Handlers," for details.

routeEvent()

JavaScript 1.2+

Nav4+

Syntax

```
document.routeEvent(eventObj)
```

The `routeEvent()` method of `document` sends the event specified in the argument to the next event handler in its chain. Using this method, you cause the events thrown or fired to proceed to the next scheduled event handler for that event. See Chapter 32, "DOM-2 Events and Event Handlers," for details.

setActive()

JScript 5.5+

IE5.5+

Syntax

```
document.setActive()
```

The `setActive()` method of `document` names the active object as the document. It does not transfer focus in the process.

write()

JavaScript 1.0+, JScript 1.0+

Nav2+, IE3+

Syntax

```
document.write(HTMLString)
```

The `write()` method of `document` writes the first argument, a string, as HTML code to the document. If the document has not finished loading, it appends to the document; otherwise, it completely overwrites the document with the string of HTML code it receives.

I mentioned `document.write()` in Chapter 4, "String()." Early in my JavaScript development, it rapidly became one of my favorite tools. However, its use requires a bit of care.

One of the biggest mistakes a developer can make is to simply use `document.write()` again and again after `onload`:

```
document.write("<html><body>\n")
document.write("<p>Hello World</p>\n")
document.write("</body></html>")
```

I found out early on one of the two major browsers will execute the first `document.write()` call...and ignore the others. The reason for this is once you execute a `document.write()` method call, technically, the original document is gone—including the following `document.write()` method calls.

I also find if you omit a `document.close()` following your last `document.write()`, the browser may expect you to send it more information. This means not every element will render every time.

Therefore, I always compile a single string to hold my HTML code for `document.write()`, and immediately follow a `document.write()` with a `document.close()` whenever I'm replacing a page.

You can use `document.write()` before a page has finished loading to embed HTML code directly in a Web page that is in the process of downloading. Examples throughout this book demonstrate `document.write()` executing before `onload`.

Listing 23.2 demonstrates the correct usage of `document.write()` after the document has loaded.

Listing 23.2   *Using* `document.write()` *after* `onload`

```
<?xml version="1.0" ?>
<!DOCTYPE html PUBLIC "-//W3C//DTD XHTML 1.0 Transitional//EN"
➡ "DTD/xhtml1-transitional.dtd">
<html xmlns="http://www.w3.org/1999/xhtml" >
<head><title></title></head>
<body onload="go()">
<script language="JavaScript" type="text/javascript">
<!--
function go() {
    var HTML = '<?xml version="1.0" ?>\n'
    HTML += '<!DOCTYPE html PUBLIC "-//W3C//DTD XHTML 1.0 Transitional//EN"
    ➡ "DTD/xhtml1-transitional.dtd">\n'
    HTML += '<html xmlns="http://www.w3.org/1999/xhtml" >\n'
    HTML += '<head><title></title></head>\n'
    HTML += "<body>\n"
```

Listing 23.2   *(continued)*

```
   HTML += "<p>Hello World</p>\n"
   HTML += "</body>\n"
   HTML += "</html>\n"
   document.write(HTML)
   document.close()
   }
//-->
</script>
<!-- Results:
Hello World
-->
</body>
</html>
```

Event Handlers

Microsoft Internet Explorer supports the following event handlers for the HTMLDocument interface:

onactivate	ondragenter	onmouseover
onbeforeactivate	ondragleave	onmouseup
onbeforecut	ondragover	onmousewheel
onbeforedeactivate	ondragstart	onmove
onbeforeeditfocus	ondrop	onmoveend
onbeforepaste	onfocusin	onmovestart
onclick	onfocusout	onpaste
oncontextmenu	onhelp	onpropertychange
oncontrolselect	onkeydown	onreadystatechange
oncut	onkeypress	onresizeend
ondblclick	onkeyup	onresizestart
ondeactivate	onmousedown	onselectionchange
ondrag	onmousemove	onstop
ondragend	onmouseout	

HTMLBodyElement/<body>...</body>

Browser/JavaScript Version	Created By
Nav4/JavaScript 1.2	Not supported
IE4/JScript 3.0	document.body
IE5/JScript 5.0	document.body
IE5.5/JScript 5.5	document.body
Nav6/JavaScript 1.5	document.body
IE6	document.body
DOM 1 HTML	document.body

Description

The HTMLBodyElement interface contains all renderable content in the document.

Properties

aLink

JavaScript 1.5, JScript 3.0+

Nav6, IE4+

Syntax

```
[var x =] document.body.aLink [= "colString"]
```

The aLink property of document.body reflects the active-link color setting of the document. An active link is a link on which the user is clicking (the link is only active during the click, not after). Corresponds to the deprecated document.aLinkColor property.

background

JavaScript 1.5, JScript 3.0+

Nav6, IE4+

Syntax

```
[var x =] document.body.background [= imageURL]
```

The `background` property of `document.body` reflects the image URL set as a background for the Web page. Note the W3C has deprecated this property in its HTML specifications, but it remains in the W3C DOM for backward-compatibility.

bgColor

JavaScript 1.5, JScript 3.0+

Nav6, IE4+

Syntax

```
[var x =] document.body.bgColor [= colorString]
```

The `bgColor` property of `document.body` reflects the background color set for the Web page. Note the W3C has deprecated this property in its HTML specifications, but it remains in the W3C DOM for backward-compatibility.

bgProperties

JScript 3.0+

IE4+

Syntax

```
[var x =] document.body.bgProperties [= fixedString]
```

The `bgProperties` property of `document.body` is a proprietary value for specifying whether the background image scrolls with the document. When set to an empty string (the default), the background scrolls with the document. When set to "fixed," the document can scroll independent of the background; the background remains stationary.

bottomMargin

JScript 3.0+

IE4+

Syntax

```
[var x = ] document.body.bottomMargin [= pixelHeight]
```

The `bottomMargin` property of `document.body` sets a margin from the end of the document to the bottom of the scrollable window. Normally, Microsoft sets a 15-pixel margin between the bottom of the document and the bottom of the scrollable window.

innerHTML

JavaScript 1.5, JScript 5.0+

Nav6, IE5+

Syntax

```
[var x =] document.body.innerHTML [= HTMLString]
```

The `innerHTML` property of `HTMLBodyElement` interfaces retrieves or sets the HTML source code contained between, but not including, the starting and ending tags.

I personally recommend against using `innerHTML` to set the HTML inside a tag. I strongly recommend against using `innerHTML` to append to the contents of an HTML tag:

```
elem.innerHTML += "<div><p>Hello World</p></div>" // DO NOT DO THIS
```

I do like the handiness of the `innerHTML` property for retrieving HTML source code at a glance, as a companion method to the W3C Document Object Model. (The DOM provides an object structure for the source code; `innerHTML` provides the corresponding source code.)

innerText

JScript 3.0+

IE4+

Syntax

```
var x = document.body.innerText
```

The `innerText` property of `HTMLBodyElement` retrieves or sets the text contained between, but not including, the starting and ending tags.

The `innerText` property can be useful, but the DOM Level 2 `Range` interface provides far more flexibility. See Chapter 34, "DOM-2 Range," for details on text ranges.

leftMargin

JScript 3.0+

IE4+

Syntax

```
[var x = ] document.body.leftMargin [= pixelHeight]
```

The `leftMargin` property of `document.body` sets a margin from the left edge of the document to the left edge of the scrollable window. Normally, Microsoft sets a 10-pixel margin between the left edge of the document and the left edge of the scrollable window.

link

JavaScript 1.5, JScript 3.0+

Nav6, IE4+

Syntax

```
[var x =] document.body.link [= "colString"]
```

The `link` property of `document.body` reflects the unvisited link color setting of the document. Corresponds to the deprecated `document.linkColor` property.

nowrap

JScript 3.0+

IE4.0+

Syntax

```
[var x =] document.body.nowrap [= boolValue]
```

The nowrap property of document.body, when set to true, causes the text of the page to not wrap at all. The result is that unless you include hard text breaks (such as a <br /> tag), the text continues off to the right. Usually, this means scrollbars.

outerHTML

JScript 5.0+

IE5+

Syntax

```
var x = document.body.outerHTML
```

The outerHTML property of HTMLBodyElement retrieves or sets the HTML source code contained between, and including, the starting and ending tags.

I do like the handiness of the outerHTML property for retrieving HTML source code at a glance, as a companion method to the W3C Document Object Model. (The DOM provides an object structure for the source code; outerHTML provides the corresponding source code.)

rightMargin

JScript 3.0+

IE4+

Syntax

```
[var x =] document.body.rightMargin [= pixelHeight]
```

The rightMargin property of document.body sets a margin from the right edge of the document to the right edge of the scrollable window. Normally, Microsoft sets a 10-pixel margin between the right edge of the document and the right edge of the scrollable window.

tabIndex

JScript 3.0+

IE4+

Syntax

```
[ver x =] document.body.tabIndex [= numValue]
```

The `tabIndex` property of `document.body` sets where the `this` element rests in the tab order. The *tab order* is an index indicating when an element in the document receives focus as the user strikes the Tab key. When setting this value, remember it can only accept numeric integers.

A negative `tabIndex` takes the `this` element out of the tab order. Other than that, Tab key presses go to elements in this order:

- The lowest positive integer, followed by the next lowest, and so on

- After that, the source order of elements in the document

`HTMLBodyElement` is a natural stopping point for Tab key presses.

text

JavaScript 1.5, JScript 3.0+

Nav6, IE4+

Syntax

```
[var x =] document.body.text [= colorString]
```

The `text` property of `document.body` reflects the foreground, or text, color set for the Web page. Note the W3C has deprecated this property in its HTML specifications, but it remains in the W3C DOM for backward-compatibility.

topMargin

JScript 3.0+

IE4+

Syntax

```
[var x = ] document.body.topMargin [= pixelHeight]
```

The `topMargin` property of `document.body` sets a margin from the start of the document to the top of the scrollable window. Normally, Microsoft sets a 15-pixel margin between the top of the document and the top of the scrollable window.

vLink

JavaScript 1.5, JScript 3.0+

Nav6, IE4+

Syntax

```
[var x =] document.body.vLink [= "colString"]
```

The `vLink` property of `document.body` reflects the visited link color setting of the document. Corresponds to the deprecated `document.vLinkColor` property.

Methods

The `HTMLBodyElement` interface provides no methods beyond those defined in the `HTMLElement` interface.

Event Handlers

Internet Explorer supports the following event handlers for `HTMLBodyElement`:

onactivate	onclick	ondragenter
onafterprint	oncontextmenu	ondragleave
onbeforeactivate	oncontrolselect	ondragover
onbeforecut	oncut	ondragstart
onbeforedeactivate	ondblclick	ondrop
onbeforepaste	ondeactivate	onfilterchange
onbeforeprint	ondrag	onfocusin
onbeforeunload	ondragend	onfocusout

onkeydown	onmouseout	onreadystatechange
onkeypress	onmouseover	onresizeend
onkeyup	onmouseup	onresizestart
onload	onmousewheel	onscroll
onlosecapture	onmove	onselect
onmousedown	onmoveend	onselectstart
onmouseenter	onmovestart	onunload
onmouseleave	onpaste	
onmousemove	onpropertychange	

CHAPTER 24

Head Elements

The head portion of a document contains information about the document—who wrote it, what its title is, what directory all the relative links relate to, and so on. With the exception of `HTMLHeadElement`, all the elements in this chapter are child elements of `HTMLHeadElement`.

You may wonder why I do not include `HTMLScriptElement`, `HTMLStyleElement`, and `HTMLLinkElement` in this chapter. There are two reasons. One of them is that these elements have places in other chapters (scripts in Chapter 31, "Programmable Elements," styling in Chapter 33, "Styling for HTML Elements.") The other reason is scripts can also appear in the body of a document, particularly if they actually write to the document.

Ninety percent of all JavaScripts are about interacting with the document—whether it be special effects, validating a form's inputs, or the occasional insertion of tags directly into a document. HTML documents are constrained to conform to the HTML DTD both before and after processing any script elements.

So when is it logical to place a script in the head? When the script does not directly modify the document by declaring functions for later use, or if the script is manipulating content you would normally find in the head of a document.

Listing 24.1 demonstrates a function in the head that will write to the document when called, and the corresponding function will call in the body.

Listing 24.1   *What Scripts Can Go in the Body?*

```
<?xml version="1.0" ?>
<!DOCTYPE html PUBLIC "-//W3C//DTD XHTML 1.0 Transitional//EN"
➥"DTD/xhtml1-transitional.dtd">
<html xmlns="http://www.w3.org/1999/xhtml" >
<head><title></title>
<script language="JavaScript" type="text/javascript">
<!--
function addLine() {
   document.write("<p>Hello, World</p>")
   }
// Functions themselves don't write to a document...
//-->
</script>
</head>
<body>
<p>
<script language="JavaScript" type="text/javascript">
<!--
addLine()
// ...until you actually call them.
//-->
</script>
</p>
<!-- The document remains well-formed and valid.
Results:
Hello, World
-->
</body>
</html>
```

You want to load scripts that will contain code to modify the document before onload—as soon as possible—into the head section. (This I consider a best practice.) You must load scripts which, before onload, will actually modify the document or call a function to modify the document into the body section. Script code binding an event handler to an action should also go in the body of the document—while the function bound to the event may go in the head to ensure it is there before the user can fire the event. (Basically, it's just an easy way to make sure the code that can modify the document will be loaded before the code that calls for the modification.)

Style sheet elements must go in the head for a similar reason: the W3C recommends you separate content (what the document actually says) and presentation (how the document should appear to the user). Although styling deserves a place in this chapter because it covers more than just the `HTMLStyleElement` and `HTMLLinkElement` interfaces, you will find it in Chapter 33, "Styling for HTML Elements."

HTMLHeadElement Interface/<head>...</head>

Browser/JavaScript Version	Created By
Nav4/JavaScript 1.2	<head>...</head>
IE4/JScript 3.0	<head>...</head>
IE5/JScript 5.0	<head>...</head>
IE5.5/JScript 5.5	<head>...</head>
Nav6/JavaScript 1.5	<head>...</head>
IE6	<head>...</head>
DOM Level 1	<head>...</head>

> **Note**
> Implemented in Nav1+ (HTML), IE1+ (HTML), Nav6 (DOM), IE4+ (DOM)
>
> Descends from `HTMLElement` interface (Chapter 21, "HTMLElement")
>
> Parent elements: `HTMLHtmlElement` (Chapter 22, "HTMLHtmlElement")

Description

The head tag of a document contains most of the presentation information for a document. This often includes the document's title, style sheets, an extensive collection of metadata, and possibly some scripting code. The head element can easily be accessed in DOM compliant browsers by

```
var h = document.getElementsByTagName('head')[0]
```

or in Internet Explorer 4+ browsers with

```
var h = document.all.tags('head')[0]
```

Properties

children

JScript 3.0+

IE4+

Syntax

```
var x = HTMLHeadElement.children
```

The `children` property of instances of `HTMLHeadElement` is a collection of all child elements of the `this` element. See `childNodes` in Chapter 20, "Core DOM Objects," under `Node` for a more complete description.

item

JScript 3.0+

IE4+

Syntax

```
var x = HTMLHeadElement.children.item(index)
```

For the `item` method of `children`, by supplying a number (specifically, a non-negative integer less than `this.length`) as the first argument, you can get an `element` object from the `this` object representing that `element`'s placement in the `this` object's index. Any other argument you submit to this method results in the method returning `null`.

length

JScript 5.0+

IE5+

Syntax

```
var x = HTMLHeadElement.children.length
```

The `length` property of `children` tells how many objects are in the collection.

tags

JScript 3.0+

IE4+

Syntax

```
var x = HTMLHeadElement.children.tags(tagName)
```

The `tags` method of `children` returns a subset of the `this` element comprising all elements whose `tagName` property matches the first argument.

urns

JScript 5.0+

IE5+

Syntax

```
var x = HTMLHeadElement.children.urns(behaviorName)
```

The `urns` method of `children` returns a subset of the `this` element comprising all elements possessing a DHTML behavior whose name matches the first argument.

DHTML behaviors, an Internet Explorer proprietary extension to HTML, go far beyond the scope of this book. You can find information on them via Microsoft's Web site at `http://msdn.microsoft.com/workshop/author/behaviors/overview.asp`.

innerHTML

JavaScript 1.5, JScript 5.0+

Nav6, IE5+

Read-only in IE5+

Syntax

```
[var x =] HTMLHeadElement.innerHTML
```

The `innerHTML` property of instances of `HTMLHeadElement` interfaces retrieves or sets the HTML source code contained between, but not including, the starting and ending tags. However, it is read-only in this case in Internet Explorer 5+ and changing the value in Netscape 6 does not appear to have any affect.

innerText

JScript 5.0+

IE5+

Syntax

```
var x = HTMLHeadElement.innerText
```

The innerText property of instances of HTMLHeadElement interfaces retrieves the text contained between, but not including, the starting and ending tags.

The innerText property can be useful, but the DOM Level 2 Range interface provides far more flexibility. See Chapter 34, "DOM-2 Range," for details on text ranges.

ownerDocument

JavaScript 1.5

Nav6, IE6

Syntax

```
var x = HTMLHeadElement.ownerDocument
```

The ownerDocument property of instances of HTMLHeadElement returns a reference to the HTMLDocument, which contains the this element.

profile

JavaScript 1.5

Nav6, IE6

Syntax

```
[var x] = HTMLHeadElement.profile [= URIString]
```

The profile property of instances of HTMLHeadElement refers to a metadata profile by URI, which the browser may use to validate the metadata provided.

Sadly, there is no definitive information in the W3C HTML documentation about what a valid profile looks like. Likewise, I was unable to locate such a reference at Mozilla or Microsoft's Web sites. Some information may be found at http://dublincore.org. For now, you might want to avoid using this attribute until the situation resolves itself.

uniqueID

IE5.0+

JScript 5.0+

Syntax

```
var x = HTMLHeadElement.uniqueID
```

The `uniqueID` property of instances of `HTMLHeadElement` returns a string unique to the given element. Reloading the document changes this property. Note it does not exist within the `this` element until you actually call it.

Methods

The `HTMLHeadElement` interface provides no methods beyond those defined in the `HTMLElement` interface.

Event Handlers

Internet Explorer supports the following event handlers for `HTMLHeadElement`:

`onlayoutcomplete`

`onreadystatechange`

HTMLBaseElement/<base />

Browser/JavaScript Version	Created By
Nav4/JavaScript 1.2	`<base>...</base>`
IE4/JScript 3.0	`<base>...</base>`
IE5/JScript 5.0	`<base>...</base>`
IE5.5/JScript 5.5	`<base>...</base>`
Nav6/JavaScript 1.5	`<base>...</base>`
IE6	`<base>...</base>`
DOM Level 1	`<base>...</base>`

> **Note**
> Implemented in Nav1+ (HTML), IE3+ (HTML), Nav6 (DOM), IE4+ (DOM)
>
> Descends from HTMLElement interface (Chapter 21, "HTMLElement")
>
> Parent elements: HTMLHeadElement (Chapter 24, "Head Elements")

Description

The base tag of a document sets a few basic parameters for the document—namely, what window or frame from which to aim all links, and what URI directory to base all relative links. Like the HTMLHeadElement, the base tag can easily be accessed in any DOM compliant browser with the following code.

```
var baseElements = document.getElementsByTagName('base')

If (baseElements.Length > 0)

  BaseElements = baseElements[0];
```

The getElementsByTagName() method is a convenient way to access most of the head tag's elements.

Properties

href

JavaScript 1.5, JScript 3.0+

Nav6, IE4.0+

Syntax

```
[var x =] HTMLBaseElement.href [= URIDirectory]
```

The href property of instances of HTMLBaseElement specifies the directory of a relative URI to point to, overriding the base directory of the document.

In essence, if the URI is

```
<a href="myfile.htm">See My File!</a>
```

And the `href` of the base tag is

```
<base href="http://www.jslab.org/jsdd/" />
```

This translates to an absolute URI of

```
<a href="http://www.jslab.org/jsdd/myfile.htm">See My File!</a>
```

ownerDocument

Nav6, IE6

Syntax

```
var x = HTMLBaseElement.ownerDocument
```

The `ownerDocument` property of instances of `HTMLBaseElement` returns a reference to the `HTMLDocument` that contains the `this` element.

target

JavaScript 1.5+, JScript 3.0+

Nav6, IE4.0+

Syntax

```
[var x =] HTMLBaseElement.target [= targetWin]
```

The `target` property of instances of `HTMLBaseElement` reflects the currently targeted default window for all links. You can use any valid HTML window name for this value (see Chapter 15, "window," for a description of HTML window names versus JavaScript window names).

You can also use `"_blank"` to indicate opening a new window every time, `"_parent"` for the parent window, `"_top"` for the topmost window in the parent window chain (see `top` and `parent` in Chapter 15), or `"_self"` to indicate it should load into the window of its document. (`"_self"` is the default setting.)

Internet Explorer 5.0+ introduces a new one called `"_search"`, which will target the link for the browser's search sidebar.

HTMLMetaElement/<meta />

Browser / JavaScript Version	Created By
Nav4/JavaScript 1.2	<meta />
IE4/JScript 3.0	<meta />
IE5/JScript 5.0	<meta />
IE5.5/JScript 5.5	<meta />
Nav6/JavaScript 1.5	<meta />
IE6	<meta />
DOM Level 1	<meta />

> **Note**
>
> Implemented in Nav1+ (HTML), IE3+ (HTML), Nav6 (DOM), IE4+ (DOM)
>
> Descends from HTMLElement interface (Chapter 21, "HTMLElement")
>
> Parent elements: HTMLHeadElement (Chapter 24, "Head Elements")

Description

Meta tags contain information about the document, primarily for search engines and for embedding HTTP headers in the document.

Metadata (as this is commonly called) is information about a document. The table of contents for this book is one example of metadata for this book. Metadata is such a huge topic that it would literally require another Developer's Dictionary to cover it. The best reference listing META values I am aware of is http://vancouver-webpages.com/META/. (If that reference isn't enough for you, there are plenty of links at http://dmoz.org/Computers/Data_Formats/Markup_Languages/HTML/Tutorials/Meta_Tags/.)

Metadata goes far beyond the scope of this book. However, you can set cookies with metadata (see Chapter 35, "Cookies"), control the caching of pages, and give various other information about the document.

I would actually recommend you use meta tags in your HTML documents for one reason: they allows you to expose HTTP header information to the DOM as well. (The browser typically doesn't do that.) For instance, a meta tag telling the browser when to "expire" the page from the cache is the only way the DOM will know when the page has expired. I use this as an example for this section. An easy way to access meta tags in DOM compliant browsers is

```
var x = document.getElementsByTagName('meta')[index]
```

where index is the index of the tag you want. The meta tag can also be retrieved in IE4+ with

```
var x = document.all.tags('meta')[index]
```

Properties

charset

JScript 3.0+

IE4+

Syntax

```
var x = HTMLMetaElement.charset [= charSetStr]
```

The charset property of instances of HTMLMetaElement reflects the character set encoding (basically, a designation of the element's alphabet and what characters are in said alphabet) of the this element.

content

JavaScript 1.5+, JScript 3.0+

Nav6, IE4+

Syntax

```
[var x =] HTMLMetaElement.content [= contentStr]
```

The content property of instances of HTMLMetaElement for the meta tag contains exactly what information the tag carries. The name or httpEquiv attribute describes what the browser should consider the content as.

httpEquiv

JavaScript 1.5+, JScript 3.0+

Nav6, IE4+

Syntax

```
[var x =] HTMLMetaElement.httpEquiv [= HTTPheader]
```

The `httpEquiv` property of instances of `HTMLMetaElement` indicates the HTTP header code for the `this` element. Either the `httpEquiv` or the `name` property must be used for this element, but not both.

name

JavaScript 1.5+, JScript 3.0+

Nav6, IE4+

Syntax

```
[var x =] HTMLMetaElement.name [= metaName]
```

The `name` property of instances of `HTMLMetaElement` indicates the name for the content of the `this` element—basically, assigning the content a name for search purposes. Either the `httpEquiv` or the `name` property must be used for this element, but not both.

ownerDocument

JavaScript 1.5+

Nav6, IE6

Syntax

```
var x = HTMLMetaElement.ownerDocument
```

The `ownerDocument` property of instances of `HTMLMetaElement` returns a reference to the `HTMLDocument` that contains the `this` element.

scheme

JavaScript 1.5+, JScript 1.0+

Nav6, IE6

Syntax

```
[var x =] HTMLMetaElement.scheme [= metaName]
```

The `scheme` property of instances of `HTMLMetaElement` implies to the browser the structure of the data in the content. For instance, dates can be expressed as MM-DD-YY (common in the United States of America) or in DD-MM-YY (common in Europe). Microsoft's example, using the value "USA" for this property, sets the date in MM-DD-YY format.

Methods

The `HTMLMetaElement` interface provides no methods beyond those defined in the `HTMLElement` interface.

Event Handler

Internet Explorer supports the following event handler for `HTMLMetaElement`: `onlayoutcomplete`.

Example: Automatic Refreshing

With meta tags, you can describe a lot, including when the current page is no longer current. You could then use `setTimeout()` (which I describe in Chapter 15) to force the browser to retrieve a new version of the page on schedule. (The reference at the beginning of this element's section states Netscape supports refreshing by meta tags as well. Internet Explorer has deprecated the `http-equiv="refresh"` attribute value, but it still works as of version 5.5.) Listing 24.2 is a page that reloads every 10 seconds.

Listing 24.2 *Automatically Refreshing a Page*

```
<?xml version="1.0" ?>
<!DOCTYPE html PUBLIC "-//W3C//DTD XHTML 1.0 Transitional//EN"
"DTD/xhtml1-transitional.dtd">
<html xmlns="http://www.w3.org/1999/xhtml" >
<head>
<title>This is a test of meta refreshing</title>
<meta name="Author" content="Alexander J. Vincent" />
<meta http-equiv="Refresh" content="10" id="metarefresh" />
</head>
```

Listing 24.2   *(continued)*

```
<body>
<p>The time now is 
<script language="JavaScript" type="text/javascript">
<!—
If (document.getElementByID) {
document.write(new Date()+"<br/ >")
document.write(document.getElementById('metarefresh').httpEquiv)
document.write(" in 10 seconds.")
}
//—>
</script>
</p>
<!— Note:
This example will not work in IE4
Or Nav4
Results:
The time now is (date string)
Refresh in 10 seconds.
—>
</body>
</html>
```

Although this particular example isn't very useful, it does allow you to create an HTML-based chat room. Imagine two visible frames, a receive frame and a send frame. The receive frame receives the most recent signals from the server.

An even smoother design, now possible with the DOM, would be using a three-frame arrangement: a send frame, a display-receive frame, and a "system" receive frame (zero-pixel height). In this scheme, the system receive frame automatically refreshes, specifying for the server the last received message number. The server responds with a new page containing the newest messages. The system receive frame, onload, then uses the DOM to add new messages to the display-receive frame. More work for the client, less for the server—and it would render far smoother without losing older messages from the receive window.

HTMLTitleElement Interface/<title>...</title>

Browser/JavaScript Version	Created By
Nav4/JavaScript 1.2	<title>...</title>
IE4/JScript 3.0	<title>...</title>
IE5/JScript 5.0	<title>...</title>
IE5.5/JScript 5.5	<title>...</title>
Nav6/JavaScript 1.5	<title>...</title>
IE6	<title>...</title>
DOM Level 1	<title>...</title>

> **Note**
>
> Implemented in Nav1+ (HTML), IE3+ (HTML), Nav3/4 (Javascript read-only), Nav6 (DOM), IE4+ (DOM)
>
> Descends from `HTMLElement` interface (Chapter 21, "HTMLElement")
>
> Parent elements: `HTMLHeadElement`

Description

The `HTMLTitleElement` contains as a text string the title of the document. This element may not have child elements. Like the other children of `HTMLHeadElement`, you can access `HTMLTitleElement` in DOM compliant browsers with

```
var x = document.getElementsByTagName('title')[0]
```

and in Internet Explorer 4 it can be accessed with

```
var x = document.all.tags('title')[0]
```

Given that this is a rather popular element to manipulate the DOM, it also provides a title property for the document object that makes for a little more readable code. This property dates back to the beginnings of JavaScript so compatibility with older browsers should not be a problem.

Properties

innerHTML

JavaScript 1.5, JScript 5.0+

Nav6, IE5+

Read-only in Nav6, IE5+

Syntax

```
[var x =] HTMLTitleElement.innerHTML
```

The `innerHTML` property of `HTMLTitleElement` instances retrieves the HTML source code contained between, but not including, the starting and ending tags. As the `text` property (and `this.childNodes[0].nodeValue`) cover these as well, you may not need to use this property. Ultimately, `innerHTML` is just another alternative to `document.title` for retrieving the title of a document.

innerText

JScript 5.0+

IE5+

Syntax

```
var x = HTMLTitleElement.innerText
```

The `innerText` property of `HTMLTitleElement` interfaces retrieves or sets the text contained between, but not including, the starting and ending tags. As the `text` property (and `this.childNodes[0].nodeValue`) cover these as well, you may not need to use this property. This property is supposed to be read/write, but I encountered problems with trying to write to it for the title element. If you want to change the title of the document, I would highly recommend using `document.title` instead.

The `innerText` property can be useful, but the DOM Level 2 `Range` interface provides far more flexibility. See Chapter 34, "DOM-2 Range," for details on text ranges.

ownerDocument

JavaScript 1.5+

Nav6, IE6

Syntax

```
var x = HTMLTitleElement.ownerDocument
```

The ownerDocument property of instances of HTMLTitleElement returns a reference to the HTMLDocument which contains the this element.

text

JavaScript 1.5+, JScript 3.0+

Nav6, IE4+

Syntax

```
[var x =] HTMLTitleElement.text [= titleString]
```

The text property of instances of HTMLTitleElement elements allows you to retrieve or set the text of the document's title. This property is another convenient option for retrieving the title of a document, but it does have some quirks in some browsers when used to set the title. The value will be updated, but on some versions of Internet Explorer the change might not be reflected in the title bar.

uniqueID

JScript 5.0+

IE5.0+

Syntax

```
var x = HTMLTitleElement.uniqueID
```

The uniqueID property of instances of HTMLTitleElement returns a string unique to the given element. Reloading the document changes this property. Note it does not exist within the this element until you actually call it.

Methods

The HTMLTitleElement interface provides no methods beyond those defined in the HTMLElement interface.

Event Handlers

Internet Explorer supports the following event handlers for `HTMLTitleElement`:

`onlayoutcomplete`

`onreadystatechange`

CHAPTER 25

Form Elements

Forms are the primary way by which a client computer sends information to the server. A form can be used for simple data storage (logging into a password-restricted area) or for complex data storage (filling out a Bugzilla bug report).

Forms take several stages: generation of the form by the server (which sometimes changes based on input from the client—such as the browser name and version), data entry by the user, often a validation by JavaScript, submittal to the server, and processing by the server. Needless to say, working with HTML forms is one of the biggest uses of JavaScript.

This chapter does not cover the most common element of forms, the `HTMLInputElement`, `<input>...</input>`. You will find that in Chapter 26. However, all other elements of forms are in this chapter.

HTMLFormElement interface/`<form>`...`</form>`

Browser / JavaScript Version	Created By
Nav4/JavaScript 1.2	`<form>`...`</form>`
IE4/JScript 3.0	`<form>`...`</form>`
IE5/JScript 5.0	`<form>`...`</form>`
IE5.5/JScript 5.5	`<form>`...`</form>`
Nav6/JavaScript 1.5	`<form>`...`</form>`
IE6	`<form>`...`</form>`
DOM Level 1	`document.createElement("form")`

> **Note**
> Implemented in Nav1+ (HTML), IE1+ (HTML), Nav6 (DOM), IE4+ (DOM)
> Descends from `HTMLElement` interface (Chapter 21, "HTMLElement")
> Parent elements: `HTMLBodyElement` (Chapter 22, "HTMLHtmlElement"), any block text element

Description

The `<form>`...`</form>` element primarily exists as a wrapper for all form elements on a page: check boxes, drop-down combo boxes, and so on. Typically, according to the W3C, these elements must be descendent elements of a form element.

Referencing a Form

There are several different ways to refer to a form in a document. One is, of course, the `document.getElementById()` method, with the first argument being the form's `id` attribute. (See Chapter 20, "Core DOM Objects," for details.) However, several other approaches predate the DOM—many of which the DOM Level 1 adapts.

You can refer to the form as `document.forms.formName`. You can also refer to the form as `document.forms[x]`, where x is the zero-based index of the forms on the page. (The first form on the page, for example, is `document.forms[0]`.)

From any element of the form, you can refer to its container form by its `form` property. This comes in handy from event handlers: `onselect="this.form.submit()"` is common for a combo box.

Finally, you can sometimes refer to a form by name directly as a property of `document`, such as `document.`*`formName`*.

Listing 25.1   *Accessing Forms in Many Ways*

```
<?xml version="1.0" ?>
<!DOCTYPE html PUBLIC "-//W3C//DTD XHTML 1.0 Transitional//EN"
➥"DTD/xhtml1-transitional.dtd">
<html xmlns="http://www.w3.org/1999/xhtml" >
<head><title></title></head>
<body onload="go()">
<form name="alpha" action="javascript:void(null)">
<p>
<input name="one" value="one" />
<input id="two" value="two" />
</p>
</form>

<form id="beta" action="javascript:void(null)">
<p>
<input name="three" value="three" />
<input id="four" value="four" />
</p>
</form>

<form action="javascript:void(null)">
<p>
<textarea name="ta" id="ta" rows="10" cols="60"></textarea>
</p>
</form>

<p>
<script type="text/javascript">
<!--
function val(objName) {
    if (eval("typeof " + objName) != "undefined") {
        document.forms[2].ta.value += (objName + ":  " + eval(objName) + "\n")
        return true
        } else {
```

Listing 25.1   *(continued)*

```
        document.forms[2].ta.value += (objName + " is undefined\n")
        return false
        }
    }

function go() {
    val("document.alpha")
    val("document.forms['alpha']")
    val("document.forms.alpha")
    val("document.forms[0]")
    val("document.beta")
    val("document.forms['beta']")
    val("document.forms.beta")
    val("document.forms[1]")
    }
//-->
</script>
</p>
<!-- Results in Internet Explorer 5.0+:
document.alpha: [object]
document.forms['alpha']: [object]
document.forms.alpha: [object]
document.forms[0]: [object]
document.beta is undefined
document.forms['beta']: [object]
document.forms.beta: [object]
document.forms[1]: [object]

Netscape 6.0+ uses [object HTMLFormElement] instead of [object].
Netscape Communicator 4.x uses [object Form].
-->
</body>
</html>
```

The XHTML 1.0 strict DTD removes the name attribute for forms. Listing 25.1 is valid XHTML 1.0 Transitional, but not XHTML 1.0 Strict or XHTML 1.1. This is why I continue to recommend using the full document.forms prefix instead of simply document as in document.*formName*.

You should also, when writing your forms, aim for XHTML 1.0 Transitional; use both name and id attributes, matching their values. Netscape Communicator 4.x recognizes only the name attribute in its DOM, and the id attribute you should include anyway, as your forms are fairly important pieces of the document. For radio buttons you likely will not be able to use identical name and ID attributes because you will probably want several with the same value for the name attribute.

Validation of Forms

JavaScript provides the onsubmit handler of forms to intercept a form's submission carried out by the user clicking on a Submit button. However, for the onsubmit handler to truly cancel a form submission, the event handler (not the function it calls) must return false. Listing 25.2 demonstrates how onsubmit must operate.

Listing 25.2   *Correct and Incorrect Use of* onsubmit

```
<?xml version="1.0" ?>
<!DOCTYPE html PUBLIC "-//W3C//DTD XHTML 1.0 Transitional//EN"
➥"DTD/xhtml1-transitional.dtd">
<html xmlns="http://www.w3.org/1999/xhtml" >
<head><title></title></head>
<body>
<script language="JavaScript" type="text/javascript">
<!--
function test() {
   return false;
   }
//-->
</script>

<form action="mailto:nobody@jslab.org" method="post" onsubmit="return test()">
<input type="hidden" value="world" name="hello" />
<input type="submit" value="Clicking this button does nothing." />
</form>

<form action="mailto:nobody@jslab.org" method="post" onsubmit="test()">
<input type="hidden" value="world" name="hello" />
<input type="submit" value="Clicking this button sends the form." />
</form>
</body>
</html>
```

Where a Form Sends Data and How

Forms can send their data to a number of places. The required `action` attribute of a form designates the URI to which the form will send its data. At the same time, the `method` attribute defines the HTTP method by which the form's contents will travel. (Do not confuse the `method` attribute with methods of an object.)

You can have several different kinds of URIs for the `action` attribute. Listing 16.2 uses the `javascript:valSubmit()` URI to validate the form before constructing a valid URI for the next document in the sequence (Listing 16.3, for reference) in the HTTP GET method style. (I will explain the two most important HTTP methods in a moment.)

Normally, people send forms to server-side scripts for processing, such as PHP, Perl, and JavaServer Pages. (For server-side languages, I recommend you read Sams *PHP Developer's Cookbook* by Sterling Hughes, with contributions by Andrei Zmievski for PHP and *Perl Developer's Dictionary* for CGI.) A typical (in this case fictional) URI would be `http://www.jslab.org/jsdd/helloworld.php`, indicating a PHP script to process the form's inputs and send an HTML page back to the browser.

You can also designate a `mailto:` URI for the form. This will tell Netscape and Internet Explorer browsers to submit the form by e-mail. (This is generally less reliable than other methods of submitting a form, and you should use it only as a last resort.) Listing 25.3, which works with Internet Explorer, shows a form that uses `mailto:`.

Listing 25.3   *Mailing a Form's Results*

```
<?xml version="1.0" ?>
<!DOCTYPE html PUBLIC "-//W3C//DTD XHTML 1.0 Transitional//EN"
➥"DTD/xhtml1-transitional.dtd">
<html xmlns="http://www.w3.org/1999/xhtml" >
<head><title></title></head>
<body>
<form action="mailto:nobody@jslab.org" method="post">
<input type="text" value="Alex Vincent" name="author" id="author" />
<input type="hidden" value="www.jslab.org" name="website" id="website" />
<input type="button" onclick="document.forms[0].submit()" value="Submit!" />
</form>
</body>
</html>
```

If you want to create similar `mailto` functionality with Netscape 4 or 6 you cannot use JavaScript, but you must use a Submit button instead.

There are a few different HTTP methods for sending information to the server, but for forms we concern ourselves with only two. One is the HTTP GET method, the default. (You use this method all the time, without query strings, to get HTML pages.) In this case, it's just a matter of requesting a properly formatted URI from the server. Forms use the query-string to send information in a *name0=value0&name1=value1&...* format. Literally, the browser will extract the name of each form input and its corresponding value and attach it to the end of the URI in this manner.

This procedure is not always the best, simply because it uses the URI. There are dangers in large URIs—a safe limit is 255 characters. Obviously, that doesn't leave a lot of room for big forms, especially when some of that URI is the pointer to the form processing script. When going from page to page using JavaScript to send information (as I describe in Chapter 16, "location"), if you have anything other than an absolutely minimal amount of information to send, passing information via the URI is not a good idea. Forget about sending files via HTTP GET.

The other useful method for submitting information to a server is the HTTP POST method. This creates a multipart HTTP message, where each field of the form has its own distinct section. This is preferable for a number of reasons (including security, especially for passwords). Files should be sent using HTTP POST. You should construct large forms with the form set to submit via HTTP POST. You can explicitly set the form's submission method using the `method` attribute of `HTMLFormElement`.

Bottom line: unless you have a really, really small form that doesn't involve a password or a file upload, use the HTTP POST method. At the same time, you should set your `enctype` attribute explicitly to `"multipart/form-data"` when using HTTP POST.

Properties

acceptCharset

JavaScript 1.5, JScript 5.0+

Nav6.0+, IE5.0+

Syntax

```
[var x =] HTMLFormElement.acceptCharset [= charSetList]
```

The `acceptCharset` property of `HTMLFormElement` objects designates a list of character sets the server expects to receive from the form. In essence, the server may choose to specify this if it so desires.

---

action
JavaScript 1.0+, JScript 1.0+

Nav2.0+, IE3.0+

Syntax

```
[var x = ] HTMLFormElement.action [= URIString]
```

The `action` property of `HTMLFormElement` objects reflects the `action` attribute, which designates the URI the form's information will submit to. Most of the time, you will want to set the accompanying method value to `"post"` in the HTML source code, and likewise set the `enctype` attribute value to `"multipart/form-data"`.

---

autocomplete
JScript 5.0+

IE5.0+

Syntax

```
[var x =] HTMLFormElement.autocomplete [= stringValue]
```

The `autocomplete` property of `HTMLFormElement` objects, when set to `"on"`, allows the browser to "fill in" certain form fields based on partial user input. You see this feature fairly often in Internet Explorer, where you type in a few characters and the browser suggests the remaining characters. (The location bar is the best place to find this feature regardless of the Web page.)

If you explicitly set the `autocomplete` property to `false` for the form, AutoComplete is disabled for all form controls.

---

children
JScript 3.0+

IE4+

See `childNodes` under the DOM `Document` object in Chapter 20, "Core DOM Objects."

---

elements

JavaScript 1.0+, JScript 1.0+

Nav2.0+, IE3.0+

Syntax

```
[var x = ] HTMLFormElement.elements
```

The `elements` property of `HTMLFormElement` objects is a collection of the form inputs (including buttons, select boxes, text areas, and so on) in the form, in numerical order of appearance within the document's source code. For instance, the first element of a form named `myForm` would be `document.forms.myForm.elements[0]`.

Netscape and Internet Explorer are generous to us, however. They allow us to refer to elements of a form directly as numerical properties of the form itself. `document.forms.myForm[0]` will also refer to the first element of the form. Listing 25.4 shows us the shorthand abbreviation in use.

Listing 25.4   *Form Elements Directly and Indirectly Named*

```
<?xml version="1.0" ?>
<!DOCTYPE html PUBLIC "-//W3C//DTD XHTML 1.0 Transitional//EN"
➥"DTD/xhtml1-transitional.dtd">
<html xmlns="http://www.w3.org/1999/xhtml" >
<head><title></title></head>
<body onload="go()">
<form name="alpha" id="alpha" action="javascript:void(null)">
<p>
<input id="one" value="one" />
<br />
<textarea rows="10" cols="60" id="ta"></textarea>
</p>
</form>

<p>
<script type="text/javascript">
<!--
function val(objName) {
    if (eval("typeof " + objName) != "undefined") {
        document.forms.alpha.ta.value += (objName + ":  " + eval(objName)
➥ + "\n")
```

Listing 25.4   *(continued)*

```
        return true
    } else {
        document.forms.alpha.ta.value += (objName + " is undefined\n")
        return false
    }
}

function go() {
    document.forms.alpha.reset()
    val("document.forms.alpha[0]")
    val("document.forms.alpha.elements[0]")
}
//-->
</script>
</p>
<!-- Results in Internet Explorer 5.0+:
document.forms.alpha[0]:  [object]
document.forms.alpha.elements[0]:  [object]

Netscape 6.0+ uses [object HTMLInputElement] instead of [object].

-->
</body>
</html>
```

encoding/enctype

JavaScript 1.0+, JavaScript 1.5 (enctype)

Nav2.0-Nav4.78, IE5+ (encoding), Nav6, IE6 (enctype)

Syntax

```
[var x =] HTMLFormElement.enctype [= mimeType]
```

The enctype property of HTMLFormElement objects reflects the mime-type of the message the client browser will send to the server onsubmit. The default for this is "application/x-www-form-urlencoded". When you do not explicitly set this value, however, Netscape will return an empty string.

When you want to submit files, it is wise to explicitly set this value to "multipart/form-data", and set the method attribute to "post".

innerHTML

JavaScript 1.5, JScript 3.0+

Nav6, IE4+

Syntax

```
[var x =] HTMLFormElement.innerHTML [= HTMLString]
```

The innerHTML property of HTMLFormElement interfaces retrieves or sets the HTML source code contained between, but not including, the starting and ending tags.

I personally recommend against using innerHTML to set the HTML inside a tag. I strongly recommend against using innerHTML to append to the contents of an HTML tag:

```
elem.innerHTML += "<div><p>Hello World</p></div>" // DO NOT DO THIS
```

I do like the handiness of the innerHTML property for retrieving HTML source code at a glance, as a companion method to the W3C Document Object Model. (The DOM provides an object structure for the source code; innerHTML provides the corresponding source code.)

innerText

JScript 3.0+

IE4+

Syntax

```
var x = HTMLFormElement.innerText
```

The innerText property of HTMLFormElement retrieves or sets the text contained between, but not including, the starting and ending tags.

The innerText property can be useful, but the DOM Level 2 Range interface provides far more flexibility. See Chapter 34, "DOM-2 Range," for details on text ranges.

length

JavaScript 1.0+, JScript 3.0+

Nav2.0+, IE4.0+

Syntax

```
[var x = ] HTMLFormElement.length
```

The `length` property of `HTMLFormElement` objects reflects the number of form control elements in the form. This property is read-only, but you can change it simply by adding or removing form control elements from the `this` object.

Perhaps surprisingly, `<input type="image" />` elements will not be counted in the `length` property in either Internet Explorer or Netscape Navigator.

method

JavaScript 1.0+, JScript 1.0+

Nav2.0+, IE3.0+

Syntax

```
[var x =] HTMLFormElement.method [= HTTPmethod]
```

The `method` property of `HTMLFormElement` objects reflects the HTTP method the client browser will use to submit the form. The default for this is `"get"`. When you do not explicitly set this value, however, Netscape will return an empty string.

It is often preferable to explicitly set this value to `"post"`. Short forms carrying a small amount of data you may set to `"get"`.

name

JavaScript 1.0+, JScript 1.0+

Nav2.0+, IE3.0+

Syntax

```
[var x =] HTMLFormElement.name [= nameString]
```

The `name` property of `HTMLFormElement` objects reflects the `name` attribute of the form. Netscape Navigator 4 will ignore an attempt to set the name property from JavaScript. (Note, XHTML 1.0 has deprecated this attribute, but at this time it is not yet deprecated in the W3C DOM.) You can explicitly set this value at any time.

outerHTML

JScript 3.0+

IE4+

Syntax

```
var x = HTMLFormElement.outerHTML
```

The outerHTML property of HTMLFormElement retrieves or sets the HTML source code contained between, and including, the starting and ending tags.

I do like the handiness of the outerHTML property for retrieving HTML source code at a glance, as a companion method to the W3C Document Object Model. (The DOM provides an object structure for the source code; outerHTML provides the corresponding source code.)

tabIndex

JScript 3.0+

IE4+

Syntax

```
[ver x =] HTMLFormElement.tabIndex [= numValue]
```

The tabIndex property of HTMLFormElement objects sets where the this element rests in the tab order. The tab order is an index indicating when an element in the document receives focus as the user strikes his Tab key. When setting this value, remember it can only accept numeric integers.

A negative tabIndex takes the this element out of the tab order. Other than that, Tab key presses go to elements in this order:

- The lowest positive integer, followed by the next lowest, and so on.

- After that, the source order of elements in the document.

target

JavaScript 1.0+

Nav2.0+

Syntax

```
[var x =] HTMLFormElement.target [= targetWin]
```

The `target` property of instances of `HTMLFormElement` reflects the currently targeted window the browser will receive its response from the server in. Any valid HTML window name (see Chapter 15, "window," for a description of HTML window names versus JavaScript window names) you can use for this value.

You can also use `"_blank"` to indicate opening a new window every time, `"_parent"` for the parent window, `"_top"` for the topmost window in the parent window chain (see `top` and `parent` in Chapter 15, "window"), or `"_self"` to indicate it should load into the window of its document. (`"_self"` is the default setting.)

Internet Explorer 5.0+ introduces a new one called `"_search"`, which will target the link for the browser's search sidebar.

Methods

reset()

JavaScript 1.0+

Nav2.0+

Syntax

```
HTMLFormElement.reset()
```

The `reset()` method of `HTMLFormElement` objects resets all values of the `this` form to the default values specified in the HTML source code. This is equivalent to clicking on an `<input type="reset" />` button for the form.

submit()

JavaScript 1.0+

Nav2.0+

Syntax

```
HTMLFormElement.submit()
```

The submit() method of HTMLFormElement objects submits the this form to the URI specified in the action property of the form. This is equivalent to clicking on an <input type="submit" /> button for the form with one significant difference—when you use a Submit button, the onsubmit handler is called and when you use the submit() method, it is not.

Event Handlers

Netscape supports the following event handlers for HTMLFormElement objects:

onreset

onsubmit

Microsoft Internet Explorer supports the following event handlers for HTMLFormElement objects:

onactivate	ondragleave	onmouseover
onbeforeactivate	ondragover	onmouseup
onbeforecopy	ondragstart	onmousewheel
onbeforecut	ondrop	onmoveend
onbeforedeactivate	onfocus	onmovestart
onbeforeeditfocus	onfocusin	onpaste
onbeforepaste	onfocusout	onpropertychange
onblur	onhelp	onreadystatechange
oncontextmenu	onkeydown	onreset
oncontrolselect	onkeypress	onresize
oncopy	onkeyup	onresizeend
oncut	onlosecapture	onresizestart
ondblclick	onmousedown	onselectstart
ondeactivate	onmouseenter	onsubmit
ondrag	onmouseleave	ontimeerror
ondragend	onmousemove	
ondragenter	onmouseout	

HTMLButtonElement Interface/<button>...</button>

Browser / JavaScript Version	Created By
Nav4/JavaScript 1.2	Not implemented
IE4/JScript 3.0	`<button>...</button>`
IE5/JScript 5.0	`<button>...</button>`
IE5.5/JScript 5.5	`<button>...</button>`
Nav6/JavaScript 1.5	`<button>...</button>`
IE6	`<button>...</button>`
DOM Level 1	`document.createElement("button")`

> **Note**
> Implemented in Nav6, IE4+
>
> Descends from `HTMLElement` interface (Chapter 21, "HTMLElement")

Description

The new `<button>...</button>` element is similar to the `<input type="button" />` element (see Chapter 26, "Form Input Elements: `HTMLInputElement`"). However, the `HTMLButtonElement` allows you to include markup for rendering the "inside" of the button. The standard HTML button from the `<input />` tag allows styled text only (see Chapter 33, "Styling for HTML Elements"). Listing 25.5 shows the contemporary button tag, and its predecessor, the `<input type="button" />`.

Listing 25.5   *Buttons and Button Inputs*

```
<?xml version="1.0" ?>
<!DOCTYPE html PUBLIC "-//W3C//DTD XHTML 1.0 Transitional//EN"
➥"DTD/xhtml1-transitional.dtd">
<html xmlns="http://www.w3.org/1999/xhtml" >
<head><title></title></head>
<body>
<form action="javascript:void(0)">
<p>
```

Listing 25.5 *(continued)*

```
<button type="button"><img src="25lst04b.gif" alt="Beaker icon" />Hello World
➥</button>
<br />
<img src="25lst04b.gif" alt="Beaker icon" /><input type="button"
➥value="Hello World" />
</p>
</form>
</body>
</html>
```

There are a few exceptions to including markup inside the button's tags. For instance, you cannot include <a>...</a> or <form>...</form> tags. Likewise, any tag in this chapter cannot be a child element of button elements. HTML 4 also prohibits <input /> tags as children of button elements. Finally, the W3C HTML 4.01 Recommendation prohibits using image maps as child elements of buttons.

> **Caution**
> You should not have these elements as descendents of the button tag either (for instance, a `<p><form>...</form></p>` scenario).

HTMLButtonElement objects typically are submit buttons—they will submit the form onclick. However, you can explicitly set the type attribute to "reset" for a reset button, or to "button" for an ordinary button.

Properties

accessKey
JavaScript 1.5

Nav6

Syntax

```
[var x = ] HTMLButtonElement.accessKey [ = "c"]
```

The accessKey property of HTMLButtonElement objects designates a shortcut key to focus. When the user presses the designated key and the Alt key (on the Windows platform) although the window for the this object has focus, the element gains focus. The nodeValue for this attribute must be one character in length.

> **Note**
> Internet Explorer 5 implements this property for all elements, as I note in Chapter 21, "HTMLElement."

children

JScript 3.0+

IE4+

See childNodes under the DOM Document object in Chapter 20, "Core DOM Objects."

disabled

JavaScript 1.5

Nav6

Syntax

```
var boolValue = HTMLButtonElement.disabled
```

The disabled property of HTMLButtonElement objects prevents the user from using the button until, for example, some necessary form elements have been completed.

> **Note**
> Internet Explorer 5 implements this property for all elements, as I note in Chapter 21, "HTMLElement."

form

JavaScript 1.5, JScript 3.0+

Nav6, IE4.0+

Read-only

Syntax

```
var x = HTMLButtonElement.form
```

The `form` property of `HTMLButtonElement` objects refers directly to the `HTMLFormElement` that contains the `this` object. If the button is not contained within a form, then it has a null value.

innerHTML

JavaScript 1.5, JScript 3.0+

Nav6, IE4+

Syntax

```
[var x =] HTMLButtonElement.innerHTML [= HTMLString]
```

The `innerHTML` property of `HTMLButtonElement` interfaces retrieves or sets the HTML source code contained between, but not including, the starting and ending tags.

I personally recommend against using `innerHTML` to set the HTML inside a tag. I strongly recommend against using `innerHTML` to append to the contents of an HTML tag:

```
elem.innerHTML += "<div><p>Hello World</p></div>" // DO NOT DO THIS
```

I do like the handiness of the `innerHTML` property for retrieving HTML source code at a glance, as a companion method to the W3C Document Object Model. (The DOM provides an object structure for the source code; `innerHTML` provides the corresponding source code.)

innerText

JScript 3.0+

IE4+

Syntax

```
var x = HTMLButtonElement.innerText
```

The `innerText` property of `HTMLButtonElement` retrieves or sets the text contained between, but not including, the starting and ending tags.

The `innerText` property can be useful, but the DOM Level 2 `Range` interface provides far more flexibility. See Chapter 34, "DOM-2 Range," for details on text ranges.

name

JavaScript 1.5, JScript 3.0+

Nav6, IE4+

Syntax

```
[var buttonName =] HTMLButtonElement.name [= newName]
```

The `name` property of `HTMLButtonElement` objects provides a name for the button by which the ancestor `HTMLFormElement` may have the button as a property.

outerHTML

JScript 3.0+

IE4+

Syntax

```
var x = HTMLButtonElement.outerHTML
```

The `outerHTML` property of `HTMLButtonElement` retrieves or sets the HTML source code contained between, and including, the starting and ending tags.

I do like the handiness of the `outerHTML` property for retrieving HTML source code at a glance, as a companion method to the W3C Document Object Model. (The DOM provides an object structure for the source code; `outerHTML` provides the corresponding source code.)

tabIndex

JavaScript 1.5, JScript 3.0+

Nav6, IE4+

Syntax

```
[ver x =] HTMLButtonElement.tabIndex [= numValue]
```

The tabIndex property of HTMLButtonElement objects sets where the this element rests in the tab order. The tab order is an index indicating when an element in the document receives focus as the user strikes the Tab key. When setting this value, remember it can only accept numeric integers.

A negative tabIndex, in Internet Explorer, takes the this element out of the tab order. Other than that, Tab key presses go to elements in this order:

- The lowest positive integer, followed by the next lowest, and so on.
- After that, the source order of elements in the document.

HTMLButtonElement is a natural stopping point for Tab key presses.

type

JavaScript 1.5, JScript 3.0+

Nav6, IE4+

Read-only

Syntax

```
var x = HTMLButtonElement.type
```

The type property of HTMLButtonElement objects reflects the type attribute of the button. Its value may be "submit", "reset", or "button".

value

JavaScript 1.5, JScript 3.0+

Nav6, IE4+

Syntax

```
[var x =] HTMLButtonElement.value [= valueString]
```

The value property of HTMLButtonElement objects reflects the value attribute of the button. The name="value" pair on a button will indicate, in a form that has more than one submit button, which button has been clicked.

Methods

blur()

JavaScript 1.5, JScript 3.0+

Nav6, IE4+

Syntax

```
HTMLButtonElement.blur()
```

The `blur()` method of `HTMLButtonElement` objects forces the form control to lose focus. What this means is it tells the browser "I'm not important; let something else take center stage." The browser reacts by assigning focus specifically to no object.

focus()

JavaScript 1.5, JScript 3.0+

Nav6, IE4+

Syntax

```
HTMLButtonElement.focus()
```

The `focus()` method of `HTMLButtonElement` objects forces the form control to gain focus. This means it tells the browser "I'm important; make sure I alone react to the keyboard." The browser reacts by assigning focus specifically to that object.

Event Handlers

Microsoft Internet Explorer supports the following event handlers for `HTMLFormElement` objects:

onactivate	onbeforepaste	oncontrolselect
onafterupdate	onbeforeupdate	oncut
onbeforeactivate	onblur	ondblclick
onbeforecut	onclick	ondeactivate
onbeforedeactivate	oncontextmenu	ondragenter
onbeforeeditfocus		

ondragleave	onkeyup	onmoveend
ondragover	onlosecapture	onmovestart
ondrop	onmousedown	onpaste
onerrorupdate	onmouseenter	onpropertychange
onfilterchange	onmouseleave	onreadystatechange
onfocus	onmousemove	onresize
onfocusin	onmouseout	onresizeend
onfocusout	onmouseover	onresizestart
onhelp	onmouseup	onselectstart
onkeydown	onmousewheel	ontimeerror
onkeypress	onmove	

HTMLFieldSetElement Interface/<fieldset>...</fieldset>

Browser / JavaScript version	Created by:
Nav4/JavaScript 1.2	Not implemented
IE4/JScript 3.0	<fieldset>...</fieldset>
IE5/JScript 5.0	<fieldset>...</fieldset>
IE5.5/JScript 5.5	<fieldset>...</fieldset>
Nav6/JavaScript 1.5	<fieldset>...</fieldset>
IE6	<fieldset>...</fieldset>
DOM Level 1	document.createElement("fieldset")

> **Note**
> Implemented in Nav6, IE4+
>
> Descends from HTMLElement interface (Chapter 21, "HTMLElement")

Description

The field set element, in tandem with the HTMLLegendElement, provides a visually appealing grouping of form controls. The field set element presents a box around the form controls its markup contains. The legend element presents a title for the field set element, over the box outline.

Listing 25.6 demonstrates the correct usage of field set and legend elements. Figure 25.1 shows what they look like when a browser renders them.

Listing 25.6   *Field Sets and Legends in Markup*

```
<?xml version="1.0" ?>
<!DOCTYPE html PUBLIC "-//W3C//DTD XHTML 1.0 Transitional//EN"
➡"DTD/xhtml1-transitional.dtd">
<html xmlns="http://www.w3.org/1999/xhtml" >
<head><title></title></head>
<body>
<form action="javascript:void(0)">
<fieldset>
<legend>This is the legend text</legend>
<p>Checkbox Zero<input type="checkbox" /></p>
<p>Checkbox One<input type="checkbox" /></p>
</fieldset>
</form>
</body>
</html>
```

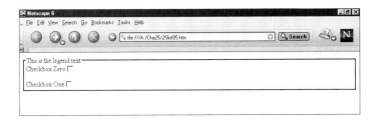

Figure 25.1

Field sets and legends on the screen.

Properties

---

align

JScript 3.0+

IE4+

Deprecated in HTML 4

Syntax

```
[var x = ] HTMLFieldSetElement.align [= alignString]
```

The `align` attribute of `HTMLFieldSetElement` objects defines where the edges of the field set border align with the HTML elements outside the field set.

---

form

JavaScript 1.5

Nav6, IE6

Read-only

Syntax

```
var x = HTMLFieldSetElement.form
```

The `form` property of `HTMLFieldSetElement` objects refers directly to the `HTMLFormElement` that contains the `this` object, when the object is contained in a form.

---

innerHTML

JavaScript 1.5, JScript 3.0+

Nav6, IE4+

Syntax

```
[var x =] HTMLFieldSetElement.innerHTML [= HTMLString]
```

The `innerHTML` property of `HTMLFieldSetElement` interfaces retrieves or sets the HTML source code contained between, but not including, the starting and ending tags.

I personally recommend against using `innerHTML` to set the HTML inside a tag. I strongly recommend against using `innerHTML` to append to the contents of an HTML tag:

```
elem.innerHTML += "<div><p>Hello World</p></div>" // DO NOT DO THIS
```

I do like the handiness of the `innerHTML` property for retrieving HTML source code at a glance, as a companion method to the W3C Document Object Model. (The DOM provides an object structure for the source code; `innerHTML` provides the corresponding source code.)

innerText

JScript 3.0+

IE4+

Syntax

```
var x = HTMLFieldSetElement.innerText
```

The `innerText` property of `HTMLFieldSetElement` retrieves or sets the text contained between, but not including, the starting and ending tags.

The `innerText` property can be useful, but the DOM Level 2 `Range` interface provides far more flexibility. See Chapter 34, "DOM-2 Range," for details on text ranges.

outerHTML

JScript 3.0+

IE4+

Syntax

```
var x = HTMLFieldSetElement.outerHTML
```

The `outerHTML` property of `HTMLFieldSetElement` retrieves or sets the HTML source code contained between, and including, the starting and ending tags.

I do like the handiness of the `outerHTML` property for retrieving HTML source code at a glance, as a companion method to the W3C Document Object Model. (The DOM provides an object structure for the source code; `outerHTML` provides the corresponding source code.)

tabIndex

JavaScript 1.5, JScript 5.0+

Nav6, IE5+

Syntax

```
[ver x =] HTMLFieldSetElement.tabIndex [= numValue]
```

The tabIndex property of HTMLFieldSetElement objects sets where the this element rests in the tab order. The tab order is an index indicating when an element in the document receives focus as the user strikes his Tab key. When setting this value, remember it can only accept numeric integers.

A negative tabIndex in Internet Explorer takes the this element out of the tab order. Other than that, Tab key presses go to elements in this order:

- The lowest positive integer, followed by the next lowest, and so on.

- After that, the source order of elements in the document.

Methods

The HTMLFieldSetElement interface provides no methods or event handlers beyond those the HTMLElement interface defines.

HTMLIsIndexElement Interface/

Browser / JavaScript Version	Created By
Nav4/JavaScript 1.2	
IE4/JScript 3.0	
IE5/JScript 5.0	
IE5.5/JScript 5.5	
Nav6/JavaScript 1.5	
IE6	
DOM Level 1	document.createElement("isindex")

> **Note**
>
> Implemented in Nav6, IE4+
>
> Deprecated in HTML 4
>
> Descends from HTMLElement interface (Chapter 21, "HTMLElement")
>
> Parent elements: HTMLBodyElement (Chapter 22, "HTMLHtmlElement")

Description

The <isindex /> tag is a holdover from earlier versions of HTML in browsers. Basically, you should not use it under any circumstances. It cannot be a child of any form, and yet it was originally intended to go with a form to the server. This does not make for very "clean" HTML.

The correct syntax for <isindex /> includes a prompt attribute. Listing 25.7 compares the current, "proper" way to retrieve information, and the deprecated <isindex /> tag's use.

Listing 25.7   *The Successor to*

```
<?xml version="1.0" ?>
<!DOCTYPE html PUBLIC "-//W3C//DTD XHTML 1.0 Transitional//EN
➥"DTD/xhtml1-transitional.dtd">
<html xmlns="http://www.w3.org/1999/xhtml" >
<head><title></title></head>
<body>
<!-- Deprecated terminology -->
<isindex prompt="What is your name?" id="customerName_0" />

<form action="javascript:void(0)">
<!-- Current terminology, inside a form -->
<p>What is your name?<input name="customerName_1" id="customerName_1" /></p>

</form>
</body>
</html>
```

Properties

---

action

JScript 1.0+

IE3+

Syntax

`[var x =] HTMLIsIndexElement.action [= postURI]`

Same as `this.form.action`.

---

form

JavaScript 1.5

Nav6, IE6

Read-only

Syntax

`var x = HTMLIsIndexElement.form`

The `form` property of `HTMLIsIndexElement` objects refers directly to the `HTMLFormElement` that contains the `this` object.

---

innerHTML

JavaScript 1.5, JScript 3.0+

Nav6, IE4+

Syntax

`[var x =] HTMLIsIndexElement.innerHTML [= HTMLString]`

The `innerHTML` property of `HTMLIsIndexElement` interfaces retrieves or sets the HTML source code contained between, but not including, the starting and ending tags. In empty elements there is, of course, no content.

I personally recommend against using `innerHTML` to set the HTML inside a tag. I strongly recommend against using `innerHTML` to append to the contents of an HTML tag:

```
elem.innerHTML += "<div><p>Hello World</p></div>" // DO NOT DO THIS
```

I do like the handiness of the `innerHTML` property for retrieving HTML source code at a glance, as a companion method to the W3C Document Object Model. (The DOM provides an object structure for the source code; `innerHTML` provides the corresponding source code.)

innerText

JScript 3.0+

IE4+

Syntax

```
var x = HTMLIsIndexElement.innerText
```

The `innerText` property of `HTMLIsIndexElement` retrieves or sets the text contained between, but not including, the starting and ending tags. In empty elements there is, of course, no element content.

The `innerText` property can be useful, but the DOM Level 2 `Range` interface provides far more flexibility. See Chapter 34, "DOM-2 Range," for details on text ranges.

outerHTML

JScript 3.0+

IE4+

Syntax

```
var x = HTMLIsIndexElement.outerHTML
```

The `outerHTML` property of `HTMLIsIndexElement` retrieves or sets the HTML source code contained between, and including, the starting and ending tags. In empty elements, of course, there is no content.

I do like the handiness of the outerHTML property for retrieving HTML source code at a glance, as a companion method to the W3C Document Object Model. (The DOM provides an object structure for the source code; outerHTML provides the corresponding source code.)

prompt

JavaScript 1.5

Nav6

Syntax

```
[var x =] HTMLIsIndexElement.prompt
```

The prompt property of HTMLIsIndexElement objects refers to the prompt attribute. This specifies, in turn, what the <isindex /> tag is to ask the user for.

tabIndex

JScript 5.0+

IE5+

Syntax

```
[ver x =] HTMLIsIndexElement.tabIndex [= numValue]
```

The tabIndex property of HTMLIsIndexElement objects sets where the this element rests in the tab order. The tab order is an index indicating when an element in the document receives focus as the user strikes his Tab key. When setting this value, remember it can only accept numeric integers.

A negative tabIndex in Internet Explorer takes the this element out of the tab order. Other than that, Tab key presses go to elements in this order:

- The lowest positive integer, followed by the next lowest, and so on.

- After that, the source order of elements in the document.

Methods

The `HTMLIsIndexElement` interface provides no methods beyond those the `HTMLElement` interface defines.

Event Handlers

Microsoft Internet Explorer supports the following event handlers for `HTMLIsIndexElement` objects:

onactivate

onbeforedeactivate

onbeforeeditfocus

onblur

oncontrolselect

ondeactivate

onfocus

onmove

onmoveend

onmovestart

onreadystatechange

onresize

onresizeend

onresizestart

HTMLLabelElement/<label>...</label>

Browser / JavaScript Version	Created By
Nav4/JavaScript 1.2	Not implemented
IE4/JScript 3.0	<label>...</label>
IE5/JScript 5.0	<label>...</label>

IE5.5/JScript 5.5	`<label>...</label>`
Nav6/JavaScript 1.5	`<label>...</label>`
IE6	`<label>...</label>`
DOM Level 1	`document.createElement("label")`

> **Note**
> Implemented in Nav6, IE4+
>
> Descends from `HTMLElement` interface (Chapter 21, "HTMLElement")

Description

The World Wide Web Consortium says it best in its HTML 4.01 Recommendation, and I quote from Section 17.2:

"Some form controls automatically have labels associated with them (press buttons) while most do not (text fields, check boxes and radio buttons, and menus)... The LABEL element is used to specify labels for controls that do not have implicit labels."

This means standard buttons have text inside of them (see `HTMLButtonElement` earlier in this chapter, and `<input type="button" />` in Chapter 26) to identify their purpose, but most other form controls have no room for an interior text. The `<label />` element fills this gap.

Unlike other form controls, you are allowed to have form controls as child elements of this element. (The `<label />` element excludes itself as a child, though.) When your label does not itself contain the form control it labels, use the `for` attribute (not to be confused with the `for` or `for...in` statements of Chapter 11, "The Global Object and Statements") as an `IDREF`. (Those of you unfamiliar with XML should know `IDREF` means a reference to an `id` attribute, where the contents of this attribute match a unique ID attribute in the document.) Listing 25.8 shows a number of different uses for the `HTMLLabelElement`.

Listing 25.8   *Labeling Text Inputs as an Example*

```
<?xml version="1.0" ?>
<!DOCTYPE html PUBLIC "-//W3C//DTD XHTML 1.0 Transitional//EN
➥"DTD/xhtml1-transitional.dtd">
<html xmlns="http://www.w3.org/1999/xhtml" >
```

Listing 25.8   *(continued)*

```
<head><title></title></head>
<body>
<form action="javascript:void(0)">
<p>
<label>
<input type="text" name="text0" id="text0" value="text0" />
Label for text0
</label>
</p>

<p>
<label>
Label for text1
<input type="text" name="text1" id="text1" value="text1" />
</label>
</p>

<p>
<input type="text" name="text2" id="text2" value="text2" />
<label for="text2">Label for text2</label>
<!-- The for attribute points to the id attribute of the text input. -->
</p>

</form>
</body>
</html>
```

Properties

accessKey

JavaScript 1.5

Nav6

Syntax

```
[var x = ] HTMLLabelElement.accessKey [ = "c"]
```

The accessKey property of HTMLLabelElement objects designates a shortcut key to focus. When the user presses the designated key and the Alt key (on the Windows platform) while the window for the this object has focus, the element gains focus. The nodeValue for this attribute must be one character in length.

> **Note**
> Internet Explorer 5 implements this property for all elements, as I note in Chapter 21, "HTMLElement."

form

JavaScript 1.5

Nav6, IE6

Read-only

Syntax

```
var x = HTMLLabelElement.form
```

The form property of HTMLLabelElement objects refers directly to the HTMLFormElement which contains the this object. If the label is not contained in a form element it has the value of null.

htmlFor

JavaScript 1.5+, JScript 3.0+

Nav6, IE4+

Syntax

```
[var idref =] HTMLLabelElement.htmlFor [= idString]
```

The htmlFor property of HTMLLabelElement objects is an ID reference, or IDREF, to another HTML element with a matching id attribute. This property tells the browser which form element the label ties in to.

innerHTML

JavaScript 1.5, JScript 3.0+

Nav6, IE4+

Syntax

```
[var x =] HTMLLabelElement.innerHTML [= HTMLString]
```

The `innerHTML` property of `HTMLLabelElement` interfaces retrieves or sets the HTML source code contained between, but not including, the starting and ending tags.

I personally recommend against using `innerHTML` to set the HTML inside a tag. I strongly recommend against using `innerHTML` to append to the contents of an HTML tag:

```
elem.innerHTML += "<div><p>Hello World</p></div>" // DO NOT DO THIS
```

I do like the handiness of the `innerHTML` property for retrieving HTML source code at a glance, as a companion method to the W3C Document Object Model. (The DOM provides an object structure for the source code; `innerHTML` provides the corresponding source code.)

innerText

JScript 3.0+

IE4+

Syntax

```
var x = HTMLLabelElement.innerText
```

The `innerText` property of `HTMLLabelElement` retrieves or sets the text contained between, but not including, the starting and ending tags.

The `innerText` property can be useful, but the DOM Level 2 `Range` interface provides far more flexibility. See Chapter 34, "DOM-2 Range," for details on text ranges.

outerHTML

JScript 3.0+

IE4+

Syntax

```
var x = HTMLLabelElement.outerHTML
```

The `outerHTML` property of `HTMLLabelElement` retrieves or sets the HTML source code contained between, and including, the starting and ending tags.

I do like the handiness of the `outerHTML` property for retrieving HTML source code at a glance, as a companion method to the W3C Document Object Model. (The DOM provides an object structure for the source code; `outerHTML` provides the corresponding source code.)

tabIndex

JavaScript 1.5, JScript 5.0+

Nav6, IE5+

Syntax

```
[ver x =] HTMLLabelElement.tabIndex [= numValue]
```

The `tabIndex` property of `HTMLLabelElement` objects sets where the `this` element rests in the "tab order." The tab order is an index indicating when an element in the document receives focus as the user strikes his Tab key. When setting this value, remember it can only accept numeric integers.

A negative `tabIndex`, in Internet Explorer, takes the `this` element out of the tab order. Other than that, Tab key presses go to elements in this order:

- The lowest positive integer, followed by the next lowest, and so on.

- After that, the source order of elements in the document.

Methods

Netscape and Internet Explorer provide no methods to `HTMLLabelElement` beyond those provided via the `HTMLElement` interface.

Event Handlers

Microsoft Internet Explorer supports the following event handlers for
`HTMLLabelElement` objects:

onactivate	ondragend	onmouseleave
onafterupdate	ondragenter	onmousemove
onbeforeactivate	ondragleave	onmouseout
onbeforecopy	ondragover	onmouseover
onbeforecut	ondragstart	onmouseup
onbeforedeactivate	ondrop	onmousewheel
onbeforeeditfocus	onerrorupdate	onmove
onbeforepaste	onfocus	onmoveend
onbeforeupdate	onfocusin	onmovestart
onblur	onfocusout	onpaste
onclick	onhelp	onpropertychange
oncontextmenu	onkeydown	onreadystatechange
oncontrolselect	onkeypress	onresize
oncut	onkeyup	onresizeend
ondblclick	onlosecapture	onresizestart
ondeactivate	onmousedown	onselectstart
ondrag	onmouseenter	

HTMLLegendElement/<legend>...</legend>

Browser/JavaScript Version	Created By
Nav4/JavaScript 1.2	Not implemented
IE4/JScript 3.0	<legend>...</legend>
IE5/JScript 5.0	<legend>...</legend>
IE5.5/JScript 5.5	<legend>...</legend>

Nav6/JavaScript 1.5   `<legend>...</legend>`

IE6   `<legend>...</legend>`

DOM Level 1   `document.createElement("legend")`

Note

Implemented in Nav6, IE4+

Descends from HTMLElement interface (Chapter 21, "HTMLElement")

Required parent element: HTMLFieldSetElement

Description

The `<legend>...</legend>` element, in tandem with the `HTMLFieldSetElement`, provides a visually appealing grouping of form controls. The field set element presents a box around the form controls its markup contains. The legend element presents a title for the field set element, over the box outline.

Listing 25.6 demonstrates the correct usage of field set and legend elements. Figure 25.1 shows what they look like when a browser renders them.

Properties

align

JavaScript 1.5, JScript 3.0+

Nav6, IE4+

Deprecated in HTML 4

Syntax

```
[var x =] HTMLLegendElement.align [= alignStr]
```

The `align` property of `HTMLLegendElement` objects refers directly to the `align` attribute of the `this` object's corresponding tag. The possible values are `"top"`, `"left"`, `"right"`, and `"bottom"`, corresponding to where the developer wants to place the legend relative to the fieldset it belongs to.

accessKey

JavaScript 1.5

Nav6

Syntax

```
[var x = ] HTMLLegendElement.accessKey [ = "c"]
```

The accessKey property of HTMLLegendElement objects designates a shortcut key to focus. When the user presses the designated key and the Alt key (on the Windows platform) while the window for the this object has focus, the element gains focus. The nodeValue for this attribute must be one character in length.

> **Note**
> Internet Explorer 5 implements this property for all elements, as I note in Chapter 21, "HTMLElement."

form

JavaScript 1.5, JScript 5.6

Nav6, IE6

Read-only

Syntax

```
var x = HTMLLegendElement.form
```

The form property of HTMLLegendElement objects refers directly to the HTMLFormElement that contains the this object.

innerHTML

JavaScript 1.5, JScript 3.0+

Nav6, IE4+

Syntax

```
[var x =] HTMLLegendElement.innerHTML [= HTMLString]
```

The `innerHTML` property of `HTMLLegendElement` interfaces retrieves or sets the HTML source code contained between, but not including, the starting and ending tags.

I personally recommend against using `innerHTML` to set the HTML inside a tag. I strongly recommend against using `innerHTML` to append to the contents of an HTML tag:

```
elem.innerHTML += "<div><p>Hello World</p></div>" // DO NOT DO THIS
```

I do like the handiness of the `innerHTML` property for retrieving HTML source code at a glance, as a companion method to the W3C Document Object Model. (The DOM provides an object structure for the source code; `innerHTML` provides the corresponding source code.)

innerText

JScript 3.0+

IE4+

Syntax

```
var x = HTMLLegendElement.innerText
```

The `innerText` property of `HTMLLegendElement` retrieves or sets the text contained between, but not including, the starting and ending tags.

The `innerText` property can be useful, but the DOM Level 2 `Range` interface provides far more flexibility. See Chapter 34, "DOM-2 Range," for details on text ranges.

outerHTML

JScript 3.0+

IE4+

Syntax

```
var x = HTMLLegendElement.outerHTML
```

The `outerHTML` property of `HTMLLegendElement` retrieves or sets the HTML source code contained between, and including, the starting and ending tags.

I do like the handiness of the outerHTML property for retrieving HTML source code at a glance, as a companion method to the W3C Document Object Model. (The DOM provides an object structure for the source code; outerHTML provides the corresponding source code.)

tabIndex

JavaScript 1.5, JScript 5.0+

Nav6, IE5+

Syntax

```
[ver x =] HTMLLegendElement.tabIndex [= numValue]
```

The tabIndex property of HTMLLegendElement objects sets where the this element rests in the tab order. The tab order is an index indicating when an element in the document receives focus as the user strikes his Tab key. When setting this value, remember it can only accept numeric integers.

A negative tabIndex, in Internet Explorer, takes the this element out of the tab order. Other than that, Tab key presses go to elements in this order:

- The lowest positive integer, followed by the next lowest, and so on.

- After that, the source order of elements in the document.

Methods

The HTMLLegendElement interface provides no methods or event handlers beyond those the HTMLElement interface defines.

HTMLOptGroupElement/<optgroup>...</optgroup>

Browser/JavaScript Version	Created By
Nav4/JavaScript 1.2	Not Implemented
IE4/JScript 3.0	Not Implemented
IE5/JScript 5.0	Not Implemented

IE5.5/JScript 5.5	Not Implemented
Nav6/JavaScript 1.5	`<optgroup>...</optgroup>`
IE6	`<optgroup>...</optgroup>`
DOM Level 1	`document.createElement("optgroup")`

> **Note**
> Implemented in Nav1+ (HTML), Nav2+ (JS), IE3+
>
> Descends from `HTMLElement` interface (Chapter 21, "HTMLElement")
>
> Required parent element: `HTMLSelectElement`

Description

The `<optgroup>...</optgroup>` element provides the markup to hold a group of option elements in a drop-down menu, also known as a *combo box*. At this time, HTML 4 does not permit nesting of `<optgroup>...</optgroup>` tags. See the section on `HTMLSelectElement`, later in this chapter, for details.

Properties

disabled

JavaScript 1.5, JScript 5.5

Nav6, IE6

Syntax

```
var boolValue = HTMLOptGroupElement.disabled
```

The `disabled` property of `HTMLOptGroupElement` objects prevents the user from modifying a group of options in a select element.

> **Note**
> Internet Explorer 5 implements this property for all elements, as I note in Chapter 21, "HTMLElement."

label

JavaScript 1.5

Nav6, IE6

Syntax

```
[var x =] HTMLOptGroupElement.label [= visibleString]
```

The `label` property of `HTMLOptGroupElement` objects provides the visual label for the `optgroup` within the select element.

Methods

The `HTMLOptGroupElement` interface provides no methods or event handlers beyond those the `HTMLElement` interface defines.

HTMLOptionElement/<option />

Browser/JavaScript Version	Created By
Nav4/JavaScript 1.2	`<option />` `var x = new Option()`
IE4/JScript 3.0	`<option />`
IE5/JScript 5.0	`<option />`
IE5.5/JScript 5.5	`<option />`
Nav6/JavaScript 1.5	`<option />` `var x = new Option()`
IE6	`<option />`
DOM Level 1	`document.createElement("option")`

> **Note**
>
> Implemented in Nav1+ (HTML), Nav2+ (JS), IE3+
>
> Descends from `HTMLElement` interface (Chapter 21, "HTMLElement")
>
> Required ancestor element: `HTMLSelectElement`
>
> Required parent element: either `HTMLSelectElement` or `HTMLOptGroupElement`

Description

The `<option />` element provides the markup to hold a single choice in a drop-down menu, also known as a combo box. See the section on `HTMLSelectElement`, later in this chapter, for details.

Netscape and Internet Explorer 4+ provide an alternative way to construct `<option />` elements: its `Option()` constructor function. This predates the DOM and has been retained for backward-compatibility. The syntax for the `Option()` constructor function is as follows:

```
var x = new Option([optText [, optValue [, optDefSelect [, optSelected] ] ] ])
```

The first argument, when given, sets the `text` property of the option. The second argument, when given, sets the `value` property of the option. The third argument, when `true`, sets the option as a default selected option in the select box it attaches to. The fourth argument, when `true`, sets the option as a selected option in the select box it attaches to. The first two optional arguments are strings; the last two optional arguments the `Option()` constructor treats as either `true` or `false`.

Properties

defaultSelected

JavaScript 1.1+, JScript 1.0+

Nav3+, IE3+

Syntax

```
var x = HTMLOptionElement.defaultSelected
```

The `defaultSelected` property of `HTMLOptionElement` objects reflects whether the option is selected by default.

disabled

JavaScript 1.5

Nav6

Syntax

```
var boolValue = HTMLOptionElement.disabled
```

The `disabled` property of `HTMLOptionElement` objects disables the form control from accepting user input.

> **Note**
> Internet Explorer 5 implements this property for all elements, as I note in Chapter 21, "HTMLElement".

form

JavaScript 1.5, JScript 5.0+

Nav6, IE5+

Read-only

Syntax

```
var x = HTMLOptionElement.form
```

The `form` property of `HTMLOptionElement` objects refers directly to the `HTMLFormElement` that contains the `this` object. The value of the property is `null` if there is no containing form element.

index

JavaScript 1.0+, JScript 1.0+

Nav2+, IE3+

Syntax

```
var x = HTMLOptionElement.index
```

The index property of HTMLOptionElement objects refers directly to the this object's position in its parent (or grandparent, in the case of a parent <optgroup>...</optgroup> element) HTMLSelectElement's options collection.

label

JavaScript 1.5

Nav6, IE6

Syntax

```
[var x =] HTMLOptionElement.label [= visibleString]
```

The label property of HTMLOptionElement objects overrides the default contents of the this element, presenting its value to the user as the selectable option value. However, this does not override the actual content of the this element.

length

JavaScript 1.0–JavaScript 1.3

Nav2-Nav4

Syntax

```
var x = HTMLOptionElement.length
```

The length property of HTMLOptionElement objects refers directly to the length of its parent (or grandparent, in the case of a parent <optgroup>...</optgroup> element) HTMLSelectElement's options collection.

selected

JavaScript 1.0+, JScript 1.0+

Nav2+, IE3+

Syntax

```
var x = HTMLOptionElement.selected
```

The selected property of HTMLOptionElement objects reflects whether the option is currently selected. Setting this property to true on an HTMLSelectElement that cannot accept multiple selections forces any other options in the select box to be unselected.

text
JavaScript 1.0 (readonly), JavaScript 1.1+, JScript 1.0+

Nav2.0 (readonly), Nav3.0+, IE3+

Syntax

```
[var x =] HTMLOptionElement.text [= newText]
```

The text property of HTMLOptionElement objects is equivalent to the text inside the this element's tags.

value
JavaScript 1.0+, JScript 5.0+

Nav2.0+, IE5+

Syntax

```
[var x =] HTMLOptionElement.value [= newText]
```

The value property of HTMLOptionElement objects reflects the this element's value attribute—what its ancestor <select>...</select> element will submit to the server onsubmit.

Methods

The HTMLOptionElement interface provides no methods beyond those the HTMLElement interface defines.

Event Handlers
Microsoft Internet Explorer supports the following event handlers for HTMLOptionElement objects:

```
onlayoutcomplete

onlosecapture

onpropertychange
```

onreadystatechange

onselectstart

ontimeerror

HTMLSelectElement/<select>...</select>

Browser / JavaScript Version	Created By
Nav4/JavaScript 1.2	<select>...</select>
IE4/JScript 3.0	<select>...</select>
IE5/JScript 5.0	<select>...</select>
IE5.5/JScript 5.5	<select>...</select>
Nav6/JavaScript 1.5	<select>...</select>
IE6	<select>...</select>
DOM Level 1	document.createElement("select")

> **Note**
> Implemented in Nav1+ (HTML), Nav2+ (JS), IE3+
>
> Descends from HTMLElement interface (Chapter 21, "HTMLElement")
>
> Required ancestor element: HTMLFormElement (Netscape 2–4)

Description

The <select>...</select> element presents either a combo box, also known as a drop-down menu, or a multiple selections box. The distinction occurs when the multiple="multiple" attribute is part of the starting tag.

Listing 25.9 demonstrates select boxes. Note the interesting effect of the option group tag in the right box in Netscape 6 and Internet Explorer 6. The word "lightcols" is bolded and italicized, but you cannot select it. This is how Netscape 6 and Internet Explorer 6 identify their groupings to the user. The options in the group itself are indented. It's also immediately obvious, by the end of the indenting, where the group ends. Figure 25.2 accompanies Listing 25.10, the rendering of two types of select boxes.

Listing 25.9   *Select-one and Select-multiple*

```
<?xml version="1.0" ?>
<!DOCTYPE html PUBLIC "-//W3C//DTD XHTML 1.0 Transitional//EN"
➥"DTD/xhtml1-transitional.dtd">
<html xmlns="http://www.w3.org/1999/xhtml" >
<head><title></title></head>
<body>
<form action="javascript:void(0)">

<select name="myselect" id="myselect">
<option>M18</option>
<optgroup label="pre-1.0">
<option>0.9.2</option>
<option>0.9.3</option>
<option>0.9.4</option>
<option>0.9.5</option>
</optgroup>
<option>1.0</option>
</select>

<select multiple="multiple" name="multiselect" id="multiselect">
<option>white</option>
<optgroup label="lightcols">
<option>red</option>
<option>green</option>
<option>blue</option>
</optgroup>
<option>black</option>
</select>

</form>
</body>
</html>
```

Getting the selected value(s) of the combo box is a bit complex—unlike other form controls you cannot, before Netscape 6, simply say *HTMLSelectElement*.value for Netscape browsers. If the user has selected only one option, you can get its value from the following line:

```
var x = HTMLSelectElement.options[HTMLSelectElement.selectedIndex].value
```

Figure 25.2
Select boxes in a screenshot.

This is because the *HTMLSelectElement* object's options property in the DOM is an array of *HTMLOptionElement* objects. If you have multiple selected options, you must iterate through each one to retrieve the values:

```
var response= new Array();
for (var x = 0; x < HTMLSelectElement.length; x++) {
    if (HTMLSelectElement.options[x].selected == true) {
        response[response.length] = HTMLSelectElement[x].value
        }
    }
```

(In most cases, you can omit the options property and refer to individual options as properties of the select box. However, this is not necessarily in compliance with the W3C DOM.)

Properties

disabled
JavaScript 1.5

Nav6

Syntax

```
var boolValue = HTMLSelectElement.disabled
```

The disabled property of HTMLSelectElement objects prevents the user selecting any options.

> **Note**
> Internet Explorer 5 implements this property for all elements, as I note in Chapter 21, "HTMLElement."

form

JavaScript 1.0+, JScript 1.0+

Nav2+, IE3+

Read-only

Syntax

```
var x = HTMLSelectElement.form
```

The `form` property of `HTMLSelectElement` objects refers directly to the `HTMLFormElement` which contains the `this` object.

length

JavaScript 1.0–JavaScript 1.3, JavaScript 1.5, JScript 1.0+

Nav2-Nav4, Nav6 IE3+

Syntax

```
var x = HTMLSelectElement.length
```

The `length` property of `HTMLSelectElement` objects refers directly to the length of its options collection.

multiple

JavaScript 1.5, JScript 5.0+

Nav6, IE5+

Syntax

```
[var boolValue =] HTMLSelectElement.multiple [= boolValue2]
```

The `multiple` property of `HTMLSelectElement` objects, when set to `true`, designates a multiple-select box. Otherwise, the `this` object is an ordinary select box, or combo box.

For Netscape browsers prior to Netscape 6, use the `type` property to distinguish a single select box from a multiple select box.

name

JavaScript 1.0+, JScript 1.0+

Nav2+, IE3+

Syntax

```
[var x =] HTMLSelectElement.name [= nameString]
```

The `name` property of `HTMLSelectElement` objects provides a name for the select element by which the ancestor `HTMLFormElement` may have the select element as a property.

options

JavaScript 1.0+, JScript 1.0+

Nav2+, IE3+

Syntax

```
var x = HTMLSelectElement.options
```

The `options` property of `HTMLSelectElement` objects is acollection of the `HTMLOptionElement` elements that are descendants of the `this` object. You use the `options` property to reach the individual options.

options.add()

JavaScript 1.5

Nav6

See the `add()` method for `HTMLSelectElement` later in this chapter.

options.item()

JScript 3.0+

IE4+

Syntax

```
var x = HTMLSelectElement.options.item(index)
```

The `item()` method of *HTMLSelectElement*`.options` returns an `HTMLOptionElement` object, corresponding to the option's placement in the `options` array.

options.length

JavaScript 1.5, JScript 3.0+

Nav6, IE4+

Syntax

```
var x = HTMLSelectElement.options.length
```

The `length` property of *HTMLSelectElement*`.options` tells how many objects are in the collection.

options.remove()

JavaScript 1.5

Nav6

See the `remove()` method for `HTMLSelectElement` later in this chapter.

options.tags()

JScript 3.0+

IE4+

Syntax

```
var x = HTMLSelectElement.options.tags(tagName)
```

The `tags()` method of *HTMLSelectElement*`.options` returns a subset of the `this` element comprising all elements whose `tagName` property matches the first argument.

options.urns()

JScript 5.0+

IE5+

Syntax

```
var x = HTMLSelectElement.options.urns(behaviorName)
```

The urns() method of *HTMLSelectElement*.options returns a subset of the this element comprising all elements possessing a DHTML behavior whose name matches the first argument.

DHTML behaviors, an Internet Explorer proprietary extension to HTML, go far beyond the scope of this book. You can find information on them via Microsoft's Web site at http://msdn.microsoft.com/workshop/author/behaviors/overview.asp.

selectedIndex

JavaScript 1.0+, JScript 1.0+

Nav2+, IE3+

Syntax

[var *x* =] *HTMLSelectElement*.selectedIndex [= *newSelectedIndex*]

The selectedIndex property of HTMLSelectElement objects is the index number of the first selected option in the this.options array.

Whenever no option is selected, this value is -1.

Do not use this property on a select box with multiple selects available. Instead, loop through the elements of the options array.

type

JavaScript 1.1+, JScript 3.0+

Nav3+, IE4+

Read-only

Syntax

var *x* = *HTMLSelectElement*.type

The type property of HTMLSelectElement objects reflects the type attribute of the this element. If the multiple property is set to true, Netscape and Internet Explorer return "select-multiple"; else, Netscape and Internet Explorer returns "select-one".

Methods

add()

JavaScript 1.5

Nav6

Syntax

HTMLSelectElement.add(HTMLOptionElement, HTMLOptionElement)

The add() method of HTMLSelectElement objects inserts the first argument, a new
<option /> element the developer creates, into the this object's options.

Internet Explorer has this method as well, but it does not work properly according to
the Document Object Model. The documentation Microsoft provides on the add()
method contradicts the W3C DOM definition. Worse, when I wrote Listing 25.10 to
test it, I discovered both scenarios would cause exception in Internet Explorer 6.
Listing 25.10, for Netscape 6 only, demonstrates correct usage of the add() and
remove() methods.

Listing 25.10   *Adding and Removing Options from a Select Box*

```
<?xml version="1.0" ?>
<!DOCTYPE html PUBLIC "-//W3C//DTD XHTML 1.0 Transitional//EN"
➥"DTD/xhtml1-transitional.dtd">
<html xmlns="http://www.w3.org/1999/xhtml" >
<head><title></title>
<script language="JavaScript" type="text/javascript">
<!--
function changeOptions() {
    var multiselect = document.forms[0].multiselect

    var yellow = document.createElement("option")
    var yellowText = document.createTextNode("yellow")
    yellow.appendChild(yellowText)

    var green = document.getElementById("green")
    multiselect.add(yellow, green)

    setTimeout("removeOptions()",1000)
    }
```

Listing 25.10   *(continued)*

```
function removeOptions() {
    var multiselect = document.forms[0].multiselect
    var blue = document.getElementById("blue")
    multiselect.remove(blue.index)
    }
//-->
</script>
</head>
<body onload="changeOptions()">
<form action="javascript:void(0)">
<select multiple="multiple" name="multiselect" id="multiselect">
<option>white</option>
<option>red</option>
<option id="green">green</option>
<option id="blue">blue</option>
<option>black</option>
</select>
</form>
<!-- The select box, onload, will have the following options:
white
red
yellow
green
black
-->
</body>
</html>
```

blur()

JavaScript 1.0, JScript 1.0+

Nav2+, IE3.0+

Syntax

HTMLSelectElement.blur()

The blur() method of HTMLSelectElement objects forces the form control to lose focus. This means it tells the browser "I'm not important; let something else take center stage." The browser reacts by assigning focus specifically to no object.

focus()

JavaScript 1.0, JScript 1.0+

Nav2+, IE3.0+

Syntax

`HTMLSelectElement.focus()`

The `focus()` method of `HTMLSelectElement` objects forces the form control to gain focus. This means it tells the browser "I'm important; make sure I alone react to the keyboard." The browser reacts by assigning focus specifically to that object.

handleEvent()

JavaScript 1.2+

Nav4+

Syntax

`HTMLSelectElement.handleEvent(eventObj)`

The `handleEvent()` method of `HTMLSelectElement` objects for Netscape takes an event object as an argument and an appropriate element handle the event. See Chapter 32, "DOM-2 Events and Event Handlers," for details.

remove()

JavaScript 1.5, JScript 3.0+

Nav6, IE4+

Syntax

`HTMLSelectElement.remove(nonNegInteger)`

The `remove()` method of `HTMLSelectElement` objects removes one option from the `this` object's `options` array and the corresponding Web page. The first argument is a number indicating the zero-based index number of the option in the `this.options` array. Listing 25.9 demonstrates one way for an `HTMLOptionElement` object to have itself removed from its parent select box.

Event Handlers

Netscape supports the following event handlers for the HTMLSelectElement interface:

onblur

onchange

onfocus

Internet Explorer supports the following event handlers for the HTMLSelectElement interface:

onactivate	ondragenter	onmousemove
onafterupdate	ondragleave	onmouseout
onbeforeactivate	ondragover	onmouseover
onbeforecut	ondrop	onmouseup
onbeforedeactivate	onerrorupdate	onmousewheel
onbeforeeditfocus	onfocus	onmove
onbeforepaste	onfocusin	onmoveend
onbeforeupdate	onfocusout	onmovestart
onblur	onhelp	onpaste
onchange	onkeydown	onpropertychange
onclick	onkeypress	onreadystatechange
oncontextmenu	onkeyup	onresize
oncontrolselect	onlosecapture	onresizeend
oncut	onmousedown	onresizestart
ondblclick	onmouseenter	onselectstart
ondeactivate	onmouseleave	

HTMLTextAreaElement/<textarea>...</textarea>

Browser / JavaScript Version	Created By
Nav4/JavaScript1.2	`<textarea>...</textarea>`
IE4/JScript3.0	`<textarea>...</textarea>`
IE5/JScript5.0	`<textarea>...</textarea>`
IE5.5/JScript5.5	`<textarea>...</textarea>`
Nav6/JavaScript1.5	`<textarea>...</textarea>`
IE6	`<textarea>...</textarea>`
DOM Level 1	`document.createElement("textarea")`

> **Note**
> Implemented in Nav1+ (HTML), Nav2+ (JS), IE3+
>
> Descends from `HTMLElement` interface (Chapter 21, "HTMLElement")
>
> Required ancestor element: `HTMLFormElement`

Description

The text area element is a multiline, multicolumn plain text typing area. You see it quite often in forums, e-mail forms—basically anywhere in which you have a large amount of text to type. I use them at JSLab myself to provide an editing interface for HTML code (and often to transport such code from the server to the client and vice versa).

I've mentioned how I use text areas to transport code in JSLab more than once in this book; I won't repeat it again here. However, there is one useful feature proprietary to both Netscape and Internet Explorer that the W3C has excluded from its HTML 4 Recommendation.

The `wrap` attribute allows a Web page to define what sort of text wrapping should take place within the text area. Without this, to prevent word-wrapping, I would have to use PHP code (or the DOM, if the browser supports it) to create a wide enough text area in the page. JavaScripters, especially those using the DOM, realize 80 characters to a line is a maximum that is not always practical to maintain.

One other thing I truly dislike about text areas is they don't provide direct JavaScript control of the cursor position. There is work ongoing at Mozilla as part of implementing DOM-2 Range, dependent on Bugzilla bug # 58850 (`http://bugzilla.mozilla.org/show_bug.cgi?id=58850`). When this bug is fixed, Mozilla will indirectly provide control of the cursor position within a text area.

Properties

accessKey

JavaScript 1.5

Nav6

Syntax

```
[var x = ] HTMLTextAreaElement.accessKey [ = "c"]
```

The `accessKey` property of `HTMLTextAreaElement` objects designates a shortcut key to focus. The element gains focus when the user presses the designated key and the Alt key (on the Windows platform) while the window for the `this` object has focus. The `nodeValue` for this attribute must be one character in length.

> **Note**
> Internet Explorer 5 implements this property for all elements, as I note in Chapter 21, "HTMLElement."

cols

JavaScript 1.5

Nav6

Syntax

```
[var x =] HTMLTextAreaElement.cols [= colsNum]
```

The `cols` property of `HTMLTextAreaElement` objects reflects the number of columns in the text area, originally set by the `cols` attribute.

defaultValue

JavaScript 1.0+, JScript 5.0+

Nav2.0+, IE5+

Syntax

```
[var x =] HTMLTextAreaElement.defaultValue [= defString]
```

The defaultValue property of HTMLTextAreaElement objects reflects the default setting of the this object. In the case of text areas, it is effectively the raw code between the <textarea> and </textarea> tags.

disabled

JavaScript 1.5

Nav6

Syntax

```
var boolValue = HTMLTextAreaElement.disabled
```

The disabled property of HTMLTextAreaElement objects prevents the user from modifying the value of the object directly or from submitting the value entered in the text area.

> **Note**
> Internet Explorer 5 implements this property for all elements, as I note in Chapter 21, "HTMLElement."

form

JavaScript 1.0+, JScript 1.0+

Nav2+, IE3+

Read-only

Syntax

```
var x = HTMLTextAreaElement.form
```

The form property of HTMLTextAreaElement objects refers directly to the HTMLFormElement that contains the this object.

innerText

JScript 3.0+

IE4+

Syntax

```
var x = HTMLTextAreaElement.innerText
```

The innerText property of HTMLTextAreaElement retrieves or sets the text contained between, but not including, the starting and ending tags.

The innerText property can be useful, but the DOM Level 2 Range interface provides far more flexibility. See Chapter 34, "DOM-2 Range," for details on text ranges.

IsMultiLine

JScript 5.5+

IE5.5+

Syntax

```
var boolValue = HTMLTextAreaElement.isMultiLine
```

The rows attribute may directly affect the setting of the isMultiLine property. However, in the absence of that the isMultiLine property of HTMLTextAreaElement will return true if there are two or more lines of text in the text area, or false if there are one or zero lines of text in the text area. (Given text areas are designed to hold multiple lines of text, you can pretty much count on this property being true.)

name

JavaScript 1.0+

Nav2+, IE3.0+

Syntax

```
[var x =] HTMLTextAreaElement.name [= nameString]
```

The name property of `HTMLTextAreaElement` objects provides a name for the text area by which the ancestor `HTMLFormElement` may have the text area as a property.

outerHTML

JScript 3.0+

IE4+

Syntax

```
var x = HTMLTextAreaElement.outerHTML
```

The `outerHTML` property of `HTMLTextAreaElement` retrieves or sets the HTML source code contained between, and including, the starting and ending tags.

I do like the handiness of the `outerHTML` property for retrieving HTML source code at a glance, as a companion method to the W3C Document Object Model. (The DOM provides an object structure for the source code; `outerHTML` provides the corresponding source code.)

readOnly

JavaScript 1.5+, JScript 3.0+

Nav6, IE4.0+

Syntax

```
[var x =] HTMLTextAreaElement.readOnly [= boolValue]
```

The `readOnly` property of `HTMLTextAreaElement` objects is a `true` or `false` value reflecting whether the value of the text area is currently read-only. Ironically, the `readOnly` property is itself not read-only. Thus, JavaScript can control whether you can change this property.

rows

JavaScript 1.5, JScript 1.0+

Nav6, IE3+

Syntax

```
[var x =] HTMLTextAreaElement.rows [= rowsNum]
```

The rows property of HTMLTextAreaElement objects reflects the number of rows in the text area, originally set by the rows attribute.

---

status

JScript 3.0+

IE4+

Syntax

`[var boolValue =] HTMLTextAreaElement.status [= selectOn]`

The status property of HTMLTextAreaElement objects indicates whether the this object is selected. A value of true indicates it is; a value of false indicates it is not. Microsoft also supports a value of null, indicating the element is not quite ready (see readyState of Chapter 21, "HTMLElement").

---

tabIndex

JavaScript 1.5, JScript 3.0+

Nav6, IE4+

Syntax

`[ver x =] HTMLTextAreaElement.tabIndex [= numValue]`

The tabIndex property of HTMLTextAreaElement objects sets where the this element rests in the tab order. The tab order is an index indicating when an element in the document receives focus as the user strikes his Tab key. When setting this value, remember it can only accept numeric integers.

A negative tabIndex, in Internet Explorer, takes the this element out of the tab order. Other than that, Tab key presses go to elements in this order:

- The lowest positive integer, followed by the next lowest, and so on.

- After that, the source order of elements in the document.

HTMLTextAreaElement is a natural stopping point for Tab key presses.

type

JavaScript 1.1+, JScript 1.0+

Nav3+, IE3.0+

Read-only

Syntax

`var x = HTMLTextAreaElement.type`

The `type` property of `HTMLTextAreaElement` objects reflects the `type` attribute of the `this` element. Netscape and Internet Explorer return a value of `"textarea"` for this property.

value

JavaScript 1.0+, JScript 1.0+

Nav2+, IE3.0+

Syntax

`[var x =] HTMLTextAreaElement.value [= newString]`

The `value` property of `HTMLTextAreaElement` objects reflects the `value` attribute of the `this` element. This is the current contents of the text area.

wrap

JScript 3.0+

IE4+

Deprecated in HTML 4

Syntax

`[var x =] HTMLTextAreaElement.wrap [= wrapString]`

The `wrap` property of `HTMLTextAreaElement` objects reflects the word wrap setting of the `this` object. Typically, it defaults to "soft," meaning words wrap naturally, and line breaks only occur when entered with an Enter key. A "hard" wrap is identical, as far as JavaScript is concerned. (The setting affects how the carriage returns and spaces will be submitted to the server.)

The "off" setting disables word wrapping entirely.

HTML 4 and XHTML 1 do not permit the wrap attribute, and HTML 4 prohibits a script from invalidating a document. This means if you wish to maintain word wrap control, you must (for now) not use the wrap property either in an XHTML document.

Methods

blur()

JavaScript 1.0+, JScript 1.0+

Nav2+, IE3.0+

Syntax

HTMLTextAreaElement.blur()

The blur() method of HTMLTextAreaElement objects forces the form control to "lose focus." What this means is it tells the browser "I'm not important; let something else take center stage." The browser reacts by assigning focus specifically to no object.

focus()

JavaScript 1.0+, JScript 1.0+

Nav2+, IE3.0+

Syntax

HTMLTextAreaElement.focus()

The focus() method of HTMLTextAreaElement objects forces the form control to "gain focus." What this means is it tells the browser "I'm important; make sure I alone react to the keyboard." The browser reacts by assigning focus specifically to that object.

handleEvent()

JavaScript 1.2+

Nav4+

Syntax

HTMLSelectElement.handleEvent(*eventObj*)

The handleEvent() method of HTMLSelectElement objects for Netscape has an event object as its argument. See Chapter 32, "DOM-2 Events and Event Handlers," for details.

select()

JavaScript 1.0+, JScript 3.0+

Nav2+, IE4.0+

Syntax

HTMLTextAreaElement.select()

The select() method of HTMLTextAreaElement objects forces the browser to select the entire contents of the text area.

Event Handlers

Netscape supports the following event handlers for the HTMLTextAreaElement interface:

onblur

onchange

onfocus

onkeyDown

onkeyPress

onkeyUp

onselect

Internet Explorer supports the following event handlers for the `HTMLTextAreaElement` interface:

onactivate	ondragenter	onmouseout
onafterupdate	ondragleave	onmouseover
onbeforeactivate	ondragover	onmouseup
onbeforecopy	ondragstart	onmousewheel
onbeforecut	ondrop	onmove
onbeforedeactivate	onerrorupdate	onmoveend
onbeforeeditfocus	onfilterchange	onmovestart
onbeforepaste	onfocus	onpaste
onbeforeupdate	onfocusin	onpropertychange
onblur	onfocusout	onreadystatechange
onchange	onhelp	onresize
onclick	onkeydown	onresizeend
oncontextmenu	onkeypress	onresizestart
oncontrolselect	onkeyup	onscroll
oncut	onlosecapture	onselect
ondblclick	onmousedown	onselectstart
ondeactivate	onmouseenter	ontimeerror
ondrag	onmouseleave	
ondragend	onmousemove	

CHAPTER 26

Form Input Elements: HTMLInputElement

Browser/JavaScript Version	Created By
Nav4/JavaScript 1.2	`<input />`
IE4/JScript 3.0	`<input />`
IE5/JScript 5.0	`<input />`
IE5.5/JScript 5.5	`<input />`
Nav6/JavaScript 1.5	`<input />`
IE6	`<input />`
DOM Level 1	`document.createElement("input")`

> **Note**
> Implemented in Nav1+ (HTML), IE1+ (HTML), Nav2+ (DOM), IE3+ (DOM)
>
> Descends from `HTMLElement` interface (Chapter 21, "HTMLElement")
>
> Required ancestor element (in Nav4): `HTMLFormElement` (Chapter 25, "Form Elements")

Description

The `<input />` element is easily the most important form control in XHTML, in that there are several different types of inputs. Because there are several properties covered in this element that are specific to certain types, each property or method will also mention the specific types that support it.

Chapter 25, "Form Elements," covers the rules of submitting form control values to the server. A quick refresher: Use both the `name` and `id` attributes, except for radio buttons where the ID value for each must differ from all others.

The Various Types of Inputs

There are several different kinds of inputs for a form. Each kind is differentiated from the others by the input's `type` attribute. The default, if you do not include it, is the `type="text"` input. This is a one-line text box. Other kinds of form inputs include the following:

- The `type="password"` input is identical to the `text` type, except to the user each character typed in it appears as asterisks. Most developers know it provides no real security, except in the sense of a user stepping away from his keyboard. (JavaScript has access to the value contained in the password, for instance.)

- The type="hidden" input is a string value the page never exposes directly to the user. JavaScript has access to this value as well (which can be exceptionally useful for "preprocessed" form values). You normally see this type as a way for the server to "remember" certain values.

- The type="radio" input, based on sharing a common name attribute (but *not* a common id attribute), allows for choosing from a group a preferred value. The radio input only allows one selected value from all radio buttons sharing the same name attribute. Note each such element will appear in the form's elements collection.

- The type="checkbox" input is a check box (simple enough).

- The type="button" input is a button. Usually these do not need a name or id attribute. (The button exists on the page, and provides no useful information to the server. Other form inputs do.) You use it primarily for executing a JavaScript command.

- The type="reset" and type="submit" inputs are buttons as well, but with a more useful native purpose; they reset and submit the forms, respectively.

- The type="image" input also submits the form, but uses an image the document refers to as its Submit button. I cover this type in Chapter 30, "Image Elements."

- The type="file" input references a file by name in a text field. It references the file the browser will submit to the server. (Once again, if you use this input, use the HTTP POST method, as I describe in Chapter 25, "Form Elements.")

Listing 26.1 demonstrates the various types of form inputs; Figure 26.1 shows a screenshot of them.

Listing 26.1   *The Ten Inputs*

```
<?xml version="1.0" ?>
<!DOCTYPE html PUBLIC "-//W3C//DTD XHTML 1.0 Transitional//EN"
➥"DTD/xhtml1-transitional.dtd">
<html xmlns="http://www.w3.org/1999/xhtml" >
<head><title></title></head>
<body>
<form action="whatever.cgi" method="post" enctype="multipart/form-data">
<p>
Text Input: <input type="text" name="author" value="Alex Vincent" /><br />
Password Input: <input type="password" name="pword" value="password" /><br />
Hidden Input:  <input type="hidden" name="workgroup" value="mozthelawns" />
```

Listing 26.1   *(continued)*

```
<br />
</p>
<hr />
<p>
Radio Button:
<input type="radio" name="towhom" value="0" checked="checked" />All Hands
<input type="radio" name="towhom" value="1" />Moderators only
<input type="radio" name="towhom" value="2" />Project owner
</p>
<hr />
<p>
Radio Button:  <input type="radio" name="codetype" value="0" />Live code
<input type="radio" name="codetype" value="1" />Test case
</p>
<hr />
<p>
Checkbox Input:  <input type="checkbox" name="validate" />Validate??<br />
Button:  <input type="button"
    value="Click me to learn how many form controls I have!"
    onclick="alert('The form has ' + this.form.length + ' elements.')" />

File:  <input type="file" name="filename" /><br />

<input type="reset" /><input type="submit" />
<input name="myImage" type="image" src="25lst04b.gif" alt="Submit the form!" />
</p>
</form>
</body>
</html>
```

Syntax specific to type=image is described in Chapter 30, "Image Elements."

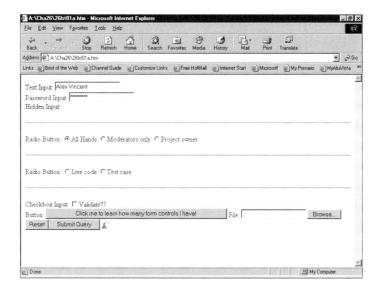

Figure 26.1
Screenshot of the ten inputs.

Properties

accept

JavaScript 1.5

Nav6

Types of inputs supported: file

Syntax

`[var x = ] HTMLInputElement.accept [= mimeTypeList]`

The accept property of HTMLInputElement objects returns a comma-separated list of mime-types the server expects to receive for the file input. The list is a string value; the browser does not attempt to do any validation of the file based on the file type or extension.

accessKey

JavaScript 1.5, JScript 5.0+

Nav6, IE5+

Syntax

```
[var x=] HTMLInputElement.accessKey
```

The accessKey property defines a single keyboard character that gives access to an input form control.

align

JavaScript 1.5, JScript 5.0+

Nav6, IE5+

Syntax

The align property aligns an HTMLInputElement with its surrounding text, horizontally or vertically.

alt

JavaScript 1.5, JScript 5.0+

Nav6, IE5+

Syntax

```
[var x=] HTMLInputElement.alt
```

The alt property provides alternative text for user agents where an input element is not supported.

checked

JavaScript 1.0+, JScript 1.0+

Nav2+, IE3+

Types of inputs supported: check box, radio

Syntax

```
[var x =] HTMLInputElement.checked [= boolValue]
[var x =] radioButton[y].checked [= boolValue]
```

The `checked` property of `HTMLInputElement` objects reflects, for check boxes, whether the box is currently checked. A `true` value means it is checked; a `false` value means it is not.

For radio buttons, the `checked` property is actually a property of individual radio options, each of which is a numbered property of the radio button. Setting `checked` to `true` for one of these options moves the selection to that option, deselecting any other radio options in that radio button.

defaultChecked

JavaScript 1.0+, JScript 1.0+

Nav2+, IE3+

Types of inputs supported: check box, radio

Syntax

```
[var x =] HTMLInputElement.checked [= boolValue]
[var x =] radioButton[y].checked [= boolValue]
```

The `defaultChecked` property of `HTMLInputElement` objects reflects, for check boxes, whether the input has the `checked="checked"` attribute set. (This attribute defines whether the default setting for the check box is checked.)

For radio buttons, the `defaultChecked` property is actually a property of individual radio options, each of which is a numbered property of the radio button. The only one for which the `defaultChecked` property will have the value of `"true"` will be the radio button with the attribute `checked="checked"`.

defaultValue

JavaScript 1.0+, JScript 1.0+

Nav2+, IE3+

Types of inputs supported: button (IE3+ only), check box (IE3+ only), file (Nav6, IE3+), hidden (IE3+ only), password, radio (IE3+ only), reset (IE3+ only), submit (IE3+ only), text

Syntax

```
[var x =] HTMLInputElement.defaultValue [= defString]
```

The `defaultValue` property of `HTMLInputElement` objects reflects a default value for the text field or form control. Unless you assign a default value, this has a value of `null`. If a user enters a value, the `defaultValue` property does not affect the input.

disabled

JavaScript 1.5, JScript 3.0+

Nav6, IE4+

Types of inputs supported: button, check box, file, password, radio, reset, submit, text, image

Syntax

```
var boolValue = HTMLInputElement.disabled
```

The `disabled` property of `HTMLInputElement` objects allows you to disable a form control when you set its value to `true`. In this setting, no user can adjust the form control's `value` property. Check boxes cannot be checked or unchecked; buttons cannot be clicked. Text input fields are locked when the control is disabled. If an object is disabled, the corresponding value is not submitted.

This property predates the `disabled` property of all HTML elements (see Chapter 21, "HTMLElement," for details) for Internet Explorer.

form

JavaScript 1.0+, JScript 1.0+

Nav2+, IE3.0+

Types of inputs supported: button, check box, file, hidden, password, radio, reset, submit, text

Read-only

Syntax

```
var x = HTMLInputElement.form
```

The `form` property of `HTMLInputElement` objects refers directly to the `HTMLFormElement` that contains the `this` object.

maxLength

JavaScript 1.5, JScript 3.0+

Nav6, IE4+

Types of inputs supported: password, text

Syntax

```
var x = HTMLInputElement.maxLength
```

The `maxLength` property of `HTMLInputElement` objects corresponds to the maximum number of characters the text field may accept.

name

JavaScript 1.0+, JScript 1.0+ (JScript 3.0+ file)

Nav2+, IE3.0+ (IE4+ file)

Types of inputs supported: button, check box, file, hidden, password, radio, reset, submit, text

Syntax

```
[var x =] HTMLInputElement.name [= nameString]
```

The `name` property of `HTMLInputElement` objects provides a name for the button by which the ancestor `HTMLFormElement` may have the button as a property.

outerHTML

JScript 3.0+

IE4+

Types of inputs supported: button, check box, file, hidden, password, radio, reset, submit, text

Syntax

```
var x = HTMLInputElement.outerHTML
```

The `outerHTML` property of `HTMLInputElement` retrieves or sets the HTML source code contained between, and including, the starting and ending tags.

> **Note**
> Because `<input />` does not have children, usually all you'll get is the input tag(s).

I do like the handiness of the `outerHTML` property for retrieving HTML source code at a glance, as a companion method to the W3C Document Object Model. (The DOM provides an object structure for the source code; `outerHTML` provides the corresponding source code.)

readOnly

JavaScript 1.5+, JScript 3.0+

Nav6, IE4.0+

Types of inputs supported: password, text

Syntax

```
[var x =] HTMLInputElement.readOnly [= boolValue]
```

The `readOnly` property of `HTMLInputElement` objects is a `true` or `false` value reflecting whether the value of the text area is currently read-only or not. Ironically, the `readOnly` property is itself not read-only. Thus, JavaScript can change this property.

size

JavaScript 1.5, JScript 1.0+

Nav6, IE3+

Types of inputs supported: button, check box, file, password, radio, reset, submit, text

Syntax

```
[var x =] HTMLInputElement.size [= numChars]
```

The `size` property of `HTMLInputElement` objects reflects the number of characters that the user can expect to be visible in the input at any given time. (For buttons, check boxes, radio, reset, and submit inputs, this is irrelevant, but it's there.)

status

JScript 3.0+

IE4+

Types of inputs supported: check box, radio

Syntax

`[var boolValue =] HTMLInputElement.status [= selectOn]`

The `status` property of `HTMLInputElement` objects indicates whether the `this` object is selected. A value of `true` indicates it is; a value of `false` indicates it is not. Microsoft also supports a value of `null`, indicating the element is not quite ready (see `readyState` of Chapter 21, "HTMLElement").

tabIndex

JavaScript 1.5, JScript 3.0+

Nav6, IE4+

Syntax

`[ver x =] HTMLInputElement.tabIndex [= numValue]`

The `tabIndex` property of `HTMLInputElement` objects sets where the `this` element rests in the tab order. The *tab order* is an index indicating when an element in the document receives focus as the user strikes his Tab key. When setting this value, remember it can only accept numeric integers.

In Internet Explorer, a negative `tabIndex` takes the `this` element out of the tab order. Other than that, Tab key presses go to elements in this order:

- The lowest positive integer, followed by the next lowest, and so on.
- After that, the source order of elements in the document.

`HTMLInputElement` objects are a natural stopping point for Tab key presses.

textLength

JavaScript 1.5

Nav6

Types of inputs supported: password, text

Read-only

Syntax

```
var x = HTMLInputElement.textLength
```

The `textLength` property of `HTMLInputElement` objects reflects the length of the text in its field. This is basically equivalent to `this.value.length`.

type

JavaScript 1.1+, JScript 1.0+

Nav3+, IE3.0+

Types of inputs supported: button, check box, file, hidden, password, radio, reset, submit, text

Read-only

Syntax

```
var x = HTMLInputElement.type
```

The `type` property of `HTMLInputElement` objects reflects the `type` attribute of the `this` element.

There are different values for different types; all are identical to the kind of input this is (for instance, "button" for a button input).

value

JavaScript 1.0+, JScript 1.0+

Nav2+, IE3.0+

Types of inputs supported: button, check box, file, hidden, password, radio, reset, submit, text

Syntax

`[var x =] HTMLInputElement.value [= newString]`

The `value` property of `HTMLInputElement` objects reflects the `value` attribute of the `this` element.

- For button, reset, and submit inputs, this is the text appearing on the button.
- For check box inputs, this has a default value of `"on"` in Netscape 4.x browsers.
- For file inputs, this reflects the URI of the file (not its contents, which nonprivileged client-side JavaScript can read but not set).
- For radio buttons, this reflects the value of the checked radio button.
- For text inputs, this reflects the current contents of the text field.

width

JScript 3.0+

IE4+

Types of inputs supported: button, check box, file, password, radio, reset, submit, text

Syntax

`[var x =] HTMLInputElement.width [= numPixels]`

The `width` property of `HTMLInputElement` objects defines how many pixels of horizontal space the `this` object should occupy on the screen. It must be a non-negative integer.

Methods

blur()

JavaScript 1.0+, JScript 1.0+

Nav2+, IE3.0+

Types of inputs supported: button, check box, password, radio, reset, submit, text

Syntax

HTMLInputElement.blur()

The blur() method of HTMLInputElement objects forces the form control to lose focus. This means it tells the browser "I'm not important; let something else take center stage." The browser reacts by assigning focus specifically to no object.

click()

JavaScript 1.0+, JScript 3.0+

Nav2+, IE4+

Types of inputs supported: button, check box, file (IE4+ only), password (IE4+ only), radio, reset, submit, text (IE4+ only)

Syntax

HTMLInputElement.click()

The click() method of HTMLInputElement objects simulates a click on the object. For button, radio, reset, and submit inputs in Netscape, it does not fire the click event.

focus()

JavaScript 1.0+, JScript 1.0+

Nav2+, IE3.0+

Types of inputs supported: button, check box, file, password, radio, reset, submit, text

Syntax

HTMLInputElement.focus()

The focus() method of HTMLInputElement objects forces the form control to gain focus. This means is it tells the browser "I'm important; make sure I alone react to the keyboard." The browser reacts by assigning focus specifically to that object.

handleEvent()

JavaScript 1.2+

Nav4.00–Nav4.78

Types of inputs supported: button, check box, file, password, radio, reset, submit, text

Syntax

HTMLInputElement.handleEvent(*eventObj*)

The handleEvent() method of HTMLInputElement objects for Netscape has an event object as its argument. See Chapter 32, "DOM-2 Events and Event Handlers," for details.

select()

JavaScript 1.0+, JScript 3.0+

Nav2+, IE4+

Types of inputs supported: button (IE4+ only), file, password, reset (IE4+ only), submit (IE4+ only), text

Syntax

document.*formName.namedInput*.select()

The select() method of HTMLInputElement objects simply selects the contents of the text field.

Event Handlers

Netscape supports the following event handlers for the HTMLInputElement interface:

onblur (button, check box, file, password, radio, reset, submit, text)

onchange (file, text, password)

onclick (button, check box, radio, reset, submit)

onfocus (button, check box, file, password, radio, reset, submit, text)

onmousedown (button)

onmouseup (button)

onselect (text)

Internet Explorer supports the following event handlers for the HTMLInputElement interface:

onactivate (button, check box, file, hidden, password, radio, reset, submit, text)

onafterupdate (check box, hidden, password, radio, text)

onbeforeactivate (button, check box, file, password, radio, reset, submit, text)

onbeforecut (button, check box, file, password, radio, reset, submit, text)

onbeforedeactivate (button, check box, file, hidden, password, radio, reset, submit, text)

onbeforeeditfocus (button, check box, file, hidden, password, radio, reset, submit, text)

onbeforepaste (button, check box, file, password, radio, reset, submit, text)

onbeforeupdate (check box, file, hidden, password, radio, text)

onblur (button, check box, file, password, radio, reset, submit, text)

onchange (text)

onclick (button, check box, file, password, radio, reset, submit, text)

oncontextmenu (button, check box, file, password, radio, reset, submit, text)

oncontrolselect (button, check box, file, hidden, password, radio, reset, submit, text)

oncut (button, check box, file, password, radio, reset, submit, text)

ondblclick (button, check box, file, password, radio, reset, submit, text)

ondeactivate (button, check box, file, hidden, password, radio, reset, submit, text)

ondrag (button, check box, file, password, radio, reset, submit, text)

ondragend (button, check box, file, password, radio, reset, submit, text)

ondragenter (button, check box, file, password, radio, reset, submit, text)

ondragleave (button, check box, file, password, radio, reset, submit, text)

ondragover (button, check box, file, password, radio, reset, submit, text)

ondragstart (button, check box, file, password, radio, reset, submit, text)

ondrop (button, check box, file, password, radio, reset, submit, text)

onerrorupdate (check box, file, hidden, password, radio, text)

onfilterchange (button, check box, file, password, radio, reset, submit, text)

onfocus (button, check box, file, hidden, password, radio, reset, submit, text)

onfocusin (button, check box, file, password, radio, reset, submit, text) onfocusout (button, check box, file, password, radio, reset, submit, text)

onhelp (button, check box, file, password, radio, reset, submit, text)

onkeydown (button, check box, file, password, radio, reset, submit, text)

onkeypress (button, check box, file, password, radio, reset, submit, text)

onkeyup (button, check box, file, password, radio, reset, submit, text)

onlosecapture (button, check box, file, hidden, password, radio, reset, submit, text)

onmousedown (button, check box, file, password, radio, reset, submit, text)

onmouseenter (button, check box, file, password, radio, reset, submit, text)

onmouseleave (button, check box, file, password, radio, reset, submit, text)

onmousemove (button, check box, file, password, radio, reset, submit, text)

onmouseout (button, check box, file, password, radio, reset, submit, text)

onmouseover (button, check box, file, password, radio, reset, submit, text)

onmouseup (button, check box, file, password, radio, reset, submit, text)

onmousewheel (button, check box, file, password, radio, reset, submit, text)

onmove (button, check box, file, hidden, password, radio, reset, submit, text)

onmoveend (button, check box, file, hidden, password, radio, reset, submit, text)

onmovestart (button, check box, file, hidden, password, radio, reset, submit, text)

onpaste (button, check box, file, password, radio, reset, submit, text)

onpropertychange (button, check box, file, hidden, password, radio, reset, submit, text)

onreadystatechange (button, check box, file, hidden, password, radio, reset, submit, text)

onresize (button, file, password, reset, submit, text)

onresizeend (button, check box, file, password, radio, reset, submit, text)

onresizestart (button, check box, file, password, radio, reset, submit, text)

onselect (text)

onselectstart (button, check box, file, password, radio, reset, submit, text)

ontimeerror (button, check box, file, hidden, password, radio, reset, submit, text)

CHAPTER 27

List Elements

Lists have been with us since at least the days of pen and paper (which thankfully haven't gone away entirely), and are present in HTML and JavaScript as well. Literally every array in JavaScript is an ordered collection of values—which matches the definition of a list pretty well. (Arrays can have properties outside the ordered collection, but this is beside the point.)

HTML and XHTML take an interesting approach to lists (and later, tables, in Chapter 29, "Table Elements"). They have a wrapper list element (<ul>...</ul>, <ol>...</ol>), which contains exclusively a special list item element (<li>...</li>). Thus, they present a one-dimensional data structure in a hierarchy, as opposed to tables, which are two-dimensional.

Also, an old and very popular practice of HTML is no longer valid according to HTML 4. (So popular I used it to write the original table of contents of this book. As I've stated in the Introduction, I've learned a lot in writing this book...) A deprecated example of HTML 4 places an <ol>...</ol> element as a direct child of an <ul>...</ul> element. The intent is to create a "multi-level" list, like an outline. Listing 27.1 shows the correct way to build such a list—by placing the inner list inside an <li>...</li> of the outer list.

Listing 27.1   *Nested Lists in XHTML*

```
<?xml version="1.0" ?>
<!DOCTYPE html PUBLIC "-//W3C//DTD XHTML 1.0 Transitional//EN"
➥"DTD/xhtml1-transitional.dtd">
<html xmlns="http://www.w3.org/1999/xhtml" >
<head><title></title></head>
<body>
<ol>
<li>Object()
    <ol>
    <li>Description</li>
    <li>Properties</li>
    <li>Methods</li>
    <li>Example</li>
    </ol>
</li>
<li>Array()
    <ol>
    <li>Description</li>
    <li>Properties</li>
    <li>Methods</li>
    <li>Example</li>
    </ol>
</li>
</ol>
</body>
</html>
```

(Normally, I don't indent HTML. I do it here for readability, to emphasize where a nested list ends and begins. Myself being an expert in JavaScript, I almost never think about indenting HTML, for fear it would confuse me to have different indentations for HTML and for scripts.)

The hierarchical structuring of the lists lends itself well to the Document Object Model. The first child element of an ordered list will be the first listed item in that ordered list.

One other item of note: HTML does not directly support continuing a numbering from one nested list to another. For instance, there is no way to tie the second inner list of Listing 27.1 to the first. We can manually set a continuation using the `value` attribute or the deprecated `start` attribute.

HTMLDirectoryElement Interface

Browser/JavaScript Version	Created By
Nav4/JavaScript 1.2	Not implemented in JavaScript
IE4/JScript 3.0	`<dir>...</dir>`
IE5/JScript 5.0	`<dir>...</dir>`
IE5.5/JScript 5.5	`<dir>...</dir>`
Nav6/JavaScript 1.5	`<dir>...</dir>`
IE6	`<dir>...</dir>`
DOM Level 1	`document.createElement("dir")`

> **Note**
> Implemented in Nav1+ (HTML), IE3+ (HTML), Nav6 (DOM), IE4+ (DOM)
> Descends from `HTMLElement` interface (Chapter 21)
> Parent elements: `HTMLBodyElement` (Chapter 22), any block text element
> Deprecated in HTML 4

HTML originally designated the `<dir>...</dir>` element to give a directory listing. The `<ul>...</ul>` element has replaced it in terms of functionality, and you should avoid use of this element.

Properties

compact

JavaScript 1.5

Nav6, IE6

Syntax

`[var x =] HTMLDirectoryElement.compact [= boolValue]`

The `compact` property of `HTMLDirectoryElement` objects reflects whether the browser should render the directory element's contents in a smaller space than normal.

innerHTML

JavaScript 1.5, JScript 3.0+

Nav6, IE4+

Syntax

```
[var x =] HTMLDirectoryElement.innerHTML [= HTMLString]
```

The innerHTML property of HTMLDirectoryElement interfaces retrieves or sets the HTML source code contained between, but not including, the starting and ending tags.

I personally recommend against using innerHTML to set the HTML inside a tag. I strongly recommend against using innerHTML to append to the contents of an HTML tag:

```
elem.innerHTML += "<div><p>Hello World</p></div>" // DO NOT DO THIS
```

I do like the handiness of the innerHTML property for retrieving HTML source code at a glance, as an alternative method to the W3C Document Object Model. (The DOM provides an object structure for the source code; innerHTML provides the corresponding source code.)

innerText

JScript 3.0+

IE4+

Syntax

```
var x = HTMLDirectoryElement.innerText
```

The innerText property of HTMLDirectoryElement retrieves or sets the text contained between, but not including, the starting and ending tags.

The innerText property can be useful, but the DOM Level 2 Range interface provides far more flexibility. See Chapter 34, "DOM-2 Range," for details on text ranges.

outerHTML

JScript 3.0+

IE4+

Syntax

```
var x = HTMLDirectoryElement.outerHTML
```

The `outerHTML` property of `HTMLDirectoryElement` retrieves or sets the HTML source code contained between, and including, the starting and ending tags.

I do like the handiness of the `outerHTML` property for retrieving HTML source code at a glance, as an alternative method to the W3C Document Object Model. (The DOM provides an object structure for the source code; `outerHTML` provides the corresponding source code.)

Methods

The `HTMLDirectoryElement` interface provides no methods beyond those the `HTMLElement` interface defines.

Event Handlers

Internet Explorer supports the following event handlers for the `HTMLDirectoryElement` interface:

onactivate	oncontrolselect	ondragstart
onbeforeactivate	oncopy	ondrop
onbeforecopy	oncut	onfocus
onbeforecut	ondblclick	onfocusin
onbeforedeactivate	ondeactivate	onfocusout
onbeforeeditfocus	ondrag	onhelp
onbeforepaste	ondragend	onkeydown
onblur	ondragenter	onkeypress
onclick	ondragleave	onkeyup
oncontextmenu	ondragover	onlosecapture

onmousedown	onmousewheel	onresize
onmouseenter	onmove	onresizeend
onmouseleave	onmoveend	onresizestart
onmousemove	onmovestart	onselectstart
onmouseout	onpaste	ontimeerror
onmouseover	onpropertychange	
onmouseup	onreadystatechange	

HTMLDListElement Interface

Browser/JavaScript Version	Created By
Nav4/JavaScript 1.2	Not implemented
IE4/JScript 3.0	`<dl>...</dl>`
IE5/JScript 5.0	`<dl>...</dl>`
IE5.5/JScript 5.5	`<dl>...</dl>`
Nav6/JavaScript 1.5	`<dl>...</dl>`
IE6	`<dl>...</dl>`
DOM Level 1	`document.createElement("dl")`

> **Note**
> Implemented in Nav1+ (HTML), IE3+ (HTML), Nav6 (DOM), IE4+ (DOM)
> Descends from `HTMLElement` interface (Chapter 21)
> Parent elements: `HTMLBodyElement` (Chapter 22), any block text element
> Deprecated in HTML 4

The definition list element in HTML originally meant to contain terms and their corresponding definitions. The idea was a `<dt>...</dt>` element would name the term to define, and a `<dd>...</dd>` element partnered with it would contain the corresponding definition. By partnering the two child elements, groups of these partnerships could form the children of the `<dl>...</dl>` element:

```
<dl>
<dt>Apple</dt>
<dd>A red fruit</dd>
```

```
<dt>Grape</dt>
<dd>A green or purple fruit</dd>
</dl>
```

Properties

blockDirection

JScript 5.0+

IE5+

Syntax

```
var x = HTMLDListElement.blockDirection
```

The blockDirection property of HTMLDListElement objects is a read-only version of the dir property, covered in Chapter 21, "HTMLElement."

compact

JavaScript 1.5, JScript 3.0+

Nav6, IE4+

Syntax

```
[var x =] HTMLDListElement.compact [= boolValue]
```

The compact property of HTMLDListElement objects reflects whether the browser should render the definition element's contents in a smaller space than normal.

innerHTML

JavaScript 1.5, JScript 3.0+

Nav6, IE4+

Syntax

```
 [var x =] HTMLDListElement.innerHTML [= HTMLString]
```

The innerHTML property of HTMLDListElement interfaces retrieves or sets the HTML source code contained between, but not including, the starting and ending tags.

I personally recommend against using `innerHTML` to set the HTML inside a tag. I strongly recommend against using `innerHTML` to append to the contents of an HTML tag:

```
elem.innerHTML += "<div><p>Hello World</p></div>" // DO NOT DO THIS
```

I do like the handiness of the `innerHTML` property for retrieving HTML source code at a glance, as a companion method to the W3C Document Object Model. (The DOM provides an object structure for the source code; `innerHTML` provides the corresponding source code.)

outerHTML

JScript 3.0+

IE4+

Syntax

```
var x = HTMLDListElement.outerHTML
```

The `outerHTML` property of `HTMLDListElement` retrieves or sets the HTML source code contained between, and including, the starting and ending tags.

I do like the handiness of the `outerHTML` property for retrieving HTML source code at a glance, as a companion method to the W3C Document Object Model. (The DOM provides an object structure for the source code; `outerHTML` provides the corresponding source code.)

Methods

The `HTMLDListElement` interface provides no methods beyond those the `HTMLElement` interface defines.

Event Handlers

Internet Explorer supports the following event handlers for the `HTMLDListElement` interface:

onactivate	ondragend	onmouseout
onbeforeactivate	ondragenter	onmouseover
onbeforecopy	ondragleave	onmouseup
onbeforecut	ondragover	onmousewheel
onbeforedeactivate	ondragstart	onmove
onbeforeeditfocus	ondrop	onmoveend
onbeforepaste	onfocus	onmovestart
onblur	onfocusin	onpaste
onclick	onfocusout	onpropertychange
oncontextmenu	onhelp	onreadystatechange
oncontrolselect	onlayoutcomplete	onresize
oncopy	onlosecapture	onresizeend
oncut	onmousedown	onresizestart
ondblclick	onmouseenter	onselectstart
ondeactivate	onmouseleave	ontimeerror
ondrag	onmousemove	

HTMLLIElement Interface

Browser/JavaScript Version	Created By
Nav4/JavaScript 1.2	Not Implemented
IE4/JScript 3.0	`<li>...</li>`
IE5/JScript 5.0	`<li>...</li>`
IE5.5/JScript 5.5	`<li>...</li>`
Nav6/JavaScript 1.5	`<li>...</li>`
IE6	`<li>...</li>`
DOM Level 1	`document.createElement("li")`

Note

Implemented in Nav1+ (HTML), IE3+ (HTML), Nav6 (DOM), IE4+ (DOM)

Descends from `HTMLElement` interface (Chapter 21)

Parent elements: `HTMLDirectoryElement`, `HTMLMenuElement`, `HTMLOListElement`, `HTMLULListElement`

The `<li>...</li>` element defines the items of the list.

Properties

blockDirection

JScript 5.0+

IE5+

Syntax

```
var x = HTMLLIElement.blockDirection
```

The `blockDirection` property of `HTMLLIElement` objects is a read-only version of the `dir` property, covered in Chapter 21, "HTMLElement."

innerHTML

JavaScript 1.5, JScript 3.0+

Nav6, IE4+

Syntax

```
[var x =] HTMLLIElement.innerHTML [= HTMLString]
```

The `innerHTML` property of `HTMLLIElement` interfaces retrieves or sets the HTML source code contained between, but not including, the starting and ending tags.

I personally recommend against using `innerHTML` to set the HTML inside a tag. I strongly recommend against using `innerHTML` to append to the contents of an HTML tag:

```
elem.innerHTML += "<div><p>Hello World</p></div>" // DO NOT DO THIS
```

I do like the handiness of the `innerHTML` property for retrieving HTML source code at a glance, as a companion method to the W3C Document Object Model. (The DOM provides an object structure for the source code; `innerHTML` provides the corresponding source code.)

innerText

JScript 3.0+

IE4+

Syntax

```
var x = HTMLLIElement.innerText
```

The `innerText` property of `HTMLLIElement` retrieves or sets the text contained between, but not including, the starting and ending tags.

outerHTML

JScript 3.0+

IE4+

Syntax

```
var x = HTMLLIElement.outerHTML
```

The `outerHTML` property of `HTMLLIElement` retrieves or sets the HTML source code contained between, and including, the starting and ending tags.

I do like the handiness of the `outerHTML` property for retrieving HTML source code at a glance, as a companion method to the W3C Document Object Model. (The DOM provides an object structure for the source code; `outerHTML` provides the corresponding source code.)

type

JavaScript 1.5, JScript 3.0+

Nav6, IE4+

Syntax

```
[var x = ] HTMLLIElement.type [= bulletStr]
```

The `type` attribute of `HTMLLIElement` objects reflects the style of list numbering the list uses. For instance, the list's numbering can be uppercase or lowercase Roman numerals (I, II, III, IV, V...), uppercase or lowercase letters (A, B, C, D, E...), numbers (1, 2, 3, 4, 5...), or a bullet (filled circle, square, empty circle).

> **Note**
> The `type` property is deprecated in HTML 4. Browsers that support CSS2 can make use of `list-style-type` and related properties of the CSS2 specification.

You can set this value to `1` for numbered bullets, `A` for uppercase letters, `I` for Roman numerals, `a` for lowercase letters, `i` for lowercase Roman numerals, `disc` for a filled circle, `circle` for an empty circle, or `square` for a filled square.

value

JavaScript 1.5, JScript 3.0+

Nav6, IE4+

Syntax

```
[var x = ] HTMLLIElement.value [= number]
```

The `value` attribute of `HTMLLIElement` objects reflects the ordinal index of the list item. For example, if the type is Roman numerals and the value is `"2"`, this element will render with a bullet of `"B"`.

Methods

The `HTMLLIElement` interface provides no methods beyond those the `HTMLElement` interface defines.

Event Handlers

Internet Explorer supports the following event handlers for the `HTMLLIElement` interface:

onactivate	ondragenter	onmousemove
onbeforeactivate	ondragleave	onmouseout
onbeforecopy	ondragover	onmouseover
onbeforecut	ondragstart	onmouseup
onbeforedeactivate	ondrop	onmousewheel
onbeforeeditfocus	onfocus	onmove
onbeforepaste	onfocusin	onmoveend
onblur	onfocusout	onmovestart
onclick	onhelp	onpaste
oncontextmenu	onkeydown	onpropertychange
oncontrolselect	onkeypress	onreadystatechange
oncopy	onkeyup	onresize
oncut	onlayoutcomplete	onresizeend
ondblclick	onlosecapture	onresizestart
ondeactivate	onmousedown	onselectstart
ondrag	onmouseenter	ontimeerror
ondragend	onmouseleave	

HTMLMenuElement Interface

Browser/JavaScript Version	Created By
Nav4/JavaScript 1.2	Not implemented
IE4/JScript 3.0	`<menu>...</menu>`
IE5/JScript 5.0	`<menu>...</menu>`
IE5.5/JScript 5.5	`<menu>...</menu>`
Nav6/JavaScript 1.5	`<menu>...</menu>`
IE6	`<menu>...</menu>`
DOM Level 1	`document.createElement("menu")`

> **Note**
> Implemented in Nav1+ (HTML), IE3+ (HTML), Nav6 (DOM), IE4+ (DOM)
>
> Descends from HTMLElement interface (Chapter 21)
>
> Parent elements: HTMLBodyElement (Chapter 22), any block text element
>
> Deprecated in HTML 4

The <menu>...</menu> element HTML originally designated to give a menu listing. The <ul>...</ul> element has replaced it in terms of functionality, and you should avoid use of this element.

Properties

blockDirection

JScript 5.0+

IE5+

Syntax

```
var x = HTMLMenuElement.blockDirection
```

The blockDirection property of HTMLMenuElement objects is a read-only version of the dir property, covered in Chapter 21, "HTMLElement."

compact

JavaScript 1.5

Nav6, IE6

Syntax

```
[var x =] HTMLMenuElement.compact [= boolValue]
```

The compact property of HTMLMenuElement objects reflects whether the browser should render the directory element's contents in a smaller space than normal.

innerHTML

JavaScript 1.5, JScript 3.0+

Nav6, IE4+

Syntax

```
[var x =] HTMLMenuElement.innerHTML [= HTMLString]
```

The `innerHTML` property of `HTMLMenuElement` objects retrieves or sets the HTML source code contained between, but not including, the starting and ending tags.

I personally recommend against using `innerHTML` to set the HTML inside a tag. I strongly recommend against using `innerHTML` to append to the contents of an HTML tag:

```
elem.innerHTML += "<div><p>Hello World</p></div>" // DO NOT DO THIS
```

I do like the handiness of the `innerHTML` property for retrieving HTML source code at a glance, as a companion method to the W3C Document Object Model. (The DOM provides an object structure for the source code; `innerHTML` provides the corresponding source code.)

innerText

JScript 3.0+

IE4+

Syntax

```
var x = HTMLMenuElement.innerText
```

The `innerText` property of `HTMLMenuElement` objects retrieves or sets the text contained between, but not including, the starting and ending tags.

outerHTML

JScript 3.0+

IE4+

Syntax

```
var x = HTMLMenuElement.outerHTML
```

The `outerHTML` property of `HTMLMenuElement` objects retrieves or sets the HTML source code contained between, and including, the starting and ending tags.

I do like the handiness of the `outerHTML` property for retrieving HTML source code at a glance, as a companion method to the W3C Document Object Model. (The DOM provides an object structure for the source code; `outerHTML` provides the corresponding source code.)

Methods

The `HTMLMenuElement` interface provides no methods beyond those the `HTMLElement` interface defines.

Event Handlers

Internet Explorer supports the following event handlers for the `HTMLMenuElement` interface:

onactivate	ondrag	onmousedown
onbeforeactivate	ondragend	onmouseenter
onbeforecopy	ondragenter	onmouseleave
onbeforecut	ondragleave	onmousemove
onbeforedeactivate	ondragover	onmouseout
onbeforeeditfocus	ondragstart	onmouseover
onbeforepaste	ondrop	onmouseup
onblur	onfocus	onmousewheel
onclick	onfocusin	onmove
oncontextmenu	onfocusout	onmoveend
oncontrolselect	onhelp	onmovestart
oncopy	onkeydown	onpaste
oncut	onkeypress	onpropertychange
ondblclick	onkeyup	onreadystatechange
ondeactivate	onlosecapture	onresize

```
onresizeend

onresizestart

onselectstart

ontimeerror
```

HTMLOListElement Interface

Browser/JavaScript version	Created by:
Nav4/JavaScript 1.2	Not implemented
IE4/JScript 3.0	`<ol>...</ol>`
IE5/JScript 5.0	`<ol>...</ol>`
IE5.5/JScript 5.5	`<ol>...</ol>`
Nav6/JavaScript 1.5	`<ol>...</ol>`
IE6	`<ol>...</ol>`
DOM Level 1	`document.createElement("ol")`

> **Note**
> Implemented in Nav1+ (HTML), IE3+ (HTML), Nav6 (DOM), IE4+ (DOM)
> Descends from `HTMLElement` interface (Chapter 21)
> Parent elements: `HTMLBodyElement` (Chapter 22), any block text element

The ordered list element is a wrapper for all `<li>...</li>` elements in the given list. The distinction here is that within this element, the list elements are intended to be numbered in the order presented within the HTML markup.

Properties

blockDirection

JScript 5.0+

IE5+

Syntax

```
var x = HTMLOListElement.blockDirection
```

The `blockDirection` property of `HTMLOListElement` objects is a read-only version of the `dir` property, covered in Chapter 21, "HTMLElement."

compact

JavaScript 1.5, JScript 3.0+

Nav6, IE4+

Syntax

```
[var x =] HTMLOListElement.compact [= boolValue]
```

The `compact` property of `HTMLOListElement` objects reflects whether the browser should render the directory element's contents in a smaller space than normal.

innerHTML

JavaScript 1.5, JScript 3.0+

Nav6, IE4+

Syntax

```
 [var x =] HTMLOListElement.innerHTML [= HTMLString]
```

The `innerHTML` property of `HTMLOListElement` objects retrieves or sets the HTML source code contained between, but not including, the starting and ending tags.

I personally recommend against using `innerHTML` to set the HTML inside a tag. I strongly recommend against using `innerHTML` to append to the contents of an HTML tag:

```
elem.innerHTML += "<div><p>Hello World</p></div>" // DO NOT DO THIS
```

I do like the handiness of the `innerHTML` property for retrieving HTML source code at a glance, as a companion method to the W3C Document Object Model. (The DOM provides an object structure for the source code; `innerHTML` provides the corresponding source code.)

innerText

JScript 3.0+

IE4+

Syntax

`var x = HTMLOListElement.innerText`

The `innerText` property of `HTMLOListElement` objects retrieves or sets the text contained between, but not including, the starting and ending tags.

outerHTML

JScript 3.0+

IE4+

Syntax

`var x = HTMLOListElement.outerHTML`

The `outerHTML` property of `HTMLOListElement` objects retrieves or sets the HTML source code contained between, and including, the starting and ending tags.

I do like the handiness of the `outerHTML` property for retrieving HTML source code at a glance, as a companion method to the W3C Document Object Model. (The DOM provides an object structure for the source code; `outerHTML` provides the corresponding source code.)

start

JavaScript 1.5, JScript 3.0+

Nav6, IE4+

Syntax

`[var x = ] HTMLOListElement.start [= startIndex]`

The `start` attribute of `HTMLOListElement` objects reflects the ordinal index of the first list item among its child elements. For example, if the type is Roman numeral and the value is `"2"`, this element will render with a bullet of `"II"`.

type

JavaScript 1.5, JScript 3.0+

Nav6, IE4+

Syntax

```
[var x = ] HTMLOListElement.type [= bulletStr]
```

The type attribute of HTMLOListElement objects reflects the style of list numbering the list uses. For instance, the list's numbering can be uppercase or lowercase Roman numerals (I, II, III, IV, V…), uppercase or lowercase letters (A, B, C, D, E…), numbers (1, 2, 3, 4, 5…), or a bullet (filled circle, square, empty circle).

Methods

The HTMLOListElement interface provides no methods beyond those the HTMLElement interface defines.

Event Handlers

Internet Explorer supports the following event handlers for the HTMLOListElement interface:

onactivate	oncopy	onfocus
onbeforeactivate	oncut	onfocusin
onbeforecopy	ondblclick	onfocusout
onbeforecut	ondeactivate	onhelp
onbeforedeactivate	ondrag	onkeydown
onbeforeeditfocus	ondragend	onkeypress
onbeforepaste	ondragenter	onkeyup
onblur	ondragleave	onlayoutcomplete
onclick	ondragover	onlosecapture
oncontextmenu	ondragstart	onmousedown
oncontrolselect	ondrop	onmouseenter

onmouseleave	onmove	onresize
onmousemove	onmoveend	onresizeend
onmouseout	onmovestart	onresizestart
onmouseover	onpaste	onselectstart
onmouseup	onpropertychange	ontimeerror
onmousewheel	onreadystatechange	

HTMLUListElement Interface

Browser/JavaScript Version	Created By
Nav4/JavaScript 1.2	Not implemented
IE4/JScript 3.0	`<ul>...</ul>`
IE5/JScript 5.0	`<ul>...</ul>`
IE5.5/JScript 5.5	`<ul>...</ul>`
Nav6/JavaScript 1.5	`<ul>...</ul>`
IE6	`<ul>...</ul>`
DOM Level 1	`document.createElement("ul")`

> **Note**
> Implemented in Nav1+ (HTML), IE3+ (HTML), Nav6 (DOM), IE4+ (DOM)
> Descends from `HTMLElement` interface (Chapter 21)
> Parent elements: `HTMLBodyElement` (Chapter 22), any block text element

The unordered list element is a wrapper for all `<li>...</li>` elements in the given list. The distinction here is that within this element, the list item elements are not intended to be in any particular order.

Properties

blockDirection

JScript 5.0+

IE5+

Syntax

```
var x = HTMLUListElement.blockDirection
```

The `blockDirection` property of `HTMLUListElement` objects is a read-only version of the `dir` property, covered in Chapter 21, "HTMLElement."

compact

JavaScript 1.5, JScript 3.0+

Nav6, IE4+

Syntax

```
[var x =] HTMLUListElement.compact [= boolValue]
```

The `compact` property of `HTMLUListElement` objects reflects whether the browser should render the directory element's contents in a smaller space than normal.

innerHTML

JavaScript 1.5, JScript 3.0+

Nav6, IE4+

Syntax

```
[var x =] HTMLUListElement.innerHTML [= HTMLString]
```

The `innerHTML` property of `HTMLUListElement` interfaces retrieves or sets the HTML source code contained between, but not including, the starting and ending tags.

I personally recommend against using `innerHTML` to set the HTML inside a tag. I strongly recommend against using `innerHTML` to append to the contents of an HTML tag:

```
elem.innerHTML += "<div><p>Hello World</p></div>" // DO NOT DO THIS
```

I do like the handiness of the `innerHTML` property for retrieving HTML source code at a glance, as a companion method to the W3C Document Object Model. (The DOM provides an object structure for the source code; `innerHTML` provides the corresponding source code.)

innerText

JScript 3.0+

IE4+

Syntax

```
var x = HTMLUListElement.innerText
```

The `innerText` property of `HTMLUListElement` objects retrieves or sets the text contained between, but not including, the starting and ending tags.

outerHTML

JScript 3.0+

IE4+

Syntax

```
var x = HTMLUListElement.outerHTML
```

The `outerHTML` property of `HTMLUListElement` objects retrieves or sets the HTML source code contained between, and including, the starting and ending tags.

I do like the handiness of the `outerHTML` property for retrieving HTML source code at a glance, as a companion method to the W3C Document Object Model. (The DOM provides an object structure for the source code; `outerHTML` provides the corresponding source code.)

type

JavaScript 1.5, JScript 3.0+

Nav6, IE4+

Syntax

```
[var x = ] HTMLUListElement.type [= bulletStr]
```

The `type` attribute of `HTMLUListElement` objects reflects the style of list numbering the list uses. For instance, the list's numbering can be uppercase or lowercase Roman numerals (I, II, III, IV, V...), uppercase or lowercase letters (A, B, C, D, E...), numbers (1, 2, 3, 4, 5...), or a bullet (filled circle, square, empty circle).

Methods

The `HTMLUListElement` interface provides no methods beyond those the `HTMLElement` interface defines.

Event Handlers

Internet Explorer supports the following event handlers for the `HTMLUListElement` interface:

onactivate	ondragenter	onmousemove
onbeforeactivate	ondragleave	onmouseout
onbeforecopy	ondragover	onmouseover
onbeforecut	ondragstart	onmouseup
onbeforedeactivate	ondrop	onmousewheel
onbeforeeditfocus	onfocus	onmove
onbeforepaste	onfocusin	onmoveend
onblur	onfocusout	onmovestart
onclick	onhelp	onpaste
oncontextmenu	onkeydown	onpropertychange
oncontrolselect	onkeypress	onreadystatechange
oncopy	onkeyup	onresize
oncut	onlayoutcomplete	onresizeend
ondblclick	onlosecapture	onresizestart
ondeactivate	onmousedown	onselectstart
ondrag	onmouseenter	ontimeerror
ondragend	onmouseleave	

CHAPTER 28

Text Formatting Elements

Text formatting elements could easily be among the most boring of subjects when it comes to the Document Object Model. Most of the time you don't even think about them. Most of them you've probably used only a few times, though a few are familiar. I know I don't use all of these very frequently.

So what is a text formatting element, anyway?

A text formatting element is simply an element describing what kind of text it contains, or how it affects its surrounding text. For instance, a `<p>...<p>` element contains normal paragraph text, whereas a `<pre>...</pre>` element contains preformatted text. A `<br />` element breaks apart the text around it.

HTML defines most of these as elements with a semantic meaning and an actual markup rendering. For instance, the `<ins>...</ins>` element indicates a change to the document of some sort, an official change with an official reason and an official date and time. This helps you track changes to the document.

The real benefit of this chapter will come when you read Chapter 33, "Styling for HTML Elements." You see, every element of HTML is styleable—you can change its appearance if you want. All other elements in this book have a specific purpose that makes styling them somewhat inappropriate except for certain conditions. The same does not apply to text formatting elements. These elements have minimal styling instructions attached to them—in the case of <div>...</div> and ..., almost none at all! Plus, the whole point of styling, the reason it was invented, was to make your text look fancy—not your forms or your tables or scripts.

Before you can make your text fancy, though, you need to know how to make—and mark up—your text in the first place.

Throughout this book, I've been making references to the innerHTML, outerHTML, innerText, and outerText properties. Listing 28.1 gives a comparison of how these properties work—and a little explanation as well.

Listing 28.1   *Exploring innerHTML, innerText, outerHTML and outerText*

```
<?xml version="1.0" ?>
<!-- Internet Explorer 5.0+ only. -->
<!DOCTYPE html PUBLIC "-//W3C//DTD XHTML 1.0 Transitional//EN"
➥ "DTD/xhtml1-transitional.dtd">
<html xmlns="http://www.w3.org/1999/xhtml" >
<head><title></title>
<script language="JavaScript" type="text/javascript">
<!--
window.onload = function() {
    var em = document.getElementsByTagName("em")[0]

    var p0 = document.createElement("p")
    p0.appendChild(document.createTextNode("innerHTML: "+em.innerHTML))
    document.body.appendChild(p0)

    var p1 = document.createElement("p")
    p1.appendChild(document.createTextNode("innerText:  "+em.innerText))
    document.body.appendChild(p1)

    var p2 = document.createElement("p")
    p2.appendChild(document.createTextNode("outerHTML: "+em.outerHTML))
    document.body.appendChild(p2)

    var p3 = document.createElement("p")
    p3.appendChild(document.createTextNode("outerText: "+em.outerText))
    document.body.appendChild(p3)
```

Listing 28.1   *(continued)*

```
    var p4 = document.createElement("p")
    em.innerText = "innerHTML works on nesting of elements"
    var p4_text = "After setting em.innerText, em.nodeType == " + em.nodeType
    p4_text += " and em.childNodes.length == " + em.childNodes.length + "."

    p4.appendChild(document.createTextNode(p4_text))
    p4.appendChild(document.createElement("br"))

    p4_text = "em.parentNode == " + em.parentNode + "."
    p4.appendChild(document.createTextNode(p4_text))
    document.body.appendChild(p4)

    var p5 = document.createElement("p")
    em.outerText = "innerHTML works on nesting of elements"
    var p5_text = "After setting em.outerText, em.nodeType == " + em.nodeType
    p5_text += " and em.childNodes.length == " + em.childNodes.length + "."

    p5.appendChild(document.createTextNode(p5_text))
    p5.appendChild(document.createElement("br"))

    p5_text = "em.parentNode == " + em.parentNode + "."
    p5.appendChild(document.createTextNode(p5_text))

    document.body.appendChild(p5)      }
//-->
</script>
</head>
<body>
<p>This is a test to see
how <em id='me'>innerHTML works <strong>on nesting </strong>of
elements</em>,
 as well as innerText, outerText, and outerHTML.</p>
<pre>Note how setting innerText and setting outerText have different results.
The first replaces all childNodes with a single child text node. The second
replaces the this element with a new text node and removes the this element
from the document entirely.</pre>
<!-- Results:
innerHTML: innerHTML works <STRONG>on nesting </STRONG>of elements
innerText: innerHTML works on nesting of elements
outerHTML: <EM id=me>innerHTML works <STRONG>on nesting </STRONG>of
➥elements</EM>
```

Listing 28.1   *(continued)*

```
outerText: innerHTML works on nesting of elements
After setting em.innerText, em.nodeType == 1 and em.childNodes.length == 1.
em.parentNode == [object].
After setting em.outerText, em.nodeType == 1 and em.childNodes.length == 0.
em.parentNode == null.
-->
</body>
</html>
```

Five Unusual But Significant Text Formatting Elements

There are five elements in particular you should be aware of, especially their impact on browsers and the standards. These five are among the strangest elements involving text, considering their special implementation (or lack thereof).

Before inline frames (see Chapter 15, "window"), Netscape 4 introduced an `src` property for a proprietary `<layer>...</layer>` element and for objects created from a corresponding `Layer()` constructor function. The result is that, effectively, these elements became floating documents, which the master document wouldn't have to flow around.

For inline documents from external sources, Netscape 4 introduced the `<ilayer>...</ilayer>` tag. (The master document has to flow around these. The `<object>...</object>` tag in Chapter 31, "Programmable Elements," is better for the purpose intended, however, as it is standardized.)

Internet Explorer browsers ignored the `<layer>...</layer>` and `<ilayer>...</ilayer>` elements entirely.

Listing 28.2 shows the best practice for a scenario of this type.

Listing 28.2   *Layers and Inline Frames Together*

```
<!-- 28lst02a.htm -->
<html>
<!-- Not valid XHTML 1.0. Netscape 4+, Internet Explorer 5+  -->
<head><title></title></head>
<body>
<p>Outer document.</p>
<iframe border="1" src="28lst02b.htm" width="100" height="100"
```

Listing 28.2   *(continued)*

```
style="position:absolute;top:200px;left:200px;">
    <layer src="28lst02b.htm" width="100" height="100" border="1"
style="position:absolute;top:200px;left:200px;">
        Test failed.
    </layer>
</iframe>
<!-- Results:
A positioned document with the words "Inner document."
-->
</body>
</html>


<?xml version="1.0" ?>
<!-- 28lst02b.htm -->
<!DOCTYPE html PUBLIC "-//W3C//DTD XHTML 1.0 Transitional//EN"
➥"DTD/xhtml1-transitional.dtd">
<html xmlns="http://www.w3.org/1999/xhtml" >
<head><title></title></head>
<body>
<p>Inner document.</p>
</body>
</html>
```

`<layer>...</layer>` and `<ilayer>...</ilayer>` elements are not valid HTML. To achieve these special effects, you effectively have to break standards. Especially when you consider positioning and z-index.

Here's where things really get ugly. With the CSS property `position:absolute`, an element effectively becomes a layer in Netscape. Thus it becomes a member of the `document.layers` array in Netscape (which I've already ranted about in Chapter 18, "navigator," for a different reason). It is also (simply by existing in the document) a property of the `document.all` collection in Internet Explorer (same rant).

Each browser's implementation of z-index was shaky, as well, and in some respects still is.

The result? Dynamic HTML was anything but standard, and anything but easy to implement effectively. Correct, standards-compliant code went out of fashion. The ugliest JavaScript code ever seen stemmed from this 4.x browser split. The differences themselves practically gave birth to browser sniffing in the first place, the wrong way (see Chapter 18).

I applaud Netscape 6's decision to stick to the standards for layers, dropping the proprietary element altogether and the `document.layers` object. Likewise, Netscape's committal to the CSS Level 2 Recommendation from the W3C makes it possible to write Web code that works in both browsers. You'll see some divergences in standards again, though, in Chapters 32 and 33 ("DOM-2 Events and Event Handlers" and "Styling for HTML Elements," respectively).

Three other unusual text formatting elements are the `<div>...</div>`, `<marquee>...</marquee>`, and `<xmp>...</xmp>` elements.

`HTMLDivElement` objects, or `<div>...</div>` elements, are special block elements for containing and styling other block elements. This may not make much sense until you see Listing 28.3 and its corresponding screenshot, Figure 28.1.

Listing 28.3   *A Document with and without* `HTMLDivElement`

```
<?xml version="1.0" ?>
<!-- Netscape 6, Internet Explorer 5.0+ only.  -->
<!DOCTYPE html PUBLIC "-//W3C//DTD XHTML 1.0 Transitional//EN"
➥"DTD/xhtml1-transitional.dtd">
<html xmlns="http://www.w3.org/1999/xhtml" >
<head><title></title>
<style type="text/css">
<!--
.invert {
    background-color:black;
    color:white;
    }
//-->
</style>
</head>
<body>
<p class="invert">This text is inside a paragraph which has white text on a
➥ black background.</p>
<p class="invert">This text is inside a paragraph which has white text on a
➥ black background.</p>
<div class="invert">
<p>This text is inside a paragraph inside a div which has white text on a black
➥ background.</p>
<p>This text is inside a paragraph inside a div which has white text on a black
➥ background.</p>
</div>
</body>
</html>
```

Five Unusual But Significant Text Formatting Elements

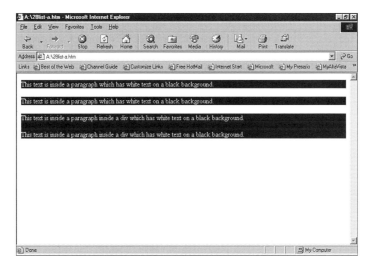

Figure 28.1
The advantages of using HTMLDivElement.

> **Note**
> Netscape 4 doesn't show any differences in Listing 28.3. Its rendering is technically incorrect.

Microsoft decided, beginning with version 3.0 of its browser, to provide a simple marquee effect in HTML. So Microsoft introduced the <marquee>...</marquee> element. There are only three problems with this idea: (1) Netscape doesn't support it, (2) it's not valid HTML, and (3) you can achieve the same effects using JavaScript and HTML anyway. A fancy special effect that looks great in Internet Explorer loses all its pizzazz (and I mean all) in Netscape browsers and Amaya. The contents don't always "degrade well" (a term I will explain in Chapter 33).

Listing 28.4 shows the <marquee>...</marquee> element in use. Screenshots do not suffice to describe this (we're talking about content constantly in motion).

Listing 28.4   *Marquee and Equivalent HTML/JS Code*

```
<html>
<!-- Not valid XHTML 1.0.  Netscape 6, Internet Explorer 5.0+ only.  -->
<head><title></title>
<script language="JavaScript" type="text/javascript">
```

Listing 28.4   *(continued)*

```
<!--
function marqueeMove() {
    var marqueeContents = document.getElementById("marqueeContents")
    var leftPix = marqueeContents.style.left
    leftPix = leftPix.substr(0, leftPix.length-2) * 1 - 5
    var widthPix = marqueeContents.style.width
    widthPix = widthPix.substr(0, widthPix.length-2) * 1
    if (widthPix + leftPix < 0) {
        leftPix = widthPix;
        }
    marqueeContents.style.left = leftPix + "px"
    }
//-->
</script>
</head>
<body onload="setInterval(marqueeMove,60)">
<marquee width="100">Hello World</marquee>
<div style="width:100px;overflow:hidden;">
<span style="position:relative;left:100px;width:100px;white-space:nowrap;"
 id="marqueeContents">Hello World</span>
</div>
</body>
</html>
```

You may need to tinker around to get it to work your way. Also, it is not properly object-oriented as I describe in Chapter 1, "Object()".

Finally, we come to one of the elements of HTML I actually miss: <xmp>...</xmp>. This element was formerly part of HTML, but is completely gone from HTML 4.0. As I will note later in the chapter, XML's CDATA sections make an almost exact substitute. I provide Listing 28.5 for this as well.

Listing 28.5   *The Father of CDATA Sections*

```
<html>
<!-- Not valid XHTML 1.0.  -->
<head><title></title></head>
<body>
<p>
<xmp>This is some sample code.</xmp><br />
<![CDATA[
```

Listing 28.5   *(continued)*

```
This is some CDATA code.]]>
</p>
</body>
</html>
```

HTMLAnchorElement/<a>...</a>

Browser/JavaScript Version	Created By
Nav4/JavaScript 1.2	<a>...</a>
IE4/JScript 3.0	<a>...</a>
IE5/JScript 5.0	<a>...</a>
IE5.5/JScript 5.5	<a>...</a>
Nav6/JavaScript 1.5	<a>...</a>
IE6	<a>...</a>
DOM Level 1	document.createElement("a")

> **Note**
>
> Implemented in Nav1+ (HTML), IE3+ (HTML), Nav2+ (DOM), IE3+ (DOM)
>
> Descends from HTMLElement interface (Chapter 21)
>
> Inline Text Formatting Element

Description

The <a>...</a> element defines a hyperlink or an HTML anchor. With an href attribute, the element is a hyperlink to another URI (including the javascript: pseudo-URI).

With a name attribute, the element is an anchor. <a name="hello"></a> is an anchor you can reference by URI as "#hello".

Netscape and Internet Explorer both make this element available via the document.anchors and document.links collections; but anchors are available only in document.anchors and links are available only in document.links.

Interestingly, the official W3C Document Object Model covers only about half the properties that Netscape and Internet Explorer both implement in common. The other half comes from extensions similar to the location object's properties. Still, the two browsers agree on a lot about anchor elements.

Properties

accessKey

JavaScript 1.5

Nav6

Syntax

```
[var x = ] HTMLAnchorElement.accessKey [= key]
```

The accessKey property of HTMLAnchorElement objects designates a shortcut key to focus. When the user presses the designated key and the meta key (on Windows, this is ALT) while the window for the this object has focus, the element gains focus. The nodeValue for this attribute must be one character in length.

> **Note**
> Internet Explorer 5.0+ implements this for all elements.

charset

JavaScript 1.5

Nav6, IE6

Syntax

```
[var x =] HTMLAnchorElement.charset [= charSetStr]
```

The charset property of HTMLAnchorElement objects indicates the standard character set name, as a string, of the object the this element references.

coords

JavaScript 1.5

Nav6, IE6

Syntax

`[var x =] HTMLAnchorElement.coords [= coordSequence]`

The coords property of HTMLAnchorElement objects is a sequence of coordinates appropriate to the shape property of the this object. Only commas separate the coordinates. (These correspond to clickable areas of an image map, and represent an alternative way to define image maps. I give more information about image maps in Chapter 30, "Image Elements.")

When shape is not specified or is "rect", the coordinates are $(x1, y1)$ and $(x2, y2)$, which are two opposite corners of a rectangle. In this format, you would see "x1,y1,x2,y2" for the coords property.

When shape is "circle", the coordinates are (cx, cy) and the radius r of the circle, where (cx, cy) represents the center of the circle. In this format, you would see "cx,cy,r".

When shape is "poly", things get a little more interesting. You get a series of points $(x1, y1), (x2, y2), (x3, y3)$… which, when you connect them from point to point with line segments, produces a polygon. The last point in such a sequence must match the first exactly; you cannot omit it. I do not recommend crossing one line segment with another; the results may be highly unpredictable. In this format, coords would resemble "x1,y1,x2,y2,x3,y3,...,xn,yn,x1,y1".

hash

JavaScript 1.0+, JScript 1.0+

Nav2+, IE3+

Read-only (Nav2, Nav3 only)

Syntax

`[var x =] HTMLAnchorElement.hash [= targetName]`

The hash property of HTMLAnchorElement objects identifies the target or anchor of the link's URI. The browser uses anchors to load a page and scroll it to a particular place

in the document automatically. Anchors you define with the `name` property of
`HTMLAnchorElement`:

```
<a name="myTarget"></a>
```

Typically, the anchor in this sense does not have an `href` property. The hash refers to
the part of the URI following (and including) the pound sign (#) but preceding (and
not including) the question mark (?). In the URI
`http://www.jslab.org/mydir/mypage.htm#mySpot?owner="AlexVincent"`, the `hash`
property is equal to `"#mySpot"`.

You can set the `this.hash` property explicitly to force the browser to scroll automatically to the given target when the link is clicked.

host

JavaScript 1.0+, JScript 1.0+

Nav2, IE3+

Read-only (Nav2, Nav3)

Syntax

```
[var x =] HTMLAnchorElement.host [= targetName]
```

The `host` property of `HTMLAnchorElement` objects joins the `this.hostname` and
`this.port` properties in one string. You can explicitly set both properties at the same
time by setting the `host` property directly.

Given a URI `http://www.jslab.org:80/mypage.htm`, `this.host` is usually
`"www.jslab.org:80"`. However, in most cases the `this.port` property is an empty
string. Most of the time, this may return `"www.jslab.org"`. Thus, `this.host` is often a
synonym for `this.hostname`.

For files local to the client machine, this is an empty string.

hostname

JavaScript 1.0+, JScript 1.0+

Nav2, IE3+

Read-only

Syntax

```
[var x =] HTMLAnchorElement.hostname [= "targetName"]
```

The `hostname` property of `HTMLAnchorElement` objects represents the server domain name from which the user called the current document. This includes any subdomains attached to the domain name. Given a URI `http://www.jslab.org/mypage.htm`, `location.hostname` equals `"www.jslab.org"`.

For files local to the client machine, this is an empty string.

href

JavaScript 1.5, JScript 1.0+

Nav2+, IE3+

Syntax

```
[var x =] HTMLAnchorElement.href [= URIString]
```

The `href` property of `HTMLAnchorElement` objects refers to the Web address of the resource itself. With this property, the `this` element becomes a hyperlink.

hreflang

JavaScript 1.5

Nav6, IE6+

Syntax

```
[var x =] HTMLAnchorElement.hreflang [= language]
```

The `hreflang` property of `HTMLAnchorElement` objects refers to the language of the document the `href` property references. This is more of an advisory property than a practical one.

innerHTML

JavaScript 1.5, JScript 5.0+

Nav6, IE4+

Syntax

```
[var x =] HTMLAnchorElement.innerHTML [= HTMLString]
```

The `innerHTML` property of `HTMLAnchorElement` interfaces retrieves or sets the HTML source code contained between, but not including, the starting and ending tags.

I personally recommend against using `innerHTML` to set the HTML inside a tag. I strongly recommend against using `innerHTML` to append to the contents of an HTML tag:

```
elem.innerHTML += "<div><p>Hello World</p></div>" // DO NOT DO THIS
```

I do like the handiness of the `innerHTML` property for retrieving HTML source code at a glance, as an alternative method to the W3C Document Object Model. (The DOM provides an object structure for the source code; `innerHTML` provides the corresponding source code.)

innerText

JScript 5.0+

IE4+

Syntax

```
var x = HTMLAnchorElement.innerText
```

The `innerText` property of `HTMLAnchorElement` retrieves or sets the text contained between, but not including, the starting and ending tags.

The `innerText` property can be useful, but the DOM Level 2 `Range` interface provides far more flexibility. See Chapter 34, "DOM-2 Range," for details on text ranges.

Methods

JScript 3.0+

IE4+

Syntax

```
[var x =] HTMLAnchorElement.Methods [= methodList]
```

The `Methods` property of `HTMLAnchorElement` objects corresponds to a comma-separated list of HTTP methods the server supports for the object to which the `this` element links.

name

JavaScript 1.5, JScript 1.0+

Nav6, IE3+

Syntax

```
[var x =] HTMLAnchorElement.name [= URITarget]
```

The `name` property of `HTMLAnchorElement` objects refers to the target the `this` element defines. Without it, you cannot use a hyperlink to scroll to it (that is, unless you're in the mood for some very convoluted scripting).

nameProp

JScript 5.0+

IE5+

Syntax

```
[var x =] HTMLAnchorElement.nameProp [= fileName]
```

The `nameProp` property of `HTMLAnchorElement` objects returns the filename of the file to which it links, excluding the path and targeting info. You can extract this info from `this.href`, though.

outerHTML

JScript 4.0+

IE4+

Syntax

```
var x = HTMLAnchorElement.outerHTML
```

The `outerHTML` property of `HTMLAnchorElement` retrieves or sets the HTML source code contained between, and including, the starting and ending tags.

I do like the handiness of the `outerHTML` property for retrieving HTML source code at a glance, as an alternative method to the W3C Document Object Model. (The DOM provides an object structure for the source code; `outerHTML` provides the corresponding source code.)

outerText

JScript 4.0+

IE4+

Syntax

```
var x = HTMLAnchorElement.outerText
```

The outerText property of HTMLAnchorElement objects is, as Listing 28.1 demonstrates, similar to the this.innerText property. The difference is in how you set the value; setting outerText replaces this with a new text node.

pathname

JavaScript 1.0+, JScript 1.0+

Nav2, IE3+

Syntax

```
var x = HTMLAnchorElement.pathname
```

The pathname property of HTMLAnchorElement objects retrieves the filename path from the server to the filename and extension. It excludes any targets and query strings, and does not include a server name.

I like to use this property sometimes to get the actual filename itself. Listing 16.1 shows this in some detail for the location object.

port

JavaScript 1.0+, JScript 1.0+

Nav2, IE3+

Read-only

Syntax

```
var x = HTMLAnchorElement.port
```

The port property of HTMLAnchorElement objects returns the port number of the server the page came through, if the server provided it. Usually, servers offer pages through specific "ports": HTTP-served pages normally go through port 80, and FTP-served pages go through port 21.

However, rarely does a server provide the port number, and Internet Explorer ignores the port number if the server sends the page by the HTTP protocol. So in all likelihood, this particular property will be an empty string.

Setting the port number can cause unusual effects if you do not set it to a port number for serving pages from. Most of the time, if you do not set it to the default port number, you will get a "404 File Not Found" page.

protocol

JavaScript 1.0+, JScript 1.0+

Nav2, IE3+

Syntax

`[var x =] HTMLAnchorElement.protocol [= protocolString]`

The `protocol` property of `HTMLAnchorElement` objects refers to what `protocol` the client will call the link by. Usually it's `"http:"` for the HyperText Transfer Protocol. Others you may see a lot of are `"ftp:"` for File Transfer Protocol, `"news:"` for newsgroup readings, and `"mailto:"` for e-mail.

A couple you will also see that technically aren't protocols are `"javascript:"`, for sending JavaScript commands to the browser, and `"about:"`, which provides information about the browser. One I particularly like is `"view-source:"`, which tells the browser to display the source code to a file.

Netscape makes this property a read/write property; Microsoft holds it as read-only. However, there is rarely any reason to tinker with this particular property. The various protocols for Internet access are not interchangeable.

rel

JavaScript 1.5, JScript 1.0+

Nav6, IE3+

Syntax

`[var x =] HTMLAnchorElement.rel [= relation]`

The `rel` property of `HTMLAnchorElement` objects refers to the kind of link the element infers.

rev

JavaScript 1.5, JScript 1.0+

Nav6, IE3+

Syntax

```
[var x =] HTMLAnchorElement.rev [= relation]
```

The rev property of HTMLAnchorElement objects refers to the kind of link the element infers from the other document to this one (in reverse, basically). For style sheets you must absolutely not use this property.

search

JavaScript 1.0+, JScript 1.0+

Nav2, IE3+

Syntax

```
[var x =] HTMLAnchorElement.search [= "targetName"]
```

The search property of HTMLAnchorElement objects describes the query-string of the link's URI. This includes the question mark of a URI and everything following.

When setting this property, be aware of correct URI syntax. For this, I strongly recommend you use the encodeURI() top-level function of Netscape 6 and Internet Explorer 5.5. For browsers prior to Netscape 6 and Internet Explorer 5.5, avoid placing spaces, question marks, colons, # characters, @ characters, and percentage marks in the query-string.

shape

JavaScript 1.5

Nav6, IE6

Syntax

```
[var x =] HTMLAnchorElement.shape [= coordSequence]
```

The shape property of HTMLAnchorElement objects, in concurrence with the coords property, determines which areas of the link are clickable, their shape and size.

When shape is not specified or is "rect", the coordinates are $(x1, y1)$ and $(x2, y2)$, which are two opposite corners of a rectangle. In this format, you would see "x1,y1,x2,y2" for the coords property.

When shape is "circle", the coordinates are (cx, cy) and the radius r of the circle, where (cx, cy) represents the center of the circle. In this format, you would see "cx,cy,r".

When shape is "poly", things get a little more interesting. You get a series of points $(x1, y1)$, $(x2, y2)$, $(x3, y3)$…which, when you connect them from point to point with line segments, produces a polygon. The last point in such a sequence must match the first exactly; you cannot omit it. I do not recommend crossing one line segment with another; the results may be highly unpredictable. In this format, coords would resemble "x1,y1,x2,y2,x3,y3,...,xn,yn,x1,y1".

tabIndex

JavaScript 1.5, JScript 3.0+

Nav6, IE4+

Syntax

```
[ver x =] HTMLAnchorElement.tabIndex [= numValue]
```

The tabIndex property of HTMLAnchorElement objects sets where the this element rests in the tab order. The tab order is an index indicating when an element in the document receives focus as the user strikes their Tab key. When setting this value, remember it can only accept numeric integers.

A negative tabIndex takes the this element out of the tab order. Other than that, Tab key presses go to elements in this order:

• The lowest positive integer, followed by the next lowest, and so on

• After that, the source order of elements in the document.

target

JavaScript 1.0+, JScript 1.0+

Nav2.0+, IE3.0+

Syntax

```
[var x =] HTMLAnchorElement.target [= targetWin]
```

The target property of instances of HTMLAnchorElement reflects the currently targeted window the browser will receive its response from the server in. Any valid HTML window name (see Chapter 15, "window," for a description of HTML window names versus JavaScript window names) you can use for this value.

You can also use "_blank" to indicate opening a new window every time, "_parent" for the parent window, "_top" for the topmost window in the parent window chain (see top and parent in Chapter 15), or "_self" to indicate it should load into the window of its document. ("_self" is the default setting.)

Internet Explorer 5.0+ introduces a new one called "_search", which will target the link for the browser's search sidebar.

text
JavaScript 1.2+

Nav4+

Syntax

```
[var x =] HTMLAnchorElement.text
```

The text property of HTMLAnchorElement objects reflects the text of the element's contents.

type
JavaScript 1.5

Nav6, IE6

Syntax

```
[var x =] HTMLAnchorElement.type [= mimeType]
```

The type property of HTMLAnchorElement objects is the mime-type of the file the src property references.

x
JavaScript 1.2+

Nav4

Syntax

```
var x = HTMLAnchorElement.x
```

The x property of `HTMLAnchorElement` objects corresponds to the distance from the left edge of the `this` element to the left edge of the document.

y

JavaScript 1.2+

Nav4

Syntax

```
var y = HTMLAnchorElement.y
```

The y property of `HTMLAnchorElement` objects corresponds to the distance from the top edge of the `this` element to the top edge of the document.

Methods

blur()

JavaScript 1.5, JScript 3.0+

Nav6, IE4+

Syntax

```
HTMLAnchorElement.blur()
```

The `blur()` method of `HTMLAnchorElement` objects forces the `this` element to lose focus. What this means is it tells the browser "I'm not important; let something else take center stage." The browser reacts by assigning focus specifically to no object.

focus()

JavaScript 1.5, JScript 3.0+

Nav6, IE4+

Syntax

```
HTMLAnchorElement.focus()
```

The focus() method of HTMLAnchorElement objects forces the this element to gain focus. What this means is it tells the browser "I'm important; make sure I alone react to the keyboard." The browser reacts by assigning focus specifically to that object.

Event Handlers

Netscape 4 supports the following event handlers for the HTMLAnchorElement object:

onclick

ondblclick

onkeydown

onkeypress

onkeyup

onmousedown

onmouseout

onmouseup

onmouseover

Internet Explorer supports the following event handlers for the HTMLAnchorElement interface:

onactivate	oncontextmenu	ondragstart
onafterupdate	oncontrolselect	ondrop
onbeforeactivate	oncopy	onerrorupdate
onbeforecopy	oncut	onfocus
onbeforecut	ondblclick	onfocusin
onbeforedeactivate	ondeactivate	onfocusout
onbeforeeditfocus	ondrag	onhelp
onbeforepaste	ondragend	onkeydown
onbeforeupdate	ondragenter	onkeypress
onblur	ondragleave	onkeyup
onclick	ondragover	onlosecapture

Description

onmousedown	onmousewheel	onresize
onmouseenter	onmove	onresizeend
onmouseleave	onmoveend	onresizestart
onmousemove	onmovestart	onselectstart
onmouseout	onpaste	ontimeerror
onmouseover	onpropertychange	
onmouseup	onreadystatechange	

HTMLBaseFontElement Interface/<basefont>...</basefont>

Browser/JavaScript Version	Created By
Nav4/JavaScript 1.2	<basefont />
IE4/JScript 3.0	<basefont />
IE5/JScript 5.0	<basefont />
IE5.5/JScript 5.5	<basefont />
Nav6/JavaScript 1.5	Not Implemented
IE6	<basefont />
DOM Level 1	document.createElement("basefont")

> **Note**
> Implemented in Nav1+ (HTML), IE3+ (HTML), Nav2+ (DOM), IE4+ (DOM)
>
> Descends from HTMLElement interface (Chapter 21)
>
> Inline Text Formatting Element
>
> Deprecated in HTML 4

Description

The <basefont /> element represents a base font style for the entire document. With the introduction of style sheets (Chapter 33, "Styling for HTML Elements"), the need for this element has gone away.

Netscape 6 and Mozilla.org have decided not to support this element. It is a part of HTML 4.0, albeit deprecated, so shame on them. You can read the debate over `<basefont />` at `http://bugzilla.mozilla.org/show_bug.cgi?id=3875`.

Netscape 4 does support this element, but it exposes no attributes as properties.

Properties

color
JScript 3.0+

IE4+

Syntax

`[var x =] HTMLBaseFontElement.color [= colorString]`

The `color` property of `HTMLBaseFontElement` objects represents the color of the standard font in the document.

face
JScript 1.0+

IE4+

Syntax

`[var x =] HTMLBaseFontElement.face [= fontName]`

The `face` property of `HTMLBaseFontElement` objects represents the name of the standard font in the document. (Verdana, for instance, is popular for Web design.)

size
JScript 3.0+

IE4+

Syntax

`[var x =] HTMLBaseFontElement.size [= sizeValue]`

The `size` property of `HTMLBaseFontElement` objects represents the size of the standard font in the document. Values without a + or - prefixed to them indicate an explicit font size. Values with a + or - prefixed to them indicate a change from the default value (which is equivalent to 4.)

Event Handlers

Internet Explorer supports the following event handlers for the `HTMLBaseFontElement` interface:

```
onlayoutcomplete
```

```
onmouseenter
```

```
onmouseleave
```

```
onreadystatechange
```

HTMLBRElement/

Browser/JavaScript Version	Created By
Nav4/JavaScript 1.2	` `
IE4/JScript 3.0	` `
IE5/JScript 5.0	` `
IE5.5/JScript 5.5	` `
Nav6/JavaScript 1.5	` `
IE6	` `
DOM Level 1	`document.createElement("br")`

> **Note**
> Implemented in Nav1+ (HTML), IE3+ (HTML), Nav6 (DOM), IE4+ (DOM)
>
> Descends from `HTMLElement` interface (Chapter 21)
>
> Inline Text Formatting Element

Description

The `<br />` element defines an intentional line break in the document. It breaks the text containing it into two different sections.

Properties

clear

JavaScript 1.5, JScript 1.0+

Nav6, IE4+

Syntax

```
[var x =] HTMLBRElement.clear [= clearString]
```

The clear property of HTMLBRElement objects denotes a continuance of text after an item on either the left or right side's bottom edge of the item. For instance, if there is an <img /> to the left and the line break occurs within the vertical dimensions of the image, the text will continue below that image with the correct clear setting.

Such line breaks apply to objects on the left if clear is set to "left" or "both". They apply to objects on the right if clear is set to "right" or "both".

The default value, "none", means a normal line break, ignoring other elements in the document entirely.

outerHTML

JScript 4.0+

IE4+

Syntax

```
var x = HTMLBRElement.outerHTML
```

The outerHTML property of HTMLBRElement retrieves or sets the HTML source code of the tag.

I do like the handiness of the outerHTML property for retrieving HTML source code at a glance, as a companion method to the W3C Document Object Model. (The DOM provides an object structure for the source code; outerHTML provides the corresponding source code.)

Event Handlers

Internet Explorer supports the following event handlers for the HTMLBRElement interface:

onlayoutcomplete

onlosecapture

onreadystatechange

HTMLDivElement/<div>...</div>

Browser/JavaScript Version	Created By
Nav4/JavaScript 1.2	<div>...</div>
IE4/JScript 3.0	<div>...</div>
IE5/JScript 5.0	<div>...</div>
IE5.5/JScript 5.5	<div>...</div>
Nav6/JavaScript 1.5	<div>...</div>
IE6	<div>...</div>
DOM Level 1	document.createElement("div")

> **Note**
> Implemented in Nav1+ (HTML), IE3+ (HTML), Nav2+ (DOM), IE4+ (DOM)
> Descends from HTMLElement interface (Chapter 21)
> Block Text Element

Description

The <div>...</div> element represents a generic block element for containing and styling other block and inline elements as a group. When you position this element absolutely, for instance, its contents go with it to the appropriate locations on the page.

> **Note**
> It is a common practice to absolutely position HTMLDivElement objects using styling and the CSS property "position:absolute;". If you do so (or if you set the position to "relative"), the Netscape 4 browser will attach the element to its document.layers array and give it all the properties of a Layer() object.It's not so common to do the same for other elements (such as <p>...</p>), but attaching such positioning has the same effect in Netscape 4.
> See Chapter 33, "Styling for HTML Elements," for more about positioning and hiding elements.

Properties

align

JavaScript 1.5, JScript 3.0+

Nav6, IE4+

Syntax

```
[var x=] HTMLDivElement.align [= alignString]
```

The `align` attribute of `HTMLDivElement` objects defines where the edges of the `this` object align with the HTML elements outside the `this` object.

innerHTML

JavaScript 1.5, JScript 3.0+

Nav6, IE4+

Syntax

```
[var x =] HTMLDivElement.innerHTML [= HTMLString]
```

The `innerHTML` property of `HTMLDivElement` interfaces retrieves or sets the HTML source code contained between, but not including, the starting and ending tags.

I personally recommend against using `innerHTML` to set the HTML inside a tag. I strongly recommend against using `innerHTML` to append to the contents of an HTML tag:

```
elem.innerHTML += "<div><p>Hello World</p></div>" // DO NOT DO THIS
```

I do like the handiness of the `innerHTML` property for retrieving HTML source code at a glance, as an alternative method to the W3C Document Object Model. (The DOM provides an object structure for the source code; `innerHTML` provides the corresponding source code.)

innerText

JScript 3.0+

IE4+

Properties

Syntax

```
var x = HTMLDivElement.innerText
```

The `innerText` property of `HTMLDivElement` objects retrieves or sets the text contained between, but not including, the starting and ending tags.

The `innerText` property can be useful, but the DOM Level 2 `Range` interface provides far more flexibility. See Chapter 34, "DOM-2 Range," for details on text ranges.

outerHTML

JScript 4.0+

IE4+

Syntax

```
var x = HTMLDivElement.outerHTML
```

The `outerHTML` property of `HTMLDivElement` objects retrieves or sets the HTML source code contained between, and including, the starting and ending tags.

I do like the handiness of the `outerHTML` property for retrieving HTML source code at a glance, as an alternative method to the W3C Document Object Model. (The DOM provides an object structure for the source code; `outerHTML` provides the corresponding source code.)

outerText

JScript 4.0+

IE4+

Syntax

```
var x = HTMLDivElement.outerText
```

The `outerText` property of `HTMLAnchorElement` objects is, as Listing 28.1 demonstrates, similar to the `this.innerText` property. The difference is in how you set the value; setting `outerText` replaces `this` with a new text node.

Event Handlers

When an `element` is positioned absolutely in Netscape and becomes part of the `document.layers` collection, it inherits event handlers from the `window` object (see Chapter 15).

Internet Explorer supports the following event handlers for the `HTMLDivElement` interface:

onactivate	ondragenter	onmousemove
onafterupdate	ondragleave	onmouseout
onbeforeactivate	ondragover	onmouseover
onbeforecopy	ondragstart	onmouseup
onbeforecut	ondrop	onmousewheel
onbeforedeactivate	onerrorupdate	onmove
onbeforeeditfocus	onfilterchange	onmoveend
onbeforepaste	onfocus	onmovestart
onbeforeupdate	onfocusin	onpaste
onblur	onfocusout	onpropertychange
onclick	onhelp	onreadystatechange
oncontextmenu	onkeydown	onresize
oncontrolselect	onkeypress	onresizeend
oncopy	onkeyup	onresizestart
oncut	onlayoutcomplete	onscroll
ondblclick	onlosecapture	onselectstart
ondeactivate	onmousedown	ontimeerror
ondrag	onmouseenter	
ondragend	onmouseleave	

HTMLFontElement Interface/<font>...</font>

Browser/JavaScript Version	Created By
Nav4/JavaScript 1.2	<font>...</font>
IE4/JScript 3.0	<font>...</font>
IE5/JScript 5.0	<font>...</font>
IE5.5/JScript 5.5	<font>...</font>
Nav6/JavaScript 1.5	<font>...</font>

IE6
DOM Level 1

`<font>...</font>`
`document.createElement("font")`

> **Note**
>
> Implemented in Nav1+ (HTML), IE3+ (HTML), Nav6 (DOM), IE4+ (DOM)
>
> Descends from `HTMLElement` interface (Chapter 21)
>
> Inline Text Element
>
> Deprecated in HTML 4

Description

The `<font>...</font>` element represents a specific font style to apply to its contents. With the introduction of style sheets (Chapter 33, "Styling for HTML Elements"), the need for this element has gone away.

Properties

color

JavaScript 1.5, JScript 1.0+

Nav6, IE3+

Syntax

`[var x =] HTMLFontElement.color [= colorString]`

The `color` property of `HTMLFontElement` objects represents the color of the specific font in the document.

face

JavaScript 1.5, JScript 3.0+

Nav6, IE4+

Syntax

`[var x =] HTMLFontElement.face [= fontName]`

The `face` property of `HTMLFontElement` objects is a comma-separated list of the specific fonts the document requests, in order, for the `this` element's contents. (Verdana, for instance, is popular for Web design.) An example might be:

```
<font face="Verdana, Times New Roman, Courier New">Hello World</font>
```

innerHTML

JavaScript 1.5, JScript 5.0+

Nav6, IE4+

Syntax

```
[var x =] HTMLFontElement.innerHTML [= HTMLString]
```

The `innerHTML` property of `HTMLFontElement` objects retrieves or sets the HTML source code contained between, but not including, the starting and ending tags.

I personally recommend against using `innerHTML` to set the HTML inside a tag. I strongly recommend against using `innerHTML` to append to the contents of an HTML tag:

```
elem.innerHTML += "<div><p>Hello World</p></div>" // DO NOT DO THIS
```

I do like the handiness of the `innerHTML` property for retrieving HTML source code at a glance, as an alternative method to the W3C Document Object Model. (The DOM provides an object structure for the source code; `innerHTML` provides the corresponding source code.)

innerText

JScript 5.0+

IE4+

Syntax

```
var x = HTMLFontElement.innerText
```

The `innerText` property of `HTMLFontElement` objects retrieves or sets the text contained between, but not including, the starting and ending tags.

The `innerText` property can be useful, but the DOM Level 2 `Range` interface provides far more flexibility. See Chapter 34, "DOM-2 Range," for details on text ranges.

outerHTML

JScript 4.0+

IE4+

Syntax

```
var x = HTMLFontElement.outerHTML
```

The outerHTML property of HTMLFontElement objects retrieves or sets the HTML
source code contained between, and including, the starting and ending tags.

I do like the handiness of the outerHTML property for retrieving HTML source code
at a glance, as an alternative method to the W3C Document Object Model. (The
DOM provides an object structure for the source code; outerHTML provides the
corresponding source code.)

outerText

JScript 4.0+

IE4+

Syntax

```
var x = HTMLFontElement.outerText
```

The outerText property of HTMLFontElement objects is, as Listing 28.1 demonstrates,
similar to the this.innerText property. The difference is in how you set the value;
setting outerText replaces this with a new text node.

size

JavaScript 1.5, JScript 3.0+

Nav6, IE4+

Syntax

```
[var x =] HTMLFontElement.size [= sizeValue]
```

The size property of HTMLFontElement objects represents the size of the specific font
in the document. Values without a + or - prefixed to them indicate an explicit font size.
Values with a + or - prefixed to them indicate a change from the default value (which
is equivalent to 4.)

Event Handlers

Internet Explorer supports the following event handlers for the `HTMLFontElement` interface:

onactivate	ondragleave	onmousemove
onbeforeactivate	ondragover	onmouseout
onbeforecut	ondragstart	onmouseover
onbeforedeactivate	ondrop	onmouseup
onbeforeeditfocus	onfocus	onmousewheel
onbeforepaste	onfocusin	onmove
onblur	onfocusout	onmoveend
onclick	onhelp	onmovestart
oncontextmenu	onkeydown	onpaste
oncontrolselect	onkeypress	onpropertychange
oncut	onkeyup	onreadystatechange
ondblclick	onlayoutcomplete	onresizeend
ondeactivate	onlosecapture	onresizestart
ondrag	onmousedown	onselectstart
ondragend	onmouseenter	ontimeerror
ondragenter	onmouseleave	

HTMLHeadingElement Interface / <h*N*>...</h*N*>

Browser/JavaScript Version	Created By
Nav4/JavaScript 1.2 <h2>...</h2> <h3>...</h3> <h4>...</h4> <h5>...</h5> <h6>...</h6>	<h1>...</h1>

IE4/JScript 3.0	`<h1>...</h1>`
	`<h2>...</h2>`
	`<h3>...</h3>`
	`<h4>...</h4>`
	`<h5>...</h5>`
	`<h6>...</h6>`
IE5/JScript 5.0	`<h1>...</h1>`
	`<h2>...</h2>`
	`<h3>...</h3>`
	`<h4>...</h4>`
	`<h5>...</h5>`
	`<h6>...</h6>`
IE5.5/JScript 5.5	`<h1>...</h1>`
	`<h2>...</h2>`
	`<h3>...</h3>`
	`<h4>...</h4>`
	`<h5>...</h5>`
	`<h6>...</h6>`
Nav6/JavaScript 1.5	`<h1>...</h1>`
	`<h2>...</h2>`
	`<h3>...</h3>`
	`<h4>...</h4>`
	`<h5>...</h5>`
	`<h6>...</h6>`
IE6	`<h1>...</h1>`
	`<h2>...</h2>`
	`<h3>...</h3>`
	`<h4>...</h4>`
	`<h5>...</h5>`
	`<h6>...</h6>`
DOM Level 1	`document.createElement("h1")`
	`document.createElement("h2")`
	`document.createElement("h3")`
	`document.createElement("h4")`
	`document.createElement("h5")`
	`document.createElement("h6")`

Note

Implemented in Nav1+ (HTML), IE3+ (HTML), Nav6 (DOM), IE4+ (DOM)

Descends from `HTMLElement` interface (Chapter 21)

Block Text Formatting Element

Description

The `HTMLHeadingElement` interface corresponds to six nearly identical elements, each of which indicates the section following as a level of certain relative importance. <h1>...</h1> elements usually correspond to the document title, whereas <h2>...</h2> elements are titles for major sections of the document, <h3>...</h3> elements are titles for normal sections of the document, <h4>...</h4> elements are titles for minor sections of the document, and so on. The concept is for each level of element to appear only within the contents of the next higher element's sections; <h2>...</h2>-level sections should only appear inside the contents of <h1>...</h1>-level sections, for example:

```
<html>
<head><title>Document Title</title>
</head>
<body>
<h1>Document Title</h1>
<p>This document describes very little.</p>
<h2>Colors</h2>
<p>There are three primary colors in the world:  red, green, and blue.</p>
<h3>Red</h3>
<p>Red you can designate in hexadecimal RGB as #ff0000.</p>
<h3>Green</h3>
<p>Green you can designate in hexadecimal RGB as #00ff00.  (However, this is
often too bright, so you'll see #007f00 for green and #00ff00 for a very
bright green.)</p>
<h3>Blue</h3>
<p>Blue you can designate in hexadecimal RGB as #0000ff.</p>
<h2>Shapes</h2>
The FooBarBaz organization will define shapes in a later revision of this
document.
</body>
</html>
```

> **Note**
> The Amaya editor has a very nice feature when you use headings like this. When you go to the Special menu and check Section Numbering, it automatically generates section headings (1, 2, 3, and so on for h2, 1.1, 1.2, 1.3, 2.1, and so on for h3 under h2, and so on.)

Properties

align

JavaScript 1.5, JScript 3.0+

Nav6, IE4+

Deprecated in HTML 4

Syntax

```
[var x = ] HTMLHeadingElement.align [= alignString]
```

The `align` attribute of `HTMLHeadingElement` objects defines where the `this` element's contents align horizontally in comparison with the body text. Normally, text aligns to the left edge of the document. There are four permissible values: `"left"`, `"center"` (for centered text), `"right"` (for text on the right edge), and `"justify"` (against both the left and right edges as much as possible).

innerHTML

JavaScript 1.5, JScript 5.0+

Nav6, IE5+

Syntax

```
[var x =] HTMLHeadingElement.innerHTML [= HTMLString]
```

The `innerHTML` property of `HTMLHeadingElement` objects retrieves or sets the HTML source code contained between, but not including, the starting and ending tags.

I personally recommend against using `innerHTML` to set the HTML inside a tag. I strongly recommend against using `innerHTML` to append to the contents of an HTML tag:

```
elem.innerHTML += "<div><p>Hello World</p></div>" // DO NOT DO THIS
```

I do like the handiness of the `innerHTML` property for retrieving HTML source code at a glance, as an alternative method to the W3C Document Object Model. (The DOM provides an object structure for the source code; `innerHTML` provides the corresponding source code.)

innerText

JScript 5.0+

IE5+

Syntax

```
var x = HTMLHeadingElement.innerText
```

The `innerText` property of `HTMLHeadingElement` objects retrieves or sets the text contained between, but not including, the starting and ending tags.

The `innerText` property can be useful, but the DOM Level 2 `Range` interface provides far more flexibility. See Chapter 34, "DOM-2 Range," for details on text ranges.

outerHTML

JScript 4.0+

IE4+

Syntax

```
var x = HTMLHeadingElement.outerHTML
```

The `outerHTML` property of `HTMLHeadingElement` objects retrieves or sets the HTML source code contained between, and including, the starting and ending tags.

I do like the handiness of the `outerHTML` property for retrieving HTML source code at a glance, as an alternative method to the W3C Document Object Model. (The DOM provides an object structure for the source code; `outerHTML` provides the corresponding source code.)

outerText

JScript 4.0+

IE4+

Syntax

```
var x = HTMLHeadingElement.outerText
```

The `outerText` property of `HTMLHeadingElement` objects is, as Listing 28.1 demonstrates, similar to the `this.innerText` property. The difference is in how you set the value; setting `outerText` replaces `this` with a new text node.

Methods

The `HTMLHeadingElement` interface provides no methods beyond those the `HTMLElement` interface defines.

Event Handlers

Internet Explorer supports the following event handlers for the `HTMLHeadingElement` interface:

onactivate	ondragenter	onmousemove
onbeforeactivate	ondragleave	onmouseout
onbeforecopy	ondragover	onmouseover
onbeforecut	ondragstart	onmouseup
onbeforedeactivate	ondrop	onmousewheel
onbeforeeditfocus	onfocus	onmove
onbeforepaste	onfocusin	onmoveend
onblur	onfocusout	onmovestart
onclick	onhelp	onpaste
oncontextmenu	onkeydown	onpropertychange
oncontrolselect	onkeypress	onreadystatechange
oncopy	onkeyup	onresize
oncut	onlosecapture	onresizeend
ondblclick	onmousedown	onresizestart
ondeactivate	onmouseenter	onselectstart
ondrag	onmouseleave	ontimeerror
ondragend		

HTMLHRElement Interface / <hr />

Browser/JavaScript Version	Created By
Nav4/JavaScript 1.2	<hr />
IE4/JScript 3.0	<hr />
IE5/JScript 5.0	<hr />
IE5.5/JScript 5.5	<hr />
Nav6/JavaScript 1.5	<hr />
IE6	<hr />
DOM Level 1	document.createElement("hr")

> **Note**
>
> Implemented in Nav1+ (HTML), IE3+ (HTML), Nav6(DOM), IE4+ (DOM)
>
> Descends from HTMLElement interface (Chapter 21)
>
> Block Text Formatting Element

Description

The <hr /> element defines a horizontal rule in the document—a horizontal line running the full width of the window or parent element. It informally defines sections of the document.

Prior to HTML 4, this element had attributes to define its style—the width of the rule, the type of lines to draw, the alignment, and so on. Once again, styling has deprecated all but the element itself.

Properties

align

JavaScript 1.5, JScript 3.0+

Nav6, IE4+

Deprecated in HTML 4

Syntax

[var x =] HTMLHRElement.align *[= alignString]*

The align attribute of HTMLHRElement objects defines where the this element aligns horizontally in comparison with the body text. This will not make sense unless you change the width property away from "100%", its default.

Normally, this element aligns to the horizontal center of the document. There are four permissible values: "left", "center" (for centered text), "right" (for text on the right edge), and "justify" (against both the left and right edges as much as possible).

color

JScript 1.0+

IE4+

Syntax

[var x =] HTMLHRElement.color *[= colorString]*

The color property of HTMLHRElement objects represents the color of the this object in the document.

noShade

JScript 1.0+

Nav6, IE4+

Deprecated in HTML 4

Syntax

[var x =] HTMLHRElement.noShade *[= boolValue]*

The noShade attribute of HTMLHRElement objects indicates to the browser it must render the this element in a single color (as opposed to two colors, which the browser uses to create a shading effect).

outerHTML

JScript4.0+

IE4+

Syntax

```
var x = HTMLHRElement.outerHTML
```

The `outerHTML` property of `HTMLHRElement` objects retrieves or sets the HTML source code contained between, and including, the starting and ending tags.

I do like the handiness of the `outerHTML` property for retrieving HTML source code at a glance, as an alternative method to the W3C Document Object Model. (The DOM provides an object structure for the source code; `outerHTML` provides the corresponding source code.)

outerText

JScript 4.0+

IE4+

Syntax

```
var x = HTMLHRElement.outerText
```

The `outerText` property of `HTMLHRElement` objects is, as Listing 28.1 demonstrates, similar to the `this.innerText` property. The difference is in how you set the value; setting `outerText` replaces `this` with a new text node.

size

JavaScript 1.5, JScript 3.0+

Nav6, IE4+

Deprecated in HTML 4

Syntax

```
[var x = ] HTMLHRElement.size [= heightPixels]
```

The `size` attribute of `HTMLHRElement` objects defines, in terms of pixels, the vertical size dimension of the `this` element.

width

JavaScript 1.5, JScript 5.0+

Nav6, IE5+

Deprecated in HTML 4

Syntax

```
[var x = ] HTMLHRElement.width [= widthString]
```

The width attribute of HTMLHRElement objects defines the width of the this element, in terms of pixels or percentages of the viewable window.

Event Handlers

Internet Explorer supports the following event handlers for the HTMLHRElement interface:

onactivate	ondragleave	onmousemove
onbeforeactivate	ondragover	onmouseout
onbeforecut	ondragstart	onmouseover
onbeforedeactivate	ondrop	onmouseup
onbeforepaste	onfocus	onmousewheel
onblur	onfocusin	onmove
onclick	onfocusout	onmoveend
oncontextmenu	onhelp	onmovestart
oncontrolselect	onkeydown	onpaste
oncopy	onkeypress	onpropertychange
oncut	onkeyup	onreadystatechange
ondblclick	onlayoutcomplete	onresize
ondeactivate	onlosecapture	onresizeend
ondrag	onmousedown	onresizestart
ondragend	onmouseenter	onselectstart
ondragenter	onmouseleave	ontimeerror

Layer()/<layer>...</layer> / <ilayer>...</ilayer>

Browser/JavaScript Version	Created By
Nav4/JavaScript 1.2	`<layer>...</layer>`
	`<ilayer>...</ilayer>`
	var x = new Layer(*width*)
IE4/JScript 3.0	Not Implemented
IE5/JScript 5.0	Not Implemented
IE5.5/JScript 5.5	Not Implemented
Nav6/JavaScript 1.5	Not Implemented
IE6	Not Implemented
DOM Level 1	Not Implemented

> **Note**
> Implemented in Nav4 (HTML/DOM)
>
> Block Text Element
>
> Not part of HTML 4

Description

Netscape 4's `<layer>...</layer>` element is a tag specifically created to allow for positioned documents and document fragments, before the HTML 4.0 standard accepted the `<iframe />` element. Listing 28.2 gives a suggested format for rendering layers in Netscape 4, Netscape 6, and Internet Explorer browsers.

Netscape 4's `<ilayer>...</ilayer>` element is a tag specifically created for inline positioned documents and document fragments, which force content to flow around them.

There are a number of tutorials around for how to handle layers in Netscape 4, and how to handle their equivalents in other browsers. The best tutorial I've seen to date comes from Dan Steinman at `http://www.dansteinman.com/dynduo`. Admittedly, if you don't know about his `DynLayer()` objects and his DynAPI project, you may get lost in these pages for a bit. (He also has a link on his page to DynAPI2, an update of his popular project for Netscape 6.)

> **Note**
>
> Any element you use absolute or relative positioning on and Netscape 4 recognizes becomes a member of the Netscape 4 `document.layers` collection, and inherits all the properties and methods of `Layer()` objects automatically.
>
> Netscape 4 does not recognize the `<iframe />` element, which is why Listing 28.2 is effective. Other browsers don't recognize `<layer />`, so it works out. Except for the DOM, of course.
>
> You activate absolute positioning with CSS, via the `"position:absolute;"` property.
>
> Also, remember to treat each layer as its own window, and its contents (if it is not a `<layer />` element) as an independent document. It is a bad idea, for example, to place form inputs inside a layer if the inputs associate directly with a form element outside the layer. (Of course, you can use JavaScript to retrieve values before submitting the form.)

`Layer()` objects created by the `<layer>`...`</layer>` element are considered `window` objects, and inherit properties appropriately. See Chapter 15, "window," for details.

Properties

above

JavaScript 1.2–1.3

Nav4

Syntax

```
var x = LayerObj.above
```

The `above` property of `Layer()` objects refers to the layer that has the next highest z-index property than this one in the document, or `this.parentLayer` if there is none.

background

JavaScript 1.2–1.3

Nav4

Syntax

```
[var x =] LayerObj.background [= imageObject]
```

The `background` property of `Layer()` objects is an `Image()` object (see Chapter 30, "Image Elements") which the `this` object uses as a background for its corresponding layer.

below

JavaScript 1.2–1.3

Nav4

Syntax

```
var x = LayerObj.below
```

The `below` property of `Layer()` objects refers to the layer that has the next lowest `z-index` property than this one in the document, or `null` if there is none.

bgColor

JavaScript 1.2–1.3

Nav4

Syntax

```
var x = LayerObj.bgColor
```

The `bgColor` property of `Layer()` objects refers to the background color of the layer. You can specify it either by name (`"cyan"`, `"red"`, `"white"`, `"navy"`, and so on) or by hexadecimal (`"#00FFFF"`). Hexadecimal is the preferred style, as color names in browsers may not be universally recognized.

clip

JavaScript 1.2–1.3

Nav4

The `clip` property of `Layer()` objects is a holding object for the viewing rectangle properties of the `this` object. You do not generally refer to this property directly, but to its properties.

bottom

JavaScript 1.2–1.3

Nav4

Syntax

```
[var x =] LayerObj.clip.bottom [= pixelNumber]
```

The `bottom` property of the `clip` object designates the bottom edge of the clipping area as a number value in pixels.

height

JavaScript 1.2–1.3

Nav4

Syntax

```
[var y =] LayerObj.clip.height [= pixelValue]
```

The `height` property of the `clip` object designates the height of the clipping area, as a number value in pixels.

left

JavaScript 1.2–1.3

Nav4

Syntax

```
[var x =] LayerObj.clip.left [= pixelString]
```

The `left` property of the `clip` object designates the left edge of the clipping area, as a number value in pixels.

right

JavaScript 1.2–1.3

Nav4

Syntax

```
[var x =] LayerObj.clip.right [= pixelValue]
```

The `right` property of the `clip` object designates the right edge of the clipping area, as a number value in pixels.

top
JavaScript 1.2–1.3

Nav4

Syntax

```
[var x =] LayerObj.clip.top [= pixelString]
```

The `top` property of the `clip` object designates the top edge of the clipping area, as a number value in pixels.

width
JavaScript 1.2–1.3

Nav4

Syntax

```
[var x =] LayerObj.clip.width [= pixelString]
```

The `width` property of the `clip` object designates the width of the clipping area, as a number value in pixels.

id, name
JavaScript 1.2–1.3

Nav4

Syntax

```
[var x =] LayerObj.id [= layerId]
[var x =] LayerObj.name [= layerId]
```

The `id` and `name` properties of `Layer()` objects reflect the `id` attribute of the `this` object.

left, x

JavaScript 1.2–1.3

Nav4

Syntax

```
[var x =] LayerObj.left [= pixelString]
[var x =] LayerObj.x [= pixelString]
```

The `left` property of `Layer()` objects reflects the distance from the left edge of the `this` object to the left edge of the `this.parentLayer` object. The `x` property references the same value.

pageX

JavaScript 1.2–1.3

Nav4

Syntax

```
[var x =] LayerObj.pageX [= pixelString]
```

The `pageX` property of `Layer()` objects reflects the distance from the left edge of the `this` object to the left edge of the window's canvas (the space the document takes up, including offscreen scrolling).

pageY

JavaScript 1.2–1.3

Nav4

Syntax

```
[var x =] LayerObj.pageY [= pixelString]
```

The `pageY` property of `Layer()` objects reflects the distance from the top edge of the `this` object to the top edge of the window's canvas (the space the document takes up, including offscreen scrolling).

parentLayer

JavaScript 1.2–1.3

Nav4

Syntax

```
[var x =] LayerObj.parentLayer [= windowObj]
```

The `parentLayer` property of `Layer()` objects reflects the `Layer()` or `window` object which contains the `this` object. In essence,

```
alert(document.layers[0].parentLayer == window) // returns true
```

siblingAbove

JavaScript 1.2–1.3

Nav4

Syntax

```
var x = LayerObj.siblingAbove
```

The `siblingAbove` property of `Layer()` objects refers to the layer that has the next higher `z-index` property in `this.parentLayer`, or `this.parentLayer` if there is none.

siblingBelow

JavaScript 1.2–1.3

Nav4

Syntax

```
var x = LayerObj.siblingBelow
```

The `siblingBelow` property of `Layer()` objects refers to the layer that has the next lower `z-index` property in `this.parentLayer`, or `null` if there is none.

src

JavaScript 1.2–1.3

Nav4

Syntax

```
[var x =] LayerObj.src [= URIString]
```

The src property of Layer() objects reflects the location of the layer's contents as a URI. By changing this property, you can affect which document renders in the this object.

top, y

JavaScript 1.2–1.3

Nav4

Syntax

```
[var y =] LayerObj.top [= pixelString]
[var y =] LayerObj.y [= pixelString]
```

The top property of Layer() objects reflects the distance from the top edge of the this object to the top edge of the this.parentLayer object. The y property references the same value.

visibility

JavaScript 1.2–1.3

Nav4

Syntax

```
[var x =] LayerObj.visibility [= visibilityString]
```

The visibility property of Layer() objects, when set to "show", makes the this object visible to the user. When set to "hide", the user cannot see the this object.

When you set the visibility to "inherit", the layer inherits the visibility property of its parent layer.

window

JavaScript 1.2–1.3

Nav4

Syntax

```
var x = LayerObj.window
```

The `window` property of `Layer()` objects refers to the `this` object:

```
alert(document.layers[0].window == document.layers[0]) // returns true
```

zIndex

JavaScript 1.2–1.3

Nav4

Syntax

```
[var z =] LayerObj.zIndex [= zIndex]
```

The `zIndex` property of `Layer()` objects identifies the layer's position above or below other elements in the third dimension (toward or away from the user), relative to other layers in the `this.parentLayer` collection.

Methods

captureEvents()

JavaScript 1.2–1.3

Nav4

Syntax

```
LayerObj.captureEvents(eventName0 [|| eventName1 ...])
```

The `captureEvents()` method of `Layer()` objects intercepts all events of the types given as arguments. (Typically, these events are referred to as `Event.EVENTNAME`, where the event name is capitalized.) Using this method, you catch the events thrown or fired before the object they apply to catches them. See Chapter 32, "DOM-2 Events and Event Handlers," for details.

handleEvent()

JavaScript 1.2–1.3

Nav4

Syntax

```
LayerObj.handleEvent(eventName)
```

The handleEvent() method of Layer() objects assigns all events of the type given as the first argument to the this object. (Typically, these events are referred to as Event.*EVENTNAME*, where the event name is capitalized.) Using this method, you force the events thrown or fired to report to a particular object's event handler. See Chapter 32, "DOM-2 Events and Event Handlers," for details.

load()

JavaScript 1.2–1.3

Nav4

Syntax

`LayerObj.load(fileURI, pixelWidth)`

The load() method of Layer() objects loads the first argument, a file URI string, into the this object, assuming a width set in the second argument, a pixel width number.

moveAbove()

JavaScript 1.2–1.3

Nav4

Syntax

`LayerObj.moveAbove(otherLayerObj)`

The moveAbove() method of Layer() objects moves the this object to become a child layer of the first argument, itself a Layer() object. The this object is just above the first argument's layer.

moveBelow()

JavaScript 1.2–1.3

Nav4

Syntax

`LayerObj.moveBelow(otherLayerObj)`

The moveBelow() method of Layer() objects moves the this object to become a child layer of the first argument, itself a Layer() object. The this object is just below the first argument's layer.

moveBy()

JavaScript 1.2–1.3

Nav4

Syntax

`LayerObj.moveBy(rightPixels, downPixels)`

The `moveBy()` method of `Layer()` objects accepts two arguments. The first tells how many pixels the `this` object is to move to the right. The second tells how many pixels the `this` object is to move down. (Negative values are acceptable, telling how far to move to the left and up, respectively.)

moveTo()

JavaScript 1.2–1.3

Nav4

Syntax

`LayerObj.moveTo(horizPixels, vertPixels)`

The `moveTo()` method of `Layer()` objects accepts two arguments. The first tells how far from the left edge of `this.parentLayer` the layer must be. The second tells how far from the top edge of `this.parentLayer` the layer must be.

moveToAbsolute()

JavaScript 1.2–1.3

Nav4

Syntax

`LayerObj.moveToAbsolute(horizPixels, vertPixels)`

The `moveToAbsolute()` method of `Layer()` objects accepts two arguments. The first tells how far from the left edge of the `window` object the layer must be. The second tells how far from the top edge of the `window` object the layer must be.

resizeBy()

JavaScript 1.2–1.3

Nav4

Syntax

LayerObj.resizeBy(*rightPixels, downPixels*)

The resizeBy() method of Layer() objects resizes the visible "clipping" of the this object (see clip earlier in this section for details) by moving the bottom-right corner of the this object. The corner moves to the right by the number of pixels in the first argument. It moves down by the number of pixels in the second argument.

resizeTo()

JavaScript 1.2–1.3

Nav4

Syntax

LyaerObj.resizeTo(*horizPixels, vertPixels*)

The resizeTo() method of Layer() objects resizes the visible "clipping" of the this object (see clip earlier in this section for details) by moving the bottom-right corner of the this object. The corner adjusts the outer width to match the number of pixels in the first argument. It adjusts the outer height to match the number of pixels in the second argument.

routeEvent()

JavaScript 1.2–1.3

Nav4

Syntax

LayerObj.routeEvent(*eventObj*)

The routeEvent() method of Layer() objects sends the event specified in the argument to the next event handler in its chain. (Typically, these events are referred to as Event.*EVENTNAME*, where the event name is capitalized.) Using this method, you cause the events thrown or fired to proceed to the next scheduled event handler for that event. See Chapter 32, "DOM-2 Events and Event Handlers," for details.

Event Handlers

Netscape 4 exposes the following event handlers for `Layer()` objects:

`onblur`

`onfocus`

`onload`

`onmouseout`

`onmouseover`

<marquee>...</marquee>

Browser/JavaScript Version	Created By
Nav4/JavaScript 1.2	Not Implemented
IE4/JScript 3.0	`<marquee>...</marquee>`
IE5/JScript 5.0	`<marquee>...</marquee>`
IE5.5/JScript 5.5	`<marquee>...</marquee>`
Nav6/JavaScript 1.5	Not Implemented
IE6	`<marquee>...</marquee>`
DOM Level 1	Not Implemented

Note

Implemented in IE3+ (HTML), IE4+ (DOM)

Descends from `HTMLElement` interface (Chapter 21)

Block Text Element

Description

The marquee element of Internet Explorer creates, for all intents and purposes, a scrolling `HTMLDivElement`. Listing 28.4 demonstrates a partial equivalent to this element using standard XHTML and DOM.

Properties

---

behavior

JScript 3.0+

IE4+

Syntax

`[var x =] marqueeObj.behavior [= behaviorString]`

The `behavior` property of `<marquee>...</marquee>` elements expresses how the marquee's contents move. A value of `"slide"` indicates the marquee should follow its direction property and stop on contact with the edge. A value of "alternate" indicates it should bounce upon contact with its walls. The default, `"scroll"`, indicates it should follow its direction property and restart when its content disappears entirely.

---

bgColor

JScript 3.0+

IE4+

Syntax

`[var x =] marqueeObj.bgColor [= color]`

The `bgColor` property of `<marquee>...</marquee>` elements refers to the background color of the marquee. You can specify it either by name (`"cyan"`, `"red"`, `"white"`, `"navy"`, and so on) or by hexadecimal (`"#00FFFF"`). Hexadecimal is the preferred style, as color names in browsers may not be universally recognized.

---

direction

JScript 3.0+

IE4+

Syntax

`[var x =] marqueeObj.direction [= dirString]`

The direction property of <marquee>...</marquee> elements tells the browser which direction to send the marquee, "up", "down", the default "left", or "right", starting from the opposite edge.

height

JScript 3.0+

IE4+

Syntax

```
[var y =] marqueeObj.height [= heightPixels]
```

The height property of <marquee>...</marquee> elements reflects the height of the marquee as rendered on the screen in pixels.

hspace

JScript 1.0+

IE3+

Syntax

```
[var x =] marqueeObj.hspace [= hSpacePixels]
```

The hspace property of <marquee>...</marquee> elements reflects the horizontal whitespace margins of the marquee as rendered on the screen in pixels.

innerHTML

JScript 3.0+

IE4+

Syntax

```
[var x =] marqueeObj.innerHTML [= HTMLString]
```

The innerHTML property of <marquee>...</marquee> elements retrieves or sets the HTML source code contained between, but not including, the starting and ending tags.

I personally recommend against using `innerHTML` to set the HTML inside a tag. I strongly recommend against using `innerHTML` to append to the contents of an HTML tag:

```
elem.innerHTML += "<div><p>Hello World</p></div>" // DO NOT DO THIS
```

I do like the handiness of the `innerHTML` property for retrieving HTML source code at a glance, as an alternative method to the W3C Document Object Model. (The DOM provides an object structure for the source code; `innerHTML` provides the corresponding source code.)

innerText

JScript 3.0+

IE4+

Syntax

```
var x = marqueeObj.innerText
```

The `innerText` property of `<marquee>...</marquee>` elements retrieves or sets the text contained between, but not including, the starting and ending tags.

The `innerText` property can be useful, but the DOM Level 2 `Range` interface provides far more flexibility. See Chapter 34, "DOM-2 Range," for details on text ranges.

loop

JScript 3.0+

IE4+

Syntax

```
[var x =] marqueeObj.loop [= loopNum]
```

The `loop` property of `<marquee>...</marquee>` elements, when set to a positive integer, determines the number of times the marquee effect shall repeat. When set to `0`, `-1`, or `""`, the `this` element will repeat eternally (or until you unload the page).

outerHTML

JScript 3.0+

IE4+

Syntax

```
var x = marqueeObj.outerHTML
```

The outerHTML property of <marquee>...</marquee> elements retrieves or sets the HTML source code contained between, and including, the starting and ending tags.

I do like the handiness of the outerHTML property for retrieving HTML source code at a glance, as an alternative method to the W3C Document Object Model. (The DOM provides an object structure for the source code; outerHTML provides the corresponding source code.)

outerText

JScript 3.0+

IE4+

Syntax

```
var x = marqueeObj.outerText
```

The outerText property of <marquee>...</marquee> elements is, as Listing 28.1 demonstrates, similar to the this.innerText property. The difference is in how you set the value; setting outerText replaces this with a new text node.

scrollAmount

JScript 3.0+

IE4+

Syntax

```
[var x =] marqueeObj.scrollAmount [= pixelNumber]
```

The scrollAmount property of <marquee>...</marquee> elements sets the number of pixels per iteration the marquee moves.

scrollDelay

JScript 3.0+

IE4+

Syntax

```
[var x =] marqueeObj.scrollDelay [= mSec]
```

The `scrollDelay` property of `<marquee>...</marquee>` elements sets the delay between iterations of the marquee.

truespeed

JScript 3.0+

IE4+

Syntax

```
[var x =] marqueeObj.truespeed [= boolValue]
```

The `truespeed` property of `<marquee>...</marquee>` elements, when set to `true`, tells the browser to render effects close to realtime, per the default `scrollDelay` and `scrollAmount` values.

Personally, I couldn't detect any difference between having it on and having it off.

vspace

JScript 3.0+

IE4+

Syntax

```
[var y =] marqueeObj.vspace [= heightPixels]
```

The `vspace` property of `<marquee>...</marquee>` elements reflects the vertical whitespace margins of the image as rendered on the screen in pixels.

width

JScript 3.0+

IE4+

Syntax

```
[var x =] marqueeObj.width [= widthPixels]
```

The width property of <marquee>...</marquee> elements reflects the width of the image as rendered on the screen in pixels.

Methods

start()

JScript 3.0+

IE4+

Syntax

```
marqueeObj.start()
```

The start() method of <marquee>...</marquee> elements restarts the this element's scrolling, but does not call the onstart event handler.

stop()
JScript 3.0+

IE4+

Syntax

```
marqueeObj.stop()
```

The stop() method of <marquee>...</marquee> elements ends the this element's scrolling.

Event Handlers

onactivate	onbeforedeactivate	onblur
onafterupdate	onbeforeeditfocus	onbounce
onbeforeactivate	onbeforepaste	onclick
onbeforecut	onbeforeupdate	oncontextmenu

oncontrolselect	onfocusin	onmove
oncut	onfocusout	onmoveend
ondblclick	onhelp	onmovestart
ondeactivate	onkeydown	onpaste
ondrag	onkeypress	onpropertychange
ondragend	onkeyup	onreadystatechange
ondragenter	onlosecapture	onresize
ondragleave	onmousedown	onresizeend
ondragover	onmouseenter	onresizestart
ondragstart	onmouseleave	onscroll
ondrop	onmousemove	onselectstart
onerrorupdate	onmouseout	onstart
onfilterchange	onmouseover	ontimeerror
onfinish	onmouseup	
onfocus	onmousewheel	

HTMLModElement Interface/<ins>...</ins>/<del>...</del>

Browser/JavaScript Version	Created By
Nav4/JavaScript 1.2	<del>...</del>
	<ins>...</ins>
IE4/JScript 3.0	<del>...</del>
	<ins>...</ins>
IE5/JScript 5.0	<del>...</del>
	<ins>...</ins>
IE5.5/JScript 5.5	<del>...</del>
	<ins>...</ins>
Nav6/JavaScript 1.5	<del>...</del>
	<ins>...</ins>

IE6	`<del>...</del>`
	`<ins>...</ins>`
DOM Level 1	`document.createElement("del")`
	`document.createElement("ins")`

> **Note**
> Implemented in Nav6 (HTML/DOM), IE4+ (HTML/DOM)
>
> Descends from `HTMLElement` interface (Chapter 21)
>
> Inline Text Formatting Elements or Block Text Formatting Elements (but not both)

Description

The `<ins>...</ins>` and `<del>...</del>` elements define areas of the document that an editor has modified from the original. This would come in very handy for chapter writing and editing, but HTML is not the standard format for editing chapters for Sams Publishing. (There are some good reasons for that; HTML doesn't offer all the simple flexibility.)

Specifically, as you might guess, `<ins>...</ins>` designates a section of the document an editor adds to the document. Likewise, `<del>...</del>` designates a section of the document an editor has marked for removal.

(Personally, I think it unfortunate HTML did not include a `<stet>...</stet>` element. For the record, the word "stet" is a term used in journalism to indicate a section of a document should remain as it was originally, that a portion of a document's change is incorrect.)

HTML 4 specifies you can use them in a document as inline text formatting elements or as block text formatting elements. However, you may not use them as both.

Technically, the following is allowable (but sloppy):

```
<p>This is <ins>a <del>questionable, but </del>valid snippet of </ins>HTML.</p>
```

> **Note**
> There's a special comparison to note here. The Core DOM in Chapter 20 allows for live but temporary alterations to a document. These two elements allow for permanent but fixed alterations to the same document.

cite

JavaScript 1.5

Nav6, IE6

Syntax

```
[var x =] HTMLModElement.cite [= URIString]
```

The `cite` property of `HTMLModElement` objects identifies the URI of the document explaining a reason for the change.

The W3C also suggests using the `title` property for short summaries of the changes.

dateTime

JavaScript 1.5

Nav6, IE6

Syntax

```
[var x =] HTMLModElement.dateTime [= exactTimeString]
```

The `dateTime` property of `HTMLModElement` objects identifies a date and time the editor included the modification to which the `this` element refers.

innerHTML

JavaScript 1.5, JScript 3.0+

Nav6, IE4+

Syntax

```
[var x =] HTMLModElement.innerHTML [= HTMLString]
```

The `innerHTML` property of `HTMLModElement` objects retrieves or sets the HTML source code contained between, but not including, the starting and ending tags.

I personally recommend against using `innerHTML` to set the HTML inside a tag. I strongly recommend against using `innerHTML` to append to the contents of an HTML tag:

```
elem.innerHTML += "<div><p>Hello World</p></div>" // DO NOT DO THIS
```

I do like the handiness of the innerHTML property for retrieving HTML source code at a glance, as an alternative method to the W3C Document Object Model. (The DOM provides an object structure for the source code; innerHTML provides the corresponding source code.)

innerText

JScript 3.0+

IE4+

Syntax

```
var x = HTMLModElement.innerText
```

The innerText property of HTMLModElement objects retrieves or sets the text contained between, but not including, the starting and ending tags.

The innerText property can be useful, but the DOM Level 2 Range interface provides far more flexibility. See Chapter 34, "DOM-2 Range," for details on text ranges.

outerHTML

JScript 3.0+

IE4+

Syntax

```
var x = HTMLModElement.outerHTML
```

The outerHTML property of HTMLModElement objects retrieves or sets the HTML source code contained between, and including, the starting and ending tags.

I do like the handiness of the outerHTML property for retrieving HTML source code at a glance, as an alternative method to the W3C Document Object Model. (The DOM provides an object structure for the source code; outerHTML provides the corresponding source code.)

outerText

JScript 3.0+

IE4+

Syntax

```
var x = HTMLModElement.outerText
```

The `outerText` property of `HTMLModElement` objects is, as Listing 28.1 demonstrates, similar to the `this.innerText` property. The difference is in how you set the value; setting `outerText` replaces `this` with a new text node.

Event Handlers

Internet Explorer supports the following event handlers for the `HTMLModElement` interface:

```
onactivate

onbeforedeactivate

onbeforeeditfocus

onblur

oncontrolselect

ondeactivate

onfocus

onmove

onmoveend

onmovestart

onreadystatechange

onresizeend

onresizestart

ontimeerror
```

<nobr>…</nobr>

Browser/JavaScript Version	Created By
Nav4/JavaScript 1.2	<nobr>...</nobr>
IE4/JScript 3.0	<nobr>...</nobr>
IE5/JScript 5.0	<nobr>...</nobr>

IE5.5/JScript 5.5	`<nobr>...</nobr>`
Nav6/JavaScript 1.5	`<nobr>...</nobr>`
IE6	`<nobr>...</nobr>`
DOM Level 1	`document.createElement("nobr")`
	`// non-standard`

Note

Implemented in Nav3+ (HTML), IE3+ (HTML)

Descends from `HTMLElement` interface (Chapter 21)

Inline Text Formatting Element

Not part of HTML 4

Description

The `<nobr>...</nobr>` element indicates a section that will have no line breaks whatsoever. Exceptionally long text blocks inside this element may force the browser to use scrollbars.

The `<wbr />` element exists to provide for a "soft" line break inside this element, if necessary.

Properties

outerHTML

JScript 3.0+

IE4+

Syntax

```
var x = noBR.outerHTML
```

The `outerHTML` property of `<nobr>...</nobr>` elements retrieves or sets the HTML source code contained between, and including, the starting and ending tags.

I do like the handiness of the `outerHTML` property for retrieving HTML source code at a glance, as an alternative method to the W3C Document Object Model. (The DOM

provides an object structure for the source code; outerHTML provides the
corresponding source code.)

outerText

JScript 3.0+

IE4+

Syntax

```
var x = noBr.outerText
```

The outerText property of <nobr>...</nobr> elements is, as Listing 28.1
demonstrates, similar to the this.innerText property. The difference is in how you set
the value; setting outerText replaces this with a new text node.

Methods

The <nobr>...</nobr> element provides no methods beyond those the HTMLElement
interface defines.

Event Handlers

Internet Explorer supports the following event handlers for the <nobr>...</nobr>
element:

onbeforeactivate	ondrag	onkeydown
onbeforecopy	ondragend	onkeypress
onbeforecut	ondragenter	onkeyup
onbeforeeditfocus	ondragleave	onlosecapture
onbeforepaste	ondragover	onmouseenter
onclick	ondragstart	onmouseleave
oncontextmenu	ondrop	onmousemove
oncopy	onfocusin	onmouseover
oncut	onfocusout	onmouseup
ondblclick	onhelp	onmousewheel

onpaste

onpropertychange

onreadystatechange

onselectstart

HTMLParagraphElement/<p>...</p>

Browser/JavaScript Version	Created By
Nav4/JavaScript 1.2	<p>...</p>
IE4/JScript 3.0	<p>...</p>
IE5/JScript 5.0	<p>...</p>
IE5.5/JScript 5.5	<p>...</p>
Nav6/JavaScript 1.5	<p>...</p>
IE6	<p>...</p>
DOM Level 1	document.createElement("p")

> **Note**
> Implemented in Nav1+ (HTML), IE3+ (HTML), Nav6 (DOM), IE4+ (DOM)
>
> Descends from `HTMLElement` interface (Chapter 21)
>
> Block Text Element

Description

The <p>...</p> element defines a standard paragraph element in HTML.

Properties

align
JavaScript 1.5, JScript 3.0+

Nav6, IE4+

Deprecated in HTML 4

Syntax

```
[var x = ] HTMLParagraphElement.align [= alignString]
```

The `align` attribute of `HTMLParagraphElement` objects defines where the `this` element's contents align horizontally in comparison with the body text. Normally, text aligns to the left edge of the document. There are four permissible values: `"left"`, `"center"` (for centered text), `"right"` (for text on the right edge), and `"justify"` (against both the left and right edges as much as possible).

innerHTML

JavaScript 1.5, JScript 3.0+

Nav6, IE4+

Syntax

```
[var x =] HTMLParagraphElement.innerHTML [= HTMLString]
```

The `innerHTML` property of `HTMLParagraphElement` objects retrieves or sets the HTML source code contained between, but not including, the starting and ending tags.

I personally recommend against using `innerHTML` to set the HTML inside a tag. I strongly recommend against using `innerHTML` to append to the contents of an HTML tag:

```
elem.innerHTML += "<div><p>Hello World</p></div>" // DO NOT DO THIS
```

I do like the handiness of the `innerHTML` property for retrieving HTML source code at a glance, as an alternative method to the W3C Document Object Model. (The DOM provides an object structure for the source code; `innerHTML` provides the corresponding source code.)

innerText

JScript 3.0+

IE4+

Syntax

```
var x = HTMLParagraphElement.innerText
```

The `innerText` property of `HTMLParagraphElement` objects retrieves or sets the text contained between, but not including, the starting and ending tags.

The `innerText` property can be useful, but the DOM Level 2 `Range` interface provides far more flexibility. See Chapter 34, "DOM-2 Range," for details on text ranges.

outerHTML

JScript 3.0+

IE4+

Syntax

```
var x = HTMLParagraphElement.outerHTML
```

The `outerHTML` property of `HTMLParagraphElement` retrieves or sets the HTML source code contained between, and including, the starting and ending tags.

I do like the handiness of the `outerHTML` property for retrieving HTML source code at a glance, as an alternative method to the W3C Document Object Model. (The DOM provides an object structure for the source code; `outerHTML` provides the corresponding source code.)

outerText

JScript 3.0+

IE4+

Syntax

```
var x = HTMLParagraphElement.outerText
```

The `outerText` property of `HTMLParagraphElement` objects is, as Listing 28.1 demonstrates, similar to the `this.innerText` property. The difference is in how you set the value; setting `outerText` replaces `this` with a new text node.

Methods

The `HTMLParagraphElement` interface provides no methods beyond those the `HTMLElement` interface defines.

Event Handlers

Internet Explorer supports the following event handlers for the `HTMLParagraphElement` interface:

onactivate	ondragenter	onmousemove
onbeforeactivate	ondragleave	onmouseout
onbeforecopy	ondragover	onmouseover
onbeforecut	ondragstart	onmouseup
onbeforedeactivate	ondrop	onmousewheel
onbeforeeditfocus	onfocus	onmove
onbeforepaste	onfocusin	onmoveend
onblur	onfocusout	onmovestart
onclick	onhelp	onpaste
oncontextmenu	onkeydown	onpropertychange
oncontrolselect	onkeypress	onreadystatechange
oncopy	onkeyup	onresize
oncut	onlayoutcomplete	onresizeend
ondblclick	onlosecapture	onresizestart
ondeactivate	onmousedown	onselectstart
ondrag	onmouseenter	ontimeerror
ondragend	onmouseleave	

HTMLPreElement Interface / <pre>...</pre>

Browser/JavaScript Version	Created By
Nav4/JavaScript 1.2	<pre>...</pre>
IE4/JScript 3.0	<pre>...</pre>
IE5/JScript 5.0	<pre>...</pre>
IE5.5/JScript 5.5	<pre>...</pre>
Nav6/JavaScript 1.5	<pre>...</pre>
IE6	<pre>...</pre>
DOM Level 1	document.createElement("pre")

> **Note**
>
> Implemented in Nav1+ (HTML), IE3+ (HTML), Nav6 (DOM), IE4+ (DOM)
>
> Descends from `HTMLElement` interface (Chapter 21)
>
> Block Text Element

Description

The `<pre>...</pre>` element defines a block of "preformatted" text. What this means, conventionally, is the browser treats carriage returns (your Enter and Return keys, typically) as line breaks, and spaces and tabs within the source code as spaces and tabs in the document itself. In other words, this element implies to the document to treat the contents almost literally.

Almost. The deprecated `<xmp>...</xmp>` element means literally; XML reinstates its equivalent with the `<![CDATA[...]]>` tags, which I describe in Chapter 20, "Core DOM Objects," under `CDATASection`. Other markup elements, such as `<em>...</em>`, still apply to the contents of `<pre>...</pre>` elements.

Properties

innerHTML

JavaScript 1.5, JScript 3.0+

Nav6, IE4+

Syntax

```
[var x =] HTMLPreElement.innerHTML [= HTMLString]
```

The `innerHTML` property of `HTMLPreElement` objects retrieves or sets the HTML source code contained between, but not including, the starting and ending tags.

I personally recommend against using `innerHTML` to set the HTML inside a tag. I strongly recommend against using `innerHTML` to append to the contents of an HTML tag:

```
elem.innerHTML += "<div><p>Hello World</p></div>" // DO NOT DO THIS
```

I do like the handiness of the `innerHTML` property for retrieving HTML source code at a glance, as an alternative method to the W3C Document Object Model. (The DOM provides an object structure for the source code; `innerHTML` provides the corresponding source code.)

innerText

JScript 3.0+

IE4+

Syntax

```
var x = HTMLPreElement.innerText
```

The `innerText` property of `HTMLPreElement` retrieves or sets the text contained between, but not including, the starting and ending tags.

The `innerText` property can be useful, but the DOM Level 2 `Range` interface provides far more flexibility. See Chapter 34, "DOM-2 Range," for details on text ranges.

outerHTML

JScript 3.0+

IE4+

Syntax

```
var x = HTMLPreElement.outerHTML
```

The `outerHTML` property of `HTMLPreElement` retrieves or sets the HTML source code contained between, and including, the starting and ending tags.

I do like the handiness of the `outerHTML` property for retrieving HTML source code at a glance, as an alternative method to the W3C Document Object Model. (The DOM provides an object structure for the source code; `outerHTML` provides the corresponding source code.)

outerText

JScript 3.0+

IE4+

Syntax

```
var x = HTMLPreElement.outerText
```

The `outerText` property of `HTMLPreElement` objects is, as Listing 28.1 demonstrates, similar to the `this.innerText` property. The difference is in how you set the value; setting `outerText` replaces `this` with a new text node.

width

JavaScript 1.5

Nav6

Syntax

```
[var x =] HTMLPreElement.width [= width]
```

The `width` property of `HTMLPreElement` objects designates the width of the window the `this` element should take up.

wrap

JScript 3.0+

IE5.5

Deprecated in HTML 4

Syntax

```
[var x =] HTMLPreElement.wrap [= wrapString]
```

The `wrap` property of `HTMLPreElement` objects reflects the word wrap setting of the `this` object. Typically, it defaults to "soft," meaning words wrap naturally, and line breaks only occur when entered with an enter key. A "hard" wrap is identical, as far as JavaScript is concerned. (The setting affects how the carriage returns and spaces will be submitted to the server.)

The "off" setting disables word wrapping entirely.

HTML 4 and XHTML 1 do not permit the `wrap` attribute, and HTML 4 prohibits a script from invalidating a document. This means if you want to maintain word wrap control, you must not (for now) use the `wrap` property either in an XHTML document.

Methods

The `HTMLPreElement` interface provides no methods beyond those the `HTMLElement` interface defines.

Event Handlers

Internet Explorer supports the following event handlers for the `HTMLPreElement` interface:

onactivate	ondragenter	onmouseout
onbeforeactivate	ondragleave	onmouseover
onbeforecopy	ondragover	onmouseup
onbeforecut	ondragstart	onmousewheel
onbeforedeactivate	ondrop	onmove
onbeforeeditfocus	onfocus	onmoveend
onbeforepaste	onfocusin	onmovestart
onblur	onfocusout	onpaste
onclick	onhelp	onpropertychange
oncontextmenu	onkeydown	onreadystatechange
oncontrolselect	onkeypress	onresize
oncopy	onkeyup	onresizeend
oncut	onlosecapture	onresizestart
ondblclick	onmousedown	onselectstart
ondeactivate	onmouseenter	ontimeerror
ondrag	onmouseleave	
ondragend	onmousemove	

HTMLQuoteElement Interface / <q>...</q>

Browser/JavaScript Version	Created By
Nav4/JavaScript 1.2	`<blockquote>...</blockquote>`
	`<quote>...</quote>`
IE4/JScript 3.0	`<blockquote>...</blockquote>`
	`<quote>...</quote>`
IE5/JScript 5.0	`<blockquote>...</blockquote>`
	`<quote>...</quote>`
IE5.5/JScript 5.5	`<blockquote>...</blockquote>`
	`<quote>...</quote>`
Nav6/JavaScript 1.5	`<blockquote>...</blockquote>`
	`<quote>...</quote>`
IE6	`<blockquote>...</blockquote>`
	`<quote>...</quote>`
DOM Level 1	`document.createElement("blockquote")`
	`document.createElement("quote")`

> **Note**
> Implemented in Nav1+ (HTML), IE3+ (HTML), Nav6 (DOM), IE4+ (DOM)
> Descends from `HTMLElement` interface (Chapter 21)
> Block Text Element (blockquote), Inline Text Element (quote)

Description

The `<blockquote>...</blockquote>` element defines a block-level quote element for quoting text from another source.

Properties

cite

JavaScript 1.5

Nav6, IE6

Syntax

```
[var x =] HTMLQuoteElement.cite [= URIString]
```

The `cite` property of `HTMLQuoteElement` objects identifies the URI of the document from where the quote came.

innerHTML

JavaScript 1.5, JScript 3.0+

Nav6, IE4+

Syntax

```
[var x =] HTMLQuoteElement.innerHTML [= HTMLString]
```

The `innerHTML` property of `HTMLQuoteElement` objects retrieves or sets the HTML source code contained between, but not including, the starting and ending tags.

I personally recommend against using `innerHTML` to set the HTML inside a tag. I strongly recommend against using `innerHTML` to append to the contents of an HTML tag:

```
elem.innerHTML += "<div><p>Hello World</p></div>" // DO NOT DO THIS
```

I do like the handiness of the `innerHTML` property for retrieving HTML source code at a glance, as an alternative method to the W3C Document Object Model. (The DOM provides an object structure for the source code; `innerHTML` provides the corresponding source code.)

innerText

JScript 3.0+

IE4+

Syntax

```
var x = HTMLQuoteElement.innerText
```

The `innerText` property of `HTMLQuoteElement` retrieves or sets the text contained between, but not including, the starting and ending tags.

The `innerText` property can be useful, but the DOM Level 2 `Range` interface provides far more flexibility. See Chapter 34, "DOM-2 Range," for details on text ranges.

outerHTML

JScript 3.0+

IE4+

Syntax

```
var x = HTMLQuoteElement.outerHTML
```

The outerHTML property of HTMLQuoteElement retrieves or sets the HTML source code contained between, and including, the starting and ending tags.

I do like the handiness of the outerHTML property for retrieving HTML source code at a glance, as an alternative method to the W3C Document Object Model. (The DOM provides an object structure for the source code; outerHTML provides the corresponding source code.)

outerText

JScript 3.0+

IE4+

Syntax

```
var x = HTMLQuoteElement.outerText
```

The outerText property of HTMLQuoteElement objects is, as Listing 28.1 demonstrates, similar to the this.innerText property. The difference is in how you set the value; setting outerText replaces this with a new text node.

Methods

The HTMLQuoteElement interface provides no methods beyond those the HTMLElement interface defines.

Event Handlers

Internet Explorer supports the following event handlers for the `HTMLQuoteElement` interface:

`onactivate`

`onbeforedeactivate`

`onbeforeeditfocus`

`onblur`

`oncontrolselect`

`ondeactivate`

`ondrag`

`ondragend`

`ondragenter`

`ondragleave`

`ondragover`

`ondragstart`

`ondrop`

`onfocus`

`onkeydown`

`onkeypress`

`onkeyup`

`onmove`

`onmoveend`

`onmovestart`

`onreadystatechange`

`onresizeend`

`onresizestart`

`onselectstart`

`ontimeerror`

<wbr />

Browser/JavaScript Version	Created By
Nav4/JavaScript 1.2	<wbr />
IE4/JScript 3.0	<wbr />
IE5/JScript 5.0	<wbr />
IE5.5/JScript 5.5	<wbr />
Nav6/JavaScript 1.5	<wbr />
IE6	<wbr />
DOM Level 1	Not implemented

> **Note**
> Implemented in Nav3+ (HTML), IE3+ (HTML)
> Inline Text Element
> Not part of HTML 4

Description

The <wbr /> element creates a "soft" line break inside a <nobr>...</nobr> element—basically, if the window is small enough for horizontal scrollbars to appear and this tag is present, the browser may create a line break. (It does not have to.)

> **Caution**
> This element, being nonstandard, does not implement all of the features of HTMLElement. Use at your own risk.

outerHTML

JScript 3.0+

IE4+

Syntax

```
var x = wbrObj.outerHTML
```

The outerHTML property of <wbr /> elements retrieves or sets the HTML source code contained between, and including, the starting and ending tags.

I do like the handiness of the outerHTML property for retrieving HTML source code at a glance, as an alternative method to the W3C Document Object Model. (The DOM provides an object structure for the source code; outerHTML provides the corresponding source code.)

outerText

JScript 3.0+

IE4+

Syntax

```
var x = wbrObj.outerText
```

The outerText property of <wbr /> elements is, as Listing 28.1 demonstrates, similar to the this.innerText property. The difference is in how you set the value; setting outerText replaces this with a new text node.

<xmp>...</xmp>

Browser/JavaScript Version	Created By
Nav4/JavaScript 1.2	<xmp>...</xmp>
IE4/JScript 3.0	<xmp>...</xmp>
IE5/JScript 5.0	<xmp>...</xmp>
IE5.5/JScript 5.5	<xmp>...</xmp>
Nav6/JavaScript 1.5	<xmp>...</xmp>
IE6	<xmp>...</xmp>
DOM Level 1	Not implemented

> **Note**
> Implemented in Nav1+ (HTML), IE3+ (HTML)
>
> Block Text Element
>
> Not part of HTML 4

Description

The `<xmp>...</xmp>` element designates, like a CDATA section, a block of code to take literally. (See Chapter 20, "Core DOM Objects", for a description of CDATA sections.)

Properties

innerHTML

JavaScript 1.5, JScript 5.0+

Nav6, IE4+

Syntax

```
[var x =] xmpObj.innerHTML [= HTMLString]
```

The `innerHTML` property of `<xmp>...</xmp>` elements retrieves or sets the HTML source code contained between, but not including, the starting and ending tags.

I personally recommend against using `innerHTML` to set the HTML inside a tag. I strongly recommend against using `innerHTML` to append to the contents of an HTML tag:

```
elem.innerHTML += "<div><p>Hello World</p></div>" // DO NOT DO THIS
```

I do like the handiness of the `innerHTML` property for retrieving HTML source code at a glance, as an alternative method to the W3C Document Object Model. (The DOM provides an object structure for the source code; `innerHTML` provides the corresponding source code.)

innerText

JScript 3.0+

IE4+

Syntax

```
var x = xmpObj.innerText
```

The `innerText` property of `<xmp>`...`</xmp>` elements retrieves or sets the text contained between, but not including, the starting and ending tags.

The `innerText` property can be useful, but the DOM Level 2 `Range` interface provides far more flexibility. See Chapter 34, "DOM-2 Range," for details on text ranges.

outerHTML

JScript 3.0+

IE4+

Syntax

```
var x = xmpObj.outerHTML
```

The `outerHTML` property of `<xmp>`...`</xmp>` elements retrieves or sets the HTML source code contained between, and including, the starting and ending tags.

I do like the handiness of the `outerHTML` property for retrieving HTML source code at a glance, as a companion method to the W3C Document Object Model. (The DOM provides an object structure for the source code; `outerHTML` provides the corresponding source code.)

outerText

JScript 3.0+

IE4+

Syntax

```
var x = xmpObj.outerText
```

The `outerText` property of `<xmp>`...`</xmp>` elements is, as Listing 28.1 demonstrates, functionally equivalent to the `this.innerText` property.

Methods

The `<xmp>`...`</xmp>` element provides no methods beyond those the `HTMLElement` interface defines.

Event Handlers

Internet Explorer supports the following event handlers for the `<xmp>...</xmp>` element:

onactivate	ondragleave	onmouseout
onbeforeactivate	ondragover	onmouseover
onbeforecut	ondragstart	onmouseup
onbeforedeactivate	ondrop	onmousewheel
onbeforeeditfocus	onfocus	onmove
onbeforepaste	onfocusin	onmoveend
onblur	onfocusout	onmovestart
onclick	onhelp	onpaste
oncontextmenu	onkeydown	onpropertychange
oncontrolselect	onkeypress	onreadystatechange
oncut	onkeyup	onresize
ondblclick	onlosecapture	onresizeend
ondeactivate	onmousedown	onresizestart
ondrag	onmouseenter	onselectstart
ondragend	onmouseleave	ontimeerror
ondragenter	onmousemove	

CHAPTER 29

Table Elements

HTMLTableElement / <table>...</table>

Browser/JavaScript Version	Created By
Nav4/JavaScript 1.2	Not implemented
IE4/JScript 3.0	`<table>...</table>`
IE5/JScript 5.0	`<table>...</table>`
IE5.5/JScript 5.5	`<table>...</table>`
Nav6/JavaScript 1.5	`<table>...</table>`
IE6	`<table>...</table>`
DOM Level 1	`document.createElement("table")`

> **Note**
>
> Implemented in Nav1.1+ (HTML), IE3+ (HTML), Nav6 (DOM), IE4+ (DOM)
>
> Descends from `HTMLElement` interface (Chapter 21)
>
> Parent elements: `HTMLBodyElement` (Chapter 22), any block text element

Description

Tables provide us with an organized format for information. Basically, with two indexes (the row number and the column number, for instance), you can find a particular piece of information in the table (the cell) without having to go through the whole table.

Let's look at how tables are implemented in HTML. Imagine taking a square and slicing it horizontally a few dozen times, and then laying the strips in a sequence, so that where one strip ends, the next begins. This is precisely how HTML organizes its tables' *cells*. The `<tr>...</tr>` elements define the rows and the `<td>...</td>` and `<th>...</th>` elements define the individual cells. This is primarily how HTML defines its "two-dimensional" data structure for tables.

The DOM and HTML Tables

In most cases, the Core DOM (discussed in Chapter 20, "Core DOM Objects") is adequate for navigating a document. Tables are a notable exception to this rule.

For one thing, (X)HTML allows `<thead>...</thead>`, `<tbody>...</tbody>`, and `<tfoot>...</tfoot>` elements, but not everybody uses them. Also, Netscape's own DOM creates a text node before the `<td>...</td>` element in the following:

```
<tr>
<td>Go Mariners</td>
</tr>
```

Needless to say, `childNodes` can get confusing. Fortunately, the HTML DOM comes to the rescue. It provides a direct access via the `rows` collection of the `<table>...</table>` element to the table's rows (including header and footer rows). For each row, there is a `cells` collection corresponding to the cells in that row. As in other collections, the first item has an index number of 0.

Caution
HTML 4 has a specific order for the possible child elements of a table. The order begins with an optional caption. Any column group elements follow this. Then comes an optional table head section. Third is an optional table foot section, followed by optional table body sections. (X)HTML prohibits a table row being a direct child of a table element by the document type definition. If you omit a `<tbody>` element in your code, a node corresponding to `<tbody>` will appear in the DOM, in conformity to the DTD as it applies to HTML tables.

Other Features of HTML Tables

Tables have a lot of flexibility to them. You can specify sizes of rows, columns, the whole table, and of individual cells. You can specify how many columns or rows a cell occupies. Before frames, tables were the only way to specify any frame-like page rendering (I believe tables preceded styling and positioned content).

In fact, the W3C resisted adding frames to the HTML standards for several years, and only did so by popular demand. Even then, the HTML 4 recommendation includes three document type definitions. Frames only appear in the loosest of them.

Properties

align

JavaScript 1.5, JScript 3.0+

Nav6, IE4+

Syntax

`[var x =] HTMLTableElement.align [= alignString]`

The `align` property of `HTMLTableElement` objects refers to the horizontal alignment of the table relative to the document—whether its left edge lines up with the left side of the main text, its right edge lines up with the right side, or the table is centered horizontally. This attribute may take values of `"left"`, `"right"`, or `"center"`, respectively.

bgColor

JavaScript 1.5, JScript 3.0+

Nav6, IE4+

Syntax

`[var x =] HTMLTableElement.bgColor [= colorString]`

The `bgColor` property of `HTMLTableElement` objects refers to the background color of the table. You can specify it either by name (`"cyan"`, `"red"`, `"white"`, `"navy"`, and so on) or by hexadecimal (`"#00FFFF"`). Hexadecimal is the preferred style, as color names in browsers may not be universally recognized.

border

JavaScript 1.5, JScript 3.0+

Nav6, IE4+

Syntax

`[var x =] HTMLTableElement.border [= pixelNumber]`

The `border` property of `HTMLTableElement` objects designates the thickness of table cell and table borders within the table, in terms of pixels.

The W3C has introduced the `frame` and `rules` attributes, which I cover as properties. These properties modify the appearance of the table's edges. Listing 29.1 combines these three properties to create Figure 29.1, a series of tables. It contains a nested table that is cloned using DOM-based JavaScript and then values for various properties may be set.

Listing 29.1   *Tables with Rules, Frames, and Borders*

```
<?xml version="1.0" ?>
<!DOCTYPE html PUBLIC "-//W3C//DTD XHTML 1.0 Transitional//EN"
➥"DTD/xhtml1-transitional.dtd">
<html xmlns="http://www.w3.org/1999/xhtml" >
<head><title></title>
<script language="JavaScript" type="text/javascript">
<!--
function copyTables() {
    var myTable = document.getElementById("myTable")
    var masterRow0 = document.getElementById("master").rows[0].cells
    var masterRow1 = document.getElementById("master").rows[1].cells

    var copy1 = myTable.cloneNode(true)
    copy1.rows[0].childNodes[0].firstChild.nodeValue = "1-pixel border"
    copy1.border = 1
    masterRow0[1].appendChild(copy1)

    var copy2 = copy1.cloneNode(true)
    copy2.rows[0].childNodes[0].firstChild.nodeValue = "frame hsides"
    copy2.frame="hsides"
    masterRow0[2].appendChild(copy2)

    var copy3 = copy1.cloneNode(true)
    copy3.rows[0].childNodes[0].firstChild.nodeValue = "frame lhs"
    copy3.frame="lhs"
    masterRow1[0].appendChild(copy3)

    var copy4 = copy1.cloneNode(true)
    copy4.rows[0].childNodes[0].firstChild.nodeValue = "rules rows"
    copy4.rules="rows"
    masterRow1[1].appendChild(copy4)

    var copy5 = copy1.cloneNode(true)
    copy5.rows[0].childNodes[0].firstChild.nodeValue = "rules groups"
    copy5.rules="groups"
```

Listing 29.1   *(continued)*

```
      masterRow1[2].appendChild(copy5)
    }
//-->
</script>
</head>
<body onload="copyTables()">

<table id="master">
<tr><td>
<!-- Original table -->
<table id="myTable">
<colgroup span="2"></colgroup>
<col />
<tbody>
<tr><td>No borders</td><td>2</td><td>3</td></tr>
<tr><td>4</td><td>5</td><td>6</td></tr>
</tbody>
<tbody>
<tr><td>7</td><td>8</td><td>9</td></tr>
</tbody>
</table>
<!-- End original table -->
</td>

<!-- Experimental tables -->
<td></td><td></td></tr>
<tr><td></td><td></td><td></td></tr>
<!-- End experimental tables -->
</table>

</body>
</html>
```

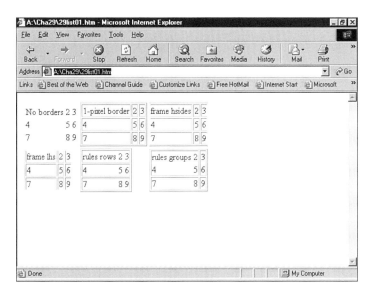

Figure 29.1
Tables with rules, frames, and borders.

caption

JavaScript 1.5, JScript 3.0+

Nav6, IE4+

Syntax

```
[var x =] HTMLTableElement.caption [= captionElement]
```

The caption property of HTMLTableElement objects refers to the table's
<caption>...</caption> element. I cover this element later in the chapter.

cellPadding

JavaScript 1.5, JScript 3.0+

Nav6, IE4+

Syntax

```
[var x =] HTMLTableElement.cellPadding [= pixelNumber]
```

The `cellPadding` property of `HTMLTableElement` objects refers to the distance in pixels between each table cell and its interior contents. This creates a whitespace margin around the contents but inside the borders of the cell.

Alternatively, you can specify a percentage for this value. In this case, the left and right margins thus become percentages of available horizontal space, and the top and bottom margins become percentages of available vertical space.

cells

JScript 5.0+

IE5+

Syntax

```
var x = HTMLTableElement.cells
```

The `cells` property of `HTMLTableElement` objects is a collection of all cells in the table, including header cells. The cells appear in this collection in order of their appearance in the document.

item

JScript 5.0+

IE5+

Syntax

```
var x = HTMLTableElement.cells.item(indexOrString[,index])
```

For the `item` method of `children`, by supplying a number (specifically, a non-negative integer less than `this.length`) as the first argument, you can get a `Node` object from the `this` object representing that `Node`'s placement in the `this` object's index. Any other argument you submit to this method results in the method returning `null`.

length

JScript 5.0+

IE5+

Syntax

```
var x = HTMLTableElement.cells.length
```

The `length` property of `children` tells how many objects are in the collection.

tags
JScript 5.0+

IE5+

Syntax

```
var x = HTMLTableElement.cells.tags(tagName)
```

The `tags` method of `children` returns a subset of the `this` element comprising all elements whose `tagName` property matches the first argument.

urns
JScript 5.0+

IE5+

Syntax

```
var x = HTMLTableElement.cells.urns(behaviorName)
```

The `urns` method of `children` returns a subset of the `this` element comprising all elements possessing a DHTML behavior whose name matches the first argument.

DHTML behaviors, an Internet Explorer proprietary extension to HTML, go far beyond the scope of this book. You can find information on them via Microsoft's Web site at `http://msdn.microsoft.com/workshop/author/behaviors/overview.asp`.

cellSpacing
JavaScript 1.5, JScript 3.0+

Nav6, IE4+

Syntax

```
[var x =] HTMLTableElement.cellSpacing [= pixelNumber]
```

The `cellSpacing` property of `HTMLTableElement` objects refers to the distance in pixels around each cell of the table. This creates a whitespace margin between cells and from the table to the cells nearest the table edge.

cols

JScript 3.0+

IE4+

Syntax

```
[var x =] HTMLTableElement.cols [= colsNumber]
```

The `cols` property of `HTMLTableElement` objects refers to the number of columns in the table. Microsoft's documentation on this claims it is part of the W3C DOM; it is not.

> **Caution**
> Setting this value directly can have unexpected and severe effects; avoid its use whenever possible.

frame

JavaScript 1.5, JScript 3.0+

Nav6, IE4+

Syntax

```
[var x =] HTMLTableElement.frame [= frameString]
```

The `frame` property of `HTMLTableElement` objects designates the sides of the table that will possess borders.

- The value `"border"`, which is the default when a `border` property is set, means all four sides shall have a border. The `"box"` value is equivalent.

- The `"void"` value, which is the default when a `border` property is not set, means no sides shall have a border.

- You can specify `"above"` for the top border only, `"below"` for the bottom border only, `"lhs"` for the left-side border only, or `"rhs"` for the right-side border only.

- You can also specify `"hsides"` for the top and bottom borders only, or `"vsides"` for the left and right borders only.

Listing 29.1 combines the `frame` property with the `rules` and `border` properties to create Figure 29.1, a series of tables.

height

JScript 3.0+

IE4+

Syntax

```
[var x =] HTMLTableElement.height [= pixelNumber]
```

The `height` property of `HTMLTableElement` objects allows you to retrieve or specify the height of the table in pixels. This is a Microsoft extension to HTML for tables, but is present in other elements.

innerHTML

JavaScript 1.5, JScript 3.0+

Nav6, IE4+

Syntax

```
[var x =] HTMLTableElement.innerHTML [= HTMLString]
```

The `innerHTML` property of `HTMLTableElement` interfaces retrieves or sets the HTML source code contained between, but not including, the starting and ending tags. In Internet Explorer `innerHTML` is read-only.

I personally recommend against using `innerHTML` to set the HTML inside a tag. This forces the browser to re-render the contents of the page. I strongly recommend against using `innerHTML` to append to the contents of an HTML tag:

```
elem.innerHTML += "<div><p>Hello World</p></div>" // DO NOT DO THIS
```

This forces the browser to retrieve the current `innerHTML` value, add new markup to it, and re-render the entire page.

I do like the handiness of the `innerHTML` property for retrieving HTML source code at a glance, as an alternative method to the W3C Document Object Model. (The DOM provides an object structure for the source code; `innerHTML` provides the corresponding source code.)

innerText

JScript 3.0+

IE4+

Syntax

```
var x = HTMLTableElement.innerText
```

The `innerText` property of `HTMLTableElement` retrieves or sets the text contained between, but not including, the starting and ending tags. In tables, the `innerText` property is read-only.

outerHTML

JScript 3.0+

IE4+

Syntax

```
var x = HTMLTableElement.outerHTML
```

The `outerHTML` property of `HTMLTableElement` retrieves or sets the HTML source code contained between, and including, the starting and ending tags.

I do like the handiness of the `outerHTML` property for retrieving HTML source code at a glance, as an alternative method to the W3C Document Object Model. (The DOM provides an object structure for the source code; `outerHTML` provides the corresponding source code.)

rows

JavaScript 1.5, JScript_3.0

Nav6, IE4+

Syntax

```
var x = HTMLTableElement.rows
```

The rows property of HTMLTableElement objects is a collection of all rows in the table, including header rows, footer rows, and body rows.

The W3C DOM does not specify the order in which table rows appear in the collection. Internet Explorer 5+ and Netscape 6 place body rows before the footer rows in the collection, as Listing 29.2 demonstrates.

Listing 29.2   *The Ordering of Rows in the* rows *Collection*

```
<?xml version="1.0" ?>
<!DOCTYPE html PUBLIC "-//W3C//DTD XHTML 1.0 Transitional//EN"
➥"DTD/xhtml1-transitional.dtd">
<html xmlns="http://www.w3.org/1999/xhtml" >
<head><title></title>
<script language="JavaScript" type="text/javascript">
<!--
function listRows() {
    var myTable = document.getElementById("myTable")
    var rowlist = document.getElementById("rowlist")
    for (var x = 0; x < myTable.rows.length; x++) {
        var newtext = document.createTextNode(myTable.rows[x].id)
        rowlist.appendChild(newtext)
        rowlist.appendChild(document.createElement("br"))
        }
    }
//-->
</script>
</head>
<body onload="listRows()">
<table id="myTable">
<thead>
<tr id="header"><td>Header row</td></tr>
</thead>

<tfoot>
<tr id="footer"><td>Footer row</td></tr>
</tfoot>

<tbody>
<tr id="bodyrow"><td>Body row</td></tr>
</tbody>
```

Listing 29.2   *(continued)*

```
</table>
<p id="rowlist">
<!-- Results:
header
bodyrow
footer
-->
</p>
</body>
</html>
```

item

JavaScript_1.5, JScript 3.0+

Nav6, IE4+

Syntax

```
var x = HTMLTableElement.rows.item(index)
```

```
var x = HTMLTableElement.rows.item('idstring'[,optionalIndex])
```

For the `item` method of `rows`, by supplying a number (specifically, a non-negative integer less than `this.length`) as the first argument, you can get a `Node` object from the `this` object representing that `Node`'s placement in the `this` object's index. Any other argument you submit to this method results in the method returning `null`.

length

JavaScript_1.5, JScript 3.0+

Nav6, IE4+

Syntax

```
var x = HTMLTableElement.rows.length
```

The `length` property of `rows` is read-only and tells how many objects are in the collection.

tags

JScript 3.0+

IE4+

Syntax

```
var x = HTMLTableElement.rows.tags(tagName)
```

The `tags` method of `rows` returns a subset of the `this` element comprising all elements whose `tagName` property matches the first argument.

urns

JScript 5.0+

IE5+

Syntax

```
var x = HTMLTableElement.rows.urns(behaviorName)
```

The `urns` method of `rows` returns a subset of the `this` element comprising all elements possessing a DHTML behavior whose name matches the first argument.

DHTML behaviors, an Internet Explorer proprietary extension to HTML, go far beyond the scope of this book. You can find information on them via Microsoft's Web site at `http://msdn.microsoft.com/workshop/author/behaviors/overview.asp`.

rules

JavaScript 1.5, JScript 3.0+

Nav6, IE4+

Syntax

```
[var x =] HTMLTableElement.rules [= rulesString]
```

The rules property of `HTMLTableElement` objects designates where lines inside the table bordering cells may appear.

- The value `"all"`, which is the default when a `border` property is set, means all cells shall have lines around them.

- The `"none"` value, which is the default when a border property is not set, means no lines shall appear within the table.

- You can specify `"rows"` for lines between rows only, or `"columns"` for lines between columns only.

- You can also specify `"groups"` to indicate groupings to receive border lines; this means all columns designated by `<colgroup>...</colgroup>` and `<col />` elements, and around `<thead>...</thead>`, `<tbody>...</tbody>`, and `<tfoot>...</tfoot>` elements.

Listing 29.1 combines the `rules` property with the `frame` and `border` properties to create Figure 29.1, a series of tables.

summary

JavaScript 1.5, JScript 5+

Nav6, IE5+

Syntax

```
[var x =] HTMLTableElement.summary [= string]
```

The `summary` property of `HTMLTableElement` objects is an optional string value summarizing the table's purpose.

tBodies

JavaScript 1.5, JScript 5.0+

Nav6, IE5+

Syntax

```
var x = HTMLTableElement.tBodies
```

The `tBodies` property of `HTMLTableElement` objects is a collection of all `<tbody>...</tbody>` objects in the table, in order of their appearance. See `HTMLTableSectionElement` for more details on `<tbody>...</tbody>`.

item

JavaScript 1.5, JScript 5.0+

Nav6, IE5+

Syntax

```
var x = HTMLTableElement.tBodies.item(index)
```

```
var x = HTMLTableElement.tBodies.item('elementId'[,optionalIndex]) (IE only)
```

For the `item` method of `tBodies`, by supplying a number (specifically, a non-negative integer less than `this.length`) as the first argument, you can get a `Node` object from the `this` object representing that `Node`'s placement in the `this` object's index. Any other argument you submit to this method results in the method returning `null`.

length

JavaScript 1.5, JScript 5.0+

Nav6, IE5+

Syntax

```
var x = HTMLTableElement.tBodies.length
```

The `length` property of `tBodies` tells how many objects are in the collection.

tags

JScript 3.0+

IE4+

Syntax

```
var x = HTMLTableElement.tBodies.tags(tagName)
```

The `tags` method of `tBodies` returns a subset of the `this` element comprising all elements whose `tagName` property matches the first argument.

urns

JScript 5.0+

IE5+

Syntax

```
var x = HTMLTableElement.tBodies.urns(behaviorName)
```

The urns method of tBodies returns a subset of the this element comprising all elements possessing a DHTML behavior whose name matches the first argument.

DHTML behaviors, an Internet Explorer proprietary extension to HTML, go far beyond the scope of this book. You can find information on them via Microsoft's Web site at http://msdn.microsoft.com/workshop/author/behaviors/overview.asp.

tFoot

JavaScript 1.5, JScript 3.0+

Nav6, IE4+

Syntax

```
var x = HTMLTableElement.tFoot [= HTMLTableSectionElement]
```

The tFoot property of HTMLTableElement objects refers to the <tfoot>...</tfoot> object in the table, if provided. See HTMLTableSectionElement for more details.

tHead

JavaScript 1.5, JScript 3.0+

Nav6, IE4+

Syntax

```
var x = HTMLTableElement.tHead [=HTMLTableSectionElement]
```

The tHead property of HTMLTableElement objects refers to the <thead>...</thead> object in the table, if provided. See HTMLTableSectionElement for more details.

width

JavaScript 1.5, JScript 3.0+

Nav6, IE4+

Syntax

```
[var x =] HTMLTableElement.width [= pixelNumber]
```

The width property of HTMLTableElement objects refers to the width of the table rendered on the screen. If expressed as a number of pixels, the table will occupy that number of pixels on the screen. If expressed as a percentage, that percentage of the horizontal viewing area (including scrolled content) will host the table.

Methods

createCaption()

JavaScript 1.5, JScript 5+

Nav6, IE4+

Syntax

```
var x = HTMLTableElement.createCaption()
```

The createCaption method of HTMLTableElement objects will, if there is currently a HTMLTableCaptionElement object for this table, return the table caption. If not, it will create and return one for the table.

createTFoot()

JavaScript 1.5, JScript 3+

Nav6, IE4+

Syntax

```
var x = HTMLTableElement.createTFoot()
```

The createTFoot() method of HTMLTableElement objects will, if there is currently a table footer for this table, return the table footer. If not, it will create and return one for the table. (See HTMLTableSectionElement, later in this chapter, for details.)

createTHead()

JavaScript 1.5, JScript 3+

Nav6, IE4+

Syntax

```
var x = HTMLTableElement.createTHead()
```

The createTHead() method of HTMLTableElement objects will, if there is currently a table header for this table, return the table header. If not, it will create and return one for the table. (See HTMLTableSectionElement, later in this chapter, for details.)

deleteCaption()

JavaScript 1.5, JScript 3.0+

Nav6, IE4+

Syntax

```
HTMLTableElement.deleteCaption()
```

The deleteCaption method of HTMLTableElement objects will, if there is currently a HTMLTableCaptionElement object for this table, remove the table caption.

deleteRow()

JavaScript 1.5, JScript 3.0+

Nav6, IE4+

Syntax

```
HTMLTableElement.deleteRow(rowIndex)
```

The deleteRow() method of HTMLTableElement objects removes the row in the this object's rows collection whose index matches the first argument, a non-negative integer. In Internet Explorer the rowIndex argument is optional and, if not passed, the last row of the table is deleted.

deleteTFoot()

JavaScript 1.5, JScript 3.0+

Nav6, IE4+

Syntax

`HTMLTableElement.deleteTFoot()`

The `deleteTFoot()` method of `HTMLTableElement` objects will, if there is currently a table footer for this table, remove the table footer. (See `HTMLTableSectionElement`, later in this chapter, for details on headers and footers.)

deleteTHead()

JavaScript 1.5, JScript 3.0+

Nav6, IE4+

Syntax

`HTMLTableElement.deleteTHead()`

The `deleteTHead()` method of `HTMLTableElement` objects will, if there is currently a table header for this table, remove the table header. (See `HTMLTableSectionElement`, later in this chapter, for details on headers and footers.)

insertRow()

JavaScript 1.5, JScript 5+

Nav6, IE5+

Syntax

`var x = HTMLTableElement.insertRow(rowIndex)`

The `insertRow()` method of `HTMLTableElement` objects inserts a new empty row into the `this` object's `rows` collection, just before the row whose index number matches the first argument, a non-negative integer.

In the case where the row being inserted borders a grouping element (header, footer, body), the row will be inserted in the same grouping as the row it will be inserted before.

I do not recommend this particular method for HTML 4. A row cannot be empty according to the HTML 4 Recommendation. Instead, create the entire row, including cells, and then use the following:

```
HTMLTableElement.rows[oldRow].parentNode.insertBefore(newRow,
➥HTMLTableElement.rows[oldRow])
```

moveRow()

JScript 5.0+

IE5+

Syntax

```
HTMLTableElement.moveRow(rowIndexToMove, toBeforeRowIndex)
```

The moveRow() method of HTMLTableElement objects moves a row from one place in the this object's rows collection to another. The row has an index number specified in the first argument, and will move to just after the row with an index number specified in the second argument.

Event Handlers

Internet Explorer supports the following event handlers for the HTMLTableElement interface:

onactivate	ondblclick	onfocusin
onbeforeactivate	ondeactivate	onfocusout
onbeforecut	ondrag	onhelp
onbeforedeactivate	ondragend	onkeydown
onbeforeeditfocus	ondragenter	onkeypress
onbeforepaste	ondragleave	onkeyup
onblur	ondragover	onlosecapture
onclick	ondragstart	onmousedown
oncontextmenu	ondrop	onmouseenter
oncontrolselect	onfilterchange	onmouseleave
oncut	onfocus	onmousemove

onmouseout	onmovestart	onresizestart
onmouseover	onpaste	onscroll
onmouseup	onpropertychange	onselectstart
onmousewheel	onreadystatechange	ontimeerror
onmove	onresize	
onmoveend	onresizeend	

HTMLTableCaptionElement/<caption>...</caption>

Browser/JavaScript Version	Created By
Nav4/JavaScript 1.2	Not implemented
IE4/JScript 3.0	`<caption>...</caption>`
IE5/JScript 5.0	`<caption>...</caption>`
IE5.5/JScript 5.5	`<caption>...</caption>`
Nav6/JavaScript 1.5	`<caption>...</caption>`
IE6	`<caption>...</caption>`
DOM Level 1	`document.table.createCaption()`

> **Note**
> Implemented in Nav1.1+ (HTML), IE3+ (HTML), Nav6 (DOM), IE4+ (DOM)
> Descends from `HTMLElement` interface (Chapter 21)
> Parent elements: `HTMLTableElement`

Description

The caption element for tables is really simple: it provides a place to store a caption for the table.

Properties

align

JavaScript 1.5, JScript 3.0+

Nav6, IE4+

Syntax

```
[var x =] HTMLTableCaptionElement.align [= alignString]
```

The `align` property of `HTMLTableCaptionElement` objects refers to the position of the caption relative to the table. This attribute may take values of `"left"`, `"right"`, `"top"` or `"bottom"`. When, for example, the value of the property is `"top"` the caption is placed at the top of the table.

innerHTML

JavaScript 1.5, JScript 3.0+

Nav6, IE4+

Syntax

```
[var x =] HTMLTableCaptionElement.innerHTML [= HTMLString]
```

The `innerHTML` property of `HTMLTableCaptionElement` interfaces retrieves or sets the HTML source code contained between, but not including, the starting and ending tags.

I personally recommend against using `innerHTML` to set the HTML inside a tag. I strongly recommend against using `innerHTML` to append to the contents of an HTML tag:

```
elem.innerHTML += "<div><p>Hello World</p></div>" // DO NOT DO THIS
```

This forces the browser to retrieve the current `innerHTML` value, add new markup to it, and re-render the entire page.

I do like the handiness of the `innerHTML` property for retrieving HTML source code at a glance, as an alternative method to the W3C Document Object Model.

innerText

JScript 3.0+

IE4+

Syntax

```
var x = HTMLTableCaptionElement.innerText
```

The `innerText` property of `HTMLTableCaptionElement` retrieves or sets the text contained between, but not including, the starting and ending tags.

outerHTML

JScript 3.0+

IE4+

Syntax

```
var x = HTMLTableCaptionElement.outerHTML
```

The `outerHTML` property of `HTMLTableCaptionElement` retrieves or sets the HTML source code contained between, and including, the starting and ending tags.

I do like the handiness of the `outerHTML` property for retrieving HTML source code at a glance.

vAlign

JScript 3.0+

IE4+

Syntax

```
[var x =] HTMLTableCaptionElement.vAlign [= alignString]
```

The `vAlign` property of `HTMLTableCaptionElement` objects refers to the vertical placement of the caption relative to the table—whether it is above or below the table. This attribute may take values of `"top"` or `"bottom"`, respectively.

Microsoft's documentation on this claims it is part of the W3C DOM; it is not.

Methods

The `HTMLTableCaptionElement` interface provides no methods beyond those the `HTMLElement` interface defines.

Event Handlers

Internet Explorer supports the following event handlers for the `HTMLTableCaptionElement` interface:

onactivate	ondragenter	onmousemove
onbeforeactivate	ondragleave	onmouseout
onbeforecopy	ondragover	onmouseover
onbeforecut	ondragstart	onmouseup
onbeforedeactivate	ondrop	onmousewheel
onbeforepaste	onfocus	onmove
onblur	onfocusin	onmoveend
onclick	onfocusout	onmovestart
oncontextmenu	onhelp	onpaste
oncontrolselect	onkeydown	onpropertychange
oncopy	onkeypress	onreadystatechange
oncut	onkeyup	onresizeend
ondblclick	onlosecapture	onresizestart
ondeactivate	onmousedown	onselectstart
ondrag	onmouseenter	ontimeerror
ondragend	onmouseleave	

HTMLTableCellElement/<td>...</td> / <th>...</th>

Browser/JavaScript Version	Created By
Nav4/JavaScript 1.2	Not implemented
IE4/JScript 3.0	`<td>...</td>`
	`<th>...</th>`
IE5/JScript 5.0	`<td>...</td>`
	`<th>...</th>`
IE5.5/JScript 5.5	`<td>...</td>`
	`<th>...</th>`
Nav6/JavaScript 1.5	`<td>...</td>`
	`<th>...</th>`
IE6	`<td>...</td>`
	`<th>...</th>`
DOM Level 1	`document.createElement("td")`

`document.createElement("th")document.table.row.insertCell(cellIndex)`

> **Note**
> Implemented in Nav1.1+ (HTML), IE3+ (HTML), Nav6 (DOM), IE4+ (DOM)
> Descends from `HTMLElement` interface (Chapter 21)
> Parent elements: `HTMLTableRowElement`

Description

The table cell elements `<td>...</td>` and `<th>...</th>` designate the actual areas where the contents of each cell of the table are. (A cell is where a row and column intersect.)

The two elements are meant for different purposes. The `<th>...</th>` element is for header cells, such as the headings of a column. The `<td>...</td>` is for normal data.

> **Note**
> In a sense, table cell elements are like <div>...</div> elements (covered in Chapter 28, "Text Elements." Both can hold additional block-level elements (such as paragraphs or tables).

Properties

abbr

JavaScript 1.5

Nav6, IE6

Syntax

```
[var x = ] HTMLTableCellElement.abbr [= abbrString]
```

The abbr property of HTMLTableCellElement objects allows a developer to specify an abbreviation of the table cell's contents in plain text. The W3C recommends use of this attribute for accessibility reasons.

align

JavaScript 1.5, JScript 3.0+

Nav6, IE4+

Syntax

```
[var x =] HTMLTableCellElement.align [= alignString]
```

The align property of HTMLTableCellElement objects refers to the horizontal alignment of the cell's contents. This attribute may take values of "left", "right", or "center", "justify", or "char" respectively. The "char" value indicates the document wants alignment based on the character designated by the char attribute. (Note both browsers currently ignore the "char" setting.) See the ch and chOff properties for details.

axis

JavaScript 1.5

Nav6, IE6

Syntax

```
[var x =] HTMLTableCellElement.axis [= axisString]
```

The `axis` property of `HTMLTableCellElement` objects is a comma-separated list, naming categories under which the cell's contents all fall, as shown in Table 29.1.

Table 29.1   *Axes of Information*

Meat	Fruit	Bread	Date
Beef	Apples	Rolls	Monday
Pork	Peaches	Biscuits	Tuesday
Chicken	Oranges	Wheat slices	Wednesday

In Table 29.1, you could say:

```
<tr>
<td axis="Meat">Beef</td>
<td axis="Fruit">Apples</td>
<td axis="Bread">Rolls</td>
<td axis="Date">Monday</td>
</tr>
```

In this scenario, the browser would have some information for its own use.

The Meat, Fruit, Bread, and Date words will not render based on the presence or absence of the `axis` attribute. This attribute is for the conveyance of meta data only—data about the data. Browsers may ignore this attribute at their own discretion. If you want to see these labels rendered, you would need to create an additional row containing these values.

bgColor

JavaScript 1.5, JScript 3.0+

Nav6, IE4+

Syntax

```
[var x =] HTMLTableCellElement.bgColor [= colorString]
```

The bgColor property of HTMLTableCellElement objects refers to the background color of the table cell. You can specify it either by name ("cyan", "red", "white", "navy", and so on) or by hexadecimal ("#00FFFF"). Hexadecimal is the preferred style, as color names in browsers may not be universally recognized.

cellIndex

JavaScript 1.5, JScript 3.0+

Nav6, IE4+

Syntax

```
var x = HTMLTableCellElement.cellIndex
```

The cellIndex property of HTMLTableCellElement objects corresponds to the cell's index number in the cells collection of its parent row. Essentially, for table cell elements,

```
this.parentNode.cells[this.cellIndex] === this
```

ch

JavaScript 1.5

Nav6, IE6

Syntax

```
[var x =] HTMLTableCellElement.ch [= characterString]
```

The ch property of HTMLTableCellElement objects refers to a common character of the cell to which the document wants the table cell aligned. (This defaults to the local decimal point.) Netscape and Internet Explorer currently ignore this attribute, as well as its counterpart, the chOff attribute. They also ignore the char setting for the align attribute. Listing 29.3 demonstrates these.

Listing 29.3   *Aligning to a Character in XHTML*

```
<?xml version="1.0" ?>
<!DOCTYPE html PUBLIC "-//W3C//DTD XHTML 1.0 Transitional//EN"
➥"DTD/xhtml1-transitional.dtd">
<html xmlns="http://www.w3.org/1999/xhtml" >
<head><title></title></head>
<body>
<table border="1">
<tr><td align="char">3.1415926535</td></tr>
<tr><td align="char">.6931471805599453</td></tr>
</table>
</body>
</html>
```

chOff

JavaScript 1.5

Nav6, IE6

Syntax

```
[var x =] HTMLTableCellElement.chOff [= characterOffset]
```

The chOff property of HTMLTableCellElement objects refers to the offset of the ch attribute's character in the table cell. Netscape and Internet Explorer currently ignore this attribute, as well as its counterpart, the ch attribute. They also ignore the char setting for the align attribute. Listing 29.3 demonstrates these.

colSpan

JavaScript 1.5, JScript 3.0+

Nav6, IE4+

Syntax

```
[var x =] HTMLTableCellElement.colSpan [= numberCols]
```

The colSpan property of HTMLTableCellElement objects refers to the number of columns of the table the table cell occupies.

Often I find setting the colspan attribute for HTML elements can cause a lot of interesting effects—shoving over a cell into a new column that didn't exist before, for example. So a bit of tinkering with this, and a few other cells, to achieve the desired results may be necessary. The same applies for the corresponding colSpan property under the DOM.

headers

JavaScript 1.5

Nav6, IE6

Syntax

```
[var x =] HTMLTableCellElement.headers [= headerString]
```

The headers property of HTMLTableCellElement objects is a string of id attributes for various other table cells in the table that are headings for this particular cell. Table 29.2's Apple cell has several headers.

Table 29.2   A Sample Table With Headers

Meat	Fruit	Bread	Date	Bill
Hamburgers	Apple	Rolls	**Monday**	
Pork Chops	Peach	Biscuits	**Tuesday**	
Chicken Legs	Orange	Wheat slices	**Wednesday**	
Meat	Fruit	Bread	Date	June
Veal	Pear	Rolls	**Thursday**	
Ham slices	Watermelon	Biscuits	**Friday**	
Chicken Thighs	Grapes	Wheat slices	**Saturday**	

In this table, you could easily create header references from Apple to Fruit, Monday, and Bill. Assuming each cell had the same id attribute as its contents, this would be:

```
<td headers="Fruit Monday Bill" id="Apple">Apple</td>
```

height

JavaScript 1.5, JScript 3.0+

Nav6, IE4+

Syntax

```
[var x = ] HTMLTableCellElement.height [= pixelNumber]
```

The `height` property of `HTMLTableCellElement` objects allows the document to recommend a cell height. The browser may fully ignore this property at its own discretion, and you should not rely on this property.

innerHTML

JavaScript 1.5, JScript 3.0+

Nav6, IE4+

Syntax

```
[var x =] HTMLTableCellElement.innerHTML [= HTMLString]
```

The `innerHTML` property of `HTMLTableCellElement` interfaces retrieves or sets the HTML source code contained between, but not including, the starting and ending tags.

I personally recommend against using `innerHTML` to set the HTML inside a tag. I strongly recommend against using `innerHTML` to append to the contents of an HTML tag:

```
elem.innerHTML += "<div><p>Hello World</p></div>" // DO NOT DO THIS
```

This forces the browser to retrieve the current `innerHTML` value, add new markup to it, and re-render the entire page.

I do like the handiness of the `innerHTML` property for retrieving HTML source code at a glance, as an alternative method to the W3C Document Object Model.

innerText

JScript 5.0+

IE5+

Syntax

```
var x = HTMLTableCellElement.innerText
```

The `innerText` property of `HTMLTableCellElement` retrieves or sets the text contained between, but not including, the starting and ending tags.

noWrap

JavaScript 1.5, JScript 3.0+

Nav6, IE4+

Deprecated in HTML 4

Syntax

```
[var x =] HTMLTableCellElement.noWrap [= wrapString]
```

The noWrap property of HTMLTableCellElement objects reflects the word wrap setting of the this object. Typically, it defaults to false, meaning words wrap automatically. The true setting disables word wrapping entirely.

HTML 4 Strict and XHTML 1 Strict do not permit the noWrap attribute, and HTML 4 prohibits a script from invalidating a document. This means if you want to maintain word wrap control, you must use styling, covered in Chapter 33, "Styling for HTML Elements."

outerHTML

JScript 3.0+

IE4+

Syntax

```
var x = HTMLTableCellElement.outerHTML
```

The outerHTML property of HTMLTableCellElement retrieves or sets the HTML source code contained between, and including, the starting and ending tags. The outerHTML property is read-only for table cells.

I do like the handiness of the outerHTML property for retrieving HTML source code at a glance, as an alternative method to the W3C Document Object Model.

rowSpan

JavaScript 1.5, JScript 3.0+

Nav6, IE4+

Syntax

```
[var x =] HTMLTableCellElement.rowSpan [= numberRows]
```

The `rowSpan` property of `HTMLTableCellElement` objects refers to the number of rows of the table the table cell occupies.

scope

JavaScript 1.5

Nav6, IE6

Syntax

```
[var x =] HTMLTableCellElement.scope [= scopeString]
```

The `scope` property of `HTMLTableCellElement` objects allows a header cell to designate itself as a header for its current row, column, row group (specified by a `HTMLTableSectionElement` object), or column group. The property, when set to `"row"`, assigns the cell to its row. When set to `"col"`, the property assigns the cell to its column. Similarly, `"rowgroup"` and `"colgroup"` result in assignments to its row group and column group, respectively.

vAlign

JavaScript 1.5, JScript 3.0+

Nav6, IE4+

Syntax

```
[var x =] HTMLTableCellElement.vAlign [= alignString]
```

The `vAlign` property of `HTMLTableCellElement` objects refers to the vertical alignment of the cell's contents. This attribute may take values of `"top"`, `"middle"`, or `"bottom"`, or `"baseline"` respectively. The first three align the contents as a whole along the top, center, or bottom of the cell respectively. The `"baseline"` value aligns them such that the first line of each cell's content is aligned.

width

JavaScript 1.5, JScript 3.0+

Nav6, IE4+

Syntax

```
[var x = ] HTMLTableCellElement.width [= pixelNumber]
```

The width property of HTMLTableCellElement objects allows the document to recommend a cell width.

Methods

The HTMLTableCellElement interface provides no methods beyond those the HTMLElement interface defines.

Event Handlers

Internet Explorer supports the following event handlers for the HTMLTableCellElement interface:

onactivate	ondragenter	onmousemove
onbeforeactivate	ondragleave	onmouseout
onbeforecopy	ondragover	onmouseover
onbeforecut	ondragstart	onmouseup
onbeforedeactivate	ondrop	onmousewheel
onbeforeeditfocus	onfilterchange	onmove
onbeforepaste	onfocus	onmoveend
onblur	onfocusin	onmovestart
onclick	onfocusout	onpaste
oncontextmenu	onhelp	onpropertychange
oncontrolselect	onkeydown	onreadystatechange
oncopy	onkeypress	onresizeend
oncut	onkeyup	onresizestart
ondblclick	onlosecapture	onselectstart
ondeactivate	onmousedown	ontimeerror
ondrag	onmouseenter	
ondragend	onmouseleave	

HTMLTableColElement/<colgroup>...</colgroup> / <col />

Browser/JavaScript Version	Created By
Nav4/JavaScript 1.2	Not implemented
IE4/JScript 3.0	`<colgroup>...</colgroup>`
	`<col />`
IE5/JScript 5.0	`<colgroup>...</colgroup>`
	`<col />`
IE5.5/JScript 5.5	`<colgroup>...</colgroup>`
	`<col />`
Nav6/JavaScript 1.5	`<colgroup>...</colgroup>`
	`<col />`
IE6	`<colgroup>...</colgroup>`
	`<col />`
DOM Level 1	`document.createElement("colgroup")`
	`document.createElement("col")`

> **Note**
> Implemented in IE3+ (HTML), Nav6 (HTML/DOM), IE4+ (DOM)
> Descends from HTMLElement interface (Chapter 21)
> Parent elements: `HTMLTableElement`, `HTMLTableColElement` (colgroup)

Description

The column group elements allow document authors to create structural divisions within a table. In XHTML 1.0, column group elements immediately follow any optional caption element.

Although the HTML Validation service does not check for a valid number of column group elements, there are rules you must follow. Your count of columns must be precise. For instance, the children of the table element that are column group elements must have their span attributes totaling the same number of columns as are in the table. (The column group elements have default span attributes equal to 1.)

Currently, Netscape 6's support of column groups for their intended purpose, styling of the columns, is a little shaky. Also, if you attempt to modify the number of columns (including by adding a key table cell) in a table containing column groups, you will inevitably break HTML compliance in the table before you fix it.

Therefore, for the time being, I recommend you clone a table using the Core DOM cloneNode(true) method (see Chapter 20, "Core DOM Objects," under Node), make your changes to the clone, and then replace the table with its clone when you've finished. This way, you can maintain your document's validity while making the necessary adjustments.

Properties

align

JavaScript 1.5, JScript 3.0+

Nav6, IE4+

Syntax

```
[var x =] HTMLTableColElement.align [= alignString]
```

The align property of HTMLTableColElement objects refers to the horizontal alignment of the cell's contents. This attribute may take values of "left", "right", or "center", "justify", or "char" respectively. The char value indicates the document wants alignment based on the character designated by the char attribute. (Note both browsers currently ignore the "char" setting.) See the ch and chOff properties for details.

ch

JavaScript 1.5

Nav6

Syntax

```
[var x =] HTMLTableColElement.ch [= characterString]
```

The `ch` property of `HTMLTableColElement` objects refers to a common character of the column to which the document wants the column's cells aligned. (This defaults to the local decimal point.) Netscape and Internet Explorer currently ignore this attribute, as well as its counterpart, the `chOff` attribute. They also ignore the `char` setting for the `align` attribute. Listing 29.3 demonstrates these for table cells.

chOff

JavaScript 1.5

Nav6

Syntax

```
[var x =] HTMLTableColElement.chOff [= characterOffset]
```

The `chOff` property of `HTMLTableColElement` objects refers to the offset to the `ch` attribute's character in the table column. Netscape and Internet Explorer currently ignore this attribute, as well as its counterpart, the `ch` attribute. They also ignore the `char` setting for the `align` attribute. Listing 29.3 demonstrates these for table cells.

innerHTML

JavaScript 1.5 (`colgroup`), JScript 3.0+ (`colgroup`)

Nav6 (`colgroup`), IE4+ (`colgroup`)

Syntax

```
[var x =] HTMLTableColElement.innerHTML [= HTMLString]
```

The `innerHTML` property of `HTMLTableColElement` interfaces retrieves the HTML source code contained between, but not including, the starting and ending tags.

I do like the handiness of the `innerHTML` property for retrieving HTML source code at a glance, as an alternative method to the W3C Document Object Model.

outerHTML

JScript 3.0+

IE4+

Syntax

```
var x = HTMLTableColElement.outerHTML
```

The outerHTML property of HTMLTableColElement retrieves the HTML source code contained between, and including, the starting and ending tags.

I do like the handiness of the outerHTML property for retrieving HTML source code at a glance, as an alternative method to the W3C Document Object Model. (The DOM provides an object structure for the source code; outerHTML provides the corresponding source code.)

span

JavaScript 1.5, JScript 3.0+

Nav6, IE4+

Syntax

```
[var x =] HTMLTableColElement.span [= colsSpan]
```

The span property of HTMLTableColElement objects designates for the table how many columns of the table the this object affects.

vAlign

JavaScript 1.5, JScript 3.0+

Nav6, IE4+

Syntax

```
[var x =] HTMLTableColElement.vAlign [= alignString]
```

The vAlign property of HTMLTableColElement objects refers to the horizontal alignment of the column's contents. This attribute may take values of "top", "middle", or "bottom", or "baseline" of each cell respectively. The first three align the contents as a whole along the top, center, or bottom, respectively. The "baseline" value aligns them such that the first line of each cell's content is aligned.

width

JavaScript 1.5, JScript 3.0+

Nav6, IE4+

Syntax

```
[var x = ] HTMLTableColElement.width [= pixelNumber]
```

The width property of HTMLTableColElement objects allows the document to recommend a column width. The browser may fully ignore this property at its own discretion, and you should not rely on this property.

Methods

The HTMLTableColElement interface provides no methods beyond those the HTMLElement interface defines.

Event Handlers

Internet Explorer supports the following event handlers for the HTMLTableColElement interface:

    onlayoutcomplete (col)

    onreadystatechange (col, colgroup)

HTMLTableRowElement/<tr>...</tr>

Browser/JavaScript Version	Created By
Nav4/JavaScript 1.2	Not implemented
IE4/JScript 3.0	<tr>...</tr>
IE5/JScript 5.0	<tr>...</tr>
IE5.5/JScript 5.5	<tr>...</tr>
Nav6/JavaScript 1.5	<tr>...</tr>
IE6	<tr>...</tr>
DOM Level 1	document.createElement("tr")

> **Note**
> Implemented in Nav1.1+ (HTML), IE3+ (HTML), Nav6 (DOM), IE4+ (DOM)
> Descends from HTMLElement interface (Chapter 21)
> Parent elements: HTMLTableSectionElement

Description

The table row element defines each row in a table. Note (X)HTML requires a table row element cannot be a child element of a table element; it must be a child of a table section element.

Properties

align

JavaScript 1.5, JScript 3.0+

Nav6, IE4+

Syntax

```
[var x =] HTMLTableRowElement.align [= alignString]
```

The align property of HTMLTableRowElement objects refers to the horizontal alignment of the row's contents. This attribute may take values of "left", "right", or "center", "justify", or "char" respectively. The "char" value indicates the document wants alignment based on the character designated by the char attribute. (Note both browsers currently ignore the char setting.) See the ch and chOff properties for details.

bgColor

JavaScript 1.5, JScript 3.0+

Nav6, IE4+

Syntax

```
[var x =] HTMLTableRowElement.bgColor [= colorString]
```

The bgColor property of HTMLTableRowElement objects refers to the background color of the table row. You can specify it either by name ("cyan", "red", "white", "navy", and so on) or by hexadecimal ("#00FFFF"). Hexadecimal is the preferred style, as color names in browsers may not be universally recognized.

cells

JavaScript 1.5, JScript 3.0+

Nav6, IE4+

Syntax

```
var x = HTMLTableRowElement.cells
```

The `cells` property of `HTMLTableRowElement` objects is a collection of all cells in the table rows, including header cells. The cells appear in this collection in order of their appearance in the document.

item

JavaScript 1.5, JScript 5.0+

Nav6, IE5+

Syntax

```
var x = HTMLTableRowElement.cells.item(index)
```

```
var x = HTMLTableRowElement.cells.item('idString'[, optionalIndex]) (IE Only)
```

For the `item` method of `cells`, by supplying a number (specifically, a non-negative integer less than `this.length`) as the first argument, you can get a `Node` object from the `this` object representing that `Node`'s placement in the `this` object's index. Any other argument you submit to this method results in the method returning `null`.

length

JavaScript 1.5, JScript 3.0+

Nav6, IE4+

Syntax

```
var x = HTMLTableRowElement.cells.length
```

The `length` property of `cells` tells how many objects are in the collection.

tags

JScript 3.0+

IE4+

Syntax

```
var x = HTMLTableRowElement.cells.tags(tagName)
```

The `tags` method of `cells` returns a subset of the `this` element comprising all elements whose `tagName` property matches the first argument.

urns

JScript 5.0+

IE5+

Syntax

```
var x = HTMLTableRowElement.cells.urns(behaviorName)
```

The `urns` method of `cells` returns a subset of the `this` element comprising all elements possessing a DHTML behavior whose name matches the first argument.

DHTML behaviors, an Internet Explorer proprietary extension to HTML, go far beyond the scope of this book. You can find information on them via Microsoft's Web site at `http://msdn.microsoft.com/workshop/author/behaviors/overview.asp`.

ch

JavaScript 1.5

Nav6, IE6

Syntax

```
[var x =] HTMLTableColElement.ch [= characterString]
```

The `ch` property of `HTMLTableRowElement` objects refers to a common character of the row the document wants the column's cells aligned to. (This defaults to the local decimal point.) Netscape and Internet Explorer currently ignore this attribute, as well as its counterpart, the `chOff` attribute. They also ignore the `char` setting for the `align` attribute. Listing 29.3 demonstrates these for table cells.

chOff

JavaScript 1.5

Nav6, IE6

Syntax

```
[var x =] HTMLTableRowElement.chOff [= characterOffset]
```

The chOff property of HTMLTableRowElement objects refers to the offset to the ch attribute's character in the table row. Netscape and Internet Explorer currently ignore this attribute, as well as its counterpart, the ch attribute. They also ignore the char setting for the align attribute. Listing 29.3 demonstrates these for table cells.

innerHTML

JavaScript 1.5, JScript 3.0+

Nav6, IE4+

Syntax

```
[var x =] HTMLTableRowElement.innerHTML [= HTMLString]
```

The innerHTML property of HTMLTableRowElement interfaces retrieves or sets the HTML source code contained between, but not including, the starting and ending tags. The innerHTML property is read-only for Internet Explorer.

innerText

JScript 3.0+

IE4+

Syntax

```
var x = HTMLTableRowElement.innerText
```

The innerText property of HTMLTableRowElement retrieves the text contained between, but not including, the starting and ending tags.

outerHTML

JScript 3.0+

IE4+

Syntax

```
var x = HTMLTableRowElement.outerHTML
```

The `outerHTML` property of `HTMLTableRowElement` retrieves the HTML source code contained between, and including, the starting and ending tags.

I do like the handiness of the `outerHTML` property for retrieving HTML source code at a glance, as an alternative method to the W3C Document Object Model. (The DOM provides an object structure for the source code; `outerHTML` provides the corresponding source code.)

rowIndex

JavaScript 1.5, JScript 3.0+

Nav6, IE4+

Syntax

```
var x = HTMLTableRowElement.rowIndex
```

The `rowIndex` property of `HTMLTableRowElement` objects corresponds to the row's index number in the `rows` collection of its ancestor table. Essentially, for table row elements, if `myTable` is the table which `rowIndex` belongs to, then

```
myTable.rows[this.rowIndex] === this
```

sectionRowIndex

JavaScript 1.5, JScript 3.0+

Nav6, IE4+

Syntax

```
var x = HTMLTableRowElement.sectionRowIndex
```

The `sectionRowIndex` property of `HTMLTableRowElement` objects corresponds to the row's index number in the rows collection of its parent element (whether it is the table, table head, table foot, or a table body). Essentially, for table row elements

```
this.parentNode.rows[this.sectionRowIndex] === this
```

Listing 29.4, which works with Internet Explorer 5+ and Netscape 6, shows it works for table elements as well, something the DOM documentation doesn't necessarily reveal. (This works because the browser assumes the presence of a table body when it is not there for this instance.)

Listing 29.4   `sectionRowIndex` *for a Parent Table Element*

```
<?xml version="1.0" ?>
<!DOCTYPE html PUBLIC "-//W3C//DTD XHTML 1.0 Transitional//EN"
➥"DTD/xhtml1-transitional.dtd">
<html xmlns="http://www.w3.org/1999/xhtml" >
<head><title></title></head>
<body onload="var x = document.getElementById('myRow');
var y = document.createTextNode(x.sectionRowIndex);
document.getElementById('p1').appendChild(y);">
<table>
<tr id="myRow"><td>1</td><td>2</td><td>3</td></tr>
</table>
<p id="p1">sectionRowIndex == </p>
<!-- Results:
sectionRowIndex == 0
-->
</body>
</html>
```

vAlign

JavaScript 1.5, JScript 3.0+

Nav6, IE4+

Syntax

```
[var x =] HTMLTableRowElement.vAlign [= alignString]
```

The vAlign property of HTMLTableRowElement objects refers to the vertical alignment of the row's cells. This attribute may take values of "top", "middle", or "bottom", or "baseline" of each cell respectively. The first three align the contents as a whole along the top, center, or bottom respectively. The "baseline" value aligns them such that the first line of each cell's content is aligned.

width

JScript 3.0+

IE4+

Syntax

```
[var x = ] HTMLTableRowElement.width [= pixelNumber]
```

The width property of HTMLTableRowElement objects allows the document to recommend a row width. The browser may fully ignore this property at its own discretion, and you should not rely on this property.

Methods

deleteCell()

JavaScript 1.5, JScript 3.0+

Nav6, IE4+

Syntax

```
var x = HTMLTableRowElement.deleteCell(rowIndex)
```

The deleteCell() method of HTMLTableRowElement objects removes the cell in the this object's cells collection whose index matches the first argument, a non-negative integer. If there is no argument Internet Explorer deletes the last row.

insertCell()

JavaScript 1.5, JScript 3.0+

Nav6, IE4+

Syntax

```
var x = HTMLTableElement.insertCell(rowIndex)
```

The `insertCell()` method of `HTMLTableRowElement` objects inserts a new empty cell into the `this` object's `cells` collection, just before the cell whose index number matches the first argument, a non-negative integer. If the row index is omitted, then Internet Explorer appends a new cell at the end of the `cells` collection.

Be careful in using this method in tables possessing column groups. As I note earlier, you are not allowed to break HTML compliance via script, and HTML compliance requires the number of columns match the defined number of columns. By adding a cell in the wrong place, you can force a table to add a column.

Event Handlers

Internet Explorer supports the following event handlers for the `HTMLTableRowElement` interface:

onactivate	ondrag	onlosecapture
onbeforeactivate	ondragend	onmousedown
onbeforecopy	ondragenter	onmouseenter
onbeforecut	ondragleave	onmouseleave
onbeforedeactivate	ondragover	onmousemove
onbeforeeditfocus	ondragstart	onmouseout
onbeforepaste	ondrop	onmouseover
onblur	onfilterchange	onmouseup
onclick	onfocus	onmousewheel
oncontextmenu	onfocusin	onmove
oncontrolselect	onfocusout	onmoveend
oncopy	onhelp	onmovestart
oncut	onkeydown	onpaste
ondblclick	onkeypress	onpropertychange
ondeactivate	onkeyup	onreadystatechange

```
onresizeend

onresizestart

onselectstart

ontimeerror
```

HTMLTableSectionElement/<thead>...</thead> / <tfoot>...</tfoot> / <tbody>...</tbody>

Browser/JavaScript Version	Created By
Nav4/JavaScript 1.2	Not implemented
IE4/JScript 3.0	`<thead>...</thead>`
	`<tfoot>...</tfoot>`
	`<tbody>...</tbody>`
IE5/JScript 5.0	`<thead>...</thead>`
	`<tfoot>...</tfoot>`
	`<tbody>...</tbody>`
IE5.5/JScript 5.5	`<thead>...</thead>`
	`<tfoot>...</tfoot>`
	`<tbody>...</tbody>`
Nav6/JavaScript 1.5	`<thead>...</thead>`
	`<tfoot>...</tfoot>`
	`<tbody>...</tbody>`
IE6	`<thead>...</thead>`
	`<tfoot>...</tfoot>`
	`<tbody>...</tbody>`
DOM Level 1	`document.createElement("thead")`
	`document.createElement("tfoot")`
	`document.createElement("tbody")`

> **Note**
>
> Implemented in IE3+ (HTML), Nav6 (HTML/DOM), IE4+ (DOM)
>
> Descends from `HTMLElement` interface (Chapter 21)
>
> Parent elements: `HTMLTableElement`

Description

The table section element defines a table section in the document. Note (X)HTML requires that a table row element cannot be a child element of a table element when the table also has a child which is a table section element. Table rows should be contained within a table section.

There's actually a very specific order of table sections in (X)HTML. You are permitted one optional `<thead>...</thead>` element, followed by one optional `<tfoot>...</tfoot>` element, and then followed by any number of optional `<tbody>...</tbody>` elements.

Properties

align

JavaScript 1.5, JScript 3.0+

Nav6, IE4+

Syntax

`[var x =] HTMLTableSectionElement.align [= alignString]`

The `align` property of `HTMLTableSectionElement` objects refers to the horizontal alignment of the table section's rows relative to the table—whether its left edge lines up with the left side of the main text, its right edge lines up with the right side, or the table section is centered horizontally. This attribute may take values of `"left"`, `"right"`, or `"center"`, respectively.

bgColor

JScript 3.0+

IE4+

Syntax

`[var x =] HTMLTableSectionElement.bgColor [= colorString]`

The `bgColor` property of `HTMLTableSectionElement` objects refers to the background color of the table. You can specify it either by name (`"cyan"`, `"red"`, `"white"`, `"navy"`, and so on) or by hexadecimal (`"#00FFFF"`). Hexadecimal is the preferred style, as color names in browsers may not be universally recognized.

ch

JavaScript 1.5

Nav6, IE6

Syntax

`[var x =] HTMLTableSectionElement.ch [= characterString]`

The `ch` property of `HTMLTableSectionElement` objects refers to a common character of the section's cells the document wants the section's cells aligned to. (This defaults to the local decimal point.) Netscape and Internet Explorer currently ignore this attribute, as well as its counterpart, the `chOff` attribute. They also ignore the `char` setting for the `align` attribute. Listing 29.3 demonstrates these for tables.

chOff

JavaScript 1.5

Nav6, IE6

Syntax

`[var x =] HTMLTableSectionElement.chOff [= characterOffset]`

The `chOff` property of `HTMLTableSectionElement` objects refers to the offset to the `ch` attribute's character in the section's cells. Netscape and Internet Explorer currently ignore this attribute, as well as its counterpart, the `ch` attribute. They also ignore the `char` setting for the `align` attribute. Listing 29.3 demonstrates these for tables.

innerHTML

JavaScript 1.5, JScript 3.0+

Nav6, IE4+

Syntax

```
[var x =] HTMLTableSectionElement.innerHTML [= HTMLString]
```

The innerHTML property of HTMLTableSectionElement interfaces retrieves the HTML source code contained between, but not including, the starting and ending tags.

innerText

JScript 3.0+

IE4+

Syntax

```
var x = HTMLTableSectionElement.innerText
```

The innerText property of HTMLTableSectionElement retrieves the text contained between, but not including, the starting and ending tags.

outerHTML

JScript 3.0+

IE4+

Syntax

```
var x = HTMLTableSectionElement.outerHTML
```

The outerHTML property of HTMLTableSectionElement retrieves the HTML source code contained between, and including, the starting and ending tags.

I do like the handiness of the outerHTML property for retrieving HTML source code at a glance, as a companion method to the W3C Document Object Model. (The DOM provides an object structure for the source code; outerHTML provides the corresponding source code.)

rows

JavaScript 1.5, JScript 3.0+

Nav6, IE4+

Syntax

```
var x = HTMLTableSectionElement.rows
```

The rows property of HTMLTableSectionElement objects is a collection of all rows in the table section, including header rows, footer rows, and body rows. The rows appear in the order of their placement in the document.

item

JScript 3.0+

Nav6, IE4+

Syntax

```
var x = HTMLTableSectionElement.rows.item(index)
```

For the item method of rows, by supplying a number (specifically, a non-negative integer less than this.length) as the first argument, you can get a Node object from the this object representing that Node's placement in the this object's index. Any other argument you submit to this method results in the method returning null.

length

JScript 3.0+

Nav6, IE4+

Syntax

```
var x = HTMLTableSectionElement.rows.length
```

The length property of rows tells how many objects are in the collection.

tags

JScript 3.0+

IE4+

Syntax

`var x = HTMLTableSectionElement.rows.tags(tagName)`

The `tags` method of `rows` returns a subset of the `this` element comprising all elements whose `tagName` property matches the first argument.

urns

JScript 5.0+

IE5+

Syntax

`var x = HTMLTableSectionElement.rows.urns(behaviorName)`

The `urns` method of `rows` returns a subset of the `this` element comprising all elements possessing a DHTML behavior whose name matches the first argument.

DHTML behaviors, an Internet Explorer proprietary extension to HTML, go far beyond the scope of this book. You can find information on them via Microsoft's Web site at `http://msdn.microsoft.com/workshop/author/behaviors/overview.asp`.

vAlign

JavaScript 1.5, IE4+

Nav6, IE4+

Syntax

`[var x =] HTMLTableSectionElement.vAlign [= alignString]`

The `vAlign` property of `HTMLTableSectionElement` objects refers to the vertical alignment of the section's cells' contents. This attribute may take values of `"top"`, `"middle"`, or `"bottom"`, or `"baseline"`, respectively. The first three align the contents as a whole along the top, center, or bottom, of each cell respectively. The `"baseline"` value aligns them such that the first line of each cell's content is aligned.

Methods

deleteRow()

JavaScript 1.5, JScript 3.0+

Nav6, IE4+

Syntax

HTMLTableSectionElement.deleteRow(*rowIndex*)

The deleteRow() method of HTMLTableSectionElement objects removes the row in the this object's rows collection whose index matches the first argument, a non-negative integer. In Internet Explorer if there is no argument the last row in the rows collection is deleted.

insertRow()

JavaScript 1.5, JScript 3.0+

Nav6, IE4+

Syntax

var *x* = *HTMLTableSectionElement*.insertRow(*rowIndex*)

The insertRow() method of HTMLTableSectionElement objects inserts a new empty row into the this object's rows collection, just before the row whose index number matches the first argument, a non-negative integer. In Internet Explorer, with no argument, a row is appended after the last row of the rows collection.

This particular method is not good for HTML 4. Instead, I suggest you create the entire row, including cells, and then use

HTMLTableSectionElement.rows[*oldRow*].parentNode.insertBefore(*newRow*,
➥*HTMLTableSectionElement*.rows[*oldRow*])

moveRow()

JScript 5.0+

IE5+

Syntax

HTMLTableSectionElement.moveRow(*rowIndexToMove, toBeforeRowIndex*)

The moveRow() method of HTMLTableSectionElement objects moves a row from one place in the this object's rows collection to another. The row has an index number specified in the first argument, and will move to just after the row with an index number specified in the second argument.

Event Handlers

Internet Explorer supports the following event handlers for the HTMLTableSectionElement interface:

onactivate	onfocus	onmouseup
onbeforeactivate	onfocusin	onmousewheel
onbeforecut	onfocusout	onmove
onbeforedeactivate	onhelp	onmoveend
onbeforepaste	onkeydown	onmovestart
onblur	onkeypress	onpaste
onclick	onkeyup	onpropertychange
oncontextmenu	onlosecapture	onreadystatechange
oncontrolselect	onmousedown	onresizeend
oncut	onmouseenter	onresizestart
ondblclick	onmouseleave	onselectstart
ondeactivate	onmousemove	ontimeerror
ondragenter	onmouseout	
ondragstart	onmouseover	

CHAPTER 30

Image Elements

HTMLImageElement/<img />

Browser/JavaScript Version	Created By
Nav4/JavaScript 1.2	`<img />`
IE4/JScript 3.0	`<img />`
IE5/JScript 5.0	`<img />`
IE5.5/JScript 5.5	`<img />`
Nav6/JavaScript 1.5	`<img />`
IE6	`<img />`
DOM Level 1	`document.createElement("img")`

> **Note**
> Implemented in Nav1+ (HTML), IE3+ (HTML), Nav3+ (DOM), IE4+ (DOM)
> Descends from `HTMLElement` interface (Chapter 21)
> Parent elements: `HTMLBodyElement` (Chapter 22), any block text element

Description

Images have been a part of hypertext for quite some time. As the World Wide Web came into the public view in the early 1990s, there were already a few ways to store an image as a file. The most popular formats then (as now) were GIF and JPEG files. These types of images are not exactly the kind you can hand-code, like an HTML or XML document, and other modules of the two major browsers handle the rendering of these files. (X)HTML included a special tag, the `<img />` tag, with an `src` attribute to tell the browser you wanted to view an image in the document.

You should not expect newer image formats, such as SVG (which you can hand-code, incidentally), to work with the `<img />` element. Instead, the HTML 4 Recommendation includes the `<object>...</object>` element, covered in Chapter 31, "Programmable Elements." The `<embed>` element is, however, the only way currently to embed an SVG image so it is viewable across browsers.

```
<embed src="MySVGImage.svg" width="300px" height="200px" type="image/svg+xml" />
```

Because these bitmap images are not HTML or XML, JavaScript's capabilities across browsers to modify them are limited. Although you can achieve some effects with filters and CSS, once the src attribute is set, just about all you can do to change the image is set a new src attribute.

For the record, all five listings featured in this chapter are available via the JavaScript Developer's Dictionary Web site at http://www.jslab.org/jsdd. Just look for www.jslab.org/jsdd/30list01.html through www.jslab.org/jsdd/30list05.html.

Animation and Caching of Images in HTML

One of the most common uses of JavaScript is to change an image onmouseover. For instance, if you have a black-and-white thumbnail, and you want to see a color version when the mouse is over it, the following code works, with Netscape 6 and Internet Explorer 4 onward:

```
<img id="thumbnail" src="thumbnail_bw.gif" alt="Sample"
onmouseover="this.src = 'thumbnail_color.gif'"
onmouseout="this.src = 'thumbnail_bw.gif'" />
```

There's only one problem with this. If the color image isn't preloaded, you'll be waiting for a moment while the browser calls the color image from the server... This is not very desirable.

Two different methods for creating and caching images exist. One is by the Image() function as a constructor. The other is by creating a new image element in the DOM and swapping it out when needed. Listings 30.1 and 30.2 show these two alternatives.

Listing 30.1 *Caching Images with* Image()

```
<?xml version="1.0" ?>
<!DOCTYPE html PUBLIC "-//W3C//DTD XHTML 1.0 Transitional//EN"
➥"DTD/xhtml1-transitional.dtd">
<html xmlns="http://www.w3.org/1999/xhtml" >
<head><title></title>
<script language="JavaScript" type="text/javascript">
<!--
var imageCache = new Array()
for (var x = 0; x < 1; x++) {
    imageCache[x] = new Image()
    imageCache[x].src = "on_" + x + ".gif"
    }
```

Listing 30.1   *(continued)*

```
function imageSwap(imgIndex) {
    var k = document.images[imgIndex].src
    document.images[imgIndex].src = imageCache[imgIndex].src
    imageCache[imgIndex].src = k
    }
//-->
</script>
</head>
<body>
<img id="thumbnail" src="off_0.gif"
onmouseover="imageSwap(0)" onmouseout="imageSwap(0)" alt="Sample" />
</body>
</html>
```

I used an image index in Listing 30.1 but, equally, you could add a name attribute to the <img/> element and use document.images['imageName'].src.

In my testing, IE5.5 always went back to the drive where I stored the image. Listing 30.2, which will work in Internet Explorer 5.0+ and Netscape 6, is much more graceful for pages with a single image, never going back to the drive.

Listing 30.2   *Caching Images with the DOM*

```
<?xml version="1.0" ?>
<!DOCTYPE html PUBLIC "-//W3C//DTD XHTML 1.0 Transitional//EN"
"DTD/xhtml1-transitional.dtd">
<html xmlns="http://www.w3.org/1999/xhtml" >
<head><title></title>
<script language="JavaScript" type="text/javascript">
<!--

var imageCache = new Array()
function go() {
    var z = document.getElementsByTagName("img")
    for (var x = 0; x < z.length; x++) {
        var y = x
        imageCache[y] = document.createElement("img")
        imageCache[y].src = "on_" + x + ".gif"
        imageCache[y].id = "on_" + x
        imageCache[y].onmouseout = function () {imageSwap(y)}
        }
    }
```

Listing 30.2   *(continued)*

```
function imageSwap(arg) {
    var x = document.getElementsByTagName("img")[0]
    var y = imageCache[arg]
    imageCache[arg] = x.parentNode.replaceChild(y, x)
    }
//-->
</script>
</head>
<body onload="go()">
<p>
<img id="thumb" src="off_0.gif" alt="Sample"
onmouseover="imageSwap(0)" />
</p>
</body>
</html>
```

This is a very rudimentary animation that JavaScript drives, based on an event. You can generate a timed animation using JavaScript, which will work in Internet Explorer 5+ and Netscape 6, as Listing 30.3 demonstrates. Notice the use of the `setTimeout()` function within the `rotateImage()` function.

Listing 30.3   *Basic Timed Animation Using JavaScript*

```
<?xml version="1.0" ?>
<!DOCTYPE html PUBLIC "-//W3C//DTD XHTML 1.0 Transitional//EN"
➥"DTD/xhtml1-transitional.dtd">
<html xmlns="http://www.w3.org/1999/xhtml" >
<head><title></title>
<script language="JavaScript" type="text/javascript">
<!--
var imageCache = new Array()
for (var x = 0; x <= 2; x++) {
    imageCache[x] = document.createElement("img")
    imageCache[x].src = "img_" + x + ".gif"
    }
x = 0

function rotateImage() {
    x++ // 1, 2, 3
    x %= 3 // 1, 2, 0
    document.getElementById("thumbnail").src = imageCache[x].src
```

Listing 30.3   *(continued)*

```
    setTimeout("rotateImage()", 1000)
    // assuring a repeat
    }

//-->
</script>
</head>
<body onload="rotateImage()">
<img id="thumbnail" src="img_0.gif" alt="Sample" />
</body>
</html>
```

Properties

align

JavaScript 1.5, JScript 3.0+

Nav6, IE4+

Syntax

```
[var x =] HTMLImageElement.align [= alignString]
```

The `align` property of `HTMLImageElement` object refers to the vertical alignment of the image relative to the baseline of the surrounding text in the document—whether the bottom edge of the image lines up with the bottom of the main text, its top edge lines up with the top of the text, or the image is centered vertically.

In Netscape 6, this attribute may take values of "bottom," "top," or "middle," respectively.

Internet Explorer 6 offers quite a few more options. "absbottom" means the absolute bottoms of the text and the image line up. "absmiddle" lines up the absolute centers horizontally. "texttop" lines up the absolute tops of the image with the text. "baseline" lines up the baselines of the text with the bottom of the image.

alt

JavaScript 1.5, JScript 3.0+

Nav6, IE4+

Syntax

`[var x =] HTMLImageElement.alt [= altTextString]`

The `alt` property of the `HTMLImageElement` object is an alternate text string in case the image cannot be loaded into the page. The W3C requires it in HTML 4 for accessibility reasons. I like it because it also helps in the case of an HTTP 404 image.

border

JavaScript 1.1+, JScript 3.0+

Nav3+, IE4+

Syntax

`[var x =] HTMLImageElement.border [= pixelNumber]`

The `border` property of `HTMLImageElement` objects specifies how many pixels of space around an image there should be. This property, though deprecated in HTML 4, is useful; often a developer wants to use an image for a link, but does not want a blue border around it. Listing 30.4 puts this to good use.

Listing 30.4   *A Clickable Image with No Blue Borders*

```
<?xml version="1.0" ?>
<!DOCTYPE html PUBLIC "-//W3C//DTD XHTML 1.0 Transitional//EN"
"DTD/xhtml1-transitional.dtd">
<html xmlns="http://www.w3.org/1999/xhtml" >
<head><title></title></head>
<body>
<a href="javascript:void(null)"
><img src="http://www.jslab.org/author/alex.jpg"
alt="My Navy photo" border="0" /></a>
<p>Note how there is no blue border around this image.</p>
</body>
</html>
```

(If you actually load this, you'll see what I looked like in 1996.)

> **Tip**
> You may notice for a moment I moved the closing portion of the link tag to the next line. This is another dirty little secret of HTML—it doesn't care where you end a tag, as long as you end it. By doing this, I prevent a whitespace text node from being in there, and it helps prevent an unwanted carriage return.

complete

JavaScript 1.1+, JScript 3.0+

Nav3+, IE4+

Syntax

```
var x = HTMLImageElement.complete
```

The `complete` property of `HTMLImageElement` objects is a Boolean value (see Chapter 5, "Boolean()," for a definition) reflecting whether the image has finished loading.

galleryImg

IE6

Syntax

```
[var x =] HTMLImageElement.galleryImg [= boolValue]
```

The `galleryImg` property of `HTMLImageElement` is an extension Microsoft Internet Explorer 6 provides for image handling by the user. When set to `true`, this value activates the Gallery Toolbar—which allows a user to save, print, or temporarily resize to fit an image on the screen.

You can learn more about this nonstandard but interesting feature at
`http://msdn.microsoft.com/workshop/misc/mypictures/mypictures_ovw.asp`.

height

JavaScript 1.1+, JScript 3.0+

Nav3+, IE4+

Syntax

```
[var x =] HTMLImageElement.height [= heightPixels]
```

The `height` property of `HTMLImageElement` objects reflects the height of the image as rendered on the screen in pixels. In Netscape 3 and 4 it is read-only. The `height` property is reliable only after the image has been loaded, as can be confirmed using an `onload` handler. (Using the `Image()` constructor, mentioned later in this chapter, results in the actual image height being this property when first set.)

hspace

JavaScript 1.1+, JScript 3.0+

Nav3+, IE4+

Syntax

```
[var x =] HTMLImageElement.hspace [= hSpacePixels]
```

The `hspace` property of `HTMLImageElement` objects reflects the horizontal whitespace margins of the image as rendered on the screen in pixels. (Using the `Image()` constructor, mentioned later in this chapter, results in this property starting as 0.) In Netscape 3 and 4 the `hspace` property was read-only.

isMap

JavaScript 1.5, JScript 3.0+

Nav6, IE4+

Syntax

```
[var x =] HTMLImageElement.isMap [= boolValue]
```

The `isMap` property of `HTMLImageElement` objects indicates to the browser whether the image is a server-side image map. Such maps must be inside an `<a href="..."></a>` element, where the map points to the server-side processor for this image map. (The coordinates the user clicks on will be appended as a query-string to the URI of the link.)

longDesc

JavaScript 1.5

Nav6, IE6

Syntax

```
[var x =] HTMLImageElement.longDesc [= descString]
```

The longDesc property of HTMLImageElement objects gives a URI to a longer description of what the image represents. This is meant to assist the alt attribute in describing the element.

lowSrc

JavaScript 1.1+, JScript 3.0+

Nav3+, IE4+

Syntax

```
[var x =] HTMLImageElement.lowSrc [= smallerImageSizeURI]
```

The lowSrc property of HTMLImageElement objects is a URI pointing to a copy of the image with a smaller file size. A browser will attempt to download the lowSrc image before downloading the src image. The idea is to allow the user to see a preview of the actual image to scale, before the actual image loads. Therefore, lowSrc images tend to have much lower file sizes, usually by decreasing resolution.

This is actually one of the most under-used features of image markup, and is very important when you have images greater than about 20 kilobytes. (That's about three seconds of download time on a 56Kbps connection.) I encourage you to spend some time creating low-resolution editions of the images on your site, just to give someone something to see while the real image loads. It is also good practice to specify the width and height attributes on all <img> elements.

name

JavaScript 1.1+, JScript 3.0+

Nav3+, IE4+

Syntax

```
[var x =] HTMLImageElement.name [= nameString]
```

The name property of HTMLImageElement objects reflects the name of the image in the document.images collection. HTML 4 did not formally deprecate the name attribute for this element, but the W3C does not recommend its use. (They have removed it from XHTML 1.0 Strict.)

This presents a similar issue to identifying forms by a name attribute; see Listing 25.1 for details.

nameProp

JScript 5.0+

IE5+

Syntax

```
[var x =] HTMLImageElement.nameProp [= imgSrc]
```

The nameProp property of HTMLImageElement objects is a read-only version of the src property. Use src instead; it's DOM-compliant and better supported.

outerHTML

JScript 3.0+

IE4+

Syntax

```
var x = HTMLImageElement.outerHTML
```

The outerHTML property of HTMLImageElement retrieves or sets the HTML source code contained between, and including, the starting and ending tags. (Note: Because <img /> does not have children, usually all you'll get is the image tag.)

I do like the handiness of the outerHTML property for retrieving HTML source code at a glance, as a companion method to the W3C Document Object Model. (The DOM provides an object structure for the source code; outerHTML provides the corresponding source code.)

protocol

JScript 3.0+

IE4+

Syntax

```
var x = HTMLImageElement.protocol
```

The `protocol` property of `HTMLImageElement` objects reflects the protocol (HTTP, FTP, and so on) used to fetch the image from the server. As this is nonstandard, you can probably be safer extracting this value from the `src` property.

src

JavaScript 1.1+, JScript 3.0+

Nav3+, IE4+

Syntax

```
[var x =] HTMLImageElement.src [= imgSrc]
```

The `src` property of `HTMLImageElement` objects reflects the location of the image as a URI. By changing this property, you can affect which image renders in the image tag. It is permissible to use a relative URL when setting the `src` property, however you should be aware that when retrieving the property it will be expressed as an absolute URL.

useMap

JavaScript 1.5+, JScript 5.0+

Nav6+, IE5+

Syntax

```
[var x =] HTMLImageElement.useMap [= mapName]
```

The `useMap` property of `HTMLImageElement` objects associates the `this` element with a map element, described later in this chapter.

vspace

JavaScript 1.1+, JScript 3.0+

Nav3+, IE4+

Syntax

```
[var x =] HTMLImageElement.height [= heightPixels]
```

The vspace property of HTMLImageElement objects reflects the vertical whitespace margins of the image as rendered on the screen in pixels. You can change the value of the vspace property in Netscape 6 and Internet Explorer 4+. (Using the Image() constructor, mentioned later in this chapter, results in this property starting as 0.)

width

JavaScript 1.1+, JScript 3.0+

Nav3+, IE4+

Syntax

`[var x =] HTMLImageElement.width [= widthPixels]`

The width property of HTMLImageElement objects reflects the width of the image as rendered on the screen in pixels. The value of the width property is reliable only after the image has finished loading and therefore it is sensible to use an onload handler to ensure that loading has completed before accessing the property. You may set the width property in Netscape 6 and Internet Explorer 4+. (Using the Image() constructor, mentioned later in this chapter, results in the actual image height being this property when first set.)

Methods

handleEvent()

JavaScript 1.2–1.3

Nav4–Nav4.78

Syntax

`HTMLImageElement.handleEvent(eventObj)`

The handleEvent() method of HTMLImageElement objects for Netscape assigns all events of the type given as the first argument to the this object. (Typically, these events are referred to as Event.EVENTNAME, where the event name is capitalized.) Using this method, you force the events thrown or fired to report to a particular object's event handler. See Chapter 32, "DOM-2 Events and Event Handlers," for details.

Netscape 6 apparently does not support this method for images.

Event Handlers

Internet Explorer supports the following event handlers for the `HTMLImageElement` interface:

onabort	ondragend	onmousemove
onactivate	ondragenter	onmouseout
onafterupdate	ondragleave	onmouseover
onbeforeactivate	ondragover	onmouseup
onbeforecopy	ondragstart	onmousewheel
onbeforecut	ondrop	onmove
onbeforedeactivate	onerror	onmoveend
onbeforepaste	onerrorupdate	onmovestart
onbeforeupdate	onfilterchange	onpaste
onblur	onfocus	onpropertychange
onclick	onfocusin	onreadystatechange
oncontextmenu	onfocusout	onresize
oncontrolselect	onhelp	onresizeend
oncopy	onload	onresizestart
oncut	onlosecapture	onselectstart
ondblclick	onmousedown	ontimeerror
ondeactivate	onmouseenter	
ondrag	onmouseleave	

HTMLInputElement/<input type="image" />

Browser/JavaScript Version	Created By
Nav4/JavaScript 1.2	`<input type="image"/>`
IE4/JScript 3.0	`<input type="image"/>`
IE5/JScript 5.0	`<input type="image"/>`

IE5.5/JScript 5.5	`<input type="image"/>`
Nav6/JavaScript 1.5	`<input type="image"/>`
IE6	`<input type="image"/>`
DOM Level 1	`document.createElement("input").`➥`setAttribute("type", "image")`

Note

Implemented in Nav1+ (HTML), IE1+ (HTML), Nav2+ (DOM), IE3+ (DOM)

Descends from `HTMLElement`

Required ancestor element: `HTMLFormElement` (Chapter 25, "Form Elements")

Description

The `type="image"` input submits a form, but uses an image the document refers to as its submit button. (Forms and form inputs fall under Chapters 25 and 26 ("Form Elements" and "Form Input Elements: HTMLInputElement," respectively).

For all intents and purposes, you can consider the `HTMLInputElement` with a type of `"image"` to have the same properties as an image element. There are a few additions, however, as follows.

Properties

form

JavaScript 1.5+, JScript 3.0+

Nav6+, IE4+

Read-only

Syntax

`var x = HTMLInputElement.form`

The `form` property of `HTMLInputElement` image objects refers directly to the `HTMLFormElement` which contains the `this` object.

name

JavaScript 1.0+, JScript 1.0+

Nav2+, IE3.0+

Syntax

```
[var x =] HTMLInputElement.name [= nameString]
```

The name property of HTMLInputElement image objects provides a name for the button by which the ancestor HTMLFormElement may have the button as a property.

The name property also reflects the name of the image in the document.images collection. HTML 4 has not formally deprecated the name attribute for this element, but the W3C does not recommend its use. (They have removed it from XHTML 1.0 Strict.)

type

JavaScript 1.5+, JScript 3.0+

Nav6+, IE4.0+

Syntax

```
var x = HTMLInputElement.type
```

The type property of HTMLInputElement image objects reflects the type attribute of the this element.

There are different values for different types; all are identical to the kind of input this is (for instance, "image" for an image input).

Methods

blur()

JavaScript 1.5+, JScript 3.0+

Nav6+, IE4.0+

Syntax

```
HTMLInputElement.blur()
```

The `blur()` method of `HTMLInputElement` image objects forces the form control to lose focus. This means it tells the browser "I'm not important; let something else take center stage." The browser reacts by assigning focus specifically to no object.

click()

JavaScript 1.5+, JScript 3.0+

Nav6, IE4+

Syntax

HTMLInputElement.click()

The `click()` method of `HTMLInputElement` image objects simulates a click on the object.

focus()

JavaScript 1.5+, JScript 3.0+

Nav6, IE4.0+

Syntax

HTMLInputElement.focus()

The `focus()` method of `HTMLInputElement` image objects forces the form control to gain focus. This means it tells the browser "I'm important; make sure I alone react to the keyboard." The browser reacts by assigning focus specifically to that object.

select()

JavaScript 1.1+, JScript 3.0+

Nav3+, IE4+

Syntax

HTMLInputElement.select()

The `select()` method of `HTMLInputElement` image objects simply selects the contents of the text field where one is present. It does not apply to the situation where there is an `HTMLInputElement` with type of "image".

Event Handlers

Internet Explorer supports the following event handlers for the `HTMLInputElement` interface:

onactivate	ondragleave	onmousemove
onbeforeactivate	ondragover	onmouseout
onbeforecut	ondragstart	onmouseover
onbeforedeactivate	ondrop	onmouseup
onbeforeeditfocus	onfilterchange	onmousewheel
onbeforepaste	onfocus	onmove
onblur	onfocusin	onmoveend
onclick	onfocusout	onmovestart
oncontextmenu	onhelp	onpaste
oncontrolselect	onkeydown	onpropertychange
oncut	onkeypress	onreadystatechange
ondblclick	onkeyup	onresize
ondeactivate	onlosecapture	onresizeend
ondrag	onmousedown	onresizestart
ondragend	onmouseenter	onselectstart
ondragenter	onmouseleave	ontimeerror

HTMLMapElement/<map>...</map>

Browser/JavaScript Version	Created By
Nav4/JavaScript 1.2	Not Implemented
IE4/JScript 3.0	<map>...</map>
IE5/JScript 5.0	<map>...</map>
IE5.5/JScript 5.5	<map>...</map>
Nav6/JavaScript 1.5	<map>...</map>

IE6   <map>...</map>

DOM Level 1   document.createElement("map")

> **Note**
> Implemented in Nav1+ (HTML), IE3+ (HTML), Nav6 (DOM), IE4+ (DOM)
>
> Descends from HTMLElement interface (Chapter 21)
>
> Parent elements: HTMLBodyElement (Chapter 22), any block text element

Description

Map elements, simply put, define a client-side group of areas on an image. The map associates with the image by matching the image's useMap attribute to the name attribute of the map. The concept is that the area elements represent clickable regions of the image.

Listing 30.5, later in this chapter under HTMLAreaElement, will demonstrate the use of maps and image areas.

Properties

areas
JavaScript 1.5, JScript 3.0+

Nav6, IE4+

Syntax

```
var x = HTMLMapElement.areas
```

The areas property of HTMLMapElement objects is a zero-based collection of all HTMLAreaElement child elements of the this object.

item
JavaScript_1.5, JScript 5.0+

Nav6, IE4+

Syntax

```
var x = HTMLMapElement.areas.item(index)
```

For the `item` method of `areas`, by supplying a number (specifically, a non-negative integer less than `this.length`) as the first argument, you can get a `Node` object from the `this` object representing that `Node`'s placement in the `this` object's index. Any other argument you submit to this method results in the method returning `null`.

length

JavaScript 1.5, JScript 5.0+

Nav6, IE4+

Syntax

```
var x = HTMLMapElement.areas.length
```

The `length` property of `areas` tells how many objects are in the collection.

tags

JScript 3.0+

IE4+

Syntax

```
var x = HTMLMapElement.areas.tags(tagName)
```

The `tags` method of `areas` returns a subset of the `this` element comprising all elements whose `tagName` property matches the first argument.

urns

JScript 5.0+

IE5+

Syntax

```
var x = HTMLMapElement.areas.urns(behaviorName)
```

The `urns` method of `areas` returns a subset of the `this` element comprising all elements possessing a DHTML behavior whose name matches the first argument.

DHTML behaviors, an Internet Explorer proprietary extension to HTML, go far beyond the scope of this book. You can find information on them via Microsoft's Web site at `http://msdn.microsoft.com/workshop/author/behaviors/overview.asp`.

name

JavaScript_1.5, JScript_3.0+

Nav6, IE4+

Syntax

```
var x = HTMLMapElement.areas.name(imageName)
```

The `name` property of `HTMLMapElement` objects provides a reference for image elements to reach the `this` object's child area elements. Note in the image you must precede the name reference with a hash mark (#).

outerHTML

JScript 3.0+

IE4+

Syntax

```
var x = HTMLMapElement.outerHTML
```

The `outerHTML` property of `HTMLMapElement` retrieves or sets the HTML source code contained between, and including, the starting and ending tags.

I do like the handiness of the `outerHTML` property for retrieving HTML source code at a glance, as an alternative method to the W3C Document Object Model. (The DOM provides an object structure for the source code; `outerHTML` provides the corresponding source code.)

Methods

The `HTMLMapElement` interface provides no methods beyond those the `HTMLElement` interface defines.

Event Handlers

Internet Explorer supports the following event handlers for the `HTMLMapElement` interface:

onbeforeactivate	ondragstart	onmouseleave
onbeforecut	ondrop	onmousemove
onbeforepaste	onfocusin	onmouseout
onclick	onfocusout	onmouseover
oncut	onhelp	onmouseup
ondblclick	onkeydown	onmousewheel
ondrag	onkeypress	onpaste
ondragend	onkeyup	onpropertychange
ondragenter	onlosecapture	onreadystatechange
ondragleave	onmousedown	onscroll
ondragover	onmouseenter	onselectstart

HTMLAreaElement/<area />

Browser/JavaScript Version	Created By
Nav4/JavaScript 1.2	Not Implemented
IE4/JScript 3.0	<area />
IE5/JScript 5.0	<area />
IE5.5/JScript 5.5	<area />
Nav6/JavaScript 1.5	<area />
IE6	<area />
DOM Level 1	document.createElement("area")

> **Note**
> Implemented in Nav1+ (HTML), IE3+ (HTML), Nav6 (DOM), IE4+ (DOM)
>
> Descends from `HTMLElement` interface (Chapter 21)
>
> Parent element: `HTMLMapElement`

Description

Area elements define the clickable regions of a client-side image map. Basically, when you click on one of these in the image, an action takes place via the href property. The area element is thus intended as a link within an image.

However, it is possible to define an area without an href property to link to. In cases like this, the event handlers would be your next bet. The noHref property exists to provide this facility.

Figuring out the exact coordinates of an image map area element can be a process of trial and error without an imaging program. I'm going to borrow and modify Listing 30.4 into Listing 30.5, to create the correct usage of map, image, and area elements into one document. The listing runs on IE5+.

Listing 30.5 *Maps, Areas, and Images, Oh My!*

```
<?xml version="1.0" ?>
<!DOCTYPE html PUBLIC "-//W3C//DTD XHTML 1.0 Transitional//EN"
➥"DTD/xhtml1-transitional.dtd">
<html xmlns="http://www.w3.org/1999/xhtml" >
<head><title></title></head>
<body onload="document.getElementById('hat').focus()">
<img src="http://www.jslab.org/author/alex.jpg"
alt="My Navy photo" border="0" usemap="#alex" />

<map name="alex" id="alex">
<area alt="hat" id="hat" coords="10,0,187,97" shape="rect"
➥href="javascript:void()" />
</map>
</body>
</html>
```

You can see what the code produces at http://www.jslab.org/jsdd/areamap.html.

Properties

accessKey

JavaScript 1.5

Nav6

Syntax

```
[var x = ] HTMLAreaElement.accessKey [ = "c"]
```

The accessKey property of HTMLAreaElement object designates a shortcut key to focus. By the user pressing the designated key and the ALT key (on the PC platform) while the window for the this object has focus, the element gains focus. The nodeValue for this attribute must be one character in length.

> **Note**
> Internet Explorer 5 implements this property for all elements, as I note in Chapter 21, "HTMLElement.")

alt

JavaScript 1.5, JScript 3.0+

Nav6, IE4+

Syntax

```
[var x =] HTMLAreaElement.alt [= altTextString]
```

The alt property of HTMLAreaElement objects is a text string to describe what the area represents.

coords

JavaScript 1.5, JScript 3.0+

Nav6, IE4+

Syntax

```
[var x =] HTMLAreaElement.coords [= coordSequence]
```

The `coords` property of `HTMLAreaElement` objects is a sequence of coordinates appropriate to the `shape` property of the `this` object. Only commas separate the coordinates.

When `shape` is not specified or is `"rect"`, the coordinates are $(x1, y1)$ and $(x2, y2)$, which are two opposite corners of a rectangle. In this format, you would see *x1,y1,x2,y2* for the `coords` property.

When `shape` is `"circle"`, the coordinates are (cx, cy) and the radius r of the circle, where (cx, cy) represents the center of the circle. In this format, you would see *cx,cy,r*.

When `shape` is `"poly"`, things get a little more interesting. You get a series of points (x1, y1), (x2, y2), (x3, y3)…which, when you connect them from point to point with line segments, produces a polygon. The last point in such a sequence must match the first exactly; you cannot omit it. I do not recommend crossing one line segment with another; the results may be highly unpredictable. In this format, `coords` would resemble *x1,y1,x2,y2,x3,y3,…,xn,yn,x1,y1*.

href

JavaScript 1.5, JScript 3.0

Nav6, IE4+

Syntax

```
[var x = ] HTMLAreaElement.href [= URIString]
```

The `href` property of `HTMLAreaElement` objects lists a URI that the user will call upon should he actually click on the area element. Without the `noHref` property set to `true`, this property becomes mandatory.

The `HTMLAreaElement` object has several additional properties in Internet Explorer similar to the ones I discuss in Chapter 16, "location." They are the hash, host, hostname, pathname, port, protocol, and search properties. Their equivalents are described in Chapter 16.

noHref

JavaScript 1.5, JScript_3.0

Nav6, IE4+

Syntax

```
[var x =] HTMLAreaElement.noHref [= boolValue]
```

The noHref property of HTMLAreaElement objects defines the this element as an area that has no URI to request from a browser. Without the href property, this property becomes mandatory.

shape

JavaScript 1.5, JScript 3.0+

Nav6, IE4+

Syntax

```
[var x =] HTMLAreaElement.shape [= stringValue]
```

The shape property of HTMLAreaElement objects, in concurrence with the coords property, determines which areas of an image are clickable, and their shape and size.

tabIndex

JavaScript 1.5, JScript 3.0+

Nav6, IE4+

Syntax

```
[ver x =] HTMLAreaElement.tabIndex [= numValue]
```

The tabIndex property of HTMLAreaElement objects sets where the this element rests in the tab order. The tab order is an index indicating when an element in the document receives focus as the user strikes his Tab key. When setting this value, remember it can only accept numeric integers.

A negative `tabIndex`, in Internet Explorer, takes the `this` element out of the tab order. Other than that, Tab key presses go to elements in this order:

- The lowest positive integer, followed by the next lowest, and so on.

- After that, the source order of elements in the document.

target
JavaScript 1.5, JScript_3.0

Nav6, IE4+

Syntax

`[var x = ] HTMLAreaElement.target [= HTMLWindowName]`

The `target` element of `HTMLAreaElement` objects tells which window, by HTML target name, to send it to (including possibly a new one).

Chapter 15, "window," explains the difference between HTML window names and JavaScript window names.

CHAPTER 31

Programmable Elements

If there's one feature of XHTML I love more than any other, it's being able to create scripts for it. I wouldn't be writing this book if I didn't love that so much. As a child I tinkered around with a small number of programming and scripting languages: LOGO, TI-99/4a BASIC, MS-DOS batch files, MS-DOS 5.0 QBASIC, and now JavaScript. I think you can understand why this particular chapter would hold a very special place for me.

As you know by now, (X)HTML supports the capability for you to script it via the `<script />` element. However, this particular element is a little more flexible than you might think. You've seen snippets of the element's flexibility here and there; in this chapter I examine it in detail.

With the `<object>...</object>`, `<applet>...</applet>`, and `<param />` elements, you can also include Java applets and special files for plug-ins, such as a background MIDI sound file in your Web page.

Netscape goes a step further and directly allows Java and JavaScript to talk to each other. Internet Explorer followed suit, at least for applets. (Netscape supports a standalone Java runtime engine.) This means Java can manipulate JavaScript, and JavaScript can manipulate Java. I'm therefore beginning this chapter with a quick introduction to Netscape's LiveConnect technology, which allows for this. (Although

Internet Explorer supports similar features, it does not support calling Java from JavaScript—which is what Listing 31.1 does.)

> **Note**
> Java and JavaScript are similar only in name and perhaps syntax. Java is a compiled language; JavaScript is interpreted. It's thus much easier to make changes to a JavaScript file than it is to a Java applet or bean. Of course, Java offers far more power than JavaScript.
>
> JavaScript is more than powerful enough for me, most of the time. Here, I'll go into the inspiration for my BigDecimal script (which I mention in Chapter 2, "Function()"), the `java.math.BigDecimal` class.

LiveConnect: Netscape's Bridge to Java

Netscape provides four top-level objects for accessing Java from JavaScript. They are the `Packages`, `java`, `netscape`, and `sun` objects. These objects mirror the Java language's `Packages`, `java`, `netscape`, and `sun` classes.

Java is an immensely complex language, especially for a developer who doesn't want to learn the whole thing. But one thing I like about Java is its support for arbitrary-precision numbers, numbers of any length of digits you want. Java calls them `BigDecimal()` objects.

You can create a `BigDecimal()` object using the Java `BigDecimal()` function (a method of the `math` "package", which is itself a property of the `java` class). But because it's an object and not a number value, Java provides special methods for handling arithmetic and comparisons between two `BigDecimal()` numbers. The `BigDecimal()` function takes one argument, either a number or a string of numerical characters that make up a valid number.

Examine Listing 31.1 for a moment. It divides 1 by 3 to produce 50 digits of the fraction 1/3.

Listing 31.1   *The* `java` *Class Unleashed in JavaScript*

```
<?xml version="1.0" ?>
<!-- Netscape 4+ browsers only. -->
<!DOCTYPE html PUBLIC "-//W3C//DTD XHTML 1.0 Transitional//EN"
➥"DTD/xhtml1-transitional.dtd">
<html xmlns="http://www.w3.org/1999/xhtml" >
```

Listing 31.1   *(continued)*

```
<head><title></title>
</head>
<body>
<p>
<script language="JavaScript" type="text/javascript">
<!--
var x = new java.math.BigDecimal(1)
var y = new java.math.BigDecimal(3)
// creating two new Java objects
var z = x.divide(y, 50, java.math.BigDecimal.ROUND_HALF_UP)
/* This is a simple arithmetic operation. The divide method takes three
arguments. The this object is the dividend. The first argument (here y) is
the divisor. The second argument tells how many digits of accuracy to return.
The third argument is a special rounding constant for when the returned
BigDecimal number has more digits than requested. (1/3 has an endless number
of digits.)
*/
document.write(x + " divided by " + y + " = " + z);
//-->
</script>
</p>
<!-- Results:
1 divided by 3 is 0.33333333333333333333333333333333333333333333333333
-->
</body>
</html>
```

HTMLAppletElement/<applet>...</applet>

Browser/JavaScript Version	Created By
Nav4/JavaScript 1.2	<applet>...</applet>
IE4/JScript 3.0	<applet>...</applet>
IE5/JScript 5.0	<applet>...</applet>
IE5.5/JScript 5.5	<applet>...</applet>
Nav6/JavaScript 1.5	<applet>...</applet>
IE6	<applet>...</applet>
DOM Level 1	document.createElement("applet")

> **Note**
>
> Implemented in Nav2+ (HTML), IE3+ (HTML), Nav3+ (DOM), IE4+ (DOM)
>
> Descends from `HTMLElement` interface (Chapter 21)
>
> Parent elements: `HTMLBodyElement` (Chapter 23), any block element
>
> Deprecated in HTML 4

Description

HTML designated the `<applet>...</applet>` element originally to hold Java applets. Its use has been discarded for the more generalized `<object>...</object>`. However, you may still use it.

By including this element in the document, the applet itself becomes a member of the `document.applets` collection. Any public properties and methods of the applet become available as properties and methods of the applet's entry in the collection. Often this includes any properties the DOM exposes on the `<applet>...</applet>` element.

The `document.applets` object becomes available in Netscape 3.0+; any applets you add to the page enter this array in that version of JavaScript.

For my examples, I will be borrowing the JavaClock applet from Sun Microsystems. You can find this at `http://java.sun.com/openstudio/applets/clock.html`. (No, you will not find the source code to the applet in this book.) This chapter assumes you have downloaded and unzipped the `demo.zip` file from the Java Web site into the same directory as the listing itself; the `demo` directory should be a child directory of the listing's directory.

Listing 31.2 calls on the applet in an XHTML page. (This assumes the applet is in the same directory as the `index.html` page, which comes in the `clock` directory of the demo file.) It also attempts to list all the properties of the applet. (In Internet Explorer 5, it stops at `width`, and then throws an exception without a reason I can explain.)

Listing 31.2   *A JavaClock Applet and Its Properties*

```
<?xml version="1.0" ?>
<!-- Netscape 6, Internet Explorer 5.0+ only. Requires Java. -->
<!DOCTYPE html PUBLIC "-//W3C//DTD XHTML 1.0 Transitional//EN"
➥"DTD/xhtml1-transitional.dtd">
<html xmlns="http://www.w3.org/1999/xhtml" >
<head><title></title>
```

Description

Listing 31.2 *(continued)*

```
<script language="JavaScript" type="text/javascript">
<!--
function go() {
  var p = document.getElementById("props")
  try {
    for (var property in document.applets[0]) {
      p.appendChild(document.createTextNode(property))
      p.appendChild(document.createElement("br"))
      }
    }
  catch(e) {
    }
  }
//-->
</script>
</head>
<body onload="go()">
<p>In case you're wondering what time it is, here is a clock
based on your computer's current time.</p>
<applet codebase="demo/clock/classes" code="JavaClock.class"
width="150" height="150">
<!-- JavaClock applet (c) 2000 Sun Microsystems, Inc. ALL RIGHTS RESERVED
Available with full permissions at
➥http://java.sun.com/openstudio/applets/clock.html
-->

<param name="delay"  value="100" />
<param name="link"   value="http://java.sun.com/" />
<param name="border" value="5" />
<param name="nradius" value="80" />
<param name="cfont"   value="Verdana|BOLD|18" />
<param name="bgcolor" value="7f7fff" />
<param name="shcolor" value="ff0000" />
<param name="mhcolor" value="000000" />
<param name="hhcolor" value="0000ff" />

<param name="ccolor" value="cccc00" />
<param name="ncolor" value="000000" />

</applet>
<p id="props">Here are the public properties and methods of this clock:<br />
```

Listing 31.2   *(continued)*

```
</p>
</body>
</html>
```

Netscape 3 and 4 implement a `mayscript` attribute for applet elements. This attribute allows the applet to access and call on JavaScript. (An applet attempting to call or access JavaScript without this attribute set will throw an exception.)

Netscape 6 does not appear to have this limitation; it certainly is not in the DOM for Netscape 6. Likewise, Internet Explorer does not support this attribute.

Properties

align

JavaScript 1.5, JScript 1.0+

Nav6, IE4+

Syntax

```
[var x =] HTMLAppletElement.align [= alignString]
```

The `align` property of `HTMLAppletElement` objects refers to the alignment of the applet relative to the surrounding text— whether its bottom edge lines up with the bottom side of the main text, its top edge lines up with the top side, or it's centered vertically.

In Netscape 6, this attribute may take values of `"bottom"`, `"top"`, or `"middle"`, respectively. Two other options, `"left"` and `"right"`, allow for text floating alongside the applet.

Internet Explorer 6 offers quite a few more options. `"absbottom"` means the absolute bottoms of the text and the image line up. `"absmiddle"` lines up the absolute centers horizontally. `"texttop"` lines up the absolute tops of the image with the text. `"baseline"` lines up the baselines of the text with the bottom of the image.

alt

JavaScript 1.5

Nav6, IE6

Syntax

```
[var x =] HTMLAppletElement.alt [= altTextString]
```

The `alt` property of `HTMLAppletElement` objects is an alternative text string in case the applet cannot be loaded into the page. The W3C requires it in HTML 4 for accessibility reasons. I like it because it also helps in the case of an HTTP 404 file.

altHTML

IE6

Syntax

```
HTMLAppletElement.altHTML = altTextString
```

The `altHTML` property of `HTMLAppletElement` objects is an alternative HTML string in case the applet cannot be loaded into the page. Microsoft states this property is write-only.

archive

JavaScript 1.5

Nav6, IE6

Syntax

```
[var x =] HTMLAppletElement.archive [= URI]
```

The `archive` property of `HTMLAppletElement` objects is a comma-separated list of URIs through which the browser can expect to search. Note these are typically `.zip` archive files.

code

JavaScript 1.5, JScript 3.0+

Nav6, IE4+

Syntax

```
[var x =] HTMLAppletElement.code [= URI]
```

The `code` property of `HTMLAppletElement` objects represents the actual URI of the applet, relative to the `codeBase` URI.

codeBase

JavaScript 1.5, JScript 4.0+

Nav6, IE4+

Syntax

```
[var x =] HTMLAppletElement.codeBase [= URI]
```

The codeBase property of HTMLAppletElement objects represents the base URI of the applet where the browser expects to find all the files associated with the applet. This is equivalent to the <base href="..." /> element, but for applets.

height

JavaScript1.5, JScript5.0+

Nav6, IE5.0+

Syntax

```
[var x =] HTMLAppletElement.height [= heightPixels]
```

The height property of HTMLAppletElement objects reflects the height of the applet as rendered on the screen in pixels.

hspace

JavaScript1.5, JScript 3.0+

Nav6, IE4+

Syntax

```
[var x =] HTMLAppletElement.hspace [= hSpacePixels]
```

The hspace property of HTMLAppletElement objects reflects the horizontal whitespace margins of the image as rendered on the screen in pixels.

name

JavaScript 1.1+, JScript 3.0+

Nav3+, IE4+

Syntax

```
[var x =] HTMLAppletElement.name [= nameString]
```

The `name` property of `HTMLAppletElement` objects reflects the name of the applet in the `document.applets` collection.

object

JavaScript 1.5, JScript 3.0+

Nav6, IE4+

Syntax

```
[var x =] HTMLAppletElement.object [= URI]
```

The `object` property of `HTMLAppletElement` objects, for Netscape 6 browsers, represents the actual URI of the applet, relative to the `codeBase` URI.

For Internet Explorer browsers, `object` refers to the actual applet itself. (This is good for finding the public methods and properties of the applet.)

src

JScript 3.0+

IE4+

Syntax

```
[var x =] HTMLAppletElement.src [= URI]
```

The `src` property of `HTMLAppletElement` objects represents the actual URI of the plug-in data. This is equivalent to the `data` property of the `HTMLObjectElement`.

vspace

JavaScript1.5, JScript 3.0+

Nav6, IE4+

Syntax

```
[var x =] HTMLAppletElement.vspace [= vSpacePixels]
```

The vspace property of HTMLAppletElement objects reflects the vertical whitespace margins of the image as rendered on the screen in pixels.

width

JavaScript1.5, JScript 5.0+

Nav6, IE5.0+

Syntax

```
[var x =] HTMLAppletElement.width [= widthPixels]
```

The width property of HTMLAppletElement objects reflects the width of the applet as rendered on the screen in pixels.

Methods

The HTMLAppletElement interface provides no methods beyond those the HTMLElement interface defines.

Event Handlers

Internet Explorer supports the following event handlers for the HTMLAppletElement object:

onactivate	ondeactivate	onmouseup
onbeforeactivate	onfocus	onmousewheel
onbeforecut	onfocusin	onmove
onbeforedeactivate	onfocusout	onmoveend
onbeforeeditfocus	onhelp	onmovestart
onbeforepaste	onkeydown	onpaste
onblur	onkeypress	onpropertychange
oncellchange	onkeyup	onreadystatechange
onclick	onload	onresize
oncontextmenu	onlosecapture	onresizeend
oncontrolselect	onmousedown	onresizestart
oncut	onmouseenter	onrowenter
ondataavailable	onmouseleave	onrowexit
ondatasetchanged	onmousemove	onrowsdelete
ondatasetcomplete	onmouseout	onrowsinserted
ondblclick	onmouseover	onscroll

HTMLEmbedElement/<embed>...</embed>

Browser/JavaScript Version	Created By
Nav4/JavaScript 1.2	`<embed>...</embed>`
IE4/JScript 3.0	`<embed>...</embed>`
IE5/JScript 5.0	`<embed>...</embed>`
IE5.5/JScript 5.5	`<embed>...</embed>`
Nav6/JavaScript 1.5	`<embed>...</embed>`
IE6	`<embed>...</embed>`
DOM Level 1	`document.createElement("embed")`

> **Note**
>
> Implemented in Nav2+ (HTML), IE3+ (HTML), Nav6 IE4+ (DOM)
>
> Descends from `HTMLElement` interface (Chapter 21)
>
> Proprietary extension to HTML

Description

The `<embed>...</embed>` element is a nonstandard extension to HTML for plug-ins. It is equivalent to `HTMLObjectElement`, but implements an entirely different feature set.

The W3C recommends you use `HTMLObjectElement` instead if possible. I agree with them mostly, as a matter of principle.

As a matter of practicality, that may not be feasible. The Scalable Vector Graphics (SVG) markup language doesn't appear to have a standardized `HTMLObjectElement` markup tag yet. SVG 1.0 (which I discuss in Chapter 36, "XML-Related Technologies and Their DOMs") recommends use of the `<embed>...</embed>` element in HTML. Other situations (particularly backward-compatibility and using the native Java VM instead of the Sun Java VM) favor the `<embed>...</embed>` element as well.

Properties

align

JavaScript 1.5, JScript 3.0+

Nav6, IE4+

Syntax

```
[var x =] HTMLEmbedElement.align [= alignString]
```

The `align` property of `HTMLEmbedElement` objects refers to the alignment of the object relative to the surrounding text. Possible values include `"top"`, `"bottom"`, `"left"`, and `"right"`.

height

JavaScript 1.5, JScript 3.0+

Nav6, IE4+

Syntax

```
[var x =] HTMLEmbedElement.height [= heightPixels]
```

The `height` property of `HTMLEmbedElement` objects reflects the height of the object as rendered on the screen in pixels.

name

JavaScript 1.5, JScript 3.0+

Nav6, IE4+

Syntax

```
[var x =] HTMLEmbedElement.name [= nameString]
```

The `name` property of `HTMLEmbedElement` objects reflects the name of the embedded object in the `document.embeds` collection.

palette

JScript 3.0+

IE4+

Syntax

`[var x =] HTMLEmbedElement.palette [= paletteObj]`

The `palette` element of `HTMLEmbedElement` objects retrieves the color palette for the `this` element.

pluginspage

JScript 3.0+

IE4+

Syntax

`[var x =] HTMLEmbedElement.pluginspage [= URIString]`

The `pluginspage` property of `HTMLEmbedElement` objects is a URI representing where the user may download the plug-in for the `this` element.

src

JavaScript 1.5, JScript 3.0+

Nav6, IE4+

Syntax

`[var x =] HTMLEmbedElement.src [= URIString]`

The `src` property of `HTMLEmbedElement` objects represents the actual URI of the plug-in data. This is equivalent to the `data` property of the `HTMLObjectElement`.

type

JavaScript 1.5

Nav6

Syntax

`[var x =] HTMLEmbedElement.type [= mimeType]`

The `type` property of `HTMLEmbedElement` objects is the mime-type of the file the `src` property references.

units

JScript 3.0+

IE4+

Syntax

```
[var x =] HTMLEmbedElement.units [= unitString]
```

The `units` property of `HTMLEmbedElement` objects refers to the measuring units used in the `height` and `width` properties.

width

JavaScript 1.5, JScript 3.0+

Nav6, IE4+

Syntax

```
[var x =] HTMLEmbedElement.height [= widthPixels]
```

The `width` property of `HTMLEmbedElement` objects reflects the width of the embedded object as rendered on the screen in pixels.

Methods

The `HTMLEmbedElement` interface provides no methods beyond those the `HTMLElement` interface defines.

Event Handlers

Internet Explorer supports the following event handlers for the `HTMLEmbedElement` object:

onactivate	onfocus	onmouseup
onbeforeactivate	onfocusin	onmousewheel
onbeforecut	onfocusout	onmove
onbeforedeactivate	onhelp	onmoveend
onbeforepaste	onload	onmovestart
onblur	onlosecapture	onpaste
onclick	onmousedown	onpropertychange
oncontextmenu	onmouseenter	onreadystatechange
oncontrolselect	onmouseleave	onresize
oncut	onmousemove	onresizeend
ondblclick	onmouseout	onresizestart
ondeactivate	onmouseover	onscroll

HTMLObjectElement/<object>...</object>

Browser/JavaScript Version	Created By
Nav4/JavaScript 1.2	`<object>...</object>`
IE4/JScript 3.0	`<object>...</object>`
IE5/JScript 5.0	`<object>...</object>`
IE5.5/JScript 5.5	`<object>...</object>`
Nav6/JavaScript 1.5	`<object>...</object>`
IE6	`<object>...</object>`
DOM Level 1	`document.createElement("object")`

> **Note**
> Implemented in Nav4+ (HTML), IE3+ (HTML), Nav6 (DOM), IE4+ (DOM)
>
> Descends from `HTMLElement` interface (Chapter 21)
>
> Parent elements: `HTMLBodyElement` (Chapter 23), any block element

Description

The `<object>...</object>` element (not to be confused with JavaScript objects, covered in Chapter 1, "Object()") denotes a generic object for embedding into a Web page. The idea is for HTML to be extensible via the `HTMLObjectElement` object to permit non-HTML objects to appear.

This has advantages over the `HTMLAppletElement` interface for its sheer flexibility. For instance, you could embed a second HTML document within the HTML document. In this respect it is a precursor to the inline frame element (Chapter 15, "window"). Listing 31.3 embeds an HTML document in this fashion.

Listing 31.3   `HTMLObjectElement` *Containing HTML Documents*

```
<!-- 31lst03a.htm -->
<?xml version="1.0" ?>
<!DOCTYPE html PUBLIC "-//W3C//DTD XHTML 1.0 Transitional//EN"
➥"DTD/xhtml1-transitional.dtd">
<html xmlns="http://www.w3.org/1999/xhtml" >
<head><title></title></head>
<body>
<p>Outer document.</p>
<table border="1">
  <tbody>
    <tr>
      <td>
      <object type="text/html" data="31lst03b.htm" width="100"
      ➥height="100">test</object>
      </td>
    </tr>
  </tbody>
</table>
<!-- Results:
The object element reveals the phrase "Inner document."
-->
</body>
</html>


<!-- 31lst03b.htm -->
<?xml version="1.0" ?>
<!DOCTYPE html PUBLIC "-//W3C//DTD XHTML 1.0 Transitional//EN"
➥"DTD/xhtml1-transitional.dtd">
<html xmlns="http://www.w3.org/1999/xhtml" >
<head><title></title></head>
<body>
<p>Inner document.</p>
</body>
</html>
```

Description

The contents of the HTMLObjectElement are available in case the browser does not load the object requested. This is for backward-compatibility purposes, and to provide a fail-safe for the object. For instance, in Netscape 3, Listing 31.3 would have the word "test" instead of the phrase "Inner document."

This also becomes important if the user does not have the plug-in for the object installed. You can provide a hyperlink to the plug-in download site.

As I mentioned earlier, <applet>...</applet> has been deprecated in favor of this element. So how do you use Java in Internet Explorer and still remain within the standards?

Sun Microsystems, which created Java and maintains the Java standard, has a plug-in available to support Java through the <object>...</object> element. You can find detailed documentation for driving a browser to run the Java VM at http://java.sun.com/products/plugin/1.3/docs/tags.html. In a nutshell, it specifies an HTMLObjectElement that receives as <param /> child elements the various attributes corresponding to the equivalent <applet>...</applet>. For example, see Listing 31.4. (This runs using Sun's Java VM, not the browser's native VM. Without Sun's Java VM, this listing does not work. Netscape 6 has special instructions for installing Java.)

Listing 31.4   HTMLObjectElement *and Applets*

```
<?xml version="1.0" ?>
<!-- Requires Sun Java Virtual Machine.
Netscape 6, Internet Explorer 5+ only. -->
<!DOCTYPE html PUBLIC "-//W3C//DTD XHTML 1.0 Transitional//EN"
➥"DTD/xhtml1-transitional.dtd">
<html xmlns="http://www.w3.org/1999/xhtml" >
<head><title></title>
<script language="JavaScript" type="text/javascript">
<!--
function go() {
  var p = document.getElementById("props")
  try {
    for (var property in document.applets[0]) {
      p.appendChild(document.createTextNode(property))
      p.appendChild(document.createElement("br"))
      }
    }
  catch (e) {
    }
```

Listing 31.4   *(continued)*

```
//-->
</script>
</head>
<body onload="go()">
<p>In case you're wondering what time it is, here is a clock
based on your computer's current time.</p>

<object classid="clsid:8AD9C840-044E-11D1-B3E9-00805F499D93"
width="150" height="150" align="baseline"
codebase="http://java.sun.com/products/plugin/1.3/
➥jinstall-13-win32.cab#Version=1,3,0,0">

<param name="codebase" value="demo/clock/classes"" />
<param name="code" value="JavaClock.class" />
<!-- JavaClock applet (c) 2000 Sun Microsystems, Inc. ALL RIGHTS RESERVED
Available with full permissions at
http://java.sun.com/openstudio/applets/clock.html
-->
<param name="delay"  value="100" />
<param name="link"   value="http://java.sun.com/" />
<param name="border" value="5" />
<param name="nradius" value="80" />
<param name="cfont"  value="Verdana|BOLD|18" />
<param name="bgcolor" value="7f7fff" />
<param name="shcolor" value="ff0000" />
<param name="mhcolor" value="000000" />
<param name="hhcolor" value="0000ff" />

<param name="ccolor" value="cccc00" />
<param name="ncolor" value="000000" />

</object>
<p id="props">Here are the public properties and methods of this clock:<br />
</p>
</body>
</html>
```

> **Caution**
> The <object> tag above must be exactly as listed in the codebase and classid
> attributes in Listing 31.4 for this to work properly.

The interesting fact about this arrangement is the movement of attributes from the
`<applet>...</applet>` element to individual `<param />` elements. This is per the Java
Plug-in specification mentioned previously.

Note

By the time you read this, Sun Microsystems may have updated its page for Gecko-based
browsers such as Netscape 6. At the time of this writing, Gecko is not formally supported
by the documentation.

Also, you should not expect this property as a member of the `document.applets`
collection.

Properties

---

align

JavaScript 1.5, JScript 3.0+

Nav6, IE4+

Syntax

```
[var x =] HTMLObjectElement.align [= alignString]
```

The `align` property of `HTMLObjectElement` objects refers to the alignment of the
object relative to the surrounding text—whether its bottom edge lines up with the
bottom side of the main text, its top edge lines up with the top side, or centered
vertically.

In Netscape 6, this attribute may take values of `"bottom"`, `"top"`, or `"middle"`, respectively. Two other options, `"left"` and `"right"`, allow for text floating alongside the
object.

Internet Explorer 6 offers quite a few more options. "absbottom" means the absolute
bottoms of the text and the image line up. "absmiddle" lines up the absolute centers
horizontally. "texttop" lines up the absolute tops of the image with the text. "baseline"
lines up the baselines of the text with the bottom of the image.

alt

IE6

Syntax

```
[var x =] HTMLObjectElement.alt [= altTextString]
```

The alt property of HTMLObjectElement objects is an alternative text string in case the object cannot be loaded into the page.

archive

JavaScript 1.5

Nav6, IE6

Syntax

```
[var x =] HTMLObjectElement.archive [= URI]
```

The archive property of HTMLObjectElement objects is a comma-separated list of URIs through which the browser can expect to search. Note these are typically .zip archive files.

border

JavaScript 1.5

Nav6, IE6

Syntax

```
[var x =] HTMLObjectElement.border [= borderPixels]
```

The border property of HTMLObjectElement objects specifies a thickness, in number of pixels, of a border around the this element.

classId

JScript5.0+

IE5+

Syntax

```
[var x =] HTMLObjectElement.classId [= classId]
```

The `classId` property of `HTMLObjectElement` objects is a string unique to the plug-in required to execute the object's contents. Although it is not read-only, setting this property to an incorrect value can have unpredictable effects.

code

JavaScript 1.5, JScript 3.0+

Nav6, IE4+

Syntax

```
[var x =] HTMLObjectElement.code [= URI]
```

The `code` property of `HTMLObjectElement` objects represents the actual URI of the object, relative to the `codeBase` URI. (This applies if the `this` element refers to an applet class file.)

codeBase

JavaScript 1.5, JScript 3.0+

Nav6, IE4+

Syntax

```
[var x =] HTMLObjectElement.code [= URI]
```

The `codeBase` property of `HTMLObjectElement` objects represents the base URI of the object where the browser expects to find all the files associated with the object. This is equivalent to the `<base href="..." />` element, but for objects.

codeType

JavaScript 1.5, JScript 3.0+

Nav6, IE4+

Syntax

```
[var x =] HTMLObjectElement.codeType [= mimeType]
```

The `codeType` property of `HTMLObjectElement` objects is the mime-type of the file which the `this` element references, if there is one.

contentDocument

JavaScript 1.5

Nav6

Syntax

```
[var x =] HTMLObjectElement.contentDocument [= mimeType]
```

The `contentDocument` property of `HTMLObjectElement` objects reflects the `document` object of the `this` element. This can be useful when you embed an XML or HTML document (including SVG images, which I'll cover in Chapter 36, "XML-Related Technologies and Their DOMs").

data

JavaScript 1.5, JScript 3.0+

Nav6, IE4+

Syntax

```
[var x =] HTMLObjectElement.data [= URI]
```

The `data` property of `HTMLObjectElement` objects represents the actual URI of the object's data, relative to the `codeBase` URI. This is typically where you'll name the object's actual location.

declare

JavaScript 1.5

Nav6, IE6

Syntax

```
[var x =] HTMLObjectElement.declare [= boolValue]
```

The `declare` property of `HTMLObjectElement` objects, when set to `true`, tells the browser to call but not activate the object. Another object must later activate this object for rendering.

form

JavaScript 1.5, JScript 3.0+

Nav6, IE4+

Read-only

Syntax

```
var x = HTMLObjectElement.form
```

The form property of HTMLObjectElement objects refers directly to the HTMLFormElement that contains the this object, if there is one. If there is not, this property returns null.

height

JavaScript1.5, JScript 3.0+

Nav6, IE4+

Syntax

```
[var x =] HTMLObjectElement.height [= heightPixels]
```

The height property of HTMLObjectElement objects reflects the height of the object as rendered on the screen in pixels.

hspace

JavaScript1.5, JScript 3.0+

Nav6, IE4+

Syntax

```
[var x =] HTMLObjectElement.hspace [= hSpacePixels]
```

The hspace property of HTMLObjectElement objects reflects the horizontal whitespace margins of the object as rendered on the screen in pixels.

name

JavaScript1.5

Nav6, IE6

Syntax

```
[var x =] HTMLObjectElement.name [= nameString]
```

The name property of HTMLObjectElement objects reflects the name of the object.

standby

JavaScript 1.5

Nav6, IE6

Syntax

```
[var x =] HTMLObjectElement.standby [= altMsg]
```

The standby property of HTMLObjectElement objects contains a plaintext message for the browser to use while it loads the object.

tabIndex

JavaScript 1.5, JScript 5.0+

Nav6, IE5+

Syntax

```
[ver x =] HTMLObjectElement.tabIndex [= numValue]
```

The tabIndex property of HTMLObjectElement objects sets where the this element rests in the tab order. The *tab order* is an index indicating when an element in the document receives focus as the user strikes the Tab key. When setting this value, remember it can only accept numeric integers.

A negative tabIndex takes the this element out of the tab order. Other than that, Tab key presses go to elements in this order:

1. The lowest positive integer, followed by the next lowest, and so on.

2. After that, the source order of elements in the document.

type

JavaScript 1.5, JScript 3.0+

Nav6, IE4+

Syntax

```
[var x =] HTMLObjectElement.type [= mimeType]
```

The type property of HTMLObjectElement objects is the mime-type of the file the data property references, if there is one.

useMap

JavaScript 1.5

Nav6, IE6

Syntax

```
[var x =] HTMLImageElement.useMap [= mapName]
```

The useMap property of HTMLObjectElement objects associates the this element with a <map>...</map> element, which I describe in Chapter 30, "Image Elements."

vspace

JavaScript 1.5, JScript 3.0+

Nav6, IE4+

Syntax

```
[var x =] HTMLObjectElement.vspace [= vSpacePixels]
```

The vspace property of HTMLObjectElement objects reflects the vertical whitespace margins of the object as rendered on the screen in pixels.

width

JavaScript 1.5, JScript 1.0+

Nav6, IE3+

Syntax

```
[var x =] HTMLObjectElement.width [= widthPixels]
```

The `width` property of `HTMLObjectElement` objects reflects the width of the object as rendered on the screen in pixels.

Methods

The `HTMLObjectElement` interface provides no methods beyond those the `HTMLElement` interface defines.

Event Handlers

Internet Explorer supports the following event handlers for the `HTMLObjectElement` object:

onactivate	ondragend	onmoveend
onbeforedeactivate	ondragenter	onmovestart
onbeforeeditfocus	ondragleave	onpropertychange
onblur	ondragover	onreadystatechange
oncellchange	ondragstart	onresize
onclick	ondrop	onresizeend
oncontrolselect	onerror	onresizestart
ondataavailable	onfocus	onrowenter
ondatasetchanged	onkeydown	onrowexit
ondatasetcomplete	onkeypress	onrowsdelete
ondblclick	onkeyup	onrowsinserted
ondeactivate	onlosecapture	onscroll
ondrag	onmove	onselectstart

HTMLParamElement/<param />

Browser/JavaScript Version	Created By
Nav4/JavaScript 1.2	<param />
IE4/JScript 3.0	<param />
IE5/JScript 5.0	<param />
IE5.5/JScript 5.5	<param />
Nav6/JavaScript 1.5	<param />
IE6	<param />
DOM Level 1	document.createElement("param")

> **Note**
> Implemented in Nav2+ (HTML), IE3+ (HTML), Nav6 IE4+ (DOM)
>
> Descends from `HTMLElement` interface (Chapter 21)
>
> Parent elements: `HTMLObjectElement`, `HTMLAppletElement`

Description

The `<param />` element represents a parameter or variable for the object or applet to use. Basically, this element normally supports a `"name = value"` structure; it has a `name` attribute and a `value` attribute. The browser will pass this information on to the object or applet in question.

This behavior can change with the `valueType` attribute. Setting `valueType` to `"ref"` means `value` is a URI pointing to a file holding the value and `type` is its mime-type. When `valueType` is set to `"object"`, the `value` property becomes an `IDREF` attribute for an `HTMLObjectElement` elsewhere in the document.

Properties

name
JavaScript 1.5, JScript 3.0+ (read-only)

Nav6, IE4+ (read-only), IE6 (read/write)

Syntax

```
[var x =] HTMLParamElement.name [= varName]
```

The `name` property of `HTMLParamElement` objects identifies the name of the variable the this element passes to the applet or object of `this.parentNode`.

type
JavaScript 1.5

Nav6, IE6

Syntax

```
[var x =] HTMLParamElement.type [= mimeType]
```

The `type` property of `HTMLParamElement` objects identifies, if `valueType` is set to `"ref"`, the mime-type of the file the `value` property references. Otherwise, `type` has no meaning.

value

JavaScript 1.5, JScript 3.0+ (read-only)

Nav6, IE4+ (read-only), IE6 (read/write)

Syntax

```
[var x =] HTMLParamElement.value [= varName]
```

The `value` property of `HTMLParamElement` objects identifies, if `valueType` is not set or set to `"data"`, the value of the variable the `this` element passes to the applet or object of `this.parentNode`.

If `valueType` is set to `"ref"`, the `value` property is a URI identifying where the value may be found.

If `valueType` is set to `"object"`, the `value` property is an IDREF identifying an object or applet elsewhere in the document containing information for `this.parentNode`.

valueType

JavaScript 1.5

Nav6, IE6

Syntax

```
[var x =] HTMLParamElement.valueType [= varName]
```

The `valueType` property of `HTMLParamElement` objects determines what kind of information the `value` property holds. There are three permissible values for `valueType`: the default `"data"`, `"ref"`, or `"object"`.

Methods

The `HTMLParamElement` interface provides no methods beyond those the `HTMLElement` interface defines.

HTMLScriptElement/<script>...</script>

Browser/JavaScript Version	Created By
Nav4/JavaScript 1.2	`<script>...</script>`
IE4/JScript 3.0	`<script>...</script>`
IE5/JScript 5.0	`<script>...</script>`
IE5.5/JScript 5.5	`<script>...</script>`
Nav6/JavaScript 1.5	`<script>...</script>`
IE6	`<script>...</script>`
DOM Level 1	`document.createElement("script")`

> **Note**
> Implemented in Nav2+ (HTML), IE3+ (HTML), Nav6, IE4+ (DOM)
> Descends from `HTMLElement` interface (Chapter 21)

Description

The `HTMLScriptElement` is a generic element for adding scripting features to a document. This is the primary (in fact, the only) element you can use to designate scripting within a document. (Event handlers, in the context of HTML, are attributes.)

There are two standard types of scripts available to Web browsers. The first is of course JavaScript, also known as JScript to Microsoft Internet Explorer browsers. The second is VBScript, a Microsoft Internet Explorer scripting language based on Visual Basic.

If you're interested in server-side scripting, you can also specify a server-side script via this element. PHP 4, for instance, scans a document it processes for `<script language="php">...</script>` elements. (For XHTML 1.0 Strict compliance, I've suggested PHP also check for the `type="application/x-httpd-php"` attribute as well. But there's always the `<?php...?>` processing instruction.)

As for manipulating scripting by the DOM, there can be numerous unexpected effects... The best way, for Internet Explorer 5.0 and Netscape 6.1+, is to set the `text` or `src` properties. Listing 31.5 uses these to add a pair of scripts to a document.

Listing 31.5 *Scripts Adding Scripts*

```
<!-- 31lst05a.htm -->
<?xml version="1.0" ?>
<!--Netscape 6.1+, Internet Explorer 5.0+ only. -->
<!DOCTYPE html PUBLIC "-//W3C//DTD XHTML 1.0 Transitional//EN"
➥"DTD/xhtml1-transitional.dtd">
<html xmlns="http://www.w3.org/1999/xhtml" >
<head><title></title>
<script language="JavaScript" type="text/javascript">
function go() {
  var scriptText = "var p0 = document.createElement('p');\n"
  scriptText += "p0.appendChild(document.createTextNode('Inline script
➥added!'));\n"
  scriptText += "document.body.appendChild(p0)"

  var script = document.createElement("script")
  script.text = scriptText
  script.setAttribute("type", "text/javascript")
  script.setAttribute("language", "JavaScript")
  document.body.appendChild(script)

  script = document.createElement("script")
  script.setAttribute("type", "text/javascript")
  script.setAttribute("language", "JavaScript")
  script.setAttribute("src", "31lst05b.js")
  document.body.appendChild(script)
  }
</script>
</head>
<body onload="go()">
<p>Document loaded normally.</p>
<!-- Results:
Inline script added!
Library script added!
-->
</body>
</html>

// 31lst05b.js
var p1 = document.createElement('p')
p1.appendChild(document.createTextNode('Library script added!'))
document.body.appendChild(p1)
```

Description

As for before `onload`, examine Listing 31.6. This time, it works in Netscape 6 and Internet Explorer 5.0+, using the DOM Level 0 method `document.write()`.

Listing 31.6   *Preloading Scripts by* `document.write()`

```
<!-- 31lst06a.htm -->
<?xml version="1.0" ?>
<!-- Netscape 6, Internet Explorer 5.0+ only. -->
<!DOCTYPE html PUBLIC "-//W3C//DTD XHTML 1.0 Transitional//EN"
➥"DTD/xhtml1-transitional.dtd">
<html xmlns="http://www.w3.org/1999/xhtml" >
<head><title></title>
<script language="JavaScript" type="text/javascript">
  var scriptText = "var p0 = document.createElement('p');\n"
  scriptText += "p0.appendChild(document.createTextNode('"
  scriptText += "Inline and library scripts added!'));\n"
  scriptText += "function go() {document.body.appendChild(p0)}"

  var script = "<script language='JavaScript' type='text/javascript'>\n"
  script += scriptText
  script += "</scr"+"ipt>" // broken up to prevent early end to this script
  document.write(script)

  var script = "<script language='JavaScript' type='text/javascript'"
  script += " src='31lst06b.js'>\n"
  script += scriptText
  script += "</scr"+"ipt>" // broken up to prevent early end to this script
  document.write(script)
</script>
</head>
<body>
<p>Document loaded normally.</p>
<!-- Results:
Inline and library scripts added!
-->
</body>
</html>

// 31lst06b.js
window.onload = go
```

I do not in any situation recommend using the DOM to remove or alter a script. The only reason you might even consider that is to edit or disable certain scripts, and there's plenty you can do in JavaScript natively to accomplish the same without calling on the browser's DOM functions.

> **Note**
> It is entirely appropriate to include <noscript>...</noscript> element tags as a sibling node to <script /> elements, for browsers with scripting disabled. I mention the <noscript>...</noscript> element in Chapter 21, "HTMLElement".

Finally, although XHTML would permit it, Internet Explorer does not like a <script src="library.js" /> element. Internet Explorer requires both the starting and ending tags.

Properties

charset

JavaScript 1.5

Nav6, IE6

Syntax

```
[var x =] HTMLScriptElement.charset [= charSetStr]
```

The charset property of HTMLScriptElement objects indicates the standard character set name, as a string, to the browser.

defer

JScript 3.0+

IE4+

Syntax

```
[var x =] HTMLScriptElement.defer [= boolValue]
```

The `defer` property of `HTMLScriptElement` objects indicates to the browser whether it may delay processing of this script until the document has finished loading. This can be useful for scripts that do not need to operate before the document loads, and can speed loading time.

> **Note**
> Mozilla currently has a bug filed against it to enable the `<script defer="defer" />` attribute. It's only a hint from the Web page, however, and not an actual requirement for implementation.

event
JScript 3.0+

IE4+

Syntax

```
[var x =] HTMLScriptElement.event
```

The `event` property of `HTMLScriptElement` objects specifies an event handler that, in partnership with the `htmlFor` property, identifies the script as an event handler for a particular element. Listing 31.7 demonstrates the use of this property, defining an event handler for an element.

htmlFor
JScript 3.0+

IE4+

Syntax

```
[var x =] HTMLScriptElement.htmlFor
```

The `htmlFor` property of `HTMLScriptElement` objects specifies an element that, in partnership with the `event` property, identifies the script as an event handler for that element. (Note this property corresponds to the `for` attribute.) Listing 31.7 demonstrates the use of this property, defining an event handler for an element.

> **Caution**
>
> Netscape 6 does not support the `htmlFor` or `event` attributes. It does have them as empty strings in the DOM.
>
> This is significant because any script element with these attributes is intended to reflect an event handler. But Netscape assumes the script is to execute immediately in the context of the window.
>
> I strongly recommend against use of these attributes. There are better ways (as I describe in Chapter 32, "DOM-2 Events and Event Handlers") to attach event handling to an element.

src

JavaScript 1.5, JScript 3.0+

Nav6, IE4+

Syntax

```
[var x =] HTMLScriptElement.src [= scriptURI]
```

The `src` property of `HTMLScriptElement` objects reflects the location of the script as a URI, if there is one. (Inline scripts will return `""`.)

text

JavaScript 1.5, JScript 3.0+

Nav6.1+, IE4+

Syntax

```
[var x =] HTMLScriptElement.text [= sourceCode]
```

The `text` property of `HTMLScriptElement` objects reflects the actual source code of the script element itself.

> **Note**
>
> Until I started on this section, I didn't even know this existed. It allows you to create a tool for isolating all the code executing when the script loads, and I for one like to collect all the little script initialization statements together into one function for modularity and ease of tracing. You'll see an example of this at the end of this chapter.

---

type

JavaScript 1.5, JScript 3.0+

Nav6, IE4+

Syntax

[var *x* =] *HTMLScriptElement*.type [= *mimeType*]

The type property of HTMLScriptElement objects reflects a mime-type for the scripting language. This property replaces the language attribute, and modern browsers may expect to use the type attribute in preference to language.

> **Note**
> However, for XHTML 1.0 Transitional documents, I continue to recommend use of the language attribute. You can use it with Netscape (and to a limited extent, Internet Explorer) browsers to specify a minimum version requirement to JavaScript. For instance, Netscape 4.x+ browsers will look for language="JavaScript1.2" attributes.
>
> This is why throughout the book you see JavaScript version numbers: knowing which version supports which, and which you can include with a given <script /> element.

Methods

The HTMLScriptElement interface provides no methods beyond those the HTMLElement interface defines.

Event Handlers

Internet Explorer supports the following event handlers for the HTMLScriptElement object:

```
onload
onpropertychange
onreadystatechange
```

Example: Reorganizing a Script

As you know by now, any JavaScript statements outside a function but inside a script execute automatically. As scripts get larger and larger (and I do write some fairly large ones), I have a habit of placing certain statements immediately after the function to which they relate. For instance, take this excerpt from Listing 1.10:

```
Object.prototype.instances = [""]

function addInstance() {
  if (!this.instanceIndex) {
   this.instanceIndex = this.instances.length
   this.instances[this.instanceIndex] = this
   }
  }
Object.prototype.addInstance = addInstance

function getInstanceName() {
  return "Object.instances["+this.instanceIndex+"]"
  }
Object.prototype.getInstanceName = getInstanceName

function testObj() {
  this.value = 0
  this.addInstance()
  }

function test(x) {
  if (x.value < 100) {
   x.value += 10
   HTML += x.value + "<br />"
   setTimeout("test(" + x.getInstanceName() + ")")
   } else {
   HTML += "Pass"
   document.write(HTML)
   }
  }

HTML = ""
k = new testObj()
test(k)
```

There's nothing really wrong with this, in terms of JavaScript code—it works fine. But at the same time, notice how the top-level statements are a bit spread out. This does not help a person who later might come upon the script and want to tinker with it; he or she would have to dig throughout the code to find the top-level statements, which aren't all that obvious to the reader. (Were my top-level statements in this excerpt obvious to you when you first saw them?)

I could rewrite it like this and lose no functionality:

```
function addInstance() {
  if (!this.instanceIndex) {
   this.instanceIndex = this.instances.length
   this.instances[this.instanceIndex] = this
   }
  }

function getInstanceName() {
  return "Object.instances["+this.instanceIndex+"]"
  }

function testObj() {
  this.value = 0
  this.addInstance()
  }

function test(x) {
  if (x.value < 100) {
   x.value += 10
   HTML += x.value + "<br />"
   setTimeout("test(" + x.getInstanceName() + ")")
   } else {
   HTML += "Pass"
   document.write(HTML)
   }
  }

function init_script_0() {
  Object.prototype.instances = [""]
  Object.prototype.addInstance = addInstance
  Object.prototype.getInstanceName = getInstanceName
  HTML = ""
  k = new testObj()
```

```
    test(k)
    }
init_script_0()
```

This has the advantage of bringing all the top-level script statements into one function, which will still execute anyway. Thus, all the master code is controllable from one source. I like this, again because of the idea of modularity.

As you'll recall, there are three ways to create a function in JavaScript. We will ignore the new Function() constructor. The other two are

```
funcName = function(argList) {...}
```

and

```
function funcName(argList) {...}
```

So, without further ado, Listing 31.7 presents a complex script to reorganize your top-level JavaScript code into pure functions and one top-level activation statement. Note none of this would be possible, really, without the Document Object Model and the text property of <script /> elements.

Listing 31.7   *Modularizing JavaScript Automatically*

```
<?xml version="1.0" ?>

<!DOCTYPE html PUBLIC "-//W3C//DTD XHTML 1.0 Transitional//EN"
➥"DTD/xhtml1-transitional.dtd">
<html xmlns="http://www.w3.org/1999/xhtml" >
<head><title></title>
<script language="JavaScript" type="text/javascript">
<!--
var go = function() {
    var reorgScript = document.getElementsByTagName("script")[0]
    document.getElementById('myCode').value = reorganizeScript(reorgScript)
    }

var sky = "#0000ff" // The sky is blue.

function reorganizeScript(script) {
    var scriptText = script.text
    var reg = /(function\s\w*)|(\w*\s*=\s*function\(\))/g
```

Listing 31.7   *(continued)*

```
// regular expression to match all literal function names
    var funcs = scriptText.match(reg), scriptTextPreview = ""
    var funcNames = []

    var scriptArray = scriptText.split("\n")
// split text into lines
    for (var m = 0; m < funcs.length; m++) {
        if (funcs[m].substr(0, 9) == "function ") {
// function myFunc() {...
            funcNames[m] = funcs[m].substr(9)
            }
        else {
// myFunc = function() {
            funcNames[m] = funcs[m].substr(0, funcs[m].indexOf("="))
            funcNames[m] = funcNames[m].substr(0, funcNames[m].indexOf(" "))
            }
// funcNames[m] == myFunc
        if (typeof window[funcNames[m]] == "function") {
// make sure it really is a top-level function
            var funcText = window[funcNames[m]].toString()
            var funcStart = funcText.indexOf(funcText.match(/\S/))
            funcText = funcText.substr(funcStart)
            var funcLength = funcText.lastIndexOf("}")
            funcLength += (funcText.substr(funcLength).length)
            var scriptIndex = scriptText.indexOf(funcs[m])
// find the function in the source and its length
            if (funcs[m].substr(0, 9) != "function ") {
                funcLength += funcs[m].indexOf("function(")
                }
            var temp = scriptText.substr(scriptIndex)
// count closing brackets
            var funcCloseBrackets = funcText.split("}")
            var tempCloseBrackets = temp.split("}")
            tempCloseBrackets.length = funcCloseBrackets.length - 1
            temp = tempCloseBrackets.join("}") + "}"
            funcLength = temp.length
// we have now reduced temp to the function

            scriptTextPreview += temp
            scriptTextPreview += "\n\n"
```

Listing 31.7   *(continued)*

```
// extracting and storing functions in original form

            var scriptTextpt1 = scriptText.substr(0, scriptIndex)
            var scriptTextpt2 = scriptText.substr(scriptIndex + funcLength)
            scriptText = scriptTextpt1 + scriptTextpt2
// remove the function from the source entirely
            }
        }

    scriptTextpt1 = scriptText.split("\n")
    scriptText = ""
    for (m = 0; m < scriptTextpt1.length; m++) {
        if (scriptTextpt1[m].length > 1) {
            scriptText += scriptTextpt1[m] + "\n"
            }
        }
// remove extraneous \n characters
    if (scriptText.substr(0,4) == "<!--") {
        scriptText = scriptText.substr(4, scriptText.indexOf("//-"+"->")-4)
        }
    if (scriptText.substr(0,9) == "<![CDATA[") {
        scriptText = scriptText.substr(9, scriptText.indexOf("]]"+">")-3)
        }
// remove comment lines and CDATA section

    if ((script.id != "")&&(script.id != null)) {
        var fInitName = script.id + "_init"
        } else {
        fInitName = "initFunc_" + Math.random().toString().substr(2)
        fInitName += "_" + (new Date() * 1)
        }
// creating initialization function name

    scriptText = "function " + fInitName + "() {" + scriptText
    scriptText += "}\n\n" + fInitName + "();"
// creating initialization function

    scriptText = scriptTextPreview + scriptText
// restoring original functions unedited

    return scriptText
```

Listing 31.7 *(continued)*

```
// return reorganized script and exit function.
    }
reorganizeScript.author = "Alex Vincent"
reorganizeScript.copyright = 2001

window.onload = go
//-->
</script>
</head>
<body>
<form action="javascript:void()">
<p>Revised code:</p>
<textarea cols="80" rows="40" id="myCode"></textarea>
</form>
</body>
</html>
```

> **Note**
> Listing 31.7 has one of the most subtle weaknesses I have ever seen. It's so subtle that you are unlikely to ever encounter it, and fixing it properly appears excessively difficult.
>
> Netscape 6 removes comments from the `Function.prototype.toString()` method. But the corresponding `script.text` property doesn't.
>
> This listing counts closing braces (`}`) to determine the end of the function. But if you have a commented-out closing brace, the count will be wrong in Netscape 6.
>
> Because of its relative improbability (how often do you include closing braces in comments?) and difficulty to fix (scanning for comments with closing braces and adjusting the count appropriately), I've decided to let it slide. The intention of the listing is as a practical example you can use and understand.

In case you want to avoid running this script, Listing 31.8 has the output of this script.

Listing 31.8 *Reorganization of Code Completed*

```
go = function() {
    var reorgScript = document.getElementsByTagName("script")[0]
    document.getElementById('myCode').value = reorganizeScript(reorgScript)
    }
```

Listing 31.8   *(continued)*

```javascript
function reorganizeScript(script) {
    var scriptText = script.text
    var reg = /(function\s\w*)|(\w*\s*=\s*function\(\))/g
// regular expression to match all literal function names
    var funcs = scriptText.match(reg), scriptTextPreview = ""
    var funcNames = []

    var scriptArray = scriptText.split("\n")
// split text into lines
    for (var m = 0; m < funcs.length; m++) {
        if (funcs[m].substr(0, 9) == "function ") {
// function myFunc() {...
            funcNames[m] = funcs[m].substr(9)
            }
        else {
// myFunc = function() {
            funcNames[m] = funcs[m].substr(0, funcs[m].indexOf("="))
            funcNames[m] = funcNames[m].substr(0, funcNames[m].indexOf(" "))
            }
// funcNames[m] == myFunc
        if (typeof window[funcNames[m]] == "function") {
// make sure it really is a top-level function
            var funcText = window[funcNames[m]].toString()
            var funcStart = funcText.indexOf(funcText.match(/\S/))
            funcText = funcText.substr(funcStart)
            var funcLength = funcText.lastIndexOf("}")
            funcLength += (funcText.substr(funcLength).length)
            var scriptIndex = scriptText.indexOf(funcs[m])
// find the function in the source and its length
            if (funcs[m].substr(0, 9) != "function ") {
                funcLength += funcs[m].indexOf("function(")
                }
            var temp = scriptText.substr(scriptIndex)
// count closing brackets
            var funcCloseBrackets = funcText.split("}")
            var tempCloseBrackets = temp.split("}")
            tempCloseBrackets.length = funcCloseBrackets.length - 1
            temp = tempCloseBrackets.join("}") + "}"
            funcLength = temp.length
```

Listing 31.8 *(continued)*

```
// we have now reduced temp to the function

        scriptTextPreview += temp
        scriptTextPreview += "\n\n"
// extracting and storing functions in original form

        var scriptTextpt1 = scriptText.substr(0, scriptIndex)
        var scriptTextpt2 = scriptText.substr(scriptIndex + funcLength)
        scriptText = scriptTextpt1 + scriptTextpt2
// remove the function from the source entirely
      }
    }

  scriptTextpt1 = scriptText.split("\n")
  scriptText = ""
  for (m = 0; m < scriptTextpt1.length; m++) {
    if (scriptTextpt1[m].length > 1) {
      scriptText += scriptTextpt1[m] + "\n"
      }
    }
// remove extraneous \n characters
  if (scriptText.substr(0,4) == "<!--") {
    scriptText = scriptText.substr(4, scriptText.indexOf("//-"+"->")-4)
    }
  if (scriptText.substr(0,9) == "<![CDATA[") {
    scriptText = scriptText.substr(9, scriptText.indexOf("]]"+">")-3)
    }
// remove comment lines and CDATA section

  if ((script.id != "")&&(script.id != null)) {
    var fInitName = script.id + "_init"
    } else {
    fInitName = "initFunc_" + Math.random().toString().substr(2)
    fInitName += "_" + (new Date() * 1)
    }
// creating initialization function name

  scriptText = "function " + fInitName + "() {" + scriptText
  scriptText += "}\n\n" + fInitName + "();"
// creating initialization function
```

Listing 31.8   *(continued)*

```
    scriptText = scriptTextPreview + scriptText
// restoring original functions unedited

    return scriptText
// return reorganized script and exit function.
    }

function initFunc_8290502790671658_1016173595830() {
var sky = "#0000ff" // The sky is blue.
reorganizeScript.author = "Alex Vincent"
reorganizeScript.copyright = 2001
window.onload = go
}

initFunc_8290502790671658_1016173595830();
```

If you're really in the mood to clean up your code, think about functions inside functions, as I demonstrated in Chapter 2, "Function()." Or think of other ways to detect patterns (such as similar fragments of code repeated), and see if you can dynamically generate additional functions to reduce and modularize your code further.

CHAPTER 32

DOM-2 Events and Event Handlers

From Chapter 21 on, you've been noticing lists of event handlers each element supports. Event handlers in JavaScript are primarily about doing something before the normal reactions to a user's actions take place. For instance, we frequently use a form onsubmit event handler for validation of the form on the client. Chapter 30, "Image Elements," featured two event-driven animations (Listings 30.1 and 30.2) with the mouse over a certain image location. In Chapter 15, "window," I covered frames and the impact of the onload event handler.

So what is an event, anyway? In JavaScript terms, an event is an object created and passed around like a hot potato to various other objects in the document when something happens. Event handlers are optional slots in each element for functions that react to specific types of events.

To give you a comparison, think of American football. You have a bunch of guys on the line of scrimmage, and then *boom*, something happens. The football flies from one guy's hands into the quarterback's. Everybody starts running, trying to get into position. The quarterback throws the ball. Sometimes another guy catches it; sometimes the ball falls to the turf. Sometimes the guy who catches it has to throw it again to someone else. Never mind the touchdown.

Think of the football as an event; it's being thrown all over the place. The people who catch it are the event handlers. The intended receiver is known as the event target. The only discrepancy between this concept and real football is that in this scenario, each player has an extra football stuffed under his shirt to throw, in case he happens to catch a football. In other words, if a particular event listener has instructions to fire an event when it catches the first event, two events are going to leave its hands.

Sound chaotic? It can be—but every event has a target. Every football in this game will be caught by the right player. Of course, some players may also have instructions to throw the ball on the ground and stop it from going any further. (This is canceling the event.)

This chapter begins with a discussion on DOM-based techniques for events, followed by a formal definition of the DOM-2 Events interfaces. Later, I will discuss procedures for browsers that don't follow the DOM-2, such as Netscape 4.x. Finally, we concern ourselves with the event handlers themselves.

DOM-2 Events Introduced: Listeners and Interfaces

In the original model of events (HTML), you have an event handler such as `onload` which has a function or string of JavaScript commands attached to it:

```
<input type="button" onclick="alert('Hello World!');" />
<input type="button" onclick="func1(this);this.value = null" value="Hi" />
```

This model hasn't gone away. It's still in effect. But these event handlers are only a piece of a much larger group known as event listeners.

Event listeners are a superset to event handlers. The biggest difference is that event listeners are available for all `Node` objects (see Chapter 20, "Core DOM Objects," for a definition of nodes).

The W3C DOM2-Events Recommendation appends the `EventTarget` interface's methods to the `Node` interface. By using the `addEventListener()` and `removeEventListener()` methods from `EventTarget` (which for browsers supporting `Events` is `Node`), you control which nodes are paying attention for which events. By using the `dispatchEvent()` method, you effectively are firing an event from that node.

Event listeners also follow a different, more formal syntax than event handlers. HTML treats event handlers as attributes; they are in the HTML DOM. All other event listeners are entirely scripted, and there is an `EventListener` interface.

Creating and Using Event Model Objects

The first step to creating an event model under the DOM is to create a function to receive the event. The function may expect to receive one argument, an Event object. The this object is the element receiving the event.

Then comes assigning the event handler. Before the DOM, you could often assign an event handler directly:

```
object.oneventname = functionName
```

With the DOM, we have the addEventListener() method:

```
object.addEventListener("eventname", functionName, bubbling)
```

Canceling the event handler is similar. Before the DOM, you simply set it to null:

```
object.oneventname = null
```

With the DOM, you have the removeEventListener() method:

```
object.removeEventListener("eventname", functionName, useCapture)
```

The third argument is new for both DOM functions; it determines whether or not an event listener will catch an event as it "bubbles" upward in the document object tree. A true value means it will. A false value means the event listener will catch the event during the capturing phase, which I explain in the next section. (I explain bubbling a little bit later in this chapter.)

Listing 32.1 demonstrates Event object properties, and identifies the this object conclusively. It also creates the element that holds the event listener, assigns, and later removes the event listener.

Listing 32.1   *DOM Event Handling 101*

```
<?xml version="1.0" ?>
<!-- Netscape 6 browsers only. -->
<!DOCTYPE html PUBLIC "-//W3C//DTD XHTML 1.0 Transitional//EN"
➥"DTD/xhtml1-transitional.dtd">
<html xmlns="http://www.w3.org/1999/xhtml" >
<head><title></title>
<script language="JavaScript" type="text/javascript">
<!--
function go() {
  var input = document.createElement("input")
```

Listing 32.1   *(continued)*

```
  input.setAttribute("type", "button")
  input.setAttribute("value", "Click Here!")
  input.setAttribute("id", "myInput")
// creating a button.

  input.addEventListener("click", respond, true)
// adding an event listener to the element.

  document.forms[0].appendChild(input)
// adding the element to the document.
  }

function respond() {
  var p = document.createElement("p")
  var p_text = document.createTextNode("The this object is " + this.id + ".")
  p.appendChild(p_text)
  document.body.appendChild(p)
// explaining which element is the this object.

// creating a table
  var table = document.createElement("table")
  table.setAttribute("border", "1")
  var tbody = document.createElement("tbody")

  var y = 0
  var tr = document.createElement("tr")
  var td = document.createElement("th")
// reusing the same variable name in the loop

// begin table heading information
  td.appendChild(document.createTextNode("Index"))
  tr.appendChild(td)

  td = document.createElement("th")
  td.appendChild(document.createTextNode("Property Name"))
  tr.appendChild(td)

  td = document.createElement("th")
  td.appendChild(document.createTextNode("Property Value"))
  tr.appendChild(td)
```

Listing 32.1   *(continued)*

```
  tbody.appendChild(tr)
// end table heading information

  for (property in arguments[0]) {
// adding a new row for each property of the event object
    tr = document.createElement("tr")
    td = document.createElement("td")
    td.appendChild(document.createTextNode(y))
// which property number it happens to be
    tr.appendChild(td)
    y++

    td = document.createElement("td")
    var td_text = document.createTextNode(property)
// the property name
    td.appendChild(td_text)
    tr.appendChild(td)

    td = document.createElement("td")
    var td_text = document.createTextNode(arguments[0][property])
// the property value
    td.appendChild(td_text)
    tr.appendChild(td)

    tbody.appendChild(tr)
    }
  table.appendChild(tbody)
  document.body.appendChild(table)

  document.getElementById("myInput").
➥removeEventListener("click", respond, true)
// removing the event listener to reduce the chance of two tables at once
  }
//-->
</script>
</head>

<body onload="go()">
<form action="javascript:void(null)" method="get">
</form>
<!--Results after clicking on the button:
```

Listing 32.1 *(continued)*

```
The this object is myInput.
Index  Property Name Property Value
0      type         click
1      target       [object HTMLInputElement]
...
-->
</body>
</html>
```

Event Capturing and Bubbling

Sometimes you'll find an event goes through several elements before reaching the
element on which the event is meant to act. For instance, the click event in Listing
32.1 goes from the window object to the myInput element, as Listing 32.2 shows.

Listing 32.2   *Capturing (and Releasing) an Event*

```
<?xml version="1.0" ?>
<!-- Netscape 6.0+ only. -->
<!DOCTYPE html PUBLIC "-//W3C//DTD XHTML 1.0 Transitional//EN"
➥"DTD/xhtml1-transitional.dtd">
<html xmlns="http://www.w3.org/1999/xhtml" >
<head><title></title>
<script language="JavaScript" type="text/javascript">
<!--
function go() {
  var input = document.createElement("input")
  input.setAttribute("type", "button")
  input.setAttribute("value", "Click Here!")
  input.setAttribute("id", "myInput")
// creating a button.

  input.addEventListener("click", respond, true)
// adding an event listener to the element.

  document.forms[0].appendChild(input)
// adding the element to the document.

  document.forms[0].addEventListener("click", respond, true)
// attempting to have the form catch the click as well.
```

Listing 32.2   *(continued)*

```
  document.addEventListener("click", respond, true)
// does the event go through the document?

  window.addEventListener("click", respond, true)
// does the event go through the window?
  }

var numberCaught = 0

function respond(evt) {
  numberCaught++
  var p = document.createElement("p")
  var objName
  if (this == document) {
    objName = "document"
    }
  if (this == self) {
    objName = "window"
    }
  if (typeof this.id != "undefined") {
    objName = this.id
    }
  var p_text = "The " + objName + " object was number "
  p_text += numberCaught + " to catch this event; event.eventPhase is "
  p_text += evt.eventPhase + "."
  p.appendChild(document.createTextNode(p_text))
  document.body.appendChild(p)
// explaining which element is the this object.
  }
//-->
</script>
</head>

<body onload="go()">
<form action="javascript:void(null)" method="get" id="myForm">
</form>
<!-- Results after clicking on the button (Netscape 6.1):
The window object was number 1 to catch this event; event.eventPhase is 1.

The document object was number 2 to catch this event; event.eventPhase is 1.
```

Listing 32.2   *(continued)*

```
The myForm object was number 3 to catch this event; event.eventPhase is 1.

The myInput object was number 4 to catch this event; event.eventPhase is 2.

-->
</body>
</html>
```

This is known as event capturing—an event trickling down from the top of the tree to the target element. (Actually, in a sense, it trickles from above the top. The window object is senior to the document object, but the DOM concerns itself with window on rare occasions. Events are one of those occasions.) All events go through event capturing (but most of the time, transparently; you usually don't set event listeners on every node). The eventPhase property reveals whether the event is undergoing capturing (a value of 1, meaning it is progressing down), or is at the target element (a value of 2).

The opposite of event capturing is event bubbling—an event trickling up from the target element to the top of the tree again. Not all events bubble; the click event does. (The eventPhase property for an event that is bubbling has a value of 3.)

The addEventListener()'s third argument determines if the node will catch the event before it reaches its target (true) or possibly after it reaches its target (false). Listing 32.3 modifies Listing 32.2 to have two nodes (the form and the document) catch the event in the bubbling phase.

Listing 32.3   *Event Capturing and Bubbling*

```
<?xml version="1.0" ?>
<!-- Netscape 6.0+ only. -->
<!DOCTYPE html PUBLIC "-//W3C//DTD XHTML 1.0 Transitional//EN"
➥"DTD/xhtml1-transitional.dtd">
<html xmlns="http://www.w3.org/1999/xhtml" >
<head><title></title>
<script language="JavaScript" type="text/javascript">
<!--
function go() {
  var input = document.createElement("input")
  input.setAttribute("type", "button")
  input.setAttribute("value", "Click Here!")
  input.setAttribute("id", "myInput")
```

Listing 32.3   *(continued)*

```
// creating a button.

  input.addEventListener("click", respond, true)
// adding an event listener to the element.

  document.forms[0].appendChild(input)
// adding the element to the document.

  document.forms[0].addEventListener("click", respond, false)
// attempting to have the form catch the click as well.

  document.addEventListener("click", respond, false)
// does the event go through the document?

  window.addEventListener("click", respond, true)
// does the event go through the window?
  }

var numberCaught = 0

function respond(evt) {
  numberCaught++
  var p = document.createElement("p")
  var objName
  if (this == document) {
    objName = "document"
    }
  if (this == self) {
    objName = "window"
    }
  if (typeof this.id != "undefined") {
    objName = this.id
    }
  var p_text = "The " + objName + " object was number "
  p_text += numberCaught + " to catch this event; event.eventPhase is "
  p_text += evt.eventPhase + "."
  p.appendChild(document.createTextNode(p_text))
  document.body.appendChild(p)
// explaining which element is the this object.
  }
//-->
```

Listing 32.3   *(continued)*

```
</script>
</head>

<body onload="go()">
<form action="javascript:void(null)" method="get" id="myForm">
</form>
<!-- Results after clicking on the button (Netscape 6.1):
The window object was number 1 to catch this event; event.eventPhase is 1.

The myInput object was number 2 to catch this event; event.eventPhase is 2.

The myForm object was number 3 to catch this event; event.eventPhase is 3.

The document object was number 4 to catch this event; event.eventPhase is 3.

-->
</body>
</html>
```

Canceling an Event's Propagation

Sometimes you want an event to stop somewhere en route to its target or away from it. The stopPropagation() method of Event objects exists for this purpose.

Suppose we want the form to stop all click events from reaching inside the form. We could create a special modification to Listing 32.2, adding the stopPropagation() method automatically. Listing 32.4 shows the results of this.

Listing 32.4   *Canceling the Event's Propagation*

```
<?xml version="1.0" ?>
<!DOCTYPE html PUBLIC "-//W3C//DTD XHTML 1.0 Transitional//EN"
➥"DTD/xhtml1-transitional.dtd">
<html xmlns="http://www.w3.org/1999/xhtml" >
<head><title></title>
<script language="JavaScript" type="text/javascript">
<!--
function go() {
  var input = document.createElement("input")
  input.setAttribute("type", "button")
  input.setAttribute("value", "Click Here!")
  input.setAttribute("id", "myInput")
```

Listing 32.4   *(continued)*

```
// creating a button.

  input.addEventListener("click", respond, true)
// adding an event listener to the element.

  document.forms[0].appendChild(input)
// adding the element to the document.

respondAndStop = function(evt) {
  respond(evt)
  evt.stopPropagation()
  }

  document.forms[0].addEventListener("click", respondAndStop, true)
// attempting to have the form catch the click as well.

  document.addEventListener("click", respond, true)
// does the event go through the document?

  window.addEventListener("click", respond, true)
// does the event go through the window?
  }

var numberCaught = 0

function respond(evt) {
  numberCaught++
  var p = document.createElement("p")
  var objName = evt.currentTarget

  var p_text = "The " + objName + " object was number "
  p_text += numberCaught + " to catch this event; event.eventPhase is "
  p_text += evt.eventPhase + "."

  p.appendChild(document.createTextNode(p_text))
  document.body.appendChild(p)
// explaining which element is the this object.
  }
//-->
</script>
</head>
```

Listing 32.4   *(continued)*

```
<body onload="go()">
<form action="javascript:void(null)" method="get" id="myForm">
</form>
<!-- Results after clicking on the button (Netscape 6.1):
The [object Window] object was number 1 to catch this event;
➡ event.eventPhase is 1.

The [object HTMLDocument] object was number 2 to catch this event;
➡ event.eventPhase is 1.

The [object HTMLFormElement] object was number 3 to catch this event;
➡ event.eventPhase is 1.

-->
</body>
</html>
```

Canceling an Event's Default Action

Sometimes you want the default action of an event to not happen at all. For some events, such as a form submission, this is possible; for others, such as a key press, this is not.

The W3C DOM-2 Events specification defines the `preventDefault()` method for this purpose. You can also use the `getPreventDefault()` method to determine if the event's default action has indeed been canceled.

Use Event Listeners Carefully

Using event listeners indiscriminately can cause some unusual effects. For instance, in Listings 32.2 through 32.4, if you click anywhere in the document pane besides the button, you'll find the event firing for the `window` and `document` elements. That can be embarrassing for the Web page developer.

Fortunately, there are properties of the `Event` interface (and subsequently, of `Event` objects) that enable you to determine in the event listener functions how to react to the event. Listing 32.5 demonstrates a safer event listening version of Listing 32.2, checking the event target node against the input element. (I will forego the `eventPhase` property here.)

Listing 32.5   *Validating Events By Target*

```
<?xml version="1.0" ?>
<!-- Netscape 6.0+ browsers only. -->
<!DOCTYPE html PUBLIC "-//W3C//DTD XHTML 1.0 Transitional//EN"
➥"DTD/xhtml1-transitional.dtd">
<html xmlns="http://www.w3.org/1999/xhtml" >
<head><title></title>
<script language="JavaScript" type="text/javascript">
<!--
function go() {
  var input = document.createElement("input")
  input.setAttribute("type", "button")
  input.setAttribute("value", "Click Here!")
  input.setAttribute("id", "myInput")
// creating a button.

  input.addEventListener("click", respond, true)
// adding an event listener to the element.

  document.forms[0].appendChild(input)
// adding the element to the document.

  document.addEventListener("click", respond, true)
// does the event go through the document?
  }

var numberCaught = 0

function respond(evt) {
  var p = document.createElement("p")
  var objName
  if (this == document) {
    objName = "document"
    }
  if (this == self) {
    objName = "window"
    }
  if (typeof this.id != "undefined") {
    objName = this.id
    }
  if (evt.target == document.getElementById("myInput")) {
    numberCaught++
```

Listing 32.5 *(continued)*

```
    var p_text = "The " + objName + " object was number "
    p_text += numberCaught + " to catch this event."
// explaining which element is the this object.
    } else {
    var p_text = "The " + objName + " object caught this event, "
    p_text += "but the author did not want that."
    arguments[0].stopPropagation()
    }
  p.appendChild(document.createTextNode(p_text))
  document.body.appendChild(p)
  }
//-->
</script>
</head>

<body onload="go()">
<form action="javascript:void(null)" method="get" id="myForm">
</form>
<!-- Results after clicking on the button (Netscape 6.1):
The document object was number 1 to catch this event.

The myInput object was number 2 to catch this event.

Results after clicking anywhere else in the document pane:
The document object caught this event, but the author did not want that.
-->
</body>
</html>
```

Of course, the safest way to ensure a node doesn't catch an event is to not add an event listener to it in the first place.

Creating and Throwing Custom Events

There are ways to create an event object from scratch as well. In the DOM, it starts with a new method of the Document node (originally introduced in Chapter 20) known as the createEvent() method. As you might suspect, it creates and returns an event. More precisely, it returns an Event object.

> **Note**
> Technically, the `createEvent()` method is a method of the `DocumentEvent` interface. However, the W3C mentions `Document` and `DocumentEvent` interfaces apply to the same object—which for us is still the `document` object.

The object you receive back from the `createEvent()` method is very likely a blank event, with only its basic type defined. (You define the basic type as the first argument of the `createEvent()` method.) There are three basic types the DOM-2 Events Recommendation defines: "UIEvents," "MutationEvents," and "HTMLEvents." (The Recommendation did not define key events in this round.)

The `initEvent()` method allows you to redefine the type, whether the `Event` object is cancelable (throwing the football to the ground), and if the `Event` object can bubble. You can also specify exactly which event type this is (a `load` event or a `click` event, for example). However, after you define the basic type, you must also define specific properties of the `Event` object, via the appropriate function. (The exception is for HTML events; in these cases, `initEvent()` is sufficient.)

The DOM defines three different methods. The `initUIEvent()` method initializes a generic user interface event. The `initMouseEvent()` method initializes a generic mouse event, which is a specific subset of user interface events. The `MutationEvent()` method initializes an event for document alterations by the DOM.

Netscape 6 defines an additional `initKeyEvent()` method. The W3C plans to include something similar in a future revision of events for the DOM.

Before the formal definitions, examine Listing 32.6. This listing is a modification of Listing 32.1, but creates the event object from scratch. (Don't worry about not understanding the arguments of the `initMouseEvents()` method yet; I cover them later in the chapter.)

Listing 32.6   *Creating an Event from Scratch*

```
<?xml version="1.0" ?>
<!-- Netscape 6+ browsers only. -->
<!DOCTYPE html PUBLIC "-//W3C//DTD XHTML 1.0 Transitional//EN"
➥"DTD/xhtml1-transitional.dtd">
<html xmlns="http://www.w3.org/1999/xhtml" >
<head><title></title>
<script language="JavaScript" type="text/javascript">
<!--
```

Listing 32.6   *(continued)*

```
function go() {
  var x = document.createEvent("MouseEvents")
  x.initMouseEvent("click", true, true, self, 1, 0, 0, 0, 0, false, false,
➥false, false, 0, null)
  document.addEventListener("click", respond, true)
  document.getElementById("hello").dispatchEvent(x)
  }

function respond() {
  var p = document.createElement("p")
  var p_text = document.createTextNode("The this object is " + this.id + ".")
  p.appendChild(p_text)
  document.body.appendChild(p)
// explaining which element is the this object.

// creating a table
  var table = document.createElement("table")
  table.setAttribute("border", "1")
  var tbody = document.createElement("tbody")

  var y = 0
  var tr = document.createElement("tr")
  var td = document.createElement("th")
// reusing the same variable name in the loop


// begin table heading information
  td.appendChild(document.createTextNode("Index"))
  tr.appendChild(td)

  td = document.createElement("th")
  td.appendChild(document.createTextNode("Property Name"))
  tr.appendChild(td)

  td = document.createElement("th")
  td.appendChild(document.createTextNode("Property Value"))
  tr.appendChild(td)

  tbody.appendChild(tr)
// end table heading information
```

Listing 32.6   *(continued)*

```
  for (property in arguments[0]) {
// adding a new row for each property of the event object
    tr = document.createElement("tr")
    td = document.createElement("td")
    td.appendChild(document.createTextNode(y))
// which property number it happens to be
    tr.appendChild(td)
    y++

    td = document.createElement("td")
    var td_text = document.createTextNode(property)
// the property name
    td.appendChild(td_text)
    tr.appendChild(td)

    td = document.createElement("td")
    var td_text = document.createTextNode(arguments[0][property])
// the property value
    td.appendChild(td_text)
    tr.appendChild(td)

    tbody.appendChild(tr)
    }
  table.appendChild(tbody)
  document.body.appendChild(table)

  document.removeEventListener("click", respond, true)
// removing the event listener to reduce the chance of two tables at once
  }

//-->
</script>
</head>

<body onload="go()">
<input type="button" id="hello" value="Dummy Button" />
<!-- Results are similar to Listing 32.1. -->
</body>
</html>
```

> **Note**
> Listing 32.6 should state the target is the input element. Instead it states the target is the document. This is a bug in the Netscape browser.

Who Supports DOM-2 Events?

Completely? No one.

Netscape 6.x has the closest support to DOM-2 Events of all the major browsers. It has a number of known bugs (event listeners firing their own events in a recursion scheme typically leads to a crash), and is currently missing the generic UI events (`onactivate`, `onfocusin`, `onfocusout`). On the other hand, it does include key events.

Events in Internet Explorer

The good news is Internet Explorer supports the original HTML event handlers as event handlers. The bad news is even with Internet Explorer 6, there is no attempt to use the DOM-2 Events model, aside from many of the specific event types being similar. The current event becomes a property of the `window` object, named `window.event`.

Microsoft includes an alternative extension to the `<script>...</script>` element for event handling. The `for` attribute reflects an element's `id` attribute somewhere in the document, and the `event` attribute is the event handler, including the `on` prefix, on which the script acts. (For the record, this sort of event handling takes place after the document has loaded; forget about using this for the `onload` event handler.)

Listing 32.7 has a simple HTML document utilizing this new feature. Unlike the DOM-2 specification, when you clone the node with a `true` argument, the event handler will attach to its fellow elements as well.

Listing 32.7   *Microsoft's Proprietary Scripted Events*

```
<html>
<!-- This document is not XHTML 1.0. Internet Explorer 5.0+ only. -->
<head><title></title>
<script language="JavaScript" type="text/javascript" for="bodyp"
➥event="onmouseover">
document.body.appendChild(this.cloneNode(true))
</script>
```

Listing 32.7   *(continued)*

```
</head>

<body >
<p id="bodyp">Move your mouse over me, and watch me appear again.</p>
</body>
</html>
```

> **Caution**
> Netscape 6 does not support the `htmlFor` or `event` attributes. It does have them as empty strings in the DOM.
>
> This is significant because any script element with these attributes is intended to reflect an event handler. But Netscape assumes the script is to execute immediately in the context of the window.
>
> I strongly recommend against use of these attributes. There are better ways to attach event handling to an element.

Event Handlers Are Also Available as Methods

Listing 32.7 could easily be an XHTML 1.0 document if instead it assigned the `onmouseover()` method of the paragraph element to a function. Note Listing 32.8, which assigns functions to methods directly, twice.

Listing 32.8   *Defining Event Handlers Directly*

```
<?xml version="1.0" ?>
<!-- Netscape 6+, Internet Explorer 5.0+ only. -->
<!DOCTYPE html PUBLIC "-//W3C//DTD XHTML 1.0 Transitional//EN"
➡"DTD/xhtml1-transitional.dtd">
<html xmlns="http://www.w3.org/1999/xhtml" >
<head><title></title>
<script language="JavaScript" type="text/javascript">
<!--
function go() {
  document.body.appendChild(this.cloneNode(true))
  }

window.onload = function () {
  document.getElementById("bodyp").onmouseover = go
  }
```

Listing 32.8   *(continued)*

```
//-->
</script>
</head>

<body >
<p id="bodyp">Move your mouse over me, and watch me appear again.</p>
</body>
</html>
```

Unlike in the previous example, the `cloneNode(true)` method of nodes does not copy the event handler. Also, using the `setAttribute()` method is useless in setting event handlers.

One fact worth noting: Listing 32.8 works in Netscape 6 browsers as well. (The only reason it does not work with Netscape 4 is Netscape 4 does not support the DOM Level 1. Listing 32.10 is for Netscape 4.x browsers, and does attach event handlers in this manner.)

Event Bubbling and Canceling in Internet Explorer

Listing 32.9 reveals bubbling applied in Internet Explorer. If you click on the first line of text, two paragraph nodes appear: one containing "P" for the original paragraph node, and one containing "BODY" for the document body. Anywhere else on the document, a click generates one paragraph node containing "BODY."

Listing 32.9   *Event Bubbling, the Old-Fashioned Way*

```
<?xml version="1.0" ?>
<!DOCTYPE html PUBLIC "-//W3C//DTD XHTML 1.0 Transitional//EN"
➥"DTD/xhtml1-transitional.dtd">
<html xmlns="http://www.w3.org/1999/xhtml" >
<head><title></title>
<script language="JavaScript" type="text/javascript">
<!--
function go() {
  var p = document.createElement("p")
  p.appendChild(document.createTextNode(this.nodeName))
  document.body.appendChild(p)
  }

window.onload = function () {
  document.getElementById("bodyp").onmousedown = go
```

Listing 32.9   *(continued)*

```
    document.body.onmousedown = go
    }
//-->
</script>
</head>

<body>
<p id="bodyp">Click anywhere on the document (especially here).</p>
</body>
</html>
```

As for popping the bubble (that is, making sure the event won't bubble up), a single line added to the go() function suffices:

```
event.cancelBubble = true
```

With this line, if you click on the paragraph element, that's the end of the event.

> **Note**
> Internet Explorer appears not to implement event capturing as the W3C DOM defines it. An event object starts at the node that fires it.

Default actions (such as submitting the form in an onsubmit event handler) cancel when the returnValue property of event (or the return value of last function the event calls) is false.

Mouse Capture in Internet Explorer

Internet Explorer introduces a new concept: mouse capturing. Basically, any element can capture mouse events on them using the setCapture() method of that element, including those which normally wouldn't. (I'm sure I don't need to explain just how useful mouse events are.)

Similarly, the releaseCapture() method allows Internet Explorer to clear the capturing of mouse events. Unfortunately, mouse capturing and event capturing are not very similar.

Mouse capturing also has a special event handler for it, the `onlosecapture` event handler. This becomes useful for cleanup of the effects of an element capturing mouse events. It fires when all the mouse events involved with a particular mouse action have cleared.

Netscape 4 and Events

Events in Netscape 4 don't match completely the procedures for Internet Explorer or Netscape 6. All three browsers support event handlers as attributes of elements or properties of their corresponding JavaScript objects. Beyond that, it's another ball game.

Caution

Netscape 4.x does not appear to implement event bubbling. An event starts from the `window` object and ends at the element with the event handler.

Compare this to Internet Explorer: Netscape 4 only lets events go "down" from the window. Internet Explorer only lets events go "up" to the window...

At least Netscape 6 is making an effort to use the standard, but this is just another area where you must be very careful in coding for multiple browsers.

Listing 32.10 incorporates the four event capturing methods that you find on most objects in the Netscape 4.x DOM. The paragraphs and lists describe a sequence of actions concerning the events and their related functions.

Listing 32.10   *Capturing Events in Netscape 4.x*

```
<?xml version="1.0" ?>
<!DOCTYPE html PUBLIC "-//W3C//DTD XHTML 1.0 Transitional//EN"
➥"DTD/xhtml1-transitional.dtd">
<html xmlns="http://www.w3.org/1999/xhtml" >
<!-- Netscape 4.x only. -->
<head><title></title>
<script language="JavaScript" type="text/javascript">
<!--
function go() {
  var x = altImage.src
  altImage.src = document.images[0].src
```

Listing 32.10   *(continued)*

```
  document.images[0].src = x
  }
altImage = new Image()
altImage.src = "on_0.gif"

document.captureEvents(Event.MOUSEOVER | Event.MOUSEOUT)

function catchEvent(evtObj) {
  alert("Event captured!")
  document.links[1].handleEvent(evtObj)
  }

function stopCatchEvent(evtObj) {
  alert("Event will no longer be captured!")
  routeEvent(evtObj)
  document.releaseEvents(Event.MOUSEOVER | Event.MOUSEOUT)
  }

function finishEvent(evtObj) {
  if (evtObj.target == document.links[0]) {
    alert("The second link is handling the event!")
    document.routeEvent(evtObj)
    }
  }

document.onMouseOver = catchEvent
document.onMouseOut = stopCatchEvent

//-->
</script>
</head>

<body onload="document.links[1].onMouseOver = finishEvent;">
<p><a href="javascript:void('FirstLink')" onmouseover="go()"
onmouseout="go()"><img src="off_0.gif" border="0" alt="Sample image" /></a>
Move your mouse through the icon <a href="javascript:void('SecondLink')" >up
 and down.</a></p>
<p>There is a specific series of actions which take place when you put your
 mouse over the image.</p>
<ol>
<li>The mouseover event fires.</li>
```

Listing 32.10   *(continued)*

```
<li>The document <b>captures</b> the mouseover event.</li>
<li>The catchEvent() function executes, receiving as an argument a Netscape
  event object.</li>
<li>catchEvent() directs the second link to <b>handle</b> the event. (The
  image is the first link.)</li>
<li>The finishEvent() function executes, receiving the event object as its
  first argument. (This comes from the onload event handler for the body.)</li>
<li>finishEvent() <b>routes</b> the event on its way to its normal
  destination.</li>
<li>As there are no more captures en route, it arrives at the firing element,
  the first link.</li>
<li>The onmouseover for the first link calls go(), which changes the image
  automatically.</li>
</ol>

<p>When the mouse moves off the image, another sequence of actions takes
place.</p>
<ol>
<li>The document <b>captures</b> the mouseout event.</li>
<li>The stopCatchEvent() function executes, receiving as an argument a
Netscape event object.</li>
<li>stopCatchEvent() <b>routes</b> the event on its way to its normal
destination.</li>
<li>As there are no more captures en route, it arrives at the firing element,
the first link.</li>
<li>The onmouseout for the first link calls go(), which changes the image
automatically.</li>
<li>stopCatchEvent() tells the document to <b>release</b> all capturing of
mouseover and mouseout events.</li>
</ol>
<p>As a result, the document only catches these events once.</p>
</body>
</html>
```

Event Interface (DOM)/Event

Browser/JavaScript Version	Created By
Nav4/JavaScript 1.2	*event handler*
IE4/JScript 3.0	*event handler*
IE5/JScript 5.0	*event handler*
IE5.5/JScript 5.5	`document.createEventObject(`*eventClass*`)`
	event handler
Nav6/JavaScript 1.5	`document.createEvent()`
	event handler
IE6	`document.createEventObject(`*eventClass*`)`
	event handler
DOM Level 2 Events	`document.createEvent()`*event handler*

> **Note**
> Implemented in Nav3+ (event handler), Nav6 (DOM)

Description

The `Event` interface is the basis for all events in the DOM—much like the `Node` interface in Chapter 20, is the basis for all nodes in the DOM. Everything else is a modification thereof.

Netscape 6 is the only browser to formally handle the DOM `Event` interface. Internet Explorer has a partial implementation, formally naming it `event`, a property of `window`.

Properties

Netscape 6's `Event` interface defines a lot of properties—most of them constants about which we need not worry. (Try running Listing 32.1 and you'll see what I mean.) The following line in Netscape 6:

```
javascript:var x = 0; for (property in Event.prototype) {x++}; alert(x)
```

returns an astonishing 191 alerts. (Don't try this at home.) Most of these, such as `DOM_VK_N`, are identical in all events. (This stands for the letter N on the keyboard, in case you're curious.)

Part III   Document Object Model for HTML Documents

Specifically, there are 151 constant properties, which Table 32.1 lists.

Table 32.1   *DOM-2 Event Constant Properties*

Property Name	Property Value	Property Name	Property Value
CAPTURING_PHASE	1	DOM_VK_B	66
AT_TARGET	2	DOM_VK_C	67
BUBBLING_PHASE	3	DOM_VK_D	68
MOUSEDOWN	1	DOM_VK_E	69
MOUSEUP	2	DOM_VK_F	70
MOUSEOVER	4	DOM_VK_G	71
MOUSEOUT	8	DOM_VK_H	72
MOUSEMOVE	16	DOM_VK_I	73
MOUSEDRAG	32	DOM_VK_J	74
CLICK	64	DOM_VK_K	75
DBLCLICK	128	DOM_VK_L	76
KEYDOWN	256	DOM_VK_M	77
KEYUP	512	DOM_VK_N	78
KEYPRESS	1024	DOM_VK_O	79
DRAGDROP	2048	DOM_VK_P	80
FOCUS	4096	DOM_VK_Q	81
BLUR	8192	DOM_VK_R	82
SELECT	16384	DOM_VK_S	83
CHANGE	32768	DOM_VK_T	84
RESET	65536	DOM_VK_U	85
SUBMIT	131072	DOM_VK_V	86
SCROLL	262144	DOM_VK_W	87
LOAD	524288	DOM_VK_X	88
UNLOAD	1048576	DOM_VK_Y	89
XFER_DONE	2097152	DOM_VK_Z	90
ABORT	4194304	DOM_VK_NUMPAD0	96
ERROR	8388608	DOM_VK_NUMPAD1	97
LOCATE	16777216	DOM_VK_NUMPAD2	98
MOVE	33554432	DOM_VK_NUMPAD3	99
RESIZE	67108864	DOM_VK_NUMPAD4	100

Table 32.1   *(continued)*

Property Name	Property Value	Property Name	Property Value
FORWARD	134217728	DOM_VK_NUMPAD5	101
HELP	268435456	DOM_VK_NUMPAD6	102
BACK	536870912	DOM_VK_NUMPAD7	103
TEXT	1073741824	DOM_VK_NUMPAD8	104
ALT_MASK	1	DOM_VK_NUMPAD9	105
CONTROL_MASK	2	DOM_VK_MULTIPLY	106
SHIFT_MASK	4	DOM_VK_ADD	107
META_MASK	8	DOM_VK_SEPARATOR	108
DOM_VK_CANCEL	3	DOM_VK_SUBTRACT	109
DOM_VK_BACK_SPACE	8	DOM_VK_DECIMAL	110
DOM_VK_TAB	9	DOM_VK_DIVIDE	111
DOM_VK_CLEAR	12	DOM_VK_F1	112
DOM_VK_RETURN	13	DOM_VK_F2	113
DOM_VK_ENTER	14	DOM_VK_F3	114
DOM_VK_SHIFT	16	DOM_VK_F4	115
DOM_VK_CONTROL	17	DOM_VK_F5	116
DOM_VK_ALT	18	DOM_VK_F6	117
DOM_VK_PAUSE	19	DOM_VK_F7	118
DOM_VK_CAPS_LOCK	20	DOM_VK_F8	119
DOM_VK_ESCAPE	27	DOM_VK_F9	120
DOM_VK_SPACE	32	DOM_VK_F10	121
DOM_VK_PAGE_UP	33	DOM_VK_F11	122
DOM_VK_PAGE_DOWN	34	DOM_VK_F12	123
DOM_VK_END	35	DOM_VK_F13	124
DOM_VK_HOME	36	DOM_VK_F14	125
DOM_VK_LEFT	37	DOM_VK_F15	126
DOM_VK_UP	38	DOM_VK_F16	127
DOM_VK_RIGHT	39	DOM_VK_F17	128
DOM_VK_DOWN	40	DOM_VK_F18	129
DOM_VK_PRINTSCREEN	44	DOM_VK_F19	130
DOM_VK_INSERT	45	DOM_VK_F20	131
DOM_VK_DELETE	46	DOM_VK_F21	132

Table 32.1   *(continued)*

Property Name	Property Value	Property Name	Property Value
DOM_VK_0	48	DOM_VK_F22	133
DOM_VK_1	49	DOM_VK_F23	134
DOM_VK_2	50	DOM_VK_F24	135
DOM_VK_3	51	DOM_VK_NUM_LOCK	144
DOM_VK_4	52	DOM_VK_SCROLL_LOCK	145
DOM_VK_5	53	DOM_VK_COMMA	188
DOM_VK_6	54	DOM_VK_PERIOD	190
DOM_VK_7	55	DOM_VK_SLASH	191
DOM_VK_8	56	DOM_VK_BACK_QUOTE	192
DOM_VK_9	57	DOM_VK_OPEN_BRACKET	219
DOM_VK_SEMICOLON	59	DOM_VK_BACK_SLASH	220
DOM_VK_EQUALS	61	DOM_VK_CLOSE_BRACKET	221
DOM_VK_A	65	DOM_VK_QUOTE	222
		DOM_VK_META	224

> **Note**
> These constants may not be very useful without a visualization of the keyboards in question. The Web site for this book (`http://www.jslab.org/jsdd`) has this information in a visual format.

Here, then, are the properties and methods not defined previously, for both Netscape 4 and Netscape 6. (Mutation event properties are not in the 151 properties, but they are here.)

altKey

JavaScript 1.5, JScript 3.0+

Nav6, IE4+

Syntax

```
var x = eventObject.altKey
```

The `altKey` property of `Event` objects reflects, for user interface events, whether the Alt key on a Windows keyboard was pressed when the event fires.

altLeft

JScript 5.5+

IE5.5

Syntax

```
var x = eventObject.altLeft
```

The altLeft property of Event objects reflects, for user interface events, if the leftside Alt key on a Windows keyboard was pressed when the event fires.

This can be useful in tandem with the altKey property. For instance, if the right Alt key is pressed, altKey will read as true while this property will read as false.

attrChange

JavaScript 1.5

Nav6

Syntax

```
var x = eventObject.attrChange
```

The attrChange property for mutation events reflects what kind of change happens to the target element's attribute. For instance, a value of 1 means the attribute's value was replaced; a value of 2 means the element gained an attribute with a new value. A value of 3 implies the element had an attribute removed.

attrName

JavaScript 1.5

Nav6

Syntax

```
var x = eventObject.attrName
```

The attrName property for mutation events reflects the name of the target element's attribute experiencing a change.

bubbles

JavaScript 1.5

Nav6

Read-only.

Syntax

```
var x = eventObject.bubbles
```

The bubbles property of Event objects reflects whether the event will continue to bubble upward from the targeted element to the document or window.

button

JavaScript 1.5

Nav6

Syntax

```
var x = eventObject.button
```

The button property of Event objects reflects, for user interface events, which mouse button the user depressed for the event. In Netscape, for a standard mouse with the left-to-right orientation, a value of 0 reflects the leftmost mouse button, 1 represents a possible center button, and 2 represents the rightmost mouse button.

Internet Explorer does it differently, allowing 1 to stand for the left mouse button, 2 for the right mouse button, and 4 for the center mouse button. If you click multiple mouse buttons, the totals for the buttons add up (the left and right mouse buttons, for example, mean 3).

cancelable

JavaScript 1.5

Nav6

Syntax

```
var x = eventObject.cancelable
```

The cancelable property of Event objects reflects whether the user can cancel the default action of the event (say, submitting a form for an event fired from an onsubmit event handler). For some events (notably mutation events) the property is always false.

cancelBubble
JavaScript 1.5, JScript 3.0+

Nav6, IE4+

Syntax

```
var x = eventObject.cancelBubble
```

The cancelBubble property of Event objects, once set to true, establishes the event will not bubble from its target element through all ancestors, to the document or window.

charCode
JavaScript 1.5

Nav6

The charCode property of Event objects, in theory, should return a character code of a key pressed. However, it appears to be partially in effect at this time. Martin Honnen (whom I thanked in the credits for this book) suggests the following line of code to retrieve a character code:

```
var keyCode = event.which ? event.which : event.keyCode ? event.keyCode :
➥ event.charCode;
```

clientX
JavaScript 1.5, JScript 3.0+

Nav6, IE4+

Syntax

```
var x = eventObject.clientX [= pixelCoord]
```

The `clientX` property of `Event` objects reflects, for user interface events, where in the client window the event took place. In this case, it represents the number of pixels from the left edge of the document's viewable space to the event's firing location.

For Netscape 6 and Internet Explorer 4, this property is read-only.

clientY

JavaScript 1.5, JScript 3.0+

Nav6, IE4+

Syntax

```
var x = eventObject.clientY [= pixelCoord]
```

The `clientY` property of `Event` objects reflects, for user interface events, where in the client window the event took place. In this case, it represents the number of pixels from the top edge of the document's viewable space to the event's firing location.

For Netscape 6 and Internet Explorer 4, this property is read-only.

ctrlKey

JavaScript 1.5, JScript 3.0+

Nav6, IE4+

Syntax

```
var x = eventObject.crtlKey
```

The `ctrlKey` property of `Event` objects reflects, for user interface events, whether the Alt key on a Windows keyboard was pressed when the event fires.

ctrlLeft

JScript 5.5+

IE5.5

Syntax

```
var x = eventObject.ctrlLeft
```

The `ctrlLeft` property of `Event` objects reflects, for user interface events, whether the left-side Ctrl key on a Windows keyboard was pressed when the event fires.

This can be useful in tandem with the `ctrlKey` property. For instance, if the right Ctrl key is pressed, `ctrlKey` will read as `true` while this property will read as `false`.

currentTarget

JavaScript 1.5

Nav6

Syntax

```
var x = eventObject.currentTarget
```

The `currentTarget` property of `Event` objects reflects the `Node` object the event is currently dealing with. It is not the eventual target of the event (covered by `target`.)

This property is an ideal way to affect the node listening for that event. (But if the node is listening for mutation events, treat it as read-only or you will generate browser crashes.)

detail

JavaScript 1.5

Nav6

Syntax

```
var x = eventObject.detail
```

The `detail` property of `Event` objects is a number giving detailed information about the event for the given specific type of event. This value varies by event. (For mouse events, it typically means the number of mouse clicks in this event sequence.)

eventPhase

JavaScript 1.5

Nav6

Syntax

```
var x = eventObject.eventPhase
```

The `eventPhase` property of `Event` objects is a number representing whether the event object is in a capturing phase, a bubbling phase, or at the node for which it aimed. A value of 1 means the event is under capturing (proceeding down from the window to the target). A value of 2 means the event is on its target node. A value of 3 means the event is bubbling up from the target node (toward the window or document).

fromElement

JScript 3.0+

IE4+

Syntax

```
var x = eventObject.fromElement
```

The fromElement property of Event objects returns the element the mouse pointer departed to reach the srcElement property. This is similar to the relatedTarget property.

You can have several different mouse-related events firing in Internet Explorer 5.5+ almost simultaneously. Because of this, the mouse events really rely on toElement. Listing 32.12 demonstrates event types, and the toElement and fromElement properties.

height

JavaScript 1.2+

Nav4+

Syntax

```
var x = eventObject.height
```

The height property of Event objects is equivalent to the y property. For instance,

```
<a href="javascript:void()" onclick="alert(arguments[0].y + '\n' +
➥arguments[0].height)">
<div style="height:200;width:200;background-color:red;">Hello<br />World</div>
</a>
```

returns identical (and changing) values for y and height in Netscape 4.

isChar

JavaScript 1.5

Nav6

Syntax

```
var x = eventObject.isChar
```

The isChar property of Event objects is a holdover from the Mozilla codebase, and conveys no useful information. The DOM Working group is creating a replacement for it in the DOM-3 Events specification (currently a working draft).

keyCode

JavaScript 1.5, JScript 3.0+

Nav6, IE4+

Syntax

```
var x = eventObject.keyCode
```

The keyCode property of Event objects, for Netscape 6, is a number equal to one of the predefined constants for Event, indicating which key on the keyboard was pressed.

For Internet Explorer browsers, it is a Unicode equivalent to the key pressed. You can find Unicode charts at http://www.unicode.org.

This property applies for key events only.

layerX

JavaScript 1.5

Nav6

Syntax

```
var x = eventObject.layerX
```

For Netscape 4.x browsers, the layerX property of Event objects refers to the number of pixels from the left edge of its Layer object to the left edge of the event's location.

Absent a `Layer` object in Netscape 4, and in Netscape 6 when not involving an absolutely positioned `<div>...</div>`, it will correspond to the `clientX` property. (As I mention in Chapter 28, "Text Formatting Elements," absolutely positioned elements often reflect like layers.)

This property is only available for mouse events.

layerY

JavaScript 1.5

Nav6

Syntax

```
var x = eventObject.layerY
```

For Netscape 4.x browsers, the `layerY` property of `Event` objects refers to the number of pixels from the top edge of its `Layer` object to the top edge of the event's location.

Absent a `Layer` object in Netscape 4, and in Netscape 6 when not involving an absolutely positioned `<div>...</div>`, it will correspond to the `clientY` property. (As I mention in Chapter 28, absolutely positioned div elements often reflect like layers.)

This property is only available for mouse events.

metaKey

JavaScript 1.5

Nav6

Syntax

```
var x = eventObject.metaKey
```

The `metaKey` property of `Event` objects reflects whether the "meta" key on the keyboard was down at the moment. Windows keyboards do not have a "meta" key; I believe it is specific to Macintosh keyboards.

modifiers

JavaScript 1.2–1.3

Nav4–4.78

Syntax

```
var x = eventObject.modifiers
```

The modifiers property of Event objects is a number value indicating the various modifier keys that apply to the event. Basically, it combines four constants (ALT_KEY, SHIFT_KEY, CTRL_KEY, and META_KEY) into one number, but only containing the values active at the moment of the event. (For instance, if the Shift key were pressed but not the Alt key, the SHIFT_KEY constant would be added to the number and the ALT_KEY constant would not.)

> **Note**
> You can find more information about the modifiers property on my Web site via a link at http://www.jslab.org/jsdd.

newValue

JavaScript 1.5

Nav6

Syntax

```
var x = eventObject.newValue
```

The newValue property for mutation events reflects the corrected value of the target element's attribute that experienced a change.

originalTarget

JavaScript 1.5

Nav6

Syntax

```
var x = eventObject.originalTarget
```

The originalTarget property of Event objects reflects a slightly more accurate targeting of the event than the target property in some cases. However, this property is meant more for XUL (which is beyond the scope of this book) than for (X)HTML. You can safely ignore this property.

pageX

JavaScript 1.2+

Nav4+

Syntax

```
var x = eventObject.pageX
```

The pageX property of Event objects reflects the current cursor horizontal position of the document in pixels.

pageY

JavaScript 1.2+

Nav4

Syntax

```
var x = eventObject.pageY
```

The pageY property of Event objects reflects the current cursor vertical position of the document in pixels.

prevValue

JavaScript 1.5

Nav6

Syntax

```
var x = eventObject.prevValue
```

The prevValue property for mutation events reflects the previous value of the target element's attribute that experienced a change.

propertyName

JScript 5.0+

IE5+

Syntax

```
var x = eventObject.propertyName [= newName]
```

The `propertyName` property, for `propertychange` events, reflects the name of the property undergoing a change as a string.

rangeOffset

JavaScript 1.5

Nav6

Syntax

```
var x = eventObject.rangeOffset
```

The `rangeOffset` property of `Event` objects indicates, relative to the `Text` node containing the event's target, on which character the event actually occurs.

Listing 32.11 demonstrates the `rangeOffset` and `rangeParent` properties. (Chapter 34, "DOM-2 Range," covers ranges in far more detail.) Note the listing catches two events, the `mousedown` and the `mouseup`. The `rangeOffset` and `rangeParent` change accordingly for each event.

rangeParent

JavaScript 1.5

Nav6

Syntax

```
var x = eventObject.rangeParent
```

The `rangeParent` property of `Event` objects indicates which `Text` node contains the event's targeted character.

Listing 32.11 demonstrates the `rangeOffset` and `rangeParent` properties. (Chapter 34, covers ranges in far more detail.) Note the listing catches two events, the `mousedown` and the `mouseup`. The `rangeOffset` and `rangeParent` change accordingly for each event.

Listing 32.11   *The Parent and Offset of a Select Range*

```
<?xml version="1.0" ?>
<!DOCTYPE html PUBLIC "-//W3C//DTD XHTML 1.0 Transitional//EN"
➡"DTD/xhtml1-transitional.dtd">
<html xmlns="http://www.w3.org/1999/xhtml" >
```

Listing 32.11   *(continued)*

```html
<head><title></title>
<script language="JavaScript" type="text/javascript">
<!--
function respond(evt) {
  var text = "type = " + evt.type + "\n"
  text += "rangeParent.nodeValue = " + evt.rangeParent.nodeValue + "\n"
  text += "evt.rangeOffset = " + evt.rangeOffset
  var pre = document.createElement("pre")
  pre.appendChild(document.createTextNode(text))
  document.body.appendChild(pre)
  }
//-->
</script>
</head>

<body onload="document.addEventListener('mouseup',respond, true);
document.addEventListener('mousedown',respond, true);
alert(document.getElementById('txt').childNodes[2].nodeValue)">
<pre id="txt">The quick <span style="color:red">red fox</span> jumped over the
➥ lazy <span
 style="color:brown">brown dog</span>.</pre>
<pre>^^^^5^^^^0    ^^^^5^^^^0^^^^5^^^^0^^    ^</pre>
<pre>    ^^^^5^^    ^^^^5^^^^</pre>
<p>Select any text in the above line.</p>
</body>
</html>
```

relatedTarget

JavaScript 1.5

Nav6

Syntax

```
var x = eventObject.relatedTarget
```

The relatedTarget property of Event objects reflects, for mouseover and mouseout events, the node the mouse pointer left or entered, respectively.

repeat

JScript 5.0+

IE5+

Syntax

```
var x = eventObject.repeat
```

The `repeat` property of Event objects returns, for key events, `true` if the depressed key is being held down.

If the key is down long enough to register two or more keystrokes of the same key, the property will return `true`. Otherwise, it will return `false`. The `repeat` property changes based on how many times the event has fired (more than once means `true`.)

returnValue

JScript 3.0+

IE4+

Syntax

```
[var x = ] eventObject.returnValue [= newReturn]
```

The `returnValue` property of Event objects reflects what the event will return upon the firing node.

Notably, this is much like the `preventDefault()` method—by setting this value to `false`, you prevent the default action of the event.

saveType

JScript 5.5+

IE5.5

Syntax

```
var x = eventObject.saveType
```

The `saveType` property of Event objects, for `contentsave` events, reflects whether the Clipboard's contents are text (`"TEXT"`) or (X)HTML markup (`"HTML"`).

screenX

JavaScript 1.2+, JScript 3.0+

Nav4+, IE4+

Syntax

```
var x = eventObject.screenX
```

The `screenX` property of `Event` objects reflects, for user interface events, where on the viewable screen the event took place.

screenY

JavaScript 1.2+, JScript 3.0+

Nav4+, IE4+

Syntax

```
var x = eventObject.screenY
```

The `screenY` property of `Event` objects reflects, for user interface events, where on the viewable screen the event took place.

shiftKey

JavaScript 1.5, JScript 3.0+

Nav6, IE4+

Syntax

```
var x = eventObject.shiftKey
```

The `shiftKey` property of `Event` objects reflects, for user interface events, whether the Shift key on a Windows keyboard was pressed when the event fires.

shiftLeft

JScript 5.5+

IE5.5

Syntax

```
var x = eventObject.shiftLeft
```

The shiftLeft property of Event objects reflects, for user interface events, whether the leftside Shift key on a Windows keyboard was pressed when the event fires.

This can be useful in tandem with the shiftKey property. For instance, if the right Shift key is pressed, shiftKey will read as true while this property will read as false.

srcElement

JScript 3.0+

IE4+

Syntax

```
var x = eventObject.srcElement
```

The srcElement property of Event objects is equivalent to the target property for Netscape 6 browsers. (However, Netscape 6's target property can apply to events targeted at any type of node; Internet Explorer only allows events on elements.)

target

JavaScript 1.2+

Nav4+

Syntax

```
var x = eventObject.target
```

The target property of Event objects is the node the event fired against. For instance, if a form has an onsubmit event handler, the form is the target of any form submission events aimed at that form (for instance, if the user clicks on the Submit button).

In Netscape 6's events model, the target is the end of the line if the event does not bubble, or the middle if the event does bubble.

For Netscape 4, the target property is an object representing the element, not the element itself.

timeStamp

JavaScript 1.5

Nav6

Syntax

```
var x = eventObject.timestamp
```

The `timestamp` property of `Event` objects should represent a number value you can use in the `Date()` constructor function (see Chapter 6, "Date()"), designating exactly when the event happened.

Unfortunately, this is not the case. I received an absurdly low number for this property—numbers that placed the events in 1970. You should therefore regard this property as unreliable in Netscape 6.

toElement

JScript 3.0+

IE4+

Syntax

```
[var x = ] eventObject.toElement [= targetElement]
```

The `toElement` property of `Event` objects reflects the element the mouse pointer is moving toward. Usually this is equivalent to the `srcElement` property of the event.

You can have several different mouse-related events firing in Internet Explorer 5.5+ almost simultaneously. Because of this, the mouse events really rely on `toElement`. Listing 32.12 demonstrates event types, and the `toElement` and `fromElement` properties.

Listing 32.12   *Mouse Events,* `toElement` *and* `fromElement`

```
<?xml version="1.0" ?>
<!DOCTYPE html PUBLIC "-//W3C//DTD XHTML 1.0 Transitional//EN"
➥ "DTD/xhtml1-transitional.dtd">
<html xmlns="http://www.w3.org/1999/xhtml" >
<!-- Internet Explorer 5.5+ only. -->
<head><title></title>
</head>
<body id="body">
<p id="paragraph">Move your mouse <em onmouseover="evtNote(this)"
  onmouseout="evtNote(this)" onmouseenter="evtNote(this)"
➥ onmouseleave="evtNote(this)"
  id="em">around <strong id="strong">the italic</strong>
```

Listing 32.12   *(continued)*

```
  text</em> for Internet Explorer events.</p>
<pre id="pre"></pre>
<script language="JavaScript" type="text/javascript">
<!--
function evtNote() {
  var evt = window.event
  var text = "evt.type = " + evt.type
  pre.appendChild(document.createTextNode(text))
  pre.appendChild(document.createElement("br"))
  try {
    text = "evt.toElement.id = " + evt.toElement.id
    pre.appendChild(document.createTextNode(text))
    pre.appendChild(document.createElement("br"))
    }
  catch(e) {
    }
  try {
    text = "evt.fromElement.id = " + evt.fromElement.id
    pre.appendChild(document.createTextNode(text))
    pre.appendChild(document.createElement("br"))
    }
  catch(e) {
    }
  pre.appendChild(document.createElement("hr"))
  }

var pre = document.getElementById("pre")
//-->
</script>

</body>
</html>
```

type

JavaScript 1.5, JScript 3.0+

Nav4+, IE4+

Syntax

```
var x = eventObject.type
```

The type property of Event objects is the specific type of event involved. For instance, a mouse click event will have the string "click" for its value.

view

JavaScript 1.5

Nav6

Syntax

```
var x = eventObject.view
```

The view property of Event objects reflects, for user interface events, a "view" of the document. Although this is a bit confusing, it's best simplified to say window.

which

JavaScript 1.2+

Nav4+

Syntax

```
var x = eventObject.which
```

The which property of Event objects reflects, for user interface events, which mouse button the user depressed for the event. For a standard mouse with the left-to-right orientation, a value of 1 reflects the leftmost mouse button, 2 represents a possible center button, and 3 represents the rightmost mouse button.

Essentially,

```
eventObject.button == eventObject.which - 1
```

width

JavaScript 1.2+

Nav4+

Syntax

```
var x = eventObject.width
```

The width property of Event objects is equal to the number of pixels horizontally in its window object. (This means the frame if the event exists in a frame.)

x

JavaScript1.2+, JScript 3.0+

Nav4+, IE4+

Syntax

```
var x = eventObject.x
```

The x property of Event objects is equal to the number of pixels from the event target's left edge to the left edge of said target's parent element. If the mouse is not in the window when the event fires, x is equal to –1.

y

JavaScript1.2+, JScript 3.0+

Nav4+, IE4+

Syntax

```
var y = eventObject.y
```

The y property of Event objects is equal to the number of pixels from the event target's top edge to the top edge of said target's parent element. If the mouse is not in the window when the event fires, y is equal to –1.

Methods

getPreventDefault()

JavaScript 1.5

Nav6

Syntax

```
var boolValue = eventObject.getPreventDefault()
```

The getPreventDefault() method of Event objects reflects whether the preventDefault() method of the this object has been called. A true response indicates preventDefault() has executed.

initEvent()

JavaScript 1.5

Nav6

Syntax

eventObject.initEvent(*type*, *bubbleBool*, *cancelBool*)

The initEvent() method of Event objects passes a few basic facts to the this object, if the event itself is waiting to fire. The first argument, a string, reflects the specific event type it is. (You create a general event type using the document.createEvent() method.)

The second argument, if true, indicates the event after arriving on its target may bubble upward back toward the document node or the window.

The third argument, if true, indicates a function listening for and receiving the event may cancel the event's default action.

For example,

eventObject.initEvent("load", false, false)

creates an HTML load event. If you use this function to initialize a key event, a mouse event, or a user interface event in general, the use of a more specific function, such as initKeyEvent(), initMouseEvent(), or initUIEvent(), is recommended.

Once the event has started its course after an event handler or listener fires it, the W3C DOM prohibits use of this method.

initKeyEvent()

JavaScript 1.5

Nav6

Syntax

eventObject.initKeyEvent(*type*, *bubbleBool*, *cancelBool*, *view*, *ctrlArg*, *altArg*, ➥*shiftArg*, *metaArg*, *keyCode*, *charCode*)

- The initKeyEvent() method of Event objects passes several facts to the this object, if the event itself is waiting to fire. The first argument (*type*), a string, reflects the specific event type it is. (You create a general event type using the document.createEvent() method.)

- The second argument (*bubbleBool*), if true, indicates the event after arriving on its target may bubble up back toward the document node or the window.

- The third argument (*cancelBool*), if true, indicates a function listening for and receiving the event may cancel the event's default action.

- The fourth argument (*view*) is considered a "view" of the event. It's best to just use window. (I briefly discuss views in Chapter 33, "Styling for HTML Elements".)

- The fifth through eighth arguments (*ctrlArg, altArg, shiftArg, metaArg*) are true or false values representing the Ctrl, Alt, Shift, and Meta keys being pressed, respectively.

- The ninth argument (*keyCode*) represents the keyCode property, which you can gather from the table of constants earlier in this chapter.

- The tenth argument (*charCode*) represents the charCode property, which as we've already discussed, is not particularly useful.

Once the event has started its course after an event handler or listener fires it, the W3C DOM prohibits use of this method.

initMouseEvent()
JavaScript 1.5

Nav6

Syntax
```
eventObject.initMouseEvent(type, bubbleBool, cancelBool, view, detail,
➥ screenX, screenY, clientX, clientY, ctrlArg, altArg, shiftArg,
➥ metaArg, button, relTarget)
```

- The initMouseEvent() method of Event objects passes several facts to the this object, if the event itself is waiting to fire. The first argument (*type*), a string, reflects the specific event type it is. (You create a general event type using the document.createEvent() method.)

- The second argument (*bubbleBool*), if true, indicates the event after arriving on its target may bubble up back toward the document node or the window.

- The third argument (*cancelBool*), if true, indicates a function listening for and receiving the event may cancel the event's default action.

- The fourth argument (*view*) is considered a "view" of the event. It's best to just use window. (Chapter 33, has a very brief description of views.)

- The fifth argument (*detail*) ties into the detail property of the event; again, I will cover this for specific events a bit later.

- The sixth through ninth arguments (*screenX, screenY, clientX, clientY*) represent the screenX, screenY, clientX, and clientY properties respectively.

- The 10th through 13th arguments (*ctrlArg, altArg, shiftArg, metaArg*) are true or false values representing the Ctrl, Alt, Shift, and Meta keys being pressed, respectively.

- The 14th (*button*) argument reflects the button property.

- The 15th (*relTarget*) argument corresponds to the relatedTarget property of the event.

Once the event has started its course after an event handler or listener fires it, the W3C DOM prohibits use of this method.

initUIEvent()

JavaScript 1.5

Nav6

Syntax

eventObject.initUIEvent(*type, bubbleBool, cancelBool,* window, *detailArg*)

- The initUIEvent() method of Event objects passes several facts to the this object, if the event itself is waiting to fire. The first argument, (*type*) is a string, reflects the specific event type it is. (You create a general event type using the document.createEvent() method.)

- The second argument, (*bubbleBool*) if true, indicates the event after arriving on its target may bubble upwards back towards the document node or the window.

- The third argument, (*cancelBool*) if true, indicates a function listening for and receiving the event may cancel the event's default action.

- The fourth argument (window) is considered a "view" of the event. It's best to just use window.

- The fifth argument (*detailArg*) represents a detail property for onactivate events.

Once the event has started its course after an event handler or listener fires it, the
W3C DOM prohibits use of this method.

preventBubble()

JavaScript 1.5

Nav6

Syntax

eventObject.preventBubble()

The preventBubble() method of Event objects should tell the this object to cancel
the bubbling of the event.

Unfortunately, this is not the case; Netscape browsers simply stop the event entirely.
Mozilla.org reports this method has actually been deprecated in favor of the
stopPropagation() method.

preventCapture()

JavaScript 1.5

Nav6

Syntax

eventObject.preventCapture()

The preventCapture() method of Event objects should tell the this object to cancel
the capturing of the event and proceed directly to the event's target.

Unfortunately, this is not the case; Netscape browsers simply stop the event entirely.
Mozilla.org reports this method has actually been deprecated in favor of the
stopPropagation() method.

preventDefault()

JavaScript 1.5

Nav6

Syntax

eventObject.preventDefault()

The `preventDefault()` method of `Event` objects cancels the default action of the event. This means the action the event would normally take on its target element will not occur.

To put it in perspective, consider the `onsubmit` event handler. This is effectively equivalent, for forms at least, to specifying `onsubmit="return false"`. The form will not submit under either condition.

stopPropagation()

JavaScript 1.5

Nav6

Syntax

```
eventObject.stopPropagation()
```

The `stopPropagation()` method of `Event` objects terminates the event's progress. Essentially it will go no further up the document node tree under any circumstances.

EventTarget Interface (DOM)

Browser/JavaScript Version	Created By
Nav4/JavaScript 1.2	Not Implemented
IE4/JScript 3.0	Not Implemented
IE5/JScript 5.0	Not Implemented
IE5.5/JScript 5.5	Not Implemented
Nav6/JavaScript 1.5	Node
IE6	Not Implemented
DOM Level 2 Events	Node

> **Note**
> Implemented in Nav3+ (event handler), Nav6 (DOM)

Description

The `EventTarget` interface extends the `Node` interface, providing a few additional methods for each node to listen for events.

Properties

The EventTarget interface provides no additional properties to the Node interface.

Methods

addEventListener()

JavaScript 1.5

Nav6

Syntax

object.addEventListener("*eventname*", *functionName*, *captureBoolean*)

The addEventListener() method of Node objects adds an event listener to the this object. The browser checks for two facts about every event that passes that listener.

The first fact the browser checks on the event is its type, against the event listener's type to watch for. You specify this in the first argument, the event name as a string. If the event names match, the check passes.

The second fact the browser checks for is whether the event is in a capturing phase (down from the document) or a bubbling phase (up from the node). If it is in a capturing phase and the third argument of this function is true, the check passes. If it is in a bubbling phase and the third argument of this argument is false, the check passes. If the event is at its target node, the check passes automatically.

If both checks pass, the Event object which the event listener "heard" will pass to the second argument, a function, as its first argument.

Note you may add as many event listener functions as you want via this method; matching arguments (except for the function) will not replace any event listeners.

dispatchEvent()

JavaScript 1.5

Nav6

Syntax

object.dispatchEvent(*eventObject*)

The dispatchEvent() method of Node objects fires the event in the first argument, targeted at the this object. The event will capture and bubble normally.

removeEventListener()

JavaScript 1.5

Nav6

Syntax

```
object.removeEventListener("EventName", functionName, captureBoolean)
```

The removeEventListener() method of Node objects removes only the event listener that addEventListener() assigned with the exact same arguments.

DocumentEvent Interface (DOM)

Browser/JavaScript Version	Created By
Nav4/JavaScript 1.2	Not Implemented
IE4/JScript 3.0	Not Implemented
IE5/JScript 5.0	Not Implemented
IE5.5/JScript 5.5	Not Implemented
Nav6/JavaScript 1.5	document
IE6	Not Implemented
DOM Level 2 Events	document

> **Note**
> Implemented in Nav3+ (event handler), Nav6 (DOM)

Description

The DocumentEvent interface extends the Document interface, providing one additional method for the document to create events.

Properties

The EventListener interface provides no additional properties to the Document interface.

Methods

createEvent()

JavaScript 1.5

Nav6

Syntax

```
var x = document.createEvent(eventClass)
```

The createEvent() property of document returns a new event, uninitialized, to the script. The first argument may be several different values: "HTMLEvents" for HTML events (load, unload, and so on), "UIEvents" for generic user interface events, "MutationEvents" for document mutation events, or "KeyEvents" for generic key events.

In any case, upon creating the event, you should use the appropriate initialization method (initEvent(), initKeyEvent(), initMouseEvent(), and so on) to correctly set the event's parameters.

Events in Netscape and Internet Explorer

This section lists all events you may typically find in a browser. The events you can use as HTML attributes, you simply prefix with the letters "on". There are only a few here that the W3C has officially approved for HTML 4 and XHTML 1. Likewise, there are only a few (all mutation events) for which no browser recognizes a corresponding HTML attribute.

To find an actual event name, simply remove the first two letters, the "on" portion (if they are in the event name). This list would be alphabetically organized, if all event handlers had the "on" prefix.

> **Caution**
> There are a lot of event handlers—and correspondingly, event types—in this section. However, not all event handlers in this section are in the W3C's HTML or XHTML Recommendations. In some cases, to maintain compliance with (X)HTML, you will have to add event listeners to the targets you have in mind in order to act on these events.

abort

JavaScript 1.1+, JScript 3.0+

Nav3+, IE4+

The abort event fires whenever a user halts the downloading of an image. Typically, this happens when the user clicks the Stop button on his browser before the image has finished loading.

activate

JScript 5.5+

IE5.5+

The activate event fires whenever the this element is set as the active element of the document. See the activeElement property of document (in Chapter 23, "HTMLDocument/document") for details.

afterprint

JScript 5.0+

IE5+

The afterprint event fires after the computer has served the document for printing or after the computer has released a Print Preview mode for the document.

The beforeprint event precedes this one; in a printing routine call (such as window.print()), the beforeprint event will fire, and then the document will print, and then the afterprint event will fire.

Microsoft recommends using these two events to prepare a document for printing, and then to restore the document to its original state.

beforeactivate

JScript 5.5+

IE5.5+

The activate event fires just before the this element is set as the active element of the document. The concept is to allow a Web page to prevent the element from becoming the active element. See the activeElement property of document (in Chapter 23) for details.

beforecopy

JScript 5.0+

IE5+

The beforecopy event fires just before copying the this object to the system Clipboard. This allows you to use Internet Explorer's proprietary methods to alter what the Clipboard receives, or alter the document itself.

beforecut

JScript 5.0+

IE5+

The beforecut event fires just before the cutting of the this object to the system Clipboard. This allows you to use Internet Explorer's proprietary methods to alter what the Clipboard receives, or alter the document itself.

beforedeactivate

JScript 5.5+

IE5.5+

The beforedeactivate event fires just before the this element stops being the active element of the document. See the activeElement property of document (in Chapter 23) for details.

beforeeditfocus

JScript 5.5+

IE5.5+

The `beforeeditfocus` event fires just before the `this` element can be edited. This applies primarily to `HTMLInputElement` and `HTMLTextAreaElement` objects, but when the `designMode` or `contentEditable` properties are set to `true` on any element, this event also applies to that element.

beforepaste

JScript 5.0+

IE5+

The `beforepaste` event fires just before the pasting from the Clipboard of the `this` object to the system Clipboard. This allows you to use Internet Explorer's proprietary methods to alter what the document receives.

beforeprint

JScript 5.0+

IE5+

The `beforeprint` event fires before the computer has served the document for printing or before the computer has released a Print Preview mode for the document.

The `afterprint` event follows this one; in a printing routine call (such as `window.print()`), the `beforeprint` event will fire, and then the document will print, and then the `afterprint` event will fire.

Microsoft recommends using these two events to prepare a document for printing, and then to restore the document to its original state.

beforeunload

JScript 3.0+

IE4+

The `beforeunload` event fires just before the document begins to unload for any reason.

There are known bugs with `window.setTimeout()` being in place even when you have a `window.clearTimeout()` in place in the `onunload` event handler. You can use the `beforeunload` event to do the cleanup in Internet Explorer, and `unload` to do the same cleanup in Netscape.

blur

JavaScript 1.0+, JScript 3.0+

Nav2+, IE4+

HTML 4

The `blur` event fires when the `this` object loses focus. (Recall that a `window` can lose focus while an element in its `document` can retain focus.)

bounce

JScript 3.0+

IE4+

The `bounce` event fires when the `this` element (a marquee element) has its text bounce off either end. See Chapter 28, "Text Formatting Elements," for details.

change

JavaScript 1.0+, JScript 1.0+

Nav2+, IE3+

HTML 4

The `change` event fires when the `value` or `selectedIndex` property of the `this` element, a form control, changes.

click

JavaScript 1.0+, JScript 3.0+

Nav2+, IE4+

HTML 4

The `click` event fires when the `this` object receives a click from the mouse. This represents a mouse click. The `mousedown` and `mouseup` events precede this event for Netscape 4.x browsers; they currently do not work for links in Netscape 6.0 browsers, but Netscape 6.1 re-enables them. For Internet Explorer browsers, `mousedown` precedes `click`, which `mouseup` follows.

The `detail` property reflects the number of clicks on the target node.

Also, the `contextmenu` event reacts to right clicks after the `click` event.

contextmenu

JavaScript 1.5, JScript 5.0+

Nav6.1+, IE5+

The `contextmenu` event fires when the `this` object receives a right-click from the mouse. The `detail` property reflects the number of clicks on the target node.

Also, the click event reacts to right clicks before the contextmenu event.

controlselect

JScript 5.5+

IE5.5+

The `controlselect` event fires on an element with `contentEditable` (see Chapter 21, "HTMLElement," for details) enabled, when the user selects the `this` element. Basically, it allows the user to select the element(s) whose content they want to edit.

copy

JScript 5.0+

IE5+

The `copy` event fires when the user copies a selection to the Clipboard from the document.

cut

JScript 5.0+

IE5+

The `cut` event fires when the user cuts a selection to the Clipboard from the document.

dblclick

JavaScript 1.2+, JScript 3.0+

Nav4+, IE4+

HTML 4

The `dblclick` event fires when the `this` object receives a pair of rapid clicks from the mouse. This event typically fires after all other mouse-related events could possibly fire on the element.

deactivate

JScript 5.5+

IE5.5+

The deactivate event fires whenever the this element is no longer the active element of the document. See the activeElement property of document (in Chapter 23) for details.

DOMAttrModified

JavaScript 1.5

Nav6

Not recognized as an HTML attribute

The DOMAttrModified event fires when the this element has an attribute, such as id, changed.

DOMCharacterDataModified

JavaScript 1.5

Nav6

Not recognized as an HTML attribute

The DOMCharacterDataModified event fires when the this object's character data (discussed in Chapter 20, "Core DOM Objects," under CDATASection) changes.

DOMNodeInserted

JavaScript 1.5

Nav6

Not recognized as an HTML attribute

The DOMNodeInserted event fires when the this object has a child node added to it.

DOMNodeRemoved

JavaScript 1.5

Nav6

Not recognized as an HTML attribute

The DOMNodeRemoved event fires when the this object has a child node removed.

drag

JScript 5.0+

IE5.0+

The `drag` event fires whenever the mouse button is down and the mouse is moving to drag a selection. Although the text you are attempting to drag may not always move with your mouse, the `drag` event continues to fire as if you were actually performing a drag.

The sequence of events for a drag and drop series of events in Internet Explorer is `dragstart`, `drag`, `dragend`, `drop`. An extra event sequence, when the mouse is passing through a drop target, is `dragenter`, `dragover`, `dragleave`.

dragdrop

JavaScript 1.2–1.3

Nav4.00–4.78

The `dragdrop` event (unrelated to all other drag and drop events in this chapter) fires whenever a user drags an item from another window into the current window. For instance, if a user drags an HTML file icon from the desktop into the browser window, the `dragdrop` event fires and the browser attempts to load the HTML file.

dragend

JScript 5.0+

IE5.0+

The `dragend` event fires whenever the mouse button releases a selection. Although the text you are attempting to drag may not always move with your mouse, the `dragend` event fires as if you were actually performing a drag.

The sequence of events for a drag and drop series of events in Internet Explorer is `dragstart`, `drag`, `dragend`, `drop`. An extra event sequence, when the mouse is passing through a drop target, is `dragenter`, `dragover`, `dragleave`.

dragenter

JScript 5.0+

IE5.0+

The `dragenter` event fires whenever the mouse pointer enters a valid drop target while the mouse is dragging something. Although the text you are attempting to drag may not always move with your mouse, the dragenter event fires as if you were actually performing a drag.

The sequence of events for a drag and drop series of events in Internet Explorer is dragstart, drag, dragend, drop. An extra event sequence, when the mouse is passing through a drop target, is dragenter, dragover, dragleave.

dragleave

JScript 5.0+

IE5.0+

The dragleave event fires whenever the mouse pointer leaves a valid drop target while the mouse is dragging something. Although the text you are attempting to drag may not always move with your mouse, the dragleave event fires as if you were actually performing a drag.

The sequence of events for a drag and drop series of events in Internet Explorer is dragstart, drag, dragend, drop. An extra event sequence, when the mouse is passing through a drop target, is dragenter, dragover, dragleave.

dragover

JScript 5.0+

IE5.0+

The dragover event fires continuously whenever the mouse pointer is over a valid drop target while the mouse is dragging something. Although the text you are attempting to drag may not always move with your mouse, the dragover event fires as if you were actually performing a drag.

The sequence of events for a drag and drop series of events in Internet Explorer is dragstart, drag, dragend, drop. An extra event sequence, when the mouse is passing through a drop target, is dragenter, dragover, dragleave.

dragstart

JScript 5.0+

IE5.0+

The dragstart event fires whenever the mouse button begins dragging a selection. Although the text you are attempting to drag may not always move with your mouse, the dragstart event fires as if you were actually performing a drag.

The sequence of events for a drag and drop series of events in Internet Explorer is dragstart, drag, dragend, drop. An extra event sequence, when the mouse is passing through a drop target, is dragenter, dragover, dragleave.

drop

JScript 5.0+

IE5.0+

The drop event fires whenever the mouse button releases a selection on a valid drop target. Although the text you are attempting to drag may not always move with your mouse, the drop event fires as if you were actually performing a drag.

The sequence of events for a drag and drop series of events in Internet Explorer is dragstart, drag, dragend, drop. An extra event sequence, when the mouse is passing through a drop target, is dragenter, dragover, dragleave.

error

JavaScript 1.1+, JScript 1.0 (window), JScript 3.0+

Nav3+, IE3 (window), IE4+

HTML 4

The error event has two different purposes. For images and programmable elements (except <script />; see Chapters 30 and 31, "Image Elements" and "Programmable Elements," respectively), the onerror event handler fires when the browser cannot load the corresponding file named by the src attribute.

For the window object, it fires for JavaScript errors in general. This can be very useful for creating generic error handling routines prior to the try...catch statement of Chapter 11, "The Global Object and Statements."

Netscape 4 and Internet Explorer give three arguments to a window.onerror event handler. The first argument is a string identifying the error message. The second is a string identifying the file registering the error. The third is a number representing the line number of the file where the error occurred.

Netscape 6 follows a different path, one I mentioned earlier. It passes one argument, an Event object. Nonetheless, for Netscape 6, the Error() object and the try...catch and throw statements are preferable. See Chapters 10 and 11, "Error()" and "The Global Object and Statements" respectively, for details.

> **Note**
> Future versions of Netscape (such as 6.5, based on Mozilla 1.0) will revert to the Netscape 4.x `window.onerror` behavior for error tracking.

However, you must watch out for using the `try...catch` statement and the `window.onerror` event handler in the same window! I have discovered, to my disappointment, a `try...catch` statement is not protected against interference by the onerror event handler. Listing 32.13 demonstrates this danger.

Listing 32.13   *Don't Mix* `try...catch` *with* `onerror`

```
<?xml version="1.0" ?>
<!DOCTYPE html PUBLIC "-//W3C//DTD XHTML 1.0 Transitional//EN"
➥"DTD/xhtml1-transitional.dtd">
<html xmlns="http://www.w3.org/1999/xhtml" >
<head><title></title>
<script language="JavaScript" type="text/javascript">
<!--
// Suppose this were in a library.js file.
errCode = 0

function errorHandler() {
  errCode++
  return true
  }

window.onerror = errorHandler
//-->
</script>
</head>
<body>
<script language="JavaScript" type="text/javascript">
<!--
errCode = 0

try {
  var x = "A".toNumber()
  }
catch(e) {
  errCode++
```

Listing 32.13   *(continued)*

```
    }

if (errCode > 0) {
  document.write("Errors detected: " + errCode)
  }
//-->
</script>
<!-- Results:
Errors detected: 2
-->
<p>Actual errors: 1</p>
</body>
</html>
```

One engineer I chatted with for mozilla.org implied this wasn't a bug worth fixing. I think he's right in the sense that this bug is avoidable. But I still personally feel allowing window.onerror to act within a try...catch is a dangerous thing. You can use one or the other in your document, but using both in the same document is not a recommended practice.

filterchange

JScript 3.0+

IE4+

The filterchange event fires when the filter, usually a transition effect, changes or completes. Filters are largely beyond the scope of this book, but you can learn about them at http://msdn.microsoft.com/workshop/author/filter/reference/properties/transition.asp.

> **Note**
> For the record, transitions of the sort listed in this link are not recommended for general Web design. They are a proprietary extension, which looks cool the first time you see it, but quickly grows irritating.

finish

JScript 5.0+

IE5+

The finish event fires when a marquee element (see Chapter 28) finishes its looping of the contents.

focus

JavaScript 1.0 (Text input), JavaScript 1.1+ (all form inputs, window), JavaScript 1.2–1.3 (Layer), JScript 3.0+

Nav2+ (Text input), Nav3+ (all form inputs, window), Nav4 (Layer), IE4+

HTML 4

The focus event fires when the this object receives focus. One of the most common uses of this event is to continuously prevent focus from staying on this:

```
targetObject.onfocus = function () { this.blur() }
```

focusin

IE6

The focusin event fires just before the this element receives focus.

focusout

IE6

The focusin event fires just as another element takes focus from the this element. Note this is not the same as the blur event, which fires when an object loses focus unconditionally.

help

JScript 3.0+

IE4+

The help event fires when the this element is the activeElement of the document, and the user presses the F1 key. (The F1 key traditionally is the help key in Windows.) I would recommend using help to present a miniature pop-up window with a detailed help section, should a ToolTip prove inadequate. (Too bad it's not part of the W3C events model.)

keydown

JavaScript 1.2+, JScript 3.0+

Nav4+, IE4+

HTML 4

The keydown event fires when the user initially depresses a key. The sequence of events for a key pressing series of events in Internet Explorer is keydown, keypress, keyup (though you may have multiple keypress events for a given key press).

keypress

JavaScript 1.2+, JScript 3.0+

Nav4+, IE4+

HTML 4

The keypress event fires repeatedly while the user has a key depressed. The sequence of events for a key pressing series of events in Internet Explorer is keydown, keypress, keyup (though you may have multiple keypress events for a given key press).

keyup

JavaScript 1.2+, JScript 3.0+

Nav4+, IE4+

HTML 4

The keyup event fires when the user releases a key. The sequence of events for a key pressing series of events in Internet Explorer is keydown, keypress, keyup (though you may have multiple keypress events for a given key press).

load

JavaScript 1.0+, JScript 3.0+

Nav2+, IE3+

HTML 4

The load event fires when the this object completes loading in the browser. This is a very important event for the window object, particularly for framed documents (see Chapter 15, "window" for details).

Unfortunately, there is no property in JavaScript telling you the page has loaded. I therefore often set a property in the `onload` event handler of the `document.body`:

```
<body onload="loaded = true">
```

Internet Explorer also exposes this event for script elements. This is a highly useful concept the W3C HTML recommendations do not support.

Note

The `onload` event handler is defined for the `HTMLBodyElement` and `HTMLFramesetElement` objects in HTML 4; when you see these, they actually apply to the `window` object.

---

losecapture

JScript 5.0+

IE5+

The `losecapture` event fires whenever the `this` element has mouse capture set on it (see "Mouse Capture in Internet Explorer" earlier in this chapter) and after all other mouse events for the `this` element have fired for the most recent mouse actions. Essentially, in the train of mouse events, the `losecapture` event is always the caboose, often providing "cleanup" for mouse capturing.

mousedown

JavaScript 1.0+, JScript 3.0+

Nav2+, IE4+

HTML 4

The `mousedown` event fires when the user's mouse button depresses on the `this` object. The `mousedown` and `mouseup` events precede the `click` event for Netscape 4.x browsers; `mouseup` currently does not work for links in Netscape 6.0 browsers, but returns for Netscape 6.1. For Internet Explorer browsers, `mousedown` precedes `click`, which `mouseup` follows.

mouseenter

JScript 5.5+

IE5.5+

The `mouseenter` event fires when the mouse pointer enters the `this` object. Note this does not fire if the mouse pointer begins over the `this` object as it renders on the screen; it is the act of entering the object that fires the event.

onmouseleave

JScript 5.5+

IE5.5+

The `mouseleave` event fires when the mouse pointer leaves the `this` object. Note this does not fire if the mouse pointer begins outside the `this` object as it renders on the screen; it is the act of leaving the object that fires the event.

> **Caution**
> This event waits until you are completely outside the `this` element before firing. By contrast, `onmouseout` fires when you move over a child element of the `this` object as well. Listing 32.12 demonstrates this.

mousemove

JavaScript 1.2+, JScript 3.0+

Nav4+, IE4+

The mousemove event fires when the mouse pointer moves over the this object. This event is not cancelable.

Because this happens very frequently, it's generally inadvisable to use code like this:

```
document.onmousemove = function() { alert("Hello World!") }
```

However, it is entirely appropriate to use this code to create mouse trails. There are several such scripts available on the World Wide Web. One of them resides at `http://www.wsabstract.com/script/script2/cursortrail.shtml`.

mouseout

JavaScript 1.1+, JScript 3.0+

Nav3+, IE4+

HTML 4

The `mouseout` event fires when the mouse pointer leaves the `this` object. The element it enters is the event's `relatedTarget`.

> **Caution**
> This event fires when you move over a child element of the `this` object as well. By contrast, `onmouseleave` waits until you are completely outside the `this` element. Listing 32.12 demonstrates this.

This event typically precedes the `mouseleave` event. You'll often see this event in "rollovers" (including much less complex versions of Listing 32.10) and for hypertext ToolTips (images, clickable links, and so on, when your mouse passes over an element).

mouseover

JavaScript 1.1+, JScript 3.0+

Nav3+, IE4+

HTML 4

The `mouseover` event fires when the mouse pointer enters the `this` object. The element it leaves is the event's `relatedTarget`.

This event typically precedes the `mouseenter` event. You'll often see this event in "rollovers" (including much less complex versions of Listing 32.10) and for hypertext ToolTips (images, clickable links, and so on, when your mouse passes over an element).

mouseup

JavaScript 1.0+, JScript 3.0+

Nav2+, IE4+

HTML 4

The `mouseup` event fires when the user's mouse button releases on the `this` object. The `mousedown` and `mouseup` event precede the `click` event for Netscape 4.x browsers; `mouseup` currently does not work for links in Netscape 6.0 browsers, but returns for Netscape 6.1. For Internet Explorer browsers, `mousedown` precedes `click`, which `mouseup` follows.

mousewheel

IE6

The mousewheel event fires when the user's mouse wheel rotates. It includes a special property, wheelDelta, to indicate the amount of scroll. (Calculus fans will recall delta means change—the mouse wheel often tells the browser to scroll the window, thus changing the y-position of the page.) Positive values for this property mean an upward scroll of the document; negative values indicate a downward scroll. The larger the property's absolute value, the more the user moved the wheel.

move

JavaScript1.2+, JScript 5.5+

Nav4+, IE5.5+

The move event fires when the this object moves. To give you an idea of how this works, try running Listing 32.14, which moves an HTMLDivElement around the screen.

Listing 32.14   *The* move *Event and Coordinates*

```html
<html>
<!-- Not XHTML 1.0. For Internet Explorer 5.5 only. -->
<head><title></title>
<style type="text/css">
<!--
     .me {
     position:absolute;
     top:100px;
     left:100px;
     width:20px;
     height:20px;
     background-color:#7f7fff;
   }
-->
</style>
<script language="JavaScript" type="text/javascript">
<!--
function mover() {
  me.style.left = event.clientX
  me.style.top = event.clientY
  }
```

Listing 32.14 *(continued)*

```
function movenote() {
  var k = document.getElementById('notes')
  k.childNodes[0].nodeValue = "Left: " + event.clientX
  k.childNodes[2].nodeValue = "Top: " + event.clientY
  }
//-->
</script>
</head>
<body onmousemove="mover()">
<p id="notes">Left: 100px<br />Top: 100px</p>
<div class="me" id="me" name="me" onmove="movenote()">test</div>
</body>
</html>
```

As you move the mouse around, the `<div>...</div>` element moves with it. The move event for that element fires as well, updating the coordinates of the element's position for you to see constantly.

moveend

JScript 5.5+

IE5.5+

The moveend event fires when the this object has stopped moving. The movestart and multiple move events fire before the moveend event fires.

movestart

JScript 5.5+

IE5.5+

The movestart event fires when the this object has stopped moving. Multiple move events and the moveend event fire after the movestart event fires.

paste

JScript 5.0+

IE5+

The paste event fires when the user pastes a selection from the Clipboard into the document.

PART III   Document Object Model for HTML Documents

propertychange

JScript 5.0+

IE5+

The propertychange event fires after the user changes any property or attribute of the this element.

You might think this would make it perfect to build an emulation of Netscape's Object.prototype.watch() method (see Chapter 1, "Object()"). Much to my disappointment, I have discovered this is not the case.

Observe Listing 32.15. It shows a listing you would expect would fire once for each change to a concealed element. It does, but once for the change away from the norm and once back. This is a bit surprising at first, but easy to understand.

Listing 32.15   *Attempting a* watch() *Using* onpropertychange

```
<html>
<!-- Not XHTML 1.0. Internet Explorer 5.0+ only. -->
<head><title></title>
<script language="JavaScript" type="text/javascript">
<!--
function watchFunc(arg) {
  var x = document.createElement("p")
  x.appendChild(document.createTextNode("Change detected"))
  document.body.appendChild(x)
  if (arg.form.watchLock_a.value != arg.form.watchLock_b.value) {
    if (arg.name == arg.form.watchLock_a.name) {
      arg.form.watchLock_a.value = arg.form.watchLock_b.value
      }
    if (arg.name == arg.form.watchLock_b.name) {
      arg.form.watchLock_b.value = arg.form.watchLock_a.value
      }
    var x = document.createElement("p")
    x.appendChild(document.createTextNode(arg.name + " restored to " +
arg.value))
    document.body.appendChild(x)
    }
  }

function test() {
  document.forms[0].watchLock_a.value = false;
```

Listing 32.15   *(continued)*

```
  document.forms[0].watchLock_b.value = false;
  document.forms[0].watchLock_a.onpropertychange = function() {};
  var x = document.createElement("p")
  var y = "onpropertychange is " +
document.forms[0].watchLock_a.onpropertychange
  x.appendChild(document.createTextNode(y))
  document.body.appendChild(x)
  }
//-->
</script>
</head>
<body onload="test()">
<form id="watchForm" action="javascript:void(null)" >
<input type="hidden" name="watchLock_a" value="true"
➥ onpropertychange="watchFunc(this)" />
<input type="hidden" name="watchLock_b" value="true"
➥ onpropertychange="watchFunc(this)" />
</form>
<!-- Results:
Change detected
Change detected
watchLock_a restored to true
Change detected
Change detected
watchLock_b restored to true
onpropertychange is function() {}
-->
</body>
</html>
```

As I've done in examples in the past, the test() function drives this page. We see the expected double "Change detected" for each of the watchLock input values changing.

But, when we change the onpropertychange property of the element, it all falls apart. The event fires on the new onpropertychange event handler, not the old one. The watch is broken, like the Object.prototype.unwatch() method would do. This is a surprising, and unfortunate, weakness in the scheme.

Note this property does not fire when the innerHTML or innerText properties change—so forget about using a parent element to watch over a group of child elements. (Likewise, changes to outerHTML and outerText based solely on changes to innerHTML and innerText will not trigger this event handler.)

readystatechange

JScript 5.0+

IE5+

The readystatechange event fires whenever the readyState property of the this object changes. Note you can expect this event handler to fire more than once while the document loads; there are five "states" of readiness for the readyState property.

reset

JavaScript 1.1+, JScript 3.0+

Nav3+, IE4+

The reset event fires when the this element, a form, resets.

resize

JavaScript 1.2+, JScript 3.0+

Nav4+, IE4+

The resize event fires when the this object, usually a window, resizes.

resizeend

JScript 5.5+

IE5.5+

The reziseend event fires on an element with contentEditable (see Chapter 21, for details) enabled, when the user finishes resizing the element.

resizestart

JScript 5.5+

IE5.5+

The rezisestart event handler fires on an element with contentEditable enabled (see Chapter 21 for details), when the user begins resizing the element.

scroll

JScript 3.0+

IE4+

The scroll event fires when the this object scrolls—either by user action (clicking on a scrollbar thumb, for instance) or when the document's scripts force a scroll (the scrollTo() method of window, for instance).

> **Note**
> At this time, Netscape 6 should support this event handler but does not.

select

JavaScript 1.5, JScript 3.0+

Nav6, IE3+

HTML 4

The select event fires when the this object receives the selection; that is, when a portion of the this object's contents are selected.

> **Note**
> The Netscape 4 documentation for JavaScript states this is available since Netscape 2. However, repeated testing shows this is not the case.

selectionchange

JScript 5.5+

IE5.5+

The selectionchange event fires when the selection within the document changes.

selectstart

JScript 5.5+

IE5.5+

The selectstart event fires when the selection of the this object begins. It thus precedes the select event in firing order.

start

JScript 4.0+

IE4+

The start event fires when a marquee element (see Chapter 28) starts each looping of its contents.

stop

JScript 5+

IE5+

The stop event fires when the document abruptly stops loading before it is completed. This can happen, for instance, if the user decides to go to another Web page before the current page completely loads. This also happens when the user clicks the Stop button.

(If you're looking for the event handler that fires when a marquee stops, try the finish event.)

submit

JavaScript 1.0+, JScript 1.0+

Nav2+, IE3+

HTML 4

The submit event fires when the this element, a form, submits. This event handler is used very frequently to allow JavaScript to perform a validation of the form's data.

unload

JavaScript 1.0+, JScript 1.0+

Nav2+, IE3+

HTML 4

The unload event fires as the document begins to unload; this happens for a new page being called or for a window closing.

I personally have found this event unreliable in Internet Explorer; often the page will unload before any functions I call via this event have a chance to execute. You may want to use the beforeunload event for Internet Explorer instead, even if it is non-standard. For Netscape and Internet Explorer, try using both.

CHAPTER 33

Styling for HTML Elements

Popular Web design involves three elements: (X)HTML, JavaScript, and styling. The three combine to create what people call Dynamic HTML, or DHTML. I've already covered XHTML and JavaScript to a very large extent. But I haven't really covered styling.

The traditional form of styling, Cascading Style Sheets (CSS), is by far the most popular. The W3C has published two levels of its CSS Recommendations, with a third level currently a Working Draft.

Netscape 4 introduced JavaScript Style Sheets (JSSS). There are no such standards for JavaScript Style Sheets per se, but in most cases it's simply using JavaScript to affect styling properties. A JavaScript style sheet could thusly go inside a `<script>...</script>` element as easily as it could go in a `<style type="text/javascript">...</style>` element. (Netscape 6 removed it, in favor of CSS.) Netscape 4 also supports CSS.

Netscape and Internet Explorer diverge wildly on the subject of styling, to the point of absurdity. Hence why the W3C created the CSS standards. Even with the standards, you often have to write one way for Netscape 4 browsers, another for Netscape 6 browsers, and still another for Internet Explorer browsers.

Fortunately, you don't need CSS to write a good Web page. If you take a browser with styling disabled to an HTML page with styling, in theory it should render just fine— maybe not with the special effects or fancy colors, but certainly legibly. If the page is legible without the CSS, it "degrades well."

Before I get started with this chapter formally, let me point out why styling is such a conundrum even today. In October 2001, Microsoft redesigned msn.com, and temporarily blocked all browsers except its own. The blockages included messages to upgrade to a "standards-compliant" browser—namely, Internet Explorer 6.

This managed to irritate a lot of people. Opera.com, which makes the Opera browser suite, knew fully well Microsoft was not "standards-compliant": not in its msn.com Web pages, and most certainly not in its browser, as Opera.com quickly proved.

Opera constructed an XHTML page with CSS, fully compliant with the W3C standards. The company touted the page very specifically as compliant, and when you ran the page through the W3C validators for CSS and XHTML, yes, it was valid and well-formed. Hopefully when you read this the link will still be valid, but you can see it for yourself at `http://www.opera.com/pressreleases/xhtml/20011026.xml`.

The Opera browser rendered it nicely. The Amaya 5.2 editor rendered it nicely (very nicely on my machine; Amaya didn't support one of the fonts the page used. I liked the "degraded" font better.) Netscape 6 rendered it nicely (see Figure 33.1).

Figure 33.1

Netscape 6 and the Opera compliance test.

Internet Explorer 6, well...see Figure 33.2.

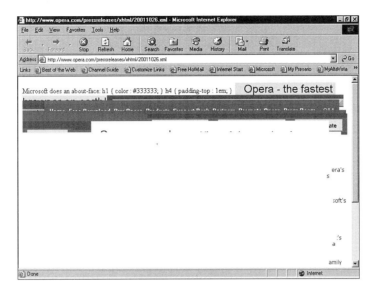

Figure 33.2
Internet Explorer 6 and the Opera compliance test.

Although you can laugh for several minutes over this one (as I did), it proves the point Opera.com intended. You can look at this point two different ways. You can either gripe about Internet Explorer's noncompliance with standards, or you can work to write your style sheets and JavaScript code to work in both browsers.

> **Note**
> I've recently discovered a workaround to let Internet Explorer 6 render this page correctly. It involves an XSL Transformations style sheet to simply copy the document, node for node, back into Internet Explorer. You can see the results of this at `http://www.jslab.org/articles/XHTML_IE.xml`.

The Basics of CSS

The W3C defines the Cascading Style Sheet language, or CSS, as the primary language for styling. The concept is simple: each individual style sheet applies on top of whatever styling was there before it. This is called the "cascade."

Before I get into the formal description, I reiterate a couple of terms from the CSS
Level 2 Recommendation: the *declaration block* and the *selector*. A declaration block is
simply a section of CSS code between and including a set of brackets. For example,

```
p {
  text-indent: 15px;
  }
```

would define a declaration block for the `<p>...</p>` element, with one styling
property to it. You separate individual style rules (the various styling code effects,
such as `text-indent: 15px`) with semicolons. The section preceding the opening brace
(in this case, the p character) is the selector, which CSS uses to define what the
declaration block applies to. The declaration, combined with its selector, makes up a
style rule.

> **Note**
>
> If you happen to notice this resembles the syntax of function code blocks and individual
> lines in Chapter 13, "JavaScript Syntax," that is intentional. JavaScript and CSS use similar
> syntax. CSS permits multi-line comments (`/*...*/`), but not single-line comments (`//`).

Simple Selectors in CSS

A CSS style rule begins by identifying the group of elements it applies to via the
selector. Sometimes it's just a single element, designated by the `id` attribute and
prefixed with a hash mark (#), as Listing 33.1 demonstrates.

Listing 33.1   *Setting Styling By ID*

```
<?xml version="1.0" ?>
<!DOCTYPE html PUBLIC "-//W3C//DTD XHTML 1.0 Transitional//EN"
➥"DTD/xhtml1-transitional.dtd">
<html xmlns="http://www.w3.org/1999/xhtml" >
<head><title></title>
<style type="text/css">
<!--
#hello {
  text-indent: 15px
  }
-->
</style>
</head>
```

Listing 33.1 *(continued)*

```
<body>
<p id="hello">Indented Text.</p>
<p>Non-indented text.</p>
<!-- Results:
 Indented Text.
Non-indented text.
-->
</body>
</html>
```

Sometimes you can set all elements of a particular element name by naming the element specifically. (Match the case of the element; although HTML allows you to not match the case, XML and XHTML force you to match case.) Listing 33.2 sets all paragraph elements as indented.

Listing 33.2 *Setting Styling for All Elements of a Type*

```
<?xml version="1.0" ?>
<!DOCTYPE html PUBLIC "-//W3C//DTD XHTML 1.0 Transitional//EN"
➥"DTD/xhtml1-transitional.dtd">
<html xmlns="http://www.w3.org/1999/xhtml" >
<head><title></title>
<style type="text/css">
<!--
p {
  text-indent: 15px
  }
-->
</style>
</head>
<body>
<p>Indented text.</p>
<p>Also indented text.</p>
<pre>Non-indented text.</pre>
<!-- Results:
 Indented text.
 Also indented text.
Non-indented text.
-->
</body>
</html>
```

You can specify all elements in the document using the asterisk (*) character as the selector. You can also specify a "class" of elements to share styling properties, as in Listing 33.3. Note the elements in this class share a common string in their `class` attributes, and the class itself has a period (.) as its prefix.

CSS supports both cascading and overriding of styling effects. By cascading, I mean you can apply multiple and separate styling effects using separate declaration blocks. By overriding, I mean the latest declaration block will take precedence over any other declaration block.

You can also specify, by class, for an element to inherit styling from two separate declaration blocks. (This works in Internet Explorer 5.0+ and Netscape 6.0+ only.) Note in Listing 33.3 the fourth paragraph element; it is both capitalized and extra-indented. In the `class` attribute for this element, a space separates the two classes.

Listing 33.3   *Cascading and Overriding Styling*

```
<?xml version="1.0" ?>
<!-- Netscape 6.0+, Internet Explorer 5.0+ only -->
<!DOCTYPE html PUBLIC "-//W3C//DTD XHTML 1.0 Transitional//EN"
➥"DTD/xhtml1-transitional.dtd">
<html xmlns="http://www.w3.org/1999/xhtml" >
<head><title></title>
<style type="text/css">
<!--
p {
  text-indent: 15px;
  }
.one {
  text-transform: uppercase;
  }
.two {
  text-indent: 30px;
  }
-->
</style>
</head>
<body>
<p>Indented text.</p>
<p class="one">Capitalized Indented text.</p>
<p class="two">Extra Indented text.</pre>
<p class="one two">Capitalized and Extra Indented Text.</p>
<pre>Not indented text.</pre>
```

Listing 33.1   *(continued)*

```
<!-- Results:
 Indented text.
 CAPITALIZED INDENTED TEXT.
  Extra Indented Text.
  CAPITALIZED AND EXTRA INDENTED TEXT.
Not indented text.
-->
</body>
</html>
```

Compound Selectors in CSS

I used .one in Listing 33.3 to demonstrate a class selector. It is a simplified form of *.one, which uses the universal selector (*) to determine a primary set of elements the declaration block applies to. *.one is a compound selector.

Compound selectors are essentially the combination of two or more simple selectors to further restrict the scope of the following declaration block. For instance,

```
pre.one {
    text-indent: 30px;
    }
```

would mean only preformatted text elements with a one class applied would receive the 30px indentation.

There are other sorts of compound selectors available. You can specify, to a limited extent, which elements in the DOM have a particular declaration block applicable.

```
p:first-child {
    color:red;
    }
```

In this code section, any paragraph element that is also the first child element of another element has a text color of red. :first-child is a pseudo-class CSS permits. (Internet Explorer 5.0 and Netscape 4.x do not support it.)

Other pseudo-classes of CSS are as follows:

- :link for unvisited links
- :visited for visited links

- `:active` for active links (mouse clicked but not released)

- `:hover` for when the mouse hovers over the selected object

- `:focus` for when the object has focus

You can specify an element descending from a senior element using a space between them.

```
html p {
    text-indent:15px;
    }
```

The preceding code means any paragraph element which descends from an `<html>...</html>` element (translation: any paragraph element in an HTML document) receives a text indentation of 15 pixels. (Netscape 4 does not support this.)

You can specify an element as a child of a parent element using a greater-than sign (>) between them:

```
body > p {
    text-indent:15px;
    }
```

This says any paragraph element that is a child of the `HTMLBodyElement` will have a text indent of 15 pixels. (Netscape 4 does not support this.)

You can specify an element following another element using a + sign. For instance, the *second* paragraph element as a child of the `HTMLBodyElement` you could refer to as:

```
body > p:first-child + p {
    color:red;
    }
```

As you can see, compounded selectors are really quite useful.

The Order of Precedence in Styling, from Elements

Generally there are four different ways to apply a styling property to an element. The first way, which almost always takes precedent (see Listing 33.9), is the `style` attribute of the element itself. This is always a CSS declaration block, but without the brackets. You can use this to override just about any other styling in place. Listing 33.4 shows this particular technique.

Listing 33.4   *Styling an Element Directly*

```
<?xml version="1.0" ?>
<!DOCTYPE html PUBLIC "-//W3C//DTD XHTML 1.0 Transitional//EN"
➥"DTD/xhtml1-transitional.dtd">
<html xmlns="http://www.w3.org/1999/xhtml" >
<head><title></title></head>
<body>
<p style="text-indent: 15px;">Indented Text.</p>
<p>Non-indented text.</p>
<!-- Results:
 Indented Text.
Non-indented text.
-->
</body>
</html>
```

The second way is to define the element as a member of a class, using the `class` attribute of the element. Each class is a string of alphanumeric characters (A–Z, a–z, 0–9, and the underscore "_"). By separating each class by spaces in the `class` attribute, you can allow each class to apply to the element. In the CSS style sheet, you define the class first by a period, and then the class name, and then the declaration block. (Listing 33.3 best demonstrates the `class` attribute.)

The third way is to refer to the element in a style sheet by its `id` attribute. In the CSS style sheet, you would prefix its `id` attribute with a hash mark (#). (Listing 33.1 best demonstrates the use of the `id` attribute.)

The fourth way is to consider all elements of that particular type (all paragraph elements, for example) as a class. In situations like this, simply naming the element type and attaching a declaration block does the trick. (Listing 33.2 best demonstrates the use of the element name as a class.)

There are other ways to refer elements to styling effects, but these should be more than enough to get you started. Generally, the order of declaration blocks in a document reflects the priority of each procedure's impact on the cascade of styling effects. Later declaration blocks take precedent over earlier ones.

The Order of Precedence in Styling, from Style Sheets

There are five ways for a style sheet to impact a document. The first is the `style` attribute, which contains a miniature style sheet every time you use it. This always takes precedent over any other way.

> **Note**
> The exception to this rule is with the `runtimeStyle` property of an element in Internet Explorer 5+. Setting values through this overrides even the `style` attribute.

The second way is using the `<style>...</style>` element of (X)HTML, which contains an inline style sheet. Generally for HTML, you should comment out the contents of this element using `<!--...-->`, just like `HTMLScriptElement` objects (see Chapter 31, "Programmable Elements"). But for XHTML served as an XML document, use CDATA sections (Chapter 20, "Core DOM Objects") instead, again like `HTMLScriptElement` objects.

The third way is using the `<link />` element of (X)HTML. This is usually the preferred method for referencing an external style sheet from (X)HTML.

The fourth way is using the `<?xml-stylesheet ?>` processing instruction. This is very similar in syntax to the `<link />` element from HTML, but specifically exists to support CSS styling of XML documents. You may only use this before the `<!DOCTYPE >` tag. It works in XHTML served as XML. The W3C Recommendation defining this special processing instruction is at `http://www.w3.org/TR/xml-stylesheet`. (I cover this special processing instruction, and version info, in the `<link />` section.)

> **Note**
> Microsoft supports a `<?xml:stylesheet ?>` processing instruction, identical in behavior. This came before the W3C Recommendation specifying `<?xml-stylesheet ?>`. Though I do not recommend this, in a pinch you can use this to specify a style sheet specifically for Internet Explorer browsers.

The fifth way doesn't involve any (X)HTML tags at all. The `@import` CSS rule allows a Web page to include another CSS style sheet. The `url()` pseudo-function is a good idea in this case; you may see it often in other languages, such as Scalable Vector Graphics (SVG). (Technically, it's not required for CSS, but it's a good practice.) Listing 33.5 shows the use of `@import`, using one XHTML document and two CSS style sheets.

Listing 33.5 *Style Sheets Importing Other Style Sheets*

```
<!-- 33lst05a.htm -->
<?xml version="1.0" ?>
<!-- Netscape 6.0+, Internet Explorer 5.0+ only -->
<!DOCTYPE html PUBLIC "-//W3C//DTD XHTML 1.0 Transitional//EN"
➥"DTD/xhtml1-transitional.dtd">
<html xmlns="http://www.w3.org/1999/xhtml" >
<head><title></title>
<link href="33lst05b.css" type="text/css" rel="stylesheet" />
</head>
<body>
<p>This text is indented and capitalized.</p>
<pre>Non-indented text.</pre>
<!-- Results:
 THIS TEXT IS INDENTED AND CAPITALIZED.
Non-indented text.
-->
</body>
</html>


<!-- 33lst05b.css -->
@import url("33lst05c.css");

p {
  text-transform: uppercase;
  }

<!-- 33lst05c.css -->
p {
  text-indent: 15px;
  }

/* End of listing */
```

Generally, the order these rules appear in a document reflects the priority of each style sheet's impact on the cascade of styling effects. Later rules override earlier ones.

Activating and Deactivating Style Sheets

Internet Explorer 5 and Netscape 6 also provide for "backup" style sheets. You can literally use JavaScript and the DOM for style sheets to turn a style sheet on or off. Listing 33.6 is a simplistic example of style sheet swapping.

Listing 33.6   *Switching Style Sheets Dynamically*

```html
<!-- 33lst06a.htm -->
<?xml version="1.0" ?>
<!-- Netscape 6.0+, Internet Explorer 5.0+ only -->
<!DOCTYPE html PUBLIC "-//W3C//DTD XHTML 1.0 Transitional//EN"
➥"DTD/xhtml1-transitional.dtd">
<html xmlns="http://www.w3.org/1999/xhtml" >
<head><title></title>
<link href="33lst06b.css" rel="stylesheet" />
<link href="33lst06c.css" rel="alternate stylesheet" title="blue" />
<script language="JavaScript" type="text/javascript">
<!--
function go(y) {
  for (var x = 0; x < document.styleSheets.length; x++) {
    if (document.styleSheets[x].disabled == false) {
      document.styleSheets[x].disabled = true
      document.styleSheets[y].disabled = false
      x = document.styleSheets.length // exit function
      }
    }
  }
//-->
</script>
</head>
<body>
<p>This Sentence Starts Out As LowerCase Letters.</p>
<p><a href="javascript:go(1)">UPPERCASE</a> <a href="javascript:go(0)"
➥>lowercase</a></p>
<!-- Results after clicking UPPERCASE link:
THIS SENTENCE STARTS OUT AS LOWERCASE LETTERS.

Results after clicking lowercase link:
this sentence starts out as lowercase letters.
-->
</body>
</html>

<!-- 33lst06b.css -->
p {
  text-transform: lowercase;
  }
```

Listing 33.6 *(continued)*

```
<!-- 33lst06c.css -->
p {
  text-transform: uppercase;
  }
/* End of listing */
```

Take a moment to consider the implications of switching and importing style sheets. The two possibilities combine to allow you to create style sheets that are a combination of individual style sheet effects; basically, you can have entire style sheets broken down into shared miniature style sheets, all of which a master style sheet calls. Change master style sheets, and you change the layout, like a Rubik's cube. Same box, a different appearance. The miniature style sheets, and the master style sheets calling them, would be modules of CSS code. Modular code is good for XHTML, it's definitely good for JavaScript… it's good for CSS too, giving you more flexibility than you've seen before.

The !important Style Sheet Attribute

Style sheet rules can always have their "importance" bumped up. By appending the word !important to a rule, it sends a message to the browser that nonimportant rules must bend to this one. This is a quick way to get around inheritance issues and assure dominance of a particular declaration you care about (unless another styling rule overriding yours also has !important attached to it).

Listing 33.7 shows how !important can dominate a style sheet arrangement.

Listing 33.7 *The* !important *Attribute Gets Attention*

```
<!-- 33lst07a.htm -->
<?xml version="1.0" ?>
<!-- Netscape 6.0+, Internet Explorer 5.0+ only -->
<!DOCTYPE html PUBLIC "-//W3C//DTD XHTML 1.0 Transitional//EN"
➥"DTD/xhtml1-transitional.dtd">
<html xmlns="http://www.w3.org/1999/xhtml" >
<head><title></title>
<link href="33lst07b.css" rel="stylesheet" />
<link href="33lst06c.css" rel="stylesheet" />
<!-- Note we are borrowing the second style sheet from Listing 33.6.
Both style sheets are active. -->
```

Listing 33.7   *(continued)*

```
</head>
<body>
<p>This sentence is entirely lowercase letters.</p>
<!-- Results:
this sentence is entirely lowercase letters.
-->
</body>
</html>


<!-- 33lst07b.css -->
p {
  text-transform: lowercase !important;
  }
/* End of listing. */
```

Style Sheet Property Names in JavaScript

One fact Netscape 4, Netscape 6, and Internet Explorer all agree on is how they name their style sheet properties in JavaScript. You cannot have a property named `text-indent`. JavaScript would read that as `text` minus `indent`. Instead, the browsers follow a JavaScript tradition of capitalizing the first letter of every word, except the first word. For the `text-indent` CSS property, for instance, you would say `textIndent`.

Beyond this localized naming, however, things get very complex...

Object Models and Cascading Style Sheets

Many people assume the `style` property of an element contains exact references to each styling effect for that element. This simply is not true, and the official documentation from both Microsoft and the W3C confirms this. The `style` property only retrieves from the `style` attribute. Listing 33.8 shows what happens when you try to retrieve this property.

Listing 33.8   *Style Sheets Do Not Reflect the* `style` *Property*

```
<?xml version="1.0" ?>
<!-- Netscape 6.x, Internet Explorer 5.0+ only. -->
<!DOCTYPE html PUBLIC "-//W3C//DTD XHTML 1.0 Transitional//EN"
➥"DTD/xhtml1-transitional.dtd">
```

Listing 33.8   *(continued)*

```
<html xmlns="http://www.w3.org/1999/xhtml" >
<head><title></title>
<style type="text/css">
p {
    color: #ff0000;
    }
</style>
<script language="JavaScript" type="text/javascript">
<!--
function go() {
    var p = document.getElementsByTagName("p")[0]
    var pre = document.createElement("pre")
    var pre_text = "p.style.color = '" + p.style.color + "'."
    pre.appendChild(document.createTextNode(pre_text))
    document.body.appendChild(pre)
    }
//-->
</script>
</head>
<body>
<p>This text is red.</p>
<pre><a href="#" onclick="go();
return false">Get the style.color property of the paragraph.</a></pre>
<!-- Results after clicking on the link:
p.style.color = ''.
-->
</body>
</html>
```

Instead, you need to know four different approaches: one for Netscape to get and one
to set, one for Internet Explorer to get and one to set. Listing 33.9 covers all four
approaches.

Listing 33.9   *Getting and Setting Styles Correctly*

```
<?xml version="1.0" ?>
<!-- Netscape6, Internet Explorer 5.0+ only-->
<!DOCTYPE html PUBLIC "-//W3C//DTD XHTML 1.0 Transitional//EN"
➥"DTD/xhtml1-transitional.dtd">
<html xmlns="http://www.w3.org/1999/xhtml" >
<head><title></title>
```

Listing 33.9   *(continued)*

```html
<style type="text/css">
p {
   color: green
   }
</style>
<script language="JavaScript" type="text/javascript">
<!--
function Nav_change() {
   var p = document.getElementsByTagName("p")[0]
   p.style.color = "blue"
   }

function Nav_read() {
   var p = document.getElementsByTagName("p")[0]
   var pStyle = document.defaultView.getComputedStyle(p, "")
   alert(pStyle.getPropertyValue("color"))
   }

function IE_change() {
   var p = document.getElementsByTagName("p")[0]
   p.runtimeStyle.color = "blue"
   }

function IE_read() {
   var p = document.getElementsByTagName("p")[0]
   var pStyle = p.currentStyle
   alert(pStyle.color)
   }

//-->
</script>
</head>
<body>
<p>The color of this paragraph is originally green.</p>
<pre>Netscape 6: <a href="#" onclick="Nav_change();
➥return false">Change color</a> or <a
href="#" onclick="Nav_read();return false">Read color</a>

Internet Explorer: <a href="#" onclick="IE_change();
➥ return false">Change color</a> or <a
```

Listing 33.9   *(continued)*

```
href="#" onclick="IE_read();return false">Read color</a>
</pre>
</body>
</html>
```

To retrieve the color in Netscape 6 (per the DOM), you actually have to reference the normal view of the document. A *view* in this case refers to a particular rendering—the brief DOM Level 2 Views Recommendation covers this. We'll stick with the `defaultView` property of `document`.

From there, use the `getComputedStyle()` method, feeding in the specific element you want to retrieve and any desired pseudo-element (such as `:first-child` from CSS). This gives you a read-only version of the current styling on that element or pseudo-element. The `getPropertyValue()` method retrieves the string value (for Netscape as a hexadecimal RBG color).

To set a value, use the `style` property of the element in question. (I said it was incorrect to use in retrieving the value. But `style` is the best way for Netscape 6 to set that value.) This sets the inline `style` attribute to have the property.

For Internet Explorer 5.0 and greater, you can retrieve the `currentStyle` property and pull the appropriate JavaScript-named property. For setting the property, you can use `style` if you wish (Internet Explorer 4 supports it as well), but it's safer to use `runtimeStyle` instead. Again, this affects only the element itself.

Caution

If the user has the `!important` CSS attribute set, you could be in trouble. I found Netscape allows for setting the `!important` attribute directly (as in `"blue !important"`), but Internet Explorer does not. My tests reveal that if the original green color has the `!important` attribute set, you will not be able to *directly* implement a blue color.

Caution

You will also be in trouble if you treat any property returned as a number (for instance, *element*`.style.left`). Both Netscape and Internet Explorer return string values for any styling properties. You cannot simply do a = 15 operation on them; you must explicitly set the value to = `"15px"`, for example.

I briefly mentioned `className` in Chapter 21, "HTMLElement." Fortunately you can directly set it. If you add the following line to Listing 33.3 as an `onload` event handler,

```
document.getElementsByTagName("p")[2].className = "one"
```

the third line becomes capitalized, but not extra indented.

As for referring to a particular styling effect from a `style sheet`, that gets a bit more complicated. First, you have to reference the correct style sheet. Any style sheet that a `<link />` or `<style>...</style>` element references directly is available as a property of the `document.styleSheets` object.

An indirect reference via the `@import` at-rule will not show up in the `document.styleSheets` collection. If you ask for `document.styleSheets.length` in Listing 33.5, the response is 1. The imported style sheet is not that one.

Instead, you must access the interior style sheet via the `imports` collection in Internet Explorer. The following line, for Listing 33.5, returns an alert of "15px" in Internet Explorer 5:

```
alert(document.styleSheets[0].imports[0].rules[0].style.textIndent)
```

Netscape 6.2 does not currently allow access to the imported style sheet from the document object.

> **Note**
> Recent Mozilla builds allow access via:
>
> ```
> alert(document.styleSheets[0].cssRules[0].styleSheet.cssRules[0].style.text
> Indent)
> ```
>
> This is per the W3C DOM Level 2 Style Recommendation. No other browser this book focuses on does it correctly in this format.

Assuming you can get to the right style sheet, the `rules` collection in Internet Explorer and the `cssRules` collection in Netscape 6 become your searching points. Each individual CSS styling block is a member of these arrays. Given the different implementations, it may be best to search through the index of rules for the one you want. Note that for you to actually reach the styling properties, you will need the `style` property in-between the property name and the collection name.

For instance, in Listing 33.5,

```
alert(document.styleSheets[0].cssRules[1].style.textTransform)
```

will return `"uppercase"` in Netscape 6 browsers. In Internet Explorer, the equivalent line is:

```
alert(document.styleSheets[0].rules[0].style.textTransform)
```

The difference stems from Internet Explorer splitting the various CSS rules into `imports`, `rules`, and `pages` collections.

> **Note**
> These properties are NOT read-only! By setting `textTransform` to "lowercase" directly, you can force the style sheet rule to change, and in most cases, this means the styling of the element itself changes. The same flexibility applies to all properties of the `style` property.

Adding and removing rules via the DOM gets slightly interesting. The `deleteRule()` method of the style sheet in question removes the rule named by index number. (The first rule you would remove with *styleSheet*`.deleteRule(0)`, for example.)

As for adding a rule, you feed the `insertRule()` method two arguments: the original unparsed string of the new rule, and the index number of the existing rule you want the new rule to precede. There is no `createCSSRule()` method, as you might expect given how other objects in the DOM are created.

Finally, the ordinary Core DOM is the best way to outright remove or insert a style sheet. Simply use `document.createElement()` to create the appropriate `<link />` element. (You could also use a few methods to insert a CDATA section into a new `<style>...</style>` element.) Make sure you set the attributes, especially the `type` attribute, appropriately, and insert such elements into the head of the HTML document. For removing the element, the `removeChild()` method of `Node` interfaces should do quite nicely.

Netscape 4 does dynamic styling effects totally differently, of course.

Netscape 4 and JavaScript Styling

Netscape 4.x exposes three collections of the `document` object for accessing and altering styling before the document finishes loading: `tags`, `ids`, and `classes`. (After `onload`, any properties of these properties become read-only.) I covered them briefly in Chapter 23, "HTMLDocument/document," but they deserve a deeper explanation here.

The `document.tags` object has styling for every type of HTML element as a property by name. Note Listing 33.10, which indents the paragraph using `document.tags`.

Listing 33.10   *Netscape and* `document.tags`

```
<?xml version="1.0" ?>
<!-- Netscape 4.x only, before onload. -->
<!DOCTYPE html PUBLIC "-//W3C//DTD XHTML 1.0 Transitional//EN"
➥"DTD/xhtml1-transitional.dtd">
<html xmlns="http://www.w3.org/1999/xhtml" >
<head><title></title>
<style type="text/css">
<!--
p {
  text-indent:15px;
  }
-->
</style>
<script language="JavaScript" type="text/javascript">
<!--
window.onload = function() {
   document.forms.form0.myField.value = document.tags.p.textIndent
   }
document.tags.p.color = "#ff0000";
//-->
</script></head>
<body>
<p>This sentence has been indented and colored red.</p>
<pre>Non-indented text.</pre>
<form action="javascript:void()" name="form0">
<pre>The text indent is precisely <input type="text" size="5"
➥ name="myField" />.</pre>
</form><!-- Results:
 This sentence has been indented and colored red.
Non-indented text.
The text indent is precisely 15px.
-->
</body>
</html>
```

Netscape 4 also breaks case-sensitivity for styling; it does not matter in Listing 33.10 if you say document.tags.p or document.tags.P.

As far as classes go, they're fairly similar. The document.classes object has every class as a property by name. However, to apply a class of styling to all elements calling that class, you must actually reference the document.classes.all object, as in Listing 33.11:

Listing 33.11   *Netscape and* document.classes

```
<?xml version="1.0" ?>
<!-- Netscape 4.x only, before onload. -->
<!DOCTYPE html PUBLIC "-//W3C//DTD XHTML 1.0 Transitional//EN"
➥"DTD/xhtml1-transitional.dtd">
<html xmlns="http://www.w3.org/1999/xhtml" >
<head><title></title>
<script language="JavaScript" type="text/javascript">
<!--
document.classes.one.all.textIndent = "30px"
//-->
</script>
</head>
<body>
<p class="one">This text is indented.</p>
<pre>Non-indented text.</pre>
<!-- Results:
 This sentence has been indented.
Non-indented text.
-->
</body>
</html>
```

Netscape 4 also allows you to reference an element by its id attribute for styling, using the attribute value as a property of the document.ids object.

Twelve CSS Properties

These twelve CSS properties are significant enough to warrant a special section in my opinion, even though this is a book on JavaScript.

background-color/backgroundColor

The background-color CSS property specifies a background color for the this element. As with other instances of colors, you can specify a color by name at your own risk. A hexadecimal color designation (such as #FFFFFF for pure white) is better.

color

The `color` CSS property specifies a foreground, or text, color for the `this` element. As with other instances of colors, you can specify a color by name at your own risk. A hexadecimal color designation (such as `#FFFFFF` for pure white) is better.

display

The `display` CSS property defines how the document should attempt to lay out the `this` element. It defines primarily whether an element appears as a block, as an inline effect, or not at all.

To explain this, consider each paragraph as a block. Then consider a code font within each block as an inline effect. In writing the draft chapters of this book, I've also included commentary to numerous people, commentary you will never see. This is considered as having a display to "none" (no one).

The `display` property has several possible values. The most obvious are `"block"`, `"inline"`, and `"none"`. However, there are several others, including `"list-item"` and `"table-cell"`. Another worth mentioning is `"inherit"`. This one means the `this` element will inherit whatever styling its `parentNode` has.

> **Note**
> You will often see this particular property in collapsible DHTML widgets; it's really quite useful there.

font-family/fontFamily

The `font-family` CSS property defines fonts, in order of preference, which the `this` element should use. Each option you separate with a comma.

```
p {
   font-family: Technical, Verdana, Arial;
   }
```

font-size/fontSize

The `font-size` CSS property defines the size of the font to use, in vertical size. From my experience in journalism, a `"10pt"` or `"12pt"` font is good for regular text; `"14pt"` or `"18pt"` for emphasis. (You can set other kinds of font sizes, including relative font sizes, but explicitly naming a number of vertical points is the norm.)

font-style/fontSyle

The font-style CSS property defines the "slant" of the font to use, such as italic (/ slant) or oblique (\ slant).

font-weight/fontWeight

The font-weight CSS property defines the heaviness or boldness of the font to use. Normal fonts are usually 400, boldfaced fonts 700. The W3C defines multiples of 100 from 100 to 900, "normal", "bold", "bolder" (up 100 points), and "lighter" (down 100 points).

left

The left CSS property specifies, for an absolutely positioned element (see position), how far from the left edge of the parent element the this element is.

position

The position CSS property specifies how the this element is positioned in the context of the document. A value of "absolute" means its coordinates are explicitly stated by the top and left properties. A value of "relative" means the coordinates specify an offset from its regular position.

text-indent/textIndent

The text-indent CSS property specifies the amount of indent the text of the first line should indent. It does not specify an indent for the entire paragraph.

top

The top CSS property specifies, for an absolutely positioned element (see position), how far from the top edge of the parent element the this element is.

visibility

The visibility CSS property specifies whether the this element is actually visible to the user.

The CSS2 W3C Recommendation states this may have values of "hidden" or "visible". Netscape 6 and Internet Explorer both use these values. Netscape 4 uses "hide" and "show". The "inherit" value, which Netscape 4+ and Internet Explorer both support, means it inherits its visibility setting from its parent element.

HTMLStyleElement/<style>...</style>

Browser/JavaScript Version	Created By
Nav4/JavaScript 1.2	`<style>...</style>`
IE4/JScript 3.0	`<style>...</style>`
IE5/JScript 5.0	`<style>...</style>`
IE5.5/JScript 5.5	`<style>...</style>`
Nav6/JavaScript 1.5	`<style>...</style>`
IE6	`<style>...</style>`
DOM Level 1	`document.createElement("style")`
DOM Level 2	`document.createElement("style")`
	`document.implementation.createCSSStyleSheet()`

> **Note**
>
> Implemented in Nav4+ (HTML), IE3+ (HTML), Nav6+ (DOM), IE4+ (DOM)
>
> Descends from `HTMLElement` interface (Chapter 21)
>
> Parent elements: `HTMLHeadElement` (Chapter 24)

The `HTMLStyleElement` defines an inline style sheet for the document.

Properties

disabled

JavaScript1.5, JScript3.0+

Nav6, IE4+

Syntax

`[var x =] HTMLStyleElement.disabled [= boolValue]`

The `disabled` property of `HTMLStyleElement` objects refers to whether a style sheet is currently inactive in the document; a `true` value indicates the style sheet is not in force on the document at this time.

innerHTML

JScript5.0+

IE5+

The `innerHTML` property of `HTMLStyleElement` objects retrieves or sets the HTML source code contained between, but not including, the starting and ending tags.

I personally recommend against using `innerHTML` to set the HTML inside a tag. I strongly recommend against using `innerHTML` to append to the contents of an HTML tag:

```
elem.innerHTML += "<div><p>Hello World</p></div>" // DO NOT DO THIS
```

I do like the handiness of the `innerHTML` property for retrieving HTML source code at a glance, as an alternative method to the W3C Document Object Model. (The DOM provides an object structure for the source code; `innerHTML` provides the corresponding source code.)

media

JavaScript1.5, JScript3.0+

Nav6, IE4+

Syntax

```
[var x =] HTMLStyleElement.media [= targetMedium]
```

The `media` property of `HTMLStyleElement` objects refers to the targeted medium the style sheet applies for. For instance, a printed version of the document may have a style sheet specifically for the document. In cases like this, you would set the `media` property to `"print"`.

outerHTML

JScript5.0+

IE5+

The `outerHTML` property of `HTMLStyleElement` objects retrieves or sets the HTML source code contained between, and including, the starting and ending tags.

I do like the handiness of the `outerHTML` property for retrieving HTML source code at a glance, as an alternative method to the W3C Document Object Model. (The DOM provides an object structure for the source code; `outerHTML` provides the corresponding source code.)

sheet

JavaScript1.5

Nav6

Syntax

```
var x = HTMLStyleElement.sheet
```

The `sheet` property of `HTMLStyleElement` objects refers to the style sheet object the `this` element defines.

styleSheet

JScript5.0+

IE5.0+

Syntax

```
var x = HTMLStyleElement.styleSheet
```

The `styleSheet` property of `HTMLStyleElement` objects refers to the style sheet object the `this` element defines.

type

JavaScript1.5, JScript3.0+

Nav6, IE4+

Syntax

```
[var x =] HTMLStyleElement.type [= targetMedium]
```

The `type` property of `HTMLStyleElement` objects refers to the mime-type of the style sheet. This also defines the type of style sheet it is. CSS style sheets have a mime-type of `"text/css"`.

Methods

The `HTMLStyleElement` interface provides no methods beyond those the `HTMLElement` interface defines.

HTMLLinkElement/<link />/<?xml-stylesheet ?>

Browser/JavaScript Version	Created By
Nav4/JavaScript 1.2	`<link />`
IE4/JScript 3.0	`<link />`
IE5/JScript 5.0	`<link />`
	`<?xml-stylesheet ?>`
IE5.5/JScript 5.5	`<link />`
	`<?xml-stylesheet ?>`
Nav6/JavaScript 1.5	`<link />`
	`<?xml-stylesheet ?>`
IE6	`<link />`
	`<?xml-stylesheet ?>`
DOM Level 1	`document.createElement("link")`
DOM Level 2	`document.createElement("link")`
	`document.implementation.createCSSStyleSheet()`

> **Note**
>
> Implemented in Nav1+ (HTML), IE3+ (HTML), Nav6+ (DOM), IE4+ (DOM)
>
> Descends from `HTMLElement` interface (Chapter 21)
>
> Parent elements: `HTMLHeadElement` (Chapter 24)

The `HTMLLinkElement`, or `<link />`, is a link between the current `document` object and another document. It has a number of uses, including providing information for search engines, but this book examines it for style sheets primarily.

The `<?xml-stylesheet ?>` processing instruction is a special case of processing instructions, specifically set in place for XML documents to have a transformation style sheet. It is modeled after the `<link />` element; its data section is a string of "pseudo-attributes" matching the syntax of the `<link />` element's attributes.

Unfortunately, there is no special DOM for the `<?xml-stylesheet ?>` processing instruction. The following code may be able to help you:

```
for (var x = 0; x < document.childNodes.length; x++) {
    var y = document.childNodes[x]
    if ((y.nodeType == 7)&&(y.target == "xml-stylesheet")) {
      var z = y.data.split(" ")
```

```
for (var w = 0; w < z.length; w++) {
  z[w] = z[w].split("=")
  y[z[w][0]] = z[w][1]
  }
 }
}
}
```

This basically takes the processing instruction's data and splits it, then reattaches each individual *name=value* to the processing instruction as properties by name. For example, this will give such a processing instruction an href property equal to the href pseudo-attribute's value.

Not every browser handles this correctly, and you will have to use CDATA sections (Chapter 20, "Core DOM Objects") for this to work consistently in an XHTML document saved as XML, so be warned. (This is why it's not a listing.) In any case, I do not recommend <?xml-stylesheet ?> for XHTML documents (except for the Internet Explorer bug patch I mentioned near the beginning of this chapter).

Properties

charSet

JavaScript1.5

Nav6

Syntax

```
[var x =] HTMLLinkElement.charSet [= charSet]
```

The charSet property of HTMLLinkElement objects specifies the character set for the document the this object links to. In terms of style sheets, I believe it is safe to ignore this property.

disabled

JavaScript1.5, JScript3.0+

Nav6, IE4+

Syntax

```
[var x =] HTMLLinkElement.disabled [= boolValue]
```

The `disabled` property of `HTMLLinkElement` objects refers to whether a style sheet is currently inactive in the document; a `true` value indicates the style sheet is not in force on the document at this time.

href

JavaScript1.5, JScript3.0+

Nav6, IE4+

Syntax

```
[var x =] HTMLLinkElement.href [= URIString]
```

The `href` property of `HTMLLinkElement` objects refers to the Web address of a loaded style sheet. (In other words, if it hasn't loaded yet, this property is `""`.)

hrefLang

JavaScript1.5, JScript3.0+

Nav6, IE4+

Syntax

```
[var x =] HTMLLinkElement.hrefLang [= language]
```

The `hrefLang` property of `HTMLLinkElement` objects refers to the language of the document the `href` property references. For style sheets, you may safely ignore this property.

media

JavaScript1.5, JScript3.0+

Nav6, IE4+

Syntax

```
[var x =] HTMLLinkElement.media [= targetMedium]
```

The `media` property of `HTMLLinkElement` objects refers to the targeted medium for which the style sheet applies. For instance, a printed version of the document may have a style sheet specifically for the document. In cases like this, you would set the `media` property to `"print"`.

rel

JavaScript1.5, JScript3.0+

Nav6, IE4+

Syntax

```
[var x =] HTMLLinkElement.rel [= relation]
```

The `rel` property of `HTMLLinkElement` objects refers to the kind of link the element infers. For style sheets, setting this property to `"stylesheet"` activates it. Setting it to `"alternate stylesheet"` makes it a preferred alternate or disables it (depending on if the `title` attribute is used).

rev

JavaScript1.5, JScript3.0+

Nav6, IE4+

Syntax

```
[var x =] HTMLLinkElement.rel [= relation]
```

The `rev` property of `HTMLLinkElement` objects refers to the kind of link the element infers from the other document to this one (in reverse, basically). For style sheets you must absolutely not use this property.

sheet

JavaScript1.5

Nav6

Syntax

```
var x = HTMLLinkElement.sheet
```

The `sheet` property of `HTMLLinkElement` objects refers to the style sheet object the `this` element defines.

styleSheet

JScript5.0+

IE5.0+

Syntax

```
var x = HTMLLinkElement.styleSheet
```

The `styleSheet` property of `HTMLLinkElement` objects refers to the style sheet object the `this` element defines.

target

JavaScript1.5+, JScript3.0+

Nav6, IE4.0+

Syntax

```
[var x =] HTMLLinkElement.target [= targetWin]
```

The `target` property of `HTMLLinkElement` objects reflects the currently targeted default window for the document the `this` element links to. You can use any valid HTML window name for this value (see Chapter 15, "window," for a description of HTML window names versus JavaScript window names).

You can also use `"_blank"` to indicate opening a new window every time, `"_parent"` for the parent window, `"_top"` for the topmost window in the parent window chain (see `top` and `parent` in Chapter 15, "window"), or `"_self"` to indicate it should load into the window of its document. (`"_self"` is the default setting.)

Internet Explorer 5.0+ introduces a new one called `"_search"`, which will target the link for the browser's search sidebar.

> **Note**
> Targets for link elements have no bearing on style sheets. The link element is useful for describing how one document relates to another, and that is the context here. For CSS style sheets, you can ignore this attribute.

type

JavaScript1.5, JScript3.0+

Nav6, IE4+

Syntax

```
[var x =] HTMLStyleElement.type [= targetMedium]
```

The `type` property of `HTMLLinkElement` objects refers to the mime-type of the style sheet. This also defines the type of style sheet it is. CSS style sheets have a mime-type of `"text/css"`.

Methods

The `HTMLLinkElement` interface provides no methods beyond those the `HTMLElement` interface defines.

CHAPTER 34

DOM-2 Range

The Core DOM regards an XML or XHTML document as a tree of nodes. Although the Core DOM enables you to manipulate this document tree on the node level, it doesn't allow for manipulating individual characters or general text across several nodes directly. To allow for that, the W3C has released the DOM Level 2 Range specification as a W3C Recommendation.

The Mozilla project tries to implement the W3C Range specification. So far the implementation is far from complete. This chapter can therefore only provide working code examples as far as Netscape 6 supports them.

Nevertheless, the parts of the specification not yet supported are listed. The introduction already indicates that ranges are useful to represent the selection a user makes with the mouse. Therefore Mozilla and Netscape 6 build on the DOM-2 Range specification to allow for scripted manipulation of content selection.

The DOM Level 2 Range specification is one half of the DOM Level 2 Traversal-Range Recommendation, at http://www.w3.org/TR/DOM-Level-2-Traversal-Range. It is clear and very well-written; you might want to read it as a companion to this chapter.

Internet Explorer 6 does not implement the W3C Range specification. Internet Explorer 4.0+ has its own implementation of ranges and manipulating selections.

Before you get into the nitty-gritty of DOM-2 Range, I'd like to take this moment to thank Martin Honnen for his contributions in editing this chapter.

What Is A Range?

A range is a contiguous selection of content in a structured XML or XHTML document. The start point and the end point of the range are the boundary points of the range.

How can a boundary point unambiguously represent the start or end point of a range? The answer lies in the representation of a document as a tree of nodes. If the document node is the trunk of the tree and each element is a branch, sooner or later you get to the leaves of the tree. These leaves are the text nodes of the document.

So how do you get to the various portions of each leaf?

In this tree a boundary point is characterized by a node, called the container of the boundary point, and an offset. The offset differs depending on the node type of the container node. For the Document node or Element nodes, the offset specifies the position between the child nodes of the container node. For Text nodes, the offset is a zero-based index, indicating which character, from the beginning, the boundary point refers to.

Boundary Points for Element and Document Nodes

Consider the following code with a HTMLDivElement node containing three child nodes, each being a HTMLParagraphElement node:

```
<div id="d0"><p>zero</p><p id="p1">one</p><p>two</p></div>
```

See Figure 34.1.

Boundary Points for Element and Document Nodes

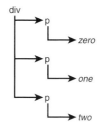

Figure 34.1
Three paragraphs and an HTMLDivElement.

If you take the HTMLDivElement node (with id="d0") as a container for our boundary point, then any offset is an offset into the child nodes of the div element. An offset of 0 is the position right before the first child node, as Figure 34.2 demonstrates:

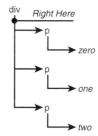

Figure 34.2
Container div, offset 0.

With the div as the container of the boundary point there are three other possible offsets. An offset of 1 marks the position immediately after the first child node, and before the second child node. Likewise, the offsets of 2 and 3 come after the second and third nodes, respectively. Figure 34.3 gives an illustration of this.

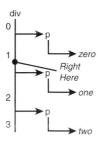

Figure 34.3
Container div, offset 1, with offsets marked.

Ranges are not about boundary points, however; they are about the contents between two boundary points. If you want a range to select the complete contents of the `HTMLDivElement` node, you need a range where both the starting and ending boundary points have the `HTMLDivElement` node as the container node. You then set the starting boundary point offset to `0` and the ending boundary point offset to `3`.

If div = `HTMLDivElement`, this is like selecting `div.childNodes[0]`, `div.childNodes[1]`, and `div.childNodes[2]`. But it does not include selecting `div.childNodes[3]` (if that node existed). The ending boundary point stops any range from taking content following that boundary point.

Boundary Points for Text Nodes

With ranges, it is especially important to grab the correct node as the container before working with the offset.

Imagine you want to select the characters `"ne"` in the text inside the second `HTMLParagraphElement`. We'll call this p. If you choose the p element itself as the container for a boundary node, you could use an offset into the child nodes of the p element.

But `p.childNodes.length == 1`.

Therefore you need to choose the `Text` node in the paragraph itself (`p.childNodes[0]`) as the container node of the boundary point.

Any offset associated with a container `Text` node is an offset into the character data of the `Text` node. If you sketch out the characters of this node, you get Figure 34.4.

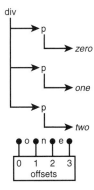

Figure 34.4
Container Text node and offsets.

So to select `"ne"` from this text node (`p.childNodes[0]`), you would need offsets of 1 and 3 for the beginning and ending boundary points, respectively.

An arbitrary range can have different container nodes for starting and ending points. For instance, if you want to select the content from the beginning of `div` to the character `"n"` in `p`, you need to choose `div` as the start container node with offset 0, and the specific `Text` node as the end container node with offset 1. This will give you `p.previousSibling`, and the characters `"on"` from `p.childNodes[0]`.

Range

Browser/JavaScript Version	Created By
Nav4/JavaScript 1.2	Not Implemented
IE4/JScript 3.0	Not Implemented
IE5/JScript 5.0	Not Implemented
IE5.5/JScript 5.5	Not Implemented
Nav6/JavaScript 1.5	`document.createRange()`
IE6	Not Implemented
DOM Level 1	Not Implemented
DOM Level 2	`document.createRange()`

> **Note**
> Implemented in Nav6

Description

The `Range` interface defines, with two boundary points, a contiguous selection of contents in the document. The selected content can be manipulated in various ways with the methods listed later.

The `Range` interface has four properties: `startContainer`, `startOffset`, `endContainer`, and `endOffset`.

There are several methods of `Range` objects for selecting contents. The `selectNode()` and `selectNodeContents()` methods set both starting and ending points together in relation to a node. The `setStartBefore()` and `setStartAfter()` methods position the start point relative to a node. The `setEndBefore()` and `setEndAfter()` methods position the end point relative to a node. Finally there are the `setStart()` and setEnd() methods, which respectively set the container node and offset of the starting and ending boundary points.

Listing 34.1 demonstrates usage of these methods in a simple example.

Listing 34.1   *Sample Ranges*

```
<?xml version="1.0" ?>
<!-- Netscape 6 and other browsers implementing W3C DOM Level 2 Range -->
<!DOCTYPE html
     PUBLIC "-//W3C//DTD XHTML 1.0 Transitional//EN"
     "http://www.w3.org/TR/xhtml1/DTD/xhtml1-transitional.dtd">
<html xmlns="http://www.w3.org/1999/xhtml">
<head><title></title>
<style type="text/css">
#d0 {
  border: 1px solid green;
}
</style>
<script type="text/javascript">
function inspectRange(range) {
  clearOutput();
  var text = 'startContainer: ' + range.startContainer
  if (typeof range.startContainer.id != "undefined") {
    text += '; id: ' + range.startContainer.id
    } else {
    text += '; nodeValue: ' + range.startContainer.nodeValue
    }
  output(text)
  output('startOffset: ' + range.startOffset);
  text = 'endContainer: ' + range.endContainer
  if (typeof range.endContainer.id != "undefined") {
    text += '; id: ' + range.endContainer.id
    } else {
    text += '; nodeValue: ' + range.endContainer.nodeValue
    }
  output(text)
  output('endOffset: ' + range.endOffset);
  output('text content: ' + range.toString());
  }

function clearOutput() {
  var range = document.createRange();
```

Listing 34.1   *(continued)*

```
    range.selectNodeContents(document.getElementById('output'));
    range.deleteContents();
    }

function output(text) {
  var output = document.getElementById('output');
  output.appendChild(document.createTextNode(text));
  output.appendChild(document.createElement('br'));
  }

function guiSelectRange(range) {
  var selection = window.getSelection();
  selection.removeAllRanges();
  selection.addRange(range);
  }

function button1() {
  var range = document.createRange();
  range.selectNodeContents(document.getElementById('d0'));
  inspectRange(range);
  guiSelectRange(range);
  }

function button2() {
  var range = document.createRange();
  range.setStart(document.getElementById('p1').firstChild, 4);
  range.setEnd(document.getElementById('p1').firstChild, 9);
  inspectRange(range);
  guiSelectRange(range);
  }

function button3() {
  var range = document.createRange();
  range.setStart(document.getElementById('d0'), 0);
  range.setEnd(document.getElementById('p1').firstChild, 9);
  inspectRange(range);
  guiSelectRange(range);
  }
</script>
</head>
<body>
```

Listing 34.1   *(continued)*

```
<div id="d0"><p>paragraph 0</p><p id="p1">paragraph 1</p><p>paragraph 2</p>
➥</div>
<form action="javascript:void()">
<input type="button" value="select content of div" onclick="button1()" />
<input type="button" value="select syllable 'graph'" onclick="button2()" />
<input type="button" onclick="button3()"
  value="select content from beginning of div till word paragraph in second p
➥ element" />
<div id="output"></div>
<!-- Results after clicking button 1:
startContainer: [object HTMLDivElement]; id: d0
startOffset: 0
endContainer: [object HTMLDivElement]; id: d0
endOffset: 3
text content: paragraph 0paragraph 1paragraph 2

Results after clicking button 2:
startContainer: [object Text]; nodeValue: paragraph 1
startOffset: 4
endContainer: [object Text]; nodeValue: paragraph 1
endOffset: 9
text content: graph

Results after clicking button 3:
startContainer: [object HTMLDivElement]; id: d0
startOffset: 0
endContainer: [object Text]; nodeValue: paragraph 1
endOffset: 9
text content: paragraph 0paragraph
-->
</body>
</html>
```

The body of Listing 34.1 features an HTMLDivElement node with three paragraphs. It also has three buttons, each one for creating a sample range. An output HTMLDivElement is also there for listing some of the properties of a created Range object.

If you click on the first button, the text of the three paragraphs is visually selected. If you have a look at the button1() function, you find the following JavaScript code:

```
var range = document.createRange();
range.selectNodeContents(document.getElementById('d0'));
inspectRange(range);
guiSelectRange(range);
```

The first line creates a `Range` object and assigns it to `range`. The second line calls the `selectNodeContents()` method of `range` with the `HTMLDivElement` node with `id="d0"` as the argument.

To check the described `startContainer`, `startOffset`, `endContainer`, and `endOffset` properties of `range`, the third line calls an `inspectRange()` function. This simply outputs those properties and the text content of the `HTMLDivElement` at the end of the page. The last line calls the function `guiSelectRange()`, so the example visually selects the range in the window. You'll see this function later in this chapter.

The second and third buttons create two other ranges. Try the buttons and check the output and you will see the container nodes and the offsets. When you execute the `button2()` function by clicking on the second button, the following code runs:

```
var range = document.createRange();
range.setStart(document.getElementById('p1').firstChild,4);
range.setEnd(document.getElementById('p1').firstChild,9);
inspectRange(range);
guiSelectRange(range);
```

The first statement again creates a range. This time you position the start point first, using the first (and only) child node, a `Text` node, of the `p` element with `id="p1"` as the container node.

We then pass in the offset 4, to indicate a starting point after four characters. Then you position the end point, again using the `Text` node as the container node, and use the offset 9 to mark the end of the range.

The third button selects contents from the beginning of the `div` element until after the word `paragraph` in the second paragraph.

The DOM-2 Traversal-Range Recommendation defines several methods to manipulate a document using a range. You can delete the contents of a range with the `deleteContents()` method. You can extract the contents of a range into a document fragment with the `extractContents()` method. You can clone the contents of a range with the `cloneContents()` method. You can insert a node or document fragment into the range with the `insertNode()` method. Or you can surround the contents of a range with the `surroundContents()` method.

Properties

---

collapsed

JavaScript 1.5

Nav6

Read-only

Syntax

```
var x = rangeObj.collapsed
```

The `collapsed` property of `Range` objects returns whether the start and end boundary points reference the same position in the document.

---

commonAncestorContainer

JavaScript 1.5

Nav6

Read-only

Syntax

```
var node = rangeObj.commonAncestorContainer
```

The `commonAncestorContainer` property of `Range` objects returns the deepest node in the document that is an ancestor of both boundary points.

In previous examples the `commonAncestorContainer` was `div` as it either was itself the container of a boundary point or contained the container of the boundary point. In Listing 34.2 you add an unordered list to the sample page, and create and position a range to span from the second paragraph in `div` to the first item in the list.

Listing 34.2   *The* `commonAncestorContainer`

```
<?xml version="1.0" ?>
<!-- NN6 and other browsers implementing
     W3C DOM Level 2 range
-->
<!DOCTYPE html
     PUBLIC "-//W3C//DTD XHTML 1.0 Transitional//EN"
```

Listing 34.2 *(continued)*

```
       "http://www.w3.org/TR/xhtml1/DTD/xhtml1-transitional.dtd">
<html xmlns="http://www.w3.org/1999/xhtml">
<head><title></title>
<style type="text/css">
#d0 {
  border: 1px solid green;
}
</style>
<script type="text/javascript">
function guiSelectRange (range) {
  var selection = window.getSelection();
  selection.removeAllRanges();
  selection.addRange(range);
}
</script>
</head>
<body>
<div id="d0"><p>paragraph 0</p><p id="p1">paragraph 1</p><p>paragraph
2</p></div>

<ul id="ul0"><li>item 0</li><li>item 1</li></ul>

<script type="text/javascript">
var range = document.createRange();
range.setStart(document.getElementById('d0'), 1);
range.setEnd(document.getElementById('ul0'), 1);
document.write('commonAncestorContainer: ' + range.commonAncestorContainer);
/* Results:
commonAncestorContainer: [object HTMLBodyElement]
*/
guiSelectRange(range);
</script>
</body>
</html>
```

The `HTMLBodyElement` node is the `commonAncestorContainer` of the range. As the `startContainer` is `div` and the `endContainer` is the list element (see Chapter 27, "List Elements"), and both are children of the body element, their deepest common ancestor is the body element.

endContainer

JavaScript 1.5

Nav6

Read-only

Syntax

```
var node = rangeObj.endContainer
```

The endContainer property of Range objects refers to the node that is the container node of the end boundary point. In Listing 34.2, this would be the list (ul) element.

endOffset

JavaScript 1.5

Nav6

Read-only

Syntax

```
var x = rangeObj.endOffset
```

The endOffset property of Range objects refers to the offset within the endContainer. For the Document node or Element nodes, the offset marks a position within the child nodes of the node. For Text nodes, the offset is within the character data of the node. Listing 34.1 is an example creating various ranges and then listing the offsets.

startContainer

JavaScript 1.5

Nav6

Read-only

Syntax

```
var node = rangeObj.startContainer
```

The startContainer property of Range objects refers to the container node of the start boundary point. In Listing 34.2, this would be the div element.

startOffset

JavaScript 1.5

Nav6

Read-only

Syntax

```
var x = rangeObj.startOffset
```

The startOffset property of Range objects refers to the offset within the startContainer node. For the Document node or Element nodes, the offset marks a position within the child nodes of the node. For Text nodes, the offset is within the character data of the node. Listing 34.1 demonstrates various ranges and the offsets of the boundary points.

Methods

cloneContents()

JavaScript 1.5

Nav 6

Syntax

```
var documentFragment = rangeObj.cloneContents();
```

The cloneContents() method of Range objects duplicates the contents of the range and returns it inside a document fragment. The document and the range do not change by calling the method. You can use it to duplicate the contents of a Range object, and then use it elsewhere.

In this respect, it is similar to the cloneNode() method of Node objects (see Chapter 20, "Core DOM Objects"). Listing 34.3 uses a HTMLDivElement from the earlier listings, and creates a range that selects its content (the three paragraph elements). It then calls cloneContents() on the range and inserts the returned document fragment at the end of the document body. The result is that the three paragraphs are duplicated and inserted at the end of the document body.

Listing 34.3   *The* `cloneContents()` *Method*

```xml
<?xml version="1.0" ?>
<!-- NN6 and other browsers implementing
     W3C DOM Level 2 range
-->
<!DOCTYPE html
     PUBLIC "-//W3C//DTD XHTML 1.0 Transitional//EN"
     "http://www.w3.org/TR/xhtml1/DTD/xhtml1-transitional.dtd">
<html xmlns="http://www.w3.org/1999/xhtml">
<head>
<title>
Listing 34list03.html -- cloneContents
</title>
</head>
<body>
<div id="d0"><p>paragraph 0</p><p id="p1">paragraph 1</p><p>paragraph
2</p></div>

<script type="text/javascript">
var range = document.createRange();
range.selectNodeContents(document.getElementById('d0'));
var docFrag = range.cloneContents();
document.body.appendChild(docFrag);
</script>
<!-- Results:
paragraph 0

paragraph 1

paragraph 2

paragraph 0

paragraph 1

paragraph 2
-->
</body>
</html>
```

cloneRange()

JavaScript 1.5

Nav6

Syntax

```
var rangeClone = rangeObj.cloneRange()
```

The cloneRange() method of Range objects returns a new Range object containing independent and complete copies of the boundary point markers for the this object.

collapse()

JavaScript 1.5

Nav6

Syntax

```
rangeObj.collapse(booleanValue)
```

The collapse() method of Range objects moves one boundary point of the this object to superimpose on the other. If the first argument is true, the end boundary point moves to the start boundary point. If the first argument is false, the start boundary point moves to the end boundary point.

compareBoundaryPoints()

JavaScript 1.5

Nav6

Syntax

```
var x = rangeObj.compareBoundaryPoints(code, rangeObj2)
```

The compareBoundaryPoints() method of Range objects returns a value indicating how one boundary point of the this object compares to a boundary point of the second argument, also a Range object. The first argument, an integer between and possibly including 0 and 3, determines which boundary points of each range this method examines.

As remembering which number refers to which comparison method is difficult, the `Range` interface defines four constants, `Range.START_TO_START`, `Range.START_TO_END`, `Range.END_TO_END`, and `Range.END_TO_START`. You can pass any of these in as the first argument to determine the comparison method. You can call for instance,

```
range1Obj.compareBoundaryPoints(Range.START_TO_START, range2Obj)
```

to compare the start points of both ranges.

If the first argument is `Range.START_TO_START`, this method compares the start boundary point of the `this` element against the start boundary point of the second argument.

If the first argument is `Range.START_TO_END`, this method compares the start boundary point of the `this` element against the end boundary point of the second argument.

If the first argument is `Range.END_TO_START`, this method compares the end boundary point of the `this` element against the start boundary point of the second argument.

If the first argument is `Range.END_TO_END`, this method compares the end boundary point of the `this` element against the end boundary point of the second argument.

The return of this method will be `1` if the `this` element's referenced boundary point comes after the second argument's referenced boundary point.

The return of this method will be `0` if the `this` element's referenced boundary point matches the location of the second argument's referenced boundary point.

The return of this method will be `-1` if the `this` element's referenced boundary point comes before the second argument's referenced boundary point.

createContextualFragment()

JavaScript 1.5

Nav6

Syntax

```
var documentFragment = rangeObj.createContextualFragment(htmlSourceCode);
```

The `createContextualFragment()` method of `Range` objects is a powerful addition in Netscape 6's implementation of the W3C Range specification. It takes one argument, a string of partial or complete HTML or XML source code, and parses it to return a `DocumentFragment` node containing the DOM tree for that source code.

Setting `innerHTML` in Netscape 6 is effectively the same as calling this method, except `innerHTML` changes a current element, while this method returns a new `DocumentFragment` node entirely.

When using `createContextualFragment()` on a `Range` object to insert the created document fragment somewhere in the document, you should position the range at that position before calling the method.

Listing 34.4 implements the Internet Explorer `insertAdjacentHTML()` method of `Element` nodes for Netscape 6 using `createContextualFragment()`.

Listing 34.4   *Using* `createContextualFragment()` *to Implement*
`insertAdjacentHTML()`

```
<?xml version="1.0" ?>
<!-- Netscape 6.0+ and Internet Explorer 4.0+ -->
<!DOCTYPE html
     PUBLIC "-//W3C//DTD XHTML 1.0 Transitional//EN"
     "http://www.w3.org/TR/xhtml1/DTD/xhtml1-transitional.dtd">
<html xmlns="http://www.w3.org/1999/xhtml">
<head><title></title>
<style type="text/css">
#d0 {
  border: 1px solid green;
}
</style>
<script type="text/javascript">
if (window.HTMLElement && HTMLElement.prototype &&
    typeof HTMLElement.prototype.insertAdjacentHTML == 'undefined')
  HTMLElement.prototype.insertAdjacentHTML = function (position, html) {
    var range = document.createRange();
    switch (position) {
      case 'beforeBegin':
        range.setStartBefore(this);
        var docFrag = range.createContextualFragment(html);
        this.parentNode.insertBefore(docFrag, this);
        break;
      case 'afterBegin':
        range.selectNodeContents(this);
        var docFrag = range.createContextualFragment(html);
        this.insertBefore(docFrag, this.firstChild);
        break;
      case 'beforeEnd':
```

Listing 34.4 *(continued)*

```
          range.selectNodeContents(this);
          var docFrag = range.createContextualFragment(html);
          this.appendChild(docFrag);
          break;
        case 'afterEnd':
          range.setStartAfter(this);
          var docFrag = range.createContextualFragment(html);
          this.parentNode.insertBefore(docFrag, this.nextSibling);
          break;
    }
    range.detach();
  };
</script>
<script language="JavaScript" type="text/javascript">
function exampleInsertBeforeBegin () {
  var html = '<p style="color: red;">To appear before div<\/p>';
  document.getElementById('d0').insertAdjacentHTML('beforeBegin', html);
  }

function exampleInsertAfterBegin () {
  var html = '<p style="color: green;">To appear after begin of div<\/p>';
  document.getElementById('d0').insertAdjacentHTML('afterBegin', html);
  }

function exampleInsertBeforeEnd () {
  var html = '<p style="color: purple;">To appear before end of div<\/p>';
  document.getElementById('d0').insertAdjacentHTML('beforeEnd', html);
  }

function exampleInsertAfterEnd () {
  var html = '<p style="color: darkblue;">To appear after end of div<\/p>';
  document.getElementById('d0').insertAdjacentHTML('afterEnd', html);
  }
</script>
</head>
<body>
<div id="d0"><p id="p0">paragraph 0</p><p id="p1">paragraph 1</p>
➥<p>paragraph 2</p></div>
<input type="button" value="insert before begin of div"
  onclick="exampleInsertBeforeBegin();" />
<input type="button" value="insert after begin of div"
```

Listing 34.4   *(continued)*

```
  onclick="exampleInsertAfterBegin();" />
<input type="button" value="insert before end of div"
  onclick="exampleInsertBeforeEnd();" />
<input type="button" value="insert after div"
  onclick="exampleInsertAfterEnd();" />
</body>
</html>
```

The body of the document contains a familiar HTMLDivElement with the three paragraphs in it. Below that are four buttons, each with an onclick handler calling an example function to insert some HTML source code into the document, relative to the div element. This uses the insertAdjacentHTML() method that usually only Internet Explorer 4.0+ provides.

However, in the first script section, you set up HTMLElement.prototype. insertAdjacentHTML(). Therefore, all HTMLElement nodes in Netscape 6 will have this method.

When you look at the implementation, you see it first creates a Range object. Then a switch statement distinguishes the different input position cases. In each case, first the range is positioned and then the createContextualFragment() method is called to convert the HTML source fragment into a document tree fragment. This DocumentFragment node is then inserted at the correct position in the document.

You should be able to run Listing 34.4 in both Internet Explorer 4+ and Netscape 6.0+ without any difference in the results when clicking the buttons.

deleteContents()

JavaScript 1.5

Nav6

Syntax

rangeObj.deleteContents()

The deleteContents() method of Range objects deletes the content selected by the range from the document. After the deletion the range is collapsed.

Internet Explorer 4+ provides the innerText property for Element nodes, which enables you to replace the content of an element with some text. Using a combination of the Range methods selectNodeContents() and deleteContents(), you can implement setting innerText for Netscape 6. See Listing 34.5.

Listing 34.5   *Setting* innerText *with Netscape 6*

```
<?xml version="1.0" ?>
<!-- Netscape 6 and other browsers implementing W3C DOM Level 2 Range.
Compatible with Internet Explorer 4+ as well. -->
<!DOCTYPE html
     PUBLIC "-//W3C//DTD XHTML 1.0 Transitional//EN"
     "http://www.w3.org/TR/xhtml1/DTD/xhtml1-transitional.dtd">
<html xmlns="http://www.w3.org/1999/xhtml">
<head><title></title>
<style type="text/css">
#d0 {
  border: 1px solid green;
}
</style>
<script type="text/javascript">
function setInnerText(elementId, text) {
  if (document.all) {
    document.all[elementId].innerText = text;
    } else if (document.implementation.hasFeature("Range", "2.0")) {
    var element = document.getElementById(elementId);
    var range = document.createRange();
    range.selectNodeContents(element);
    range.deleteContents();
    range.detach();
    } else {
    while(element.hasChildNodes()) {
      element.removeChild(element.lastChild);
      }
    }
    element.appendChild(document.createTextNode(text));
  }
</script>
</head>
<body>
<div id="d0"><p>paragraph 0</p><p id="p1">paragraph 1</p><p>paragraph
2</p></div>
<input type="button" value="set innerText of div to 'Kibology'"
  onclick="setInnerText('d0', 'Kibology');" />
<input type="button"
```

Listing 34.5   *(continued)*

```
  value="set innerText of div to 'JavaScript Developer Dictionary'"
  onclick="setInnerText('d0', 'JavaScript Developer Dictionary');" />
</body>
</html>
```

The page provides a function `setInnerText()` that takes an element's `id` as the first argument, and the text to set as the second argument. The function checks for `document.all` as part of the Internet Explorer DOM and in that case simply assigns to the `innerText` property.

> **Note**
> Earlier in this book, I ranted about object detection. However, in this instance, it's justified. You're directly using properties of `document.all`, so you need to ensure `document.all` is there.

Otherwise, the function checks for `document.implementation.hasFeature("Range", "2.0")` to find out about W3C DOM Range support.

If the support is there, the function uses the `Range` DOM to select the contents of the element, and then delete the contents.

If `Range` support is not there, the function uses the Core DOM to loop through all child nodes and remove them. At the end, the function creates and appends a `Text` node to the element.

detach()

JavaScript 1.5

Nav6

Syntax

rangeObj.detach()

The `detach()` method of `Range` objects indicates to the implementation that it can release any resources associated with the range. Any further attempts to access this object result in an exception being thrown.

You should call the `detach()` method when you are sure you do not need the range any longer. Listing 33.4 calls `range.detach()` in the `setInnerText()` function.

PART III   Document Object Model for HTML Documents

extractContents()

JavaScript 1.5

Nav6

Syntax

```
var documentFragment = rangeObj.extractContents();
```

The `extractContents()` method of `Range` objects deletes and returns the contents of
the range from the document. Listing 34.6 provides an example of `extractContents()`
to swap the contents of an element in and out.

Listing 34.6   *Example of* `extractContents()`

```
<?xml version="1.0" ?>
<!-- Netscape 6 and other browsers implementing W3C DOM Level 2 Range -->
<!DOCTYPE html
    PUBLIC "-//W3C//DTD XHTML 1.0 Transitional//EN"
    "http://www.w3.org/TR/xhtml1/DTD/xhtml1-transitional.dtd">
<html xmlns="http://www.w3.org/1999/xhtml">
<head>
<title>
Listing 34list05.html -- extractContents
</title>
<style type="text/css">
#d0 {
  border: 1px solid green;
}
#p0 {
  background-color: lightblue;
}
p.message {
  font-weight: bold;
  color: green;
}
</style>
<script type="text/javascript">
function subliminalMessage(elementId) {
  if (document.createRange) {
    var element = document.getElementById(elementId);
    element.swapped = false;
    var docFrag = document.createDocumentFragment();
```

Listing 34.6   *(continued)*

```
    var p = document.createElement('p');
    p.className = 'message';
    p.appendChild(document.createTextNode('Buy the JavaScript Developer\'s
➥ Dictionary'));
    docFrag.appendChild(p);
    element.message = docFrag;
    element.range = document.createRange();
    element.tid = setTimeout(function () { swapElement(element); }, 3000);
    }
  }


function swapElement(element) {
  element.range.selectNodeContents(element);
  if (!element.swapped) {
    element.originalContent = element.range.extractContents();
    element.appendChild(element.message);
    element.swapped = true;
    element.tid = setTimeout(function () { swapElement(element); }, 700);
    } else {
    element.message = element.range.extractContents();
    element.appendChild(element.originalContent);
    element.swapped = false;
    element.tid = setTimeout(function () { swapElement(element); }, 3000);
    }
  }
</script>
</head>
<body onload="subliminalMessage('d0'); subliminalMessage('p0');">
<div id="d0"><p>paragraph 0</p><p id=
➥"p1">paragraph 1</p><p>paragraph 2</p></div>
<p id="p0">The Range interface provides methods for accessing and manipulating
the document tree at a higher level than similar methods in the Node
interface. The expectation is that each of the methods provided by the
Range interface for the insertion, deletion, and copying of content can
be directly mapped to a series of Node editing operations enabled
by DOM Core. In this sense, the Range operations can be viewed as
convenience methods that also enable the implementation to optimize
common editing patterns.</p>
</body>
</html>
```

As you can see, there are two child elements in the body, the now familiar `div` and a paragraph. The `onload` event handler of the body calls the function `subliminalMessage()` on both elements.

This function prepares each element by creating a document fragment with the message to be swapped in, and then attaching it to the element. The function also creates a `Range` object and attaches it to the element. With the `setTimeout()` function (see Chapter 15, "window"), the `swapElement()` function is scheduled for execution.

The `swapElement()` function uses the range attached to the element to select the contents of the element. The function then extracts and stores the contents, and swaps out the message. On the next call to `swapElement()`, the reverse happens: the function extracts the message, stores that message, and restores the original contents to the element.

insertNode()

Not yet supported by Netscape 6.2 but specified by W3C

Syntax

rangeObj.insertNode(*nodeObj*);

The `insertNode()` method of `Range` objects takes a node as the argument and inserts that node at the start of the range. If the start container is a text node that node will be split into two to allow for inserting of the node argument.

This method doesn't work so far in existing Netscape releases (Netscape 6.2 being the latest). This is a bit disappointing, as an important aspect of range manipulation is missing. Perhaps (when you read this), a Netscape release supporting this method will exist.

selectNode()

JavaScript 1.5

Nav6

Syntax

rangeObj.selectNode(*node*)

The `selectNode()` method of `Range` objects takes a node as its argument, and selects the node and its content. The container node of the start and end boundary points will be the parent node of the argument, and the start offset will mark the position before the node and the end offset the position after the node.

Listing 34.7 takes the familiar `div` and demonstrates the `selectNode()` method and the `selectNodeContents()` method (which I explain later).

Listing 34.7 *Comparison of* `selectNode` *Versus* `selectNodeContents`

```
<?xml version="1.0" ?>
<!-- Netscape 6 and other browsers implementing W3C DOM Level 2 Range -->
<!DOCTYPE html
    PUBLIC "-//W3C//DTD XHTML 1.0 Transitional//EN"
    "http://www.w3.org/TR/xhtml1/DTD/xhtml1-transitional.dtd">
<html xmlns="http://www.w3.org/1999/xhtml">
<head><title></title>
<style type="text/css">
#d0 {
  border: 1px solid green;
}
</style>
<script type="text/javascript">
function inspectRange (range) {
  clearOutput();
  output('startContainer: ' + range.startContainer +
         (range.startContainer.id ?
         '; id: ' + range.startContainer.id : ''));
  output('startOffset: ' + range.startOffset);
  output('endContainer: ' + range.endContainer +
         (range.endContainer.id ?
         '; id: ' + range.endContainer.id : ''));
  output('endOffset: ' + range.endOffset);
  output('text content: ' + range.toString());
  }

function clearOutput () {
  var range = document.createRange();
  range.selectNodeContents(document.getElementById('output'));
  range.deleteContents();
  }

function output (text) {
  var output = document.getElementById('output');
  output.appendChild(document.createTextNode(text));
```

Part III   Document Object Model for HTML Documents

Listing 34.7   *(continued)*

```javascript
  output.appendChild(document.createElement('br'));
  }

function guiSelectRange (range) {
  var selection = window.getSelection();
  selection.removeAllRanges();
  selection.addRange(range);
  }

function button1() {
  var range = document.createRange();
  range.selectNode(document.getElementById('d0'));
  inspectRange(range);
  guiSelectRange(range);
  }

function button2() {
  var range = document.createRange();
  range.selectNodeContents(document.getElementById('d0'));
  inspectRange(range);
  guiSelectRange(range);
  }
</script>
</head>
<body>
<div id="d0"><p>paragraph 0</p><p id="p1">paragraph 1</p><p>paragraph 2</p>
➥</div>
<form action="javascript:void()">
<input type="button" value="select the div" onclick="button1()" />
<input type="button" value="select content of div" onclick="button2()" />
</form>
<div id="output"></div>
<!-- Results after clicking first button:
startContainer: [object HTMLBodyElement]
startOffset: 1
endContainer: [object HTMLBodyElement]
endOffset: 2
text content: paragraph 0paragraph 1paragraph 2
```

Listing 34.7 *(continued)*

```
Results after clicking second button:
startContainer: [object HTMLDivElement]; id: d0
startOffset: 0
endContainer: [object HTMLDivElement]; id: d0
endOffset: 3
text content: paragraph 0paragraph 1paragraph 2
-->
</body>
</html>
```

selectNodeContents()

JavaScript 1.5

Nav6

Syntax

rangeObj.selectNodeContents(*node*)

The selectNodeContents() method of Range objects takes one node as an argument and selects the content of that node. The node itself becomes the start and the end container nodes of the range. The offsets are positioned at 0 and *node*.childNodes.length respectively: the beginning and end of the node contents.

Listing 34.7 demonstrates the selectNodeContents() method, when you click the second button.

setEnd()

JavaScript 1.5

Nav6

Syntax

rangeObj.setEnd(*node*, *offset*)

The setEnd() method of Range objects sets the endContainer property to the first argument, a node, and the endOffset property to the second argument, a non-negative integer. Listing 34.1 uses this method in positioning a range.

setEndAfter()

JavaScript 1.5

Nav6

Syntax

rangeObj`.setEndAfter(`*node*`)`

The `setEndAfter()` method of `Range` objects takes one argument, a node, and positions the end boundary point after the node. The parent node of the argument becomes the end container and the offset marks the position after the argument node.

Listing 34.8 demonstrates the `setEndAfter()` method together with the corresponding methods `setEndBefore()`, `setStartBefore()`, and `setStartAfter()`.

Listing 34.8   *Setting Boundary Points Directly*

```
<?xml version="1.0" ?>
<!-- Netscape 6 and other browsers implementing W3C DOM Level 2 range -->
<!DOCTYPE html
     PUBLIC "-//W3C//DTD XHTML 1.0 Transitional//EN"
     "http://www.w3.org/TR/xhtml1/DTD/xhtml1-transitional.dtd">
<html xmlns="http://www.w3.org/1999/xhtml">
<head><title></title>
<style type="text/css">
#d0 {
  border: 1px solid green;
}
</style>
<script type="text/javascript">
var range;
function inspectRange(range) {
  clearOutput();
  var text = 'startContainer: ' + range.startContainer
  if (typeof range.startContainer.id != "undefined") {
    text += '; id: ' + range.startContainer.id
    }
  output(text);
  output('startOffset: ' + range.startOffset);
  text = 'endContainer: ' + range.endContainer
  if (typeof range.endContainer.id != "undefined") {
    text += '; id: ' + range.endContainer.id
    }
```

Listing 34.8   *(continued)*

```
  output(text);
  output('endOffset: ' + range.endOffset);
  output('collapsed: ' + range.collapsed);
  output('text content: ' + range.toString());
  }

function clearOutput() {
  var r = document.createRange();
  r.selectNodeContents(document.getElementById('output'));
  r.deleteContents();
  }

function output(text) {
  var output = document.getElementById('output');
  output.appendChild(document.createTextNode(text));
  output.appendChild(document.createElement('br'));
  }

function guiSelectRange(range) {
  var selection = window.getSelection();
  selection.removeAllRanges();
  selection.addRange(range);
  }

function button1() {
  range.setStartBefore(document.getElementById('p0'));
  inspectRange(range);
  guiSelectRange(range);
  }

function button2() {
  range.setStartAfter(document.getElementById('p0'));
  inspectRange(range);
  guiSelectRange(range);
  }

function button3() {
  range.setEndBefore(document.getElementById('p1'));
  inspectRange(range);
  guiSelectRange(range);
  }
```

Listing 34.8   *(continued)*

```
function button4() {
  range.setEndAfter(document.getElementById('p1'));
  inspectRange(range);
  guiSelectRange(range);
  }

function go() {
  range = document.createRange();
  range.selectNode(document.getElementById('d0'));
  inspectRange(range);
  }
</script>
</head>
<body onload="go()">
<div id="d0"><p id="p0">paragraph 0</p><p id=
➥"p1">paragraph 1</p><p>paragraph 2</p></div>
<input type="button" value="set start before first paragraph"
➥ onclick="button1()" />
<input type="button" value="set start after first paragraph"
➥ onclick="button2()" />
<input type="button" value="set end before second paragraph"
➥ onclick="button3()" />
<input type="button" value="set end after second paragraph"
➥ onclick="button4()" />
<div id="output"></div>
</body>
</html>
```

As opposed to earlier listings, Listing 34.8 uses a global `Range` object. This is so you can test the different methods and see meaningful results.

You can test the `setEndAfter()` method by clicking the fourth button in Listing 34.8.

setEndBefore()

JavaScript 1.5

Nav6

Syntax

rangeObj.setEndBefore(*node*)

The setEndBefore() method of Range objects takes one argument, a node, and positions the end boundary point of the range before the argument node. The parent node of the argument node becomes the end container node, and the end offset marks the position before the argument node.

Listing 34.8 demonstrates this method, when you click the third button.

setStart()
JavaScript 1.5

Nav6

Syntax

```
rangeObj.setStart(node, offset)
```

The setStart() method of Range objects sets the startContainer property to the first argument, a node, and the startOffset property to the second argument, a non-negative integer. Listing 34.1 uses this method in positioning a range.

setStartAfter()
JavaScript 1.5

Nav6

Syntax

```
rangeObj.setStartAfter(node)
```

The setStartAfter() method of Range objects takes one argument, a node, and positions the start boundary point after the argument node. The parent node of the argument node becomes the start container, and the offset marks the position after the argument node.

Listing 34.8 demonstrates this method, when you click the second button.

setStartBefore()
JavaScript 1.5

Nav6

Syntax

```
rangeObj.setStartBefore(node)
```

The `setStartBefore()` method of Range objects takes one argument, a node object, and positions the start boundary point before the argument node. The parent node of the argument node becomes the start container, and the offset marks the position before the argument node.

Listing 34.8 demonstrates this method, when you click the first button.

surroundContents()

Not yet implemented in Nav6 but specified by W3C

Syntax

```
rangeObj.surroundContents(nodeObj);
```

The `surroundContents()` method of Range objects takes one argument, a node, and inserts the node as a parent node of the range's contents. However, if your range contains the beginning or ending tags of an element, but not both tags of the same element, this method will throw an exception.

This powerful method for range manipulation is not supported in Netscape 6.2.

toString()

JavaScript 1.5

Nav6

Syntax

```
var x = rangeObj.toString()
```

The `toString()` method of Range objects returns the current text between the two boundary points of the `this` object as a string value.

If you will recall from Chapter 1, "`Object()`," you do not necessarily need to call this method. If you simply call for the range to become part of a string expression, or if you call the range in a prompt window, `this.toString()` automatically executes.

Listing 34.1 uses the `toString()` method in the `inspectRange()` function to output the text content of the range.

DocumentRange Interface (DOM)

Browser/JavaScript Version	Created By
Nav4/JavaScript 1.2	Not Implemented
IE4/JScript 3.0	Not Implemented
IE5/JScript 5.0	Not Implemented
IE5.5/JScript 5.5	Not Implemented
Nav6/JavaScript 1.5	Document
IE6	Not Implemented
DOM Level 2 Traversal-Range	Document

Description

The DocumentRange interface extends the Document interface, providing one additional method for the document to create ranges.

Properties

The DocumentRange interface provides no additional properties to the Document interface.

Methods

createRange()

JavaScript 1.5

Nav6

Syntax

```
var rangeObj = document.createRange()
```

The createRange() property of document returns a new Range object to the script. The range is collapsed; both start and end container nodes are the Document node, while the start and end offset are 0. This means the range is positioned before all content in the document.

nsISelection Interface

Browser/JavaScript Version	Created By
Nav4/JavaScript 1.2	Not Implemented
IE4/JScript 3.0	Not Implemented
IE5/JScript 5.0	Not Implemented
IE5.5/JScript 5.5	Not Implemented
Nav6/JavaScript 1.5	window.getSelection()
IE6	Not Implemented
DOM	Not Implemented

Description

Throughout this chapter, the listings use a function, guiSelect(), to visualize the contents' selection of a range. Basically, Netscape 6 will select the text in the old definition of the word (you can use cut and paste operations on the selected text).

On the other hand, ranges use the terminology "selecting contents" to mean defining start and end boundary points, not actually selecting those contents for cut and paste operations.

However, the DOM-2 Range specification states that these two definitions of "selection" are interchangeable. A range might result from a user selection, or vice versa.

Netscape 6 implements that with the nsISelection interface. It specifies an object Netscape returns when you call window.getSelection() (which I briefly defined in Chapter 15).

This selection object is based on ranges. However, to account for selections of text in all possible languages, a selection might contain several ranges. You can check how many ranges are in the selection with the rangeCount property.

```
var numberOfRanges = selection.rangeCount;
```

Or, you can access a single range with the method `getRangeAt()`:

```
var selectedRange = selection.getRangeAt(0);
```

This range, and thereby the selection, can then be manipulated with all the methods listed previously in the `Range` interface. Listing 34.9 is an example using `onmouseup` to read the range corresponding to the selection and inspect it.

Listing 34.9   *The Browser Selection as a* `Range` *Object*

```
<?xml version="1.0" ?>
<!-- Netscape 6+ only -->
<!DOCTYPE html
      PUBLIC "-//W3C//DTD XHTML 1.0 Transitional//EN"
      "http://www.w3.org/TR/xhtml1/DTD/xhtml1-transitional.dtd">
<html xmlns="http://www.w3.org/1999/xhtml">
<head><title></title>
<style type="text/css">
#d0 {
  border: 1px solid green;
}
</style>
<script type="text/javascript">
function inspectRange (range) {
  clearOutput();
  var text = 'startContainer: ' + range.startContainer;
  if (typeof range.startContainer.id != "undefined") {
    text += '; id: ' + range.startContainer.id;
    } else {
    text += '; nodeValue: ' + range.startContainer.nodeValue;
    }
  output(text);
  output('startOffset: ' + range.startOffset);
  text = 'endContainer: ' + range.endContainer
  if (typeof range.endContainer.id != "undefined") {
    text += '; id: ' + range.endContainer.id
    } else {
    text += '; nodeValue: ' + range.endContainer.nodeValue
    }
  output(text)
  output('endOffset: ' + range.endOffset);
  output('text content: ' + range.toString());
  }
```

Listing 34.9   *(continued)*

```javascript
function clearOutput () {
  var range = document.createRange();
  range.selectNodeContents(document.getElementById('output'));
  range.deleteContents();
  }

function output (text) {
  var output = document.getElementById('output');
  output.appendChild(document.createTextNode(text));
  output.appendChild(document.createElement('br'));
  }

function button1() {
  var selection = window.getSelection();
  if (selection.rangeCount) {
    var range = selection.getRangeAt(0);
    if (range.endContainer.nodeType == 1) {
      range.setEndAfter(range.endContainer.lastChild);
      } else if (range.endContainer.nodeType == 3) {
      range.setEnd(range.endContainer, range.endContainer.nodeValue.length);
      }
    }
  }

function button2() {
  var selection = window.getSelection();
  if (selection.rangeCount) {
    var range = selection.getRangeAt(0);
    range.deleteContents();
    }
  }

document.onmouseup = function (evt) {
  var selection = window.getSelection();
  if (selection.rangeCount) {
    inspectRange(selection.getRangeAt(0));
    }
  }
</script>
</head>
<body>
<h3>select some contents with the mouse</h3>
```

Listing 34.9 *(continued)*

```
<div id="d0"><p id="p0">paragraph 0</p><p id="p1">paragraph 1</p><p>paragraph
2</p></div>
<form action="javascript:void()">
<input type="button" value="extend selection to end of endContainer"
  onclick="button1()" />
<input type="button" value="remove selection" onclick="button2()" />
</form>
<div style="border: 1px solid purple">
<h3>range inspection output</h3>
<div id="output"></div>
</body>
</html>
```

When running Listing 34.9 in Netscape 6, you can select some text in the page with the mouse. Then, onmouseup, the browser inspects the range corresponding to the selection, as in Listing 34.1.

The two buttons are examples on manipulation of a range from the selection object. The first button extends the selection to the end of the endContainer by using the setEndAfter method or the setEnd method of the range.

> **Note**
> With Netscape 6.2, the change only becomes visible when you blur the window and refocus it.

The second button deletes the selected contents by calling the deleteContents() method of the range.

You can also make a range the current selection. The guiSelectRange() function from Listing 34.1 does that:

```
function guiSelectRange (range) {
  var selection = window.getSelection();
  selection.removeAllRanges();
  selection.addRange(range);
  }
```

As you can see, the function accesses the selection in the window. Then it removes all ranges in the selection by calling the removeAllRanges method. Finally it adds its first argument, a range passed to the function, to the selection by calling the addRange() method.

You have already experienced the results of that function if you have tried Listing 34.1 or several other listings in this chapter.

Properties

rangeCount
JavaScript 1.5

Nav6

Syntax

```
var numberOfRanges = window.getSelection().rangeCount;
```

The rangeCount property of nsISelection objects gives the number of ranges in the selection. For Western languages, there is usually exactly one range in the selection. This might differ for other languages.

Methods

addRange()
JavaScript 1.5

Nav 6

Syntax

```
selectionObj.addRange(rangeObj);
```

The addRange() method of nsISelection objects takes one argument, a Range object, and adds it to the current selection.

getRangeAt()
JavaScript 1.5

Nav6

Syntax

```
var range = window.getSelection().getRangeAt(rangeIndex) ;
```

The getRangeAt() method of nsISelection objects takes one argument, a non-negative integer indicating a zero-based index, and returns the Range object with that index in the selection.

In a sense, this is similar to the item() method of NodeList objects (see Chapter 20).

You should check the rangeCount property of this before to make sure you pass in an existing index.

removeAllRanges()

JavaScript 1.5

Nav6

Syntax

```
window.getSelection().removeAllRanges();
```

The removeAllRanges() method of nsISelection objects removes all ranges from the selection. It clears the selection in the process.

removeRange()

JavaScript 1.5

Nav6

Syntax

```
window.getSelection().removeRange(rangeObj);
```

The removeRange() method of nsISelection objects takes one argument, a Range object, and removes that range from the selection.

toString()

JavaScript 1.5

Nav6

Syntax

```
var selectedText = window.getSelection().toString();
```

The toString() method of nsISelection objects returns the selected text as a string.

CHAPTER 35
Cookies

Cookies are easily one of the "dark horses" of JavaScript. They are snippets of information the browser stores for the Web domain name they come from. They can be exceptionally useful, if the client browser has them enabled. Not everybody likes them, however; not the developer, not the end-user.

Cookies can store strings for the next time a site from that particular domain appears again in the browser. They thus offer what almost no other feature of JavaScript offers—persistent storage of data. However, quite a few businesses have misused cookies in the past. Hence, not everybody trusts them. Often it's better to use server-side code for business purposes.

> **Note**
> Internet Explorer does support a few proprietary behaviors for persistence of data, particularly `userData`. See `http://msdn.microsoft.com/workshop/author/persistence/overview.asp` for details.

I'm not saying cookies should be a last resort; there are times when having a cookie to read can be exceptionally useful. Session cookies, which end when you close out your browser, can spare you a lot of code in trying to send and receive information (as I cover in Chapters 15 and 16, "window" and "location," respectively). If your site requires cookies and you make this clear to your visitors, by all means trust they will be there and use them. (I'll provide a listing on this a little bit later.)

For the record, I want to express my thanks to John Krutsch, a fellow JavaScript Programming Help Forum moderator at Website Abstraction. John contributed a lot of expertise to this chapter, and in much of this chapter you'll be reading his words instead of mine. (He's much stronger at cookies than I am, and I'm not afraid to say it.)

Cookies, HTTP, and JavaScript

When working with Web pages, you constantly employ the use of the HyperText Transport Protocol (HTTP), a stateless protocol. This means once you make a request from the server and the server responds to that request, the slate is wiped clean and the browser cannot remember anything from the previous page. Cookies provide a way for the browser to remember this information between requests.

> **Note**
> After a Web file leaves the server, the server effectively forgets about it (it has a lot of other files to serve). Cookies and forms become doubly important in this aspect: to remind the server which client is which, when attached to an HTTP request.

There are two types of cookies to help achieve this, the session cookie and the persistent cookie. A session cookie lasts only as long as the current browser session. As soon as the browser shuts down, the cookies are forgotten. However, until then you can access them at any time.

A persistent cookie has the potential to last much longer. This type of cookie survives because the browser stores the cookie on the client hard drive. (This may be a bit alarming, but the restrictions on cookies are quite severe. For the most part a cookie by itself is harmless. It is how a Web page uses them that provides the security risk.) The client browser sends them back to the server when the URL path matches the path stored with the cookie.

The browser destroys persistent cookies only when the user explicitly deletes it, when it reaches the expiration date you explicitly set, or in some cases, when the browser reaches its limit on the amount of cookies it can store.

> **Note**
>
> You can read and manipulate cookies both from the client and the server. The focus of this book is on client-side JavaScript, of course, but most server-side programming language books (such as the *PHP Developer's Dictionary* from Sams Publishing) include functions or sections on manipulating cookies from the server. This can be useful as well.

The document.cookie property, which I mention briefly in Chapter 23, "HTMLDocument/document," is unique. It is a collection, but not the kind of collection you've seen elsewhere in this book. To JavaScript, it reflects a string of all currently set cookie *name* = *value* pairs for the document (not when they expire, however). Ironically, setting document.cookie to a particular *name* = *value* string does not eliminate other cookies in the document; it merely appends to the current list of them. Furthermore, as Listing 35.1 demonstrates, you're only allowed to set one *name* = *value* pair per statement.

Listing 35.1 *Setting a Basic Cookie*

```
<?xml version="1.0" ?>
<!-- Netscape 6, Internet Explorer 5.0+ only -->
<!DOCTYPE html PUBLIC "-//W3C//DTD XHTML 1.0 Transitional//EN"
➥"DTD/xhtml1-transitional.dtd">
<html xmlns="http://www.w3.org/1999/xhtml" >
<head><title></title>
<script language="JavaScript" type="text/javascript">
<!--
function go() {
    document.cookie = "roses = red;violets = blue;"
    document.cookie = "dandelions = yellow;"
```

Listing 35.1   *(continued)*

```
    var p = document.createElement('p')
    p.appendChild(document.createTextNode(document.cookie))
    document.body.appendChild(p)
    }
//-->
</script>
</head>
<body onload="go()">
<!-- Results:
roses=red; dandelions=yellow
-->
</body>
</html>
```

If you run this code from a Web server that sets its own cookies, you'll find the cookies for the server as well in `document.cookie`. (This is an unavoidable side effect.)

Also, the `document.cookie.length` property reflects only the length of the `document.cookie` string; it is not an array of the cookies for the document.

The Syntax of Cookies

Setting a cookie in JavaScript includes one required section and several optional ones:

```
document.cookie = "name=value[; expires=GMTDate][; domain=domainName]
➥[; path=pathName][; secure]"
```

As elsewhere in this book, arguments within square brackets ([]) are optional. Each of these optional arguments has a default value if omitted.

name = value

The *name* = *value* syntax is most similar to the HTTP GET method (which I mention briefly in Chapter 25, "Form Elements").

The *name* of a cookie is a string of (almost) any characters designating the cookie's name. When naming your cookies, you need to take some things into consideration. The use of semicolons, commas, or whitespace is not allowed. If you plan on using these in the *name* of your cookie, run them through the `escape()` or `escapeURIComponent()` functions (covered in Chapter 11, "The Global Object and Statements").

When naming cookies, use alphanumeric (A–Z, a–z, 0–9) characters and possibly the underscore (_) character for the sake of readability. There are almost no reserved words or variable name limits when assigning cookie names. "Fred", "All_Your_Base", and "Ali92" would all be valid cookie names. (The exceptions are "expires", "domain", "path", and "secure", each of which defines a particular statistic about the cookie.)

The `value` of a cookie is also a string of any characters without semicolons, commas, or whitespace, designating the value of the cookie. Again, if you plan on using semicolons, commas, or whitespace as part of your value, run it through the `escape()` or `escapeURIComponent()` function (covered in Chapter 11, "The Global Object and Statements").

The `name` and `value` strings together can be no more than 4KB per cookie. You cannot set the `value` of a cookie to `undefined` or `null`, but you can set it to `""`. `"rock"`, `"hello%20world"`, and `""` are all valid cookie values.

expires = *UTCDateString*

The `expires` argument of a cookie indicates when the cookie should expire. Setting the `expires` argument is optional. If you omit this argument, the cookie will expire at the end of the current browser session. (This defines it as a session cookie.) If you want your cookies to be persistent, assign a value to the `expires` argument.

This value needs to be in Universal Coordinated Time, which you can easily set using JavaScript's `toGMTString()` or `toUTCString()` methods of `Date()` objects (see Chapter 6, "Date()").:

```
var x = new Date();
x.setMonth(x.getMonth() + 1);
x = (x.toGMTString() || x.toUTCString())
document.cookie = "roses = red;expires = " + x + ";"
```

domain = domainURLString

The `domain` argument of a cookie indicates the domain name to which the cookie belongs. In most cases, the domain argument isn't used because it defaults to the domain of the cookie's document. In some cases, however, you may want to be able to access your cookie on other pages that reside in different domains on the same server. To allow this, simply remove the characters of the domain name that restrict your cookie's domain scope.

Consider this example:

```
http://www.example.code.com
```

A cookie created with its domain attribute set to .code.com will be readable from any of the documents in the "example" domain as well as the "code" domain. If the domain attribute was set to .example.code.com, only documents within the "example" domain would be able to see the cookie.

When specifying the value of the domain attribute, the leading full stop is necessary when not specifying a fully qualified domain name. You must specify at least two levels of the domain name.

```
document.cookie = "violets = blue;domain = jslab.org;"
```

path = *pathName*

The path argument of a cookie indicates to the Web server which part of its directory structure uses the cookie. Paths represent directories, not the individual files in those directories. When setting the path for a cookie, use forward slashes ("/") instead of back slashes ("\"). Avoid the use of trailing slashes also.

The domain root directory can be indicated by a zero-length string, "", or the traditional "/". If not given, the path of the document setting the cookie is the default value.

The following forces the path to the jsdd directory:

```
document.cookie = "violets = blue; domain = jslab.org;path = /jsdd;"
```

secure

The secure attribute, when specified, sets the cookie as a restricted cookie. This means it is for use only with connections employing Secure Socket Layer (SSL) protection through the https:// protocol. Otherwise, the cookie will be accessible to nonsecure documents as well. (SSL is beyond the scope of this book; in a nutshell, it refers to encryption and signed documents.)

Using Cookies

When you request the cookies for a specific document, you receive a list of semicolon-separated *name=value* pairs. To see if a Web page has any cookies set for it, type the following code into the location bar:

```
javascript:alert(document.cookie.replace(/;/g,"\n"))
```

Listing 35.2 extracts all the cookies for the document into an array.

John Krutsch's Cookie Jar

Listing 35.2 *An Array of Cookies*

```
<?xml version="1.0" ?>
<!DOCTYPE html PUBLIC "-//W3C//DTD XHTML 1.0 Transitional//EN"
➥"DTD/xhtml1-transitional.dtd">
<html xmlns="http://www.w3.org/1999/xhtml" >
<head><title></title></head>
<body>
<script language="JavaScript" type="text/javascript">
<!--
function go() {
    document.cookie = "trees = green;"
    document.cookie = "roses = red;"
    document.cookie = "violets = blue;"
    var cookies = document.cookie.split(";")
    var HTML = ""

    for (var index = 0; index < cookies.length; index++) {
        HTML += cookies[index] + "<br />\n"
        }
    document.write(HTML)
    }

go()
//-->
</script>

<!-- Results:
trees=green
roses=red
violets=blue
-->
</body>
</html>
```

John Krutsch's Cookie Jar

The key to using cookies effectively relies upon the cookie functions you use.
Experienced JavaScripters can create their own functions to read and manipulate
cookies. John Krutsch, for instance, prefers to use his set of cookie functions, which he

has graciously donated for this book. Pay close attention to the documentation within the code; it explains what each function cdoes.

Listing 35.3   *Standard Functions For Setting, Getting, and Deleting Cookies*

```
<?xml version="1.0" ?>
<!DOCTYPE html PUBLIC "-//W3C//DTD XHTML 1.0 Transitional//EN"
➥ "DTD/xhtml1-transitional.dtd">
<html xmlns="http://www.w3.org/1999/xhtml" >
<head><title></title>
<script language="JavaScript" type="text/javascript">
<!--// The Cookie Jar
////// Standard Functions for Setting, Getting, and Deleting Cookies
////// John Krutsch, john@xcentrixlc.com

/* Alterations by Alexander J. Vincent (Nov. 2001)

(1) Streamlined comments.
(2) Unescape cookie values in GetCookie added.
(3) Added alerts and "escape hatch" returns for missing required arguments.
*/

/*
To set a cookie pass in the name, value SetCookie("name", "value")
The 'name' and 'value' are the only required arguments.

If you want the cookie to persist past the current browser session, you can
specify the length of time you want to store the cookie in milliseconds:
SetCookie("name", "value", 15768000000) would store the cookie for six months.

When working with milliseconds you can calculate very specific expiration
dates; for example, you would calculate one month of milliseconds like so:

31 * 24 * 60 * 60 * 1000=2678400000

By omitting the expiration date the cookie will only last for the current
browser session.

To specify the domain which can use and affect this cookie specify it as
the fourth argument:

SetCookie("name", "value", 15768000000, ".xcentrixlc.com")
```

Listing 35.3 *(continued)*

```
If the domain argument is omitted the domain of the document that set the
cookie will be used.

To specify the path which can use and affect this cookie specify it as the
fifth argument:

SetCookie("name", "value", 15768000000, ".xcentrixlc.com", "/myPath")

If the path argument is omitted the path of the document that set the
cookie will be used.

To set a secure cookie simply set the flag to true by including it as the
sixth argument:

SetCookie("name", "value", 15768000000, ".xcentrixlc.com", "/myPath",1)

If the secure argument is omitted the default of false is used.

To get or delete a cookie simply pass in the name of the cookie you want
to affect

GetCookie("name")
DeleteCookie("name")

If you ask for a cookie that does not exist it will return "".
*/

function GetCookie(cookieName) {
    if (arguments.length < 1) {
        alert("Not enough arguments!");
        return false;
    }
    var regX = new RegExp("\\b" + escape(cookieName) + "=([^;]*)");
    var found = regX.exec(document.cookie);
    return (found) ? unescape(found[1]): false;
}

function SetCookie(name, value, expires, domain, path, secure) {
    if (arguments.length < 2) {
        alert("Not enough arguments!");
        return false;
```

Part III Document Object Model for HTML Documents

Listing 35.3 *(continued)*

```javascript
    }

    var cstr = escape(name) + "=" + escape(value);

    if (expires>0){
        var expdate = new Date();
        expdate.setTime(expdate.getTime() + expires);
        expdate = expdate.toGMTString();
        cstr+="; expires=" + expdate;
    }

    if(domain) cstr+="; domain=" + domain;
    if(path || path=="") cstr+="; path=" + path;
    if(secure) cstr+="; secure";

    document.cookie = cstr;
}

function DeleteCookie(name) {
    if (arguments.length < 1) {
        alert("Not enough arguments!");
        return false;
    }

    var exp = new Date();
    exp.setTime(exp.getTime() - 1000 * 60 * 60 * 24);
    document.cookie = escape(name)+"="+escape(name)+";
expires="+exp.toGMTString();
}

//-->
</script>
</head>
<body>
<script language="JavaScript" type="text/javascript">
<!--
document.write("<p>Adding author cookie...</p>\n")

SetCookie("author", "Alex Vincent")
```

Listing 35.3 *(continued)*

```
document.write("<p>Author:" + GetCookie("author") + "</p>\n")

document.write("<p>Removing author cookie...</p>\n")
DeleteCookie("author")

document.write("<p>Author:" + GetCookie("author") + "</p>\n")
//-->
</script>
<!-- Results:
Adding author cookie...

Author:Alex Vincent

Removing author cookie...

Author:
-->
</body>
</html>
```

Best Practices for Using Cookies

Different browsers impose different limitations on cookies. Always keep these standard restrictions according to RFC 2109 ("HTTP State Management Mechanism", `http://www.ietf.org/rfc/rfc2109.txt`) in mind:

- 300 total cookies

- 4KB per cookie, for the sum of both the cookie's name and value.

- 20 cookies per server or domain (completely specified hosts and domains are treated as separate entities and have a 20-cookie limitation for each, not combined).

- Users can turn cookies off or disallow them on a case-by-case basis.

Cookies are a useful resource. However, when you take their limitations into consideration, they can hardly be considered the panacea of data persistence. This is especially true if your only need for them is to employ the use of session cookies.

You can check to see if a user has his browser set up to accept cookies. This can also help you decide if you should set a cookie or use an alternative method. In Internet Explorer 4.0+ and in Netscape 6.0+, you can use the `navigator.cookieEnabled` property (covered in Chapter 18, "navigator") to determine whether cookies are enabled.

For Netscape 4 (and for backward-compatibility), set a cookie, and then check for its existence. If the cookie exists, you can assume the browser will accept cookies. (I do this in Listing 35.3.)

Once again, if a user disallows cookies, you have the option of using frames (Chapter 15, "window"), pop-up windows (Chapter 15, "window"), or the `location` object (Chapter 16, "location").

PART IV

The Future

CHAPTER 36

XML-Related Technologies and Their DOMs

I stated in the Introduction we are in a transitional period. We are transitioning in Web technologies from HTML to XML and HTML's twin brother, XHTML. This affects JavaScripters because XML documents have the Core DOM (see Chapter 20, "Core DOM Objects") available to us, and more than one such technology has its own Document Object Model extension.

I call them technologies, but they are for the most part just XML languages for which the various browsers have started implementations. These implementations are the cutting edge of Web design as I write this, the basis for these new technologies.

I will, in wrapping up this book, mention at least one standards-compliant way to associate a JavaScript with an XML document. There are some non-standard ways to do this as well (think of an XML document wrapped inside an HTML document). But before we get to that, there's a sizable amount of background to cover.

> **Note**
> XML is primarily meant as a standard for exchanging information between applications. As such, its scope goes well beyond Web browsers. This chapter restricts its approach to XML to Web browsers. JavaScript becomes available in a few limited contexts.

Note the examples in this chapter are just that: examples. In each case, I strongly recommend you make your own independent study of each subject. That's why I'm writing this final chapter, to introduce to you technologies you should keep your eye on, and be excited about. (If I've left one or two out, please accept my apologies.)

XML 1.0

XML stands for the eXtensible Markup Language specification, a document describing how to write an XML language and an XML document. There are actually two intermixed portions of the XML 1.0 Recommendation from the W3C. One of them is validation by Document Type Definition files, which I cover in the next section. The other is well-formedness, a relatively new concept in Web design.

Well-formedness is mainly a concept of crossing your t's and dotting your i's. It's an attempt to make sure your documents follow a particular format as closely as possible, without imposing too many strict rules on the document.

Elements

Elements with child nodes must have both an opening tag and a closing tag. For instance, if you have text in a paragraph, a `<p>` tag must precede the text, and a `</p>` tag must follow the text.

Elements without child nodes may close themselves using a slash inside the opening tag, and thus omit the closing tag. The image element you write in XHTML as `<img src="imgfile.gif" />`.

Attributes

Attributes in XML take a *name*="*value*" format, like HTML does. The difference here is XML requires this format; HTML makes it optional, allowing for attributes to simply be a *name*. You are permitted to use single quotes in place of double quotes, but they must match (no *name*='*value*", for instance) for a valid attribute name.

Document Structure

XML documents must have exactly one root element. This element, in the Core DOM, is considered `document.documentElement`. In XHTML documents this would be the `<html>...</html>` element. You are forbidden from having two `<html>...</html>` elements at the same level of the hierarchy. The same concept applies, more generally, to XML documents.

You may prefix the root element with a "prolog" of an optional XML declaration, followed by various comments and processing instructions, whitespace, an optional document type declaration, and more comments and or processing instructions.

I will explain the XML declaration in a moment. Comments are the same as in HTML. Document type declarations, or doctype tags, specify by name the root element of the document, a location where the DTD file for validating the XML document resides, and an optional short string describing the language the DTD file defines. You've seen dozens of XHTML 1.0 Transitional's document type tags throughout this book:

```
<!DOCTYPE html PUBLIC "-//W3C//DTD XHTML 1.0 Transitional//EN"
➥"http://www.w3.org/TR/xhtml1/DTD/xhtml1-transitional.dtd">
```

> **Note**
> This is the complete URI for the XHTML 1.0 Transitional DTD. Throughout this book, I've used the abbreviation the W3C uses.

The `PUBLIC` keyword means the next part will be a human-readable string describing the language, and the part following is the location of the actual DTD file. If the `SYSTEM` keyword is used instead, the human-readable string is omitted:

```
<!DOCTYPE html SYSTEM "DTD/xhtml1-transitional.dtd">
```

You can also include preemptive modifications to the document type definition by enclosing them in brackets:

```
<!DOCTYPE html SYSTEM "DTD/xhtml1-transitional.dtd"
[<!ENTITY % Hello "World">
]>
```

Processing instructions in XML follow the format `<?target ...?>`. For instance, I send instructions to PHP via the `<?php ... ?>` processing instruction. The XML declaration tag is a special exclusion to processing instructions. It resembles a processing instruction, except its target is `xml`. You've seen this tag dozens of times as well in this book:

```
<?xml version="1.0" ?>
```

The XML 1.0 specification restricts the targets available for processing instructions, but only slightly. You cannot use a processing instruction beginning with the characters "X," "M," and "L," in that order without it being a W3C-approved processing instruction. (To date, there are only two such sequences approved: `<?xml ?>` and `<?xml-stylesheet ?>`.)

The XML 1.0 specification is much more strict about what can come before the XML declaration tag: nothing. No spaces, no carriage returns, nothing.

> **Note**
> This presents an obvious problem for some server-side code developers, who often like to send HTTP headers from within a script. The problem is HTTP headers must be sent before anything in the document itself, such as an XML declaration tag. One workaround, perfectly valid, is to omit the XML declaration tag. I describe another on my Web site, at `http:// www.jslab.org/articles/php+xml.html`.

Any content not inside a markup tag (but always between markup tags of elements) is considered character data. This includes all the text of a document, for instance. You can also use the XML `<![CDATA[...]]>` tags to define a character data section, where any markup tags become character data as well. The browser applies no special rendering to character data, except what it inherits from the character data's parent node.

Netscape 6 and Internet Explorer 5.0+ have excellent parsers for well-formedness in documents. Netscape by default renders no elements, exposing an XML document via the Core DOM. Internet Explorer offers a default stylesheet that transforms the XML into HTML, if the XML document does not have a style sheet associated with it. The style sheet allows for color coding of various features of the language, and for collapsing the document's contents by element.

DTD

Here's where things get a little dicey. Document Type Definition files, or DTDs, loosely define the language of an XML document. From a browser perspective, DTDs give us something to check the document against for validity. A well-formed XML document not matching the constraints of a DTD associated with it is considered invalid. (At this time, neither Internet Explorer nor Netscape browsers validate using the DTD.)

I, as a Web page developer, look at DTDs in a different way. I use them as a way to define the basic structure of an XML language, from which I can construct numerous XML documents as I see fit. In a sense, they become notes for me. Of course, if an XML document I generate does not validate against its corresponding DTD, then I did something wrong—either in generating the XML document, or in the DTD file.

Elements

Defining an element is a two-step process. The first step is to name the child nodes the element may have. You accomplish this with a DTD `<!ELEMENT >` tag. Here's a couple tag>sample tags of this sort:

```
<!ELEMENT datacell (input, op, input, output*)>
<!ELEMENT output (#PCDATA)>
```

`#PCDATA` is an abbreviation for parsed character data. Basically, this means text. More importantly, any entities you have in the XML document it transforms via the DTD, and any markup is treated as markup.

The other `<!ELEMENT >` tag above defines a specific sequence of elements: one `<input />` element, followed by one `<op />` element, followed by one `<input />` element, followed by any number of `<output />` elements.

Following a child element name with `*` means any number of that element. A + means one or more of that element, and a ? means zero or one of that element. A | character means either what precedes that character or what follows it. A set of parentheses containing elements you can treat as an element itself, with regards to these special characters. This means (input | output)* indicates any ordering of `<input />` and `<output />` elements, in any number, for example.

Note this does not define these child elements as empty elements; you do that with the keyword EMPTY instead of any child element declarations:

```
<!ELEMENT nochildren EMPTY>
```

Similarly, using the keyword ANY in this place defines the tag as placing no constraints on whatever child elements and character data it may have.

Attributes

The second tag>step to defining an element is defining the attributes the element may have. You do this with a DTD `<!ATTLIST >` tag.

```
<!ATTLIST output
    source CDATA #REQUIRED
    timestamp CDATA #REQUIRED
    >
```

The first word following `!ATTLIST` names the element with which you are associating attributes. Each following line, until the end of the tag, defines attribute names, basic types, whether they will be required or implied for validity, and a possible default value.

The first word of any such attribute name line is the attribute name. This you then follow with a keyword or a set of acceptable values.

Keywords include CDATA for unparsed character data (markup inside an attribute is treated as character data, not markup), ID for an attribute that uniquely identifies the element (think `document.getElementById()` in Chapter 20, "Core DOM Objects"), and IDREF for an attribute referring to another element by its ID. A few other options are ENTITY for names of parsed entities the DTD defines, ENTITIES for whitespace separated entity names, NMTOKEN for a name token (a subset of character data restricted mainly to letters, numbers, and a few punctuation marks), and NMTOKENS for whitespace separated name tokens. One last keyword is NOTATION, which refers to a notation in the DTD.

You can define permissible values much like you define choices between elements: with a set of parentheses containing valid values, separated by a | character.

```
color (red | blue | green) #IMPLIED
```

After the acceptable values or keyword, you use `#REQUIRED` to indicate the XML document must have the attribute in question, or `#IMPLIED` to suggest the XML document may have the attribute in question. You may then include a default value following the `#REQUIRED` or `#IMPLIED` if you wish.

> **Note**
> XML 1.0 also permits a `#FIXED` keyword, where the next word, in quotes, designates a mandatory setting for the attribute value.

Entities

Entities are tag>defined or referenced with the `<!ENTITY >` tag. HTML and XML support a few known parsed entities already. From XML 1.0, you get the following entities (I've added the comments to explain what they are)

```
<!ENTITY lt      "&#38;#60;"> <!-- < character -->
<!ENTITY gt      "&#62;">      <!-- > character -->
<!ENTITY amp     "&#38;#38;"> <!-- & character -->
<!ENTITY apos    "&#39;">      <!-- ' character -->
<!ENTITY quot    "&#34;">      <!-- " character -->
```

You use them in an XML document like you would in an HTML document. When you want to say `<hello />` literally, you mark that up as `&lt;hello /&gt;`. Parsed entities do not apply inside a character data section, however.

> **Note**
> XML 1.0 also allows you to refer to individual character entities, as it does above, by the ampersand sign, followed by the pound sign, followed by either an x and a hexadecimal number, or ordinary digits alone without the x. These allow reference to Unicode characters. (The official character set name is ISO/IEC 10646 for these entities.)

You can also reference entities in other DTD files using the `PUBLIC` and `SYSTEM` keywords. A sample, again from XML 1.0, is as follows:

```
<!ENTITY open-hatch
        PUBLIC "-//Textuality//TEXT Standard open-hatch boilerplate//EN"
        "http://www.textuality.com/boilerplate/OpenHatch.xml">
```

The `PUBLIC` and `SYSTEM` keywords designate human-readable and URI strings for the entity location, just as they do for `<!DOCTYPE >` tags. However, in the file you reference by URI, there must be another entity by that name which defines it.

Another form of entity is the parameter entity, exclusively for use within DTD files. These you create by prefixing the entity name with a percentage sign and a space (`% `). You then reference them as the percentage sign, followed by the name of the entity, and then a semicolon (`%entityName;`). You can also have them in external files, as I described previously.

You can use entities as portions of the value of other entities as well. However, entities are prohibited from ultimately referencing themselves. Sooner or later, each entity must have a final explicit value defined for it.

One thing to note about entities: after you define them, or anything else in a DTD for that matter, later revisions do not override their values. The earliest incidence of an entity name takes priority over any later definitions. (This is the reverse of traditional programming approaches, which assume the last instance of an object name encountered during execution takes priority.)

Conditional Sections

Entities, and the capability to define them early with an overriding value, come in handy in creating conditional sections of a DTD. A conditional section of a DTD will take effect if it is enclosed in `<![INCLUDE[...]]>` tags. It will not take effect if it is enclosed in `<![IGNORE[...]]>` tags.

Consider the following, then:

```
<!ENTITY % includeSection "IGNORE" >
<![%includeSection;[
<!ATTLIST shirt
    color (red | blue | green) #IMPLIED
    >
]]>
<!ATTLIST shirt
    size (small | medium | large) #IMPLIED
    >
```

As is, the `<shirt />` element would have only one attribute, `size`. But if the `<!DOCTYPE>` tag included an entity that set the `%includeSection;` entity to `"INCLUDE"`

```
<!DOCTYPE shirt SYSTEM "http://www.jslab.org/doctypes/shirt"
[<!ENTITY % includeSection "INCLUDE">
]>
```

Then the `<shirt />` element would allow two attributes, `color` and `size`.

Netscape 6 currently ignores document type declarations and DTD files; Internet Explorer will load only the DTD file named in a document type declaration. Internet Explorer ignores external entities that the DTD file references, which is why XHTML 1.1, another W3C Recommendation, does not work in Internet Explorer.

XHTML 1.0: eXtensible HyperText Markup Language

XHTML 1.0 is HTML 4.01 rebuilt as an XML language. By enforcing XHTML compliance, you enforce a stable and reproducible Document Object Model across multiple browser platforms.

There are some specific features to XHTML you should be aware of. For instance, the requirements of XML have led the HTML working group to recast XHTML as entirely lowercase. XML is not as forgiving of case differences as HTML: `<html>` and `<HTML>` would be the same tag in HTML, but different tags in XML.

Here, in Listing 36.1, is a minimally compliant XHTML document I've used as a template throughout the writing of this book.

Listing 36.1   *minXHTML.xml*

```
<?xml version="1.0" ?>
<!DOCTYPE html PUBLIC "-//W3C//DTD XHTML 1.0 Transitional//EN"
➥ "DTD/xhtml1-transitional.dtd">
<html xmlns="http://www.w3.org/1999/xhtml" >
<head><title></title></head>
<body>
</body>
</html>
```

Given the complexity of the first three lines, I think you can understand why I use a template…technically, the XML declaration tag `<?xml version="1.0" ?>` is not required, but I leave it in there for good measure. You could also technically compress the `<title></title>` and `<body></body>` elements into `<title />` and `<body />`, respectively, but that leads to unexpected problems in Internet Explorer. (Besides, there are very few XHTML documents with an empty body.)

A few features about XHTML: all the elements and attributes are lowercase and must be closed. (No more `<img src="me">` tags without `</img>` or rewriting as `<img src="me.gif" />`.) Attributes which in HTML could be simply *name* now must be *name*="*name*". (This reflects in the DOM as a property name with a value of `true`. Without that attribute, the corresponding property has a value of `false`.) Every attribute value must have a pair of single quotes or a pair of double quotes around it.

There are some funny effects with a couple other changes. For instance, XML allows an XML parser to completely ignore comment sections. Every listing in this book comments out JavaScript source code. So, every XHTML listing in this book, viewed

as XML, you cannot expect to work. The workaround for that is to use
`<![CDATA[...]]>` tags in place of `<!--...-->` tags. You pretty much have to do this
anyway, as the first < character in your script will cause your script to break, due to the
rules of XML.

When you serve the document again as HTML with the `<![CDATA[...]]>` tags
though, this causes a JavaScript error.

Note

This discrepancy is the source of some debate at Mozilla.org. See bug #27403 at
`http://bugzilla.mozilla.org`.

In the meantime, I recommend you outsource your JavaScripts into library files and use the
`src` attribute of `<script></script>` elements. (Internet Explorer expects a closing tag for
script elements as well.) XML treats event handlers, which are attributes, as character data
and permits markup characters directly.

Also, as I note in Chapter 33, "Styling for HTML Elements," Internet Explorer
receiving XHTML as XML will ignore the HTML aspects of it entirely. You can see
my workaround for that at `http://www.jslab.org/articles/XHTML_IE.xml`.

One other nice fact about XHTML is it has a special mime-type specific to it,
`application/xhtml+xml`. This signifies to a browser that it is both HTML and XML
at the same time: XHTML. However, support for this mime-type in current browsers,
especially for the DOM, is stronger for the Core DOM than it is for the HTML
DOM.

Namespaces in XML

One fact the original XML 1.0 Recommendation overlooked was mixing multiple
XML languages in the same document. This may not seem like much of a problem at
first, until you realize two XML languages may have the same name for two different
elements.

For instance, SVG (a language I cover later in this chapter) includes a
`<font>...</font>` element, which differs significantly from the XHTML
`<font>...</font>` element (especially because the XHTML version is deprecated, and
the SVG version is not).

The W3C compensated for this with its Namespaces in XML Recommendation,
which you can find at `http://www.w3.org/TR/REC-xml-names`.

What is a namespace, anyway? A namespace is a URI to which all elements within a particular XML language can point. It does not need to point to an existing file; in many cases, it's simply a string to separate and distinguish its associated language from all others.

The namespaces in XML Recommendation introduce a new attribute. The new attribute is xmlns. This attribute indicates the default namespace of the document. For instance, the official namespace for XHTML is in the third line of Listing 36.1:

```
<html xmlns="http://www.w3.org/1999/xhtml" >
```

A qualified name is a prefix followed by a colon followed by the element name local to its native language. Elements and attributes may have qualified names. For instance, we could say an <img /> element from XHTML had a prefix of html and rename the element <html:img />.

As for associating the prefix with the namespace, the Namespaces in XML Recommendation also creates an xmlns namespace. You use the prefix you want for your document elements as the local name for the xmlns namespace in the document root element. Listing 36.2 shows two namespaces in the same XML document.

Listing 36.2   *Namespaces and Prefixes*

```
<?xml version="1.0" ?>
<a:root xmlns:a="http://www.jslab.org/namespaces/a"
        xmlns:b="http://www.jslab.org/namespaces/b"
        >
<!-- Note the xmlns:a attribute defining a namespace for all elements using
"a:" as a prefix. This includes a:root, the root element of the document.
The xmlns:b attribute defines a namespace for all elements using "b:" as a
prefix. -->
  <a:elem color="red">
    <a:empty size="0" />
    <b:test color="blue" a:type="foreign">
<!-- The b:test element comes inside a different namespace. The color
attribute of this element applies to the "b" namespace. The a:type attribute
applies to the "a" namespace.  -->
    </b:test>
<!-- We close out the element using the full prefix and local name.  -->
  </a:elem>
</a:root>
```

For every element properly namespaced, only the attributes not belonging to that namespace need their own namespace prefix. Similarly, any element in the same namespace as the root element may omit the namespace prefix and colon (and the root element may itself omit its namespace prefix and colon).

Listing 36.3 is almost the same as the minimal XHTML document, but with namespaces in place. (Served as text/html, the paragraph is normal. As XML, Netscape gives it the correct HTML italic.)

> **Note**
> Technically, Listing 36.3 is not XHTML 1.1, which I describe a little later in this chapter. According to a literal reading of the XHTML 1.1 specification, the root element may not have a name of `html:html`, but only `html`. (XHTML 1.1 Recommendation, Section 2.2.1)
>
> However, it is valid XML, and it does conform to the Modularization of XHTML Recommendation. Without the namespaces, it would be XHTML 1.1. It is my opinion that the omission of namespaces in this sense is an error in the specification.

Listing 36.3   *Namespaces and XHTML*

```
<?xml version="1.0" encoding="iso-8859-1"?>
<!DOCTYPE html:html PUBLIC "-//W3C//DTD XHTML 1.1//EN"
 "http://www.w3.org/TR/xhtml11/DTD/xhtml11.dtd" [
                <!ENTITY % XHTML.prefixed "INCLUDE" >
                <!ENTITY % XHTML.prefix "html" >
]>
<html:html xmlns:html="http://www.w3.org/1999/xhtml">
<html:head><html:title></html:title></html:head>
<html:body>
</html:body>
</html:html>
```

Namespaces are not an excuse to break XML compliance. An element you start as a child node of another element must close as a child node of that element no matter what namespace. XML parsers will check for well-formedness based on the qualified name. The following, for instance, is *not* well-formed:

```
<?xml version="1.0" ?>
<html:html
  xmlns:html="http://www.w3.org/1999/xhtml"
  xmlns:jsl="http://www.jslab.org/namespaces/jsl">
<html:head><html:title /></html:head>
```

```
<html:body>
<html:p><jsl:author>Alexander J. Vincent</html:p></jsl:author>
</html:body>
</html:html>
```

Likewise, the root element and the <!DOCTYPE > tag's root element declaration must match.

Namespaces, when taken into consideration with XML and HTML, provide support for one of the most useful (and personally appealing) quirks of XML page design I've ever seen.

Scripting an XML Document: <html:script />

Yes, you can use JavaScript with XML documents! The requirements are fairly modest: a namespace and the element. Unfortunately, only Netscape 6 browsers support it. Listing 36.4 uses a namespace to enable scripting.

> **Note**
> Outside of browsers, it is not typical to add HTML scripting to an XML document. I do so here because I examine XML documents from the scope of a Web browser.
>
> Also, some XML languages have JavaScript or ECMAScript support built in natively. SVG is one such language; the <html:script /> element is not necessary or advisable in these circumstances.

Listing 36.4   *Using the XHTML Namespace to Script XML*

```
<?xml version="1.0" ?>
<root xmlns="http://www.jslab.org/namespaces/root">
<script type="text/javascript" id="test" xmlns="http://www.w3.org/1999/xhtml">
<![CDATA[
window.onload = function() {
    alert("Hello World")
    }
]]>
</script>
<!-- Result:
alert window containing the string "Hello World"
-->
</root>
```

Internet Explorer and XML Data Islands

Microsoft Internet Explorer permits an alternative approach to XML in the Web browser. It implements a proprietary element to HTML, `<xml>...</xml>`. This element enables you to insert an XML document as a *data island* into your HTML document.

What is an XML data island? In short, it's a well-formed XML document fragment attached to a parent HTML document.

Why do you want an XML data island in an HTML document? That's a tougher question. However, it's the same question, really, as asking, "Why do you want an XML document?" More often than not, you're looking for a document written in a particular XML language. The language itself defines, to an extent, the context in which you intend to use the document.

Listing 36.5 has a simple XML data island embedded in an HTML document. The XML document fragment is accessible as the `XMLDocument` property of the XML element. (Internet Explorer permits using the `id` attribute's value as a property of the `window` object to directly access the XML element.)

Listing 36.5   *An XML Data Island in HTML*

```
<html>
<!-- Not XHTML 1.0 Transitional. IE5.0+ only. -->
<head><title></title>
<script language="JavaScript" type="text/javascript">
<!--
function go() {
  var fruits_doc = fruits.XMLDocument
  var fruitList = fruits_doc.getElementsByTagName("fruit")
  var x = 0;
  for (x = 0; x < fruitList.length; x++) {
    var p = document.createElement("p")
    var p_text = "There are " + fruitList[x].getAttribute("quantity")
    p_text += " " + fruitList[x].getAttribute("color")
    p_text += " " + fruitList[x].getAttribute("name") + "s in the basket."
    p.appendChild(document.createTextNode(p_text))
    document.body.appendChild(p)
    }
  }
//-->
</script>
</head>
```

Listing 36.5   *(continued)*

```
<body onload="go()">
<xml id="fruits">
  <basket type="wicker">
    <fruit name="apple" color="red" quantity="3" />
    <fruit name="orange" color="orange" quantity="2" />
    <fruit name="grape" color="green" quantity="40" />
  </basket>
</xml>
<h1>Inventory of fruits:</h1>
<!-- Results:
There are 3 red apples in the basket.
There are 2 orange oranges in the basket.
There are 40 green grapes in the basket.
-->
</body>
</html>
```

Internet Explorer treats the inline XML data island as pure data primarily; the browser makes no attempts to render this document whatsoever. That's up to you and the DOM.

There is an alternative syntax for the `<xml>...</xml>` element. With an `src` attribute, you can reference the XML document like you would a script for the `<script />` element. With that format, child elements for the XML element would be ignored.

XML, DTD, and Namespaces in XML all add up to create a new concept in the design of XML languages. Combined with XHTML, the result is yet another, vital W3C Recommendation: Modularization of XHTML.

Modularization of XHTML and XHTML 1.1

Explaining how to modularize your XML languages in the Document Type Definition files is beyond the scope of this book. Instead, I will briefly explain how Modularization of XHTML has impacted namespacing.

The point of modularization is to use as many entities as possible in the definition of the language to give maximum flexibility without changing the semantic definitions of the languages. You can switch on and off namespaces for the whole document, or for a particular XML language in the document. You can preset the prefix for a namespace as you see fit. You could even build your own XHTML language just from the various components of XHTML, put together with external entities.

To give you a taste of what is possible, examine Listing 36.6, an XHTML 1.1 + MathML 2.0 document constructed according to an experimental DTD the W3C provides. (XHTML 1.1 is almost the same as XHTML 1.0 Strict; the biggest differences are in the DTDs, which we Web page authors normally should not worry about. Of course, I specialize in pushing the boundaries…)

Listing 36.6   *XHTML Plus MathML as XML*

```
<?xml version="1.0" ?>
<!DOCTYPE html:html PUBLIC "-//W3C//DTD XHTML 1.1 plus MathML 2.0//EN"
  "http://www.w3.org/TR/MathML2/dtd/xhtml-math11-f.dtd"
[<!ENTITY % NS.prefixed "INCLUDE" >
<!ENTITY % XHTML.prefix "html" >
<!ENTITY % MATHML.prefix "math" >
]>
<html:html xmlns:html="http://www.w3.org/1999/xhtml"
    xmlns:math="http://www.w3.org/1998/Math/MathML">
<html:head><html:title /></html:head>
<html:body>
<html:p>An elementary equation in algebra is
<math:math>
  <math:mi>y</math:mi>
  <math:mo>=</math:mo>
  <math:mi>a</math:mi>
  <math:msup>
    <math:mi>x</math:mi>
    <math:mn>2</math:mn>
  </math:msup>
  <math:mo>+</math:mo>
  <math:mi>bx</math:mi>
  <math:mo>+</math:mo>
  <math:mi>c</math:mi>
</math:math>
.</html:p>
</html:body>
</html:html>
```

Currently, neither Netscape nor Internet Explorer correctly renders this example. You'll need to use the latest Amaya editor from the W3C.

I'll explain MathML later in this chapter.

XLink

HTML is HyperText Markup Language, and the one item that really makes HTML (HyperText Markup Language) hypertext was linking. Forget the image markup, forget all the other markup, hyperlinks defined Web documents in the early years. With a W3C Recommendation called XLink, we now have hyperlinks for XML.

XLink works by using a special `xlink` namespace (`xmlns:xlink="http://www.w3.org/1999/xlink"`) on any element you apply it to in an XML document. Theoretically, you can create any kind of link from one Web file to another with XLink (say, from one XML document to another XML document, or to an image file). You could also theoretically specify if the file the element links to is a clickable link or a file the document loads automatically in place of the element (think images). You can even specify whether a clickable link opens its targeted file in the current window or a new window.

Theoretically.

In practice, it's a whole different ballgame. Netscape 6 has support for "simple" links, and even then omits the capability to embed an XLink-ed file in the XML document (such as an image). Plus, the links themselves may not look like the blue underlined links you expect without styling, but they are links. Listing 36.7 shows a simplistic XLink model.

Listing 36.7   *XLink in XML*

```
<?xml version="1.0" ?>
<!-- COlst06a.xml -->
<root xmlns:xlink="http://www.w3.org/1999/xlink">
<click xlink:type="simple"
       xlink:actuate="onRequest"
       xlink:show="replace"
       xlink:href="COlst06b.htm">Click here!</click>
</root>


<?xml version="1.0" ?>
```

Listing 36.7   *(continued)*

```
<!-- COlst06b.htm -->
<!DOCTYPE html PUBLIC "-//W3C//DTD XHTML 1.0 Transitional//EN"
➥ "DTD/xhtml1-transitional.dtd">
<html xmlns="http://www.w3.org/1999/xhtml" >
<head><title></title></head>
<body>
<p>If you clicked on the link, you should arrive here!</p>
</body>
</html>
```

Internet Explorer, because it treats the XML document natively with a default XML stylesheet, ignores XLink at this time.

XSLT 1.0: eXtensible Stylesheet Language, Transformations

Here we get to some real meat and potatoes of XML Web design. XSLT defines a language for transforming an XML document from one language to another. Personally, I like this concept because I can create a single XML language, and from that XML language, generate XHTML, MathML, and SVG if I so desire. Or I can transform to any other language appealing to me at the moment.

I mention in Chapter 33, "Styling for HTML Elements," the format for the `<?xml-stylesheet ?>` processing instruction you use to associate a style sheet with a document. XSLT stands for eXtensible Stylesheet Language, Transformations. (Its cousin is XSL-FO, a language beyond the scope of current browsers and this book.) In essence, XSLT is an XML language for writing style sheets, totally different than CSS. You still use the `<?xml-stylesheet ?>` processing instruction, but for the `type` pseudo-attribute, you use `"text/xsl"`.

XSLT supports a wide range of facilities: templates, output as XML or HTML, conditional processing, and so on. Again, I use a brief XSLT document at `http://www.jslab.org/articles/XHTML_IE.xml`.

XML Schemas

This, I think, is one of the most exciting concepts out there: an XML language to define other XML languages. The language is known formally as the W3C Recommendation XML Schemas, and it has, at the time of printing, two parts: structures and data types.

XML Schemas even takes the time to use its own language to define itself. You might think this a circular argument with no basis, but that's not the case. What really happens is a two-part process. The XML Schemas language validates against a DTD for the language. This confirms it as a valid XML language by DTD. Then the XML Schemas validator takes the XML Schemas language for XML Schemas and checks it against itself for validity. It passes.

However, the true beauty of XML Schemas lies in its ability to rigorously define the validity constraints for an XML document. DTD, as you know, cannot define the difference between a number, a date, and a string. XML Schemas can (and does!) do exactly this.

You can define complete validation rules for a document, rules which state exactly what formatting an element's contents or attribute value may take. XML Schemas even enables you to define new types of formatting for content, beyond the data types XML Schemas itself provides.

Again, I see XML Schemas for more than just validation. Personally, I am of the opinion that if an XML document can come from a database's records, an XML Schemas document can define the structure of that database. (Okay, that's a bit of a stretch, but still…) Another approach is to think of them as instructions on how to construct a valid document for that language.

XML Schemas is an incredibly complex language (it has to be, to support all the power it offers). I'm not going to attempt defining XHTML in XML Schemas (there is currently a W3C Working Draft for Modularization of XHTML in XML Schemas, so I don't need to), but Listing 36.8 is a sample XML Schemas document for the XML file in Listing 36.7. The extension, in this case, is .xsd.

Listing 36.8 *A Simple XML Schemas Document*

```
<xsd:schema xmlns:xsd="http://www.w3.org/2001/XMLSchema">
  <xsd:complexType name="root">
    <xsd:sequence>
      <xsd:element name="click" type="xsd:string" />
```

Listing 36.8   *(continued)*

```
      </xsd:sequence>
    </xsd:complexType>
  </xsd:schema>
```

Associating an XML schema with a particular XML language is easy. The XML Schemas Structures Recommendation provides for the `xsi:schemaLocation` and `xsi:noNamespaceSchemaLocation` attributes for the root element. The contents of these attributes are sets of pairs of URIs. The first URI in such a pair is the namespace URI for the language. The second URI in the pair is the schema document location matching that language.

Borrowing from the Structures Recommendation, I recommend the following format, applied to the root element of the document:

```
<html:html xmlns:html="http://www.w3.org/1999/xhtml"
  xmlns:xlink="http://www.w3.org/1999/xlink"
  xmlns:xsi="http://www.w3.org/2001/XMLSchema-instance"
      xsi:schemaLocation="
        http://www.w3.org/1999/xhtml        http://www.w3.org/1999/xhtml.xsd
        http://www.w3.org/1999/xlink        http://www.w3.org/1999/xlink.xsd
        ">
```

This enables you to place the namespaces in one column, and the XML Schemas for the language in another.

(These XSD documents have not been formally named or created by the W3C; the proposed locations may not reflect the actual locations of such schema for XHTML and XLINK.)

Currently, only Internet Explorer implements XML Schemas checking in any form. I'm not yet able to test how good Microsoft's implementation of XML Schemas is.

MathML 2.0: Mathematics Markup Language

One of the first efforts of the W3C I followed closely is MathML. It is basically a language for defining a structure to mathematics content, or the presentation of a mathematics equation, within a document.

MathML is rarely alone; each MathML document describes, at best, one mathematical formula. Therefore, you will often find multiple MathML documents embedded in an XHTML document, each one describing an equation or value.

Listing 36.6 shows the use of one MathML document within an XHTML document. As you can see by looking at the source code, MathML is not a tiny language, for all the functionality it has to impart. In fact, this level of complexity is often necessary in advanced mathematics.

> **Note**
> There is one area of MathML I am decidedly unhappy about: the omission of mathematical geometry from the specification. MathML was written for scientific formulae, but you will not see a coordinate or a line segment described in any MathML 2.0 document.

Incidentally, MathML also provides a special Document Object Model to extend upon the Core DOM in Chapter 20, "Core DOM Objects." This MathML DOM does for MathML what the HTML DOM does for HTML and XHTML documents. So yes, you can script a MathML document directly.

Currently, neither Netscape nor Internet Explorer support MathML directly. You can view MathML via a plug-in, however. IBM provides the TechExplorer plug-in for MathML, hosted at `http://www.software.ibm.com/network/techexplorer`. The introductory edition of the plug-in is free. (The Mozilla project is working on enabling MathML. As an alternative, consider the Amaya editor from the W3C.)

SVG 1.0: Scalable Vector Graphics

SVG is easily the most surprising XML language the World Wide Web Consortium has put out to date. Simply put, it is an XML language for defining images.

Now that's cool. Because it's XML, you can tweak an effect that's slightly "off" here and there, and get it exactly the way you want it. Sweeping and tiny changes are both possible simultaneously. Ever hear of hand-coding a newspaper cartoon? With SVG, it's possible.

SVG does text, lines, curves, circles, ellipses, rectangles and Bezier curves (whatever those are), all natively within its own language. It provides support for gradient effects, for shading and light positioning effects, for any kind of simplistic artwork. (Often it supports not-so-simplistic artwork as well.)

Adobe makes an excellent plug-in for Netscape 4.x and Internet Explorer 5.0+ to render SVG, including partial SVG DOM support. The plug-in is available via `http://www.adobe.com/svg`.

Note SVG is *not* a language for displaying a true-color image. SVG is fundamentally different than GIF and JPEG, which are raster image formats recording the picture pixel by pixel. There are tools to "rasterize" SVG, and there are a couple of tools for converting a raster image to SVG (though the latter are not very efficient).

SVG also provides a special Document Object Model to extend upon the Core DOM in Chapter 20, "Core DOM Objects." This SVG DOM does for SVG what the HTML DOM does for HTML and XHTML documents. So yes, you can script an SVG image document directly.

In fact, I've already done this. I've written a function curve plotter, currently hosted at `http://www.jslab.org/svg/grapher2.htm`. It uses JavaScript to create the function curve plot in SVG markup, with a healthy dose of linear mathematics to back it up. No matter the version, I will gladly make source code available to anyone who asks.

For Listing 36.9, I'm including half of the plotter: the SVG image with inline scripting. I regret I was not able to actually use the SVG-specific DOM in this example; the third version of the Adobe SVG Viewer does not support all the methods I need directly. The Core DOM will have to suffice.

Nonetheless, even a scripted zoom and pan is interesting.

Listing 36.9   *SVG and JavaScripting*

```
<?xml version="1.0" standalone="no"?>
<!DOCTYPE svg PUBLIC "-//W3C//DTD SVG 20010904//EN"
 "http://www.w3.org/TR/2001/REC-SVG-20010904/DTD/svg10.dtd">
  <svg width="500px" height="360px" contentScriptType="text/javascript"
➥ id="master">
  <script>
<![CDATA[
function moveGraphBy(x,y) {
  var graph = document.getElementById("graph")
  var graph_translate = graph.getAttribute("transform").split(" ")[0]

  var graph_x = graph_translate.substr(10,graph_translate.indexOf(",") - 10) * 1
  var graph_y = graph_translate.substr(graph_translate.indexOf(",") + 1,
    graph_translate.length - graph_translate.indexOf(",") - 2) * 1
  var response = "translate(" + (graph_x + x) + "," + (graph_y + y) + ") "
  response += graph.getAttribute("transform").split(" ")[1]
  graph.setAttribute("transform", response)
  }
```

Listing 36.9 *(continued)*

```
function zoomGraphIn(z) {
  var graph = document.getElementById("graph")
  var graph_zoom = graph.getAttribute("transform").split(" ")[1]

  var graph_z = graph_zoom.substr(6,graph_zoom.indexOf(",") - 6) * z
  var response = graph.getAttribute("transform").split(" ")[0] + " "
  response += "scale(" + graph_z + "," + graph_z + ")"
  graph.setAttribute("transform", response)
  }

function zoomGraphOut(z) {
  var graph = document.getElementById("graph")
  var graph_zoom = graph.getAttribute("transform").split(" ")[1]

  var graph_z = graph_zoom.substr(6,graph_zoom.indexOf(",") - 6) / z
  var response = graph.getAttribute("transform").split(" ")[0] + " "
  response += "scale(" + graph_z + "," + graph_z + ")"
  graph.setAttribute("transform", response)
  }
]]>
</script>
  <desc>Gridlines</desc>
  <defs>
    <line id="gridline" x1="-10" y1="0" x2="10" y2="0" style="stroke:grey;" />
    <g id="partialAxis">
      <use x="0" y="10" xlink:href="#gridline" />
      <use x="0" y="9" xlink:href="#gridline" />
      <use x="0" y="8" xlink:href="#gridline" />
      <use x="0" y="7" xlink:href="#gridline" />
      <use x="0" y="6" xlink:href="#gridline" />
      <use x="0" y="5" xlink:href="#gridline" />
      <use x="0" y="4" xlink:href="#gridline" />
      <use x="0" y="3" xlink:href="#gridline" />
      <use x="0" y="2" xlink:href="#gridline" />
      <use x="0" y="1" xlink:href="#gridline" />
      </g>
    <g id="moveTri">
      <path d="M -5 -5 L 5 0 L -5 5 Z" />
      </g>
```

Listing 36.9   *(continued)*

```
    <clipPath id="gridClip">
      <rect x="-10.5" y="-10.5" width="21" height="21" />
      </clipPath>

  </defs>
  <g transform="translate(180,180) scale(16,-16)"  clip-path="url(#gridClip);"
style="fill:none; stroke:black; stroke-width:.1">
    <g id="graph" transform="translate(0,0) scale(1,1)">
      <g id="Axis">
        <line x1="-10" y1="0" x2="10" y2="0" style="stroke:black;" />
        <line x1="-10" y1="0" x2="10" y2="0" style="stroke:black;"
          transform="rotate(90)" />
        <circle cx="0" cy="0" r=".5" />
        </g>
      </g>
    <g id="grid">
      <use x="0" y="0" xlink:href="#partialAxis" />
      <use x="0" y="0" xlink:href="#partialAxis" transform="rotate(90)" />
      <use x="0" y="0" xlink:href="#partialAxis" transform="rotate(180)" />
      <use x="0" y="0" xlink:href="#partialAxis" transform="rotate(270)" />
        <line x1="-10" y1="0" x2="10" y2="0" style="stroke:grey;" />
        <line x1="-10" y1="0" x2="10" y2="0" style="stroke:grey;"
          transform="rotate(90)" />
      </g>
    </g>
  <text x="180" y="15" style="fill:black;">y</text>
  <text x="345" y="180" style="fill:black;">x</text>
  <g id="moveGrid" transform="translate(400,80)">
    <use x="0" y="0" transform="translate(40,0)"
      xlink:href="#moveTri" onclick='moveGraphBy(-1,0)' />
    <use x="0" y="0" xlink:href="#moveTri"
      transform="translate(0,20) rotate(90)" onclick='moveGraphBy(0,1)' />
    <use x="0" y="0" xlink:href="#moveTri"
      transform="translate(-40,0) rotate(180)" onclick='moveGraphBy(1,0)' />
    <use x="0" y="0" xlink:href="#moveTri"
      transform="translate(0,-20) rotate(270)" onclick='moveGraphBy(0,-1)' />
    <text x="-33" y="5">Move Graph</text>
    </g>
  <g transform="translate(400,240)">
    <use x="0" y="0" xlink:href="#moveTri"
      transform="translate(0,80) rotate(90)"  onclick="zoomGraphOut(5)"/>
```

Listing 36.9   *(continued)*

```
    <use x="0" y="0" xlink:href="#moveTri"
      transform="translate(0,-80) rotate(270)" onclick="zoomGraphIn(5)" />
    <use x="0" y="0" xlink:href="#moveTri"
      transform="translate(0,60) rotate(90)"  onclick="zoomGraphOut(4)"/>
    <use x="0" y="0" xlink:href="#moveTri"
      transform="translate(0,-60) rotate(270)" onclick="zoomGraphIn(4)" />
    <use x="0" y="0" xlink:href="#moveTri"
      transform="translate(0,40) rotate(90)"  onclick="zoomGraphOut(3)"/>
    <use x="0" y="0" xlink:href="#moveTri"
      transform="translate(0,-40) rotate(270)" onclick="zoomGraphIn(3)" />
    <use x="0" y="0" xlink:href="#moveTri"
      transform="translate(0,20) rotate(90)"  onclick="zoomGraphOut(2)"/>
    <use x="0" y="0" xlink:href="#moveTri"
      transform="translate(0,-20) rotate(270)" onclick="zoomGraphIn(2)" />
    <text x="-34" y="5">Zoom Factor</text>

    <text x="5" y="-20">2x</text>
    <text x="5" y="-40">3x</text>
    <text x="5" y="-60">4x</text>
    <text x="5" y="-80">5x</text>
    </g>
</svg>
```

> **Note**
> Again, I am decidedly unhappy about the omission of mathematical geometry from the SVG
> specification. You can define a line segment in SVG by end-coordinates, but they do not
> have a point-slope or slope-intercept line definition, to borrow terms from elementary
> geometry.
>
> I am thinking about creating a custom XML language for transformation into XHTML +
> MathML + SVG, specifically for mathematical proofs. Currently, however, I do not have a
> DTD for the three languages combined. MathML already exists as a module, and I expect
> the 1.1 version of SVG to be an SVG module that plugs into XHTML as well.

XForms

XForms is a W3C Working Draft for defining a generic form language in XML, and
also in sending the server an XML document containing the form's submitted data.
Because both the form and its submitted data are XML, they lend themselves easily to

manipulation by the Core DOM. The datatypes of XML Schemas provide an arrangement for basic form validation—validating a date, for instance, to make sure it is legitimate.

Currently, no browser implements XForms in any fashion. I don't know of any plug-ins or servers for XForms either. Nonetheless, this technology is on my watch list.

XQuery

XQuery is a W3C Working Draft for an XML-based querying language. Typically, a query exists to retrieve information from a database. Same thing, only the query is an XML document.

XQuery is really not a language for client browsers at all, but for server-side databases. Again, it is not essential for a JavaScript developer to know it, but it's interesting enough in its own right.

SOAP: Simple Object Access Protocol

Given how important objects are to JavaScript, SOAP is an XML language we would do well to watch very closely. Microsoft first introduced it using Internet Explorer and Web services as a way to exchange objects between the client and the server in a mutual language.

Microsoft has a SOAP 1.0 and a SOAP 1.1. The W3C has adopted Microsoft's SOAP languages as Notes, and has begun work on a SOAP 1.2 standard. It is currently in Working Draft status.

Other XML Languages

Netscape 6 supports two proprietary languages, XUL and XBL. XUL stands for eXtensible User-interface Language. It essentially is a language for defining user interfaces in a much tighter space than HTML makes possible, and with a great deal of flexibility. Netscape 6 skins are built from a combination of XUL and JavaScript; it's pretty interesting. `http://www.xulplanet.com` has tutorials on this language.

XBL is a W3C Note Netscape has submitted for the eXtensible Bindings Language. I know I said earlier in this book it is beyond the scope of this book, and it is.

Netscape 6 uses it to bind information in one source to another, or to attach event handlers to an element. Again, fairly interesting.

Conclusion to the *JavaScript Developer's Dictionary*

Whether it is HTML, XHTML, or XML, JavaScript is an incredibly powerful language. Hopefully this book has taught you a few things about what JavaScript can do. I know I've learned a lot in writing it.

And now, a last thought: As you are well aware of by now, the HTML DOM I covered in Part III of this book corresponds very closely to HTML attributes. In that sense, you can often look at the properties I name in this book and tie them directly to HTML. XHTML has deprecated many of them, so watch out for them. But by and large, I hope this book is not just a JavaScript Developer's Dictionary for you. I hope it serves as an (X)HTML Developer's Dictionary in the process as well.

Respectfully Yours,

Alexander James Vincent

Symbols

A

B

H

M

P

W

SAMS DEVELOPER'S LIBRARY

Cookbook   Handbook   Dictionary

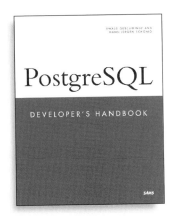

PHP
DEVELOPER'S COOKBOOK

Sterling Hughes and
Andrei Zmievski

ISBN: 0-672-32325-7
$39.99 US/$59.95 CAN

PostgreSQL
DEVELOPER'S HANDBOOK

Ewald Geschwinde and
Hans–Jürgen Schönig

ISBN: 0-672-32260-9
$44.99 US/$67.95 CAN

Perl
DEVELOPER'S DICTIONARY

Clinton Pierce

ISBN: 0-672-32067-3
$39.99 US/$59.95 CAN

OTHER DEVELOPER'S LIBRARY TITLES

PHP
DEVELOPER'S DICTIONARY

Allen Wyke,
Michael J. Walker,
and Robert M. Cox

ISBN: 0-672-32029-0
$39.99 US/$59.95 CAN

mod_perl
DEVELOPER'S COOKBOOK

Geoffrey Young,
Paul Linder, and
Randy Kobes

ISBN: 0-672-32240-4
$39.99 US/$62.95 CAN

PHP
DEVELOPER'S HANDBOOK

Luke Welling and Laura
Thomson

ISBN: 0-672-32292-7
$39.99 US/$59.95 CAN
(Available Summer 2002)

Python
DEVELOPER'S HANDBOOK

André Lessa

ISBN: 0-672-31994-2
$44.99 US/$67.95 CAN

ALL PRICES ARE SUBJECT TO CHANGE

SAMS
www.samspublishing.com